HEARING THE NEW TESTAMENT

Hearing the New Testament

Strategies for Interpretation

Edited by Joel B. Green

WILLIAM B. EERDMANS PUBLISHING COMPANY
GRAND RAPIDS, MICHIGAN

THE PATERNOSTER PRESS
CARLISLE

© 1995 Wm. B. Eerdmans Publishing Co.

Published jointly 1995 in the United States of America by
Wm. B. Eerdmans Publishing Co.
255 Jefferson Ave. S.E., Grand Rapids, Michigan 49503
and in the U.K. by
The Paternoster Press
P. O. Box 300, Carlisle, Cumbria CA3 0QS

Printed in the United States of America

00 99 98 97 96 95   7 6 5 4 3 2 1

Library of Congress Cataloging-in-Publication Data

Hearing the New Testament: strategies for interpretation /
    edited by Joel B. Green.
        p.   cm.
    Includes bibliographical references and indexes.
    ISBN 0-8028-0793-3 (paper: alk. paper)
    1. Bible. N.T. — Hermeneutics. I. Green, Joel B., 1956-   .
BS2331.H43 1995
225.6′01 — dc20   95-17637
                                               CIP

British Library Cataloguing in Publication Data

Hearing the New Testament: Strategies for Interpretation
    I. Green, Joel B.
    225.6

ISBN 0-85364-687-2

Contents

CONTENTS

Contributors

LOVEDAY C. A. ALEXANDER, Lecturer in New Testament, Department of Biblical Studies, University of Sheffield, England

JAMES L. BAILEY, Professor of New Testament, Wartburg Theological Seminary, Dubuque, Iowa, U.S.A.

STEPHEN C. BARTON, Lecturer in New Testament, Department of Theology, University of Durham, Durham, England

C. CLIFTON BLACK, Associate Professor of New Testament, Perkins School of Theology, Southern Methodist University, Dallas, Texas, U.S.A.

RICHARD BAUCKHAM, Professor of New Testament Studies, St. Mary's College, University of St. Andrews, St. Andrews, Scotland

BRUCE CHILTON, Bernard Iddings Bell Professor of Religion, Bard College, Annandale-on-Hudson, New York, U.S.A.

BART D. EHRMAN, Associate Professor of Religious Studies, The University of North Carolina at Chapel Hill, Chapel Hill, North Carolina, U.S.A.

STEPHEN E. FOWL, Associate Professor of Theology, Loyola College in Maryland, Baltimore, Maryland, U.S.A.

JOEL B. GREEN, Associate Professor of New Testament, American Baptist Seminary of the West and Graduate Theological Union, Berkeley, California, U.S.A.

RICHARD B. HAYS, Professor of New Testament, The Divinity School, Duke University, Durham, North Carolina, U.S.A.

JOHN R. LEVISON, Research Scholar in Residence, The Divinity School, Duke University, Durham, North Carolina, U.S.A.

EDGAR V. McKNIGHT, William R. Kenan Jr. Professor of Religion, Furman University, Greenville, South Carolina, U.S.A.

PRISCILLA POPE-LEVISON, Assistant Professor of the Practice of Evangelism, The Divinity School, Duke University, Durham, North Carolina, U.S.A.

MARK ALLAN POWELL, Associate Professor of New Testament, Trinity Lutheran Seminary, Columbus, Ohio, U.S.A.

SANDRA M. SCHNEIDERS, Professor of New Testament Studies and Christian Spirituality, The Jesuit School of Theology at Berkeley and Graduate Theological Union, Berkeley, California, U.S.A.

ANTHONY C. THISELTON, Professor of Christian Theology and Head of the Department of Theology, University of Nottingham, England, and Canon Theologian of Leicester Cathedral

MAX TURNER, Director of Research and Senior Lecturer in New Testament, London Bible College, Northwood, Middlesex, England

KEVIN J. VANHOOZER, Lecturer in Theology, New College, University of Edinburgh, Edinburgh, Scotland

ROBERT W. WALL, Professor of Biblical Studies, Seattle Pacific University, Seattle, Washington, U.S.A.

Abbreviations

GENERAL

§(§)	paragraph(s) or section(s)
κτλ	*καὶ τὰ λοιπά*, and the remainder
BCE	Before the Common Era (BC)
ca.	*circa*, about (with dates)
CE	Common Era (AD)
cf.	*confer*, compare
ch(s).	chapter(s)
d.	date of death
ed.	edition; editor(s), edited by
e.g.	*exempli gratia*, for example
esp.	especially
ET	English Translation
i.e.	*id est*, that is
LXX	Septuagint
ms(s)	manuscript(s)
MT	Masoretic Text
n(n)	note(s)
no.	number
NT	New Testament
OT	Old Testament
p(p).	page(s)
pace	with due respect to, but differing from
S1, S2 . . .	(Illustrative) Sentence 1, Sentence 2, etc.
Theod	Theodotion (a Greek version of the OT)

trans.	translated by
v(v).	verse(s)
vol(s).	volume(s)

ANCIENT LITERATURE

The Bible

Old Testament

Gen	Genesis	Cant	Song of Solomon
Exod	Exodus	Isa	Isaiah
Lev	Leviticus	Jer	Jeremiah
Num	Numbers	Lam	Lamentations
Deut	Deuteronomy	Ezek	Ezekiel
Josh	Joshua	Dan	Daniel
Judg	Judges	Hos	Hosea
Ruth	Ruth	Joel	Joel
1-2 Sam	1-2 Samuel	Amos	Amos
1-2 Kgs	1-2 Kings	Obad	Obadiah
1-2 Chr	1-2 Chronicles	Jonah	Jonah
Ezra	Ezra	Mic	Micah
Neh	Nehemiah	Nah	Nahum
Esth	Esther	Hab	Habakkuk
Job	Job	Zeph	Zephaniah
Ps(s)	Psalm(s)	Hag	Haggai
Prov	Proverbs	Zech	Zechariah
Eccl	Ecclesiastes	Mal	Malachi

Apocrypha/Deuterocanonical Books

Add Esth	Additions to Esther	Pr Azar	Prayer of Azariah
		Pr Man	Prayer of Manasseh
Bar	Baruch		
Bel	Bel and the Dragon	Sir	Sirach (Ecclesiasticus)
1-2 Esdr	1-2 Esdras	Sus	Susannah
4 Ezra	4 Ezra	Tob	Tobit
Jdt	Judith	Wis	Wisdom of Solomon
Ep Jer	Epistle of Jeremiah		
1-4 Macc	1-4 Maccabees		

ABBREVIATIONS

New Testament

Matt	Matthew	1-2 Thess	1-2 Thessalonians
Mark	Mark	1-2 Tim	1-2 Timothy
Luke	Luke	Tit	Titus
John	John	Phlm	Philemon
Acts	Acts	Heb	Hebrews
Rom	Romans	Jas	James
1-2 Cor	1-2 Corinthians	1-2 Pet	1-2 Peter
Gal	Galatians	1-3 John	1-3 John
Eph	Ephesians	Jude	Jude
Phil	Philippians	Rev	Revelation
Col	Colossians		

Pseudepigrapha and Noncanonical Early Christian Writings

2 Apoc. Bar.	Syriac *Apocalypse of Baruch*
3 Apoc. Bar.	Greek *Apocalypse of Baruch*
1 Clem	1 Clement
Ps(s). Sol.	*Psalms of Solomon*
T. Job	*Testament of Job*

Dead Sea Scrolls and Related Texts

CD	Cairo (Genizah text of the) *Damascus Document/Rule*
1QH	*Hôdāyôt* or Thanksgiving Hymns from Qumran Cave 1
1QM	*Milḥāmāh* or War Scroll from Qumran Cave 1
1QS	*Serek hayyaḥad* or *Rule of the Community, Manual of Discipline* from Qumran Cave 1
4Q185	Exhortation to Seek Wisdom from Qumran Cave 4

Targums

Tg. Ps.-J.	*Targum Pseudo-Jonathan*

Rabbinic Literature

b.	Babylonian Talmud
Ber.	*Berakot*
B. Meṣ	*Baba Meṣiʿa*

Other Ancient Writings

Josephus
    Ant.   *Jewish Antiquities*
    J.W.   *Jewish War*
    Life   *Life of Flavius Josephus*
Origen
    Hom. in   *Homilia in Lucam*
      Luc.
Philo
    Cong.   *De Congressu quaerendae Eruditionis gratia*
    Leg. Alleg. *Legum Allegoria*
    Leg. Gai.   *De Legatione ad Gaium*
    Migr.   *De migratione Abrahami*
    Praem.   *De Praemiis et Poenis*
    Spec. Leg. *De Specialibus Legibus*
    Vit. Mos.   *De Vita Mosis*
Tacitus
    Ann.   *Annals*
    Hist.   *Historiae*

MODERN LITERATURE

AB	Anchor Bible
ABD	*The Anchor Bible Dictionary.* 6 Vols. Edited by David Noel Freedman. New York: Doubleday, 1992.
ABRL	Anchor Bible Reference Library
AJS	*American Journal of Semiotics*
AnBib	Analecta biblica
ANRW	*Aufstieg und Niedergang der römischen Welt.* Edited by Hildegard Temporini and Wolfgang Haase. Berlin: Walter de Gruyter, 1972-.
AS	Advances in Semiotics
BAGD	Bauer, W., *A Greek-English Lexicon of the New Testament and Other Early Christian Literature.* Translated and revised by W. F. Arndt, F. W. Gingrich, and F. W. Danker. Chicago: University of Chicago, 1979.
BBR	*Bulletin for Biblical Research*
BDF	Blass, F., and A. Debrunner. *A Greek Grammer of the New Testament and Other Early Christian Literature.* Translated

	and revised by Robert W. Funk. Chicago: University of Chicago, 1979.
Bib	*Biblica*
BibInt	*Biblical Interpretation*
BibIntS	Biblical Interpretation Series
BJS	Brown Judaic Studies
BR	*Biblical Research*
BS	Biblical Seminar
BT	*Bible Translator*
BTB	*Biblical Theology Bulletin*
CAH	*Cambridge Ancient History*
CBQ	*Catholic Biblical Quarterly*
CRINT	Compedia rerum iudaicarum ad novum testamentum
CTL	Cambridge Textbooks in Linguistics
DJG	*Dictionary of Jesus and the Gospels.* Edited by Joel B. Green and Scot McKnight. Downers Grove and Leicester: InterVarsity, 1992.
DPL	*Dictionary of Paul and His Letters.* Edited by Gerald F. Hawthorne, Ralph P. Martin, and Daniel G. Reid. Downers Grove and Leicester: InterVarsity, 1993.
EDNT	*Exegetical Dictionary of the New Testament.* 3 vols. Edited by Horst Balz and Gerhard Schneider. Grand Rapids: Eerdmans, 1990-93.
ERT	*Evangelical Review of Theology*
ESW	Ecumenical Studies in Worship
ETL	*Ephemerides theologicae lovanienses*
EvQ	*Evangelical Quarterly*
ExpTim	*Expository Times*
FCI	Foundations of Contemporary Interpretation
FF	Foundations and Facets
FRLANT	Forschungen zur Religion und Literatur des Alten und Neuen Testaments
GBS	Guides to Biblical Scholarship
GNS	Good News Studies
GP	Gospel Perspectives
HeyJ	*Heythrop Journal*
HTR	Harvard Theological Review
Int	*Interpretation*
ISBL	Indiana Studies in Biblical Literature
JBL	*Journal of Biblical Literature*
JETS	*Journal of the Evangelical Theological Society*
JLT	*Journal of Literature and Theology*

JRH	*Journal of Religious History*
JRS	*Journal of Roman Studies*
JSNT	*Journal for the Study of the New Testament*
JSNTSS	Journal for the Study of the New Testament Supplement Series
JSOT	*Journal for the Study of the Old Testament*
JSOTSS	Journal for the Study of the Old Testament Supplement Series
JSPSS	Journal for the Study of the Pseudepigrapha Supplement Series
JTS	*Journal of Theological Studies*
LCBI	Literary Currents in Biblical Interpretation
LCL	Loeb Classical Library
LEC	Library of Early Christianity
LLL	Longman Linguistics Library
LS	Language in Society
LSJ	Liddell, Henry George and Robert Scott. *A Greek-English Lexicon.* Revised by Henry Stuart Jones. 9th ed., Oxford: Clarendon, 1940.
MHT	Moulton, James Hope; Wilbert Francis Howard; and Nigel Turner. *A Grammar of New Testament Greek.* 4 vols. Edinburgh: Clark, 1908-76.
NABPRBS	National Association of Baptist Professors of Religion Bibliographic Series
NAB	New American Bible
NCV	New Century Version
NIBC	New International Biblical Commentary
NICNT	New International Commentary on the New Testament
NIDNTT	*New International Dictionary of New Testament Theology.* 3 vols. Edited by Colin Brown. Grand Rapids: Zondervan, 1975-78.
NIV	New International Version
NLH	*New Literary History*
NovTSup	Novum Testamentum Supplements
NRSV	New Revised Standard Version
NTS	*New Testament Studies*
NTT	New Testament Theology
NTTS	New Testament Tools and Studies
OBT	Overtures to Biblical Theology
OCD	*Oxford Classical Dictionary.* Edited by N. G. L. Hammond and H. H. Scullard. 2d ed. Oxford: Clarendon, 1970.
PTMS	Pittsburgh Theological Monograph Series

ABBREVIATIONS

QJS	*Quarterly Journal of Speech*
RevExp	*Review and Expositor*
RelSRev	*Religious Studies Review*
RSV	Revised Standard Version
SBLAS	Society of Biblical Literature Aramaic Studies
SBLCP	Society of Biblical Literature Centennial Publications
SBLDS	Society of Biblical Literature Dissertation Series
SBLMS	Society of Biblical Literature Monograph Series
SBLSCS	Society of Biblical Literature Septuagint and Cognate Studies
SBT	Studies in Biblical Theology
SD	Studies and Documents
SHM	Studies in the History of Mission
SIHC	Studies in the Intercultural History of Christianity
SJLA	Studies in Judaism in Late Antiquity
SJT	*Scottish Journal of Theology*
SNTSMS	Society for New Testament Studies Monograph Series
SR	*Studies in Religion*
ST	*Studia theologica*
TDNT	*Theological Dictionary of the New Testament*. 10 vols. Edited by Gerhard Kittel and Gerhard Friedrich. Grand Rapids, Eerdmans, 1964-76.
TJ	*Trinity Journal*
TLG	*Thesaurus Linguae Graecae*
UBS	United Bible Societies
VE	*Vox Evangelica*
WBC	Word Biblical Commentary
WM	The World of Man
WTJ	*Wesleyan Theological Journal*
WUNT	Wissenschaftliche Untersuchungen zum Neuen Testament

1. *The Challenge of Hearing the New Testament*

JOEL B. GREEN

1. Reading as Communication

The challenge of understanding texts like the Gospel of Luke or Paul's First Letter to the Corinthians is both similar to and more pressing than that of understanding day-to-day discourse. Conversation about Mozart or world hunger over a cup of coffee involves an addresser (one who speaks), an addressee (one who hears), a context for communication, and a message; so also does our reading of 1 Corinthians. Moreover, in either case, one may account for a medium of communication — verbal and non-verbal exchange on the one hand; direct or indirect contact with the written page on the other.[1] In both, one may factor in various kinds of "noise" — things that disturb "hearing" — like a difficult translation of the Gospel of Luke, the siren of an emergency vehicle passing outside, the overlay of centuries of interpreting a passage from Paul or a sonata from Mozart, restaurant chatter breaking in on the interchange, and so on.

Reading texts is thus participation in a form of communication and can be diagrammed in the same manner as other forms of communication:

---

1. What follows is indebted to the approach of Cesare Segre with Tomaso Kemeny, *Introduction to the Analysis of the Literary Text,* AS (Bloomington/Indianapolis: Indiana University, 1988) §1.1.

context

addresser → message → addressee

medium

In either case, oral or written, the addresser assumes that he or she will be understood and, presumably, articulates the message so as to be understood. In either case, the effect of this "understanding" is more than simply the passing on of information. Rather, an addressee will be influenced by the engagement — perhaps toward more deeply held convictions, toward consideration of revising previously held views, to attitudinal shifts, to hearing Mozart (or Paul) differently in the future, to new forms of behavior, or the like.

Interactions like conversation or reading a biblical text share a further common feature: They are all open to numerous ambiguities. We may understand "hunger" differently, depending on whether we have actually experienced more than the odd missed meal. We may understand the causes or effects of world hunger along different lines or differ in our views of local responsibility for global affairs. Corresponding ambiguities reside in our attempts to "hear" the message of Paul as presented in 1 Corinthians.

And here lies a major distinction between these two arenas of communication. Over coffee one can ask "Did I hear you correctly?" or "Are you kidding?" For this reason the simple diagram of the process of communication laid out above would need to be revised to allow for ongoing clarification and mutual exchange. But in almost every case of literary communication, and certainly when we read NT texts, the act of "sending" (i.e., writing) is distant in time and space from the act of "receiving" (i.e., reading the text or hearing it read). Luke cannot adjust the presentation of his message in order to accommodate our reactions. Nor can we directly check our understanding against his intended message, as one might in face-to-face communication. We can interrogate the Gospel of Luke in order to ascertain whether our understanding coheres with the text, but we cannot directly ask its author "Did we get it right?" Although it cannot be doubted, then, that the addresser has articulated a particular message in written form, what is available to us in literature is the text itself, and it is now the medium from which addressees — those who read the NT text, for instance — infer meaning.

This does not negate our premise that the act of reading is an act of communication, but it does complicate matters somewhat. On the one hand, this way of putting things reminds us that the act of reading Luke's

Gospel (for example) is already *an act of interpretation.* Communication consists in part in generating messages via a medium for presentation to an addressee *and the interpretation of that medium to surmise a message.* In reading, we decipher marks on the page and understand them as meaningful, and we do so in ways that reflect what we have learned before — for example, about other similar marks on pages (and, so, about word and sentence construction, argument formation, and the like), about the world reflected in this Gospel, about the nature of "the Jews" or of this "Jesus" about whom the Evangelist writes, and indeed about the Gospel of Luke itself.

Moreover, the act of reading the Gospel of Luke is always, at least potentially, an encounter with the Evangelist as a partner in conversation. That conversation might be taking place in the text itself. Or it is happening behind the text if we attempt to get at the intention of the author or the author's community (or both). Or it may be going on in our own imagination and experience. Where we locate that conversation will depend largely on what we are aiming for in our interpretation of the text and what tools and approaches we use to achieve that aim. Nonetheless, as an *act of communication* our reading is not simply dispassionate, "for information only," but has the capacity to shape us in some way.

When we read rather than engage in face-to-face conversation, the events or processes of generation and interpretation of meaning are not present together. This makes our engagement with literary texts as communicative acts problematic. The writer — the addresser — is not present for consultation, and we cannot measure our construal of the text's meaning against such paralinguistic phenomena as gestures, countenance, intonation, and so on. For instance, should 1 Cor 11:19 ("Indeed, there must be factions among you, for only then will it become clear who among you are genuine") be read with a serious tone of voice or a sarcastic tone of voice?

And reading is more susceptible to ethnocentrisms, that is, to the reading of our own culture into a text which has come to us from another culture, imagining that all persons at all times and in all places experience life the way we do. This is true especially with such texts as those collected in our NT, since they are distant from all of us temporally and, to varying degrees, culturally.

Such difficulties are not without their remedies; indeed, in the chapters that follow, we will be exploring a number of ways of hearing NT texts. First, however, it may be helpful to explore further some of the obstacles we are up against.

2. Language Problems

Analyses of literary texts like the Book of Revelation or the Letter of James must first confront the problems inherent in language itself.

2.1 Language Is Linear

First, we must come to terms with the reality that texts present information in a specific sequence. In English (and Greek) we read "from left to right." When we read a text or hear one read, we are unable to get the whole picture at once and must rely on progressive revelation of information, so to speak, as one chapter gives way to another, and on our memories of information increasingly distant from what we have previously read. Perhaps it is partly in this way that "a picture is worth a thousand words," since in a landscape portrait we are able to see the whole at once. But describing that landscape to someone else in words introduces a certain linearity. What will we describe first? Second? Third?

With NT texts the problem of linearity can actually be a boon to interpretation since it raises immediately the question of the arrangement of material. What comes first? Last? Do the Gospels report events in chronological order, or do they arrange events in a sequence that draws attention to particular connections and that opens up new interpretive possibilities? Was Jesus actually baptized *after* John was imprisoned (Luke 3:18-22), or is this evidence of Luke's interest in "order," which he asserted earlier (1:1-4)? Similarly, in Revelation 5, John paints a picture with his words, first describing the one worthy to open the scroll as "the Lion of Judah," only then introducing in this role "a Lamb standing as if it had been slaughtered" (Rev 5:5-6). What direction of interpretation of both Lion and Lamb is encouraged by this sequence and by this consequent creative mix of images?

2.2 Language Is Selective

Second, an addresser cannot say everything. Not every detail can be presented, with the result that addressees — in our case, readers — are left with work to do. In fact, one can trace an inverse relationship between the amount of detail and cohesiveness provided by the writer and the degree of interpretive work required of the reader.[2]

2. Gillian Brown and George Yule, *Discourse Analysis*, CTL (Cambridge: Cambridge University, 1983) 266, 269-70.

Some gaps in literary detail occur because of the assumptions of the writer. Paul may assume that his audience at Corinth understands his reference to the death of some within the community as a consequence of Corinthian practices in the common meal (1 Cor 11:30), even if this remark has puzzled numerous commentators since. Perhaps James has in mind a particular "righteous person" who has been condemned and murdered by rich people (Jas 5:6), though modern English translations struggle with whether to take ὁ δίκαιος *(ho dikaios)* as a reference to a particular righteous person (so NRSV and NAB; Jesus? James?) or several people (so NCV and NIV; "righteous people" as a collective? the poor whom James addresses?). (On some occasions a writer provides background information of this sort to fill in potential gaps; see, e.g., the narrative asides in John 4:8, 9b.) Other gaps might function as invitations for readers to participate imaginatively in the production of meaning. For example, what reason has been given in Luke 3 for John to castigate "the crowds" for coming out to be baptized by him? What have they done to deserve being called "offspring of poisonous snakes" (Luke 3:7)?

2.3 Language Is Ambiguous

Words (or better, lexemes) often carry multiple meanings, giving rise to potential ambiguities whether one is reading or hearing someone read. Umberto Eco illustrates the ambiguity of symbols with reference to a picture of a ranch-style house with an old wagon wheel leaning against the front exterior wall. Is this a picture of a movie set for a western film? A snapshot from a ghost town? A restaurant serving country-style food? The workshop of a blacksmith? An actual ranch house? An antique shop? Like this picture, language is capable of many and diverse readings, and a way must be found for sorting through the possibilities.

2.4 Language Is Culturally Embedded

A fourth problem with language, and one that we have already hinted at, is its cultural embeddedness. In fact, alongside the benefits of modern translations of the NT is an important liability. Since we have access to the NT writings in English (and today in plain English), we often easily assume that these words, these sentences, these books are immediately available to us in our own cultural contexts. Often with little or no deliberation, we read our experience of the world into the world of these texts, failing to account for the reality that every reading of the NT today is an exercise in cross-cultural communication and understanding. As a consequence, we easily conscript selected texts to our own interests and find in them justification for our sometimes comfortable practices in the world.

Do we too easily find "the Eucharist" in 1 Cor 11:17-34? How do our practices relate to the notion of "community meal" Paul discusses? Do we understand the nature of John's baptism in Luke 3 from our contemporary practices of baptism? How do our practices, sanctioned by the church and often located within church buildings, relate to John's prophetic wilderness activity, far from the temple in Jerusalem?

*   *   *

In their various ways, the chapters that follow address such questions. They also raise other questions, all in an attempt to explore how it is that we may engage in faithful and transformative readings of the NT.

3. Looking Ahead

Every discussion of NT interpretation is grounded in a particular chronologically and socially determined moment, and the chapters collected here provide no exception to this axiom. The perspectives and approaches gathered here may seem sometimes to rest uncomfortably next to one another, taking as some do different points of departure and moving toward sometimes rival aims. That reflects the present historical moment, a time and place where methodological imperialism is passing from the scene and students of the NT (and indeed of literary texts in general) are free to bring with them all sorts of questions and interpretive strategies. How we have arrived at this state of affairs is helpfully surveyed by Anthony Thiselton in Chapter 2, which also considers the possibilities and challenges that all this brings to us.

One useful typology for the range of methods championed in NT interpretation today employs categories based on where the interpreter or interpretive method seeks to locate meaning: behind the text, in the text, or in front of the text.[3]

3. For a more sophisticated model, with interesting relevance for NT study, see M. H. Abrams, *The Mirror and the Lamp: Romantic Theory and the Critical Tradition*

Behind-the-text approaches to interpretation have occupied the ener-
gies of NT students for some two centuries, and are well represented in the
standard commentary series. Readings of this sort are generally interested
in such questions as: What did Paul intend to accomplish by writing
1 Corinthians? By what route did the tradition concerning John the Baptist
develop, and in what form(s) did it come to Luke's attention? Was Jesus
actually baptized by John, and if he was, what did that event mean historically? What did this text mean *then*, in its historical provenance and in the
world of the author? According to this way of conceiving the interpretive
task, the text of the Gospel of Luke or of 1 Corinthians is not itself the
primary focus of investigation; rather, the text is a *window* into the intent
of the author, into the history of traditions by which the materials collected
by the Evangelist were formed, or into the (possibly) historical events
reported by the text.

A number of the chapters that follow are explicitly concerned with such
questions, for example, Chapter 3 ("Traditio-Historical Criticism and the
Study of Jesus") and Chapter 4 ("Historical Criticism and Social-Scientific
Perspectives"). Others are concerned with the various ways in which the
literature and theology of the NT documents might be situated within their
first-century environments. The chapters on "The Relevance of Extra-
Canonical Jewish Texts" (5) and "The Relevance of Greco-Roman Literature
and Culture" (6) are oriented along these lines. Such historical questions
as those related to how words and modes of argument might have been
perceived (Chapters 8-9, 13), what literary forms were available to early
Christian writers and how they might have been employed to shape meaning (Chapter 10), and the use of Scripture in order to make sense of God's
work in recent history (Chapter 11) — these, too, are concerned with behind-the-text interpretation, even if not exclusively so.

In-the-text readings of the NT locate the fundamental interpretive enterprise not in the world behind the text, but in the text itself. Such readings
may sometimes grow out of a contemporary lack of interest in the historical
rootedness of the text in first-century exigencies and *may* grow out of
growing unease with the search for the ever elusive intent of the author.
More to the point, however, is the heightened interest on the text as cultural
product or artifact and as literature, with the consequence that the validity

---

(London/Oxford/New York: Oxford University, 1953) esp. 3-29; cf. the application of
Abrams's work to biblical studies in Tremper Longman III, *Literary Approaches to Biblical
Interpretation,* FCI 3 (Grand Rapids: Zondervan, 1987) 13-45.

of varying readings of a text is adjudicated not with reference to a reconstructed history behind the text but with reference to the evidence provided by the text itself. For example, the "world" of importance in these approaches is not so much "the world of Mediterranean antiquity in general" as "the world of Mediterranean antiquity as it has been actualized in this literary text." That is, "the (reconstructed) real world to which the text may witness" is highlighted over against "the world of the text itself."

Readings that accord privilege to the text in this way might benefit from reflection on the insights garnered through study of other texts from the time of the NT. Therefore, the historical questions emphasized in Chapters 5 and 6 may well be of interest here. More particularly, however, these more literary approaches are represented by Chapter 8 ("Linguistics"), Chapter 9 ("Discourse Analysis"), Chapter 10 ("Genre Analysis"), Chapter 11 ("The Use of the Old Testament by New Testament Writers"), Chapter 12 ("Narrative Criticism"), and Chapter 13 ("Rhetorical Criticism"). That several of these chapters (esp. 8-11 and 13) also appear under the heading of behind-the-text investigations suggests the degree to which these categories overlap and, indeed, how more literary-oriented explorations of NT texts are themselves interested in history.

The role of the reader or reading community also needs investigation as a vital component of the communicative act inherent in the analysis of literary texts. And this draws to our attention those approaches that focus more on meaning as it is located *in front of the text*. Such approaches highlight the reality that interpretation is not foremost the passing on of objective information from text to reader. Rather, different readers read differently. Different reading communities are situated in distinctive cultural settings and work from diverse presuppositions, and therefore "hear" or construe the same text differently. These concerns are represented by Chapter 14 ("Presuppositions in New Testament Study") and Chapter 15 ("The Reader in New Testament Study"), then explored further and illustrated in Chapter 16 ("Global Perspectives on New Testament Interpretation") and Chapter 17 ("Feminist Hermeneutics"). Other Chapters (e.g., 4, 9, 11, and 13) raise questions appropriate to reader-oriented approaches, too, again illuminating the lack of firm boundaries between the various perspectives on the aims of interpretation.

Foundational to any reading of the NT is the establishment of the text to be read, and this is the subject of Chapter 7 ("Textual Criticism"). Chapters 18-20 direct attention to some of the additional contexts in which NT texts are read — centered in the canon of the NT (and of the Bible as a whole) and in the believing community seeking to form its faith and life around wise and transformative readings of the NT.

Today, no one interpretive method can claim to provide the one authentic understanding of any given NT text. Instead, within the community of interpretation, all of these approaches (and more) will have their champions. Some readers will work to combine perspectives, some will find some approaches more appropriate to a given text than others, and some will find that in individual cases the approaches outlined here seem incompatible with one another. The purpose of juxtaposing these various methods and perspectives in this collection is not to suggest that a valid interpretation must somehow combine all of them (even if that were possible). Rather, it is to outline something of the range of questions that might be posed to particular texts and to demonstrate how different interpretive aims rely on different interpretive tools.

In order to display this variety, contributors to this volume have been asked to work with a handful of "set texts": Luke 3:1-20; John 4:1-42; 1 Cor 11:2-34; Jas 4:13–5:6; and Revelation 5. These texts represent distinct challenges to the interpreter, have their own histories of interpretation, and represent a range of literary forms or genres. No chapter treats all of these texts in detail, but each chapter on method[4] exhibits how that method might work itself out in practice with reference to one or more of these texts.

"Suggestions for Further Reading" are given at the close of most chapters for those desirous of pursuing further the various approaches discussed.

---

4. That is, all but chapters 2 and 14.

2. New Testament Interpretation in Historical Perspective

ANTHONY C. THISELTON

There have been two great paradigm shifts in NT interpretation.[1] The first, in the eighteenth century and later, was toward a single preoccupation with historical method, and the second, in the late twentieth century, has been toward a methodological pluralism.

1. The First Paradigm Shift: The Freedom of Historical Inquiry

If the beginnings of modern biblical criticism can be traced to any individual thinker or book, the strongest candidate would be Johann Salomo Semler and his four-volume *Treatise on the Free Investigation of the Canon*

1. Among standard treatments of the history of NT interpretation that as far as possible avoid a selective ideology or theological tendency see esp. Werner Kümmel, *The New Testament: The History of the Investigation of Its Problems* (Nashville: Abingdon, 1972/London: SCM, 1973); F. F. Bruce, "The History of New Testament Study," in *New Testament Interpretation,* ed. I. Howard Marshall (Exeter: Paternoster/Grand Rapids: Eerdmans, 1977) 21-59; Robert M. Grant with David Tracy, *A Short History of the Interpretation of the Bible,* 2d ed. (Philadelphia: Fortress, 1984); Stephen Neill and Tom Wright, *The Interpretation of the New Testament 1861-1986,* 2d ed. (Oxford/New York: Oxford University, 1988); and Barnabas Lindars, "The New Testament," in John W. Rogerson, Christopher Rowland, and Barnabas Lindars, *The Study and Use of the Bible* (Grand Rapids: Eerdmans/Basingstoke: Marshall Pickering, 1988) 229-397. Several essays in *The Cambridge History of the Bible,* esp. vol. 3, ed. Stanley L. Greenslade (Cambridge: Cambridge University, 1963) remain useful.

10

(1771-75).[2] Negatively, Semler reacted against the "pietistic sanctimonious-
ness" that he encountered in certain church circles. Positively, initially under
Siegmund Jakob Baumgarten at Halle, he was drawn into the liberating
experience of rationalist inquiry. Though both Baumgarten and Halle retained a relatively conservative stance and adherence to Lutheran theology,
it was in the Baumgarten home that Semler met Voltaire and Wolff. Voltaire
opposed any notion of privileged power or knowledge, whether in the form
of state hierarchy or church hierarchy. The "special" authority of Bible or
church was anathema to him, as it was to Rousseau.

It is essential to view both this attraction of rationalism and the call
for free inquiry *within their own historical context*. It is "only towards the
end of the eighteenth century" that we see the influence of John Locke
(1632-1704).[3] But his pointed observations that sheer intensity of personal
conviction offers no guarantee of truth must be understood against the
background of the religion and preaching of his own time. Against contemporary Quaker appeals that find the voice of God in the inner light of
the Spirit and Anglican sermons expounding Paul as if Paul were a legalistic
Anglican bishop of the period, Locke asserts: "Reason must be our last judge
and guide in everything."[4] "Religious enthusiasm takes away both reason
and revelation and substitutes in place of them the ungrounded fancies of
a man's own brain, and assumes them for a foundation both of opinion
and conduct."[5]

There is a parallel to Locke in the response of Thomas Hobbes (1588-
1679) to royalist appeals to Christian theology to support the divine right
of kings and to parliamentarian appeals to a doctrine of the priesthood of
all believers to support a more egalitarian political order. Locke and Hobbes
approached theological issues independently against a theologically or
ecclesially manipulative background. Locke produced a painstaking critical
apparatus of notes on Paul to serve the single "plain meaning," which was
to cut across all social and religious attempts to commandeer Pauline texts

2. *Abhandlung von freier Untersuchung des Canon*, 4 vols. (Halle: Hemmerde, 1771-
75). Important extracts in English are conveniently collected in Kümmel, *New Testament*,
62-69.

3. Henning Graf Reventlow, *The Authority of the Bible and the Rise of the Modern
World* (London: SCM/Philadelphia: Fortress, 1984) 247 (see 243-85 on Locke in his
historical context).

4. *An Essay Concerning Human Understanding* (1690; London: Collins, 1964)
IV.19.14, 432.

5. Locke, *Essay* IV.19.3, 429.

for manipulative purposes.[6] His motivation was not a "secular world view" as such; he was a religious man. The issue was not an assimilation of Christian faith into his empirical or rationalist philosophy. Too often Locke has been seen through the eyes of the ecclesiastical writers of his own time who formulated counterattacks against his use of common sense "reason" and his appeals to the "plain sense" of the Bible. But he appealed to reason, not against genuine faith as such, but against *manipulative* religion, whether from the political and religious left or from the political and religious right.

Semler was influenced by the English Deists and by Richard Simon and Johann Jacob Wettstein, but his view of Moravian pietism and Lutheran orthodoxy also had parallels with Locke's view of "enthusiasm" and Anglicanism.[7] Indeed these parallels give rise to two distinct strands in Semler: The constructive strand reflected Locke's concern to "free" biblical inquiry from the constraints of manipulative forces. Against those who sought to manipulate biblical material to support their prior ecclesial interests, Semler stressed the role of the NT as "a witness to its own time and not primarily as intended for today's reader."[8] Semler urged: "The most important factor in hermeneutical skill is that one both know the linguistic range of the Bible quite surely and exactly, and also distinguish the historical circumstances of a biblical discourse and be able to reconstruct them."[9] The more negative strand in Semler's thinking, which stood closer to Deism, made certain assumptions about the nature of divine activity in the world (or its absence from the world) on the basis of the problematic Deist maxims, which were themselves in no way value-neutral.

This leads to an ambivalence in Semler's desire to free all historical inquiry from issues of theology and doctrine.[10] His rationalism combines a positive corrective against manipulation, with which we may sympathize, with a negative concession to Deist or a-theistic worldviews that make illusory claims to be value-neutral or "objective." He argued against theo-

6. Cf. Reventlow's comment concerning "the different Locke" of *The Reasonableness of Christianity,* in which "the most amazing thing is the comprehensive knowledge of the New Testament that he shows in the detailed arguments for his central thesis: the philosopher has been replaced by an exegete who is quite remarkable by the standards of his time" (Reventlow, *Authority,* 259).

7. Cf. Kümmel, *New Testament,* 62-65; Lindars, "The New Testament," 327.

8. Kümmel, *New Testament,* 65.

9. ET in Kümmel, *New Testament,* 66.

10. Cf. John C. O'Neill, *The Bible's Authority: A Portrait Gallery of Thinkers from Lessing to Bultmann* (Edinburgh: Clark, 1991) 39-53.

logical interests that might impede "free inquiry," and he also effectively set aside any practical belief in biblical inspiration and dismissed any possible relevance to the present of extensive biblical passages and materials. If the first strand in his thinking might be viewed as a legitimate reaction in a specific sociotheological context, the second may perhaps be viewed as an extension of this methodological reaction into an a-theological doctrine or worldview. If the first concern is that theology should neither constrain nor distort historical inquiry, the second seems to suggest that theology retains no role at all in hermeneutics, as if to imply that a postivist-causal account remains value-neutral.

As Semler's approach began to become habituated into what amounted to a tradition, the crucial distinction between these two strands steadily fell from sight. The very success and acceptance of a large segment of Semler's conclusions facilitated this process. In this respect his work, by comparison, virtually placed in the shade that of his near contemporary Johann August Ernesti of Leipzig (1707-81). Ernesti also believed in freedom of historical inquiry and in the importance of liberating NT origins and exegesis from eighteenth-century ecclesial assumptions. But he retained a strong theological belief in the unique authority and special inspiration of the NT and remained unwilling to leave theology out of the picture in every aspect of NT interpretation.

2. The Quest for Freedom Ends in Constraint: The Historical Method Becomes Institutionalized into a Universal Paradigm

The work of several major figures established Semler's preoccupation with historical inquiry on a firm and unshakeable footing for some two hundred years. Semler's contemporary Johann David Michaelis (1717-91), who like Semler had been Baumgarten's student at Halle, had also studied in England when the legacy of Deism still held considerable sway and when Robert Lowth was preparing his work *On the Sacred Poetry of the Hebrews*, examining biblical poetry as a literary form. In 1750, as a professor at the newly founded University of Göttingen, Michaelis published his *Introduction to the Divine Scriptures of the New Covenant*, which formed part of a multi-volume "Introduction" to biblical literature. His *Introduction to the Old Testament* subsumed within it Richard Simon's earlier pioneering work on source criticism. The fourth edition of Michaelis's *Introduction to the New*

Testament (1788) constituted, arguably, the first of the genre of modern studies that from the late eighteenth century have usually been published under the same title. In this work Michaelis examined the origins, date, authorship, purpose, and text history of each book of the NT. In the words of Edgar Krentz, with the 1788 fourth edition "a new discipline was born, Introduction to the Old/New Testament."[11]

If Semler's historical approach in his work of 1771-75 was critically confirmed and consolidated in Michaelis's *Introduction,* this "historical paradigm" underwent further consolidation and development in the work of Semler's pupil Johann Jakob Griesbach (1745-1812).[12] Two major advances are especially associated with Griesbach's name. First, in his work on textual criticism (1774-75), he developed Bengel's earlier classification of textual witnesses into three main families — Alexandrian, Western, and Constantinopolitan — acknowledging the superiority of the first two over the third. Second, in his *Synopsis Evangeliorum* of 1776, he attempted a new approach to what he appears to have been the first to term "the pattern of the 'Synoptic Gospels.'"

With the benefit of hindsight after nearly two centuries, it is arguable that Wilhelm M. L. de Wette (1780-1849) should be ranked together with Semler as the second key figure in the establishment and institutionalization of the so-called historical-critical methods of modern NT study. But for the sake of chronological accuracy brief mention should first be made of Hermann S. Reimarus (1694-1768), Gotthold E. Lessing (1729-81), Johann G. Herder (1744-1803), and Michaelis's pupil Joannes G. Eichhorn (1752-1827).

Reimarus's Wolfenbüttel *Fragments* (1774-78), published posthumously and anonymously through Lessing's initiative, not only approached the NT in a-theological historical terms, but also explicitly claimed that every hint of supernatural or other-worldly agency in the NT represented an addition imposed by sheer illusion. If the interpretation of NT data could be manipulated by ecclesial interests, these interests included not only those of eighteenth-century pietism or orthodoxy, but also those of the earliest disciples and of the first-century Christian communities. The apos-

11. Edgar Krentz, *The Historical-Critical Method,* GBS (London: SPCK/Philadelphia: Fortress, 1975) 19.
12. Robert Morgan with John Barton, *Biblical Interpretation* (Oxford: Oxford University, 1988) 44-129, traces the emergence of this "historical paradigm"; Bruce ("History of NT Study," 38) regards Griesbach as marking the key point of transition "from the 'post-Reformation' to the 'modern' age of New Testament study."

tles and Evangelists themselves were manipulative.[13] They thought of Jesus "during his life-time and until his death as nothing other than a worldly ruler and savior." After his death they "changed their previous doctrine of his teaching and deeds." With the Evangelists they then formulated for the first time "the doctrine of a spiritual suffering savior of all mankind."[14]

On this new basis the earliest Christians created a new Jesus in the image of the apostolic church. They falsified fictitious accounts of his birth, ministry, miracles, death, resurrection, and ascension in the interest of promoting an early Christian theology of their own.[15] Reimarus does not hesitate to use the word "fraud" of the disciples and Evangelists.[16] Although the beginnings of modern ideological criticism of biblical texts most clearly go back to F. C. Baur, insofar as Reimarus sees the NT church as distorting the history of Jesus to sustain its own power interests, he perhaps offers a prior claim.

Lessing, in "On the Proof of the Spirit and Power" (1777), elaborated on the radically different truth-status of logically necessary propositions (such as the propositions of mathematics) and contingent statements of history, whose claims to truth can at best be no more than a matter of probability. But if no historical truth can be absolutely demonstrated, he said, "then nothing can be demonstrated by historical truths. That is, accidental truths of history can never become the proof of necessary truths of reason."[17] In itself this may seem to reverse the model of historical inquiry followed by Semler, Michaelis, Griesbach, and Reimarus by giving privilege not to history but to the nonhistorical truth of logic. But in practice it merely served to confirm the impossibility of gaining "certain" knowledge from documents whose truth could be established only by historical inquiry. It thus absolutized the growing divorce between history and theology. Between these two modes of inquiry Lessing's "ugly ditch" seemed to lie.[18]

---

13. Graham Shaw's recent arguments to this effect (*The Cost of Authority: Manipulation and Freedom in the New Testament* [London: SCM, 1983]), even though they are now put forward on the basis of literary theory, arguably reflect a view expounded by Reimarus on the basis of historical interpretation in the eighteenth century.

14. Hermann Samuel Reimarus, *Fragments*, ed. Charles H. Talbert (Philadelphia: Fortress 1970/London: SCM, 1971) 128-29.

15. Reimarus, *Fragments*, esp. I, §§10-13 (on the birth and title "Son of God"), §§22-23, 31-33; II, §§5-8 (on miracles and the cross), §§9-16 (on the falsification of the resurrection); and passim.

16. Reimarus, *Fragments*, e.g., p. 167.

17. G. E. Lessing, "The Proof of the Spirit and of Power," in *Lessing's Theological Writings*, ed. Henry Chadwick (London: Black/Stanford: Stanford University, 1956) 53.

18. In addition to Chadwick's edition and to other standard discussions, see espe-

Lessing also propounded a theory about the existence of a primitive Aramaic gospel source utilized by the authors of the canonical Gospels. This theory was taken up and developed by J. G. Herder (1796-97) and J. G. Eichhorn (1752-1827), though the principle can be traced back behind Lessing to Jean LeClerc (1657-1736), who originated it on the basis of a comment in Jerome.[19] It is arguable that in 1794 Eichhorn anticipated the notion of "Q" in some broad sense, since he urged that material peculiar to Matthew and Luke presupposes some common and distinctive source.[20] It may also be argued that Herder, in some preliminary measure, anticipated the later rise of redaction criticism. For he insisted — against earlier orthodox attempts to harmonize the Synoptic Gospels — that the interpreter should seek to understand what distinctive contribution each Evangelist made.[21]

It was left to de Wette to elucidate further distinctions of theological outlook and content within the NT itself and also (as is more widely appreciated today) within the OT. In the NT, he said, the Synoptic Gospels and a substantial portion of other writings (including James, 1-2 Peter, and Jude) reflect a broadly "Jewish" Christian theology; Hebrews and the Johannine writings represent an "Alexandrian" theological tradition; and the major Pauline letters constitute the third, "Pauline," strand. On one side de Wette's work thus set the stage for F. C. Baur in the next generation, with Baur's stress on conflicting trends within the NT. On the other side, de Wette saw a positive aesthetic and spiritual richness in theological diversity. Most notable, however, was the impact of this kind of critique on OT interpretation: De Wette "inaugurated a new era in critical Old Testament scholarship."[22] His work on the major differences between Kings and

---

cially Colin Brown, "Lessing and the Relevance of History," in his *Jesus in European Protestant Thought 1778-1860* (Grand Rapids: Baker, 1985, 1988) 16-29.

19. So John C. O'Neill, "The Study of the New Testament," in *Nineteenth Century Religious Thought in the West,* 3 vols., ed. Ninian Smart, John Clayton, Patrick Sherry, and Steven T. Katz (Cambridge: Cambridge University, 1985) 159 (cf. 143-78); Brown, *Jesus,* 174.

20. J. G. Eichhorn's "Concerning the First Three Gospels" (1794) is quoted in a brief extract in English together with extracts from his *Introduction to the New Testament* in Kümmel, *New Testament,* 78-79; on Eichhorn and Q, see further Brown, *Jesus,* 174-75.

21. Cf. Kümmel, *New Testament,* 79-83, which includes extracts from Herder on these issues.

22. John W. Rogerson, *Old Testament Criticism in the Nineteenth Century: England and Germany* (London: SPCK, 1984) 28.

Chronicles led to a new historical reconstruction of the development of Israelite history and religion and the composition of its sacred texts that constitutes an almost axiomatic account of a wide range of key institutional assumptions in twentieth-century OT scholarship.

De Wette's reconstructed history of Israelite religion and the development of NT theologies (plural) steadily became institutionalized as a basis for new theological evaluations. What began as a search for freedom from whatever might inhibit inquiry, namely church dogma or manipulative ecclesial interests, itself became transformed into a new institutional structure. So monolithic does this structure at times appear to have become that some writers speak, though questionably, of "*the* historical-critical method."[23]

Yet in today's intellectual climate, it is precisely this supposedly monolithic appearance of "modernity" — that is, of the period from the eighteenth century to roughly the end of the 1960s — that has come under attack. A hermeneutic of suspicion now seeks to dethrone all monolithic claims to represent a scientific "value-neutral" stance outside or above history, and it calls for the breakup of such hitherto respected institutional traditions of modernity into a new pluralism that reflects differing community interests.

3. The Second Paradigm Shift: The Reactive Quest for a Freedom of Pluralism and Attention to Textual Effects

The second great paradigm shift in NT interpretation can be illustrated by comparison of the content and scope of three books that are similar in format, one being the present volume. More than half of the eighteen essays in a 1977 collection of essays, *New Testament Interpretation*, edited by I. Howard Marshall and published in 1977,[24] address aspects of historical interpretation such as source criticism, form criticism, tradition history, and so forth. Only a relative handful take up areas such as demythologizing or the new hermeneutic. By contrast, the present volume addresses a wide variety of approaches, relatively few of which concern specific aspects of

---

23. So, e.g., Krentz, *The Historical-Critical Method*.

24. I. Howard Marshall, ed., *New Testament Interpretation: Essays on Principles and Methods* (Grand Rapids: Eerdmans/Exeter: Paternoster, 1977).

historical methods. In the same way, *Text and Interpretation: New Approaches in the Criticism of the New Testament*,[25] published in 1991, contains essays on semiotics, discourse analysis, narrative criticism, speech-act theory, reception theory, rhetorical criticism, deconstruction, sociology and sociohistory, ideology, feminism, liberation theology, and Marxism.

Evidence abounds everywhere in NT interpretation of a new search for a plurality of methods and approaches that are not tied to the historical model of critical inquiry that has characterized "modernity" in NT interpretation. The most succinct argument of this point can be found in Morgan's *Biblical Interpretation* (1988). He sums up the effects of the institutionalization of historical method into a general biblical hermeneutic:

> "Aims" and "methods" are clearly different, but the word "tasks" *(Aufgaben)*, which was prominent in German theoretical discussions, stands close to both. It led such brilliant scholars as Wrede and Wellhausen to slide from using historical methods in fulfilling historical tasks to the more questionable assumption that these are the only proper aims and goals of biblical scholarship.
>
> Historical study of the Bible thus gained a life of its own. . . . The step from using historical *methods* to defining the *aims* of biblical scholarship in exclusively historical terms set it at odds with the interests of most other readers and students of the Bible, for whom both historical and literary approaches are important only because they subserve religious (including theological) aims.[26]

As his argument proceeds, Morgan defends a pluralism of aims and interests as a legitimate deversification of the traditional agenda. He declares: "Texts, like dead men and women have no rights, no aims, no interests. They can be used in whatever way readers or interpreters choose."[27] He concludes: "The polemic implied here is directed only against the uncritical assumption that the inevitable prominence of historical *methods* in studying these ancient texts means that historical *aims* are the only ones that are respectable. Interpreters choose their aims."[28]

The notion that communities of readers "choose their aims" inevitably means that they also thereby choose their criteria of hermeneutical

---

25. Ed. P. J. Hartin and J. H. Petzer (Leiden: Brill).

26. Morgan, *Biblical Interpretation*, 171, some italics added.

27. Morgan, *Biblical Interpretation*, 7.

28. Morgan, *Biblical Interpretation*, 287, italics added in the second sentence.

"success," "edification," or "usefulness." But this hovers on the brink of the abyss of a postmodernist worldview, and it is not clear that Morgan wishes to step over the brink. He concedes that while "pluralism . . . allows scriptures to illuminate the great diversity of human experience," we do not want sheer anarchy; for "a Bible that can mean anything means nothing."[29]

It is commonplace today to use Paul Ricoeur's distinction between the historical processes that may lie "behind" a biblical text in terms of its background and origination and what occurs "in front of" the text in terms of the operative effects that it sets in motion in or for the reader, for the hearer, or for a community of readers and hearers.[30] This concern for effects is most explicit in speech-act theory and in reader-response criticism in literary theory. Morgan advocates what he terms "the literary paradigm" for bridging the gap between historical inquiry and religious concerns.[31] But theological interpretation also takes its place "in front of" the text if it reflects a perspective of listening, openness, and perhaps "consent," to use Peter Stuhlmacher's term. Indeed, as we have noted, it was precisely to eliminate theology that Semler saw the NT texts as almost exclusively witnesses to their own times rather than to ours. So the modern distinction between the history "behind" the text and interpretation "in front of" the text has a parallel already in the earlier paradigm shift of the eighteenth century.

Nevertheless as pre-Kantian rationalism gave way in the nineteenth century first to romanticism and then to post-Hegelian historical idealism, it became apparent that the unfolding of historically conditioned texts could no longer be credibly insulated from the historical process itself, which continues into the present to embrace present acts of interpretation. Past texts do more than witness objectively to brute "facts" that are past and over and done with. The legacy of Hegel left seeds of a notion of understanding that somehow enfolded interpreter and text, not as isolated

---

29. Morgan, *Biblical Interpretation*, 198, 13. I have discussed the details of Morgan's book and of his proposals in my "On Models and Methods: A Conversation with Robert Morgan," in *The Bible in Three Dimensions: Essays in Celebration of Forty Years of Biblical Studies in the University of Sheffield*, ed. David J. A. Clines, Stephen E. Fowl, and Stanley E. Porter, JSOTSS 87 (Sheffield: JSOT, 1990) 337-56; and more briefly in *New Horizons in Hermeneutics: The Theory and Practice of Transforming Biblical Reading* (London: HarperCollins/Grand Rapids: Zondervan, 1992) 57-58, 500-501.

30. Paul Ricoeur, *Hermeneutics and the Human Sciences* (Cambridge: Cambridge University, 1981) 142-44.

31. Morgan, *Biblical Interpretation*, 192-200, 214-63, and passim.

and unrelated elements, but as differentiated poles within an embracing dialectic.[32]

For David F. Strauss and other post-Hegelians it seemed worth asking whether Hegel's notion of preconceptual pictorial representations (*Vorstellungen*, not the critical philosophers' "concept," *Begriff*) might offer a "value" dimension that could re-present "facts" in such a way as to appear to clothe them with religious "value" for the present-day reader.[33] Parallels may be found between concerns of today about what occurs "in front of" the text and the categories that were thought to express the "value" pole in post-Kantian, post-Hegelian NT criticism of the nineteenth century.

A sense of due historical perspective can demonstrate the disastrous consequences of abstracting this "value" pole from serious concerns about history. Today, just as earlier, history is split apart from theology, and the Jesus of history from the Christ of faith.

4. Different Consequences for Theology of the Flight from History

4.1 Strauss

Strauss (1808-74) is a key example for our appreciation of the difficulties of this issue. On one side he seeks to strip away myths, which he attributes to theological evaluation rather than to historical reporting on the part of the earliest Christian communities. In this sense he opts for history and

32. Georg Wilhelm Friedrich Hegel, *Lectures on the Philosophy of Religion*, 3 vols. (ET; London: Kegan Paul, Trench, Trübner, 1895); cf. his *The Philosophy of History* (ET; London: Colonial, 1899); and *The Phenomenology of Mind*, 2d ed. (ET; London: Macmillan, 1931). For the contrast between his hermeneutical "integration" and Schleiermacher's more "reconstructive" approach, together with their common areas of overlap, which are usually underestimated, see James O. Duke, *The Prospects for Theological Hermeneutics: Hegel Versus Schleiermacher* (Ph.D. Diss., Vanderbilt University, 1975).

33. See Hegel, *Lectures on the Philosophy of Religion;* and the expositions of the notion in Malcolm Clark, *Logic and System: A Study of the Transition from "Vorstellung" to Thought in the Philosophy of Hegel* (The Hague: Nijhoff, 1971); and "Meaning and Language in Hegel's Philosophy," *Revue Philosophique de Louvain* 58 (1960) 557-78. More briefly, see Peter C. Hodgson, "Hegel," in *Nineteenth Century Religious Thought in West* (n. 19 above) 1:81-121, esp. 102-5; and in summary Alister McGrath, *The Making of Modern German Christology* (Oxford: Blackwell, 1986) 32-35; and John Macquarrie, *Jesus Christ in Modern Thought* (London: SCM/Philadelphia: Trinity, 1990) 212-24.

historical reconstruction. The texts serve as a vehicle for a reconstruction of the historical Jesus, who is revealed as such only when all "myth" has been stripped away. On the other side, however, Strauss locates the source of Christian theological truth not in the history of Jesus but in the early church's constructs of theology, which have laid a mythological frame over a historical core.[34] In the terminology of later interpreters, including Martin Kähler and Rudolf Bultmann, the real Christ is not the "so-called historical Jesus" but the Christ who is proclaimed in the present through some modality other than that of rational inquiry, such as the risk of faith.[35] History and faith are split apart.

The serious consequences and untenability of such an approach can be fully grasped only when we recall in detail how they unfolded in the life, career, and changing thought of Strauss himself. He was a pupil of F. C. Baur at Tübingen, though his eagerness to rush into print was such that most of his influential work was published before that of Baur. In his undergraduate days Strauss had been encouraged by Baur to read Schleiermacher, whose attempt to offer a "humanist" or "non-supernatural" christology initially impressed him. But his studies of Kant and then more especially of Hegel, including Hegel's *Phenomenology of Mind,* made a deeper and more lasting impression on him.

Strauss published his massive two-volume life of Jesus at the age of twenty-six in 1835, with a second, virtually unchanged, edition in 1836. In the face of considerable criticism he offered some concessions in a third edition of 1838, but returned to his earlier views in the fourth edition of 1840, which was translated into English by George Eliot as *The Life of Jesus Critically Examined* (1846). A fifth edition appeared in 1864, which was virtually a new study and was later translated into English as *A New Life of Jesus.* The most important category used by Strauss was arguably Hegel's careful distinction between the anthropomorphic imagery of religion, which at best relies on modes of "representing" spiritual realities through pictorial model or image *(Vorstellung),* and the critical "historical reason" of the philosopher, who understands radical historical finitude within his-

34. David F. Strauss, *The Life of Jesus Critically Examined* (ET; London: SCM, 1973); cf. esp. Macquarrie, *Jesus Christ,* 224-30; Kümmel, *New Testament,* 120-33; Brown, *Jesus,* 183-204; Claude Welch, *Protestant Thought in the Nineteenth Century,* 2 vols. (New Haven: Yale University, 1972) 1:147-54; and Hans Frei, "David Friedrich Strauss," in *Nineteenth Century Religious Thought in the West* (see n. 19 above) 1:215-60.

35. Martin Kähler, *The So-Called Historical Jesus and the Historic, Biblical Christ,* ed. Carl E. Braaten (Philadelphia: Fortress, 1964) esp. 57, 62, 94-97.

tory but can also (*pace* Kierkegaard) transcend this through *conceptual abstraction (Begriff)*. *Begriff* demands a level of logical and historical abstraction, distance, and sophistication unthinkable for the religious communities and writers of the first century. "By 'myth' Strauss meant the expression of an Idea in the form of a historical account."[36]

Anticipating much in twentieth-century debates, Strauss distinguished "pure" myths, that is, the apparatus of messianic ideas and expectations that already lay fully to hand in Judaism, from "evangelical" myths, which reflected the impression made by Jesus on the early Christian community and are expressed in narrative about Jesus rather than in confessional evaluations of Jesus as Christ. Here virtually all the basic tools of the "Jesus of history versus Christ of faith" debate are available from Strauss or even Kant, until the beginnings of a healing of the Kantian breach in Pannenberg and some more recent writers.

In Strauss's view a (supposedly) value-neutral reading of the history of Jesus makes no claim and gives no description of any redemptive significance. The notion of redemptive significance emerged as the early communities begin to conflate the pure myths of messianic expectation in Judaism with narrative accounts of Jesus' ministry and death. Evangelical myths became absorbed into the narrative account. Thus Strauss partly anticipates the principle in Bultmann's *History of the Synoptic Tradition* and in similar writings that any ascriptions to Jesus of messiahship or of prediction of the cross are *vaticinia post eventum*, "read back" into the history of Jesus by the later Christian community. Strauss also partly anticipates aspects of Bultmann's call for demythologizing the kerygma in his own demand to dehistoricize the spiritual.[37] Dehistoricizing in Strauss anticipates (although for different philosophical and theological reasons) deobjectifying in Bultmann.

36. Welch, *Protestant Thought*, 148. This interpretation is not only clear from Strauss's work but is also corroborated by Macquarrie, Kümmel, Brown, and Frei (cited in n. 34); and by McGrath, *Modern German Christology*, 35-38.

37. Rudolf Bultmann, *The History of the Synoptic Tradition* (ET; Oxford: Blackwell, 1963); *idem, Jesus Christ and Mythology* (London: SCM, 1960); *idem*, "New Testament and Mythology," in H.-W. Bartsch, ed., *Kerygma and Myth* (London: SPCK/New York: Harper, 1961) 1-44. On the link between Strauss and Bultmann, see James D. G. Dunn, "Demythologizing — The Problem of Myth in the New Testament," in *New Testament Interpretation* (see n. 1 above) 285-307; and on the connection between Bultmann's attitude to history and his whole hermeneutical program, see Anthony C. Thiselton, *The Two Horizons: New Testament Hermeneutics and Philosophical Description* (Grand Rapids: Eerdmans/Carlisle: Paternoster, 1980, 1993) 205-92.

The consequences of all this for christology have been fatal. In the conclusion of his fourth edition Strauss concedes this and asserts: "This is the key to the whole of Christology. . . . We place instead of an individual an idea, but an idea that exists in reality, and not a Kantian unreal one."[38] Yet this is not a "Christ" of corporate Christian experience, one who bears some interactive relation or even "loose fit" (a term that came into use later in English theology) with the Jesus of history. A year after the fifth edition (or second version) of his *Life of Jesus* (1864), Strauss explicitly attacked even Schleiermacher's christology as suggesting too close a relation between historical inquiry and ecclesial theology. He regarded Schleiermacher's major work, *The Christian Faith*, as the last great work of ecclesial theology.

A curious contradiction arose, of which Strauss became increasingly aware and which made him increasingly uncomfortable. In his "Concluding Dissertation" to the *Life of Jesus*, Strauss "claims that faith can survive unscathed the collapse of the historical record," even if to a greater or lesser extent he may perhaps partly be "speaking tongue in cheek."[39] Certainly his assessment of the results of historical reconstruction was not entirely unlike that of Reimarus. Like Reimarus he was prepared to see Jesus as a historical figure who opposed the legalism of Jewish Pharisaism, and like Reimarus he saw the theological and supernatural frame implied by the Gospels as no more than a "reading back" of OT prophecies and messianic expectations. But in the early stages of his work, as Kümmel observes, Strauss saw himself as "free" to reach such conclusions because on philosophical grounds he could "restore the dogmatic significance" of the eternal truth of faith in Christ *as idea*.[40] Here again, the ghost of Lessing hovers in the background, aided by a selective interpretation of Kantian dualism and Hegel's philosophies of history and language.

Nevertheless as time passed, Strauss acknowledged with increasing openness that he had cut the ground out from under the possibility of authentic Christian faith, in any meaningful or adequate sense of the term. It is instructive to compare the verdicts of three very different writers on this situation. O'Neill recognizes that Strauss abandoned Christian faith and opted for "a new faith based on Darwin's principle of the struggle for life, with literature and the music of Mozart and Beethoven replacing the church. . . . There is something refreshingly honest and open about

38. Strauss, *Life of Jesus*, §149 (780).
39. Macquarrie, *Jesus Christ*, 229.
40. Kümmel, *New Testament*, 121.

Strauss."[41] This is what attracted George Eliot in her dislike of ecclesial pietism. Macquarrie, by contrast, writes of "the tragedy" that characterizes "a theologian who has become an unbeliever: for all to behold and without denying it."[42] Karl Barth offers a harsher verdict: Strauss was driven largely by ambition, lack of humility, and a desire to manipulate theology through philosophy; he was "not a tragic figure . . . there was no tragic quality in him." And he was not a historian of the competence of even F. C. Baur.

> He was much more concerned, . . . upon his own confession, with the dream-image of his own existence than with the historical material as such. "I am not a historian: with me everything has proceeeded from dogmatic (or rather anti-dogmatic) concerns." . . . All Strauss was able to do, was to steer the ship of dogmatics carefully on to the rocks of a somewhat facile confrontation with Spinoza's and Hegel's philosophy and have it founder there with all hands.[43]

Whatever our own verdict, Strauss stands as a reminder of what is likely to occur if historical inquiry is divorced from theology or if biblical texts are divorced from history. If texts are regarded as mere "constructs" of early believing communities of readers designed only to project "worlds" for faith regardless of whether they are interwoven with any extralinguistic states of affairs, the so-called "Christ of faith" collapses, as if the Jesus of history had little or nothing to do with this construct.

4.2 Kähler and Bultmann

We do not suggest that the path taken by Strauss must end this way for every NT interpreter that follows it. O'Neill is probably correct in his observation that Strauss was simply more honest than most in working out the consequences of disengaging theology or "value" from supposedly value-neutral historical inquiry about empirical data. Indeed in the line of development that moves through Kähler (1835-1912) to Bultmann (1884-1976), the emphasis on "the preached Christ" (Kähler) or on Jesus as "the proclaimed" rather than the historical "proclaimer" (Bultmann) acquires special privilege in the interests of a pietistic or kerygmatic theology. Kähler

41. O'Neill, The Bible's Authority, 115.
42. Macquarrie, Jesus Christ, 228.
43. Karl Barth, Protestant Theology in the Nineteenth Century (ET; London: SCM, 1972) 543, 544-45; see 542-45.

and Bultmann both similarly seek to disengage the eventful and kerygmatic word "in front of" the text from the contingencies and "objectifying" consequences that characterize exploration "behind" the text.

In Kähler's view, any emphasis on critical historical reconstruction demands an "expert," and this requirement threatens to replace the rejected privilege of church papacy with a new papacy of critical scholarship. Both papacies place the ordinary reader at a distance from the text. Hence, anticipating Schweitzer and Bultmann, Kähler begins his work, titled *The So-Called Historical Jesus and the Historic, Biblical Christ* (1892), with this declaration: *"The historical Jesus of modern authors conceals from us the living Christ."* He goes on to say: "I regard the entire life-of-Jesus movement as a blind alley."[44] The link with Bultmann's later Lutheran concerns is made clear by Paul Tillich's Foreword to the English translation: "Kähler was a strictly systematic thinker who developed his ideas under the principle of the Reformers — 'justification through faith by grace.' "[45]

The basis for Bultmann's distinctive approach to the relation between "history" and "faith" arises still more explicitly from a deep suspicion of the "objective" or "descriptive" as somehow undermining a genuinely Pauline or Lutheran notion of faith. It risks, that is, transposing faith into observation or reason and turning Jesus and God into mere "objects" within a Kantian (or more strictly, neo-Kantian) conceptual world of human categories and constructs. The Jesus of historical "reconstructions" is precisely that: a humanly achieved construct, an intellectual "work," parallel to a moral "work." Hence Bultmann observes: "Our radical attempt to demythologize the New Testament," that is, to deobjectify it, "is in fact a perfect parallel to St Paul's and Luther's doctrine of justification by faith alone apart from the works of the Law," that is, justification apart from generalizing categories that produce constructs. "Like the doctrine of justification it destroys every false security," that is, all trust in historical probability.[46] Therefore Jesus is not a "world phenomenon" who can be part of "a mere reckoning with the objects in the world," not a "what" for Paul, but only "the that."[47] Similarly, God also, is not part of "a system of cognitions (universal truths) . . . ," because, if that were the case, "God would be objectively given; and knowledge of that *given object* would be accessible to

44. Kähler, *The So-Called Historical Jesus,* 43, 46.
45. Paul Tillich, Foreword to Kähler's *The So-Called Historical Jesus,* xi.
46. Bultmann, "Bultmann Replies to His Critics," in *Kerygma and Myth,* 210-11.
47. Rudolf Bultmann, *Faith and Understanding* (ET; London: SCM, 1969) 238.

us and could be achieved at will."[48] Christology arises not from reflection on the Jesus of history, but "because he [Christ] helps me."[49]

All this seeks to move from "behind" the NT to take up a position "in front of" the text — but now in the name of a pietist quasi-Lutheran faith. The NT, Bultmann concludes at the end of his *Theology of the New Testament,* may be regarded for certain purposes as "sources" to be "interrogated" by the historian "in order to reconstruct a picture of primitive Christianity as a phenomenon of the historical past."[50] But the more important task is to allow reconstruction to stand "in the service of the interpretation of the New Testament writings under the presupposition that they have *something to say to the present.*"[51]

4.3 The Appeal to Literary Methods

Strauss disengaged myth from history in a way that led him toward a collapse of Christian faith. Kähler and Bultmann disengaged proclamation "in front of" the text from history "behind the text," supposedly to make room for more authentic faith in the bare word of divine address. But in the end, they, along with Strauss, withdrew theology and faith from the public domain of debatable inquiry. They can appeal only to the kind of principle concerning which Locke complained that sheer intensity of conviction becomes indistinguishable for the critical inquirer from mere human fancy or, as we would more likely say today, from human interest.

This suggests that we should regard as ambivalent Morgan's optimistic belief that a "switch" from historical to literary paradigms as such will assist dialogue between biblical texts and religious faith. Morgan is entirely right to argue, negatively, that the impact of texts for faith necessarily becomes suppressed and sterile when an institutionalized paradigm of modern critical study subsumes historical method within the imperializing and institutionalized goal of historical aim alone. Many diverse hermeneutical aims may be legitimate. Those, however, that serve Christian faith embrace and include historical methods for certain genres of biblical texts, whether or

---

48. Rudolf Bultmann, "What Does It Mean to Speak of God?" in *Faith and Understanding,* 60.

49. Rudolf Bultmann, *Essays Philosophical and Theological* (London: SCM, 1955) 280.

50. Rudolf Bultmann, *Theology of the New Testament,* 2 vols. (London: SCM, 1955) 2:251.

51. Bultmann, *Theology,* 2:251, italics added.

not some genres (for example, consciously fictional narrative worlds or functional uses of symbols) may not in every case necessitate even historical method.

Nevertheless, the appeal to literary methods and concerns becomes no less capable of swallowing up the whole hermeneutical enterprise into a study of intralinguistic relations and semiotic forces generated by intertextuality alone than historical method has proved itself capable time and time again of similarly subsuming everything under historical aims alone. The startling parallel between Strauss and Bultmann shows that this reduction can be connected equally with quasi-secular or quasi-pietist stances. Both spring from a valid recognition that a hermeneutics preoccupied only with what lies "behind the text" is not enough. Hence the current concern is to elaborate a variety of approaches that place emphasis on the operative effects that the text sets in motion in front of it. All this is to the good, *provided that interpreters do not turn their backs on traditional questions about history.*

Again, the new hermeneutical pluralism represented by Morgan needs to be placed in the historical perspective under which we can view, with hindsight, the initial gains and subsequent losses, first, of the freedom won by Semler and others from the constraints and manipulations of purely ecclesial interests, and, second, of the awareness of Strauss and of Bultmann and others concerning the limits of historical inquiry alone.

5. Calls for a More Integrated Approach: Bypassing "Failed Conversations of Yesterday"

Several recent writers have urged the importance of a more integrated approach. At the level of a basic textbook W. Randolph Tate has produced a volume whose title speaks for itself: *Biblical Interpretation: An Integrated Approach.*[52] Mere historical interpretation views NT texts as sources of information, and literary reading alone reflects a concern for textual productivity. But Tate rightly observes that a "model of *communication* sets the agenda for our discussion."[53] I have argued at length elsewhere that while a minority of biblical texts may be primarily "productive," most are *communicative* or "transmissive," whether or not they also include a productive dimension.[54]

52. Peabody: Hendrickson, 1991.
53. Tate, *Biblical Interpretation,* xx (italics added).
54. Thiselton, *New Horizons,* 20, 41, 501, 525-26, 544, 583-85. The work of Umberto

Tate's approach coheres with Morgan's insofar as he wishes (rightly) to "advocate the method that most nearly correlates with the interpretive aims."[55] But he recognizes the need for a multi-angled or integrated set of methods since "text-centered methods tend to treat the text as a literary artifact," "reader-centered methods" encourage "interaction between the reader and the text . . . in a dialogue." But in addition to asking "what actually takes place" when a text is read, an interpreter needs to ask about the situation of the writer who produced the text: "The locus of meaning is not to be found exclusively in . . . any two of the worlds, but in the interplay between all three worlds. . . ."[56]

A second writer, one whose contribution is more substantial, more detailed, and more creative, is N. T. Wright.[57] Wright fully acknowledges not only the limitations of the institutionalized historical paradigms of "modernity," but also the tendency of flirtations with postmodernism to slide into hermeneutical anarchy. He traces "the natural hostility between 'history' and 'theology' " that has all too often institutionalized a "split . . . now enshrined in the rubrics of many a university syllabus."[58] In its place, he outlines a careful path that allows for the rootedness of NT texts in the historical life-worlds of Jesus and of the early Christian communities, but also avoids, on one side, the pseudo-objectivism and institutional constraints of the paradigms and methods of "modern" NT interpretation and, on the other side, the anarchic pluralism of so-called postmodernist approaches that collapse authors into texts, texts into readers, and theological content into the goals and interests that drive the aims of modern readers.

We find a third example in the work of Peter Stuhlmacher, who expresses no less disquiet over attempts to reinstate a supposed autonomy of historical exegesis as a first-stage project than does Wright.[59] While it is

---

Eco, partly following Jurij Lotman, becomes important in this context. See Eco, *Semiotics and the Philosophy of Language* (London: Macmillan, 1984) 68-86; cf. also his earlier work, *The Role of the Reader: Explorations in the Semiotics of Texts* (London: Hutchinson, 1981); Jurij Lotman, *The Structure of the Artistic Text* (Ann Arbor: University of Michigan, 1977); and Thiselton, *New Horizons*, 524-29.

55. Tate, *Biblical Interpretation*, 205.

56. Tate, *Biblical Interpretation*, 205, xx.

57. In *The New Testament and the People of God* (Minneapolis: Fortress/London: SPCK, 1992), the first volume of a five-volume enterprise on Christian origins and the question of God.

58. Wright, *New Testament*, 13.

59. Peter Stuhlmacher, *Biblische Theologie des Neuen Testaments. Band I: Grundlegung von Jesus zu Paulus* (Göttingen: Vandenhoeck und Ruprecht, 1992) 33-34.

undeniably possible to approach the NT within a history-of-religions frame, Stuhlmacher insists, the interpreter will with that approach lose the very dimension of kerygmatic address and claim that genuinely arises from the nature of the NT texts. To miss that is to miss a key part of what these writings historically were and authentically are. With Stuhlmacher's earlier work it is perhaps natural also to call attention to that of Ferdinand Hahn.[60] Both writers call for greater openness and dialogue between historical exegesis and the concerns of systematic theology.

Similarly, Karl Josef Kuschel not only laments the breakdown of dialogue between historical exegetes dealing with the historical Jesus and systematic theologians dealing with christology, but also describes Lessing's legacy of "a gulf between the language of the New Testament and the language of dogmatics" as "the problem of all modern theology. How is it possible to get from historical statements about Jesus Christ to statements about his metaphysical being that are in turn only historical statements by human beings?"[61] Kuschel views the agenda set up by Lessing and Kant and addressed by Harnack, Barth, and Bultmann as "Failed Conversations of Yesterday."[62]

This brings us to the very heart of the issue: Kuschel concludes that the only kind of conversation that can avoid the same failure is one that "represents a questioning of men and women that is critical of modernity: this illusion of autonomy, the plausibilities they create for themselves, their immanentist rationality."[63]

I have argued elsewhere that we can identify some important similarities, but also some critical differences, between premodern interpretation in the ancient and medieval periods and certain current trends, especially in postmodernist approaches to texts.[64] First and foremost among the

60. Peter Stuhlmacher, *Von Verstehen des Neuen Testaments: Eine Hermeneutik* (Göttingen: Vandenhoeck und Ruprecht, 1979); *idem, Historical Criticism and Theological Interpretation of Scripture: Towards a Hermeneutic of Consent* (Philadelphia: Fortress, 1977); *idem,* "Thesen zur Methodologie gegenwärtiger Exegese," in *Schriftauslegung auf dem Wege zur biblischen Theologie* (Göttingen: Vandenhoeck und Ruprecht, 1975); and Ferdinand Hahn, *Historical Investigation and New Testament Faith: Two Essays* (Philadelphia: Fortress, 1983).

61. Karl Josef Kuschel, *Born before All Time? The Dispute over Christ's Origin* (London: SCM, 1992) 30.

62. Kuschel, *Born before All Time?*, 35-176.

63. Kuschel, *Born before All Time?*, 488.

64. Thiselton, *New Horizons*, 142-48.

similarities, whereas the emphasis in modern critical methods lies on the individual reader (especially the individual interpreter or scholar, but also in most cases the individual biblical editor or writer), in postmodern approaches we can detect a strong affinity with the emphasis in the patristic period and in medieval tradition on the role of a community of readers. In negative terms, especially when a postmodernist account of the individual conscious self becomes allied with axioms in psychoanalysis since Freud, the opaqueness of the individual self and its conscious modes becomes problematic as a point of departure for hermeneutical inquiry. Psychoanalytical literary theory, partly that of Julia Kristeva but more especially of Jacques Lacan, exemplify this point.[65]

The patristic writers, especially Irenaeus, stressed the continuity of a given community of readers in time and place as a frame for interpretation that comes to constitute a tradition. Irenaeus was fully aware that an iconoclasm of tradition that discards what is inherited from predecessors in the name of the individual may appear superficially to offer a point of departure *de novo,* but in practice it constitutes only a willful and misguided rejection of "the very method of discovery," which builds on developing understanding.[66] As has been observed in another context, a pigmy standing on the shoulders of a giant can see more than one who begins at ground level. But this is extremely close to Hans-Georg Gadamer's argument when he rejects the starting point of Descartes as futile and illusory and calls for "the re-habilitation of authority and tradition."[67] Such an appeal, Gadamer insists, is not contrary to reason, as if reason and tradition could be opposed, as they were in the Enlightenment. It rests on "an act of reason itself that, aware of its own limitations, accepts that others have better understanding."[68]

This approach differs fundamentally from the more simplistic notion of conceiving "objectivity" by shaking off "tradition" and by according privilege to the isolated consciousness of the individual as a solitary inquiring subject. "Critical" understanding does not entail discarding cumulative wisdom and attempting to begin *de novo.* Even Descartes saw that such a

65. Julia Kristeva, *In the Beginning Was Love: Psychoanalysis and Faith* (New York: Columbia University, 1987); and *The Kristeva Reader,* ed. Toril Moi (New York: Columbia University, 1986); Jacques Lacan, *The Four Fundamental Concepts of Psychoanalysis* (London: Penguin, 1979).

66. Irenaeus *Adversus Haereses* 2.27.

67. Hans-Georg Gadamer, *Truth and Method* (New York: Crossroad, 1982) 245-58.

68. Gadamer, *Truth and Method,* 248.

method had limited application, remaining more relevant to mathematics, sciences, and ahistorical logic (*pace* Hegel) than to issues of Christian faith. Ricoeur has attacked the individualism of Descartes and his isolated "consciousness" as incompatible with hermeneutics. It merely perpetuates, again, "failed conversations of yesterday," to borrow Kuschel's phrase.[69]

6. The Need for a More Subtle Hermeneutic of the History of Interpretation: A Warning against Decontextualized Generalizations

Biblical hermeneutics offers increasingly subtle and nuanced perspectives for the interpretation of the NT. But in contrast many accounts of historical theology, including narrative accounts of the history of NT interpretation, often categorize writers and trends under crude stereotypes that ignore the hermeneutical particularities of the kind that might have been brought into play if the interpreter had been seeking to understand NT texts rather than Schleiermacher, Semler, or other interpreters of the NT. These stereotypes usually depend on decontextualizing a writer of the past from the writer's own agenda and recontextualizing the writer in terms of our own current agenda. On this basis a narrative becomes selective and distorted. From time to time, for example, certain conservative writers ascribe "the" historical-critical method to "the rise of rationalism" or to "the method of Descartes," while more liberal or radical scholars ascribe "modern biblical criticism" simply to freedom from ecclesial dogma.

Each diagnosis is as simplistic and misleading as the other. But each derives plausibility and force from the fact that every explanatory hypothesis seems to fit certain selected thinkers well enough but does not necessarily account for the shape of some supposed overarching movement or trend of which these thinkers are said to be examples.

Klaus Scholder and Edgar Krentz are among those who attribute the initial momentum of "*the* historical-critical method" to the role of meth-

---

69. A firm contrast can be drawn between Gadamer's notion of hermeneutical *freedom* as *absence of manipulation* (which emerges first in his earlier studies of Plato) and the *anarchic "freedom" of postmodern theories* of meaning as necessarily indeterminate, plural, and produced by *manipulative community interests.* I hope to elaborate these issues in the *Scottish Journal of Theology Lectures* (University of Aberdeen, 1994), probably to be published under the title *Theology, Meaning, and Truth* (Edinburgh: Clark).

odological doubt in the rationalist philosophy of Descartes.[70] Scholder describes this method as a commitment "never to accept anything as true that I did not know to be evidently so. . . . Reason has nothing but itself on which it can rely."[71] This methodological principle, which Descartes actually formulated as a method relevant to the sciences, is thus associated with Locke's maxim that "reason must be our last judge and guide in everything."[72] But we have noted that Locke addresses a different social context. He remains troubled by the special pleading with which Quaker enthusiasts and Anglican bishops made the NT no more than a manipulative mouthpiece for their own convictions. To speak airily in both cases of the same "rationalism" not only violates hermeneutics but all too readily becomes recontextualized into a modern agenda in which "reason" appears as an ally of secularism and unbelief. The caricature facilitates the very opposition between "reason" and "tradition" that Gadamer exposes as superficial and as often geared too narrowly to issues of the Enlightenment.

6.1 Schleiermacher

Some writers quite remarkably not only see this "rationalism" in the eighteenth century, which indeed did become obsessively over-concerned with "reason," but also extend it into the first half of the nineteenth century, when romanticism began to overtake rationalism and when Kant's three *Critiques* had exposed devastating flaws in pre-Kantian assumptions about reason. Thus even Bruce, otherwise always meticulous and precise, attributes the principle of interpreting the NT like any other set of human documents, held by Schleiermacher (1768-1834), as arising "because he could not free himself from a basic rationalism."[73] But few thinkers have done more than Schleiermacher to call into question the priority of reason over an immediacy of relationship with God.

For Schleiermacher, doctrine and ideas remain derivative from experience rather than primary. He suspects "supernatural" elements in the NT, but not because he is a rationalist. Quite the reverse: Like Herder and the great romanticist theorists of the era, he sees the NT as a product or residue

70. Klaus Scholder, *The Birth of Modern Critical Theology: Origins and Problems of Biblical Criticism in the Seventeenth Century* (London: SCM/Philadelphia: Trinity, 1990) 108-32, esp. 112-21; Krentz, *The Historical-Critical Method*, 10-14.

71. Scholder, *The Birth of Modern Critical Theology*, 112.

72. Locke, *Essay* IV.19.14.

73. Bruce, "History of NT Study," 40.

of a formerly creative and living vision, which transcended rational thought. The interpreter needs to pierce through "behind" this textual residue in order to recapture the fire of living experience that gave rise to the text. For this, the interpersonal "feminine" quality of divinatory perception of a whole remains fundamental.[74] The "rational" dimension comes into its own mainly as a checking process of comparative critical judgments that treat language and history as human systems of vocabulary, grammar, genre, sequence, and so forth. But as one who appreciated the force of Kant's transcendental critique of reason, this rational dimension belonged for Schleiermacher to the task of making understanding the text of the NT possible as a creative process of interpretation rather than as a mere reproduction of the views of earlier interpreters.[75]

Schleiermacher's aims and concerns are so distinctive and creative that we cannot simply regard him as a milestone along the road of "rationalist criticism" without doing hermeneutical violence to his work. Moreover, to see Schleiermacher merely as an example of "historical" or "genetic" interpretation is to miss the point entirely. He was long ahead of his time in seeing that whether we attend to the situation *behind* the text or to the *effects* that it sets in motion, and whether we concern ourselves with language-system or language-utterance, remains entirely a matter of hermeneutical strategy, one that depends on the particular question being addressed. The term "rationalist" certainly seems curious for one who writes in his *Speeches on Religion* (1799): "Ideas, principles, are all foreign to religion"; "religion and art stand together like kindred beings";[76] we see the eternal "in all growth and change."[77] Or in *The Christian Faith* (1821) Schleiermacher writes that no consciousness of God is possible "which has not bound up with it a relation to Christ."[78] In his rejection of the purely analytical he stands with Blake and with his contemporary William Wordsworth — not with Newton or Semler. Religion is false "if it is a copy of an idea."[79] It may be too simple to conclude that in *The Christian Faith*

74. F. D. E. Schleiermacher, *Hermeneutics: The Handwritten Manuscripts,* ed. H. Kimmerle (Missoula: Scholars, 1977) 150-51 and passim.

75. I have given a detailed exposition and critique of Schleiermacher's hermeneutics in *New Horizons,* 204-47.

76. F. D. E. Schleiermacher, *On Religion: Speeches to Its Cultured Despisers* (New York: Harper, 1958) 46.

77. Schleiermacher, *On Religion,* 160.

78. F. D. E. Schleiermacher, *The Christian Faith* (Edinburgh: Clark, 1928) 261.

79. Schleiermacher, *On Religion,* 72.

Schleiermacher merely rejects, rather than reinterprets, the idea of the supernatural in his christology.[80]

6.2 Baur

F. C. Baur (1792-1860) may, as we have seen, be regarded with some plausibility as the first writer to apply ideology-criticism to the NT. He was initially more deeply influenced by Semler than by Hegel, especially in his strictly historical or sociological study of the Petrine and Pauline "parties" at Corinth, done largely on the basis of 1 Cor 1:12 ("The Christ Party in the Corinthian Church," 1831). He postulates a conflict between a Jewish Christian community-theology that reflected a "Petrine" tradition and a more liberated and radical "Pauline" community-tradition. His key point was that theological conflict and development arose from contingent historical and social causes.[81]

Baur argued that Paul genuinely reflected the law-free gospel of Jesus, but Peter and James, he held, had compromised with narrower Judaizing tendencies, and Paul, in the major authentic Epistles, appealed to his "apostleship" commissioned by the risen Christ to oppose the Judaizing communities. "Apostleship" and anti-legalist polemic became for Baur criteria for distinguishing authentic Pauline letters from the deutero-Pauline material falsely attributed to Paul. In his *History of the Christian Church of the First Three Centuries* (1853), Baur argued that the Jesus-Paul *thesis,* which stood in conflict with the Judaizing *antithesis,* reached a *synthesis* that sought to blend, or to paper over, the earlier conflict in an emergent "catholicism." Thus Ephesians and Colossians enlarged Jewish foundations universally to include Gentiles, the Epistle to the Hebrews offered some liberation to Judaistic forms, and the Pastoral Epistles and Acts represented institutionalizing responses to an emergent Gnosticism in the second century.

The periods of Hegel's greatest influence on Baur are keenly debated.[82] Baur's earliest work was not inspired by Hegel's dialectic of conflict and synthesis, but it probably lay behind his work on Paul, published in 1845,

80. Schleiermacher, *The Christian Faith,* esp. 388-95.
81. Christophe Senft, "Ferdinand Christian Baur: Methodological Approach and Interpretation of Luke 15:11-32," in *Exegesis: Problems of Method and Exercises in Reading,* ed. François Bovon (Pittsburgh: Pickwick, 1978) 77-96.
82. Horton Harris, *The Tübingen School: A Historical and Theological Investigation of the School of F. C. Baur* (Oxford: Oxford University, 1975; Leicester: Apollos 1990) esp. 155-88, examines the issues of chronology, witnessses, and disclaimers in detail.

though whether as corroboration or as inspiration remains difficult to prove. In later years Baur sought to disengage himself from Hegel's shadow, but by then the formative period of his ideas had become established. Like Strauss and, earlier, like Reimarus, Baur excluded supernatural factors from any historical data. His early disciples, those who constituted "the Tübingen School," regarded him, to quote Eduard Zeller, his closest admirer, as "the model of a scientific mind."[83] This is one reason that Zeller attempts to play down the philosophical influence of Hegel on Baur, and it strengthens Harris's doubts about the reliability of Zeller's verdict.[84]

Even in Baur's lifetime, however, one of his own disciples and admirers came to express dissatisfaction and suspicion of a social scientific account that neglected the possibility of more complex multiple causes than a straightforward socioempirical analysis might seem to suggest. Albrecht Ritschl remained closely associated with the Tübingen School for no less than eleven years before he broke with Baur on the ground that both complexities of local community situations and issues of ethical value added levels of explanation (or even hermeneutical factors?) that could not be contained strictly within Baur's more generalized theory of historical and social forces.[85] Ritschl saw that Baur's approach did not possess the strictly scientific value-neutral status that many of its supporters claimed for it.

Baur himself readily conceded that, if he concluded that Acts had falsified earlier history in the interests of a sociotheological *Tendenz,* his own judgment about "altered history" itself depended on a point of departure that was far from value-neutral. "A false picture of the individual character of the apostle Paul we should obtain if we had no other source than the Acts of the Apostles," and this appears to emerge in the context of "the single interest of objective historical truth."[86] Yet during the period when he was most influenced by Hegel's *Philosophy of Religion,* Baur recognized the illusory nature of a value-neutral standpoint, as if the historian or interpreter stood outside or above the historical process. Apart from Horton Harris's careful study, however, and the judicious comments of such

83. Harris, *Tübingen School,* 62.

84. Harris, *Tübingen School,* 155-56.

85. Philip Hefner, *Faith and the Vitalities of History: A Theological Study Based on the Work of Albrecht Ritschl* (New York: Harper and Row, 1966), discusses Ritschl's criticisms of the Tübingen school in his *Die Enstehung der altkatholischen Kirche* (Bonn, 1850; 2d ed., 1857).

86. Baur, excerpted in Kümmel, *New Testament,* 131, 135.

interpreters as Kümmel, the portrait of Baur found in most histories of NT interpretation tend to sidestep the hermeneutical complexities, which resist neat schemes and categorizations. A plea must be made for the application of hermeneutics to the history of interpretation with no less rigor and sensitivity than is invited by the study of biblical texts.[87]

*   *   *

But even that point remains only an adjunct to more fundamental considerations. In the first great paradigm shift of the rise of historical method, a split appeared between historical and theological inquiry that constrained and fragmented creative understanding. Ironically, the quest for non-manipulatory freedom came to defeat its own aims through new constraints. But in the more recent paradigm shift, which seeks now to break the spell of institutionalized historical inquiry, a repetition of this very same mistake, though for entirely different reasons, threatens to occur by according privilege to iconoclasm and pluralism, with the risk of anarchy.

One step forward is to view emancipatory hermeneutics as neither a pull toward nor a flight from history as such, but as a call to renounce manipulative interpretation of all kinds. Our task is to seek to diagnose and to expose every instance where manipulation controls the hermeneutical agenda, even in our own community. These lessons emerge when we place current NT interpretation in due historical perspective.

---

87. I have urged this principle in an article on James Barr's interpretation of Barth on "natural theology": Anthony C. Thiselton, "Barr on Barth and Natural Theology: A Plea for Hermeneutics in Historical Theology," *SJT* (47 [1994] 519-28).

3. *Traditio-Historical Criticism and Study of Jesus*

BRUCE CHILTON

1. The Necessity of a Traditio-Historical Reading

Because the NT is a collection of documents, it seems natural to treat its contents as produced by its authors for an audience. For most of its history, Christianity has accepted the primacy of written communication: Texts have been preserved, collected, annotated, translated, expounded, and otherwise interpreted. Once the canon was agreed on, between the second and the fourth centuries, recourse to a fixed group of writings was formalized. Even while arguments concerning the canon were still being pursued, the underlying assumption was that a consensus regarding *written* texts was required.

But what about the period that led up to the composition of written texts, and the process of preserving traditions that resulted in the documents of the canon? Just as textual criticism is designed to elucidate the history of texts, so traditio-historical criticism is designed to elucidate the history of the traditions that made up those texts. What was there *before* the time early Christian authors could write for a relatively stable constituency, the formative period during which local churches emerged without the benefit of a published canon?

By definition, the period with which traditio-historical criticism concerns itself is briefer than the period with which textual criticism concerns itself. The Gospels became available as documents in the period between the destruction of the Temple (a probable incentive for the composition of Mark) and around 100 CE (in the case of John). But it is obvious that some traditions incorporated within the Gospels are much older. Later in this chapter we will consider Paul's teaching concerning Jesus' last meal with his disciples (1 Cor 11:23-26), which is comparable to the presentation of the Synoptic Gospels. Paul wrote to the Corinthians in *ca.* 56 CE, and he states in the passage that he received his tradition "from the Lord" (v. 23). How did early Christians such as Paul receive, frame, and transmit traditions concerning Jesus? Traditio-historical criticism focuses on the relatively brief period between Jesus and the first documents of the NT.

It is as well that the period in question is short, because the analysis involved in traditio-historical work is complex. There are two related reasons for this necessary complexity. First, because the concern is with what preceded written evidence, we have by definition no external check on the processes that resulted in the writing of the Gospels. Second, we gain access to those processes only by means of our hypotheses regarding how the traditions that are crystallized in the NT were formed.

Both elements of complexity bring with them temptations to reduce the problems they pose by oversimplification. Not infrequently, students (and even some scholars) will invoke a theory of early authorship by eyewitnesses in order to short-circuit the task of traditio-historical criticism. Sadly, for such theorists, the Gospels themselves refer to earlier traditions and their importance. Luke 1:2 refers to the previous witness of "eyewitnesses and servants of the word," and John 20:30; 21:25 refer to traditions that might have been included in that Gospel but were not. As early as *ca.* 53 CE, Paul warned the Galatians of the dangers of "a different gospel" (Gal 1:6): Evidently, there were distinct, sometimes conflicting, strategies of preaching within the early church. We cannot say from the outset what precisely their contents were, but neither can we critically deny their existence.

Hypotheses regarding how traditions concerning Jesus were shaped is an unavoidable part of our study. Only by understanding the traditions that produced the text can the text itself be understood. When a document is produced as literature, by a single person, reading the text involves getting to know the author; in the case of the Gospels, the authorships that produced the texts are communities. It is those communities that we become familiar with as we identify the traditions of the Gospels. For that reason, it is misleading to speak of "Matthew," "Mark," "Luke," and "John" as if they were people we knew. The Gospels "according to" those four (as they are designated in the Greek titles of the texts) are the triumphal news of God's victory in Christ[1] as promulgated in their various communities. The precise role of those figures "according to" whom a Gospel was written, be it as creators of material, collectors, editors, local historians, and the like is simply unknown.

Gospels are texts of churches, and faith in Christ — a faith that varied greatly in character and definition during the period — is often of greater concern within them than the understanding of Jesus in anything like a historical sense. The Gospels are also in the position of translating the traditions of Jesus, in both linguistic and cultural terms, into social environments unlike his own. The simple identification of the historical Jesus with the Jesus of the Gospels is not tenable.

Nonetheless, the Gospels do refer back to Jesus as their source. We cannot understand what the texts are saying unless we appreciate the Jesus they refer to, whether or not we conclude in a given instance that their literary Jesus may be identified with the historical Jesus whom we construct. Jesus is what every Gospel refers to, the principal figure of their literary history. Understanding the traditions that make up the Gospels will put us in a position to evaluate the Jesus of their literary history. The historical Jesus, in other words, only emerges as we infer what Jesus, within the environment of early Judaism, must have said or done that produced the traditions of the NT as we understand them.

Traditio-historical criticism is an engagement with the text of the NT designed to uncover the processes and the stages by which that text emerged. Although Jesus and the Gospels have been particular concerns among historians of tradition, the approach is appropriate in respect of any document that is not simply the product of a single author. In order to emphasize that, our initial example will be drawn from the work of Paul (although comparison with the Synoptic Gospels will naturally come into play). Before we proceed to an exegetical discussion, however, a brief description of the evolution of the traditio-historical approach is in order.

2. The Development of a Critical Method

Martin Dibelius and Rudolf Bultmann are usually, and rightly, identified as the scholars who pioneered inquiry into the roots of the Synoptic tradi-

---

1. The modern fashion of rendering εὐαγγέλιον *(euangelion)* as "good news" overlooks the military resonance of the Greek term as reflected in the Septuagint.

tion.[2] Their concern was not with documents that may or not have existed before the Gospels were written but with the forms of oral tradition that fed into the formation of the Gospels. The idea was that, over the course of time, a tradition would be passed on within a community, and the community would shape that tradition into certain well-defined forms. For example, a tradition might be used to celebrate the power of a deity or to give point to a particular teaching. Bultmann treated the transfiguration (Mark 9:2-8) as an instance of the first category and the dispute over fasting (Mark 2:18-22) as an instance of the second.[3]

Particularly as developed by Bultmann, form criticism has been roundly criticized.[4] Three principal faults have been identified. First, the notion of a community that created definite forms has been attacked. In the development of the Hebrew Bible, institutions such as the Temple, the monarchy, and prophetic schools were in a position to shape traditions, and production of cycles of tradition over the course of generations and even centuries would have been possible. A definite correspondence between the form of traditions and the influence of public institutions is plausible under those conditions. That length of the time and (equally important) that formality of social structure are simply not present in the situation in which the NT emerged.

Second, insofar as the development of oral tradition within the culture and period of the NT has been attested, the picture of isolated passages (pericopae) circulating in free-floating fashion has not been confirmed. Traditions seem rather, from the outset, to have emerged within cycles and were often associated with influential teachers and schools within early Christianity.

Third and finally, the analogy with tradition as it was emerging within early Judaism confirms the importance of prominent teachers in the formation of tradition, who are known by name. This analogy also makes it seem apparent — contrary to Bultmann's assumption — that a link be-

2. See Martin Dibelius, *From Tradition to Gospel* (Cambridge: Clarke, 1971) and Rudolph Bultmann, *The History of the Synoptic Tradition* (New York: Harper and Row, 1971).

3. Cf. the discussion in Vincent Taylor, *The Formation of the Gospel Tradition* (London: Macmillan, 1945) 63-87, 142-67.

4. In addition to Taylor's book, see Thorleif Boman, *Die Jesus-Überlieferung im Lichte der neueren Volkskunde* (Göttingen: Vandenhoeck und Ruprecht, 1967); Birger Gerhardsson, *Memory and Manuscript: Oral Tradition and Written Transmission in Rabbinic Judaism and Early Christianity* (Uppsala/Lund: Gleerup, 1964); idem, *The Origins of the Gospel Traditions* (London: SCM, 1979); Harald Riesenfeld, *The Gospel Tradition* (Philadelphia: Fortress, 1970); Rainer Riesner, *Jesus als Lehrer: Eine Untersuchung zum Ursprung der Evangelien-Überlieferung* (Tübingen: Mohr, 1981).

tween such traditions and what we would call history is not to be excluded from the outset. Traditions may bear the marks of their historical development, including the people and events that initiated them; however much communities may have influenced the traditions they handed on, there is virtually no evidence that they arbitrarily created such traditions.

Form criticism in its Bultmannian form should be regarded as a method that has been superseded. Since the end of World War II, students of tradition have not been limited by its presuppositions. Increasingly, following the example of Heinz Schürmann,[5] they have seen the process of the formation of the Gospels to have been one in which traditions were formed, collected, and ultimately crystallized in writing in the documents we can read today. Tradition was the foundation on which redaction, the editorial procedures followed at the stage of writing, could take place. For that reason, it is fundamentally misleading (however fashionable) to imagine that the "Evangelists" were "authors" in the sense that they alone originated their materials. Whether the paradigm of such authorship is that of a novelist or a historian, the equation of the Gospels with "literature" (self-consciously published writing) is erroneous. The materials included in the Gospels were used as instruments of teaching in churches long before documents containing them were published. The materials the documents contain draw from the riches of earlier instruction and were spoken before they were written and believed before they were spoken.

Because we have evidence only of the last stage, when traditions — whether oral or written (or some combination of the two) — were composed in documentary form, it is all too easy to fall into the trap of imagining that Gospels were composed in a purely scribal manner. Among documentary theories, the most popular has it that Mark was written first and was used in the production of Matthew and Luke. But even that theory supposes an additional source of Jesus' teaching (commonly called "Q") and is embarrassed by cases in which Matthew and Luke agree in presenting Markan material in a form different from Mark's own wording. So even the most widespread scribal theory of the origins of the Gospels in fact assumes that scribal and oral media were combined in the production of

5. See, for example, Schürmann, *Das Geheimnis Jesu. Versuche zur Jesusfrage,* Die Botschaft Gottes 2 (Leipzig: St. Benno, 1972); Bruce Chilton, *God in Strength: Jesus' Announcement of the Kingdom,* BS (Sheffield: JSOT, 1987); Matti Myllykoski, *Die letzten Tage Jesu. Markus und Johannes, ihre Traditionen und die historische Frage* (Helsinki: Suomalainen Tiedeakatemia, 1991).

the documents and acknowledges the limits of our certainty in deciding what was written and what was oral when each Gospel was composed. The principal scholar of the most frequently cited documentary theory, B. H. Streeter, openly appreciated the role of nonwritten sources in the production of the Gospels. Unfortunately, that aspect of his theory has sometimes been lost in the retelling.[6] We can say with some precision how one Gospel compares with another, but we can only guess at the precise manner in which the material within one Gospel came to be known to the community in which another Gospel was produced.

3. Cycles of Tradition

Once it has been appreciated that the writing of each Gospel is a late stage in a process in which traditions were generated, traditio-historical study takes on its proper importance. The writings of the NT were produced at different times and at discrete stages within the development of early Christianity. They all assume that an initial, usually oral, preaching about Jesus has been heard and accepted at some point in the past, whether recently or long ago. That predominantly oral message, the triumphal news or "gospel" *(euangelion)* of God's victory, is only indirectly attested in the documents of the canon. The term "Gospel" came to be applied to specific documents because they presuppose and build on the message concerning Jesus.

The first three Gospels represent a second stage following acceptance of the message of the initial gospel that their audiences have already heard. They are written as catechesis (elementary instruction), in order to prepare sympathetic hearers of the gospel of Jesus for genuine membership, marked by baptism, in their churches. The Pauline correspondence represents the degree to which baptism was only a beginning in the life of disparate churches. For all their differences, churches of differing communities and places felt an identity with one another, not least because they shared common (although not identical) traditions. The attempt to address common problems and questions as communities in contact with one another made controversy a characteristic feature of primitive Christian history.

6. Cf. Bruce Chilton, *Profiles of a Rabbi: Synoptic Opportunities in Reading about Jesus,* BJS 177 (Atlanta: Scholars, 1989) 34-43. The relevant works of Streeter are *The Four Gospels* (London: Macmillan, 1924) and three articles in *Studies in the Synoptic Problem,* ed. W. Sanday (Oxford: Clarendon, 1911).

Since the first three Gospels thus emerge from the catechetical stage of the movement, when candidates were being prepared for baptism, they provide the best indications of the governing concerns of the movement as it initiated new members. These Gospels are commonly called "synoptic," because they may be viewed together when they are printed in columns. Unfortunately, their obviously literary relationship has caused scholars to presume that they were composed by scribes working in isolation and copying from each other. A comparative approach served by an understanding of the development of tradition into documents within both early Judaism and Christianity has brought us to the point where deviations of one document from another related document are not assumed to be purely scribal changes. Rather, agreement and disagreement provide opportunities to grasp accurately the social function and meaning of a given document by referring to the distinct ways it construes material that it shares with comparable documents.

Within such an approach, agreement among the Gospels is no surprise, because documents of early Judaism and Rabbinic Judaism also present synoptic relationships, sometimes with greater verbal similarity, and often with more than three documents involved. What *is* notable in the synopticity of the first three Gospels is that the order of passages, one after another, can generally be compared; that justifies their literary characterization as the "Synoptics" in a distinctive sense. Once their function within catechesis is appreciated, the cause of their agreements (including a commonly programmatic order) and their deviations becomes evident: What we see in the first three Gospels are the methods of baptismal initiation followed in three influential, nearly contemporaneous, but separate churches. There is a reasonable degree of consensus that Mark was the first of the Gospels to be written, around 71 CE in the environs of Rome. As convention has it, Matthew was subsequently composed, near 80 CE, perhaps in Damascus (or elsewhere in Syria), while Luke came later, say in 90 CE, perhaps in Antioch.

For reasons that have been explained, the cycles of tradition that fed the Gospels, and the relationships of these cycles to early teachers such as Paul, must be matters of inference and hypothesis. The strength of any traditio-critical theory is both its inclusion of the available evidence, and its power to explain the texts as they may be read today. Certain figures within the early church are named repeatedly in those texts as bearers of authoritative tradition. Simon, called Peter (or Cephas, the original, Aramaic form of his cognomen), is presented as a witness with James and John (the sons of Zebedee) of the transfiguration (see Mark 9:2-8 and parallels); apart from their transmission of the material, there would be no such story. Other stories in which Peter is named as a key witness are cited below. James (the brother of Jesus) is named by Paul as a figure whose rules of fellowship influenced practices in churches as far from Jerusalem as Antioch (Gal 2:11-13); Luke also presents him as the highest authority on the question of purity, one who revised Peter's views in the light of the interpretation of Scripture (Acts 15:13-21). The Twelve not only are commissioned in sayings of Jesus to take on some of his characteristic activities (Matt 10:1-15; Mark 3:13-19; 6:6b-13; Luke 6:13-16; 9:1-6; 10:2-12), but are also promised thrones on which they will judge the twelve tribes of Israel (Matt 19:28; Luke 22:28-30). Only one example of a complex of tradition that Peter, James, the Twelve, and Paul influenced will be discussed here, but as we proceed it will be helpful to bear in mind some of the cycles of tradition they produced.

The Petrine cycle must have been available in Aramaic by *ca.* 35 CE, in time for Paul to be informed of it at the time of his visit to Jerusalem (see Gal 1:18). But the very name "Peter" attests early translation into Greek, in association with the wider field of preaching for which that apostle accepted responsibility. The Petrine cycle within the Synoptics may be identified by the appearance within its stories of Peter, James, and John, among whom Peter is the chief representative; the cycle substantially included the initial call of the first disciples, the healing of Jairus's daughter, the confession at Caesarea Philippi, the transfiguration, the eucharist, and the struggle in Gethsemane. By design and in fact, the Petrine use of narrative for the purpose of catechesis established a paradigm in the primitive church; the Synoptic Gospels are a monument to that narrative strategy. The genesis of the Gospels was a function of a uniquely Christian program: baptism in the name of Jesus.[7]

In its earliest phase, "Q" was a collection of sayings in the nature of a mishnah. In Judaism "mishnah" refers to that which is repeated, the distinctive teaching of a master, learned by his disciples. Jesus' mishnah in an initial form was virtually contemporaneous with the Petrine cycle. From its origins in Jesus' movement as instruction of the Twelve, the source known as "Q," made up of material in proverbial form, developed in a markedly apocalyptic direction in the environment of Galilee and Syria. This cycle is generally held to have focused on rules of discipleship, generalized in order to regulate communities, and it is widely held to have been developed by around 45 CE.[8]

The cycle of James was in the nature of a version of the Petrine cycle

---

7. Cf. also Acts 10:34-43 and the reflection of a baptismal setting in vv. 44-48.

8. Cf. John S. Kloppenborg with Leif E. Vaage, eds., *Early Christianity, Q and Jesus,* Semeia 55 (Atlanta: Scholars, 1992).

and "Q" for the apostolic group around Jesus' brother, which was centered in Jerusalem. Both the Petrine cycle and the Jacobean revision of that cycle were known in Antioch prior to the council in Jerusalem, which took place *ca.* 49 CE (see Galatians 2). The Jacobean revision itself may be dated ca. 40 CE, since it went through some development before Paul became acquainted with it in Antioch, although he was not apprised of it at the time of his visit with Peter *ca.* 35 CE. This revision would have included the insistence that the Twelve alone could provide the sense of the parables, a collection of such parables, a note concerning rejection of Jesus by his neighbors, a commissioning of the Twelve, a discussion of purity, and (as we shall see) the paschal interpretation of the eucharist within a more detailed story of the passion than the Petrine cycle had offered. Apocalyptic addenda (most prominently, the discourse in Mark 13) were included at a later stage.

The primitive cycles or revisions of tradition (Petrine, Jacobean, and instructional ["Q"]) were amalgamated into the Hellenistic catechesis reflected in the Synoptic Gospels, probably first of all in Antioch. The relationship among the sources of the catechesis is represented schematically in the first diagram below. The most likely exponent of the unified catechesis is Barnabas. His standing is consistent with the wide acceptance of the Synoptic tradition, and the greater accommodation to Jacobean influence in the Synoptics as compared to Paul would be characteristic of Barnabas (see Gal 2:13).

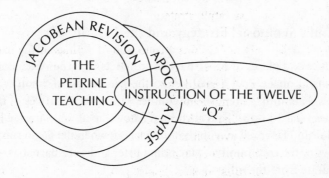

The Synoptic catechesis was a paradigm that was then developed and published in Rome (Mark), Damascus (Matthew), and Antioch itself (Luke). The spine of each Gospel is the narrative catechesis of the Petrine cycle, supplemented by Jacobean revision of that catechesis and the instruction of the Twelve ("Q"). Their similarities and differences are best understood as functions of the particular sort of catechesis (preparation of catechumens for baptism) that was current in each community. None of the Gospels is simply a copy of another; rather, each represents the choices among varying traditions, written and oral, and the development of those traditions that had taken place in a given locality, as represented in this second diagram:[9]

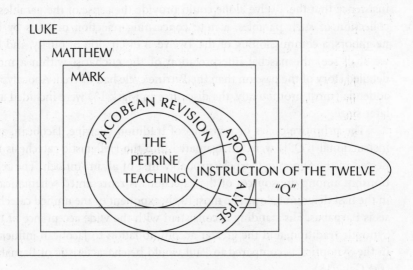

4. Paul's Symposial Strategy and the Last Supper

The times and places of his activity, his contacts, and the vehemence of his opinions all make Paul a vital key to the generation of traditions in the Gospels. Paul himself reports his conflict with representatives of the circle of James (Gal 2:11-13). Paul advocated fellowship at table among Jews and Gentiles, and Peter fell in with the practice. But when the Jacobeans arrived, the Jews of the community — including Peter and even Barnabas — began to separate from the others.

Traditio-historical criticism, in order to describe cycles of material,

9. These diagrams are schematic and are intended to show only general relationships of inclusion and intersection, not details of omission. So, for example, all of Mark and the Jacobean cycle are shown within Luke, but some of those materials were not fully incorporated within the Third Gospel.

associates passages that develop similar policies in regard to fellowship. The policy of separation, named as that of James, is consistent with the portrayal of Jesus' last meal as a Seder, the meal of Passover. The link with Passover is clearly artificial. The chronology of John excludes such an understanding (see 18:28; 19:14, 31), since Jesus dies on the day of preparation, the day before Passover. Even in the Synoptics, the authorities decide to deal with Jesus before the feast (Mark 14:1-2; Matt 26:1-5). (Luke 22:15 [probably from "Q"] should similarly be taken as the expression of an *unfulfilled* desire to eat the Passover.) In any case, the lamb, the unleavened bread, the bitter herbs required for a Seder (see Exod 12:8) are notable only for their absence from any primitive account of the Last Supper.

What makes the Last Supper a Seder is a single passage from the circle of James, in which Jesus is depicted as arranging for the paschal celebration (Matt 26:17-20/Mark 14:12-17/Luke 22:7-14); this passage presses the action into an improbably cramped space of time, but it makes the paschal setting of Jesus' meal — and therefore the eucharist — incontestable. Such an extension of the Torah to Jesus' last meal as a Seder meant that "no uncircumcised person shall eat of it" (Exod 12:48). Eucharists modeled on Jesus' meal would therefore be exclusively Jewish, as well as tied to the liturgical practice of Judaism.

The Jacobean program as a whole did not go unchallenged in Antioch, as Paul's correspondence attests. Paul, we have already seen, reports his own resistance to James's program in regard to purity. A few years later (*ca.* 56 CE), in the course of writing to the Corinthians concerning appropriate behavior during the Lord's supper, he also develops a line of resistance to the Jacobean understanding of eucharist (1 Cor 11:17-34).

It is well known that Paul's overall concern in 1 Corinthians 11 is with the practical good order of the congregation during fellowship at meals (vv. 17-22, 33, 34). In light of that purpose, the solemn assurance toward the beginning of the passage that he is passing on the tradition he received (v. 23) has seemed somewhat out of place.[10] The insistence on precision in regard to what Jesus did and said is not obviously in keeping with the simple purpose of maintaining decorum at the "dominical supper" (κυριακὸν δεῖπνον [*kyriakon deipnon*], v. 20). But in the context of the success of the Jacobean program, Paul's valiant effort to resist any paschal restriction becomes explicable.

---

10. For discussion, and a suggestion that anticipates the present treatment, see Oscar Cullmann, "The Lord's Supper and the Death of Christ," *Essays on the Lord's Supper,* ESW 1 (with F. J. Leenhardt; Richmond: John Knox, 1958) 17-20.

Paul insists on the older Petrine tradition in opposition to the paschal program of the Jacobean tradition. Paul's own reference in Gal 1:18 to a period of fifteen days during which he visited with Cephas in Jerusalem confirms what his language in 1 Cor 11:23 attests: He indeed "received from the Lord" (1 Cor 11:23), through Cephas (Gal 1:18), what he "handed over" (1 Cor 11:23) to his hearers, the Petrine model of eucharist. In writing to the Corinthians some seven years after the meeting in Jerusalem, which agreed on his sphere of interest in relation to that of the "pillars" (Gal 2:1-10),[11] Paul resisted the emerging influence of the annual Passover ritual on eucharist, which was a hallmark of the Jacobean tradition. In Pauline teaching, frequent repetition was a commandment: "Do this *as often as you drink* for my memorial" (1 Cor 11:25c). The plain meaning of Paul's clause is softened by the habit of adding "it" after "drink" in translations. But taken at face value, Paul's paradigm involves the recognition that any festive meal is an appropriate occasion of the "memorial."

Paul resists the Jacobean paradigm of eucharist in 1 Corinthians as much as he deplores the Jacobean program of purity in Galatians. He confirms the Petrine teaching because that tradition allows the eucharist to be accessible and repeated.[12] He reminds his hearers of what he has already taught as authoritative, a teaching "from the Lord" and presumably warranted by the earliest witness:[13] In that sense, what he hands on is not his own, but derives from his highest authority, "the Lord" (1 Cor 11:23). The meaning of the eucharist is not found in limiting it to Passover but in the solidarity of all believers in the memory of the Lord's death "until he comes" (vv. 26-29). That interpretation is expressed in those words only by Paul

11. For a plausible reconstruction of Paul's relationship to James, Peter, Barnabas, and the communities they represented, see Nicholas Taylor, *Paul, Antioch and Jerusalem: A Study in Relationship and Authority in Earliest Christianity,* JSNTSS 66 (Sheffield: JSOT, 1992).

12. Xavier Léon-Dufour, *Le partage du pain eucharistique selon le Nouveau Testament* (Paris: Editions du Seuil, 1982) 118, 119, also acknowledges the possibility of Paul's familiarity with what he calls the Markan tradition and I call the Petrine tradition. Cf. the translation of his work, *Sharing the Eucharistic Bread: The Witness of the New Testament* (New York: Paulist, 1987).

13. The formulation may also imply that Paul values his teaching as a revelation. But its similarity to that of the Synoptics suggests that he is not claiming unmediated verbal inspiration here. Comparison might be made with 1 Cor 7:25, 40, where Paul distinguishes traditional teaching from the more subjective guidance of the Spirit; cf. W. D. Davies, *Paul and Rabbinic Judaism: Some Rabbinic Elements in Pauline Theology* (Philadelphia: Fortress, 1980[4]) 140, 141, 194 n.5.

among the extant witnesses, and his presentation of the wording of the Petrine tradition is also unique. He illustrates both the diversity and the relatedness of catechetical materials within early Christianity.

5. The Tradition of the Petrine Circle

The similar presentations of the Synoptic Gospels suggest they rely on a common tradition. But their differences from one another (and from the wording of Paul) indicate that they are not simply copies from a single written source. Their wordings are distinctive:[14]

Matthew 26:26-28	Mark 14:22-24	Luke 22:19-20
While they were eating	And while they were eating	
Jesus took	he took	And he took
bread and blessed it,	bread, blessed it,	bread, gave thanks,
broke it, and gave	broke it, and gave	broke it and gave
to his disciples.	to them	to them,
He said,	and said,	saying,
"Take, eat;	"Take;	
this is my body."	this is my body."	"This is my body, which is given on behalf of you. Do this for my memorial."
And taking a cup	And taking a cup	And the cup similarly after they had supped,
and giving thanks,	and giving thanks,	
he gave to them,	he gave to them,	
saying,		saying,
"Drink from it, all of you.	and they all drank from it. And he said to them,	
For this is my blood	"This is my blood	"This cup is the new covenant
of the covenant,	of the covenant,	in my blood,
which is poured out	which is poured out	which is poured out
for many	on behalf of many."	on behalf of you."
for the forgiveness of sins."		

Although the uniqueness of each Gospel is striking (especially as compared to what a theory of literal documentary dependence would lead us to

14. My translation here is offered to facilitate comparison. Still, reference to a synopsis in Greek is the only way to appreciate both the distinctiveness and the coherence of the Gospels at this point.

expect), there is also a coherence that needs to be appreciated within the Judaic context of Petrine Christianity.

Within the Petrine tradition, Jesus' last meal began with the Judaic custom of blessing bread (cf. Mishnah *Berakoth* 6:5-8; Babylonian Talmud *Berakoth* 42a-46a), and its meaning was conveyed by the statement that Jesus' blood was "of the covenant." The blood poured out is deliberately reminiscent of the covenant sacrifice offered by Moses in Exodus 24 (vv. 6-8): Jesus is strongly associated with Moses in the Petrine tradition (cf. Matt 17:1-9/Mark 9:2-10/Luke 9:28-36).

Prior to the identification of Jesus' last meal with the Seder in the circle of James, the circle of Peter came to terms with the centrality of the Temple in its own way. Given that Jesus was executed in Jerusalem as a consequence of a dispute concerning the Temple, a considerable change must have occurred to enable his followers to organize in Jerusalem and to worship in that same Temple. The picture provided in Acts is clear and consistent: Under the leadership of Peter and a group of twelve, the followers of Jesus lived commonly, broke bread together regularly in their homes, and participated in the cult (see Acts 1:12-26; 2:46; 3:1-26; 4:1-37).

It is acknowledged widely that the picture of a smooth transition, entirely within the ambit of Jerusalem, and from deadly persecution to relative acceptance, is an example of Lukan idealization. The matter of appearances of the risen Jesus in Galilee is left out entirely.[15] But even Luke relates stories in which the mention of Jesus' name within the precincts of the Temple leads to arrest and interrogation at the hands of priestly authorities (see Acts 4:1-22; 5:12-42), so that the pivotal question of the compatibility between Jesus' movement and ordinary practice of the cult is marked. The Petrine tradition of the eucharist enabled the followers of Jesus both to celebrate him as a figure of Mosaic importance and to worship in the Temple with other faithful Jews.

6. The Synoptic Symposia

The abstraction of the eucharist from communal meals was attractive in Hellenistic Christianity. Eucharist became sensible and commendable within the practice of philosophical symposia. Such symposia were distin-

---

15. That is the point of departure for the analysis of F. J. Foakes Jackson and Kirsopp Lake, "The Disciples in Jerusalem and the Rise of Gentile Christianity," in *The Beginnings of Christianity*, vol. 1 (reprint, Grand Rapids: Baker, 1979) 300-20.

guished from others by a formal transition from meal to the symposium proper or "drinking party"[16] and by an avoidance of less than philosophical entertainments.[17] Philo attests to the extent to which the institution needed to be protected from abuse (*De Continentia* 57, 64). The Pauline phrase, "after supper," coordinates the supper with a well-ordered and comparatively sober philosophical symposium.

The generally Synoptic portrayal of the "last supper" implies a similar degree of sobriety, and the Lukan presentation expressly limits the consumption of wine that may take place in connection with any commemoration of the meal. In Matthew and Mark the action unfolds "while they were eating" (Matt 26:26/Mark 14:22) — and presumably drinking as well. The present form of the Lukan text manages to reduce the amount of drinking that may be imagined in connection with the meal by means of a more specific order of events: reference to the Passover (22:15, 16), sharing of wine with reference to the kingdom (vv. 17, 18), eating bread in remembrance (v. 19), and drinking again "after they supped" (μετὰ τὸ δειπνῆσαι, *meta to deipnēsai*) in view of the new covenant and the kingdom (v. 20).[18] Two cups, and two cups only, are associated with the meal in Luke.

Paul prefaces the identification of the wine in 1 Cor 11:25a with what at first seems a clumsy introduction: "In the same way he took the cup also,

---

16. See Dennis E. Smith, "Table Fellowship as a Literary Motif in the Gospel of Luke," *JBL* 106 (1987) 613-38, here 630, citing Plato *Symposium* 176A; Xenophon *Symposium* 2.1; Athenaeus *Deipnosophists* 11.462c-d. The passage from Xenophon also refers to more popular entertainments involving a female flute-player, a female dancer-acrobat, and a young man who played the zither and danced. The passage from Athenaeus shows how the usage of συμπόσιον *(symposion)* differs from that of δεῖπνον *(deipnon)*. *Deipnosophists* 462-63 attests to the extent to which drinking great quantities was held to be a virtue. For further discussion of the symposium see Baruch M. Bokser, *The Origins of the Seder: The Passover Rite and Early Rabbinic Judaism* (Berkeley: University of California, 1984) 50-66.

17. Smith, "Table Fellowship," 621; citing Plato *Symposium* 176E; Athenaeus *Deipnosophists* 5.186a. The Plato passage (immediately prior to the reference Smith has in mind) also attests the greater attention to the consumption of wine that should distinguish a philosophical symposium from others. Likewise, Athenaeus's observations may be gathered better, in their criticism of drinking too much, by reading from 5.179e-190a.

18. Smith, "Table Fellowship," 628, argues that a "short version" of the Lukan eucharistic text (vv. 15-19a) better suits the Gospel's theology than the inclusion of the longer reading. What he fails to consider is that his proposal results in reversing symposial order in relation to the meal and that control of the consumption of wine was of concern in the Hellenistic world generally and in the early church in particular.

after they supped. . . ." Jesus' identification of the bread is said simply to have taken place "on the night when he was betrayed" (v. 23b). The statement that the cup came "in the same way" at first appears equally vague, but then the clause "after they supped" seems to insist on a particular moment. If the actions indeed unfolded "in the same way," then both the bread and the cup were identified by Jesus "after supper."[19] Whenever exactly Paul understood the bread to have been eaten in relation to other foods, his abstraction of the "dominical supper" from an actual meal by means of his rendering of the Petrine tradition is evident.[20]

Hellenistic innovations in the Petrine teaching that Paul and Luke handed on went further. First, the clause "this is my blood of the covenant" became "this cup is the new covenant in my blood" (1 Cor 11:25; cf. the comparable phrasing in Luke). The linguistic changes involve several substantive consequences. The fuller phrase, simply in terms of its structure, is more stately. The thought is more developed than the direct metaphor, "This (is) my blood"; the assertion is explicated so as to avoid misunderstanding Jesus' actual blood as a repeated offering. That misunderstanding, in turn, can only have arisen after the "supper" had ceased to be viewed as comparable to the sacrifice of Exodus 24. Instead, Jesus' blood was sometimes seen within Hellenistic Christianity as comparable to that of the heroic martyrs, in the manner of 4 Macc 6:28-29; 17:21-22 (see Heb 9:11-14). The notion of the necessary repetition of human bloodshed was therefore an inference to be avoided, and the new wording precludes just that inference.

At the same time, the correctly taken cup is now made a covenant in the sense of a rite to be replicated correctly. Zech 9:11 provides a key to the grammatical structure and the sense of the Hellenistic version of Petrine tradition that Paul and Luke hand on. God in Zechariah had promised to

---

19. The wording of Luke 22:20a, which employs the same phrase, is within a better defined narrative context, which distinguishes the cup after the meal from the cup that precedes; Paul's presentation is less lucid.

20. The effect of the introduction concerning the cup is to distinguish the drinking of wine from a single cup — and perhaps even the eating of bread — from any meal that might occasion the "dominical supper." Indiscriminate eating and drinking were practices that particularly concerned Paul (1 Cor 11:21, 22); by emphasizing the Petrine order, he could address local abuses at Corinth and at the same time claim unity with the practice in the primitive church warranted by Petrine authority. The price of Paul's formulation was to abstract the "supper" from the sorts of meals that had inspired it in the ministry of Jesus.

rescue the captives of of Zion "by the blood of your covenant":[21] The older, Petrine emphasis on covenant (in association with Exodus 24) is now linked to the salvific value of blood in the new wording. Most strikingly, the covenant itself is now "new." The use of language from Jer 31:31 is less important for its biblical pedigree than for its insistence, within the innovative grammatical form of the statement, that Jesus' act amounts to a *covenantal requirement* that is to be discharged "as often as you drink, in remembrance of me" (1 Cor 11:25). Unlike the Jacobean limitation to Passover, Paul's appropriation of the Petrine tradition envisages frequent celebration by all those who could eat together. As far as Paul was concerned, *pace* James, that included *all* baptized persons. For him as well as for Luke, the meal was to be repeated for Jesus' "memorial" (1 Cor 11:24; Luke 22:19).

The repetition enjoined in 1 Cor 11:25 is, then, by no means incidental for Paul. "As often as you drink," within the tradition of the Petrine circle, is used as a bulwark against the limitations implicit within the association of eucharist with Passover, and especially the paschal chronology, of the Jacobean tradition. Paul's assumption is that Jesus' last meal, the paradigm of the Lord's Supper, was of covenantal significance, a sacrificial "memorial" that was associated with the death of Jesus in particular. The wording of that later version of Petrine tradition agrees most closely with Luke, the Synoptic Gospel that has the strongest associations with Antioch. It is likely that Paul's version of the Petrine tradition derived from his period in Antioch, his primary base by his own testimony (in Galatians 2) until his break with Barnabas.

By the Antiochene phase of the Petrine tradition "the cup" is doubly symbolic. It stands for the new covenant that Jesus mediates by his death, and it also takes the place of the blood that seals Jesus' death. Neither transfer of meaning would have been possible without the previous understandings that the wine in the cup was in some sense Jesus' blood and that the blood was of covenantal significance. In both of these aspects, 1 Cor 11:25 and Luke 22:20 give the appearance of being developed forms of Petrine tradition, the usage that developed in Antioch. Paul's symposial strategy is to apply the authority of eucharistic practice in Antioch, prior to the influence of James' circle, against the influence of the Jacobean identification with Passover and its attendant (in Paul's view, limited) insistence on purity.

The perspective of Antioch, attested in the symbolism of the cup in both

21. The sense of the phrase is "my covenant with you," as in the NRSV. The LXX omits the pronoun altogether.

Paul and Luke, involves a fresh conception of the place of "blood" in eucharist. The earlier form of the Petrine tradition (which was closely related to Jesus' practice) simply had it that the wine was blood, a surrogate of covenantal sacrifice. In the Hellenistic environment of Antioch, such a meaning could easily be confused with the notion of drinking a deity's blood in one of the mysteries. The association of Jesus' last meal with his execution, which was already a feature of the Petrine tradition, would have further encouraged the confusion. The Antiochene wording avoided any confusion of that kind by making the cup the point of comparison with the new covenant and by describing the covenant as achieved "in" or "by" (ἐν, en) Jesus' blood.

Although the phrase "in my blood" (1 Cor 11:25; Luke 22:20) excludes a possible misunderstanding of the Petrine eucharist, it also conveys a positive appraisal of Jesus' own "blood," that is, his death. The offering commemorated in the bread and wine is not simply a covenantal sacrifice in the general sense established within the Petrine cycle, but the particular form of the sacrifice known as the sacrifice for sin, or חַטָּאת (ḥaṭṭā't; cf. Leviticus 4). When Paul conceives of Jesus' death sacrificially, he conceives of it as such a sacrifice "to deal with sin" (or "as a sin offering," περὶ ἁμαρτίας [peri hamartias], Rom 8:3). Indeed, by the time he came to compose Romans, Paul had been referring to Jesus' death in that way for some five years: In Gal 1:4, Jesus is also described as having given himself for our sins.

In sum, by reading Paul from a traditio-historical point of view, together with the Synoptic Gospels, several models of eucharist become apparent, all in the form of narratives of Jesus' last meal with his disciples. For the Petrine tradition, the meal was a form of blessing and breaking bread that established Jesus' Mosaic stature in mediating the covenant. The circle of James developed the paschal associations of the meal, in order to insist on its strict limitation to the circumcised, that is, to Christian Jews. Paul insisted upon the authority of Peter/Cephas over James and accepted the characterization of the meal in Antioch as a form of symposial solidarity with a heroic martyr.

In this instance as in others, a straightforwardly historical question is raised by traditio-historical inquiry. The development of traditions within their various cultural contexts forces us to ask about the impetus that occasioned that process. What may be attributed to Jesus as a teacher within early Judaism such that his teaching and activity gave rise to traditions that, in their various transformations, generated the meanings and texts that we can interpret today?

7. Jesus' Meals and His Occupation of the Temple

The sacrificial associations of Jesus' last meal — with the covenant in the Petrine cycle, with Passover in the Jacobean, with Jesus' personal and atoning death in the catechesis of Antioch — point back toward the generative meaning of Jesus' act, the meaning that produced such conceptions. If we proceed with the traditional reading, which sees the "body" and "blood" as Jesus' own in a biographical sense, it is virtually impossible to understand the development of the traditions within their Judaic contexts.

The Mishnah, in an effort to conceive of a heinous defect on the part of a priest involved in slaughtering the red heifer, pictures him as intending to eat the flesh or drink the blood (*Para* 4:3). Because people had no share of blood, which belonged only to God, even the thought of drinking it was blasphemous. To imagine drinking human blood, consumed with human flesh, could only make the blasphemy worse. So if Jesus' words are taken with their traditional autobiographical meaning, his last meal can only be understood as a deliberate break from Judaism. Either Jesus himself promulgated a new religion, or his followers did so in his name and invented the last meal themselves. Both those alternatives find adherents today among scholars, and the debate between those who see the Gospels as literally true reports and those who see them as literary fictions shows little sign of progress. But in either case, the question remains: If the generative act was anti-sacrificial, how did the cycles of traditions and the texts as they stand come to their sacrificial constructions?

There is another, more historical way of understanding how eucharist emerged in earliest Christianity, an approach that takes account of the cultural changes that the development of the movement involved. Interest in the social world of early Judaism and in how Christianity as a social movement emerged within Judaism and then became distinct from it has been growing for most of this century. The result is that we are no longer limited to the old dichotomy between the "conservative" position that the Gospels are literal reports and the "liberal" position that they are literary fictions. Critical study has revealed that the Gospels are composite products of the various social groups that were part of Jesus' movement from its days within Judaism to the emergence of Christianity as a distinct religion. When we place eucharistic practices within the social constituencies that made the Gospels into the texts we can read today, we can understand the original meaning Jesus gave to his last meal and how his meaning generated others.

Jesus' last supper was not the only supper, just the last one.[22] In fact, his last meal would have had no meaning apart from his well-established custom of eating with people socially. There was nothing unusual about a rabbi making social eating an instrument of his instruction, and it was part of Jesus' method from the first days of his movement in Galilee.

In Judaism meals were regular expressions of social solidarity and of common identity as the people of God. Many sorts of meals are attested in the literature of early Judaism. From Qumran we learn of banquets at which the community convened in order of hierarchy; from the Pharisees we learn of collegial meals shared within fellowships *(ḥaburôt)* at which like-minded fellows *(ḥaberim)* would share the foods and the company they considered pure. Ordinary households might welcome the coming the Sabbath with a prayer of sanctification *(kidduš)* over a cup of wine, and open a family occasion with a blessing *(berakâ)* over bread and wine.

Jesus' meals were similar in some ways to some of these meals, but they were also distinctive. He had a characteristic understanding of what the meals meant and of who should participate in them. For him, eating socially with others in Israel was a parable of the feast in the kingdom that was to come. The idea that God would offer festivity for all peoples on his holy mountain (see Isa 2:2-4; 25:6-8) was a key feature in the fervent expectations of Judaism during the first century, and Jesus shared that hope, as may be seen in a saying from the source of his teaching known as "Q" (see Matt 8:11/Luke 13:28-29):

> Many shall come from east and west,
> and feast with Abraham, Isaac, and Jacob
> in the kingdom of God.[23]

Eating was a way of enacting the kingdom of God, of practicing the generous rule of the divine king. As a result, Jesus avoided exclusive practices, which divided the people of God from one another; he was willing to accept as companions people such as tax agents and other suspicious characters and to receive notorious sinners at table. The meal for him was a sign of

22. I owe the phrasing to Hershel Shanks, who in a personal conversation used it to help summarize my position.

23. Because my interest here is in the traditional form of the saying, before the changes introduced in Matthew and Luke, I give a reconstructed form; see Chilton, *God in Strength,* 179-201.

the kingdom of God, and all the people of God, assuming they sought forgiveness, were to have access to it.

Jesus' practice of fellowship at meals caused opposition from those whose understanding of Israel was exclusive. To them, he seemed profligate, willing to eat and drink with anyone, as Jesus himself observed in a saying also from "Q" (see Matt 11:19/Luke 7:34):

> A man came eating and drinking, and they complain:
> "Look, a glutton and drunkard,
> a fellow of tax agents and sinners."

Some of Jesus' opponents saw the purity of Israel as something that could only be guarded by separating from others, as in the meals of their fellow-ships *(ḥaburôt)*. Jesus' view of purity was different. He held that a son or daughter of Israel, by virtue of being of Israel, could approach his table, or even worship in the Temple. Where necessary, repentance beforehand could be demanded, and Jesus taught his followers to pray for forgiveness daily, but his understanding was that Israelites as such were pure and were fit to offer purely of their own within the sacrificial worship of Israel.

As long as Jesus' activity was limited to Galilee, he was involved in active but essentially inconsequential disputes. Slightly deviant rabbis in Galilee were far from uncommon. But Jesus also brought his teaching into the Temple, where he insisted on his own teaching (or *halakhah*) of purity. The incident that reflects the resulting dispute is usually called the cleansing of the Temple (Matt 21:12-13/Mark 11:15-17/Luke 19:45-46/John 2:13-17). From the point of view of the authorities there, what Jesus was after was the opposite of cleansing. He objected to the presence of merchants who had been given permission to sell sacrificial animals in the vast outer court of the Temple. His objection was based on his own peasant's view of purity: Israel should offer not priest's produce, which they handed over money for, but their own sacrifices, which they themselves brought into the Temple. He believed so vehemently what he taught that he and his followers drove the animals and the sellers out of the great court, no doubt with the use of force.[24]

Jesus' interference in the ordinary worship of the Temple might have been sufficient by itself to bring about his execution. After all, the Temple was the center of Judaism as long as it stood. Roman officials were so

24. For a full discussion, see Bruce Chilton, *The Temple of Jesus: His Sacrificial Program within a Cultural History of Sacrifice* (University Park: Pennsylvania State University, 1992) 91-111.

interested in its smooth functioning at the hands of the priests they appointed that they were known to sanction the penalty of death for sacrilege.[25] Yet there is no indication that Jesus was arrested immediately. Instead, he remained at liberty for some time and was finally taken into custody just after one of his meals, the last meal. The decision of the authorities of the Temple to move against Jesus when they did is what made the last supper last.

Why did the authorities wait and why did they act when they did? The Gospels portray them as fearful of the popular backing that Jesus enjoyed, and his inclusive teaching of purity probably did bring enthusiastic followers into the Temple with him. But in addition, there was another factor: Jesus could not simply be dispatched as a cultic criminal. He was not attempting an onslaught on the Temple as such; his dispute with the authorities concerned purity within the Temple. Other rabbis of his period also engaged in physical demonstrations of the purity they required in the conduct of worship. One of them, for example, is said once to have driven thousands of sheep *into* the Temple, so that people could offer sacrifice in the manner he approved of (Babylonian Talmud *Beṣa* 20a, b). Jesus' action was extreme but not totally without precedent, even in the use of force.

The authorities' delay, then, was understandable. We could also say it was commendable, reflecting continued controversy over the merits of Jesus' teaching and whether his occupation of the great court should be condemned out of hand. But why did they finally arrest Jesus? The last supper provides the key; something about Jesus' meals after his occupation of the Temple caused Judas to inform on Jesus. Of course, "Judas" is the only name that the traditions of the NT have left us. We cannot say who or how many of the disciples became disaffected by Jesus' behavior after his occupation of the Temple.

However they learned of Jesus' new interpretation of his meals of fellowship, the authorities arrested him just after the supper we call last. He continued to celebrate fellowship at table as a foretaste of the kingdom, just as he had before. But he also added a new and scandalous dimension of meaning. His occupation of the Temple having failed, Jesus said over the wine "This is my blood" and over the bread "This is my flesh" (Matt 26:26, 28/Mark 14:22, 24/Luke 22:19-20/1 Cor 11:24-25/Justin *Apology I* 66.3).

In Jesus' context, the context of his confrontation with the authorities of the Temple, his words can have had only one meaning. He cannot have

25. See Josephus *Ant.* 15 §417.

meant, "Here are my personal body and blood"; that is an interpretation that only makes sense at a later stage. Jesus' point was rather that, in the absence of a Temple that permitted his view of purity to be practiced, wine was his blood of sacrifice, and bread was his flesh of sacrifice. In Aramaic, "blood" (דְּמָא; *dᵉmā'*) and "flesh" (בִּסְרָא; *bisrā'*, which may also be rendered as "body") can carry such a sacrificial meaning, and in Jesus' context that is the most natural meaning.

The meaning of "the last supper," then, actually evolved over a series of meals after Jesus' occupation of the Temple. During that period, Jesus claimed that wine and bread were a better sacrifice than what was offered in the Temple: At least wine and bread were Israel's own, not tokens of priestly dominance. No wonder the opposition to him, even among the Twelve (in the shape of Judas, according to the Gospels), became deadly. In essence, Jesus made his meals into a rival altar, and we may call such a reading of his words a ritual or cultic interpretation.

This cultic interpretation has two advantages over the traditional autobiographical interpretation as the meaning Jesus attributed to his own final meals. The first advantage is contextual: The cultic interpretation places Jesus firmly with the Judaism of his period and at the same time accounts for the opposition of the authorities to him. The second advantage is the explanatory power of the cultic interpretation: It enables us to explain sequentially subsequent developments in the understanding of eucharist within early Christianity. The cultic sense of Jesus' last meals with his disciples is the generative meaning that permits us to explain its later meanings as eucharistic covenant, Passover, and heroic symposium.

8. Suggestions for Further Reading

For an accessible introduction to traditio-historical criticism in the hands of a masterful exegete, the student may consult C. H. Dodd, *The Apostolic Preaching and Its Developments* (New York: Harper, 1960). Although form criticism as a method has been superseded in many ways, the traditio-historical insights of Martin Dibelius and Rudolf Bultmann remain both valuable and fundamental. Of the two, Dibelius is more lucid and discursive (see *From Tradition to Gospel* [Cambridge: Clarke, 1971]) while Bultmann is more detailed and analytic (some might say dogmatic; see *The History of the Synoptic Tradition* [New York: Harper and Row, 1971]). A critical appraisal that remains useful is offered by Vincent Taylor in

The Formation of the Gospel Tradition (London: Macmillan, 1945). A more philosophical consideration is available in Erhardt Güttgemanns, *Candid Questions concerning Gospel Form Criticism,* PTMS 26 (Pittsburgh: Pickwick, 1979).

Several scholars have moved beyond a critique of form criticism to develop alternative portraits of primitive Christian traditions. Among them are Birger Gerhardsson, *Memory and Manuscript: Oral Tradition and Written Transmission in Rabbinic Judaism and Early Christianity* (Uppsala/Lund: Gleerup, 1964) and *The Origins of the Gospel Traditions* (London: SCM, 1979); Harald Riesenfeld, *The Gospel Tradition* (Philadelphia: Fortress, 1970); Rainer Riesner, *Jesus als Lehrer: Eine Untersuchung zum Ursprung der Evangelien-Überleiferung* (Tübingen: Mohr, 1981). In varying ways, all three scholars have been justly criticized for imagining that rabbinic rules of handing on tradition were normative during the first century. Once allowance is made for the greater pluralism of early Judaism, many of their insights remain useful.

The task of relating the Synoptic Gospels to the pattern of oral and written tradition in the early church was already recognized by B. H. Streeter, whose *The Four Gospels* (London: Macmillan, 1924) should still be consulted from that angle. More recent attempts to explain the emergence of the Synoptics from the point of view of traditio-historical criticism are Bo Reicke, *The Roots of the Synoptic Gospels* (Fortress: Philadelphia, 1986), and Bruce Chilton, *Profiles of a Rabbi: Synoptic Opportunities in Reading about Jesus,* BJS 177 (Atlanta: Scholars, 1989). A range of representative positions in the discussion of "Q" may be found in John S. Kloppenborg with Leif E. Vaage, eds., *Early Christianity, Q and Jesus,* Semeia 55 (Atlanta: Scholars, 1992).

The most recent phase in the investigation of traditions of Jesus' last meal in their relationship to eucharistic practice is examined in Xavier Léon-Dufour, *Sharing the Eucharistic Bread: The Witness of the New Testament* (New York: Paulist, 1987), and Bruce Chilton, *A Feast of Meanings: Eucharistic Theologies from Jesus through Johannine Circles,* NovTSup 72 (Leiden: Brill, 1994).

4. *Historical Criticism and Social-Scientific Perspectives in New Testament Study*

STEPHEN C. BARTON

1. The New Testament and Historical Criticism

Reading the NT today is a necessarily — though by no means exclusively — historical task. This is not to say that only trained historians can read the NT or that the NT can be read only as a source of historical information. Both inferences are patently untrue. As part of the canon of Christian Scripture, the NT is read above all by members of the various Christian faith communities as a constitutive part of their worship and discipleship, because the Bible is the book of the church. As such, it is read with the primary goal, not of discovering historical data, but of growth in the knowledge and love of God. This goal is pursued on the well-founded theological assumption that the overriding function of Scripture is to bear witness to God and to the self-revelation of God in Jesus Christ, a revelation that is enlivened and made effective by God's Spirit.[1]

Nevertheless, it has long been taken for granted — except in certain fundamentalist circles and among the practitioners of particular forms of structuralist interpretation — that wise or apt readings of the NT and of the Bible as a whole must include the application of historical skills and sensitivity toward the past. There are many reasons for this, but perhaps the most important are as follows.

---

1. See further, Robert Morgan with John Barton, *Biblical Interpretation* (Oxford: Oxford University, 1988) ch. 1; also Charles M. Wood, *The Formation of Christian Understanding* (Philadelphia: Westminster, 1981) ch. 2.

1.1 The Place of Historical Criticism in Our Culture

The first reason is historical and cultural, because historical interpretation itself has a history. Historical reading of texts or documents from the past is a practice that goes back to antiquity and lies at the roots of Western culture and civilization. For the historiographers of antiquity, many of whom were trained in law and rhetoric, the use of historical criticism was an important means of testing the truth claims of the reports they heard and the documents they used.[2] In the NT itself, good examples of the sensitivity of its authors to the issue of the reliability of sources (whether oral or written) come *inter alia* in the prologue of the Gospel of Luke (Luke 1:1-4) and in the writings of the Johannine circle (e.g., John 19:35; 21:24-25; 1 John 1:1-4; Rev 1:1-11).

The import of this is that reading with historical awareness as a way of assessing both the meaning and truth of texts has a long and distinguished pedigree both outside the church and within it. Such historical awareness is evident in the biblical literature itself and in the process of the formation of the biblical canon — for instance, in the appeal to the apostolic authorship of the NT documents. It is demonstrated also in the biblical interpretation of the writers of the patristic period, particularly in the theologians of the Antiochene School.[3] It was also accepted as an important ingredient of medieval biblical exegesis. With the Renaissance came a flourishing of the human sciences, a rediscovery of the Greek and Roman classics, and an acceptance of the principle of the "return to the sources" *(ad fontes)* in their original languages as an important principle of validity in interpretation. This lies behind the major development in historical philology and textual criticism represented by Erasmus's edition of the Greek NT. It also lies behind the return to the Bible and the principle of *sola scriptura* ("Scripture alone") as the hermeneutical basis on which Luther and his fellow reformers challenged the teaching and practice of the Catholic Church and instituted far-reaching political, institutional, and doctrinal changes.

This setting of Scripture over against tradition and institution characteristic of the Reformation was a feature of the Enlightenment as well, but now historical reason was used as a tool of skepticism to undermine tradi-

---

2. See F. Gerald Downing, "Historical-Critical Method," in *A Dictionary of Biblical Interpretation,* ed. R. J. Coggins and J. L. Houlden (London: SCM/Philadelphia: Trinity, 1990) 284-85.

3. See further, James L. Kugel and Rowan A. Greer, *Early Biblical Interpretation* (Philadelphia: Westminster, 1986) 178-84.

tional faith itself.[4] Under the impact of various forms of Enlightenment foundationalism (such as the rationalism of René Descartes and the empiricism of John Locke and David Hume), historical criticism was used with devastating effect by David Friedrich Strauss and others to question the veracity of the Gospel miracle stories. It was the basis also for the principle enunciated in the mid-nineteenth century by Benjamin Jowett that Scripture should be read "like any other book" and that its single objective sense was to be located in the historical reconstruction of the authors' original meanings.[5]

For most of the twentieth century, as a result, historical criticism in its various modes — the "history of religions" school, textual criticism, traditio-historical criticism, redaction criticism, and so on — has dominated as the primary method of NT interpretation. Historical reason has, in large measure, set the terms of validity in interpretation for the Bible as a whole. This means that, whether or not the application of historical reason to the Bible is the most appropriate way of understanding Scripture, it is essential that it remain an important ingredient in responsible readings of the text. Otherwise, biblical interpretation is open to the danger of becoming cut off from the public understanding of validity in interpretation and closed to what the common culture recognizes as rational. What the text means must include — even if it is not limited to — historical judgments about what the text meant.

1.2 The Nature of the NT Documents

Another reason for the widespread acceptance of the importance of historical awareness in NT interpretation arises from hermeneutics (that is, the theory of interpretation). Here the general point is that appropriate methods for interpreting a text are governed to some extent at least by the kind of text being interpreted and by the aims of the interpreter.[6] To the

---

4. See Jon D. Levenson's essay, "Historical Criticism and the Fate of the Enlightenment Project" in his *The Hebrew Bible, the Old Testament, and Historical Criticism* (Philadelphia: Westminster, 1993) 106-26.

5. For a critical assessment of this principle of interpretation see David C. Steinmetz, "The Superiority of Pre-Critical Exegesis," *Theology Today* 37 (1980) 27-38, reprinted in *Ex Auditu* 1 (1985) 74-82, and in *A Guide to Contemporary Hermeneutics: Major Trends in Biblical Interpretation*, ed. Donald K. McKim (Grand Rapids: Eerdmans, 1986) 65-77.

6. See in general, Sandra M. Schneiders, *The Revelatory Text* (San Francisco: HarperCollins, 1991) esp. ch. 4.

extent that the texts of the NT are historical documents and the aim of the interpreter is to gather or utilize historical information, the use of historical-critical methodology is not just appropriate but obligatory.

That the NT texts are historical documents, whatever else they may be, cannot be doubted. They come to us from the ancient past. They are written in the *koinē* Greek of antiquity. Their form and content are indebted to the language and thought-forms of an even more ancient text, the Hebrew Bible and its Greek version, the Septuagint, and to the character and worldview of Greco-Roman antiquity in general. What is more, their own concerns are (in part) intrinsically historical: to preserve, pass on, and interpret the traditions — including the biblical traditions — about Jesus. As the author of 1 John 1:1-3 puts it: "That which was from the beginning, which we have heard, have seen with our eyes, have looked on, and have touched with our hands, . . . we proclaim also to you, so that you may have fellowship with us."

Because the NT texts are documents from the past with their own ways of interpreting the past, there is a distance that separates them from us — a distance of chronology, language, thought-forms, culture, social patterns, and the like. Historical criticism has developed as a method of interpretation for deciphering or decoding texts from the past and for mediating between the past and the present. It enables us to understand the texts in their own historical context and helps us to avoid the misunderstandings that come from anachronistic interpretation in which the sense of distance separating the ancient text from the modern reader is lost.

Of course, it is possible to overemphasize the historical "gap" between the NT and today in such a way that a proper sense of historical distance turns into a negative feeling of alienation.[7] It is possible likewise to use historical-critical tools in such a way that other reading strategies are marginalized and the text is allowed to function only as an historical source in aid of a rather positivist kind of search for "objective facts." But to acknowledge the limits of historical interpretation and to be aware of its dangers should by no means lead us to dispense with it altogether. If, as Christians believe, true knowledge of God is bound up inextricably with the attempt to understand God's self-revelation in history and if the Christian Scriptures are the primary testimony to that divine self-revelation, then the task of

7. One study that has attracted criticism on these grounds is Dennis Nineham, *The Use and Abuse of the Bible: A Study of the Bible in an Age of Rapid Cultural Change* (London: Macmillan, 1976).

historical criticism according to the best available historical tools is a necessary part of the art of NT interpretation and of theological inquiry in general.[8]

If we turn to Luke 3:1-20 by way of illustration, a good case can be made that our understanding of Luke's account of the ministry of John the Baptist is likely to be seriously deficient if we pay insufficient attention to historical matters. Without the historical awareness that historical method fosters and clarifies, John is likely to become a two-dimensional cardboard cutout or a plasticine model pressed into shapes of any kind so that we are left with no controlled way of making sense of his life and mission, whether we are talking about the significance of the water baptism he practiced, the practical implications of the moral reformation he demanded, or the meaning of the messianic hope and judgment that he preached. What is more, it can hardly be claimed that a historical reading runs against the grain of Luke's narrative about John, since Luke (more than any of the other Evangelists) goes to considerable lengths to set John's ministry in a historical setting, a setting that includes information of a variety of kinds — chronological, political, sociological, geographical, prosopographical, and religious (3:1-3).

1.3 The Theological Importance of Historical Criticism

Historical criticism is also important theologically. For a start, it makes possible the claim that the biblical narrative is not merely realistic fiction — even if it has fictional elements — but refers to realities outside or behind the narrative, in relation to which the narrative functions as a testimony or witness. Contrary to the extreme claims of certain forms of literary interpretation, the text is not all there is. On the contrary, the text bears witness with conspicuous particularity to persons and events in history, the most important for Christians, of course, being the life, death, and resurrection of Jesus of Nazareth. To the extent that the significance of Jesus for Christian faith depends on our historical knowledge of him, historical criticism is important. This is the main theological justification for the ongoing scholarly "quest of the historical Jesus."

For example, the Johannine narrative of Jesus' encounter with the

---

8. The nature and purpose of historical knowledge in NT interpretation are discussed in N. T. Wright, *The New Testament and the People of God* (London: SPCK/Minneapolis: Fortress, 1992) ch. 4.

Samaritan woman in John 4:1-42 provides historical warrant for the Christian theological claim that the significance of Jesus for human salvation extends beyond the bounds of Judaism to the Samaritans and (by implication) to people of any race. Without texts like this, Christians would be hard put to justify their belief in the universal significance of Jesus, especially in view of other texts that appear to point in a more parochial, inner-Jewish direction (e.g., Matt 10:5-6). Similarly, without texts like this, Christians would also be hard put to justify their claim that the "eternal life" Jesus offers is intended for women as much as it is for men, especially when so much of early Christian tradition is written (whether wittingly or not) from an androcentric perspective (cf. John 4:27!) and has been interpreted as supporting patriarchal social patterns.[9] In other words, this important narrative, whether historical or history-like — and which it is is a matter that historical criticism helps to adjudicate — provides a warrant for specific theological claims about the meaning of Jesus for today. Such claims would be so much the weaker without the historical evidence that it is the job of historical criticism to sift and evaluate.

On the other hand, historical criticism is important theologically because it has the potential for making us aware of the culturally conditioned nature of both the NT text *and* of subsequent interpretations of the text, including our own. Once we recognize this, we are less likely to confuse the words of the text with the living Word of God, to which the text testifies and in whom Christians believe. Christians, after all, are summoned not to believe in the Bible but to believe in Christ, as the creeds of the church make clear. Further, historical awareness makes it less likely that we will confuse the meaning(s) of the text with the meaning(s) ascribed to it by any single church or interpretative community, even the one to which we ourselves might belong.

For example, the use of historical reason makes it possible to put a question mark against readings of 1 Cor. 11:2-16 that assume that the hierarchical ordering of the relation of man and woman (and the particular interpretation of the creation narrative to which Paul appeals as his warrant for that hierarchy) are true testimony to the will of God for all time. Many interpreters would argue contrariwise, on the basis of historical reasoning, that what Paul says is context-specific pastoral advice, culturally determined by the socioreligious significance of veils (or of particular hairstyles).[10] Seen

9. See further in ch. 17 below.

10. A good example from a massive secondary literature is Gerd Theissen, *Psychological Aspects of Pauline Theology* (Philadelphia: Fortress/Edinburgh: Clark, 1987) 158-75.

in these terms, the religious significance of the text for Christians today is relativized in a way that is proper on historical grounds. At the same time, however, it needs to be said that historical reason also makes it possible for us to question readings of 1 Corinthians 11 that render it theologically mute by labeling it either "misogynist" (and therefore dispensable as politically incorrect) or a "post-Pauline interpolation" (and therefore secondary material not worth bothering about). Historical reason has the potential, in other words, to relativize not just the text but also the relativizers!

Putting the more general point in terms analogous to the christological controversy of the early Christian centuries, historical criticism enables us to recognize that the NT has, so to speak, "two natures."[11] Along with the Bible as a whole, it is a unique witness to God and a unique source of knowledge of God. At the same time, it is treasure in earthen vessels, a text conditioned *in toto* by the historical, cultural, and linguistic circumstances in which it was produced and which shaped its long process of formation into a scriptural canon. This is crucial theologically since it follows that the "plain meaning" of the text is by no means necessarily identifiable in a straightforward way with the *Christian theological meaning* of the text. It means that the understanding of a text for what it may contribute to the knowledge and love of God is something that can be discerned only after the rigorous application of the canons of Christian judgment, a judgment itself informed in part at least by historical sensibilities.

2. Social-Scientific Perspectives in New Testament Interpretation

Once it is recognized that NT interpretation is a necessarily historical enterprise (whatever else it may be), then it is a short step to recognizing that other disciplines from the human sciences have a part to play as well, not least the social sciences. Conventionally, these include sociology, social (or cultural) anthropology, and psychology. These disciplines have the potential for throwing new light on the world behind the text (the world of the author), the world within the text (the narrated world of characters, intentions, and events), and the world in front of the text (the world of the reader).

The main presupposition that underpins the use of the social sciences

11. See further, Schneiders, *The Revelatory Text*, 27-61.

in NT interpretation is that the text of the NT is a product, not just of historical conditioning, but of social and cultural conditioning as well. To the extent that cultural factors and social forces played a part in the lives of the individuals and groups that produced the NT or to which the NT refers, sociological analysis is legitimate and necessary. If it is possible to write a social history of early Christianity using the NT as a prime source, is it not possible to engage in social-scientific analysis as well?[12]

This awareness, indebted at least in part to the sociology of knowledge coming from theorists like Peter Berger and Thomas Luckmann,[13] has given rise to a method known commonly as "sociological exegesis." This method has been characterized by one of its leading exponents, John H. Elliott, as

> the analytic and synthetic interpretation of a text through the combined exercise of the exegetical and sociological disciplines, their principles, theories and techniques. The method is *sociological* in that it involves the employment of the perspectives, presuppositions, modes of analysis, comparative models, theories and research of the discipline of sociology. It is *exegetical* in that it focuses centrally upon a biblical document and through the employment of all the subdisciplines of exegesis attempts to determine the meaning and impact of that text within its various contexts. . . . Sociological exegesis asks not only what a text said "then and there" but also how and why that text was designed to function, and what its impact upon the life and activity of its recipients and formulators was intended to be. A more comprehensive designation of the method would be a "literary-historical-sociological-theological analysis" with each aspect of the exegesis understood as interrelated with the other.[14]

The advantages of a social-scientific approach to NT interpretation, as a refinement of historical method generally, have been demonstrated at the purely practical level by the very wide range of innovative studies that have been written in the past three decades and have opened up new insights

---

12. For an example of the debate between opponents and protagonists of the viability of social-scientific analysis of the NT, see Philip F. Esler, *Community and Gospel in Luke-Acts* (Cambridge: Cambridge University, 1987) 12-16; Bengt Holmberg, *Sociology and the New Testament: An Appraisal* (Minneapolis: Fortresss, 1990) 6-17.

13. See, e.g., Peter L. Berger and Thomas Luckmann, *The Social Construction of Reality* (Harmondsworth: Penguin/Garden City: Doubleday, 1966); Berger, *The Social Reality of Religion* (Harmondsworth: Penguin, 1973).

14. John H. Elliott, *A Home for the Homeless: A Sociological Exegesis of I Peter, Its Situation and Strategy* (Philadelphia: Fortress, 1981/London: SCM, 1982) 7-8.

on old problems and introduced a significantly different cultural and communal dimension to the understanding of NT texts.[15] In part, this high level of productivity has been made possible by the posing of different kinds of questions from those traditionally posed. Howard Kee has grouped these in seven categories: boundary questions, authority questions, status and role questions, ritual questions, literary questions with social implications, questions about group functions, and questions concerning the symbolic universe and the social construction of reality.[16] It would not be claiming too much to say that putting these kinds of questions to NT texts has revitalized the art of NT interpretation and the historical study of early Christianity.

2.1   The Contribution of Social-Scientific Approaches

In general terms, the advantages of social-scientific exegesis may be summarized as follows:

First, while historical criticism focuses the interpreter's attention on relations of cause and effect over time (often referred to as "diachronic" relations) and the primary aim of the historian is to tell a story drawing on precedents and analogies, the social sciences focus attention on "synchronic" relations, that is, on the way meaning is generated by social actors related to one another by a complex web of culturally-determined social systems and patterns of communication. The difference has been compared to that between interpreting a motion picture, in which meaning arises in the viewer's response to a succession of images in sequence, and interpreting a photograph, where meaning is found in the relation of the subjects to each other caught and frozen in a single frame. The latter, synchronic analysis, makes possible what anthropologist Clifford Geertz calls "thick description" in interpretation and has great potential for increasing our understanding beyond the level of a simple, linear, cause-and-effect model of reality.[17]

15. Useful surveys include Stephen C. Barton, "The Communal Dimension of Earliest Christianity," *JTS* 43 (1992) 399-427; John H. Elliott, ed., *Social-Scientific Criticism of the New Testament and its Social World*, *Semeia* 35 (1986); Holmberg, *Sociology and the New Testament*; Carolyn Osiek, *What Are They Saying about the Social Setting of the New Testament?* (rev. ed., New York: Paulist, 1992).

16. Howard C. Kee, *Knowing the Truth: A Sociological Approach to New Testament Interpretation* (Minneapolis: Fortress, 1989) 65-69.

17. See Clifford Geertz, *The Interpretation of Cultures* (New York: Basic, 1973) ch. 1.

For example, applied to Luke 3, social-scientific analysis forces us to go beyond interpretation of the Baptist episode in terms of the sequence of events as they are narrated and to ask questions like: What is significant culturally and geopolitically about the wilderness as the location of John's revelatory experience (v. 2)? Why are tax collectors and soldiers specifically identified as responsive to John's apocalyptic preaching (vv. 12-14)? What is it about John's status and social location that makes him appear as a threat to the Herodian dynasty (vv. 19-20)? What part is this disturbing tradition about the prophetic activity of John meant to play in Luke's own act of communication in writing his Gospel?[18]

In dealing with 1 Corinthians 11 historical analysis focuses on such questions as how Paul composed the letter, the possible identities of the "trouble-makers" in Corinth, what could have happened to the churches after Paul left them to preach elsewhere, and so on. But social-scientific analysis asks questions of a different kind, to do more with social forces and the dynamics of specific cultural patterns: Why are hair covering or hairstyle causes of such acute anxiety for Paul and others? Why have meals become a source of group instability and faction? Is there any link other than in the sequence of the text between the controversies over hair and over meals? The implications of social-scientific analysis do not run counter to historical analysis. On the contrary, such "thick description" aids historical awareness by opening up new dimensions of the reality to which the text testifies. The two approaches are complementary. As social anthropologist Julian Pitt-Rivers puts it: "To understand the past is like understanding another culture."[19]

Second, social-scientific analysis is useful also in helping the interpreter of the NT fill the gaps in understanding created by the fragmentariness of the texts as sources of historical information. By offering models of interpretation that have been tried and tested on analogous data, social-scientific methodology makes it possible for the fragments to be pieced together into a larger, explanatory whole that, though hypothetical, is subject nevertheless to the controls of the interpretive models themselves.

For example, modern social dissonance theory has been used to help

---

18. For one major attempt to answer questions like these about Luke's Gospel see Jerome H. Neyrey, ed., *The Social World of Luke-Acts: Models for Interpretation* (Peabody: Hendrickson, 1991).

19. Julian Pitt-Rivers, *The Fate of Shechem: or, The Politics of Sex* (Cambridge: Cambridge University, 1977) 169.

explain why the apparent disconfirmation of early Christian eschatological hope for the return of Christ did not lead to the failure of the Christian movement as a whole.[20] Max Weber's theory of charisma and its routinization has been used to explain the apparent trend in the second and third generations of Christianity toward ever greater preoccupation with church order and the institutionalization of authority.[21] The sociology of sects has been deployed to help analyze *inter alia* the ethos of the earliest Christian conventicles, what it was like to become a Christian in the first century, how family and other social ties were affected by conversion to Christianity, and why the language and thought forms of apocalyptic are so prevalent in the NT literature.[22] By drawing attention to the importance of boundary definition and boundary maintenance for the survival of small religious groups, sect theory in combination with conflict theory makes possible a more holistic understanding of the historical data about Jesus and the first Christians than might be possible otherwise.

A third contribution of social-scientific criticism is that it makes possible what Wayne Meeks calls "a hermeneutics of social embodiment."[23] Put otherwise, it offers a corrective to the strong tendency to "theological docetism" in many circles, that is, to the assumption that what is important about the NT are its theological propositions, abstracted somehow from their literary and historical setting, and that true understanding has to do with the interpretation of words and ideas rather than, or to the neglect of, the embodiment and performance of NT faith in the lives of the people and communities from whom the text comes or for whom it was written. In particular, social-scientific methodology draws attention to the fact that beliefs and doctrines help constitute systems of communication and patterns of action within a society. As such, they are cultural artifacts that

20. See John G. Gager, *Kingdom and Community: The Social World of Early Christianity* (Englewood Cliffs: Prentice-Hall, 1975) 37-49.

21. See Gager, *Kingdom and Community,* 67-76, and, more recently, Margaret Y. MacDonald, *The Pauline Churches: A Socio-Historical Study of Institutionalization in the Pauline and Deutero-Pauline Writings* (Cambridge: Cambridge University, 1988).

22. A good example is Wayne Meeks's outstanding analysis of Paul's churches, *The First Urban Christians: The Social World of the Apostle Paul* (New Haven/London: Yale University, 1983). For some reservations about the use of the sect model, see Stephen C. Barton, "Early Christianity and the Sociology of the Sect," in *The Open Text: New Directions for Biblical Studies?* ed. Francis Watson (London: SCM, 1993) 140-62.

23. Wayne A. Meeks, "A Hermeneutics of Social Embodiment," *HTR* 79 (1986) 176-86.

shape and are in turn shaped by the societies and groups that develop them and pass them on.

Robin Scroggs made this point well in a programmatic address of 1978:

> To some it has seemed that too often the discipline of the theology of the New Testament (the history of *ideas*) operates out of a methodological docetism, as if believers had minds and spirits unconnected with their individual and corporate bodies. Interest in the sociology of early Christianity is no attempt to limit reductionistically the reality of Christianity to social dynamic; rather it should be seen as an effort to guard against a reductionism from the other extreme, a limitation of the reality of Christianity to an inner-spiritual, or objective-cognitive system. In short, sociology of early Christianity wants to put body and soul together again.[24]

On this basis, it comes as no surprise that John the Baptist's call of the people to repentance is accompanied by a demand that repentance be embodied in reformed social relations (Luke 3:10-14) and that John's criticism of Herod for his marital alliance with Herodias and for his other "evil deeds" is what so alarmed Herod and prompted his retaliation (3:19-20). Nor should it surprise the interpreter of the Fourth Gospel that the revelation of Jesus as the Messiah in John 4 has as its inevitable corollary anticipations of a new socio-religious world in the making: The Samaritans are being wooed back into the people of God by Jesus the divine bridegroom (cf. 3:29); worship of God is being redefined in non-cultic terms independent of the temple (4:16-26); and gender roles and relations appear to be in process of transformation (4:27-39). And in 1 Corinthians 11 Paul's theological concerns are not developed in the abstract, as if the Corinthian church was a kind of theological academy. On the contrary, the doctrine he enunciates and the instruction he gives are the products of engagement in the very practical, political, and material business of leading and building a Christian group in the wider context of a society whose values and ways (ought to) have become alien.[25]

---

24. Robin Scroggs, "The Sociological Interpretation of the New Testament: The Present State of Research," *NTS* 26 (1980) 165-66. For other comments along the same lines, see, e.g., Bengt Holmberg, *Paul and Power* (Lund: Gleerup, 1978/Philadelphia: Fortress, 1980) 205-7 (on "the fallacy of idealism"); Gerd Theissen, *The Social Setting of Pauline Christianity* (Edinburgh: Clark/Philadelphia: Fortress, 1982) *passim*.

25. On the political dimension of Paul's dealings with the Corinthians, see L. L. Welborn, "On the Discord in Corinth: 1 Corinthians 1–4 and Ancient Politics," *JBL* 106 (1987) 85-111.

Fourth, if social-scientific analysis assists our ability to understand historically both the world behind the text and the narrative world within the text, it also offers the possibility of increasing our understanding of ourselves as readers of the text. This is so because, in social-scientific terms, it is not only the text that is a product of a particular social and cultural milieu, but we ourselves also as readers and members of reading communities.

Since the nineteenth century, the social sciences have developed, often in tandem with historical interpretation (especially in the work of Marx and Weber), as an aspect of what Paul Ricoeur calls the "hermeneutics of suspicion."[26] In other words, in pointing to ways in which a religious tradition might be conditioned by social forces or organized to meet psychological needs, the social sciences "demystify" or unmask the tradition, turning up powerful hidden dimensions that engender a false consciousness on the part of adherents. Thus Marx focused on the hidden relation between ideology and domination and interpreted religion as a coded language of domination and submission in relations between social classes. For Freud, the central issue was the relation between religion and desire, that is, the extent to which religion is a pathological expression of frustration, prohibition, inhibition, or fear. For Durkheim, "religion is something eminently social," and he called our attention to the ways in which religious ideas and ritual actions ground society in the sacred. Feminism, more recently, has drawn attention to the relation between religion and the patriarchal domination of women — that is, the manifold ways in which religious beliefs, practices, and institutions serve to legitimize misogyny and sustain hierarchical power relations in which women are subordinated to men.[27]

Such considerations from the social sciences are as relevant to understanding ourselves as readers of the NT as to understanding the text itself. They have a direct bearing on interpretation because meaning is not something that is simply discovered in the text or "read off" the surface of the text. It is, rather, created in the encounter between text and reader. The social sciences help us to recognize that our acts of interpretation are not neutral. They are affected by who we are and to whom we belong. As Elliott

26. For a useful discussion of Ricoeur's hermeneutics see Anthony C. Thiselton, *New Horizons in Hermeneutics* (London: HarperCollins/Grand Rapids: Zondervan, 1992) ch. 10.

27. For further discussion and evaluation, see John Bowker, *The Sense of God: Sociological, Anthropological and Psychological Approaches to the Origin of the Sense of God* (Oxford: Clarendon, 1973). For the feminist critique, see Rosemary Radford Ruether, *Sexism and God-Talk* (London: SCM/Boston: Beacon, 1983).

puts it: "What we see in the text, especially in its implications, is what our experience, our gender, our social position, and our political affiliations have prepared us to see."[28] Awareness of this kind can help us as readers to avoid unconscious ethnocentric or "tribal" interpretations of the NT in which the text serves only as a reflection of our own individual or group image.

2.2 Limitations of Social-Scientific Approaches

But if social-scientific approaches offer certain contributions of a positive kind to NT interpretation, they also have their problems and limitations. In many cases, such problems are the "flip side" of the very strengths just outlined. Discussion of the problems is now widespread and is an encouraging sign of the increasing maturity of sociological exegesis.[29] Here, only a few of the main issues will be discussed.

First, there is the danger of anachronism. This may occur when methods and models that have been developed in the study of organizations, groups, or societies in the modern Western world are applied to the interpretation of texts that come from the world of Mediterranean antiquity as if no significant differences separate those two worlds. The danger here is that the data from antiquity, while they are becoming intelligible and accessible to the modern reader, are also becoming fundamentally distorted into just another instance of what we know about already.

From the point of view of historical analysis the effect can be that the text and world of the NT lose their distinctiveness and individuality as phenomena from the unique and unrepeatable past. From the point of view of theology the effect can be that the text and world of the NT lose their revelatory otherness and particularity. Jesus becomes just another charismatic leader, the early church just another millenarian movement, developments in early church life become just what is to be expected in the progress of a new religious movement from "sect" to "church," the formation of the biblical canon becomes merely an exercise in ecclesiastical control and power politics, and so on. The end result is

28. Elliott, *A Home for the Homeless,* 12.
29. See, e.g., Jonathan Z. Smith, "Too Much Kingdom, Too Little Community," *Zygon* 13 (1978) 123-30; Stanley Kent Stowers, "The Social Sciences and the Study of Early Christianity," in *Approaches to Ancient Judaism,* ed. W. S. Green, vol. 5 (Missoula: Scholars, 1985) 145-81.

74

that NT interpretation becomes at best an act of domestication and at worst an act of distortion.[30]

This leads directly to a second danger of social-scientific exegesis: its proneness to claim too much, the result of which is to reduce a particular historical-religious phenomenon to its purported sociological determinants. This happens, for example, when the meaning of a NT text is identified without remainder with the function served by that text in the hypothetical group or community that generated or preserved the text. Rather than accepting that the social sciences offer an interestingly different map of the same ground with the potential for throwing new light on possibly hidden or neglected dimensions of the text, the tendency in certain quarters is to make the rather imperialistic claim that the social sciences provide the only map worth considering. Now, in place of the "idealistic fallacy" arises what critics of sociological exegesis like to refer to as the "sociological fallacy."

For example, according to the broadly functionalist sociological methodology of Wayne Meeks, the clue to the language of riddles and the motif of misunderstanding in the Fourth Gospel lies primarily, not in the Gospel's theology of revelation, spiritual discernment, and election, but in its social function of excluding outsiders and sustaining insiders. Similarly, according to another study by Meeks, conversion to the conventicles founded by Paul was especially attractive to women and slaves, not so much because they recognized the truth of the gospel that Paul preached, but rather because they found in the conventicles an ethos and identity that resolved the psychosocial tensions of the "status inconsistency" that they felt acutely in their domestic and social relations in the outside world.[31]

It could be argued that the (usually unintentional) tendency of such interpretations is reductionist. They draw attention away from the original participants' ways of seeing things. They play down the individual and the particular in favor of the social norm and what is typical for the group. They bypass the spiritual or mystical dimension of reality in favor of the

---

30. For arguments against sociological exegesis along these lines see Edwin A. Judge, "The Social Identity of the First Christians: A Question of Method in Religious History," *JRH* 11 (1980) 201-17; Cyril S. Rodd, "On Applying a Sociological Theory to Biblical Studies," *JSOT* 19 (1981) 95-106.

31. Wayne Meeks, "The Man From Heaven in Johannine Sectarianism," *JBL* 91 (1972) 44-72; *idem*, "The Social Context of Pauline Theology," *Int* 37 (1982) 266-77. The argument in the latter is taken further in *The First Urban Christians*, the methodological weaknesses of which are discussed in Stowers, "The Social Sciences."

political and ideological. Finally, they give greater prominence to what is often least accessible (because submerged or unconscious) in ways that distract attention from the author's intention or from the (apparently) more obvious meanings of the text. At its worst, reading between the lines becomes a preoccupation stronger than reading the lines themselves.

Underlying these first two problems is a third problem that is even more fundamental: the danger of using methods and models and remaining unaware that their philosophical roots lie in Enlightenment epistemological atheism. As John G. Gager put it in an essay on interdisciplinary approaches significantly entitled, "Shall We Marry Our Enemies?":

> In the late nineteenth and early twentieth centuries, many pioneers of the social sciences were consumed by a missionary zeal to explain, indeed to explain away, all aspects of human behavior, including and especially religious behavior, as nothing more than the aftereffects of childhood and evolution.[32]

In this kind of ideological framework, theology and religion are seen as having an epiphenomenal status only as the products of other forces and interests, whether the human unconscious (Freud), economic relations and class conflict (Marx), the maintenance of society (Durkheim), or the legitimation of patriarchal domination (feminism).

This genealogy of the social sciences by no means rules out their potential value for the interpreter of the NT. On the contrary, insofar as atheism and the hermeneutics of suspicion have developed as a corrective to what have been called religion's "licensed insanities" or as a reaction against willful refusals to engage with dimensions of the biblical testimony that are uncongenial for one reason or another, then the wise interpreter is likely to welcome hermeneutical insights that make possible a more clear-sighted engagement with the truth of the NT testimony and with perversions of it. Nevertheless, awareness of this genealogy should also act as a safeguard against unwittingly allowing the agenda of interpretation to shift in a secularizing direction, away from the evangelical imperatives native to the NT itself and central to the concerns of those who read the NT with a view to growing in the knowledge and love of God.

---

32. John G. Gager, "Shall We Marry Our Enemies?" *Int* 37 (1982) 256-65, here 257. For further discussion of this point in relation to a wide range of literature, see Holmberg, *Sociology and the New Testament*, 146-53; Edwin A. Yamauchi, "Sociology, Scripture and the Supernatural," *JETS* 27 (1984) 169-92.

3. Historical and Social-Scientific Criticism Applied: The Case of 1 Cor 11:2-34

Paul's letters to the members of the Christian house churches in Corinth provide an excellent place for demonstrating the value of historical and social-scientific perspectives for the art of NT interpretation. In 1 Corinthians in particular Paul addresses a wide range of issues having to do with Christian morality and lifestyle in a pagan environment. His concerns lie not just at the level of individual morality and behavior but at the communal and societal levels as well.

Furthermore, what Paul says has a highly occasional character. It is addressed to particular problems that have been reported to him by envoys from the Christian associations in Corinth or concerning which the Corinthians themselves have written to him (cf. 1 Cor 1:11; 5:1; 7:1; 11:18; 12:1; 16:17).[33] The issues include problems of factionalism and rivalry (chs. 1–4); questions of sexual morality, marriage rules, and church discipline (chs. 5–7); matters relating to food and eating customs, especially in the context of cultic worship (chs. 8–11); matters relating to the practice of worship, including the respective authority and roles of men and women in the gatherings (chs. 11–14); the fate of believers who have died (ch. 15); and so on.

The occasional character of the letter and the wide range of moral and social issues it addresses leave no doubt that the utilization of historical tools and social-scientific perspectives for its interpretation is legitimate and necessary. This has been vindicated in practice by interpreters of 1 Corinthians such as Wayne Meeks, Jerome Neyrey, Gerd Theissen, and Antoinette Clark Wire, to name but a few.[34] The observations on 1 Corinthians 11 that follow will focus attention primarily upon the contribution of social-scientific exegesis to the interpretation of the text.

3.1 The Body

Perhaps the most important point is that a social-scientific perspective helps the interpreter to discern a unity and an underlying logic in the otherwise

33. For a highly plausible reconstruction of how 1 Corinthians came to be written see Martinus C. De Boer, "The Composition of 1 Corinthians," *NTS* 40 (1994) 229-45.

34. The relevant works of Meeks and Theissen have been cited already. See also Jerome H. Neyrey, *Paul, In Other Words: A Cultural Reading of His Letters* (Louisville: Westminster/John Knox, 1990); Antoinette Clark Wire, *The Corinthian Women Prophets* (Minneapolis: Fortress, 1990).

rather disparate series of issues that Paul addresses from at least 1 Corinthians 5 on. It could well be asked: Why does Paul appear to move so breathlessly from a case of incest to the question of judicial competence in matters of community discipline, to the practice of consorting with prostitutes, to rules about marriage, divorce and celibacy, to a controversy about eating meat sacrificed to idols, to the apostolic right to financial support, to scriptural exegesis on the theme of Israel's idolatry, to the question of appropriate head-covering in worship, to instructions about communal meal practice and the Lord's Supper? — and this by no means completes the list!

If we look at this material in the light of Scroggs's plea to "put body and soul together again," what strikes us immediately is how much of this material has to do in one way or another with human bodiliness. In particular, there is a recurring concern with matters relating to sex and food, a more-than-passing interest in who sleeps with whom and who eats with whom. Speaking in theological terms, it could be said that 1 Corinthians addresses the centrally important issue of the relation between grace and nature.[35] It shows what difference belief in the crucified and risen Christ — beliefs set out respectively in the opening (chs. 1–4) and concluding (ch. 15) parts of the letter — ought to make to believers' bodily existence both in the church community and in society at large.

But the theological categories of "grace" and "nature," while obviously legitimate and extremely important for allowing Paul's writing to work for us in systematic theological terms as Christian Scripture, are not the only way of mapping the ground of what Paul is trying to say. Indeed, it has been shown that other categories help us to define the contours of the ground in interestingly complementary ways, some of which expose aspects of the topography that theological categories leave relatively untouched.[36]

In particular, given that so much of the letter is devoted to socioreligious questions about bodiliness, sex, and food, the use of social science perspectives has become an integral part of interpreting what Paul says. This is so because the social sciences are well equipped to help in the

35. See further, Timothy Radcliffe, "Paul and Sexual Identity: 1 Corinthians 11.2-16," in *After Eve: Women, Theology and the Christian Tradition*, ed. Janet Martin Soskice (London: Marshall Pickering, 1990) 62-72.

36. In certain circles, for example, Paul's ethics in 1 Corinthians are allowed to become focused on the problem of Christian freedom and "the weaker brother" in ways that are rather individualistic and that tend to neglect the political, social, and ecclesial dimensions of the letter.

task of understanding the ways in which nature becomes a vehicle for culture. The contribution of the British social anthropologist Mary Douglas, to name but one, has been particularly noteworthy in this area. She has shown both the ways in which the body, sex, and food are made to carry a heavy cultural and metaphysical freight in particular social locations and the ways in which rules governing physical, bodily processes like sexual intercourse and the ingestion of food serve as cultural symbols of group identity and group boundaries.[37] In her early work, *Purity and Danger,* she writes, for example:

> Even more direct is the symbolism worked upon the human body. The body is a model which can stand for any bounded system. Its boundaries can represent any boundaries which are threatened or precarious. The body is a complex structure. The functions of its different parts and their relation afford a source of symbols for other complex structures. We cannot possibly interpret rituals concerning excreta, breast milk, saliva and the rest unless we are prepared to see in the body a symbol of society, and to see the powers and dangers credited to social structure reproduced in small on the human body.[38]

In this light, the at-first-sight rather arbitrary series of instructions Paul gives about the body, sex, and food — instructions that invariably have to do with exchanges between bodies or the crossing of bodily boundaries and orifices — assume a much clearer significance. They have to do with how individual physical bodies are to represent and grow together as an identifiable social body and how that social body (the church) is to conduct itself as the body of the crucified and risen Christ in the city of Corinth.

3.2 The Head

If the social sciences help us discern more clearly an important dimension of the underlying logic in Paul's instructions about the body, sex, and food

---

37. Of Mary Douglas's many works, the most pertinent for biblical interpretation are: *Purity and Danger* (London: Routledge, 1966); *Rules and Meanings* (Harmondsworth: Penguin, 1973); *Natural Symbols* (2d ed., London: Barrie and Jenkins, 1973); *Implicit Meanings* (London: Routledge and Kegan Paul, 1975); and *In the Active Voice* (London: Routledge, 1982). Extensive use is made of her work by Neyrey in his *Paul, In Other Words.* See also Sheldon R. Isenberg and Dennis E. Owen, "Bodies, Natural and Contrived: The Work of Mary Douglas," *RelSRev* 3 (1977) 1-17.

38. Douglas, *Purity and Danger,* 115.

at the general level, they also help more specifically in the interpretation of 1 Corinthians 11. In vv. 2-16, Paul gives instruction about what he considers appropriate head covering/hair style for the Corinthian women prophets. From what Paul says, it is quite clear that symbolic and religious significance attaches to a particular part of the physical body, the head, the κεφαλή (kephalē), along with how the head or the hair of the head is (or is not) adorned. This significance is obviously due, at least in part, to the metaphorical associations of the head (and other parts of the body) in discussions in antiquity about patterns of authority in the social body.

Reading between the lines, it appears that the Corinthian women prophets are expressing freely their new authority as people who, by dying and rising with Christ in baptism, have been remade as God's new creation (cf. 12:13; Gal 3:27-28). In the context of communal worship, they are doing this by disregarding conventional symbols of female identity and subordination. They pray and prophesy with their heads uncovered or their hair loose.[39] Paul resists this innovation in no uncertain terms and appeals to a whole battery of (to the modern reader rather obscure) arguments as warrants for his opposition.

This is not the place to adjudicate between Paul and the Corinthian women prophets or to give a detailed exegesis. What is pertinent here is to point out, first, that the women's sense of new spiritual identity and authority "in Christ" manifested itself in body symbols, specifically, symbols of head-covering or hairstyle; second, that these innovations surrounding the physical bodies of the women generated tensions and anxiety in the social body of the church; and third, that Paul responds to these anxieties by attempting to reimpose the conventional symbols of women's identity for the sake of propriety and orderliness in the social body, while at the same time providing arguments that would not detract from the women's legitimate authority and, more positively, would encourage the Corinthians as a whole in their worship, in the company of the angelic hosts, of the one true God.

Historical criticism makes us aware of possible analogies from Jewish and Greco-Roman culture that help to explain both why the Corinthian women prophets prayed and prophesied with their heads uncovered or their hair loose and why these innovations generated anxiety in the churches. For example, Elisabeth Schüssler Fiorenza points to a range of

---

39. There is no scholarly unanimity over how to translate the verses where Paul refers to how the women are adorning their heads or wearing their hair. For the main alternatives and a bibliography, see Wire, *Corinthian Women Prophets,* Appendix 8.

evidence showing Greek women in the mystery cults engaging in acts of worship with their heads uncovered or their hair hanging loose or both:

> Such a sight of disheveled hair would be quite common in the ecstatic worship of oriental divinities. . . . Disheveled hair and head thrown back were typical for the maenads in the cult of Dionysos, in that of Cybele, the Pythia at Delphi, the Sibyl, and unbound hair was necessary for a woman to produce an effective magical incantation. . . . Flowing and un-bound hair was also found in the Isis cult, which had a major center in Corinth.[40]

Against this kind of historical background, Paul's anxieties could be explained as a legitimate concern that the worship of the Corinthian Christians could become indistinguishable (especially to outsiders) from that of pagan idolaters.

Historical criticism also helps us interpret the position of the Corinthian women prophets. In particular, traditio-historical investigation of the pre-Pauline Christian baptismal formula cited by Paul first in Gal 3:27-28 gives us grounds for believing that, although Paul subsequently plays down the dissolution of gender boundaries effected by baptism into Christ (cf. 1 Cor 12:13 and Col 3:10-11, where "not male and female" is omitted!), the Corinthian women rejoiced in their new identity and authority, which they had been taught to think of as no longer determined by their relation to men but as determined instead by their relation to the risen Lord.[41]

The import of social-scientific exegesis does not run counter to these historical and literary perspectives but complements them and and takes them further. In particular, it draws attention to, and helps make sense of, the enormous social and religious significance accorded in the text to the physical body — specifically, to the head covering/hairstyles of the women prophets — and shows the variety of ways in which the physical body served as a symbolic map of the social body that, in turn, conveyed a range of understandings about what it meant for women and men to belong to the body of Christ.

There is, furthermore, the important issue of social control. Mary

---

40. Elisabeth Schüssler Fiorenza, *In Memory of Her: A Feminist Theological Reconstruction of Christian Origins* (New York: Crossroad/London: SCM, 1983) 227.

41. See especially, Wire, *Corinthian Women Prophets*, 122-28; also Fiorenza, *In Memory of Her*, ch. 6.

Douglas suggests that control of the social body is commonly expressed symbolically through controls exercised over the surface and orifices of the physical body.[42] Seen in this light, the uncovered heads or unloosed hair of the women prophets expresses their newfound sense of freedom and authority in the social body of the church, which is the body of Christ. Paul's instructions, replete as they are with (what the social anthropologist would call) honor and shame language designed to induce conformity,[43] seek to reassert a variant upon the social status quo by demanding that traditional body symbols of gender differentiation be reinstated.

3.3 Eating

At first sight, the shift Paul makes from the controversy over the women's head coverings/hairstyles (11:2-16) to the disorderliness of the Corinthians' meal practices (11:17-34) is abrupt and opaque. But social-scientific perspectives together with standard historical-exegetical methods show the way toward a link between these apparently disparate issues.

In brief, what the two passages have in common, at least at one level, is an underlying concern about identity and order in the Corinthian house churches, a socioreligious concern that finds its symbolic focus in rules governing the control of body surfaces and bodily orifices. In the former case, the symbolic focus is the head and hair of the women prophets; in the latter, it is ingestion into the mouth of food and drink in the course of the Corinthians' common meals.

In fact, 1 Cor 11:2-34 is part of a larger complex of moral instruction that begins in 8:1, where Paul turns to the question of "food offered to idols" (εἰδωλόθυτων, *eidōlothytōn*).[44] Paul's expectation that the women

---

42. Douglas, *Purity and Danger*, 124:

When rituals express anxiety about the body's orifices the sociological counterpart of this anxiety is a care to protect the political and cultural unity of a minority group. The Israelites were always in their history a hard-pressed minority. In their beliefs all the bodily issues were polluting, blood, pus, excreta, semen, etc. The threatened boundaries of their body politic would be well mirrored in their care for the integrity, unity and purity of the physical body.

This hypothesis is developed at much greater length in Douglas's *Natural Symbols.*

43. On honor and shame as "pivotal values of the first-century Mediterranean world," see Bruce J. Malina, *The New Testament World: Insights from Cultural Anthropology* (Atlanta: John Knox/London: SCM, 1983) ch. 2.

44. On the Hellenistic practice of cult meals as the historical context for what Paul

prophets will accept the discipline of restricting their spiritual authority (ἐξουσία, *exousia*) in the assemblies by wearing conventional head coverings/hair fashions is of a piece with Paul's overall teaching from 8:1 on that those believers who are "strong" on the basis of their special "knowledge" (γνῶσις, *gnōsis*) should limit their freedom (ἐξουσία, *exousia*) for the sake of their brothers and sisters in the faith whose consciences are "weak."

At the spiritual and religious level, the danger Paul is seeking to protect the Corinthians from is the danger of apostasy from service of the one true God through falling (back) into idolatry. In relation to their eating habits, idolatry is a threat arising both from possible moral compromise in eating food sacrificed to idols (chs. 8, 10) and from eating the Christian common meal in arrogant disregard for the fact that the meal is "the Lord's" (11:17-34, esp. v. 20) and not their own. In relation to the women prophets, idolatry is a danger caused by the threat to the glory of God posed, first, by women adopting a style of clothing or hair commonly linked with sexual immorality (cf. 11:5-6), which was itself associated with idol worship; second, by those women praying and prophesying adorned in a way that (from the dominant, male point of view) apparently drew attention to themselves as "the glory of man" (11:7); and third, by the women provoking the angels present with the believers to turn their attention away from their worship of God to attend to glory of a different kind (11:10).[45]

At the social level, Paul is attempting to protect the Corinthians from the danger of "divisions" (σχίσματα, *schismata*) and "factions" (αἱρέσεις, *haireseis*, 11:18-19). In Scroggs's terms, threats to the "soul" of the Corinthian community (idolatry) have as their corollary and counterpart threats to the "body" as well; and Paul tries to counteract these threats to the social body by calling for controls of a potent and symbolic kind on the members' physical bodies. We have seen already what this entails in relation to the heads/hair of the women prophets. In relation to the common meal, it is clear that what should have been a ritual of incorporation and group solidarity as members together of the one "body of Christ" has degenerated into a ritual of social rivalry and competition threatening to split the

---

says about meat sacrificed to idols, see Wendell Lee Willis, *Idol Meat in Corinth: The Pauline Argument in 1 Corinthians 8 and 10* (Chico: Scholars, 1985).

45. For this understanding of the way in which Paul's concern about the threat of idolatry unifies the material running from 8:1 to 11:34 I am indebted to Wire's brilliant analysis in *The Corinthian Women Prophets*, chs. 5-6.

fellowship apart (11:17-22).[46] The rich householders distinguish themselves from the poor by the timing of their meal — they eat first and without waiting for the others to arrive (11:21, 33); by its quantity and quality (11:21); and by their refusal to share (11:21). In this way the rich may be seen also as attempting to extend their influence in the church. Their eating practices are a demonstration of social status and an attempt to dominate by imposing shame (11:22). Drawing specific attention to the aspect of body symbolism, Neyrey puts the matter thus:

> The crisis over the orifice of the mouth reflects a crisis over the boundaries of the social body. Discriminatory eating and drinking manifest distinctions among the social levels of those present, thus establishing artificial boundaries within the group to exclude the poor, the hungry, or the weak: "Do you despise the church of God and humiliate those who have nothing?" (11:22 . . .). Paul perceives the breakdown of table manners (i.e., the deregulation of the oral orifice) as a threat to the boundaries of the social body. Lack of control of the orifice of the body manifests a serious disregard of the social body's integrity and purity.[47]

Paul's response represents an attempt to restructure the social patterns of the fellowship by controlling its members' eating habits. He does this above all by replacing their own meals, which are marked by profane rivalry and polluting disorderliness, with a meal of a different kind in which all can share equally (11:23-26). The new meal has a sacred name, which gives it also a transcendent point of reference: It is "the Lord's meal" (χυριαχὸν δεῖπνον, kyriakon deipnon). It is linked with authoritative tradition "received from the Lord" and "delivered" in formal catechesis to the Corinthians. This tradition infuses the meal with meaning and danger and is intended to function as a control on the practice of the meal, for it states how participants are to think about the meal, what order the meal is to follow, and what consequences will follow if the meal becomes an occasion for idolatry (i.e., for failure to "discern the body"; 11:23-32). Furthermore, Paul draws a line between this sacred "Lord's meal" and eating for the sake of merely satisfying hunger. The Corinthian Christians are to eat this meal

---

46. For much fuller sociological exegesis along these lines, see Gerd Theissen, *The Social Setting of Pauline Christianity*, ch. 4; Stephen C. Barton, "Paul's Sense of Place: An Anthropological Approach to Community Formation in Corinth," *NTS* 32 (1986) 225-46.

47. Neyrey, *Paul, In Other Words*, 123.

together, with members waiting until everyone is present; the other kind of meal is to be eaten "at home" (11:33-34). If these instructions are followed, the common meal of the Corinthians will function as it should: to incorporate individual physical bodies into the social body of the church under the lordship of Christ.

It is worth asking, in conclusion, why Paul's instructions about eating "things offered to idols" come to a conclusion — or at least a semi-colon — with these admonitions about the "Lord's meal." The socioreligious logic of his argument appears to be that the way in which the Corinthian believers conduct their bodily activities and relations, including their eating habits, expresses in a fundamental way who they are and who they belong to. The basic issue is one of allegiance: Is their allegiance to Christ or to idols? These are not just spiritual or religious concerns having to do with the individual believer, though they are certainly that. Rather, social-scientific exegesis helps us to see that they are matters of social embodiment as well. It helps us to recognize more clearly that, according to Paul, the lordship of Christ is meaningless unless the marks of that lordship are borne in the individual bodies of believers and in the corporate body of those — women and men, "strong" and "weak" — who claim to be themselves the body of Christ.

4. Suggestions for Further Reading

4.1 The Significance of Historical Inquiry for Biblical Interpretation

Theoretical and applied reflection on the nature of historical inquiry and its significance for biblical interpretation is a vast field. Helpful routes into the literature are provided by Peter Stuhlmacher, *Historical Criticism and Theological Interpretation of Scripture* (ET London: SPCK/Philadelphia: Fortress, 1979); Robert Morgan with John Barton, *Biblical Interpretation* (Oxford: Oxford University, 1988) chs. 2-6; Sandra M. Schneiders, *The Revelatory Text* (San Francisco: HarperCollins, 1991) ch. 4; W. Randolph Tate, *Biblical Interpretation: An Integrated Approach* (Peabody: Hendrickson, 1991) unit 1; N. T. Wright, *The New Testament and the People of God* (London: SPCK/Minneapolis: Fortress, 1992) part 2; and Jon D. Levenson, *The Hebrew Bible, the Old Testament, and Historical Criticism* (Philadelphia: Westminster, 1993).

4.2 The Social Sciences

Turning to the social sciences, among the major practitioners whose work has been influential in NT interpretation are the following: Max Weber has had an enormous impact through works such as *The Sociology of Religion* (ET Boston: Beacon, 1963) and *The Theory of Social and Economic Organization* (ET New York: Free, 1947). For the study of ritual and symbolic action, mention must be made of Victor Turner, *The Ritual Process* (Harmondsworth: Penguin/Ithaca: Cornell University, 1969) and *Dramas, Fields, and Metaphors* (Ithaca: Cornell University, 1974).

The social significance of purity rules and body symbolism is heavily indebted to Mary Douglas's work — in particular, *Purity and Danger* (London: Routledge, 1966); *Rules and Meanings* (Harmondsworth: Penguin, 1973); and *Natural Symbols* (2d ed., London: Barrie and Jenkins, 1973). Outstanding also have been the contributions of two other anthropologists: Edmund Leach, in *Culture and Communication: The Logic by Which Symbols Are Connected* (Cambridge: Cambridge University, 1976); and Clifford Geertz, in *The Interpretation of Cultures* (New York: Basic, 1973).

Influential for the application of sect theory and studies of millenarianism to early Christianity are the works of Bryan R. Wilson, for example, *Religious Sects: A Sociological Study* (London: Weidenfeld and Nicolson, 1970) and *Magic and the Millennium* (London: Heinemann, 1973). On the sociology of knowledge, major contributions are represented by Peter L. Berger and Thomas Luckmann, *The Social Construction of Reality* (Harmondsworth: Penguin/Garden City: Doubleday, 1966); and Peter L. Berger, *The Social Reality of Religion* (Harmondsworth: Penguin, 1973).

4.3 Social-Scientific Exegesis

In NT studies, there have been many contributors to social-scientific interpretation. A useful bibliography of work up to 1988 is Daniel J. Harrington, "Second Testament Exegesis and the Social Sciences: A Bibliography," *BTB* 18 (1988) 77-85. To this can be added David M. May, *Social Scientific Criticism of the New Testament: A Bibliography*, NABPRBS 4 (Macon: Mercer University, 1991). But the following contributions are among the most important:

Of European scholars, Gerd Theissen's work has been the most innovative and wide-ranging. His studies include: *The First Followers of Jesus* (ET; London: SCM, 1978), a broadly structural-functionalist approach to what he calls the "Jesus movement" as reflected in the Gospel traditions; *The Social Setting of Pauline Christianity* (ET; Edinburgh: Clark, 1982), a collection of highly influential sociological essays on Paul's mission and Christianity at Corinth; a ground-breaking application of psychological models to Pauline interpretation entitled *Psychological Aspects of Pauline Theology* (ET; Edinburgh: Clark/Philadelphia: Fortress, 1987); and *Social Reality and the First Christians: Theology, Ethics, and the World of the New Testament* (ET; Edinburgh: Clark, 1992), his most recent collection of essays on the Jesus tradition, Pauline theology, and questions of method in sociological exegesis.

Most of the other major contributors to sociological exegesis of the NT have come from North America. Wayne Meeks has made effective use of an eclectic approach to social-scientific models, both in a much-discussed essay on the Fourth Gospel, "The Man from Heaven in Johannine Sectarianism," *JBL* 91 (1972) 44-72, and in his major synthesis of Pauline interpretation, *The First Urban Christians: The Social World of the Apostle Paul* (New Haven: Yale University, 1983). Another leader in the field has been John H. Elliott. His book, *A Home for the Homeless. A Sociological Exegesis of 1 Peter, Its Situation and Strategy* (Philadelphia: Fortress, 1981/London: SCM, 1982) is a methodologically sophisticated study that has become a reference point for much subsequent discussion. He has followed up the methodological issues, as well as engaging in critical evaluation of Theissen's work, in his essay, "Social-Scientific Criticism of the New Testament and Its Social World: More on Method and Models," in *Semeia* 35 (1986), which he also edited. Most recently he has written *What is Social-Scientific Criticism?*, GBS (Minneapolis: Fortress, 1993).

Some would argue that among the social sciences the insights and methods of social (or cultural) anthropology are more germane to interpreting the Mediterranean world of the NT than those of sociology or psychology. Certainly, the hermeneutical potential of social or cultural anthropology has been well demonstrated by Bruce J. Malina in several books and many essays, including: *The New Testament World: Insights from Cultural Anthropology* (Atlanta: John Knox, 1981/London: SCM, 1983; rev. ed., 1993); *Christian Origins and Cultural Anthropology: Practical Models for Biblical Interpretation* (Atlanta: John Knox, 1986), which draws heavily upon the broadly structuralist "grid-group" theory of British anthropologist Mary Douglas; and with Richard Rohrbaugh, *A Social-Science Commentary on the Synoptic Gospels* (Minneapolis: Fortress, 1992), which sets Synoptic traditions in the context of ancient Mediterranean life and culture. A number of his essays and essays by others in the social-scientific field have appeared in the journal *Biblical Theology Bulletin.*

Another scholar to make wide use of anthropological and other social-scientific approaches is Jerome Neyrey. His *Paul, In Other Words: A Cultural Reading of his Letters* (Louisville: Westminster/John Knox, 1990) draws, like Malina's work, on Mary Douglas's important work on body symbolism and the social meaning of purity rules, as does his essay on "The Idea of Purity in Mark's Gospel," in *Semeia* 35 (1986) 91-128. Neyrey has also written on the Fourth Gospel in *An Ideology of Revolt: John's Christology in Social-Science Perspective* (Philadelphia: Fortress, 1988). More recently, he has edited a major collection of social-scientific essays on Luke-Acts (several coauthored by himself and Malina) entitled *The Social World of Luke-Acts: Models for Interpretation* (Peabody: Hendrickson, 1991).

A beginning has been made in exploring how social-scientific perspectives affect the interpretation of NT ethics. Noteworthy here is L. William Countryman, *Dirt, Greed and Sex: Sexual Ethics in the New Testament and Their Implications for Today* (Philadelphia: Fortress, 1988/London: SCM, 1989), which focuses on purity rules. Also important is Wayne Meeks's study, *The Moral World of the First Christians* (London: SPCK/Philadelphia: Westminster, 1987), which draws on the work of anthropologist Clifford Geertz and seeks to understand the moral formation of the early Christians in the context of the symbolic and social worlds they shared with their contemporaries in the villages and cities of the Mediterranean world. Another sociological study with implications for ethics is that of the Australian scholar, Philip F. Esler, *Community and Gospel in Luke-Acts: The Social and Political Motivations of Lucan Theology* (Cambridge: Cambridge University, 1987).

Finally, it is worth mentioning works that discuss at a more theoretical level the viability of social-scientific interpretation of the NT. Apart from the writings of Theissen in this area, an early contribution was John G. Gager's experimental study, *Kingdom and Community: The Social World of Early Christianity* (Englewood Cliffs: Prentice-Hall, 1975). Also important are two books by Howard Clark Kee: *Christian Origins in Sociological Perspective* (Philadelphia: Westminster, 1980) and *Knowing the Truth: A Sociological Approach to New Testament Interpretation* (Minneapolis: Fortress, 1989). Bengt Holmberg's study of power and authority relations in the early church, *Paul and Power* (Lund: Gleerup, 1978/Philadelphia: Fortress, 1980), broke new ground, and he has followed up his methodological reflections in *Sociology and the New Testament: An Appraisal* (Minneapolis: Fortress, 1990).

4.4 Implications in Other Directions

The links between social-scientific approaches and political hermeneutics are explored in the major collection of essays edited by Norman K. Gottwald and Richard A. Horsley, *The Bible and Liberation: Political and Social Hermeneutics* (2d ed., Maryknoll: Orbis/London: SPCK, 1993). Feminist interpretation has drawn on sociological insights also — see Elisabeth Schüssler Fiorenza's *In Memory of Her: A Feminist Theological Reconstruction of Christian Origins* (New York: Crossroad/London: SCM, 1983). Of general relevance at the foundational level of theoretical hermeneutics is Anthony Thiselton's magnum opus *New Horizons in Hermeneutics: The Theory and Practice of Transforming Biblical Reading* (London: HarperCollins/Grand Rapids: Zondervan, 1992).

5. *The Relevance of Extracanonical Jewish Texts to New Testament Study*

RICHARD BAUCKHAM

Jesus was a Galilean Jew whose ministry took place almost entirely within Jewish Palestine. The earliest Christian churches were composed of Palestinian Jews (including some Jews from the diaspora who were resident in Jerusalem). When Christianity spread outside Palestine, it was among Jewish communities in the diaspora that it first made converts. Even when large numbers of Gentile converts entered the church in the course of the NT period, the leadership of the churches still remained largely in the hands of Jewish Christians. Most of the writers of the NT were Jews. The Hebrew Bible in Greek translation became the Bible of Gentile Christians, and although they read it from the perspective of their faith in Jesus, they also read it within the Jewish traditions of interpretation that they learned from Jewish Christians. Furthermore, even Jewish religious literature that they did not regard as canonical Scripture must have been read and valued by Gentile Christians. It is very striking that apart from the Hebrew Bible itself, the Dead Sea Scrolls, and a few other Jewish documents that have been recovered by archaeologists in recent times almost all of the Jewish literature that has survived from the period before 200 CE was preserved, not by Jews, who ceased to use it, but by Christians. Even Jewish works that were not written until the Christian church was already well established and most of the NT writings had already been written, such as the apocalypses of Ezra (4 Ezra = 2 Esdras) and Baruch (2 Apocalypse of Baruch and 3 Apocalypse of Baruch), were appropriated by Christians.

All this clearly suggests not only that first-century Judaism was the principal religious context of Christian origins, but also that the character of early Christianity was decisively determined by these origins, so much so that, in terms of the history of religions, the Christianity of the NT period must be seen, not as something quite different from Judaism, but as a distinctive form of Judaism. The fact that by the end of the first century the majority of Christians were probably Gentiles who had not adopted the full observance of the law of Moses does not contradict this description, though it is one of several reasons why Christianity was coming to be seen by most non-Christian Jews as something other than a legitimate form of Judaism. Yet even this "parting of the ways" between Christianity and Judaism was essentially a dispute between divergent interpretations of a common religious heritage.

None of this is meant to deny that both Jews and Christians were strongly influenced by the culture of the Greco-Roman world. Both Jews and Christians shared, in many respects, a common cultural world with their pagan neighbors. It would be a serious mistake to isolate the Jewish context of early Christianity from the wider Greco-Roman context. Nevertheless, Jews of this period had a strong sense of their religious distinctiveness and of the necessity to preserve it, and Christians, by worshiping the God of Israel, retained the core of this distinctiveness while relaxing its strict connection with observance of the law of Moses. In recent decades of NT study older theories that attributed a determinative influence on early Christianity to non-Jewish religious cults or ideas such as the mystery cults or pre-Christian Gnosticism have largely lost credibility (though very recently the parallels between the Gospel traditions and Cynicism, which was not a religious cult, but a school of Greco-Roman philosophy, have attracted fresh attention). The thoroughly Jewish character of the NT literature has been constantly demonstrated by the intensive study of this literature in relation to relevant Jewish literature.

Moreover, such study has taken place in a period in which the study of early Judaism and its literature has itself blossomed. New discoveries, especially the Dead Sea Scrolls; serious study of works that have long been known but largely neglected, such as many of the so-called Pseudepigrapha; properly critical work on the extent to which traditions of the NT period may be preserved in the Targums (Aramaic translation-interpretations of texts from the Hebrew Bible) and the rabbinic literature; and major works of historical analysis and synthesis, such as Martin Hengel's influential work on the hellenization of Palestinian Jewish culture,[1] have transformed the

---

1. Martin Hengel, *Judaism and Hellenism* (ET London: SCM/Philadelphia: Fortress,

study of early Judaism. The resources now available to the NT student for understanding the Jewish context of early Christianity are abundant. There are introductory textbooks and major reference works. Editions, translations, commentaries, and studies of texts make them available and more accurately usable than ever before.

At the same time, there is much to be done. Important texts still await editing. Some have still been very little studied. Major issues of interpretation are highly debated. Students of the NT who take the Jewish context of early Christianity seriously cannot expect to find simply uncontroversial facts and agreed conclusions. They will encounter major debates between the leading scholars, such as that over the character of Pharisaism in the first century. They will have to learn that, as in the study of the NT, the textbooks sometimes make unqualified assertions, for example about the date of a work, which in fact rest on the slenderest of evidence and are highly debatable. They will find themselves trying to understand puzzling texts without the kind of help that is readily available in the commentaries for interpreting difficult NT texts. They will have to realize the uncertainties involved in relying, for example, on an English translation of a badly transmitted Old Slavonic version of a no longer extant Greek text that might have been translated from a Semitic original.

This may make the use of noncanonical Jewish literature in NT study seem a dauntingly difficult task. It is! The study of early Judaism is a complex and constantly developing field of study, in reality composed of a variety of highly technical and specialized disciplines. Advanced students who wish to make original contributions to this aspect of NT study will have to gain some understanding of the skills and tools of these disciplines, even if only to understand the way they are deployed by the scholars they read. In fact, many NT researchers who have turned to Jewish texts to compare them with the NT have found themselves involved in major projects of interpretation of the Jewish texts for their own sake. Some firsthand work of this kind on Jewish material should now be virtually a prerequisite for competent historical research in NT studies. But students who are only beginning NT study or who have no expectation of doing original work in the field should not be deterred from reading Jewish texts of the period along with the excellent introductory literature now available. They cannot

---

1974); *idem, Jews, Greeks and Barbarians* (ET London: SCM/Philadelphia: Fortress, 1980); *idem, The "Hellenization" of Judaea in the First Century after Christ* (ET London: SCM/Philadelphia: Trinity, 1989).

in any case avoid the extensive references to Jewish parallels and discussions of the Jewish context in virtually all literature about the NT. Even a small degree of firsthand acquaintance with the Jewish texts will make a considerable difference to students' appreciation of such references and discussions.

1. Using the Literature

The general usefulness of the extracanonical Jewish literature for NT interpretation is obvious. Insofar as the context of Jesus, the early church, and the NT writings was Jewish, these writings provide us with most of what we know about that context (along with archaeological evidence and some references to Judaism and Jewish history in pagan literature). Of course, we must understand the historical context here in the most comprehensive sense. It involves not only the religious, but (insofar as the distinctions are valid in a religious culture) also the political, social, economic, and cultural life of the Jews in Palestine and in the western diaspora. To take a very simple example, if we did not have Josephus's indispensable political history of first-century Jewish Palestine, we would not know who the "king Herod" of Acts 12:1 was, we might well confuse him with the tetrarch Herod of Luke's Gospel, and we might then accuse Luke of inaccuracy in attributing to him authority in Jerusalem at this time.

However, since most of the surviving Jewish literature is religious in purpose and content, as is the NT, it will not be surprising if the religious dimension of life (including the religious dimension of political, social, economic, and cultural life) predominates in the value of the former to illuminate the context of the latter. To take a much less simple example, every serious student of the Gospels wants to know who the Pharisees were, since, although the NT offers some indications (e.g., Acts 26:5), for the most part it refers to them without explaining who they were. The Gospels are interested solely in the Pharisees' interaction with Jesus, and so, even if their account of the Pharisees were entirely accurate, it could still be very incomplete and onesided. But the Gospels could also be suspected of having polemically distorted their picture of the Pharisees or of having retrojected onto pre-70 CE Pharisaism concerns belonging to the late first century.

Unfortunately, the other main sources of information about the Pharisees — Josephus and rabbinic traditions about the Pharisees — are also problematic: Josephus because he had his own agenda that made him very selective and (some would say) not wholly accurate in what he records about the Pharisees; the rabbinic evidence because the selection, preservation, and redaction of rabbinic traditions about the Pharisees was controlled by the concerns of the post-70 rabbinic movement. It is not surprising, therefore, that reconstructing the nature of Pharisaism in the NT period is a complex historical task with no fully agreed conclusions, but one of vital importance to NT scholarship.

One important methodological point for NT interpretation is that clearly it will not do for NT scholars simply to plunder the Jewish evidence to illustrate what the various NT texts say about the Pharisees. Of course, it is true that, for example, Matt 19:3 can be greatly illuminated by the rabbinic traditions about the debate between the schools of Hillel and Shammai over the grounds for divorce. But if we are to discuss the relationship of Jesus or the early Christians to the Pharisees in broader terms, we need as rounded and accurate an understanding of the Pharisees as a Jewish religious movement as we can gain. For this purpose, we cannot allow the NT material to control the agenda, but must study the Pharisees for their own sake with the full range of evidence available, problematic though it is. Having said that, of course, we should not forget that the NT is, among other things, itself evidence of early Judaism, including Pharisaism. If the Gospels are problematic as evidence for Pharisaism, so are the other sources.

What is true of the Pharisees is true of the whole subject. The NT student and scholar must use the Jewish literature in the first place to understand Judaism. Only someone who understands early Judaism for its own sake will be able to use Jewish texts appropriately and accurately in the interpretation of the NT. The famous warning issued by Samuel Sandmel against "parallelomania" in NT studies[2] has its most general application here. Someone who knows the Jewish literature only in the form of isolated texts selected for the sake of their apparent relationship to NT texts will not understand those texts in their own contexts (literary and otherwise) and so will not know whether they constitute real or only apparent parallels and, even supposing they are real parallels, will not be able to use them properly. A principle that NT students and even NT scholars rarely take to heart is that, for the sake of a balanced view of the relationship of Christianity to early Judaism, it is just as important to study Jewish texts that are least like anything in the NT as it is to study those with which the NT writings have most affinity.

2. Samuel Sandmel, "Parallelomania," *JBL* 81 (1962) 1-13.

Of course, it would be a mistake to wait until one has mastered the broad picture — whether of early Judaism or of early Christianity's relationship to Judaism — before studying the detailed ways in which Jewish texts can illuminate specific NT texts. In this as in most fields of study, one's understanding of the general will be enhanced by study of particulars, and the two will be constantly interrelating. What is important in the study of particular Jewish parallels to particular NT texts is never to forget that the former have a context that is essential to their meaning and relevance. This context will need to be explored in a variety of ways. The theme may need to be traced in other Jewish texts, or related to other themes. A particular word or expression or image may have to be traced in a variety of texts before the significance of its occurrence in one can be evaluated. It is usually also important to know as a whole the particular Jewish work that is being used. (Compared with modern books, all ancient Jewish works are short, most extremely short. It does not take long to read one through!) No NT student would quote a verse from a Pauline epistle, without further ado, as evidence of early Christianity in general, because Paul was a highly individual and creative thinker, and even what he shared with other Christians, which was certainly a great deal, would not have been shared equally with all Christians. But early Jewish writers were also individual and creative writers, and early Judaism was more diverse than early Christianity. Precisely in what sense a Jewish text constitutes evidence of the Jewish context of early Christianity needs to be more carefully considered than it often is.

It is extremely probable that all the NT writers read some extracanonical Jewish literature and that some of them were very familiar with some of that literature. (In addition, many of them would have known Jewish oral traditions, such as the legal traditions of the Pharisees and the exegetical traditions of the synagogues.) However, it is seldom possible to prove that a particular NT writer knew a particular Jewish writing that we know. We know that the letter of Jude explicitly quotes (in v. 14) part of the collection of Enoch literature that we know as *1 Enoch* and makes several allusions to other parts of the Enoch literature. But this is very unusual. In most cases we cannot treat the Jewish literature as sources the NT writers used, but must see them as evidence of the ideas and terminology with which NT writers were familiar. And at this point we must raise two problems.

One problem is the kind of Judaism of which a particular Jewish writing is evidence. In the unusual case of the Dead Sea Scrolls, we know at least that these writings all belonged to the library of the Qumran community. Some of the literature was written within the community and is unlikely to have been known outside the community, except by other Essenes, but clearly the community also read extracanonical religious literature that was not peculiarly its own and had wide or limited circulation among other Jews. These categories cannot always be easily distinguished. In the case of most other prerabbinic Jewish literature we do not know who wrote it or read it. For a text to be relevant to NT interpretation, we need to be able to suppose (from various kinds of evidence, including the NT) either that Christianity was influenced by (or, in relevant cases, opposed) the particular kind of Judaism represented by the text, or that in relevant respects what the text says was not peculiar to the group that produced and read it, or that the writing in question was not restricted to a particular Jewish group but circulated widely. Such judgments cannot be made in isolation from current discussion of the extent of variety in early Judaism. The current trend to emphasize diversity to such an extent as to speak of "Judaisms" in the plural[3] has rightly been challenged by E. P. Sanders's claim that it makes sense to speak of a "common Judaism" that most Jews shared and in which even those Jews who belonged to the parties, such as the Pharisees, participated.[4] Much of the literature that has survived may well have circulated quite widely and may well have been read by Jews who differed from each other on some issues. Even literature that belonged rather exclusively to particular groups, such as the Qumran community's own writings, shared many themes, traditions, and concerns with wider Jewish circles. This makes virtually all the literature of the period potentially relevant to NT interpretation, but it does not enable us to shirk the difficult questions about the extent to which a particular text in any particular case is representative or idiosyncratic.

But this reference to "literature of the period" raises the second problem, that of the date of the literature. In the past, many scholars made rather indiscriminate use of evidence from the rabbinic literature (all of which was written a century or more after the NT) as evidence for pre-70 CE Judaism. In this they were influenced by a misleading historical model, according to which Pharisaism was "normative Judaism" and later rabbinic

---

3. E.g., Jacob Neusner, William Scott Green, and Ernest S. Frerichs, eds., *Judaisms and Their Messiahs at the Turn of the Christian Era* (Cambridge: Cambridge University, 1987); Gabriele Boccaccini, *Middle Judaism: Jewish Thought 300 B.C.E. to 200 C.E.* (Minneapolis: Fortress, 1991).

4. E. P. Sanders, *Judaism: Practice and Belief 63 BCE–66 CE* (London: SCM/Philadelphia: Trinity, 1992). On this issue see also Richard Bauckham, "The Parting of the Ways: What Happened and Why," *ST* 47 (1993) 135-39.

Judaism essentially a continuation of Pharisaism. This model, along with the uncritical acceptance of all ascriptions of traditions to early rabbis in the literature, is no longer credible. In reaction, some NT scholars are reluctant to admit the relevance of any Jewish literature that cannot be shown to have been written before the NT.

But this seeming methodological stringency is a spurious kind of purism. Judaism changed after 70 CE, but not in such a way as to destroy all continuity with its past. Many of the Targums, though of uncertain date, can be shown to preserve exegetical traditions from the NT period. Their evidence must be used with care, but it is not unusable. Similarly, many of the so-called OT Pseudepigrapha are of very uncertain date — and not a few included in the now standard collection edited by James H. Charlesworth[5] are much later than the NT and even of Christian origin — but that they preserve early Jewish traditions can often be argued. They cannot be used in the same way as those that are certainly pre-Christian in date, but they are not unusable. Sometimes a striking parallel between the NT and a later Jewish work can itself show (since the influence of Jesus or Christian literature on the Jewish work is not, in such cases, usually plausible) that the Jewish work here preserves an old tradition. The use of Jewish sources later than the NT for NT interpretation requires careful and informed historical judgment by a scholar well acquainted with the literature, but it cannot be ruled out.

Sometimes parallels are instructive irrespective of date. This is sometimes the case, for example, in one of the most important areas of relationship between NT writings and Jewish literature: exegesis of the Jewish Scriptures. Evidence from early writings, especially the Qumran *pesharim* (commentaries on Scripture), shows that, despite some important differences, many of the techniques of exegesis known from rabbinic midrash (scriptural interpretation) and the Targums were already in use in the NT period. A later Jewish writing may therefore be able to illuminate the way in which a Jewish exegete is likely to have read a particular OT text, even if we cannot be confident that it preserves an ancient piece of exegesis. But this, too, is a field where it is important to go beyond parallels to an understanding of how Jewish exegetes worked and thought. Sometimes NT

5. James H. Charlesworth, ed., *The Old Testament Pseudepigrapha*, 2 vols. (London: Darton, Longman and Todd/Garden City: Doubleday, 1983, 1985). For discussion of some of the problems created by the scope of this collection, see Richard Bauckham, "The Apocalypses in the New Pseudepigrapha," *JSNT* 26 (1986) 97-117.

writers and the Christian exegetical traditions they used followed Jewish traditions of exegesis of particular texts, as we can demonstrate from parallels, but sometimes their exegesis was original. In the latter cases, however, they were still engaged in a Jewish kind of exegesis, with Jewish exegetical presuppositions and methods. In these cases, it is not particular parallels, but real understanding, gained from study of Jewish exegesis, of how Jewish exegesis was done, that will enable us to understand the NT texts in their Jewish context.

3. An Example: James 4:13–5:6

How the letter of James is related to Jewish religious traditions is an important issue in determining the character of this NT writing. Some scholars have stressed its affinities with and indebtedness to wisdom traditions and have therefore seen James as a Christian wisdom writing. Others have pointed out its resemblance to prophetic-apocalyptic material (especially in 5:1-8). Interpretation of the law of Moses also has a significant place in the letter (especially in 2:8-13). Study of Jas 4:13–5:6 in the light of Jewish literary parallels will enable us to see how these three elements coexist and cohere within the letter.

This passage is in two sections, introduced by the two parallel addresses in 4:13 and 5:1, denouncing in turn two different categories of wealthy people: merchants (4:13-17) and landowners (5:1-6). These two categories are not only distinct, they are also condemned in quite different terms. The merchants are denounced for their arrogant self-confidence, treating their lives as though they were entirely within their own control, without reference to God. The landowners are denounced for their oppression of the poor, at whose expense they have accumulated wealth and lived in luxury. The most obvious affinities of the first section are with wisdom literature, while the second section resembles prophetic-apocalyptic traditions. This is in keeping with their respective themes. Like the rich fool in Jesus' parable (Luke 12:16-20), which also has affinities with the wisdom literature, the merchants are fools to think that they can make plans for themselves without reference to God's will. They lack the religious wisdom to take into account even the obvious fact that they cannot tell what will happen tomorrow. The landowners, on the other hand, are threatened with the eschatological judgment, when justice will at last be done for the righteous whom they have defrauded and murdered.

Confirming the wisdom character of the first section is the fact that Prov 27:1 ("Do not boast about tomorrow, for you do not know what a day may bring")[6] certainly lies in the background to it. Another wisdom theme is the transience of life, to which v. 14b calls attention. By contrast with 1:10-11, which uses a similar image, the point in 4:14 does not seem to be that the life of the wicked will be cut short by God's judgment, whether at death or at the end time, but rather that all human life is transient. The general thought is therefore not unlike Ben Sira's reflection that, when the rich man ". . . says, 'I have found rest, and now I will feast on my goods,' he does not know how long it will be until he leaves them to others and dies" (Sir 11:19).

The image that James uses — mist or (more probably) smoke that appears for only a little while before vanishing completely — is one of a traditional set of images of transience that were frequently used in Jewish literature (biblical and post-biblical) both for the transience of human life in general and for the short life left to the wicked, who will soon perish under God's judgment. (It is important in a case like this to take note of the full range of parallel material rather than focusing prematurely on one or two texts, preempting the decision as to which are most relevant to the interpretation of James.) The most popular such image of transience was that of grass or flowers withering, which James uses in 1:10-11. This image is used of the transience of mortal life (Job 14:1; Pss 90:5-6; 103:15-16; Isa 40:6-8) and of the fate of the wicked (Job 15:30; Ps 37:20; 1QM 15:11; 4Q185 1; *2 Apoc. Bar.* 82:7). But the image of smoke that soon vanishes is also found frequently and is used of the transience of mortal life (4 Ezra 4:24; an apocryphal quotation in 1 Clem 17:6)[7] and of the fate of the wicked (Pss 37:20; 68:2; Hos 13:3; Wis 5:14; 1QM 15:10; 4 Ezra 7:61; *2 Apoc. Bar.* 82:6).[8] However, the distinction between the transience of all human life and the judgment coming to the wicked is not as clear as might at first appear, especially in the later texts.[9] In 4 Ezra 4:24, Ezra, who is preoccupied

---

6. Cf. Pseudo-Phocylides 116-17: "Nobody knows what will be after tomorrow or after an hour. Death is heedless of mortals, and the future is uncertain." But the best manuscripts of Pseudo-Phocylides lack these lines.

7. "I am as smoke from a pot": the speaker is Moses, and the source probably a lost Jewish work.

8. For other images of transience, see, e.g., 1 Chr 29:15; Pss 37:6; 109:23; 144:4; Eccl 6:12; Hos 13:3; Sir 14:17-19; 4 Ezra 4:24; 13:20; *2 Apoc. Bar.* 14:10; 82:8-9.

9. It is worth noting that the Targum to Isa 40:6-8 interprets this passage as referring to the judgment of the wicked.

with the sinfulness even of the righteous, closely connects this with the transience of life ("we pass from the world like locusts, and our life is like a mist, and we are not worthy to obtain mercy").

What becomes clear in some texts (2 Apoc. Bar 14:10-14; Wis 5:7-16) is that the expectation of reward and punishment after death made a considerable difference to the significance of such traditional images of transience. The transience of this mortal life, though true of the righteous as well as the wicked, is of real consequence only for the wicked, who have set all their hopes on the worldly goods they enjoy in this life and face only judgment after death, while for the righteous, who expect eternal life and reward in the next life, it is insignificant. Ezra therefore discovers (4 Ezra 7:61) that the image of the mist that vanishes is properly applied only to the wicked, who will be consumed by the fire of judgment.

Especially interesting for our purposes is Wis 5:7-16, where the wicked discover at the last judgment that their arrogance and wealth (5:8) have done them no good, because all such things have proved as transient as their own lives (5:9-14), while the righteous whom they have oppressed receive eternal life and glory (5:15-16). This passage helps us to see that the point in Jas 4:13-16 is not only that the merchants do not reckon with the transience of life, but that their plans are preoccupied with obtaining wealth that they will only be able to enjoy for the uncertain length of their transient life.

The later Jewish literature enables us to see therefore that, while the primary force of the image in Jas 4:14b is to highlight the transience of mortal life, it carries the overtone of judgment for those who set their hopes on this mortal life. The meaning is therefore much closer than it first appears to that of the parallel image in 1:10-11, where it is only the life of the rich that is depicted as transient. It is also closer than it first appears to the corresponding feature of the denunciation of the landowners in 5:1-6, where eschatological judgment is very clearly in view.

It is also noteworthy that these traditional images of transience were never confined to wisdom literature, but already occur in the OT prophets (Isa 40:6-8; Hos 13:3). In later Jewish literature they are found in apocalyptic and related literature (1QM 15:10-11; 2 Apoc. Bar. 14:10-11; 82:6-9; 4 Ezra 7:61) and in wisdom literature (4Q185; Wis 5:9-14; cf. Sir 14:17-19). Especially when wisdom literature takes on the notion of eschatological judgment, as in Wisdom 5, and wisdom motifs appear in apocalyptic, as in 2 Apoc. Bar. 14:8-9, it is clear that in the Jewish literature of NT times wisdom and apocalyptic are by no means completely distinct traditions.

Although there is truth in the observation that Jas 4:13-16 is related to the wisdom tradition and 5:1-6 to the prophetic-apocalyptic tradition, this distinction does not mean that there is any incongruity in their juxtaposition.

The second section (5:1-6) uses the style of prophetic oracles of judgment (compare 5:1 especially with Isa 13:6).[10] In 5:5 ("you have fattened your hearts for the day of slaughter")[11] there is a specific allusion to a prophetic text, Jer 12:3, where the prophet, having complained of the prosperity of the wicked, prays:

> Pull them out like sheep for the slaughter,
> and set them apart for the day of slaughter.

There is an allusion to this same text in 1QH 15:17:

> But the wicked you created
> for [the time] of your [wrath].
> You set them apart from the womb
> for the day of slaughter.

The Qumran psalmist shares James's interpretation of the Jeremiah text as referring to the eschatological day of God's judgment on the wicked. But in other respects the two authors have been attracted to the text for quite different reasons. The context in 1QH is a strongly predestinarian passage that contrasts the righteous, created by God for eternal salvation, with the wicked, created by God for eternal judgment. The righteous are the members of the community; the wicked are the rest of humanity. The author has seen predestinarian significance in the words of Jer 12:3, "set them apart (הַקְדִּשֵׁם, *haqdišēm*) for the day of slaughter." This predestinarian exegesis of the text is not James's interest. He has been attracted to the metaphor that Jeremiah uses: animals selected from the flock for slaughter. Since he applies it specifically to the rich, he is able to make a highly effective extension of the metaphor. By their luxurious living the rich have fattened themselves as domestic animals are fattened in readiness for slaughter.

This contrast between 1QH and James illustrates how relatively unhelpful it is when commentators merely give references to extracanonical

---

10. Cf. also Isa 14:31; 23:1, 6, 14; Jer 48:20; Mic 2:4.

11. Since "the day of slaughter" is certainly the eschatological day of judgment, ἐν must be used with the sense of εἰς.

Jewish literature as texts to be compared with a NT text. It is important to study both texts before establishing precisely where the point of comparison lies. In this case, that both texts allude to Jer 12:3 with reference to the eschatological judgment of the wicked is probably not coincidental: It shows that current Jewish exegesis interpreted this verse of Jeremiah eschatologically. But it is unlikely that "the day of slaughter" had become simply a stock phrase for the day of judgment, used independently of its source in Jer 12:3, since both 1QH and James make use of further, though different, features of Jer 12:3. Both authors are exegetes, making their own use of the verse within a common exegetical tradition of referring this verse to the eschatological judgment.

At first sight, such a tradition may be a little surprising, since Jer 12:3 is not a prophecy but Jeremiah's prayer for the judgment of the wicked. However, there are features of the text that would have made it attractive to Jewish apocalyptic eschatology. The phrase "the day of slaughter" would naturally be associated with other phrases using "day" that were taken to refer to the day of judgment (e.g., "the day of the Lord"). "Slaughter" (הֲרֵגָה, $h^a r\bar{e}g\hat{a}$), a rare noun (with only five occurrences in the OT), is used twice elsewhere in Jeremiah (7:32; 19:6) in prophecies that the valley of the son of Hinnom will be renamed "the valley of slaughter." This is the valley that gave its name to Gehenna, because these prophecies were interpreted as referring to the eschatological judgment of the wicked. The common Jewish exegetical practice, known as גְּזֵרָה שָׁוָה ($g^e z\bar{e}r\hat{a}$ $\check{s}\bar{a}w\hat{a}$, "equivalent regulation"), of associating, for purposes of interpretation, scriptural passages that use the same words or phrases, would easily lead to an association of Jer 12:3 with Jer 7:32 and 19:6. James himself probably made this association, since Jer 7:33 and 19:7 both state that the wicked who are slaughtered in "the valley of slaughter" are to become food for the birds and animals. Interpreting Jer 12:3 in connection with these texts, he depicts the rich as fattening themselves in order to provide the food for this gruesome eschatological feast (cf. Ezek 39:17-20; Rev 19:17-18). The connection would be all the more appropriate since, according to Ezek 39:17, the feast is a sacrificial feast, and when Jer 12:3 asks God to "set apart" the wicked for the day of slaughter, it uses a verb that indicates that they are to be devoted, like sacrificial animals, to sacrificial use. This conclusion that behind Jas 5:5b lies an exegesis of Jer 12:3 in connection with Jer 7:32; 19:6; Ezek 39:17 is only partly based on comparison with 1QH 15:17, but it is made very plausible by our general knowledge of methods of Jewish exegesis in this period.

Somewhat closer than 1QH 15:17 to James's use of Jer 12:3 is *1 Enoch* 94:9, if we could be sure that it alludes to Jer 12:3. The rich, it says,

are ready for the day of the outpouring of blood
and for the day of darkness and for the day of judgment.[12]

Unfortunately, since neither the original Aramaic nor the Greek translation of this verse is extant, we rely on the Ethiopic version alone. The phrase "the day of the outpouring of blood"[13] may allude to "the day of slaughter" in Jer 12:3, but we cannot be sure. However, there are much broader resemblances between Jas 5:1-6 and chs. 94–99 of the so-called Epistle of Enoch (*1 Enoch* 91-108). These chapters address alternately the wicked, who are portrayed especially as wealthy and as oppressors of the righteous (94:8–95:2; 96:4-8), and the persecuted righteous (95:3; 96:1-3; 97:1), just as James addresses first the rich oppressors (5:1-6) and then their victims (5:7-11), who are said to be righteous (5:6, cf. v. 16). Both Enoch and James address prophetic oracles of denunciation and judgment to the rich, though the literary form differs (Enoch uses "woe" oracles). In Enoch this direct address to the wicked is a rhetorical device that does not indicate that they are expected to be among the readers (cf. *1 Enoch* 92:1). We should almost certainly assume that the same is true in James. In Enoch, the rich are condemned for exploiting the poor (96:5) and for accumulating wealth that will not last (94:7-8; 97:8-10; 98:2-3). They will "groan and weep" (96:2). Their ill-gotten wealth will be "a testimony against you" or "a reminder against you for evil" (96:4, 7; 97:7; cf. Jas 5:3). The parallels cannot prove that James was inspired by these chapters of *1 Enoch*, though this is certainly quite possible. But they go considerably beyond what would result from common dependence on OT prophecy.[14] They must show that James writes in a continuing tradition of prophetic denunciation of the rich.

Finally we must consider Jas 5:4. Throughout his letter James is expounding the implications of the law of the love of one's neighbor (Lev 19:18b; Jas 2:8) by alluding to the more detailed commandments in its

12. The translation is from Michael A. Knibb, *The Ethiopic Book of Enoch*, vol. 2 (Oxford: Clarendon, 1978) 227.

13. Cf. other phrases used in these chapters of *1 Enoch* for the coming day of judgment on the wicked: 96:8; 97:1; 98:10; 99:4, 6; 102:5.

14. They are also more extensive than the resemblances between Jas 5:1-6 and the woes in Luke 6:24-25.

context in Lev 19:11-18.[15] In 5:4 he alludes to Lev 19:13 ("you shall not keep for yourself the wages of a laborer until morning") as well as to the fuller law on the same subject in Deut 24:14-15, and to Isa 5:9 (LXX). But this is another case where James's allusion to an OT text is illuminated by allusions to the same text in other Jewish literature. References to the law in Lev 19:13 and Deut 24:14-15 are surprisingly frequent (Mal 3:5; Sir 34:27; Tob 4:14; *T. Job* 12:4; Pseudo-Phocylides 19; *b. Baba Meṣi'a* 111a; cf. Job 31:39; Jer 22:13). The reason it was taken so seriously is made apparent in Sir 34:25-27:

> The bread of the needy is the life of the poor;
>   whoever deprives them of it is a murderer.
> To take away a neighbor's living is to commit murder;
>   to deprive an employee of wages is to shed blood.

The day laborer, who neither owned nor rented land, but worked on the estates of others and was paid his wages at the end of each day's work, was, of all peasant workers, in the most vulnerable position. His employment could be terminated at a few hours' notice. He had no security. He might often be unemployed. His wages were too small to make saving any money possible. He lived from hand to mouth. He could well need his day's wages to feed himself and his family that very day. Withholding his wages even until the morning was a serious matter. An employer who delayed paying his employees might without hyperbole be accused of murder. This may partly explain James's accusation of murder in 5:6, though (especially in view of "condemned") the reference may also be to misuse of the courts in order to deprive smallholders of their land and to absorb their farms into the big estates.

It is worth noting that allusions to the duty not to withhold the wages of the day laborer are found in both prophetic (Mal 3:5) and wisdom (Sir 34:27; Pseudo-Phocylides 19) contexts. Both prophetic and wisdom literature, of course, were concerned with moral instruction, and in the late biblical and post-biblical periods the teaching of the law of Moses was readily drawn on for this purpose in both contexts. Once again, we see that there is nothing incongruous in the conjunction of prophetic-apocalyptic,

---

15. See Luke T. Johnson, "The Use of Leviticus 19 in the Letter of James," *JBL* 101 (1982) 391-401. For a passage of Jewish ethical paraenesis that is extensively based on Leviticus 19 see Pseudo-Phocylides 9-21.

wisdom, and halakhic material in James. In various ways this conjunction was quite typical of contemporary Jewish literature that shared James's concern with practical religion.

4. Suggestions for Further Reading

This bibliography does not attempt to provide guidance on the study of the Jewish literature as such, but is confined to studies relating the Jewish literature and the NT. Two general books survey the relevant Jewish literature and offer guidance on its use in NT interpretation: Martin McNamara, *Palestinian Judaism and the New Testament,* GNS 4 (Wilmington: Glazier, 1983); and Craig A. Evans, *Noncanonical Writings and New Testament Interpretation* (Peabody: Hendrickson, 1992). Evans, who also includes extracanonical Christian and Gnostic literature, provides much more bibliographical guidance; both offer many examples of the relevance of each category of literature to NT study. For excellent introductions and commentary on relevant Jewish writings (except Targums), students should consult *Cambridge Commentaries on Writings of the Jewish and Christian World 200 BC to AD 200* (4 vols., Cambridge: Cambridge University, 1985-89).

Fuller treatments of the relevance of particular bodies of Jewish literature to NT study are also available, though there is more systematic help in some areas than in others. The Targums are well served in this respect by Martin McNamara, *Targum and Testament* (Shannon: Irish University/Grand Rapids: Eerdmans, 1972); *idem, The New Testament and the Palestinian Targum to the Pentateuch,* AnBib 27 (2d ed., Rome: Pontifical Biblical Institute, 1978). Access to studies relevant to particular NT passages may be had through Peter Nickels, *Targum and Testament: A Bibliography together with a New Testament Index* (Rome: Pontifical Biblical Institute, 1967); and J. Terence Forestell, *Targumic Traditions and the New Testament: An Annotated Bibliography with a New Testament Index,* SBLAS 4 (Chico: Scholars, 1979). In this regard see also Bruce D. Chilton, *A Galilean Rabbi and His Bible* (London: SPCK/Wilmington: Glazier, 1984); Isabel Ann Massey, *Interpreting the Sermon on the Mount in the Light of Jewish Tradition as Evidenced in the Palestinian Targums of the Pentateuch* (Lewiston/Queenston/Lampeter: Edwin Mellen, 1991). *The Aramaic Bible* (Collegeville: Liturgical, 1987-) will make the targumic literature available in English translation, with many volumes now available.

Perhaps the most accessible entry into the Dead Sea Scrolls is Geza Vermes, *The Dead Sea Scrolls in English* (4th ed., London/New York: Penguin 1995). More complete is *The Dead Sea Scrolls Translated: Qumran Texts in English,* by Florentino García Martínez (Leiden: Brill, 1994).

Among many studies relating the Dead Sea Scrolls to Jesus and early Christianity, see Herbert Braun, *Qumran und das Neuen Testament* (Tübingen: Mohr, 1966); William S. LaSor, *The Dead Sea Scrolls and the New Testament* (Grand Rapids: Eerdmans, 1972); James H. Charlesworth, ed., *John and Qumran* (London: Chapman/New York: Crossroad, 1972); Jerome Murphy-O'Connor and James H. Charlesworth, eds., *Paul and the Dead Sea Scrolls* (New York: Crossroad, 1990); James H. Charlesworth, ed., *Jesus and the Dead Sea Scrolls* (New York: Doubleday, 1992).

For Josephus, Steve Mason, *Josephus and the New Testament* (Peabody, Massachusetts: Hendrickson, 1992), is a very useful introduction, though it leaves important aspects of Josephus's many-sided value for NT studies untouched. See also Louis H. Feldman and Gohe Hata, eds., *Josephus, Judaism, and Christianity* (Detroit: Wayne State University, 1987); Gregory Sterling, *Historiography and Self-Definition: Josephos, Luke-Acts and Apologetic Historiography* (Leiden: Brill, 1992); and for exhaustive bibliography, Louis H. Feldman, *Josephus and Modern Scholarship (1937-1980)* (Berlin/New York: de Gruyter, 1984). The standard translation in English is provided in 10 vols. in the LCL; the older edition by Whiston, though often reprinted, is undependable and should be avoided.

The LCL is also the place to turn for the works of Philo in English (10 vols.). New Testament studies notable for their use of Philo's works include Peter Borgen, *Bread from Heaven: An Exegetical Study of the Concept of Manna in the Gospel of John and the Writings of Philo* (2d ed., Leiden: Brill, 1981); Wayne A. Meeks, *The Prophet-King: Moses Traditions and the Johannine Christology* (Leiden: Brill, 1967); Ronald Williamson, *Philo and the Epistle to the Hebrews* (Leiden: Brill, 1970).

For the Pseudepigrapha, James H. Charlesworth has edited *The Old Testament Pseudepigrapha,* 2 vols. (Garden City: Doubleday, 1983, 1985), though he includes material that falls outside the usual boundaries for studying the NT in the context of contemporary Jewish literature. Also available in English is *The Apocryphal Old Testament,* edited by H. F. D. Sparks (Oxford: Clarendon, 1984). Charlesworth has also written *The Old Testament Pseudepigrapha and the New Testament,* SNTSMS 54 (Cambridge: Cambridge University, 1985), though its treatment of the Pseudepigrapha's relevance to the NT is quite limited. But Charlesworth's invaluable bibliography, *The Pseudepigrapha and Modern Research with a Supplement*, SBLSCS 7S (Chico: Scholars, 1981), provides a list of items that focus especially on the relationship of pseudepigraphal texts to the NT (pp. 45-46, 253). Most of the introductions to the texts in Charlesworth's *Old Testament Pseudepigrapha*, 1983/1985) include a section on "relation to canonical books," though the usefulness of these sections varies greatly. Several articles in James H. Charlesworth and Craig A. Evans, eds., *The Pseudepigrapha and Early Biblical Interpretation*, JSPSS 14 (Sheffield: JSOT, 1993), explore the relationship between the Pseudepigrapha and the NT.

The great work of Hermann Strack and Paul Billerbeck, *Kommentar zum Neuen Testament aus Talmud und Midrasch*, 4 vols. (Munich: Beck, 1922-28; in fact it was almost entirely Billerbeck's work), though much criticized for encouraging misuse of rabbinic parallels, remains an invaluable resource for tracking down relevant material in the rabbinic literature. For access to the rabbinic literature in English translation, the student may refer to the following volumes. For the Mishnah: *The Mishnah: Translated from the Hebrew, with Introduction and Brief Explanatory Notes*, by Herbert Danby (London: Oxford University, 1933), and *The Mishnah: A New Translation*, by Jacob Neusner (New Haven: Yale University, 1988). Neusner has also provided editions of *The Talmud of Babylonia* (Atlanta: Scholars, 1984-93); *The Talmud of the Land of Israel* (Chicago: University of Chicago, 1982-91); and Midrash Rabbah (Atlanta: Scholars, 1985-91). These may be consulted alongside the older editions: *The Babylonian Talmud*, ed. Isidore Epstein (London: Soncino, 1935-59), and *The Midrash Rabbah*, ed. Harry Freedman (London: Soncino, 1939). H. L. Strack and G. Stemberger have written an *Introduction to the Talmud and Mishnah* (rev. ed., Edinburgh: Clark, 1991), which may be consulted for information on other translations. Also worthy of note is Neusner's *The Rabbinic Traditions about the Pharisees before 70* (3 vols., Leiden: Brill, 1971), which collects in translation every rabbinic passage attributing traditions to Pharisees before the fall of Jerusalem in 70 C.E.

Claude G. Montefiore, *Rabbinic Literature and Gospel Teachings* (London: Macmillan, 1930), and Samuel T. Lachs, *A Rabbinic Commentary on the New Testament: The Gospels of Matthew, Mark, and Luke* (Hoboken: Ktav, 1987), provide much more limited material. The appendix in Gustav Dalman, *Jesus-Jeshua* (London: SPCK, 1989), provides the material for comparing Jesus' aphorisms with those in rabbinic literature, while Harvey K. McArthur and Robert M. Johnston, *They Also Taught in Parables*

(Grand Rapids: Zondervan, 1990), contains a large collection of rabbinic parables in translation and is a good introduction to comparing them with Jesus' parables. W. D. Davies, *Paul and Rabbinic Judaism* (4th ed., London: SPCK/Philadelphia: Fortress, first published in 1948) remains of basic importance.

For relating traditional Jewish liturgical texts to the NT, an excellent place to start is Jakob J. Petuchowski and Michael Brocke, *The Lord's Prayer and Jewish Liturgy* (London: Burns and Oates, 1978), which includes translations of the texts and a bibliographical essay.

6. The Relevance of Greco-Roman Literature and Culture to New Testament Study

LOVEDAY C. A. ALEXANDER

1. Why Study Greco-Roman Literature and Culture?

As I travel to work in Sheffield, my train passes through a dramatic landscape of limestone peaks and dales. Isolated farms and stone-built villages nestle on the hillsides. Beneath them, invisible to the casual passer-by, is a honeycomb network of limestone caverns and underground rivers. These are dangerous hills for the unwary rambler: A hollow in the ground may lead to a hundred-foot drop into an abandoned mineshaft or a natural "swallet-hole" where a mountain-top stream vanishes underground to reappear in the cave system hundreds of feet below.

In many ways England's limestone Peak District makes a good analogy for the relationship between NT studies and the study of the Greco-Roman world. Because most NT commentaries begin with a brief survey of the "historical background" to the text, many readers imagine that "background" is something simple and uncomplicated that can be treated quickly before getting on with the real business of exegesis. It is not. Like the underground cave system beneath those homely Derbyshire farmhouses, it is complex and fascinating and has a life of its own. It may even be dangerous: Certainly one needs the services of expert guides if one is to explore it safely and with profit.

First, as readers of the NT we need to remind ourselves that *"Bible history" is part of "real history."* Dorothy Sayers records a moment of astonishment in discovering that Bible characters could have an existence in another cultural world. Cyrus, first encountered in *Tales from Herodotus,*

109

was (as she puts it) "pigeon-holed in my mind with the Greeks and Romans" until "one day, I realised with a shock as of sacrilege, that . . . he had marched clean out of Herodotus and slap into the Bible." And Ahasuerus was "a good Old-Testament-sounding name, . . . reminding one of Ahab and Ahaz and Ahaziah" — until

> I came across the astonishing equation, thrown out casually in a passing phrase, "Ahasuerus (or Xerxes)." Xerxes! — but one knew all about Xerxes. He was . . . real history; it was against Xerxes that the Greeks had made their desperate and heroic stand at Thermopylae. . . . . I think it was chiefly Cyrus and Ahasuerus who prodded me into the belated conviction that history was all of a piece, and that the Bible was part of it.[1]

This is particularly evident in the Gospels, where the events of sacred history are tied down to specific, datable periods of time: Jesus is not a timeless, mythic hero but a person who associates with characters who have a history apart from the text, who are known from secular history books: "He was crucified under Pontius Pilate." Luke's Gospel provides a good illustration, with the list of known historical figures that begins the account of John's ministry at 3:1-2. This comparative dating provides one of the few indicators of absolute chronology in the NT: It is pivotal for the whole dating of John's and Jesus' ministries and thus of the rest of the NT. So it is important to know whether it makes sense. Who are all these people? Is Luke's accounting accurate? How does this chronology tie in with other chronological indicators in the NT? Luke uses an ancient method of dating that requires outside knowledge of other dating systems, principally those of the Roman emperors. Collecting and understanding historical information of this kind has been part of the competence of the commentator from earliest times.

But there is more to history than dates, and other aspects of the narrative history of the Greco-Roman world form a necessary part of the exegete's equipment. The Corinth to which Paul wrote two of his letters, to take just one example, was a Greek city with a history going back to prehistoric times. But before Paul visited the city it had undergone a major trauma (destruction by the Romans in 146 BCE) followed by refoundation as a Roman colony (44 BCE). It is a real question to what degree Paul's

---

1. Dorothy L. Sayers, "A Vote of Thanks to Cyrus," in *Unpopular Opinions* (London: Gollancz, 1946) 23-28, here 24-25.

Corinth was Roman and how much it had retained (or reverted to) its Greek character. And the answer to this question affects our picture of the church's problems in all sorts of ways: Social composition (1 Corinthians 1), the position of women (1 Corinthians 7, 11, 14), and the religious practices of the city (1 Corinthians 8, 10) could all be estimated differently according to which cultural influence seems to predominate at any one time. Moreover a little historical awareness can save the exegete from the common anachronism of applying descriptions of the ancient Greek city wholesale to its Roman successor.[2]

But we also need to be reminded that *the Bible is part of "real" literature.* There has always been a tendency to treat biblical texts as a special kind of literature. Of course in one sense that is quite correct: The texts that make up the NT form a cohesive group, and they have much more in common with each other than they do as a group with other kinds of literature. But it is easy to forget that none of them was written as a chapter of "The Bible": The collection came later, not as part of the original concept. The literary contexts that shaped the NT texts are those of the diverse cultural worlds in which their authors and first readers lived, and that means, among others, the cultural world of Greco-Roman literature. So when Paul hears of problems within the church he founded at Corinth, his reaction is to sit down and write (or dictate) a letter. *Letter-writing* is a form of literary activity well understood in the Greco-Roman world: It has its own conventions governing phrasing and structure, and an educated person writing in Greek in the first century will be aware of those conventions, even if he or she wants to mold them in a new direction.[3] Moreover, well-developed strategies of persuasion were known and used by the orators and philosophers who dominated much of the public discourse of the cities that Paul's churches were in. NT scholars are increasingly finding that the techniques of ancient *rhetoric* and *philosophy* can help to illuminate Paul's tumultuous negotiations with the congregations he founded.[4]

2. Jerome Murphy-O'Connor, *St. Paul's Corinth,* GNS 6 (Collegeville: Glazier, 1983).

3. John Lee White, *Light from Ancient Letters* (Philadelphia: Fortress, 1986); Stanley Kent Stowers, *Letter-Writing in Greco-Roman Antiquity,* LEC 5 (Philadelphia: Westminster, 1986).

4. E.g., Abraham J. Malherbe, *Paul and the Thessalonians* (Philadelphia: Fortress, 1987); *idem, Moral Exhortation: A Greco-Roman Sourcebook,* LEC 4 (Philadelphia: Westminster, 1986); Burton L. Mack, *Rhetoric and the New Testament* (Minneapolis: Fortress, 1990).

Similarly Luke, when he sets out to write the gospel story, does not write in a literary vacuum. Others have written Gospels before him (Luke 1:1), and their work will certainly influence the shape of his own. But there is also a wider world of literature, and simply by choosing to write in Greek, Luke (like the other NT writers) becomes part of that world. If he wants to communicate his message to that wider world, he must in some sense shape his narrative according to its cultural conventions. But the precise form of the *narrative strategies* he uses — and the reasons for their ultimate success in communicating — can only be appreciated if we ourselves are prepared to enter the literary world of Luke's Greek and Roman readers.

Third, *New Testament writers and readers live in a real social world.* Paul's letters take us very directly into the kind of issues that demand exploration of the social worlds of his first readers. Behind the debates of 1 Corinthians, for example, lies a whole labyrinth of social custom and assumption that informs both the apostle's arguments and his readers' reactions. The issue of women's headgear in 1 Cor 11:2-16 raises questions about the use of the veil and its implications for the status of women in Greek and Roman society, as well as about the participation of women in religious activity.[5] The second half of the same chapter (vv. 17-34) highlights the issue of dining customs and their relation to social stratification.[6] This passage also has implications for our understanding of the Pauline churches as social groups in their own right: Do the customs surrounding the Lord's Supper have any relation to Greco-Roman religious custom, or do they simply reflect the familiar social models of the household or of the private dining club?[7]

Luke's third chapter illustrates social issues of a different sort. First, there is the social world of the characters in the narrative: Who are the "tax collectors" (3:12) and "soldiers" (3:14)? What are the social dynamics presupposed in the narrative? What social attitudes are conveyed by John's advice?[8] And second, there is the social world (or worlds) of the document itself: The task of investigating the linguistic and literary affinities of the

5. Ben Witherington, *Women in the Earliest Churches*, SNTSMS 59 (Cambridge: Cambridge University, 1988).

6. Gerd Theissen, *The Social Setting of Pauline Christianity* (Edinburgh: Clark/ Philadelphia: Fortress, 1982) chs. 2 and 4.

7. Wayne A. Meeks, *The First Urban Christians* (New Haven: Yale University, 1983) ch. 3.

8. *The Social World of Luke-Acts*, ed. Jerome H. Neyrey (Peabody: Hendrickson, 1991), contains a good sample of views (see the index).

text may also be used as a point of access to the social location of its writer and first readers.[9]

Finally, it is good to remember that *Bible people faced real political dilemmas.* As Dorothy Sayers observes, keeping the NT in a separate compartment from its world encourages a sense that its writers and characters moved in a moral and political vacuum. But by putting the Jesus story into a chronological framework, Luke also implicitly gives it a political framework. The events of the Gospel happened in the Roman Empire, not just in the unnamed space beside the river Jordan, where they are placed in Mark.

Luke uniquely forces his readers to confront this aspect of their salvation story from the outset (cf. 2:1) — though all the Gospels will face it eventually as Jesus faces Pontius Pilate in the passion narratives. But what is its significance for Luke? More than one scholar would analyze Luke's use of the imperial dating system in terms of a distinctive political stance. "His perspective on the great world is . . . attested by the notes with which he inserts the events he is describing into world history"; and this perspective lies behind a presentation that "leads him to suppress violence that originated from the centre and to see only the 'sunny side' of the reality of Rome."[10] Is Luke presenting his story to Roman readers as an *apologia* for the Christian proclamation? Or to Christian readers as an apologia for the empire?[11] Does John's advice to the soldiers and tax collectors address the concerns of a later readership that saw the professions of soldier and tax collector as incompatible with being a Christian?[12] These are all questions raised by the narrative. Looking for answers means looking not only at the historical data on which the text is based but also at more subtle questions about its ideology — about the parameters of political debate in the empire and the literary means available for carrying on that debate.

---

9. Vernon K. Robbins, "The Social Location of the Implied Author of Luke-Acts," in Neyrey, *Social World,* 305-32; Loveday C. A. Alexander, *The Preface to Luke's Gospel,* SNTSMS 78 (Cambridge: Cambridge University, 1993) ch. 8.

10. Klaus Wengst, *Pax Romana and the Peace of Jesus Christ* (London: SCM, 1987) 102.

11. Paul W. Walaskay, *"And So We Came to Rome": The Political Perspective of St. Luke,* SNTSMS 49 (Cambridge: Cambridge University, 1983).

12. Wengst, *Pax Romana,* 90-91.

2. Studying Greco-Roman Literature and Culture

First, the name. The term *"Greco-Roman"* is a relatively recent coinage that seeks to reflect the political and cultural complexities of the first-century world in which the NT texts were written. It was a world dominated in political and military terms by the Roman Empire. In the frontier zones (as Palestine was in the first century) the confrontation with Roman power was particularly acute. But before the Romans came, Palestine had for centuries been under the sway of the Hellenistic kingdoms of the successors of Alexander the Great. The language of the eastern half of the Roman Empire was and remained Greek, not Latin. Greek was the international language of trade and commerce, of government and administration, of education and culture. Most of all, Greek was the language of literature and philosophy, the language that had produced the acknowledged classics of poetry and prose. Homer, Sophocles and the poets, and Demosthenes and the stars of Attic rhetoric formed the basis of the school curriculum for anyone seeking a Greek education, while philosophers looked back to Plato, Epicurus, and other philosophical giants of the past. Rome had her own literary classics, and the tumultuous century that saw the end of the Republic and the beginning of the Empire was also a golden age of literary achievement in rhetoric, in philosophy, even in epic verse, in a newly invigorated Latin that sought to match the heights of the Greek past.

This stress on using the literary "classics" as a basis for education persisted thoughout antiquity and on into the Renaissance and the beginnings of modern scholarship.[13] This is why the study of the Greco-Roman world was for many years known simply as the study of the "Classics" and why the heart of "Classics" as a discipline has always been the study of texts. In this it has much in common with biblical studies: The arts of commentary, exegesis, lexicography, and textual criticism are part of the common patrimony of the two disciplines and were often practiced in both fields by the same people. Before the twentieth century, in fact, it would probably be true to say that the majority of NT commentators in Britain and Germany had studied classical literature at least to some extent in their schooldays, and the effect of this can be seen in the effortless observation of classical parallels that can be found in the older commentaries.

For the NT student today who wants to find her or his way into this

13. Henri Irenee Marrou, *A History of Education in Antiquity* (New York: Sheed and Ward, 1956).

fascinating field, this has the advantage that the field itself is well signposted and thoroughly researched. All the major *classical texts* may be read in critical editions based on firsthand study of manuscripts.[14] Most may be read in English translation,[15] and many have extensive coverage in commentary form (though classical commentaries tend to focus primarily on linguistic problems). Massive scholarly enterprises have produced invaluable collections of those texts that survive only in fragmentary form. Jacoby's collection of the fragments of the Greek historians is a good example.[16] Greek texts are also available in *Thesaurus Linguae Graecae (TLG)*, which opens up the potential for electronic searches for words and phrases. But *TLG* word-searches can become a bottomless pit for the unwary; *TLG* is best used in conjunction with other reference guides, especially *Oxford Classical Dictionary (OCD)* (for selecting authors of relevant dates — half of those in *TLG* are Christian authors) and LSJ (only some of the meanings of any given word may be relevant to NT study).

Reference guides to classical literature are plentiful and good, from the accessible, one-volume *OCD* (an excellent starting point for the basic information on any classical author) to the massive multi-volume *Paulys Real-Encyclopädie (RE* for short), begun in the nineteenth century and still the last and best resort for many of the minutiae of the classical world.[17] The explorer is equally well provided with *lexical aids.* Liddell and Scott's *Greek-English Lexicon* (LSJ) is an invaluable guide in which lexical usage is profusely illustrated by quotations and references from classical texts. Looking up a single word in this marvelous dictionary can give instant access to a whole system for anyone who has the patience to work through an entry

14. The major series are the Teubner texts (Leipzig/Stuttgart: Teubner) and the *Oxford Classical Texts* (Oxford: Clarendon). The *Loeb Classical Library* (LCL; Cambridge: Harvard University) provides Greek and Latin texts with facing translation, but not all of the texts are critically edited.

15. The LCL series is invaluable for reference. The *Penguin Classics* series (Harmondsworth: Penguin/New York: Viking) provides livelier translations in paperback form, handy for browsing but not always providing chapter numbers for detailed reference.

16. Felix Jacoby, *Die Fragmente der griechischen Historiker* (Leiden: Brill, 1957-).

17. Pauly-Wissowa-Kroll, *Real-Encyclopädie der classiscchen Altertumswissenschaft* (Stuttgart: Metzler, 1893-; more recently Munich: Druckenmüller). *Der Kleine Pauly,* ed. Konrat Ziegler and W. Sontheimer (Stuttgart: Druckenmüller, 1964-75) is a superb five-volume digest. But the *Oxford Classical Dictionary,* ed. Nicholas G. L. Hammond and Howard H. Scullard (2d ed., Oxford: Clarendon, 1970) is the best place to start for most purposes.

noting which authors use the word, when, and in what contexts.[18] *Journals*, finally, provide an entrée into the continuing world of classical research: *Classical World, Greece and Rome*, and *Gnomon* are all good for reviews, and *L'Année Philologique* provides an annual bibliographical survey.

If texts are at the heart of the discipline, the *narrative history* that provides a thread to string them together is also well covered at a variety of levels. Introductory surveys that tell "the story of Greece and Rome" are easily obtained[19] and provide a good starting-point for the beginner. A good story (and these are some of the best) is always easier to remember than a series of abstract social observations, and having an idea of the basic outline of ancient history makes it easier to find your way around. But ancient history, like the study of classical texts, does not conveniently stand still so that the NT student can master it: It is a discipline in its own right, developing its own agenda and throwing up new questions all the time, and researching the historical context of the NT means being prepared to move beyond the introductions and challenge accepted positions. Major *journals* in ancient history, like *Historia* or the *Journal of Roman Studies*, are a good source for up-to-date publications and research, as are the more recent *reference* series like the revised *Cambridge Ancient History* and the (topically organized) *Aufstieg und Niedergang der römischen Welt*, which includes articles in English.[20]

Getting a grasp of the narrative outlines of ancient history may well be the best place to begin for the biblical student. But for insight into the everyday lives of the first Christians we need to turn to a different kind of history that has made increasing progress in recent years, in ancient history as in other disciplines: *social history*. Crucial to this development was the discovery in the nineteenth century and into the twentieth of huge numbers of contemporary documents in the form of *inscriptions* (documents and records carved on stone and intended for public display, from epitaphs to senatorial decrees) and *papyri* (public documents and private letters written on papyrus and surviving mostly in the dry sands of Egypt). Patient scholarship over the last century has resulted in an impressive body of published

---

18. Liddell-Scott-Jones, *Greek-English Lexicon* (9th ed., Oxford: Clarendon, 1940).

19. E.g., Edward Togo Salmon, *A History of the Roman World from 30 B.C. to A.D. 138* (London/New York: Routledge, 1968); Howard H. Scullard, *From the Gracchi to Nero* (5th ed., London: Routledge, 1988).

20. *ANRW*, ed. Hildegard Temporini and Wolfgang Haase (Berlin/New York: Walter de Gruyter, 1972-).

texts of these documents, some with English translation and notes, others accompanied by the minimum of information (which may be provided in Latin). The emphasis has generally been on making the texts available to scholarship rather than on producing definitive editions.[21] It is worthwhile getting some hands-on experience of these texts by looking up the original publications wherever possible and learning the conventions by which scholars indicate the gaps and guesses that lie behind the published text. The University of Macquarie has performed a valuable service in recent years in scanning new publications of papyri and inscriptions for anything relevant to the NT.[22]

Assimilating and digesting this body of documentary material has taken longer than publishing the texts, but the effects have made themselves felt in a number of ways throughout the discipline during the twentieth century. The massive *documentation of government,* both local and imperial, has given ancient historians an unparalleled opportunity both to confirm the picture built up from narrative history of the Greco-Roman world and to deepen it. The survival of so many documents of the Greek city-states, of the Egyptian administration, and of the Roman Empire has made it possible both to ask and to answer a whole range of new questions beyond the bounds of narrative history. The detailed workings of the political system and the day-to-day decisions of administrators are often far more revealing than the stories deemed newsworthy by ancient historians. Scholars have also been able to use the many *private documents* (especially from Egypt) to supplement the evidence of the literary sources in order to build up detailed profiles of *economic and social systems* in the empire. Pioneering here was the monumental study by Rostovtzeff,[23] but many fine studies have continued the process.[24] Recent years have seen a proliferation of studies and source-books on more topical concerns such as *slavery* or the position of *women* in Greek and Roman society.[25]

---

21. It is impossible here to list all the editions of inscriptions and papyri. Lists can be found in major reference works like LSJ. For papyri an invaluable expert guide is E. G. Turner, *Greek Papyri: An Introduction* (Oxford: Clarendon, 1968).

22. *New Documents Illustrating Early Christianity,* ed. G. H. R. Horsley (Ancient History Documentary Research Centre, Macquarie University, 1981-).

23. Mikhail I. Rostovtzeff, *The Social and Economic History of the Roman Empire* (2d ed., 2 vols., Oxford: Clarendon, 1957).

24. E.g., Peter Garnsey and Richard Saller, *The Roman Empire: Economy, Society, and Culture* (London: Duckworth, 1987).

25. E.g., Keith R. Bradley, *Slaves and Masters in the Roman Empire* (Oxford: Oxford

Two things should be clear from this introduction. The first is that the study of the Greco-Roman world was not created by the needs and interests of NT exegesis and is not dependent on it, any more than the cave systems of the Peaks were created by the tourist village that exploits them — though in both cases there may be a mutually beneficial symbiosis. It is salutary for the NT student just to take a look at the sheer size of the body of texts known as "the classics" and to realize that the NT is simply one not-so-large volume on the library shelf of the Greco-Roman world. Better still, one may take time to explore a little some of the Greek and Roman texts and savor the variety of classical poetry, plays, philosophy, history, and rhetoric — not to mention the multitudinous polymathy of the Greek scientists and antiquarians. One may get to know some of the writers who were operating at around the time the NT was being written: Seneca, Plutarch, Epictetus, Dio, Tacitus, or Lucian may be maddening or fascinating by turns, but they all form part of the public world that the first Christians had to address.

Second, "Greco-Roman literature and culture" is not a single discipline and has no single methodology. Literary criticism, exegesis, and lexicography are as important here as historical or social-scientific skills. Some of these approaches will be very familiar to the NT student, others may require some practice. As in any discipline, there are specialists and generalists, recognized landmark studies and potboilers. One should learn to recognize the guides who really know their way around the system, rather than the ones who are just summarizing what they have been told. The beauty of it is that virtually any point of entry can be used as a way to get access to the system as a whole, if one looks for the right kind of guide. Many introductory guides to the Greco-Roman context of the NT, like the tourist guides to the Castleton caves, follow well-trodden paths. These are safe but predictable: The tourist walks a route that leads firmly back to the surface. If one wants to explore for oneself, it is essential to find a guide who can point to the skills and equipment needed, with precise references to texts, translations, journal articles, and classical reference works.

University, 1987); Thomas Wiedemann, *Greek and Roman Slavery* (Baltimore/London: Johns Hopkins University, 1981); *Images of Women in Antiquity,* ed. Averil Cameron and Amelia Kurht (London: Routledge, 1993); *Women's Life in Greece and Rome,* ed. Mary R. Lefkowitz and Maureen B. Fant (London: Duckworth, 1982).

3. What Does It Look Like in Practice?

In this section we will focus on Luke 3:1-2 to illustrate the variety of approaches to the NT text that can be informed by a study of Greco-Roman literature and culture and to explore some of the ways in which a NT text can be used as an access point to the whole network of "Greco-Roman literature and culture." Luke's third chapter opens with an impressive synchronistic dating that anchors the story of Jesus in the wider world of the Roman Empire. This formal and impressive opening directs our attention first of all to *the historical framework of the narrative*. The obvious questions relate to the historical data contained in the text: Who? Where? What? When? Following up the names in these verses is as good a way as any of exploring the complex political history that provides the setting for the Gospel. But they lead in their turn to How? and Why? questions about the construction of narrative history: How do historians get to know these things? What are their sources of information? And whose point of view do they presuppose?

The first point that strikes the reader is that, among all the tetrarchs and high priests, only the emperor actually has a precise chronology. In fact the commentaries give us not only the year but the day of the month for the death of Tiberius' predecessor: August 19, 14 CE. What lies behind this astonishing accuracy? The answer has to do both with location and with status. Central Rome had a highly-organized and stable administrative system in which the years of office of the annual magistrates were recorded and therefore could be used for the purposes of chronology. It is the survival of some at least of these *archival sources* that enables the historian to be precise about this particular date: Both the Calendar and the Fasti record the date of Augustus' death, in typically telegraphic style:[26]

[. . . XI]V k. Sept. Augustus [excessit]
August 19 (xiiii k. Sept.): dies tristissi(mus)/Augustus excess(it)

Clearly the interpretation of such sources demands a certain amount of technical expertise. But note also their political implications: Only the deaths of those the state considers important will be recorded in this way.

---

26. Victor Ehrenberg and A. H. M. Jones, *Documents Illustrating the Reigns of Augustus and Tiberius* (Oxford: Clarendon, 1949), 40, 50. Inscriptional sources are also important for the title of Pilate and the date of Lysanias: See Joseph A. Fitzmyer, *The Gospel according to Luke I–IX*, AB 28 (Garden City: Doubleday, 1981) 455-58.

It is no accident that history for so many centuries confined itself largely to monarchs and other public institutions.

Besides the archives, however, there are *literary sources* in the shape of the Roman historians themselves. Tacitus' detailed year-by-year account of the politics and the scandals of the capital forms the basis for detailed historical reconstruction of the few weeks following Augustus's death and suggests a reason for the four weeks' delay before the formal ratification of Tiberius's succession in the Senate.[27] A glance at Tacitus's report, however, makes it clear that his *Annals* is very different from the archival sources from which it receives its name:

> Meanwhile at Rome people plunged into slavery — consuls, senators, knights. The higher a man's rank, the more eager his hypocrisy, and his looks the more carefully studied, so as neither to betray joy at the decease of one emperor nor sorrow at the rise of another, while he mingled delight and lamentations with his flattery. (*Ann.* 1.7)[28]

The *Annals* is in fact a highly charged political history written some hundred years after the event. Its ironic presentation of the opening scenes of Tiberius's reign is a reminder that the narrative of history — even of such apparently routine matters as chronology — depends on a variety of sources that will inevitably have their own perspective and their own agenda, political or otherwise.

The potential variation in *point of view* across the empire becomes even more evident when we look at the other figures in Luke's list. *Pontius Pilate* was a Roman official whose years of office would presumably have been recorded in the central archives; but these records (their subject being of considerably less importance than the emperor) are now lost. He warrants only a brief mention by Tacitus (*Ann.* 15.44) as the procurator responsible for the execution of the "Christus" from whom the "mischievous superstition" of the *Christiani* took its name. The episode is not thought worth recording at its correct place in the chronological sequence of the *Annals*, but appears under the year 64, at the point where central Rome began to take notice of the Christian sect.

Most of our information about both Pilate and the *Herod family* comes

---

27. *CAH* 10:607-12.

28. ET from A. Church and W. Brodribb, *Annals of Tacitus* (London: MacMillan, 1895.

not from Tacitus but from the Jewish historian Josephus, who (unlike his Roman contemporary) had every reason to record the smallest details of Roman involvement with the province of Judea in the years leading up to the war of 66-70 CE. For Josephus, the Jewish War was "the greatest not only of the wars of our own times, but, so far as accounts have reached us, well nigh of all that ever broke out between cities or nations" (*J.W.* 1.1, LCL). For Tacitus, by contrast, it is only of interest as a background to the Roman civil conflicts over the imperial succession after the death of Nero. From this perspective, the year 69 can be summed up in the words, "The East was still quiet" (*Hist.* 1.10).

Even on the informational level, then, following up some of the detail in these first two verses reveals the intricate connections between narrative history and its sources, both literary and documentary. Both the ancient historian and the modern historian need access to good sources of information, and Luke was no exception. Clearly in this passage he has access to some kinds of public information on dates and officials that were not part of the Gospel tradition itself. Whether correct or incorrect, information of this type is not conjured out of thin air, so these opening verses raise the question *how* Luke had access to it. Moreover all historical sources, contemporary or not, have their own point of view: Tacitus's perspective is different from Josephus's, but even the Roman archives have a principle of selection governed by the interests of their compilers. This does not mean that the writing of history is impossible: Historians of antiquity are used to weighing the different viewpoints of their sources.[29] But it does mean that we should try to be aware of the particular interests and perspective of our "sources" — and should learn to read the NT writers as representatives of one among a number of competing and complementary interests in the Greco-Roman world.

The dating in Luke 3:1-2 also raises questions about *the text as part of Greco-Roman literature.* Why did Luke (alone of the Evangelists) choose to put this multiple dating here? What is its significance in literary terms? Most commentators cite as a parallel the multiple dating used by Thucydides to mark the beginning of his main narrative (2.2.1). This is much more precise than Luke's dating, but otherwise the parallel is a good one; it is echoed by Josephus (*J.W.* 2.284). Josephus is widely acknowledged to have been consciously modeling his own work on that

---

29. A. N. Sherwin-White, *Roman Society and Roman Law in the New Testament* (Oxford: Clarendon, 1963) 187-88.

of Thucydides,[30] and if Josephus why not Luke? Many commentators have argued that Luke here shows his aspirations (perhaps even his ability) to write as a "real" historian in the manner of the great Greek and Roman historians, and this could have a number of significant implications for our reading of his work. It could encourage us to claim the same standards of historical accuracy for Luke-Acts as are generally claimed for Thucydides; or we might begin to read other aspects of Luke's work, like the speeches of Acts, in the light of Thucydidean practice (which could lead to a rather less flattering estimate of Luke's accuracy as a reporter).[31] Either way, pursuing the literary parallel means reading Luke alongside the classical writers and paying attention to details of form, narrative structure, tone, and point of view. And this means reading not only Thucydides but also his critics and imitators: What did Luke's contemporaries think of Thucydides? When they used him as a literary model, what elements struck them as characteristically "Thucydidean"?[32]

But literary history also has *social implications*. If "history was not in the curriculum of Greco-Roman schools,"[33] who was reading Thucydides in the first century? For Luke to have read Thucydides well enough to imitate his work would imply a specialist literary education of a high order, with a correspondingly high social standing: Literary education can fairly be coupled with social privilege. To write history at all, in the terms of Greco-Roman culture, was to attempt one of the most ambitious of prose genres, in a literary world where failure merited only scorn: The second-century satirist Lucian has no mercy on the would-be "Thucydideses, Herodotuses, and Xenophons" who flocked to recount the Parthian War of 162-165 CE (*How to Write History* 2).

There is more to a literary parallel, in other words, than simply noting a similarity between texts: The text is simply the surface manifestation of a whole web of connections between culture and social world. Access to the network is relatively easy. But one must be prepared to explore a multiplicity of connections rather than settling for an oversimple solution. And one must also bear in mind the wider cultural network in which all the NT writers operate. Multiple datings like those of Luke 3:1-2 are not

30. See Thackeray's introduction to the LCL edition of Josephus's works (2:xiv-xix).
31. Martin Dibelius, *Studies in the Acts of the Apostles* (London: SCM, 1956) ch. 9.
32. Emilio Gabba, "True History and False History in Classical Antiquity," *JRS* 71 (1981) 50-62.
33. David E. Aune, *The New Testament in Its Literary Environment*, LEC 8 (Philadelphia: Westminster, 1987) 83.

unique to the Greek historians: They occur regularly in papyrus documents, and are common in another literary model to which we know Luke had access, the Greek Bible.[34] Synchronistic datings were a feature of life in the East long before the Romans appeared on the scene. Their appearance in the Jewish Scriptures is one of the marks of a national history lived for centuries under the shadow of great empires. But note the difference in literary terms. Thucydides and Josephus use the formal synchronism to mark the beginning of the quintessential subject of Greek and Roman history: a major war. Luke's subject is very different: the words and deeds of a teacher (Acts 1:1), operating within the framework of the empire yet far removed from its sources of power. (This fact alone might give reason to pause before trying to classify his work as "history" in the terms understood by Greco-Roman literature.) But as Cadbury observes, it is not even the ministry of Jesus that Luke dates in this formal way, but an event much more familiar to readers of the Hebrew Bible and its Greek translations: "The word of the Lord came to John the son of Zechariah in the wilderness."[35] Jeremiah, Zechariah, and Daniel are certainly as relevant to Luke as Thucydides — and a lot more accessible. Moreover, this presentation of John the Baptist as a successor to the prophets can be seen as part of a wider program in which Luke roots his narrative in the biblical past, a program that can be analyzed in terms of the sociological concept of "legitimation," by which the second generation of a religious sect seeks to create a past for itself in relation to the community from which it sprang.[36]

So, finally, the dating also brings us to the question of *the political ideology of the text.* Luke's insistence on articulating the imperial framework, here and elsewhere in his narrative, must cause the reader to wonder about the stance of the text toward the empire. In ascribing to Luke "a standpoint that makes him consider reality more from a perspective 'from above,'" Wengst simply gives forceful expression to a view of Luke that has become standard. It depends partly on an assessment of certain literary phenomena in terms of social status, but the same phenomena may be read in a very different way.[37] But even as a political assessment, we may ask whether such

---

34. H. J. Cadbury, *The Making of Luke-Acts* (New York: Macmillan, 1927) 205-8.

35. Cadbury, *Making of Luke-Acts,* 208-9.

36. Philip Francis Esler, *Community and Gospel in Luke-Acts,* SNTSMS 57 (Cambridge: Cambridge University, 1987).

37. For a detailed discussion, see Alexander, *Preface,* esp. ch. 8.

a view is fair. It is clear, of course, that Luke does not share the view of the empire expressed in the book of Revelation. But it is too easy to assume that there is no middle ground between John's outright condemnation of the empire and collaboration. We need look no further than the narrative portions of the book of Daniel, source of so much of the imagery of Revelation, in which the world empires are treated as a fact of life, subject to God, and owing allegiance to God. For Daniel, as for Luke, there is no reason for a believer to refuse participation in the processes of government, so long as they do not conflict with his or her prior religious loyalties. This last proviso is the key: Both Daniel and Luke explicitly reject any attempt to absolutize the claims of any human monarch over against the sovereignty of God (cf. Luke 20:25; Acts 4:19-20).

In this broader context it seems unnecessarily dogmatic to insist that Luke's use of the emperor as a chronological indicator entails a "pro-empire" position. As far as the reader is concerned, at this point in the narrative the options are still open. The word of God initiates action in a world that contains (among other things) tetrarchs and emperors. It is not yet clear (though it will become clearer by the end of Acts) how, if at all, the prophetic word and the potentates are connected (though the historian may note that Roman emperors were by no means insensitive to the prophecies that circulated among their eastern subjects).

The alert reader may well find a clue to Luke's stance later in this same chapter. Empowered by the word of God, John preaches "good news" (εὐαγ-γέλιον [euangelion], v 18). The word has already been used by an angelic messenger in connection with Jesus' birth at 2:10, in another passage framed by an emperor and his underlings (2:1-2), and it is hard to believe in either case that it is a politically innocent term. In the public propaganda of the empire, "good news" was associated with the emperor's birthday, adopted by decree as the basis of the civic calendar for all the cities of Asia in a decree from 9 BCE: "The birth date of our God signalled the beginning of Good News for the world because of him."[38] Far from expressing a craven subservience to the Empire, it may be argued, Luke's careful choice of language here is part of a political strategy that identifies Jesus as "the

38. From the Priene inscription, lines 40-41. The Greek text (traced via LSJ) is in *Die Inschriften von Priene*, ed. F. Hiller von Gaertringen (Berlin: Reimer, 1906) no. 105. The English translation is in Frederick W. Danker, *Luke*, Proclamation Commentaries (Philadelphia: Fortress, 1987) 29-30; full discussion of the text is in *idem, Benefactor* (St. Louis: Clayton, 1982) no. 33.

Superstar of superstars," in direct competition with the saviors and bene-factors proclaimed by imperial propaganda.[39]

4. Suggestions for Further Reading

I have tried to provide a (very selective) "walk-through" guide to scholarship on Greco-Roman literature and culture in the footnotes to the previous sections. Here I shall simply indicate a few books of special interest to NT readers.

On the *social world* of the NT, good introductions are: John E. Stam-baugh and David L. Balch, *The New Testament in Its Social Environment*, LEC (Philadelphia: Westminster, 1986); Wayne A. Meeks, *The Moral World of the First Christians*, LEC 6 (Philadelphia: Westminster, 1986). See also Abraham J. Malherbe, *Social Aspects of Early Christianity* (2d ed., Philadel-phia: Fortress, 1983) — pioneering and still stimulating; and Wayne A. Meeks, *The First Urban Christians* (New Haven: Yale University, 1983), a magisterial study whose footnotes open up whole tracts of Greco-Roman culture. Jerome H. Neyrey, ed., *The Social World of Luke-Acts* (Peabody: Hendrickson, 1992), gives access to more specifically social-science oriented work.

On links with Greco-Roman *literature*, see especially David E. Aune, *The New Testament in Its Literary Environment*, LEC 8 (Philadelphia: West-minster, 1987). For readers of German, Klaus Berger, "Hellenistische Gat-tungen im neuen Testament," *ANRW* 2.25.2 (1984) 1031-1432, is a treasury of detailed bibliography. Commentaries and special studies of NT books against a background of Greco-Roman literature are appearing all the time; note esp. Richard Burridge, *What Are the Gospels?* SNTSMS 70 (Cambridge: Cambridge University, 1992), for a fresh and provocative approach to an-cient genres; and *The Book of Acts in Its Ancient Literary Setting*, ed. Bruce W. Winter and Andrew D. Clarke (Grand Rapids: Eerdmans, 1993), which has a number of useful survey articles.

Finally, one or two *classic studies* are worth reading as a way of getting the "feel" of Greco-Roman literature and culture. Such a list is bound to be highly personal, but mine would include H. J. Cadbury's *The Making of Luke-Acts* (New York: Macmillan, 1927), which is especially valuable for its

---

39. Danker, *Luke*, 28-46, esp. 46.

sensitive approach to literary parallels; Arthur Darby Nock's *Conversion* (Oxford: Oxford University, 1933), for its perceptive handling of Greco-Roman modes of religious experience; and Ramsay MacMullen's *Enemies of the Roman Order* (Cambridge: Harvard University, 1966), for its pioneering insights into the discourse of alienation in the empire.

7. Textual Criticism of the New Testament

BART D. EHRMAN

Unlike other methods discussed in this book, textual criticism is not an "option" for interpreters of the NT. Whereas other approaches presuppose the wording of the text under consideration, textual criticism determines that wording. To put the matter somewhat differently, we cannot begin to explore what a text means until we know what it says. Rather than interpreting the text, textual criticism decides which words belong in the text. For this reason, textual criticism is a foundational discipline — indeed, *the* foundational discipline — for NT studies.

1. Why Textual Criticism Is Needed

We need the discipline of textual criticism because we do not have the original manuscripts of any of the books of the NT. What we have are copies that were made much later than the originals, in most instances many centuries later. These later copies were not themselves made from the autographs;[1] they were instead made from copies of copies of copies of the autographs. The problem with these later copies, the ones that have survived to our day, is that they all differ from one another to a greater or lesser

---

1. The term "autograph" comes from the Greek *auto-graphos,* meaning literally, "written with one's own hand." It is used to refer to the original manuscript produced by an author.

extent. Textual criticism examines these surviving manuscripts[2] — and there are thousands of them — and tries to decide on the basis of established critical principles what the originals themselves must have said.

Only with the invention of moveable type four hundred years ago was it possible to mass-produce literature with absolute accuracy, one copy appearing exactly like another. In antiquity, exact replications of texts were virtually impossible. When an author produced a book, he or she had to have it copied by hand; anyone else wanting a copy needed to produce it for himself or herself or hire a professional scribe to do so. Thus, to use an illustration from the NT, whoever wrote the Gospel of Matthew no doubt produced his text for his own community. If other members of the community wanted a copy for themselves, they would have to go through the laborious and painstaking process of copying it, one word at a time. Or if a Christian from a neighboring community wanted a copy, he or she would have to go through the same process. We can assume that Christians from different locations did in fact want to have copies of such valuable works. This led to a proliferation of copies, made by different Christians from different places, most of them private individuals rather than professional scribes, with differing aptitudes for the task.

The difficulty with making handwritten copies of such a long text as Matthew, or even shorter ones, is that it is nearly impossible to do so without making mistakes. (Anyone who doubts this should try to copy the Gospel of Matthew by hand, a text of about thirty-four pages in my NRSV Bible.) Moreover, anyone who makes a copy not of the original text, but of a copy of the original, will not only make new mistakes, but will also reproduce the mistakes created by the person who made the copy being used. In this way, mistakes multiply from copy to copy. Sometimes, of course, a copyist may detect a mistake in the manuscript he or she is using (for example, when the previous scribe has accidentally left out a word or an entire verse — a fairly common occurrence in our manuscripts). When this happens, the scribe producing the new copy may try to correct the error. Unfortunately, if the original is not available for checking, the "correction" may not restore the reading of the original, but introduce a new error, which will then be copied by the next copyist. And so it goes. Copies of copies of copies, each with its own errors and the errors of the copy from which it was produced.

---

2. The term "manuscript" is Latin, meaning "hand-written" (*manus* = hand; *scriptum* = something written). It typically refers to any handwritten text.

Moreover, we know from a study of ancient manuscripts that errors were not always accidental. Sometimes scribes felt inclined to change the text that they read. For example, copyists who came to a verse like Matt 24:36 — which indicates that no one, not even the Son of God himself, knows when the end will come — could well take offense at the idea that Christ did not know the time of his own return (this was especially a problem for scribes who were convinced that Christ was none other than God). This might lead a scribe to modify the text. Indeed, in this case it often *did* lead to a modification: A number of our manuscripts omit the words "not even the Son" from Matt 24:36. Scribes who made this change no doubt saw it as a "correction" or an "improvement," but textual critics, concerned to know what Matthew himself wrote, would label it a "corruption."[3]

To this point we have been speaking chiefly in the abstract about scribes inadvertently and intentionally modifying the texts of the NT that they copied. What, though, are the concrete realities? Were there in fact a large number of such errors? For us to realize the extent of the problem, some basic data may prove useful. At present, we have over 5360 manuscripts of all or part of the NT in Greek (the language in which all its books were originally written).[4] These manuscripts range in size from tiny fragments the size of a credit card to hefty volumes that include all twenty-seven books of the NT. They range in date from the early second century[5] to the sixteenth century (some copies were made by hand even after the invention of moveable-type printing). What is striking is that among these thousands of manuscripts, with the exception of the smallest fragments, no two are exactly alike in all of their particulars.

The manuscripts themselves thus leave no question that scribes made changes in their texts, and many such changes. How many differences are

3. The term "corruption" is used by textual critics to refer to any modification of the original text, whether intentional or accidental.

4. Newly discovered manuscripts are numbered at the Institute for New Testament Textual Research in Münster, Germany, which was founded by Kurt Aland and is now directed by Barbara Aland. For the numbers of the surviving manuscripts and brief descriptions of many of them, see the Alands' book *The Text of the New Testament: An Introduction to the Critical Editions and to the Theory and Practice of Modern Textual Criticism* (2d ed., Grand Rapids: Eerdmans/Leiden: Brill, 1987).

5. The oldest surviving fragment is the tiny p^{52}, which contains several verses from John 18. It is usually dated to the first half of the second century, i.e., some 30-50 years after the Gospel itself was written.

there among our surviving manuscripts? While estimates typically put them in the hundreds of thousands, no one knows the real number for certain because no one has yet been able to count them all. What we can say with confidence is that there are more differences among the manuscripts than there are words in the NT.

This is not to say that we are totally at a loss when trying to decide what the *original* text of the NT was. In fact, the vast majority of the differences in our manuscripts are insignificant, irrelevant, and easy to explain. Far and away the most common mistakes involve differences in spelling; many others involve accidental omissions of words and phrases by careless scribes.

There are, however, a large number of cases where the wording of a passage differs significantly among our manuscripts in ways that are critical for exegesis. In these instances, textual critics have to balance the arguments for one form of the text over those for another and then render a judgment as to which appears to be the original text and which a corruption of it by a later scribe.

To illustrate the potential significance of such differences, we might consider some of the more famous and striking examples. Did the author of the Gospel of Mark end his narrative at 16:8 with the women fleeing Jesus' empty tomb in fear, telling no one what they had seen? Or did the author write the final twelve verses found in some of our manuscripts but not in others, verses in which the resurrected Jesus appears to his disciples and tells them that those who believe in him will be able to handle deadly snakes and drink poison without suffering harm? Did the author of the Fourth Gospel write the famous story of the woman taken in adultery, or was this a later addition to the Gospel by a well-meaning scribe? The story is found in many of our later manuscripts between chapters 7 and 8, but in none of the early manuscripts. Did the voice at Jesus' baptism in the Gospel of Luke originally declare "You are my beloved Son, in whom I am well pleased" (exactly the words found in Mark's account), or did it proclaim "You are my Son, today I have begotten you" (as the text is worded in some of our earliest witnesses)? The latter version, a quotation of Psalm 2, proved acceptable to second-century Christians who denied that Jesus was God by insisting that he came to be "adopted" as God's Son at his baptism. As a final example, did the author of 1 John include the famous "Johannine comma" (5:7-8), the only passage in the entire Bible that explicitly affirms the trinitarian views of later Christians — that the Godhead consists of three persons and that "these three are one"? Even though the passage is part of the Latin Bible and found its way into the King James Version, it does not occur in any Greek manuscript of the NT earlier than the fourteenth century.

2. The Theory and Practice of Textual Criticism

Since all of our surviving manuscripts have mistakes, scholars must decide the original wording of the text on a case-by-case basis. The process of making this decision in view of the whole range of evidence is sometimes called the "eclectic" method.[6] In rough terms, the textual evidence is classified either as "external" — that is, based on the kinds of manuscripts that support one reading or the other — or "internal" — that is, based on the likelihood of a reading going back to the original author or to an error introduced by a scribe.

2.1 External Evidence

Since our only access to the words of the NT authors comes through the flawed manuscripts of their writings, it is important to understand how critics use these witnesses when trying to reconstruct the original text. First it is necessary to know about the kinds of manuscript evidence that are available.

a. Greek Manuscripts. The more than 5360 Greek manuscripts of all or part of the NT range in date, as we have seen, from the early second century through the sixteenth. Very few, however, are from the earlier period, down to about the year 400.

Greek manuscripts are normally divided into three main categories.[7] The papyri, that is, those written on papyrus,[8] are the earliest available witnesses, most of them dating from the second to the fifth centuries; the majuscules were written on parchment or vellum in uncial letters — com-

---

6. From the Greek word ἐκλέγω *(eklegō)*, "choose."

7. For more detailed information see Bruce M. Metzger, *The Text of the New Testament: Its Transmission, Corruption, and Restoration* (3d ed., New York/Oxford: Oxford University, 1993) ch. 1.

8. Papyrus was a reed that grew in Egypt from which was manufactured the principal writing material of antiquity, analogous in texture to a very rough grade of paper. For a more precise description, including a brief discussion of the manufacturing process itself, see Metzger, *Text of the New Testament*, 3-4.

parable to our English "capitals" — from roughly the fourth to the ninth centuries; the minuscules were written on parchment or vellum, but in minuscule (= small) letters — comparable to our English "cursive" — after the ninth century.

b. Early Versions. In addition to the Greek witnesses, we have a large number of NT manuscripts produced in other languages. Christians from the second century on recognized the need for translations of the Scriptures into other languages for those who did not read or speak Greek. The earliest translations were probably into Syriac and Latin, perhaps as early as the late second or early third centuries; sometime thereafter the NT was translated into Coptic, and eventually into Armenian, Ethiopic, Georgian, Gothic, and other languages. Like the Greek NT, each of these versions survives in a number of manuscripts, all of which, again, appear to contain mistakes.[9]

It is possible to compare the various manuscripts of any of the versions to decide what the earliest form of the translation was, to take that form and translate it back into Greek, and on that basis to decide what form of the Greek text was available to the original translator. Needless to say, this is an arduous and technical process, but it does produce useful results for scholars concerned to learn what Greek manuscripts were available in the early period when the versions were made — the period from which, unfortunately, very few actual Greek manuscripts survive.

c. Patristic quotations. Finally, we have numerous Christian writings from the second century on; the authors of these works frequently quote the NT, making it theoretically possible to reconstruct the wording of the manuscripts that they themselves were using. This particular kind of external evidence is especially fraught with uncertainty, as it is not always easy to decide whether an author is quoting exactly or simply paraphrasing; moreover, these early writings have also been handed down to us only in manuscripts produced by scribes who sometimes changed quotations found in their texts in conformity with the wording of the Scriptures as they themselves knew them. Nonetheless, when this kind of evidence is studied carefully, it can prove quite valuable; unlike the scribes of our surviving Greek manuscripts and the early versions, the patristic writers can be fixed in time and space. We know exactly when and where most of

9. Since Latin became the official language of Western Christendom, there are a particularly large number of Latin manuscripts, nearly twice the number of Greek manuscripts.

them lived; their quotations can therefore indicate with relative certainty how the text of the NT had been changed in different times and places.

How can these thousands of bits of data be used to determine the original text wherever there are differences among our witnesses? Over the years, scholars have devised a number of principles of criticism, some of which, as we will see, are of greater use than others. These principles can be expressed in terms of questions that a critic will bring to a passage that is attested in a variety of ways among different witnesses.

a. How many witnesses support each reading? For some critics, this is the all-important question; others, however, discount it entirely. Those who support this principle argue that if a passage is worded in one way in three hundred manuscripts but differently in only three, it is more likely that the majority text is original and that the three aberrant witnesses have simply incorporated a mistake.

The problem with this logic is that it overlooks an important feature of our manuscript evidence. All of our witnesses were copied from one another. Suppose that at some time during the second century there were two manuscripts with a different reading for a particular verse. One was in a remote area, and came to be copied three times before being destroyed in a fire. The other was in a major metropolitan area with a large Christian population; it was copied thirty times, and each of the copies made from it was copied ten times. At the end of this process, there would be three hundred and one manuscripts with one reading and three with the other. Does that mean that the three hundred and one are correct and the three are in error? Not necessarily! In fact, the numerical difference in the manuscript support for the two readings is not three hundred and one to three, but one to one. Each reading goes back to a solitary manuscript of the same time period. For this reason, simply counting the number of manuscripts supporting a reading is not the best way to decide the original text.

b. Which reading is supported by the most ancient manuscripts? The same illustration shows the importance of knowing the *date* of the witnesses supporting each variant reading. If there are two hundred manuscripts from the fifth to the sixteenth centuries with a particular form of the text, but two from the third century with a different form, then the form supported by the two may well be superior to that found in the two hundred. The logic here is that since manuscripts become *increasingly* corrupt with the passage of time (since copyists reproduce the mistakes of their predecessors as well as create some of their own), the earlier manuscripts as a rule will be better than the later ones.

Although this argument is generally valid, it, too, is not entirely fool-proof. Suppose there are two manuscripts with different forms of the text, one from the third century and the other from the fifth. A critic might naturally think that the third-century witness is superior since it is older. But we cannot always be certain about the age of each manuscript's *exemplar*, that is, the copy that the scribe used to produce the manuscript. It is entirely possible, for example, that the third-century manuscript had as its exemplar a manuscript made ten years earlier, still in the third century, whereas the copyist of the fifth-century manuscript had access to a very old copy preserved in his church library, say, from the second century. In this case, ironically enough, the fifth-century manuscript would reproduce an older form of the text than the third-century manuscript! For this reason, even though the age of a manuscript can be important in determining the quality of its text, it is by no means a failsafe guide.

c. How geographically diverse is the attestation for each reading? Less problematic is the matter of the geographic distribution of a reading. Here again the principle can be stated simply. If manuscripts support two different forms of a passage, with one of the forms restricted to witnesses produced in only one geographical area (Italy, for instance), whereas the other is found in witnesses spread throughout the Mediterranean (e.g., Northern Africa, Alexandria, Syria, Asia Minor, Gaul, and Spain), then the former is more likely a local variation reproduced by scribes in the region, and the other is more likely older since it was more widely known. If witnesses supporting a reading are *both* early and widespread, a strong case can be made that this reading is original.

d. What is the "quality" of the supporting witnesses? As in a court of law, there are some textual witnesses that are more reliable than others. The general principle of external evidence is that witnesses that are *known* to produce an inferior text — when the case can be decided with a high degree of certainty (on the "internal" grounds discussed below) — are also likely to produce an inferior text where the internal evidence is more ambiguous. Witnesses, like people, can be trusted or suspected, and through years of careful study scholars have decided that certain manuscripts (for example, some of the papyri, like $\mathfrak{p}^{75}$, and some of the majuscules, like Codex B) can be trusted more than others.

e. Which "groups" of witnesses support the variant readings? Scholars have long recognized that some manuscripts are closely related to one another in the sense that they typically support the same wording of the text in a large number of passages. Witnesses can thus be grouped together in light of their resemblances. Today three major groups are widely recognized: The "Alexandrian" witnesses, which include most of the earliest and "best" manuscripts as judged by their overall quality, may ultimately go back to the form of text preserved among scholars in Alexandria, Egypt; the "Western" witnesses, which are misnamed since some of them derive from the East, are manuscripts associated with codex D in the Gospels and Acts and appear to preserve an early but generally unreliable form of the text;[10] the "Byzantine" witnesses, which include the vast majority of later manuscripts, are almost universally judged by scholars to preserve an inferior form of the text.[11] The general rule of thumb for most critics is that readings attested only in Byzantine or only in Western witnesses are highly suspect; readings found among the Alexandrian witnesses are more likely to be given the benefit of the doubt, especially when they are also attested by witnesses of the other two groups.

In summary, it usually does not matter how many manuscripts support one or another reading (unless there is literally only one supporting witness, in which case we can almost always suspect that an individual scribe made a mistake). It is much more important to know the *age* of the supporting witnesses: the more ancient the better. But what matters even more is the geographical diversity, general quality, and textual grouping of the witnesses that support a reading. Readings found in the oldest, most widespread, and best manuscripts are more likely to be original than their variants.

2.2 Internal Evidence

With "internal" evidence we turn from considering the strength of the manuscript support for a reading to evaluating the competing merits of the variant readings in and of themselves. If a verse is found in two or more different forms in the manuscript tradition, which can be judged to be corruptions? And which is the original? Since these are two different questions — even though they eventually lead to the same result — scholars have identified two basic kinds of internal evidence. The first considers

10. One of the major debates among textual critics over the past century has been the overall quality of the "Western" witnesses. Some specialists continue to argue that the Western text is generally superior to the Alexandrian text. This continues, though, to be the opinion of only a small minority.

11. Some advocates of the King James Version continue to contend that the Byzantine witnesses more reliably represent the original text. None of the leading textual scholars in North America or Europe, however, takes this stance.

"transcriptional probabilities," by asking which readings were more likely to appeal to the interests and concerns of scribes (and thus to have been created by them when they "transcribed," and sometimes changed, the text); the other considers "intrinsic probabilities" by asking which readings appear to conform more closely with the language, style, and theology of the NT author and are thus intrinsically more likely to be original.

First we consider a range of issues relating to *transcriptional probabilities*. As already indicated, the majority of changes in our manuscripts can be ascribed not to the intentional manipulations of the copyists but simply to scribal accidents occasioned, for instance, by fatigue or carelessness. Transcriptional probabilities can come into play in determining where these kinds of changes have occurred. Apart from mistakes in spelling, one of the most common kinds of transcriptional error involves the accidental omission of words, phrases, or even lines. This kind of mistake is quite understandable: Not only was transcribing a Greek text slow and arduous work, but it also had to be done from exemplars that were often difficult to read. The oldest Greek manuscripts do not include punctuation or paragraph divisions; indeed, there are not even spaces left between words. As a result, when a scribe copied a word or a phrase, his eye would sometimes return to the page at the wrong place — alighting, for example, on the same word repeated later in the sentence. By resuming his copying at that point, then, the scribe would accidentally leave out the entire text between the two occurrences of the word. We have instances of scribes omitting not only phrases and lines in this way, but also entire pages!

Conversely, if the scribe's eye returned to the page at an *earlier* occurrence of a word, he could inadvertently repeat everything he had already copied. While these kinds of accidental errors are intriguing because they show how difficult it must have been to transcribe texts, they are for the most part unimportant for knowing what the originals were. They can be easily detected and disposed of as corruptions.

Far more interesting are changes that scribes appear to have made intentionally. Based on both common sense and hard data, scholars have been able to show that scribes were more likely to create certain kinds of readings than others. That is to say, when scribes changed their texts, they appear to have done so in detectable ways. The basic principle at work under transcriptional probability is the famous dictum, which may initially appear somewhat backward, that "the more difficult reading is to be preferred as original." The logic behind this principle is that Christian scribes, who had a vested interest in the texts they were copying, were more likely to make a passage easier to understand than more difficult. That is, if and when scribes were actually thinking about what they were doing, they were more likely, on average, to produce a text that made better sense rather than worse sense.

A careful study of the manuscripts of the NT reveals that scribes characteristically made several kinds of changes to "improve" the sense of the text. As is the case for many modern Christians, scribes were often puzzled or disturbed by the presence of parallel passages in the NT, especially in the Gospels, in which the same story is worded in different (sometimes contradictory) ways. When scribes were more conversant with one of the Gospel accounts, they would sometimes modify the text of the others, making them agree word for word. In Luke 3:16, for example, John the Baptist declares "I baptize you in water." Several scribes appear to have been familiar with the longer statement that John makes in Matt 3:11 and have added the appropriate final phrase to their copies of Luke so that the Baptist is more explicit, saying: "I baptize you in water *unto repentance.*" Three verses later we learn of John's reproach of Herod "for Herodias, his brother's wife." Some manuscripts have conformed this text to the parallel passage found in both Mark 6:17 and Matt 14:3 by adding the brother's name. The harmonized text now has John reproach Herod "for Herodias, his brother *Philip's* wife."

Sometimes scribes changed a verse by making it conform with a phrase that was *not* found in a parallel passage but was nonetheless familiar in popular Christian usage. This happens, for example, in Luke 3:10, where the crowds ask John "What then shall we do?" Several scribes, perhaps instinctively reflecting their knowledge of the famous scene of the Philippian jailor in Acts 16:30, added a clause that probably struck them as natural, so that now John is asked "What then shall we do, *that we might be saved?*"

Scribes sometimes added a graphic detail or a rhetorical flourish to a text they copied. An example occurs in one manuscript, the famous codex D, in Luke 3:16. Here, rather than stating that "John answered, saying to all of them," the text makes the more striking statement that "John, knowing what they were thinking, said. . . ." Yet more frequently, scribes sometimes "improved" a passage by changing its grammar. This is especially common in passages that preserve unusual or incorrect Greek syntax; but it also occurs in places where the change simply appears to help the sense. In his quotation of Isaiah 40 in Luke 3:5, John states that "the crooked ways shall be made into a straight (path)." The word "path" is not actually found in the Greek text, but, as with other occurrences of the adjective "straight," has to be supplied in our English translations from the context. The difficulty is that while the adjective ("straight") is singular, the noun that precedes it is plural ("crooked ways"). The grammar is not incorrect, but nonetheless appears to have puzzled some scribes, who changed the text simply by making the adjective plural as well, so that the (numerous) crooked ways are not transformed into a solitary straight path, but into "straight paths."

Probably the most interesting kinds of changes that scribes made in their texts are theological in nature. On occasion scribes modified their texts either to eliminate a doctrinally troublesome reference (as in Matt 24:36, mentioned above) or to insert a notion that was theologically significant.[12] This kind of motivation may lie behind the change made by several scribes of the Syriac text of Luke 3:4. In these manuscripts, rather than saying "prepare the way of the Lord, make straight his paths," John is said to have proclaimed "prepare the way of the Lord, make straight the paths *of our God*." This modified reading is interesting because it conforms John's proclamation more closely to the passage in Isaiah 40 that he quotes. What is yet more significant, however, is how the modified text functions within the context of Luke's Gospel. In the original text, John is said to announce the coming of Jesus, the Lord. For the scribes of these Syriac manuscripts, however, Jesus is more than the Lord; he is now said to be "our God."[13]

In view of the kinds of changes scribes appear likely to have made (judging not only from common sense, but also from the evidence that we have available to us), transcriptional probabilities can be set forth as guidelines for deciding which variant readings represent corruptions and which the original text. Scribes were more likely to harmonize two passages than to make them differ; they were more likely to make a passage more graphic than less; they were more likely to improve the grammar of a passage than to make it worse; they were more likely to bring a passage into conformity with their own theological views than to contradict them. As a result, the critic can employ a general rule of thumb when considering transcriptional probabilities: The more difficult reading — that is, the less harmonized, graphic, grammatical, and theologically "correct" reading — is to be preferred as original.

12. I have produced an exhaustive study of this kind of variant by looking at instances in which scribes in the second and third centuries changed their texts for christological reasons, making them conform more closely with the orthodox belief that Jesus was fully God and fully human, yet one being instead of two. See Bart D. Ehrman, *The Orthodox Corruption of Scripture: The Effect of Early Christological Controversies on the Text of the New Testament* (Oxford: Oxford University, 1993).

13. See below for a fuller discussion of this variant and the problems it raises.

Whereas in dealing with transcriptional probabilities we ask which readings were most likely to have been created by scribes in the process of transcription, in dealing with *intrinsic probabilities* we ask which reading is most likely to have been created by the author of the NT book, that is, which reading coincides with the author's language, style, and theology.

The questions raised by such considerations are more closely aligned with traditional issues of exegesis. The first question is that of language. One of the ways that the authorship of ancient texts is established is on the basis of vocabulary preferences of a writer, when these can be known. Thus, for instance, the Pastoral Epistles are commonly judged not to be Pauline, in no small measure because of the inordinately large number of words that occur in them but nowhere in the undisputed Paulines (over one-third of the entire vocabulary of the Pastorals). Similar arguments can be applied to text-critical problems. If there are two variant readings of a passage, with one of them containing words characteristic of an author and the other containing words found nowhere else in that author's writings, the latter is less likely to be original.

Similarly with arguments from style. Every author has a characteristic way of phrasing things. Moreover, most of the time, stylistic conventions are somewhat unconscious. Rarely, for example, do authors give a good deal of thought to the kinds of subordinate clauses or coordinating conjunctions that they use or to the typical length of their sentences. Once a person has developed a literary competence, these stylistic forms come more or less naturally. Since everyone has a slightly different style, though, it is sometimes possible to detect the hand of an editor when the work of an author has been modified by someone else. This basic principle has a text-critical payoff. It sometimes happens that when a passage occurs in two different forms in our manuscript tradition, one of them conforms to the style attested elsewhere for an author, whereas the other does not. In such instances, intrinsic probabilities favor the former reading.

Finally, and perhaps most critically, each author of a NT book has a distinct theological perspective that can, theoretically, be uncovered by a careful exegesis of that author's writings. There are instances, particularly in some of the most exegetically significant variants preserved for us in the manuscript tradition, in which different readings support different theological perspectives. Intrinsic probabilities demand that the theological perspective that coincides most closely with that which can otherwise be established for an author is more likely to be original.

In summary, textual critics are concerned not only to determine which

139

readings are more likely to have appealed to (and therefore, to have been created by) scribes, but also to establish which readings are more likely to have been created by the authors of the NT books themselves. Intrinsic probabilities involve establishing the original text on the basis of the language, style, and theology of a given author.

3. Applying the Principles

At this point of our discussion, an astute reader may be wondering what happens when the various kinds of evidence we have discussed conflict with one another, or in the worst of cases, appear to cancel one another out. What can the critic do, for example, when the reading that conforms most closely with the language and style of an author (and is therefore more likely original, based on intrinsic probabilities) is also the one more closely harmonized to a parallel passage (and is therefore less likely original on the basis of transcriptional probabilities)? Or, expanding the question yet further, how do critics resolve a problem when the external evidence clearly goes one way, and the internal evidence the other?

We are fortunate not to have thousands upon thousands of such cases thrust upon us. Indeed, as nearly everyone at work in this field will concede, the vast majority of all textual problems are easily resolved, so that there is a consensus on most of the variant readings preserved in our manuscripts. This is not at all to say, however, that no significant problems remain. On the contrary, many of the remaining problems *are* significant; in most instances they continue to be problems precisely because scholars disagree on how to evaluate the competing kinds of evidence. To my knowlege, all textual scholars today acknowledge that the trinitarian statement found in the "Johannine comma" (1 John 5:7-8) is not original to the Epistle. Moreover, the vast majority agree that the final twelve verses in many manuscripts (and English translations) of Mark represent a later addition to the text, as does the story of the woman taken in adultery in the later manuscripts of John. There are far fewer critics, however, willing to concede that the voice at Jesus' baptism in Luke said "Today I have begotten you."[14]

14. I am a member of the vocal minority who think that this *was* the original text, even though it is not found in many of our manuscripts. For a full discussion, which attempts to balance the various arguments pro and con, see Ehrman, *The Orthodox Corruption of Scripture*, 62-67.

In this instance, the evidence is not as clear-cut, and scholars weigh the various kinds of arguments differently.

What this means is that textual criticism is not some kind of objective science (as if any historical discipline ever could be!), but a matter of evaluating historical evidence as conscientiously and cogently as possible. Arguments have to be made for the original text on a case-by-case basis, as scholars choose to prefer the reading found in some manuscripts over that found in others.[15] Ideally, the decisions will be based on a cumulative argument that appeals to the most weighty issues of a case. We can illustrate the process by evaluating more fully two of the textual problems found in Luke 3:1-20.

We have seen that a theological issue was at stake when Luke 3:4 was changed from "Make straight his paths," to "Make straight the paths of our God." The latter text emphasizes the deity of Christ in a way that would be particularly amenable to early Christian scribes. But that is not the entire story, and there may be some countervailing evidence since the shorter text ("his paths"), which I have argued is original, happens also to be found in the parallel passages in Mark 1:3 and Matt 3:3. Moreover, the longer text, which I have judged to be theologically attractive to scribes, happens also to be more closely aligned with Isa 40:3, the verse that is quoted here. Since it is more faithful to the OT text and is less harmonized with the other Synoptics, is not the longer text more likely to be original?

These in fact would be good internal arguments for the reading that I have rejected as a corruption. But as it turns out, there is little debate among scholars in this instance as to the original text. Luke, of course, received this story from Mark (who reads "his paths" rather than "the paths of our God"). We know that there may have been a reason for *scribes* to have changed the text (to promote their beliefs in Jesus' divinity), but is there a reason for *Luke* to have done so? What is striking in this connection is that throughout his entire narrative, Luke nowhere else gives any firm indication that he understands Jesus to be "God." To be sure, Jesus is God's Son; but never, for Luke, is he simply God. Thus the longer reading both conforms to the views of early Christian scribes (Jesus' divinity: a transcriptional argument) and fails to conform to the perspective of Luke (an intrinsic argument). Since Luke would have had to go out of his way to incorporate such a view into his text (that is, he would not have been simply reproducing

---

15. This element of informed decision and choice, as I have previously indicated, is why the method is called "eclectic."

Mark here, but would have had to change the text before him to incorporate the new theological perspective), it appears unlikely that the change to "the paths of our God" was made by Luke.

This judgment is rendered altogether certain when one considers the external evidence for both readings. It is to be recalled that good external support requires that a reading be attested in the earliest, most geographically diverse, and best witnesses. In this instance, the variant reading that is at odds with Luke's own theology ("the paths of our God") is found in only one Latin and three Syriac manuscripts. *All* of our most valuable sources — that is, the entire Greek manuscript tradition — attest the other reading; thus it is found in the earliest (as well as nearly all of the latest!) and the best witnesses, and it is attested throughout the entire Mediterranean, wherever manuscripts were produced. This kind of overwhelming external attestation is almost impossible to explain if the reading is not original. Here we can see, then, how a confluence of arguments, internal and external, can work together to establish with relative certainty the original text of Luke.

Five verses later another interesting textual problem occurs, one that is somewhat harder to resolve. Luke 3:9 appears in several different forms in our manuscripts; here we will restrict ourselves to only one of the textual problems. Does John the Baptist indicate that "every tree that does not bear *good fruit* will be cut down and cast into the fire," or did the original text leave out the adjective, so that the Baptist spoke of "every tree that does not bear *fruit*"? In this instance, the general consensus among textual critics is that the longer reading ("good fruit") is original. But a strong case can be made that this consensus is wrong. Exploring some of the points in favor of the shorter reading will help us see again how various text-critical arguments can work together.

The external evidence is overwhelmingly in favor of the longer reading. This is probably the main reason that scholars have generally preferred it: It is attested in almost all of our witnesses. But it is striking that the earliest Greek witness to preserve the passage, $\mathfrak{p}^4$, from the third century, appears to attest the shorter reading.[16] Moreover, it is found in quotations of the passage in writings of the third-century Alexandrian theologian Origen,

16. When critics say that a manuscript "appears" to attest a reading, it usually means that there is a hole in the manuscript at the relevant point, but that by counting the number of letters that would have taken up the space created by the hole, they are reasonably certain what the manuscript must have read before it was damaged.

who is one of our best witnesses to the text of the NT during the earliest period of transmission. It is also found somewhat earlier in the writings of Irenaeus, the bishop of Lyons in Gaul (near the end of the second century). Finally, it is attested in several Latin manuscripts. Thus, while the longer reading has *more* documents in its favor, the shorter reading has the earliest and some of the best; and these are not at all localized, but are scattered around the Mediterranean.

It is difficult to apply intrinsic probabilities to these readings, as both appear to make good sense in a Lukan context. The transcriptional probabilities, on the other hand, are intriguing. First, the longer reading is clearly the one that scribes would know from parallel passages; not only the preaching of John in Matt 3:10, but also the even more familiar account of Jesus' own words in Matt 7:19, speak of believers bearing "good fruit." If the less harmonized reading is more likely original, then the adjective should probably be considered a scribal addition. Second, the longer reading is less susceptible of misunderstanding, which also argues against its being original. And third, as I have already intimated, one can readily imagine another reason for scribes choosing to modify the passage, if the shorter text were original: According to the short form of the text, John states that barren trees alone — those that do not bear any fruit — will be destroyed in the day of apocalyptic wrath. What, though, about trees that bear "bad" or "rotten" fruit? Will they not be judged as well?

The point is that one can readily imagine scribes adding the adjective "good" to the text if it were not originally there. But what could be the motivation for deleting it if it *were* there? It should be pointed out, in this connection, that the word is *not* omitted by scribes in the parallel passages in Matthew, which shows that scribes did not find it at all puzzling. Given the circumstance that the shorter text is attested in the earliest witnesses, which also happen to be among the best witnesses, we may be inclined to consider it original.[17]

*   *   *

As should be obvious, textual criticism is on one level a complex and demanding discipline. Only someone with a good knowledge of the Greek

---

17. Those who would argue that the external evidence is overwhelmingly in favor of the longer text would probably have to explain that the adjective was omitted accidentally by several scribes.

language in which the NT was written can be expected to delve deeply into the problems raised by the NT manuscripts and the variant forms of the text that they preserve. On the other hand, the methods that scholars use to adjudicate among the competing virtues of these textual variants are not in themselves particularly difficult and should become familiar working principles for anyone who is serious about NT interpretation. These principles are used in the better critical commentaries, and the student with only a brief introduction such as I have provided here should be able to evaluate their use for himself or herself. To restate those principles briefly: Readings that are preserved in our earliest, most widely distributed, and best witnesses are more likely to be original; so, too, are those that are judged, on a variety of grounds, to be the "more difficult" readings; and so, too, finally, are readings that conform to the language, style, and theological perspective of their author.

4. Suggestions for Further Reading

A useful college-level introduction to textual criticism is J. Harold Greenlee, *An Introduction to New Testament Textual Criticism* (rev. ed., Peabody, Massachusetts: Hendrickson, 1995). A more substantial treatment, rightly hailed as the authoritative and classic introduction, is Bruce M. Metzger, *The Text of the New Testament: Its Transmission, Corruption, and Restoration* (3d ed., New York/Oxford: Oxford University, 1993). Also valuable, particularly for the student interested in learning to use the critical apparatuses found in the printed editions of the Greek New Testament (especially the Nestle-Aland 26th edition), is Kurt and Barbara Aland, *The Text of the New Testament: An Introduction to the Critical Editions and to the Theory and Practice of Modern Textual Criticism* (2d ed., Grand Rapids: Eerdmans/Leiden: Brill, 1989).

For an up-to-date survey of developments in text criticism over the past fifty years, see the essay by Eldon Jay Epp, "Textual Criticism," in *The New Testament and Its Modern Interpreters*, ed. Eldon J. Epp and George W. MacRae (Philadelphia: Fortress/Atlanta: Scholars, 1989) 75-126. Full essays on each of the major aspects of the discipline (all the various kinds of Greek manuscripts, each of the early versions, the Patristic citations in Greek, Latin, and Syriac, and various methods and tools used by textual scholars) are now available in *The Text of the New Testament in Contemporary Research: Essays on the* Status Quaestionis, ed. Bart D. Ehrman and Michael W. Holmes, SD 46 (Grand Rapids: Eerdmans, 1995).

For an exhaustive discussion of all the major early versions, see Bruce M. Metzger, *The Early Versions of the New Testament: Their Origin, Transmission, and Limitations* (Oxford: Clarendon, 1977). A useful introduction to the Greek biblical manuscripts (of both Old and New Testaments) can be found in Metzger's *Manuscripts of the Greek Bible: An Introduction to Greek Paleography* (New York/Oxford: Oxford University, 1981).

A particularly useful tool that shows textual critics "at work" is Bruce M. Metzger's volume, *A Textual Commentary on the Greek New Testament* (Stuttgart: United Bible Societies, 1971). Here Metzger indicates the reasons behind the major textual decisions made by the five-person editorial committee responsible for producing the United Bible Societies' *Greek New Testament*, the standard Greek text available today.

Finally, those interested in the importance of textual criticism not only for establishing the original text but also for seeing how and why the text came to be changed by theologically invested scribes can consult Bart D. Ehrman, *The Orthodox Corruption of Scripture: The Effect of Early Christological Controversies on the Text of the New Testament* (New York/Oxford: Oxford University, 1993).

8. *Modern Linguistics and the New Testament*

MAX TURNER

1. The Relevance of Modern Linguistics to the Study of New Testament Texts

At first sight it may seem unnecessary to attempt any apology for careful use of linguistics in the study of NT texts. Linguistics embraces the scientific study of *all* aspects of the phenomenon of "language," from the smallest linguistic units to the largest:

phonology	the study of the individual sounds of a language, how they are generated, and how they contribute to meaning,
morphology	the study of word formation,
syntax	the ways words are combined into clauses or sentences,
structure analysis	the logical and argumentative relations of the propositions embedded in a sentence or paragraph, and
discourse analysis	how whole texts and contexts structure meanings.

As such, a study of linguistics is potentially relevant to the elucidation of *every* aspect of a text. And to judge by the enormous amount of linguistic detail the larger theological dictionaries offer on each word and the critical commentaries offer on each clause and sentence, the potential contribution of linguistic studies is largely taken for granted.

But the inclusion of the adjective "modern" in the title of this chapter is deliberate and mildly polemical. Since Ferdinand de Saussure's pioneering lectures, published posthumously in 1916,[1] a revolution has occurred in the understanding of how language and meaning are structured. The modern discipline of linguistics was thereby launched, and has become an academic growth area, particularly since the 1960s. Fueled by studies in philosophy, anthropology, psychology, and sociology, it is today a wide-ranging discipline embracing a number of specialized fields.

And yet — despite the alarm sounded by James Barr's *The Semantics of Biblical Language*[2] — modern linguistics has had relatively little influence on NT exegesis. NT study remains largely dominated by the prescientific "linguistics" encapsulated in the standard (but now dated) grammars, lexicons, and theological "dictionaries" and mediated to each new generation of theological students by commentaries and NT Greek primers. This is not to suggest that the older works have nothing to offer — they are crammed with an immensity of important data and many insightful classificatory and interpretive comments. But modern linguistics suggests a more refined and often quite different analysis of the material, leading to a host of individual exegetical adjustments. It also examines dimensions of linguistic and textual meaning that were not even touched by pre-Saussurian linguistics, for example, transformational grammar, theoretical semantics, literary-semantic analysis of paragraphs, text linguistics, pragmatics, etc.

There are now hopeful signs that this state of affairs is beginning to change. This is true especially with the arrival of such important works as Stanley Porter's *Verbal Aspect in the Greek of the New Testament*[3] and the new *Greek-English Lexicon of the New Testament Based on Semantic Domains*,[4] not to mention a host of semipopular introductions to modern linguistics written for theological students.[5]

It should be clear from what we have said that "linguistics" does not provide a single "approach" to individual texts in anything like the way that, for example, "genre criticism" or "text criticism" does. The latter are unidimensional areas of study that pose a narrow range of questions of the

---

1. Ferdinand de Saussure, *Course in General Linguistics* (ET; London: Owen, 1960).

2. Oxford: Oxford University, 1961.

3. Bern: Peter Lang, 1989.

4. Johannes P. Louw and Eugene A. Nida, *Greek-English Lexicon of the New Testament Based on Semantic Domains*, 2 vols. (New York: UBS, 1988).

5. See especially, David A. Black, *Linguistics for Students of New Testament Greek* (Grand Rapids: Eerdmans, 1988); Peter Cotterell and Max Turner, *Linguistics and Biblical Interpretation* (London: SPCK/Downers Grove: InterVarsity, 1989).

text being studied. Modern linguistics, on the other hand, is a broad field-encompassing discipline (like "science" or "theology"). While it is largely *based* on the study of actual languages, it attempts to provide general theories of language that are applicable to all languages, and it seeks to generate specific, more circumscribed hypotheses about particular groups of languages or even single dialects. We may examine some of the relevance of linguistics for NT study when we have more briefly outlined the structure of the discipline.

2. The Cardinal Principles of Modern Linguistics

Earlier linguistics tended to be concerned with particular languages, not the phenomenon of language (and meaning) in general, and was also often *prescriptive* rather *descriptive* (telling us *how* good Greek "should" be written rather than *what* sort of variations of pattern were "normal"). There were little agreement on a method of study, little formal discussion of how language in general functions, and few agreed fundamentals.

By contrast, modern linguistics is first *descriptive*, and then attempts to derive general theories. De Saussure established three fundamental and related principles on which much of the rest of the discipline rests:

(1) the structurally *arbitrary* and so purely *conventional* nature of the word-to-meaning relationship,
(2) the primary need for synchronic (rather than etymological) study of language systems, and
(3) the significance of *structure* for meaning.

2.1 The Relationship of Word and Meaning

When we say the word-to-meaning relationship is "arbitrary" we mean that generally speaking there is no transparent relationship between the sound of the word and the sort of thing it "means." There are words that "sound like" the thing denoted, like the English word "buzz" for the noise made by bees, but they belong to a very small class of words. There is nothing about the sound of the word "tree" to suggest a particular sort of plant rather than, for instance, a vehicle or a kinship relation. Other words containing the same sound are not similarly related to the vegetable world (e.g., street, treat, treacle, etc.), and the French manage just as well with a word that

148

sounds quite different, *arbre;* the Germans manage with *Bau,* and the Greeks with δένδρον *(dendron).* If there is not a "natural" relationship between the sound of a word and its sense, how are we to explain the association? Answer: The association is purely *conventional.* As we grow up, we simply learn the associations in our own language from the structured communications of those around us.

De Saussure did not by any means imply that all word-meaning relationships are entirely arbitrary. He fully recognized that the lexeme "trees" is related to "tree" and that the lexeme "truth" is related to "true," "truthful," "truly," etc. But these relations are themselves conventionally structured. A suffix "-ly" in English regularly signals an adverbial relationship as with "quick" and "quickly." But once again this is "arbitrary" and merely "conventional." The French use, for example, the quite different-sounding suffix *-ment* — as in *rapide* and *rapidement* — for the same purpose.

Like other modern European languages, Hellenistic Greek conventionalized various types of meaning in its word formation in regular ways. We find some four hundred "roots" with different combinations of prefixes and suffixes providing the lexical stock (the "vocabulary") of the language. For example, from the root βαπτ- (*bapt-,* "dip"), we get a verb βάπτω (*baptō,* "I dip") and inflected forms like βάπτει (*baptei,* "he dips"). The suffix -ιζω (*-izō*) often connotes causation, and when it is added to βαπτ- the result is βαπτίζω (*baptizō,* "I sink [something] into [some medium]" or "I baptize" ["cause to dip"]). The suffix -(σ)μος (*-[s]mos*) often connotes an event, action, or process, whence βαπτισμός (*baptismos,* "a washing"). A -(σ)μα (*-[s]ma*) suffix regularly denotes the *result* of an action, whence βάπτισμα (*baptisma,* originally "the thing washed or dipped," later "baptism"). A good knowledge of roots and of the usual force of prefixes and suffixes facilitates learning of the language and often gives a rough guide to the possible sense of unfamiliar words.[6]

6. For elementary guides see Black, *Linguistics,* 58-94; Bruce M. Metzger, *Lexical Aids for Students of New Testament Greek* (Princeton: Princeton University, 1974); Thomas Rogers, *Greek Word Roots* (Grand Rapids: Baker, 1981); Thomas A. Robinson, *Mastering Greek Vocabulary* (Peabody: Hendrickson, 1990); Matthias Stehle, *Greek Word-Building* (Missoula: Scholars, 1976); Robert E. Van Voorst, *Building Your New Testament Greek Vocabulary* (Grand Rapids: Eerdmans, 1990). For a more complex treatment see MHT, vol. 2, part 3.

2.2 *Synchronic Study of Language*

As the senses of words change with time and usage only a *synchronic* analysis of language, that is, study of the meanings words have at a given point in time, is relevant to word meaning in a particular discourse. De Saussure offered an analogy from chess: One can understand the state of the game without knowing its history. So also with language: We know what, for example, "parliament" means today without necessarily being aware it derived from a word meaning "speaking"; and one is more likely to be confused than helped by being told that "nice" originally meant "simple or ignorant." *The meanings of words change through time.*

Because word senses cannot always accurately be inferred from their formation (the meaning of "blackbird" may be relatively transparently related to its elements, but that of "ladybird" is not), and because word senses change with time and extension of use, the "original" meaning, if we can recover it, is no sure guide to later meaning. The senses of a word in Classical Greek are no safe guide to the senses of the same word in the Hellenistic Greek of Paul's day.

2.3 *Structure and Meaning*

Much linguistics following de Saussure has been called "structural linguistics," a description that highlights the significance he attributed to structure in language systems. But what is meant by this term needs clarification.

At one level we all appreciate the significance of structure in language for meaning: a structureless string of words such as

S1 question or be to that be to the not is

makes little sense. Restructured, we may discover Hamlet's

S2 To be, or not to be, that is the question.

The words now make sense because they take their places in a recognizable structured pattern.

What de Saussure emphasized, however, is that structure dictates meaning at every level from the smallest distinct sound up to the sentence. For example, the phonological unit *-ick* can be considered an incomplete structure with an open "slot" at the front. Various phonemes (or larger units) can be fitted into that slot — for example, *t-*, *k-*, *l-*, *p-*, *s-*, *w-*, *st-*, *ch-*, or

War(w)-. The choice of any one of these gives a different word from what the others would yield. For de Saussure, *it is this set of contrasting possibilities that is decisive in the conventionalizing of meaning.*

This is true, he argued, not merely at the phonetic level of word recognition, but for the understanding of word meaning in sentences. The linguistic sense of the word "cat" is largely determined by what sort of slots it can fill in a variety of sentences without being regarded as semantically anomalous. In the sentence

S3 The cat licked up the milk

the sense of the word "cat" is determined by its relationships with other words, and these relationships operate in two dimensions, "horizontal" and "vertical."

"Cat" has a horizontal "linear" relationship with the verb "lick up." Such "horizontal" relations are usually called "collocational" or "syntagmic" relations. To "lick up" is something only animals with tongues can do, and so that gives part of the sense of "cat." The collocational relationship here excludes, for example, that the word "cat" represents some kind of inanimate object, such as a stone, or some human artifact, such as a machine. It can only be an animal. Syntagmic relations thus remove the possibility of taking the word "cat" in two of its quite well-attested senses: It cannot be "cat_3" = cat-o'-nine-tails, a sort of whip with nine lashes, or "cat_4" = beam for hoisting an anchor. Similarly, in

S4 He flayed him with the cat

the sense "cat_3" is virtually demanded by the collocational relationship with the verb "flay."

But the meaning of "cat" in, for example, S3 is not merely established by its "horizontal" collocational relationship but partly also by the "vertical" relationship ("substitutional" or "paradigmatic") it sustains with other words that could have filled the same slot ("girl," "mouse," "animal," "lion," "thief," etc.). These other words could fill the slot in the sequence "the X licked up the milk" to make normal utterances, and they all exist in different sorts of relationships to the word "cat." It is these different relationships that largely define the "sense" of the word "cat."

Thus the word "cat" is a subordinate member of the class "animal," which is in turn a hyponym of the word "creature"; "cat" stands in a contrasting relationship, however, with "girl" and "mouse" (which are also "animal" and "creature"). How it stands to "lion" would depend on whether the utterer meant "cat_1" = member of the cat family including lion, tiger, leopard, domestic cat, etc., or "cat_2" = domestic feline animal.

For de Saussure, "cat_2" thus takes its sense both from the range of collocations it can stand in (we can say "He stroked the cat" but not "he cats the stroke" or "he breathes cat") and from the different relations (subordinations, antonyms, synonyms, etc.) it has with other words like "dog," "pet," "man," "animal," "stone," "mouse," and the like, in a variety of English sentences. With this in mind we may well appreciate how John Lyons introduces a chapter that he entitles "Webs of Words: The Formalization of Lexical Structure":

> People often think of the meanings of words as if each of them had an independent and separate existence. But . . . no word can be fully understood independently of other words that are related to it and delimit its sense. Looked at from a semantic point of view, the lexical structure of a language — the structure of its vocabulary — is best regarded as a large and intricate network of sense-relations: it is like a huge, multidimensional spider's web, in which each strand is one such relation and each knot in the web is a different lexeme.[7]

And in the context of this understanding, Lyons can tersely define sense: "The *sense* of an expression is, quite simply, the set of sense-relations that hold between it and other expressions."[8]

This is part of what de Saussure meant by calling meaning in language "structural." What fixes a word's meaning is *usage* — particularly how the word compares and contrasts with other possible substitutes in potential sentences and how it collocates with other words in given sentences. People as a whole learn their native languages not by acquiring dictionary or etymological meanings but by picking up patterns of synonymy and contrast in actual usages.

But "structure" determines meaning at higher levels of language as well. De Saussure went on to ask how sentences structure meaning. He thus opened the way to transformational-generative grammars, which attempt to show how all our complex sentences and meanings are produced from a small core of a dozen or so simple types of sentence.[9]

---

7. John Lyons, *Language, Meaning and Context* (London: Fontana, 1981) 75.

8. Lyons, *Language,* 58.

9. See, e.g., Ruth Kempson, *Semantic Theory* (Cambridge: Cambridge University, 1977) ch. 7; Cotterell and Turner, *Linguistics,* ch. 6.

2.4 Linguistics since De Saussure

Linguistics has come a long way since de Saussure's day. It has spawned a whole set of subdisciplines, such as semantics (the relationship of language to meaning)[10] and discourse analysis,[11] and these in turn have proliferated new areas of interest, so that discourse analysis would now be broadly divided into *text linguistics* (which looks, e.g., at how markers indicate shifts of topic or focus in a discourse),[12] *pragmatics* (which studies the interaction between speech and unarticulated shared presuppositions in communication), and so forth. Then there is *sociolinguistics* (the study of social influence on language, and vice versa), *psycholinguistics* (the study of the relationship of mind and language, including not merely how we learn language, but how we perceive ideas and meanings, and how our psychological makeup interplays with our usage), etc.

. Inevitably it would be impossible in the scope of a short chapter to describe these various disciplines of linguistics and illustrate the bearing of each on NT exegesis. We propose, instead, to look at one area in greater depth, one that is proving its worth in biblical studies — namely, *lexical semantics,* which is the study of the meaning(s) of words and expressions in a language.

3. Lexical Semantics and New Testament Study

Barr's *Semantics of Biblical Language* shook the foundations of the many attempts to do theology in the form of word studies, most notably the *Theological Dictionary of the New Testament,*[13] and has been described as nothing less than "a trumpet blast against the monstrous regiment of shoddy linguistics."[14] Barr took to task the widespread confusion between

---

10. See Kempson, *Theory,* or John Lyons, *Semantics* (Cambridge: Cambridge University, 1977).

11. See Gillian Brown and George Yule, *Discourse Analysis,* CTL (Cambridge: Cambridge University, 1983) for an introductory guide. Cf. also Cotterell and Turner, *Linguistics,* chs. 6-8.

12. Cf. Wolfgang U. Dressler, ed., *Current Trends in Textlinguistics* (Berlin: Walter de Gruyter, 1978).

13. Gerhard Kittel and Gerhard Friedrich, *Theological Dictionary of the New Testament,* 10 vols. (Grand Rapids: Eerdmans, 1964-76).

14. Moises Silva, *Biblical Words and Their Meanings* (Grand Rapids: Zondervan, 1983) 18. See Cotterell and Turner, *Linguistics,* ch. 4, on Barr's criticism and responses to it.

words (and their meanings) and "concepts." Many thought they could show how the NT writers brought entirely new and deep theological meanings to the words they used. Thus, for example, in an article on ἀγαπάω (agapaō, "I love") Stauffer happily tell us that "Johannine ἀγάπη is quite explicitly condescending love, or rather a heavenly reality which in some sense descends from stage to stage into this world," and that this love is "the principle of the world of Christ which is being built up in the cosmic crisis of the present."[15]

This sort of thing was perhaps fine, Barr was able to point out, as a description of John's *concept* of "the love of God": Stauffer may be quite right to say that for John *real* "love" is modeled on God's selfless love demonstrated in Christ. But he was absolutely wrong to imply that this is what the word *agapaō* has come to mean in John, or that for the author of John it now means, for example, some special Christian self-giving love. To make this kind of claim one simply has to ignore the inconvenient fact that John uses the verb ἀγαπάω *(agapaō)* and the noun ἀγαπή *(agapē)* in sentences such as "But people loved darkness more than the light" (John 3:19), "They loved praise from humans more than praise from God" (12:43), and "Whoever loves the world, the love of the Father is not in that person" (1 John 2:15).

Stauffer's mistake was to assume that each word had substantially just one meaning and that everything John tells us about God's love in Christ (i.e., John's "concept" of divine love) fundamentally changed the sense of the word *agapē* itself.[16] But the sense of a word is (by definition) the (usually minimal) linguistic bundle of meaning regarded as *linguistically necessary* to, or conventionally strongly associated with, a word. The "sense" of *agapē* is, therefore, some kind of "concept" because it is a bundle of coherently related meanings, namely, something like "a person's relation to someone or something involving a committing affection or attraction greater than would normally be lexicalized by 'like.'" But it is still a very different and minimal concept compared with what we mean by "John's concept of '[divine] love.'"[17] The latter is not a linguistic entity at all, though language may be used to articulate it, but a comparatively much larger and complex pattern of concepts based mainly on analysis, reflection, and meditation on

15. Ethelbert Stauffer, "ἀγαπάω κτλ," in *TDNT,* 1:21-55, here 53, 52.

16. On this problem see Barr, *Semantics,* 216-17; Cotterell and Turner, *Linguistics,* 119-20 and ch. 4.

17. On the relation between word senses and concepts, see Cotterell and Turner, *Linguistics,* chs. 4-5, pp. 139-55, 164-67.

things Jesus said and did and on what John understood these things to reveal of God. John does not transform a *word* to convey this much larger "concept." He uses whole narrative paragraphs and discourses, which might or might not contain the word *agapē*, to convey this concept.

Strangely, Barr's criticisms, though widely acclaimed and often quoted, have actually had little effect on how the majority have continued to do word studies. This was partly because although Barr himself understood lexical semantics, he did not seriously try to introduce his colleagues to the field. Excellent introductions have been written by linguists and Bible translators,[18] but they have not been published in the standard theological series.[19]

In what follows, I will discuss two examples that illustrate a number of the methods and problems of determining word meanings in the NT and the contribution linguistics makes to clarifying the issues. The first example concerns the word χάρισμα *(charisma)* and is chosen because it so well illustrates important principles of lexical semantics. The second example concerns the use of the word κεφαλή *(kephalē)* in 1 Cor 11:3. A fierce debate is raging between those who claim it means "source" and those who claim it means "authority," so it provides a helpful illustration of the need for careful attention to semantics.

4. The Sense of χάρισμα(τα) *(charisma[ta])* in Paul

This is an unusual case because we do not have *any* definite pre-Pauline uses of the word to inform our analysis. The occurrences in the Greek OT (Sir 7:33; 38:30 LXX; Ps 30:20 Theod) and Philo (*Leg. Alleg.* 3.78) are post-Christian (and in the latter case interpolated). Of the seventeen NT occurrences, one is in 1 Peter, two in the Pastorals, the rest in the universally accepted Paulines; so Paul is our first witness to the use of the lexeme. Scholars are nevertheless cautious about suggesting that Paul coined the

18. One thinks above all of Eugene A. Nida and Charles R. Taber, *The Theory and Practice of Translation* (Leiden: Brill, 1969); Nida, *Componential Analysis of Meaning* (The Hague: Mouton, 1975); *idem, Exploring Semantic Structures* (Munich: Fink, 1975).

19. The best introduction (but written for linguistics students) is probably D. A. Cruse, *Lexical Semantics*, CTL (Cambridge: Cambridge University, 1986). Another good resource, especially for students of NT Greek, is Eugene A. Nida and Johannes P. Louw, *Lexical Semantics of the Greek New Testament* (Atlanta: Scholars, 1992). Cf. also Cotterell and Turner, *Linguistics*, ch. 5.

word, and rightly so, for he uses it when writing to the Romans (who did not know his teaching) without any explanation of its sense. He appears to assume, in other words, that his readers are acquainted with its use.

But how do *we* establish what it means? The obvious avenues of approach are to examine what we can learn from its word formation, how the word relates paradigmatically to available near-synonyms, and how it is used in specific sentences in Paul. A considerable amount has been written on the basis of the first and third of these three approaches, but sadly some of the more influential accounts are seriously flawed by linguistic confusions.

4.1 Word Formation

As we have indicated, study of word formation can mislead, especially when a word has had a long history, but with a newer word it should at least afford some guide; hence, it is the appropriate starting point for Schatzmann's study of *charismata*.[20] Under the heading "etymology," Schatzmann tells us quite unequivocally: "χάρισμα is derived from the root χάρις."[21] He then provides a quick summary of his understanding of χάρις *(charis)* in Paul, and concludes that "this understanding of χάρις, then, leads to its correlate, χάρισμα."[22] A similar position was held earlier by J. D. G. Dunn in his widely quoted section on χάρισμα *(charisma)* in *Jesus and the Spirit*.[23] While Dunn does not actually make the claim in the form of an explicit statement about the linguistics of the word, the same etymological understanding emerges both from the structure of his study[24] and from regular references such as *"charisma is the inevitable outworking of charis"* or *"Charisma can only be understood as a particular expression of charis."*[25]

The nearest Dunn comes to a formal comment on the linguistics concerned is when he offers a slightly different argument, justifying his claim that

---

20. Siegfried S. Schatzmann, *A Pauline Theology of Charismata* (Peabody: Hendrickson, 1987).

21. Schatzmann, *Theology*, 1.

22. Schatzmann, *Theology*, 2.

23. James D. G. Dunn, *Jesus and the Spirit* (London: SCM, 1975) 199-256.

24. His analysis of *charis* in Paul (Dunn, *Jesus and the Spirit*, §37) provides the foundation for and leads directly to the discussion of *charisma* (§38). A similarly structured analysis is present in *NIDNTT*, where χάρισμα *(charisma)* is dealt with under the heading "Grace, Spiritual Gifts" (Hans-Helmut Esser, "Grace, Spiritual Gifts," *NIDNTT*, 2:115-24), not under "Gift."

25. Dunn, *Jesus and the Spirit*, 254, 253, his emphasis.

charisma is a particular expression of *charis* on the grounds that "this is implied . . . by the semantic relation between the two pairs of words, [that is,] by the fact that *charisma* overlaps with the latter end of the range of meaning of *charis*. . . ."[26] But this is not a safe argument at all, for two reasons. First, of the several distinct senses of χάρις *(charis)* one is "gift,"[27] and within it we may distinguish two polysemes, χάρις$_a$ = "act of giving," and χάρις$_b$ = "thing given." Dunn may be right to suggest that χάρις$_b$ can be viewed as a result of χάρις$_a$, but quite wrong to suggest that one can read Paul's theology of grace into χάρις$_a$ and then make χάρις$_b$ "an event or result of 'grace.'" This is the word/concept confusion Barr strove to correct. χάρις$_b$ is an ordinary secular word meaning "gift (the thing given)." We must avoid reading other senses of χάρις into it, just as we must avoid collapsing contextual assertions about the things called χάρις$_b$ into the sense of the lexeme itself.

Second, χάρισμα "overlaps" with χάρις only when the latter is used in the sense χάρις$_b$, but this is a straightforward case of partial synonymy, and it would be a fundamental linguistic error to suggest that any lexeme that is a partial synonym of χάρις$_b$ (as is the case with χάρισμα) is also, *ipso facto*, semantically a result or event of χάρις$_a$. Careful linguistic studies have amply clarified that partial synonyms share some (but usually not all) of their components of meaning. Just because χάρις$_b$ means "gift," with the (optional) additional component of meaning "the result of χάρις$_a$," in no way guarantees that this optional component of meaning attaches to partial synonyms of χάρις$_b$ as well. Various words in Greek for "gift" are all, like χάρισμα, partial synonyms of χάρις$_b$ (words like δόμα [*doma*], δῶρον [*dōron*], δωρεά [*dōrea*], δώρημα [*dōrēma*], κορβᾶν [*korban*, "vowed gift"], προσφορά [*prosphora*, "sacrificial gift"], etc.); but no linguist would seriously claim that any of these words mean "an event of grace" on the basis of their partial synonymy with χάρις$_b$.

The derivation of χάρισμα from χάρις leads Dunn to the further assertion that *"charisma* is an *event"* of grace,[28] or, as he has put it more recently, *"charisma* means, by definition, manifestation, embodiment of grace *(charis)*."[29] This "event" character of *charisma* has far-reaching sig-

26. Dunn, *Jesus and the Spirit*, 253.

27. See Louw and Nida, *Lexicon,* 2:262, or their discussion in Nida and Louw, *Lexical Semantics,* 62-68.

28. Dunn, *Jesus and the Spirit*, 254.

29. James D. G. Dunn, "Ministry and the Ministry: The Charismatic Renewal's Challenge to Traditional Ecclesiology," in *Charismatic Experiences in History,* ed. Cecil M. Robeck (Peabody: Hendrickson, 1985) 81-101, here 82.

nificance for Dunn's whole theology of ministry. It means for him that ministry — which he thinks for Paul is always simply the exercise of *charismata* — must be the actual deed or word in which God's Spirit becomes manifest (and charismata are understood as short-term *functions*, never persons or human abilities or talents).[30] For this reason Dunn finds it difficult to accept that Paul would have condoned any concept of church "offices": *Charisma*, for him, cannot be institutionalized, so the Pastorals represent an "early catholic" fading of the Pauline vision.[31] Evidently a considerable amount of theological freight is being carried on the back of apparently innocent linguistic assertions and assumptions!

But both the derivation of χάρισμα from χάρις and the claim that it means an "event" of *charis* are entirely implausible. In the first place the -μα (-*ma*) ending would regularly connote *result*, not "event."[32] Indeed, that "event" (of *charis*) is not one of the components of the sense of the word χάρισμα for Paul should be clear enough from Rom 6:23, where he speaks of "the free gift" (χάρισμα) that God gives us, and identifies this as "eternal life in Christ Jesus." Similarly, in 1 Cor 7:7 Paul refers to the ability to remain chaste without marrying as a χάρισμα, and here the word must connote the (enduring) enabling that is given, not an event of giving.

More significantly, χάρισμα should not be derived directly from χάρις but from the verb χαρίζομαι (*charizomai*, "give graciously").[33] The deriva-

---

30. Dunn, *Jesus and the Spirit*, 253.

31. Dunn, *Jesus and the Spirit*, §57. For criticisms of Dunn, see, e.g., M. M. B. Turner, "Spiritual Gifts: Then and Now," *VE* 15 (1985) 7-64, esp. 26-37 (and the literature cited there). For criticism of Käsemann's very similar views, see Ronald Y.-K. Fung, "Charismatic versus Organized Ministry: An Examination of an Alleged Antithesis," *EvQ* 52 (1980) 195-214; *idem*, "Function or Office? A Survey of the New Testament Evidence," *ERT* 8 (1984) 16-39.

32. The regular suffixes signifying "event" or "process" are -σις (-*sis*, e.g., κρίσις [*krisis*], "judgment"), -μος (-*mos*, e.g., βαπτισμός [*baptismos*], "dipping in water"), -εια (-*eia*, e.g., προφητεία [*prophēteia*], "act of prophesying"), and -μη (-*mē*). This is recognized by Schatzmann, *Theology*, 2. Cf. the comment by Nigel Turner: "The characteristic Ionic ending in -*ma* denotes the result of the action — the 'gift' is the result of favour" (*Christian Words* [Edinburgh: Clark, 1980] 430; Turner adds that the distinction may be less applicable in Koine); cf. also BDF §109 (2).

33. So correctly MHT, 2:354; Louw and Nida, *Lexicon*, 1:569; Hans Conzelmann, "χάρισμα," *TDNT*, 9:402-6, here 402 (though note that just three lines later Conzelmann states that "[Χάρισμα] denotes the result of χάρις viewed as an action . . ." [403]). Schatzmann's proposal (*Theology*, 2) that the verb χαρίζομαι itself derives from the noun χάρισμα is not possible; the noun is not attested before Paul's day but the verb was in regular use from Homer on!

tion of a neuter noun ending with *-ma* from another noun ending with *-is* would be unusual; nouns with *-ma* derive rather from verbs, and the *-sma* ending more specifically indicates formation by contraction from a verb ending in *-izō* or *-azō*. In short, χάρισμα is derived from χαρίζομαι and belongs to a subclass of nouns of similar formation such as κτίσμα (*ktisma*, "creature," from κτίζω [*ktizō*], "create"), σχίσμα (*schisma*, "that which is parted, a crack, division," from σχίζω [*schizō*], "split, cleave"), and the like.[34]

The outcome is this: The formation of χάρισμα as a resultative noun from the verb χαρίζομαι would suggest the sense "thing (graciously) given," "gift," rather than "event of grace."

4.2 Synonyms for χάρισμα

A writer chooses which of several words she or he considers will most adequately fill a particular "slot" in his or her sentence. Most of these choices concern words with overlapping meaning. Speaking of the death of Charles I, one might say, "They killed King Charles." But other words that overlap in meaning with "kill" could have been chosen instead, for example, annihilate, assassinate, behead, decapitate, bump off, butcher, dispatch, exterminate, execute, liquidate, murder, martyr, slaughter, slay, etc. Each shares the central component of meaning, "terminate life," but with either slightly different *senses* (e.g., "execute" = *judicially* terminate life; contrast "murder" or "martyr"; "behead" = terminate life *by decapitation;* contrast, e.g., "hang"), or different *levels of formality of discourse* ("bump off" is slang [and unspecific as to the method of killing]; "behead" is middle register, "decapitate" more formal), or different *connotations* ("slaughter" suggests "as one would an animal"). On the whole words only survive in a language if they have some clear distinctive sense, register, or connotation. Words have their meanings precisely in contrast to other possibilities.

In working with the linguistics of χάρισμα, we will want to know how it contrasts in sense, register, and connotation with other partially synonymous lexemes meaning "gift" such as δόμα (*doma*), δόσις (*dosis*), δῶρον (*dōron*), δωρεά (*dōrea*), δώρημα (*dōrēma*), διαίρεσις (*diairesis*, "distribution"), κορβᾶν (*korban*), προσφορά (*prosphora*), and χάρις (*charis* — when it is used in the sense "gift").

34. For a similar subclass of nouns from -αζω (*-azō*) verbs, see MHT, 2:354. There is a much larger class of nouns based on other verbs that generate -μα (*-ma*) endings rather than -σμα (*-sma*) endings.

Not enough serious study has been devoted to this, but we may offer the following greatly simplified guidelines: (1) For "gift" (= thing given), δόμα is semantically the most neutral term, though it would often be difficult to distinguish from δῶρον and δωρεά (both of which may focus slightly more on the semantic trait "free" in the "gift"). (2) δώρημα is slightly more formal than these words (= "something bestowed"), but not so markedly that it could not be exchanged for them as a stylistic variant in contexts where the others had been used already. (3) χάρις, when used in the sense "gift," and χάρισμα, by contrast, focus on the trait of *gracious* or *generous* giving, with the implication of *good will* or *favor* on the part of the giver. χάρισμα is always the *thing given* (graciously), and so may contrast with χάρις, which can be used in the sense of the "event" of giving as well as the "thing given."

In sum, the choice of χάρισμα over against δόμα, δῶρον, δωρεά, and δώρημα as a word for "gift" probably emphasizes that the thing described is "a gracious and generous gift and a sign of the giver's good will and favor." In Paul's discourses the "giver" is always God, but that does not mean that he thinks the word χάρισμα itself carries the sense "*divine* gift" (far less that it carries the sense "events or expressions of divine grace"). That would be to commit the all-too-common error of confusing word-sense with word-reference. But this leads us to our third approach to understanding the meaning of χάρισμα.

4.3 Usage of χάρισμα

In the Pauline letters we have the following uses of χάρισμα (in chronological order): 1 Cor 1:7; 7:7; 12:4, 6-7, 9, 28, 30, 31; 2 Cor 1:11; Rom 1:11; 5:15, 16; 6:23; 11:29; 12:6; 1 Tim 4:14; and 2 Tim 1:6. Once again, Schatzmann is effectively a spokesman for a majority of scholarship when he maintains that the term is distinctively Pauline and that the apostle uses it in a number of senses:[35] (1) in a "nontechnical" *general* sense (Rom 5:15, 16; 6:23), (2) in a nontechnical *specific* sense, for gifts given to the believer (1 Cor 7:7; 2 Cor 1:11), (3) in a *technical* sense to denote manifestations of grace within the community (Rom 12:6-8 and 1 Corinthians 12–14 are clear; cf. Rom 1:11 and 1 Cor 1:7; but Schatzmann includes also Rom 11:29), and (4) in a *technical* and *institutional* sense (1 Tim 4:14; 2 Tim 1:6). It is hardly surprising that he then thinks that "the term's distinctive-

35. Schatzmann, *Theology,* 4-5, 15-52.

ness . . . comes to light both in its adaptability to general and particular usage and in its ability to express thematic unity (grace) and diversity (gifts)," that he can speak of the "wide range of meaning" that the apostle invests in it, that he should conclude that for Paul χαρίσματα is "a complex concept [sic] with a wide range of application," and that it is impossible to give a simple definition for this "complex concept."[36]

But linguistics would suggest a quite different analysis. From the perspective of semantics, most of what Schatzmann and others like him argue betrays essentially the same confusion of words, word-senses, and concepts that Barr attacked so aggressively. Most semanticists would doubt that Paul has added *any* special meaning to the *term* χάρισμα at all and would be suspicious of the claim that he has actually introduced a whole *proliferation* of different senses. On what does such a claim rest?

That Paul uses χάρισμα in a range of expressions to refer to such different entities as his own preaching and teaching of the gospel (Rom 1:11), justification and its benefits (Romans 5), eternal life (Rom 6:23), the ability to remain a chaste unmarried person (1 Cor 7:7), and various manifestations of the Spirit *could* mean that he has developed some new profound but complex overarching theological "concept," or a complicated network of connected concepts, that unites all these uses and that can be signaled linguistically by the word χάρισμα. But linguistically it is much more likely to mean *exactly the opposite* — namely, that for Paul the term has rather *minimal content* and therefore *general meaning*.

Let us take the English use of the word "gift" as an analogy. In one of its senses it means simply "a thing given" and may have the connotation "for which one should be grateful." It is clear that this English word can be used for a very wide variety of things in the world without that suggesting that there is any special mystical "unity" in the things themselves or that the sense of the word "gift" is itself becoming more complex by virtue of such uses.

Were I now to write a discourse on school education, and apply the word "gift" in unexpected ways (referring, e.g., to homework, disciplinary structures, particular teachers, etc. as "gifts") no one would assume that I am developing new *senses* (or even a new general concept) of "gift." The English reader will perceive that I am instead simply relying on a standard sense (and connotation) of the word "gift" in a creative way to invite my readers to see certain entities (things they might normally have complained about) as things to be grateful for.

36. Schatzmann, *Theology,* 5, 10, 9, 7.

My analogy is, of course, not entirely innocent. I intend virtually the equivalent explanation of Paul's uses of χάρισμα. Linguistics requires that we do not proliferate supposed new senses where utterances can be explained adequately in terms of *known* senses. We have already noted that χάρισμα means "gift" and that it may be distinguished from other Greek words for gift by such connotations as "gracious and generous gift" and "sign of the giver's good will and favor." I suggest that this sense (and these connotations) satisfactorily explains all of Paul's uses of the word. We can see this by reviewing Schatzmann's proposed Pauline senses for χάρισμα:

First, the known sense and connotations should be the obvious explanation of Rom 5:15, 16 and 6:23. In these contexts Paul uses a variety of "gift" terms to emphasize that justification and its benefits are *freely, generously,* and *graciously* given (despite our sin and alienation, and to overcome them), and χάρισμα naturally lexicalizes this. The same applies in Rom 11:29: Paul's use of χαρίσματα here to refer (probably) to Israel's covenant benefits (cf. 9:4) — he could have used more neutral words like δόματα — stresses that these things are God's generous provision and signs of divine favor, and it thereby rhetorically underscores Israel's accountability.

Second, there should be no problem with 1 Cor 7:7 or Rom 1:11, where Paul invites his readers to perceive the teaching that he intends to give (and some of which he outlines in his letter) as God's gracious (strengthening) gift to the church, enabled through the Spirit (and if they do they will be the readier to support his ongoing mission to Spain). Again, there is no argument for a "technical" sense here.

Third, some have detected a new special technical sense where Paul uses χαρίσματα with reference to what 1 Cor 12:5 describes as "acts of service," 12:6 as "workings of God," and 12:7 as "manifestations of the Spirit." But once again the more natural explanation is Paul's *tactical* use of the common and general sense. Where the Corinthians understand their tongues, healings, prophecies, and so forth (1 Cor 12:8-10) as indications of *their own* deeply *"spiritual"* nature, and in pride are using these things selfishly and divisively, Paul (in 12:4-7) describes the same phenomena in such a way as to invite his readers to see them instead as *God's* generous gifts and self-disclosing workings and as divinely given abilities to serve.[37] No one seriously tries to persuade us that we should posit a new technical

37. K. S. Hemphill, "The Pauline Concept of Charisma: A Situational and Developmental Approach" (Ph.D. diss., University of Cambridge 1977), has made a similar suggestion.

sense for διαχονίαι (*diakoniai,* "acts of service"), ἐνεργήματα (*energēmata,* "workings"), or φανέρωσις (*phanerōsis,* "manifestation") simply because these words are used of the phenomena that the Corinthians have in mind, and there is similarly no reason to assume a new sense for χαρίσματα either. The word has not come to have a new "sense" ("*spiritual* gift") — indeed Rom 1:11 has to add the adjective πνευματικόν (*pneumatikon,* "spiritual") to χάρισμα to provide such a meaning. We should point out that even in his discussion with the Corinthians Paul does not restrict the term χάρισμα to the kind of phenomena mentioned in 12:8-10. The latter passage, no doubt, gives a fair sample of what the *Corinthians* regard as the *"spiritual things"* (which is why Paul starts with them), but the whole point of the body analogy that Paul goes on to supply is to say that God has also "given" other parts in the "body" to which the Corinthians are failing to give due recognition (12:18, 23-24, 28-31): They are to count among God's χαρίσματα some of the "parts" that they have tended to look down on (cf. 12.31), including the administrative and support functions mentioned in 12:28, as well as, for example, teachers, prophets, and apostles. *All* these — not merely the narrow list in 12:8-10 — the Corinthians are to regard as God's provision, indeed, as God's gracious and generous gifts to the church.

So χάρισμα is not a technical term in this context. The rhetorical force of Paul's use of this lexeme in 1 Corinthians 12 amounts to something like the following: "Listen, you Corinthians, who pride yourselves as *"spiritual"* for your tongues, prophecies, and healings! I want you to see these simply as God's generous gifts, along with the many other good things God generously provides, but for which you seem less grateful."

Χάρισμα does not appear to be a "(semi-)technical term" for a class of "spiritual gifts" (special manifestations of the Spirit) elsewhere in Paul's letters either.[38] In Rom 12:6-8 we again find a mixed list of what the Corinthians would have regarded as "spiritual gifts" combined with simple acts of service, generosity, and leadership, and *all* are described as χαρίσματα (12:6). Paul may indeed have thought that within Christian life one could identify a grouping of experiences that together were, in some special sense, "overt manifestations of the Spirit" (though it would inevitably be a group with very fuzzy borders), but such a group are only called χαρίσματα insofar as they are specific cases of a much broader range of God's "gracious

38. In this respect the *NIDNTT* was entirely misleading in putting the entry on *charismata* under "Grace, Spiritual Gifts," rather than under "Gift" where it belonged (see above, n. 24).

163

gifts," within which the distinction between what God "gives" through creation of a person and his or her capacities in relation to God, and what God "gives" in more immediate inspiration, would often be difficult to decide. Paul's use of the lexeme χάρισμα in Rom 12:6-8 is not meant to indicate a new special class of entities ("spiritual gifts"); the point is simply that the church (as Israel before it — cf. 11:29) receives God's graciously bestowed benefits and signs of divine favor, and should do what God has enabled, responsibly and wholeheartedly.

Ephesians 4:7-8 uses three other lexemes meaning "gift" (χάρις, δωρεά, and δόμα) for some of the same functions described in 1 Cor 12:28-30 and Rom 12:6-8, but no one claims that these, too, are "technical terms" that have developed in the same way as the (alleged) technical term χάρισμα. The Pastorals use the noun phrase τὸ χάρισμα (to charisma) to refer to some special enabling for ministry that came to Timothy in the spiritually charged context of prophecy and laying on of hands (hardly institutionalized ordination, as Dunn thinks). But this hardly requires any new understanding of the *sense* of χάρισμα (here too it means a gracious, generous gift — so all the more reason why Timothy should exercise it carefully).

In all we have no evidence whatever for a series of new "senses" of χάρισμα. Such an argument simply confuses the general sense of the word with the variety of things to which it might be applied. We have the one general sense "(gracious and generous) gift," stable connotations ("token of the giver's good will and favor"), and a fairly regular implication of these ("to be received gratefully and treated accordingly").[39] We are not saying that Paul could not have thought of the gifts listed in 1 Cor 12:8-10 as a coherent group, an identifiable subclass of "spiritual gifts" in general; we are merely saying he does not lexicalize such a distinction in his use of χάρισμα.

We have noted the frequent attempt to tie χάρισμα in sense to χάρις (*charis*, "grace"). Three points may be made in this respect. First, we have seen that χάρισμα is derived not from χάρις but from one of the several senses of the verb χαρίζομαι (*charizomai*) — namely "give generously or graciously"; any *direct* relationship to χάρις goes too far back in the history of the verb to be relevant to discussion of the meaning of χάρισμα.

Second, Paul himself makes no attempt to relate χάρισμα to χάρις. In only one of his uses of χάρισμα (Rom 12:6) is there any close connection, and there is no need to assume that the connection has a direct bearing on

39. Likewise Philo *Leg. Alleg.* 3.78; cf. also Alciphron 3.17.4 (a 2d-century CE secular source).

the sense of χάρισμα (as if Paul could not have used δόματα *[domata]* or δωρήματα *[dōrēmata]* where he has in fact chosen χαρίσματα — perhaps for assonance, or as the most suitable lexeme to emphasize that the gifts are tokens of God's generosity and good will).

Third, the Greek noun χάρις *(charis)* is regularly translated "grace," despite the fact that for many English-speaking people "grace" "has little or no religious content."[40] Because normal English does not inform our understanding of the sense, there is a tendency to read it as a vague word with positive connotations, or (worse) to read into uses of it what we know of the Reformation debates over the theology of "grace." The tendency almost ubiquitously to render χάρις by "grace" also hides the fact that in the NT χάρις has at least four main but different senses: a favorable attitude toward someone, demonstration of kindness toward someone, that which is generously and freely given (= gift), and "thanks." Armed with this observation the reader will perceive that while Paul's writings articulate a deep "theology of grace," it does not especially attach to the lexeme χάρις and that many statements one finds in scholarly studies on χάρις, for example, that "grace is *God's eschatological deed*" or " 'Grace' was for Paul a tangible and verifiable reality as much as its correlative 'Spirit' "[41] — are semantically back-to-front.

Such talk is in danger of reifying χάρις, and it would be more accurate to say: "Paul sees God's eschatological deed as a/the supreme example of χάρις$_b$ ("an act of showing kindness")" or "Paul had many tangible and verifiable transforming experiences, and he used the word χάρις$_c$ (or χάρις$_b$) to describe them so that his readers would perceive them as God's gracious gifts or as God's acts of showing kindness." If a reader wishes to hold that χάρισμα is related to χάρις, she will need to define which *occasion* of χάρισμα she is speaking of, which *sense* of χάρις she is speaking of, and what *relationship* she envisages between the two. General statements about "the relationship" are liable to mislead.

5. Ascertaining the Sense of κεφαλή (*kephalē*, "Head") in 1 Cor 11:3

The debate surrounding the sense of the word "head" (κεφαλή [*kephalē*]) in 1 Cor 11:3 concerns whether this term carries the sense "one in authority

40. Nida and Louw, *Lexical Semantics*, 66.
41. Dunn, *Jesus and the Spirit*, 202 (citing Bultmann), 203.

over" (e.g., "ruler," "captain," "lord") or "source of." It is possible to make sense of Paul's rather difficult argument from 11:3 onward on either hypothesis. He could be saying that the woman should not dishonor her husband (in matters of her headcovering) because man (Adam) is the *source* of woman and she is his "glory" (v. 7). Certainly part of Paul's argument is that woman was created from the man and for the sake of the man (vv. 8-9).[42]

Paul, however, may be arguing a little more than that — namely, in addition, that the woman should not dishonor her husband because he is her *master in marriage* (as her father was before her marriage). Perhaps this makes easier sense of 11:3 itself, for there would be no problem with saying (in Paul's society) that as Christ is the "lord" over every male, so wives were in some sense under the authority of their husbands (cf. 1 Pet 3:1-6), or that Christ in turn is under God's authority (cf. 1 Cor 15:28!). But the statements become problematic if the sequence is "Christ is the source of every man," "man is the source of the woman," and "God is the source of Christ."[43] After the use of the generic singular (Christ is the head) "of every male," the immediately following statement would naturally be understood also to be a generic singular, and so to mean "(every) man (husband?) is the head of (every) woman (wife?)," not a reference back to the one man Adam and the one woman Eve. But if that is so, "head" can hardly mean "source" without leading to apparent nonsense.

Furthermore, "head" = "in authority over" makes better sense of the relationship of 11:3 to vv 11-12, for the contrasting emphatic "nevertheless" (in the Lord the man and woman are interdependent, etc.) of 11:11 only provides a real contrast with 11:3 if the latter were stating that the man is the woman's marital master.[44]

Because 1 Cor 11:3 *could* be read on either postulated sense of the word

42. See Gordon D. Fee, *The First Epistle to the Corinthians,* NICNT (Grand Rapids, Michigan: Wm. B. Eerdmans, 1987) 498-524.

43. If the statement "Christ is the head of every man" means "Christ is the *origin* of every man," then we face these problems: (1) Paul was more likely to say that *God* is the origin of every man *through* Christ (or "in Christ"). (2) It is strikingly odd to hear Paul call Christ the origin of "every *male*" (*anēr;* why did he not use the generic term *anthrōpos* [humanity] instead?), especially if (as Fee argues) this is a reference to new creation in Christ (in which, Paul says in Gal 3:28, there is "neither male nor female").

44. See Cotterell and Turner, *Linguistics,* 316-28. Most other possible metaphorical senses of "head" are ruled out by the threefold assertion in 11:3. The nearest plausibility, perhaps, is that "head" means the especially "honored" member or "preeminent part" of a body. But the Father and the Son are not said to constitute a "body" of which the Father is the more honored or preeminent part.

"head," there has been a major battle over which (if either) metaphorical sense is actually already attested in Paul's day and so liable to be known to his readers. If, for example, it could be shown that one of the two senses was well established while the other was rare or unheard of, that would more-or-less settle the exegetical argument. As it happens, recent research has established that κεφαλή was indeed used in the sense "one in authority over," both in the LXX and also in a range of other writings.[45] Accordingly both the new edition of Bauer's lexicon (BAGD) and the new semantically competent lexicon by Louw and Nida (see n. 4 above) include "superior (rank or authority)" among the established meanings.[46] Fitzmyer argues that we should admit that κεφαλή occasionally (albeit much more rarely) meant "source" (though not in 1 Cor 11:3), but this is not recognized by the lexicons,[47] and we should consider it linguistically unsound.

Constraints of space permit us only to comment on some of the more important linguistic principles and arguments involved in the debate.[48]

(1) Lexical semantics has rightly emphasized the astonishingly wide range of distinct senses any one "word" (more accurately "word-form" or "lexical form") may have. In our earlier comments we distinguished four senses of the lexical form "cat" (and there are others). Two were related (cat = domestic cat and cat = class of mammals including lions). When a lexical form has two or more related meanings, this is called *polysemy* (and each meaning is called a *polyseme*). The other senses of cat (cat = whip and cat = anchor hoist) are not related to the first two senses. Where a lexical form has unrelated senses this is called *homonymy*.

---

45. Cf. Judg 10:18 (Alexandrinus); 11:8-9 (Alexandrinus), 11; 2 Sam 22:44; Ps 18:43; Isa 7:8-9; Jer 38:7, etc; also Josephus, *J.W.* 4.4.3 §261; Plutarch *Cicero* 14.6; *Galba* 4.3; Hermas *Similitudes* 7.3.

46. Richard S. Cervin, "Does *Kephalē* Mean 'Source' or 'Authority' in Greek Literature? A Rebuttal," *TJ* 10 (1989) 85-112, vigorously denied both, and argued that κεφαλή in Paul means "preeminence" (but effectively conceded that in Paul's male-dominant culture that would virtually mean "having authority over"). Cervin discounts the LXX examples because they reflect not idiomatic Greek but Hebraisms. Whatever their *origin*, however, the point remains that in this most influential Hellenistic Jewish writing κεφαλή does mean "ruler"; reading and rereading of the LXX was bound to make this a current usage. For a critique of Cervin see Wayne Grudem, "The Meaning of *Kephalē* ("Head"): A Response to Recent Studies," in *Recovering Biblical Manhood and Womanhood*, ed. John Piper and Wayne Grudem (Wheaton: Crossway, 1991) 425-68; Joseph A. Fitzmyer, "Kephalē in 1 Corinthians 11:3," *Int* 47 (1993) 52-59.

47. Its appearance in LSJ for "source" is under the general heading "of things, extremity"; here the word does not carry the sense "source" at all (see below).

48. See further Cotterell and Turner, *Linguistics*, ch. 5.

Most of the vocabulary of any language, other than proper names, particles, etc., consists of homonyms and polysemes, and this is true of Greek. Therefore we must be very careful of statements referring to, for example, "the meaning of σάρξ (*sarx*, "flesh") in Paul" or "the meaning of ἀρχή (*archē*, "beginning, power") in the NT." It is all too easy to assume that because we are dealing with a single lexical form, ἀρχή, for instance, we have therefore just one sense, or at least one *basic* meaning common to all the senses. But native speakers will know that the facts are otherwise. English speakers will not be prone to think brandy has much to do with ghosts just because both are called "spirits."

We need similar caution when we approach the NT. We shall find that we have to speak of at least three homonyms of *archē* — ἀρχή$_1$ = "beginning," ἀρχή$_2$ = "rule," and ἀρχή$_3$ = "corner." And each contains several closely related meanings (polysemes). Under ἀρχή$_1$ we would include the polysemes

- ἀρχή$_{1a}$ = "beginning" (aspect [including "source"]),
- ἀρχή$_{1b}$ = "beginning (time),
- ἀρχή$_{1c}$ = "first cause," and
- ἀρχή$_{1d}$ = "beginning" (aspect ["elementary"]).

Under ἀρχή$_2$ we would include the polysemes

- ἀρχή$_{2a}$ = "human ruler,"
- ἀρχή$_{2b}$ = "supernatural power," and
- ἀρχή$_{2c}$ = "sphere of authority."

The homonyms ἀρχή$_1$, ἀρχή$_2$, and ἀρχή$_3$ should be regarded as quite independent words. No Greek speaker would confuse them and mingle their meanings, any more than an English speaker would confuse cat$_4$ (anchor hoist) with cat$_2$ (domestic cat) simply because the words have the same form. The reason for this is that from the point of view of the native or competent speaker of the language, cat$_4$ is more closely related to quite different words in the semantic domain of machinery terminology (words like "tackle," "hoist," and the like) than it is to any of the other senses of the word "cat."

It is partly to bring out this point most sharply that the lexicon edited by Louw and Nida is organized quite differently from other lexicons. Instead of lumping together the different senses of ἀρχή in one entry under that head noun, they treat ἀρχή$_{1a}$ (as "source of a river") in the semantic domain of terms for bodies of water (along with "river," "pool," "bay," "spring," etc.), while ἀρχή$_{2a}$ appears in the semantic domain of terms for rule (govern), along with words for "lord," "king," "master," magistrate," etc.). For the native Greek speaker, ἀρχή$_{2a}$ is much closer to words with such completely different forms as δεσπότης (*despotēs*, "master"), ἡγεμών (*hēgemōn*, "leader"), and the like than it is to ἀρχή$_{1a}$. The two could not be confused.

Yet when Bedale's influential article attempted to argue that κεφαλή came to bear the meaning "source" he relied principally on the probability of just such a confusion.[49] The essence of his argument is as follows: In the LXX, Hebrew שׁאר (*rō'š*, "head," in a variety of senses) was sometimes translated κεφαλή and sometimes ἀρχή. As the *latter* word could carry the sense "source," it is natural to suppose that κεφαλή (*kephalē*) could come to take this meaning too.

Unfortunately this is very misleading. In fact, κεφαλή is used only as an alternative for ἀρχή$_2$ ("ruler," "chief," "head over"). It is not used to translate שׁאר where it might plausibly mean "source" (e.g., Gen 2:10), and it is not found as an alternative for ἀρχή$_1$ ("beginning," including "source"). That observation reinforces the unlikelihood that the LXX translators were at all prone to confuse the two homonyms and makes it virtually impossible that κεφαλή came to mean "source" by the complicated route of confusion of ἀρχή$_2$ with ἀρχή$_1$ and the seeping of the confusion across to κεφαλή.

(2) Semantics has underscored the difference between properties of a thing in the world that a word is used to refer to and elements intrinsic to the sense of that word. Curiously, one of the main arguments used by Catherine Kroeger in the attempt to demonstrate that κεφαλή can mean "source" is that in classical literature the head of an animal or human is so often described as the source of certain physiological fluids or life influences.[50] But this again represents linguistic confusion: My college is the source of my income, work, and some recreational resources, but that does not lead me to assume that "source" is a possible *sense* of the lexeme "college"!

(3) Another related confusion is between metaphorical senses of a *word* and discourse *similes*. A number of the cases that Fitzmyer quotes as evi-

---

49. Stephen Bedale, "The Meaning of κεφαλή in the Pauline Epistles," *JTS* 5 (1954) 211-15.

50. Catherine Kroeger, "The Classical Concept of *Head* as 'Source,'" in *Equal to Serve*, ed. G. G. Hull (Old Tappan: Revell, 1987) 267-83.

dence of κεφαλή = "authority over" concern instances where the anatomical head is regarded as the governing member of the body[51] and where various leaders are said, in this respect, to be *like* heads.[52] These instances are, of course, of significance for the argument because they may show how it is that "head" may have come to mean "ruler." But clearly to say the head governs the body and that rulers are *like* the head in that respect is not evidence of a new sense of the word "head" at all.

Fitzmyer makes the same kind of mistake when he cites Artemidorus Daldiani (2d century C.E.) *Oneirocritica* 1.2, 35; 3.66 as evidence of κεφαλή as "source." Artemidorus says that the head *"resembles"* parents in that it is the cause of one's living (1.35), and that parents are *"like"* a literal head in being the source of life and light (1.2), etc. But to say that a head is a source of something (as we have noted above) is not the same as saying that the word "head" itself means (that is, has the sense) "source." For that we need to find utterances like, "the head (anatomical) is the head (metaphorically "source") of life and light." We do not find such usages.

(4) Similarly, lexical semantics has emphasized the difference between coreferentiality and synonymy. Another argument offered to support the view that κεφαλή could mean "source" is that Herodotus (4.91) spoke once of the κεφαλαί (*kephalai*, "heads") of the Tearus River, referring thereby to those parts of the river that he might as easily have called its ἀρχαί ("sources"; he in fact uses πηγαί [*pēgai*, "springs"). But that does not mean that κεφαλή carries the sense "source." It can be used of an extremity and so came to denote either "end" of a line — and the plural here simply has the sense "the ends" of the Tearus.[53] Of course, it is true that one "end" of a river is certainly its source, but the other "end" is the mouth, and Callimachus (*Aetia* 2.46) can later use κεφαλή of that too! Both "end" and "source" can refer to the beginning of a river without "end" having the sense "source": Two words that apply to the same entity (that is, are coreferential) by no means necessarily have the same sense; they are not necessarily *synonyms*. If we hear someone exclaim "The bike has a puncture; the beast always lets me down!" it would be reasonable to assume that the phrase "the beast" refers to the speaker's bicycle, but that does not mean that "two-wheeled, chain-driven vehicle" has become a sense of the word "beast."[54]

51. Cf. Plato *Timaeus* 44d; Philo *Spec. Leg.* 3.33 §184.
52. E.g., Plutarch *Pelopidas* 2.1; Philo *Vit. Mos.* 2.5 §30; *Praem.* 19 §114.
53. See Grudem, "Meaning of *Kephalē*," 432-33.
54. On the difference between "sense," "denotation," and "reference" see Lyons,

(5) Another principle in lexical semantics is that a new sense should not be claimed unless it is clear that an utterance cannot naturally be explained by established senses. In each of the remaining cases where κε-φαλή is to said mean "source" it is possible to provide an alternative understanding from the known senses of the word:

(a) *Orphic Fragment* 21a. In this fifth-century B.C.E. fragment, Zeus is called κεφαλή ("Zeus was first, Zeus is last with white vivid lightening: Zeus the head, Zeus the middle, Zeus from whom all things are perfected"). An alternative text has ἀρχή instead, and so it is inferred that "source" is what κεφαλή must have meant here. But this could be an instance of ἀρχή₁ ("beginning," "head of time"), a sense already recognized in Classical Greek.

(b) *Testament of Reuben* 2:2. Here seven spirits are established over against humankind and are said to be the κεφαλαί of certain wicked deeds. Contextually "source" or "origin" is evidently a possible sense, and this is how H. C. Kee translates it.[55] But R. H. Charles translated it "leaders" (of the works of innovation/rebellion).[56] That the seven spirits are called κε-φαλαί because they are the ruling powers that promote these things is certainly just as possible if not more probable than that they are being called the "source" of such things (for which other lexemes would be much clearer).

(c) *Life of Adam and Eve* 19:3. "For covetousness is the κεφαλή of very sin" probably means that covetousness is the "first" or "chief representative" of all sins rather than that it is the "source" of them (in the sense that all other sins flow from it).

The two remaining places where κεφαλή is claimed to mean "source" appear to rest on mistaken readings,[57] so it must be said that we have no

---

Semantics, ch. 7; James R. Hurford and Brendan Heasley, *Semantics: A Coursebook* (Cambridge: Cambridge University, 1983) chs. 1-2; Cotterell and Turner, *Linguistics*, ch. 3.

55. "Testaments of the Twelve Patriarchs," in *The Old Testament Pseudepigrapha*, vol. 1: *Apocalyptic Literature and Testaments*, ed. James H. Charlesworth (Garden City: Doubleday, 1983) 775-828, here 782.

56. R. H. Charles, "The Testaments of the XII Patriarchs," in *The Apocrypha and Pseudepigrapha of the Old Testament in English*, 2 vols., ed. R. H. Charles (Oxford: Clarendon, 1913) 2:282-367, here 297.

57. Fitzmyer offers Philo *Praem.* 20 §25, claiming that "head" is used allegorically there "as the 'source' of the spiritual life of good people" ("Kephalē," 54). But if anything it is a clearer example of κεφαλή as "ruler," for the virtuous are said to be the head of the human race in the sense that the body will be animated (controlled by) the powers

good evidence of κεφαλή meaning "source" in the public domain of Paul's day. Those who wish to protest that "head" as "authority over" is relatively rare should at least be prepared to admit that "head" as "source" is considerably rarer (probably to the point of vanishing altogether).

In such circumstances it would be unsafe to argue that κεφαλή means "source" in 1 Cor 11:3 unless there are very good contextual indicators that Paul has been innovative in his use of the word. We would need to be persuaded not only that taking κεφαλή as "source" made sense of the argument in the context (and Fee has perhaps made a credible attempt there)[58] but also that Paul has adopted textual strategies that alert his reader to his neologism and that prevent the more usual senses of κεφαλή (already in the public domain if only through the reading of the LXX) from being read into the text. It does not appear to this reader that he has done so. A first-century reader assuming that κεφαλή means something like "authority over" would not find any *semantic* problems created for this sense in 1 Corinthians 11, or any textual indicators to mark that some new sense should be preferred.[59] For such reasons the attempt to read κεφαλή in 1 Cor 11:3 as "source" remains problematic.

6. Suggestions for Further Reading

Secular linguistics is far too large an area for us to provide meaningful bibliographical guidance here. The following works, however, can be recommended as giving elementary (but authoritative) student-oriented introductions to the areas referred to.

Perhaps the most useful *general* introduction is John Lyons, *Language and Linguistics* (Cambridge: Cambridge University, 1982). Another excellent introduction to one of the most important areas of linguistics for theological purposes (and given in the form of highly readable text and stimulating exercises) is James R. Hurford and Brendan Heasley, *Semantics:*

---

in and above the head. The other example offered by Fitzmyer is Philo *Cong.* 12 §125, where Esau is described as progenitor of his clan and " 'head' as it were to the whole creature." This might seem to make Esau seminal head of his tribe. But the "whole creature" Philo has in mind is made up not of physical descendants but of like characters, and Esau was not the "source" of these, but their first and chief representative.

58. Fee, *First Corinthians*, 498-524.
59. Cf. Cotterell and Turner, *Linguistics*, 316-28.

A Coursebook (Cambridge: Cambridge University, 1983). The most comprehensive and authoritative guide is undoubtedly John Lyons, *Semantics*, 2 vols. (Cambridge: Cambridge University, 1977).

On more specialized topics (but still written as student introductions) the following may be noted: Gillian Brown and George Yule, *Discourse Analysis*, CTL (Cambridge: Cambridge University, 1983); D. A. Cruse, *Lexical Semantics*, CTL (Cambridge: Cambridge University, 1986); Herbert H. Clark and Eve V. Clark, *Psychology and Language: An Introduction to Psycholinguistics* (New York: Harcourt, Brace and Jovanovich, 1977); R. A. Hudson, *Sociolinguistics*, CTL (Cambridge: Cambridge University, 1980); and Stephen C. Levinson, *Pragmatics*, CTL (Cambridge: Cambridge University, 1983).

James Barr's *The Semantics of Biblical Language* (Oxford: Oxford University, 1961) was probably the first work to make the relevance of semantics for biblical studies crystal clear. The first works to mediate linguistics to those interested in the linguistics of the Bible were by professional Bible translators. These works are marked by lucidity and profundity, and this is perhaps most notably the case of two works: Eugene A. Nida and Charles R. Taber, *The Theory and Practice of Translation* (Leiden: Brill, 1969), covering much of the area of semantics (including some discourse analysis); and Kathleen Callow, *Discourse Considerations in Translating the Word of God* (Grand Rapids: Zondervan, 1974). The former has effectively been extended and updated in different areas by later works by Nida (see nn. 18 and 19 above) and by Johannes P. Louw's *Semantics of New Testament Greek* (Philadelphia: Fortress, 1982). Callow's book needs supplementing by Wilbur N. Pickering's *A Framework for Discourse Analysis* (Dallas: SIL, 1980), which examines the text of Colossians in detail from this perspective. Two of these authors (Nida and Louw) have now provided the best single introduction and workbook on NT lexical semantics in *Lexical Semantics of the Greek New Testament* (Atlanta: Scholars, 1992) as an introduction to their two-volume semantic lexicon of the NT (see n. 4 above).

Semipopular attempts to mediate the findings of linguistics to *theological* students (rather than to Bible translators) include David A. Black's *Linguistics for Students of New Testament Greek* (Grand Rapids: Eerdmans, 1988); and Peter Cotterell and Max Turner's *Linguistics and Biblical Interpretation* (London: SPCK/Downers Grove: InterVarsity, 1989). Black's volume is a better general guide to the whole area of linguistics (including morphology, phonetics, tense and aspect, etc.) and, as the title suggests, is aimed primarily at helping students who are learning Greek; Cotterell and

Turner is much fuller and concentrates on different theoretical aspects of semantics and discourse analysis and on the relevance of these for the task of interpretation.

The only major scholarly contribution to NT studies (other than articles and books of collected essays) in English on the basis of linguistic theory is Stanley E. Porter's *Verbal Aspect in the Greek of the New Testament* (Bern: Lang, 1989). This book challenges much of the way the verbal system and its "tenses" have been explained in the grammars to date (and so implicitly challenges a very large number of exegetical claims based on observations about the tense usage in the NT). Porter's findings are mediated at a more accessible level in his *Idioms of the Greek New Testament* (Sheffield: JSOT, 1992). There are several helpful monographs on specialized aspects of discourse analysis — for example, Stephen H. Levinsohn, *Textual Connections in Acts,* SBLMS 31 (Atlanta: Scholars, 1987).

9. Discourse Analysis and New Testament Interpretation

JOEL B. GREEN

1. What Is Discourse Analysis?

Among the several "methods" discussed in this volume, the focus of "discourse analysis" may be the least self-evident. This is due in part to the relative youth of discourse analysis in the general world of language analysis,[1] but it also arises from the relatively infrequent identification of discourse analysis *as a discrete approach* in NT studies. According to one of the most helpful introductions to the subject, "in discourse analysis . . . we are concerned with what people using language are doing and [we are] accounting for the linguistic features in the discourse as the means employed in what they are doing."[2] As we will see, this definition needs slight emendation to include, along with linguistic features, *paralinguistic features* as well, but already we see that discourse analysis is focused on "language in use."

This is a key aspect of the significance of discourse analysis in NT interpretation since it provides a potentially fruitful way for navigating between apparently competing modes of interpretation that focus on either the history behind the text, the world of the text, or the reading community in front of the text. It is true that discourse analysis made its debut in NT study as NT interpretation was undergoing a paradigm shift from a primary

---

1. The term first appears in Zellig S. Harris, "Discourse Analysis: A Sample Text," *Language* 28 (1952) 1-30, 474-94.

2. Gillian Brown and George Yule, *Discourse Analysis*, CTL (Cambridge: Cambridge University, 1983) 26.

focus on questions of a historical nature to approaches that privileged the NT text *qua* text. As a consequence, discourse analysis in NT study has largely been practiced in the form of *text-linguistics*, which works under the assumption that a close tie exists between the way a text is structured and the meaning of the text.[3] More recent work on discourse has underscored the broader contexts and sets of relationships in which communication must be understood and, thus, the multiple levels for which discourse analysis is appropriate.

In an examination of a narrative text like Luke 3:1-20, for example, discourse analysis might focus on at least the following relationships:

(1) discourse within the narrative itself, that is, the interchange between John and the crowds, toll collectors, and soldiers (3:10-14).

For example, why does Luke write "*even* (χαί [*kai*]) toll collectors came to be baptized" (3:12)? What significance should be credited to the toll collectors' addressing John with the appellation "Teacher" (διδάσκαλε [*didaskale*], 3:12)?

(2) discourse between the addresser and addressee, that is, between Luke as narrator and the audience to which the Third Gospel is directed — taking into account the place of 3:1-20 in the larger "discourse unit" of the Gospel of Luke (or Luke-Acts) as a whole.

For example, what is the textually and culturally grounded effect of juxtaposing John and the religious and political leadership of John's larger world (3:1-3)?

(3) discourse between the text of the Third Gospel, now understood not simply as an object of inquiry but as a subject in a communicative interchange, and new generations of readers, including ourselves.

3. Cf., e.g., Johannes P. Louw, "Discourse Analysis and the Greek New Testament," *BT* 24 (1973) 108-18; Eugene A. Nida, *Toward a Science of Translating* (Leiden: Brill, 1964); *idem, Componential Analysis of Meaning* (The Hague: Mouton, 1975); and more recently, e.g., Peter Cotterell and Max Turner, *Linguistics and Biblical Interpretation* (London: SPCK/Downers Grove: InterVarsity, 1989) 230-56; A. N. Snyman, "Discourse Analysis: A Semantic Discourse Analysis of the Letter to Philemon," in *Text and Interpretation: New Approaches in the Criticism of the New Testament,* ed. P. J. Hartin and J. H. Petzer (Leiden: Brill, 1991) 83-99; David Alan Black, et al., eds., *Linguistics and New Testament Interpretation: Essays on Discourse Analysis* (Nashville: Broadman, 1992).

It will be immediately transparent from these examples that by "discourse" we do not mean simply "the text." Rather, "texts" (like Luke's Gospel) are both *cultural products* providing witness to a (past) discourse between Luke and his (first-century) "model readers"[4] and, when engaged in a close reading by readers today, *partners* in a new discourse situation. Taken seriously, discourse analysis points at one level to the artificiality of all analysis, since every engaged reading is already participation in a communicative event whereby we join in the generation of meaning and are shaped in the give and take of active discourse. On another level, though, discourse analysis is interested in *how* language-in-use invites such participation and formation.

It will already be clear how intertwined discourse analysis is with other areas of study — for example, anthropology, rhetoric, semiotics, sociology, literary analysis, reader response, and so on. This opens any discussion of "discourse analysis" to a wonderful eclecticism since it draws on insights from other interpretive approaches. At the same time, this reality suggests how discourse analysis might function as a set of doors opening the interpreter to multitudinous ways of construing a discourse[5] or as an arena for the interaction of insights generated by other means.

This fuzziness of the boundaries between disciplines also means that any introductory discussion of discourse analysis is necessarily incomplete and one-sided. Discourse analysis is now often divided into two subfields: *text-linguistics* and *pragmatics.* The former examines textual cohesion and argument development, the latter the interaction between speech and unarticulated shared presuppositions in a discourse. One can also think of discourse analysis as *sociolinguistics,* which studies the use of language in human interaction and the achievement of social objectives, and *psycholinguistics,* the focus of which is the cognitive and affective reception of communication. The introduction to discourse analysis in NT study being

---

4. The designation "model reader" is borrowed from Umberto Eco, *The Role of the Reader: Explorations in the Semiotics of Texts,* AS (Bloomington: Indiana University, 1979), and refers to the reader "supposedly able to deal interpretively with the expressions in the same way as the author deals generatively with them" (7). Compare the notion of "implied reader" in ch. 12 below.

5. One might prefer to say "text" at this point, but that designation would only be correct if understood in the broader sense of "life as text" or "text as interpretable social interchange" and not only as "document." On this expanded notion of text, cf. Clifford Geertz, "Blurred Genres: The Refiguration of Social Thought," in *Local Knowledge: Further Essays in Interpretive Anthropology* (New York: Basic, 1983) 19-35, here 30-33.

presented here will be especially characterized by its refusal to focus narrowly on text-linguistics.

2. Central Assumptions

2.1 Setting the Stage

Discourse analysis has developed in relationship to three shifts in hermeneutics ("hermeneutics" understood in broad terms). The first, which we have already mentioned, is the move away from a concentration of the interpretive agenda *behind the text* to a greater interest in the text itself. For some two centuries, biblical studies has been dominated by *historical questions* in their various guises: Did the event recounted here actually happen? To what sources did the final editor of this text have access? Were those sources tendentious or reliable? And so on. With an increasing preoccupation with the text itself, such questions have sometimes been set aside, but more often they are set alongside other issues related to how a text has been shaped, consciously or otherwise, by its author so as to generate meaning.

Discourse analysis thus examines texts as acts of communication and not as windows into a historical past. This does not mean that questions of history and tradition are obliterated in discourse analysis; rather, the weight of interest shifts. Now the question is not "Did it happen?" or "In what community was this tradition formed?" but "How and to what end is the tradition being used?"

Second, interpreters have learned more and more to account for the multiplicity of possible readings of a text. Umberto Eco illustrates this shift with reference to Claude Lévi-Strauss, who described a work of art as an object endowed with precise properties — an object, once created, with the rigidity of a crystal. Eco remarks of a text, "If it were a crystal, the cooperation of the reader would be part of its molecular structure."[6] Eco thus works against earlier attempts to objectify the text in analysis by accounting for the role of the addressee.

In Gospels research, Clifton Black has similarly pointed out the subjective, readerly assumptions that determine interpretations of the concept of discipleship in Mark, even when interpreters are working within a historical-critical paradigm. Even when using analogous procedures, asking

6. Eco, *Role of the Reader*, 3-4, 37.

parallel questions, and examining the same texts, redaction critics, Black observes, have reached embarrassingly divergent views on the role of the disciples in the Second Gospel.[7]

Today, hermeneuts often speak of the multiplicity of possible readings, focusing less on the text's "meaning," that is, its supposed one correct meaning. Some go so far as to speak less of "meaning," understood in its singularity, and more of the "uses" of a text, understood as the various ways a text is construed in given reading situations. In discourse analysis, this multiplicity of *possible meanings* is a function of the emphasis on the discourse *event*, the temporal moment when a text is realized or actualized. Discourse analysis admits a certain unpredictability of interpretation as "the right of the reader and the right of the text converge in an important struggle that generates the whole dynamic of interpretation."[8]

Also of importance for discourse analysis is the way in which "meaning" is textually constrained. As we will explore further momentarily, the full potential polysemy of our words is modulated by a series of textual relations. Discourse analysis participates in this second interpretive shift by seeking to account both for textual constraints on meaning and for the ongoing interplay of text and readers.

Third, and most recently, interpreters have begun to struggle more with discourse in its relations of power: "Utterances are not only . . . signs to be understood and deciphered; they are also *signs of wealth*, intended to be evaluated and appreciated, and *signs of authority*, intended to be believed and obeyed."[9] On the one hand, hermeneuts have been growing in their openness to the act of reading as more than the deciphering of information codes, but rather as a communicative event whereby the text is in a sense activated so as to achieve certain aims in its audience. The transformative power of texts is thus acknowledged. On the other hand, discourse is understood today as profoundly shaped by socially embedded extralinguistic factors. That is, language is used not only to get another person to understand one's thoughts and feelings, but also to define relationship, to identify location in a social group.[10]

7. C. Clifton Black, *The Disciples according to Mark: Markan Redaction in Current Debate*, JSNTSS 27 (Sheffield: JSOT, 1989).

8. Paul Ricoeur, *Interpretation Theory: Discourse and the Surplus of Meaning* (Fort Worth: Texas Christian University, 1976) 32.

9. Pierre Bourdieu, *Language and Symbolic Power* (Cambridge: Harvard University, 1991) 66.

10. Ralph Fasold, *The Sociolinguistics of Language*, LS 6 (Cambridge, Massachusetts/Oxford: Blackwell, 1990) 1.

For example, the culturally determined status of the person speaking or writing shapes how that utterance might be perceived and what effect it might have. Suppose the following is spoken in a classroom:

S1 Robin, isn't it warm in this room?

If spoken by the professor, it may well have the (perhaps intended) effect of prompting Robin to open a window. If vocalized by a fellow student, however, it is unlikely to produce the same result.

Within the NT, an important illustration of the power issues involved in discourse is found in the form of address used in narrative and epistolary literature. Typically, forms of address serve one of two general purposes: to achieve or communicate solidarity, intimacy, and/or shared fate ("Brothers and fathers, listen to me" [Acts 7:2]; "Beloved" [1 John 4:1]) and to achieve or communicate power or control, or otherwise to signal differences of social status ("Paul and Timothy, servants of Christ Jesus" [Phil 1:1]).[11] Understanding this is another concern of discourse analysis.

Contemporary discourse analysis grows out of these developments. It is also based on three closely related assumptions:

2.2 Communication Is Social, Transcending Sentences

Discourse analysis proceeds under the assumption that communication occurs at a level that transcends words, clauses, or even sentences. Utterances only rarely if ever occur in isolation; they are embedded in ongoing social interaction between human beings, and it is from this interaction that utterances take their meaning. For this reason, the same words, uttered in two different settings or among different people, will not necessarily or even likely carry the same meaning. This assumption has a number of ramifications, two of which should be mentioned here.

First, words, clauses, sentences, and even paragraphs in a text like 1 Cor 11:17-34 are already situated in an ongoing discourse situation and therefore should not be interpreted apart from that discourse situation. Even though Paul's words, "Now in the following instructions I do not commend you" (11:17), suggest the onset of a fresh *discourse unit*, we cannot help but notice the immediate contrast with 11:2: "I commend you because you remember me in everything and maintain the traditions just as I handed

---

11. Cf. Fasold, *Sociolinguistics*, 1-38.

them on to you." That is, 11:17-34 is part of a larger unit roughly corresponding to ch. 11, which is itself part of the whole of the letter that we refer to as 1 Corinthians, which is itself part of an ongoing literary exchange between Paul and the Corinthians (cf. 5:9; 7:1), which is itself part of the ongoing interchange (carried out by literary and other means) between Paul and the Corinthian church (cf. Acts 18:1-11), which is itself set within the larger cultural milieu of the Roman world as it was experienced in the region of Achaia in Greece. The Corinthians' factionalism, the significance of the communal meal, the importance of the Last Supper tradition, the play on the word "body" (σῶμα [sōma]) — these and other aspects of 11:17-34 are already situated in an ongoing conversation and tradition of meaning, and it is within this "discourse" that they have meaning.

Second, the social nature of communication underscores the relations of power on which utterances depend and draw. In discourse analysis today, *who* says *what* to *whom* and *to what end* become critical, since language in use is always more than the passing on of information. What is more, whatever power or effect a speech act has is a power or effect ascribed to it by social institutions external to the actual words employed. In 1 Corinthians 11 Paul cites a tradition regarding the Last Supper (vv. 23-25), no doubt in part thus placing himself into a larger body of Christian tradition and thus basing his appeal for behavioral changes among the Corinthian believers on the word of the Lord himself. In this social setting, appeals to tradition and to the Lord apparently lend extra weight to Paul's utterances, with the result that the net effect of his writing transcends the authority carried by the words themselves.

Of course, Paul's words are *already* the words of *an apostle* (1 Cor 1:1), so that the whole of the Paul-Corinth discourse is set within the boundaries of his relationship of authority to them. Why, we might ask, was it necessary for Paul the apostle to add to his own status the added weight of the tradition and of revelation?

2.3 Language-in-Use Is Always Culturally Embedded

"There is no use of language which is not embedded in the culture. . . ."[12] This simple and self-evident reality has often been overlooked. For example, analyses of wealth and poverty in the NT are littered with attempts to locate

---

12. Michael Stubbs, *Discourse Analysis: The Sociolinguistic Analysis of Natural Language*, LS 4 (Chicago: University of Chicago/Oxford: Blackwell, 1983) 8.

Jesus as a member of the "low" or "middle class." But this is a patent instance of the transferral of terminology from industrial and postindustrial society back into Palestinian antiquity, neglecting the possibility that "class" is a culturally determined nomenclature whose meaning in the first century might have been quite different.[13]

This illustration points to an important reality about communication — namely, that communication often proceeds on the basis of *assumed* common knowledge and experience. That is, we often listen to one another and read materials even from cultures foreign to our own, unconsciously assuming that all are operating with the same cultural background. It is for this reason, at least, that discourse analysis is interested not only in discourse *within the text*, but also with the communicative interchange between the ancient text and the contemporary reader. How are we decoding culturally embedded meaning from a time and place in many ways quite different from our own?

2.4 Humans Are Meaning-Making

Finally, discourse analysis proceeds on the assumption that we human beings have a powerful urge to make sense out of whatever is presented us. "The natural effort of hearers and readers alike is to attribute relevance and coherence to the text they encounter until they are forced not to."[14]

All language is polysemous, of course; it is capable of infinite uses. The same may not be said of discourse, however, since the multiplicity of possible meanings of language are tamed by a number of factors — some linguistic, others paralinguistic — that provide its coherence.[15] In discursive interchange, we presume coherence and relevance. For example, if we overhear from another room

S2 Quit pulling my leg!

we may well wonder whether it is to be taken metaphorically or literally. But this question would not arise for a participant in the discourse. A

---

13. Cf. Joel B. Green, "Good News to Whom? Jesus and the 'Poor' in the Gospel of Luke," in *Jesus of Nazareth: Lord and Christ. Essays on the Historical Jesus and New Testament Christology*, ed. Joel B. Green and Max Turner (Grand Rapids: Eerdmans, 1994) 59-74.

14. Brown and Yule, *Discourse Analysis*, 66.

15. Cf. Stubbs, *Discourse Analysis*, 19; Umberto Eco, *The Limits of Interpretation*, AS (Bloomington/Indianapolis: University of Indiana, 1990) 21.

participant would be privy to the attempt at humor just preceding this exclamation, or would have observed a makeshift attempt at a wrestling match, and so would know how to construe the exclamation.

3. Central Coordinates

Discourse analysis brings to the fore for investigation the social and linguistic webs within which speech occurs and derives its significance. These "webs" are of various kinds and can be outlined with reference to the relationship of a given text to its co-text, intertext, and context. *Co-text* refers to the string of linguistic data within which a text is set, the relationship of, say, a sentence to a paragraph or a pericope in Luke's Gospel to the larger Lukan narrative. *Intertext* refers to the location of a text within the larger linguistic frame of reference on which it consciously or unconsciously draws for meaning; for example, Luke's narrative builds especially on the Greek version of what we have come to call the OT (i.e., the LXX). *Context* refers to the sociohistorical realities within which the Lukan text, for example, is set.

3.1 Text and Co-Text

"The only way we can make sense of the world is to see the connections between things, and between present things and things we have experienced before or hear about."[16] This precept functions in a variety of ways in the process of reading: Readers bring with them to the reading task, for example, a basic dictionary, assumptions about genre, experience with other texts, and so on, without which texts cannot be actualized. The statement

S3 The NP is in fact a *use NP* for *S2*

taken from Greimas' *The Social Sciences: A Semiotic View*,[17] is readily understood by those already inducted into this particular "vocabulary." For the noninitiated, however, S3 may still be perceptible if one has only read

16. Deborah Tannen, "What's in a Frame? Surface Evidence for Underlying Expectations," in *Framing in Discourse*, ed. Deborah Tannen (New York/Oxford: Oxford University, 1993) 14-56, here 14-15.
17. Algirdas Julien Greimas, *The Social Sciences: A Semiotic View* (Minneapolis: University of Minnesota, 1990) 167.

this statement in its own *co-text* (conspicuously absent here). Texts appear to us in linear fashion, in English from left to right, and our present sense-making is guided by what has gone on before.

In the narrow sense *co-text* refers to previous discourse material. "Any sentence other than the first in a fragment of discourse . . . will have its interpretation forcibly constrained by the preceding text. . . ."[18] Words, sentences, and entire discourse units are shaped in their significance by the larger co-texts in which they appear; previous definitions, previous meaning systems can be nuanced, renewed, and even destroyed in new co-texts.

A text's *immediate (or local) co-text*, that is, the immediately preceding material, is often of paramount importance in shaping how a text is received. This is because of memory limitations: As reading or listening progresses, comprehension of past utterances become more and more summary.[19]

Also of significance is *staging*, that is, the prominence given a particular discourse element in relation to other elements. Which elements come prior to which others, the placement of certain characters but not others in the subject position, the repetition of words or concepts, the positioning of an actor at the center of a narrative scene, and so on — such aspects of staging as these help the reader or hearer determine the "aboutness" of a given text.

More broadly, *co-text* may refer to what comes after as well as before a text. It is true that the presence of linearization (we read from left to right) generates progressive expectations in the reading experience. We expect promises made in a narrative text (e.g., John will make ready a people, Luke 1:17) to be fulfilled (cf. Luke 3:1-20). At the same time, it is not always clear *how* those expectations will be fulfilled, or even what shape their fulfillment might take. Therefore, expectations can be reshaped or even set aside by subsequent co-text. Particularly with texts like those contained in the NT, where reading and rereading are not only possible but encouraged by those faith communities in which they are regarded as Scripture, expectations are constantly being recast as readers relate and re-relate a text to its co-text.

3.2 Discourse Situation

By *discourse situation* we mean the temporal moment of a communication act. In a text like the Third Gospel this has two primary referents. First, in

---

18. Brown and Yule, *Discourse Analysis,* 46.

19. Cf. Cesare Segre with Tomaso Kemeny, *Introduction to the Analysis of the Literary Text,* AS (Bloomington/Indianapolis: Indiana University, 1988) 163.

discourse analysis we appreciate the fact that the Third Evangelist was himself situated in a particular sociohistorical context. His narrative participates first in that (now foreign) world, and the discourse analyst must take into account that world. Second, as we read the Third Gospel a new discourse situation is realized, since we read out of our own histories.

Just as concern with *co-text* invites a close reading of the text for its structural elements and argumentative development, so attention to *discourse situation* invites social-scientific analysis. In the latter case, investigation needs to proceed along two lines simultaneously, so that readers come to understand both the values they take for granted and the (sometimes quite different) values taken for granted in the discourse situation in which the text was produced.

3.3 Presuppositions

A variety of *presuppositions* affect discourse. One thinks of *logical presuppositions*, for example, activated when a given text actively presupposes undisclosed information. The famous question

S4 Have you stopped beating your wife?

presupposes at least that one has a wife and that one has struck her at some point in the past.

Also of significance is a quite different set of presuppositions that are not so easily unveiled at the level of logic demanded by the text. We refer here to *presupposition pools,* that is, the pool of knowledge one assumes to be possessed by one's audience. Such knowledge takes the forms of "general knowledge of the world" and of the exigencies giving rise to the discourse. Each participant in a discourse has a presupposition pool, to which more is added as the discourse proceeds; that is, presupposition pools expand as new information is shared.

In his (first-century) discourse situation, for example, Luke apparently believed that he could assume a knowledge of Greek on the part of at least some of his audience, sufficient knowledge of the LXX to allow him to draw on its vocabulary and themes without often calling explicit attention to his use of it, and so on. Recent use of insights from cultural anthropology has underscored numerous other ways in which Luke has drawn on cultural values and behaviors taken for granted in the Mediterranean world — sometimes merely as the backdrop of the interactions he recounts, sometimes in order to affirm those practices, and sometimes to undermine them.[20]

It is precisely here that discourse analysis might draw on the insights of tradition criticism. Even though it may be problematic to regard, say, the first-century readers and hearers of Luke's Gospel as having personal copies or intimate knowledge of another canonical Gospel, Luke does allude to his knowledge of other traditions (1:1-4). Presumably his own narrative will be meaningful in part for the way it reshapes those traditions. An ingredient of any concern with *presuppositions* is intertextuality, since any text is built up from and assumes other texts.[21] This may relate to stock forms, recognizable story patterns, and particular uses of language as well as to the more obvious direct or indirect use of other texts. A number of NT authors were especially adept at drawing their texts into interpretive webs with the LXX, so that the ongoing story of divine redemption sheds light on the present, just as the story of Jesus is allowed to interpret the story of Israel.

Finally it should be observed that one of the key problems with presuppositions is that each participant in a discourse typically behaves as though his or her presupposition pool were shared by all. We tend to assume, for example, that the supper to which Paul refers in 1 Cor 11:17-34 is on the model of the celebration of the Supper (Eucharist, Communion, or the like) in our tradition. Discourse analysis of NT texts, then, must be actively engaged in the exploration of the presupposition pools (especially the sociohistorical context) of the Mediterranean communities in which those texts were formed.

---

20. See Joel B. Green, *The Theology of the Gospel of Luke*, NTT 3 (Cambridge: Cambridge University, 1995); *idem*, "The Social Status of Mary in Luke 1,5–2,52: A Plea for Methodological Integration," *Bib* 73 (1992) 457-71. More generally, cf. Jerome H. Neyrey, ed., *The Social World of Luke-Acts: Models for Interpretation* (Peabody: Hendrickson, 1991).

21. Cf. Jonathan Culler, *The Pursuit of Signs: Semiotics, Literature, Deconstruction* (London: Routledge and Kegan Paul, 1991) esp. ch. 5; Michael Worton and Judith Sill, eds., *Intertextuality: Theories and Practices* (Manchester: Manchester University, 1990) esp. Still and Worton's Introduction (1-44). On intertextuality and biblical studies, cf. esp. Daniel Boyarin, *Intertextuality and the Reading of Midrash*, ISBL (Bloomington/Indianapolis: Indiana University, 1990); Richard B. Hays, *Echoes of Scripture in the Letters of Paul* (New Haven/London: Yale University, 1989).

4. Toward a Discourse Analysis of Luke 3:1-20

By way of illustrating the sorts of questions and insights that might be generated by an approach to a NT text as "language in use" (i.e., from the perspective of discourse analysis), we will locate Luke 3:1-6 in its larger co-text, then examine this unit in more detail.

4.1 Luke 3:1-6: A Wide-Angle View

Although John and his followers will appear later in Luke-Acts (e.g., Luke 7:18-35; Acts 19:1-7), Luke's presentation of the public career of John appears here in Luke 3:1-6. Both the introduction and conclusion of this passage are clear, with the result that we have here a fine example of Luke's concern with dramatic staging[22] — joining John in the wilderness for his prophetic mission at the outset, removing him from the public stage and indeed from the narrative itself at the finish. On the other hand, 3:1-20 is closely tied to material regarding John in ch. 1. John's public ministry of preparing the way for Jesus has been promised, and by means of the empowering of the Holy Spirit even before his birth he has been prepared for this service; here, the narrative cycle is completed by the carrying out of his ministry and by its results. The outcome of John's ministry takes two forms: He attracts hostility leading to his imprisonment, and he paves the way for Jesus' ministry by provoking an eschatological crisis and directing popular hopes to the coming of a future deliverer. Significantly, in spite of the opposition to John and even his removal from the public sphere, the divine aim to which he committed his service continues.[23] These verses concerning John are themselves suggestive of the pattern of Jesus' experience: public ministry, then attraction of opposing forces and imprisonment, but also the continuation of God's purpose. Hence, although 3:1-20 appears in the Gospel as a discrete unit, it is tightly woven into the fabric of Luke's narrative strategy.

Luke's presentation of John's public career introduces John by placing him in sociopolitical and salvation-historical context (3:1-6), illustrates the content of his message (3:7-18), and concludes by reporting how opposition to John led to his imprisonment (3:19-20). Thus Luke draws to its finale the narrative cycle related to John by demonstrating that what was antici-

22. See Luke's concern with "order" in 1:1-4.
23. Cf. Green, *Theology of Luke*, ch. 2.

187

pated concerning him by angelic and Spirit-inspired voices (Luke 1) has been realized. Eschatological judgment, with its promise of blessing, woe, and division, has already begun; the stage is set for the public ministry of God's agent of salvation, Jesus, Son of God.

4.2 A Closer Look at Luke 3:1-6

Zechariah had prophesied that his son John would be called "prophet of the Most High" and that he would "go before the Lord to prepare his ways" (1:76; cf. 1:16-17), and now John takes up his role. In other ways, too, 3:1-6 is tied back into the material of Luke 1 — for example, analogous geopolitical markers (1:5; 3:1-2), the motifs of conversion and forgiveness (1:16-17, 77; 3:3), the wilderness setting (1:80; 3:2, 4), the identification of John as Zechariah's son, and so on. These apparent redundancies serve a vital function in the Lukan narrative and are in no way artificial. The strict concentration on Jesus' birth and childhood in Luke 2 has created a lengthy hiatus in the account concerning John, set aside after 1:80. These points of contact, then, serve as important connectives back to the earlier narrative. Although 3:1-2 obviously signals the beginning of John's public ministry, this public appearance is itself the realization of earlier promises.

Luke 3:1-6 also opens up new possibilities for development. Of special interest are the relation of this fresh work of God to the political figures introduced in 3:1-2 and the nature of John's ministry, "proclaiming a baptism of repentance for the forgiveness of sins" (3:3). Most importantly, though, 3:1-6 locates John in the anticipated public arena and on the stage of salvation history. Verses 1 and 2 present John as a prophet, the significance of whose ministry could hardly be relegated to a corner of the world. Verses 4-6 link John's mission with the eschatological consolation of God. Verses 1-2 and 4-6 thus frame and focus attention on the summary characterization of John's mission in v. 3, while that mission is at the same time interpreted in sociopolitical and redemptive-historical terms.

On the one hand, the universal scope of the coming salvation is suggested by the list of civic and religio-political leaders in 3:1-2;[24] seen in this way, this list forms a conceptual *inclusio* with "all flesh" in 3:6, a repetition of the concept at the beginning and end of the passage. But this observation must not be allowed to overshadow the apparent tensions resident in these introductory verses. For example, what does it mean to juxtapose mention

---

24. Cf. Origen *Hom. in Luc.* 21.

of Emperor Tiberius, well known for his tyrannical reign, with the preparation of the way of the Lord? What are we to make of the deliberate
juxtaposition of institutional religion, embodied in Annas and Caiaphas,
to the anointing of a prophet with the word of God? What significance
should we find in the fact that God's word has come to Zechariah "in the
wilderness" — a locale both pregnant with revolutionary meaning from
Israel's past and distant from the direct influence of the urban power elite?
Clearly, John's "wilderness" is not outside the public eye and these observations portend a coming collision between him and those who possess
power and privilege in his world.[25] All of this, it is clear, is God's doing, for
John bears the word of God and his ministry is firmly grounded in "the
book of the words of the prophet Isaiah."

The focal point of the lengthy sentence opening this unit (3:1-2) appears in its final clause, where the main verb is found: "the word of God
came to John. . . ." Together with earlier anticipations of John's prophetic
ministry (1:16-17, 76), this affirmation and the geopolitical markers in
3:1-2a identify John as a prophet in the tradition represented by Israel's
Scriptures. The sentence as a whole is reminiscent of numerous prophetic
texts — including those that also situate a prophet in a historical context
with reference to national leaders, those that declare the coming of the
divine word to the messenger, and, as in Luke 3:1-2, those combining both
of these elements. Similar lists are found in ancient historiography, and this
will have had some significance for Luke's audience as it attempted to locate
the events Luke has narrated in the real world of Roman Palestine.[26] However, the extent to which Luke has already shown his concern to read the
story of God's redemptive work in John and Jesus against the backdrop of
the Scriptures encourages in particular our hearing of scriptural echoes
here. The introduction of John is grounded in the past story of anointed
persons who speak on God's behalf and proclaim his coming judgment.

This is not to imply that Luke's sole interest in the lineup of rulers he
provides in 3:1-2a is to paint John in prophetic garb. Nor can it be said
that Luke's primary purpose is to provide data for a precise dating of the
beginning of John's prophetic work. After all, the conjunction of the rulers

---

25. Cf. Walter Brueggemann, "An Exposition of Luke 3:1-4," *Int* 30 (1976) 404-9,
here 405-8.

26. National leaders: Isa 1:1; Amos 1:1; prophets: Joel 1:1; Jonah 1:1; both elements:
Jer 1:1-4; Ezek 1:1-3; Hos 1:1; Mic 1:1; Zeph 1:1; Hag 1:1; Zech 1:1. Ancient historiographers: Thucydides 2.2; Polybius 1.3; Josephus *Ant.* 18.4.6 §106.

specifies the chronology of John's ministry only in a general sense. Presumably, the onset of John's ministry should be fixed to the period 28-29 CE, but concern with *chronological* specificity is for Luke clearly eclipsed by his interest in portraying the *sociohistorical* climate within which John ministered. Otherwise, it would be difficult to explain why he continues his list beyond Tiberius to mention Pilate, Herod, Philip, Lysanias, Annas, and Caiaphas.

What is the importance of these figures and their domains to the Lukan narrative? For some — Pilate, Herod, Annas, and Caiaphas — this is the first mention of persons who will play important roles elsewhere in the narrative. The most important to the immediate co-text is Herod, who places John in prison (3:19-20). Pilate, Annas, and Caiaphas will have similar roles of opposition to God's purpose (cf. 22:54; 23:1-25; Acts 4:5-6, 27). The others — Tiberius, Philip, and Lysanias — are otherwise absent from Luke-Acts, so it is less clear why they deserve mention at all. But even the four who figure elsewhere in the narrative are only introduced here in connection with their spheres of authority and otherwise undergo no character development apart from being juxtaposed to John.

Hence, we should recall that the presupposition pool shared by Luke and his audience consists not only of information he has provided but also of "common knowledge" that he can assume. This suggests that 3:1-2a must be read within the interpretive matrix of earlier material, such as the critique of "the powerful" and "the rich" in Mary's Song (1:52-53); that is, having read the preceding narrative, we now have a bias against any rulers who enter the narrative. And this inclination is generally supported by the juxtaposition of these rulers to John.

What of the reputations of these rulers? Does information in that regard further develop our understanding of their possible role here? The reign of Tiberius may be best remembered for the numerous treason and sedition trials that took place, during many of which he had direct and indirect influence, and his deportation of Jews from Rome.[27] Nevertheless, when his reign was still recent history, and so in Luke's discourse situation, Tiberius is likely to have been infamous for his last years as emperor: Following personal tragedy, his mental health declined, and those final years have been characterized as a period of pure terror.

---

27. See the rehabilitating treatment of Tiberius in Albino Garzetti, *From Tiberius to the Antonines: A History of the Roman Empire, AD 14-92* (London: Methuen, 1974) 3-79.

Pilate, prefect of the Roman province of Judea from 26-36/37 CE, is known from Jewish sources as "inflexible, a blend of self-will and relentlessness," one whose administration was marked by briberies, insults, robberies, outrages, wanton injuries, frequent executions without trial, and endless savage ferocity.[28] Unlike his predecessors, Pilate apparently held Jewish religious sensibilities in low esteem; for example, he introduced tokens of emperor worship into Jerusalem and took money from the temple treasury.[29] Perhaps of equal or greater importance, Pilate would have been known to Luke's audience, as he was to the Latin historiographer Tacitus,[30] as the Roman provincial ruler under whom Jesus was executed. Hence, his introduction at this juncture does not serve merely to provide "a Roman and Palestinian ambience,"[31] but itself adds to the growing sense of tension.

By "Herod" Luke means Herod Antipas, tetrarch of Galilee and Perea from 4 BCE to 39 CE. Antipas came to power following the death of his father, Herod the Great (cf. 1:5). He is remembered for overstepping Jewish sensibilities by constructing his new capital city, Tiberias, on a graveyard (thus on unclean ground) and for placing images in public places.[32] In general, however, he seems to have avoided offending his Jewish subjects in obvious ways, even if his own Jewish religiosity was vitiated by his primary commitments to Rome and Hellenism. It was this loyalty to Rome and concomitant concerns of a political nature that led to his unpopular imprisonment and execution of John the Baptist[33] — an action likely preserved in the memory of Luke's audience already and in any case noted in the immediate co-text (3:19-20). This, together with Herod's role in the execution of Jesus (cf. 23:6-12; Acts 4:27), may well have been resident in the presupposition pool assumed by Luke.

It is less clear why Luke includes Philip and Lysanias in this list of rulers. Philip reigned from 4 B.C.E to 34 CE in a largely Gentile area situated in the northeastern section of the former kingdom of Herod the Great. Because of his locale and the make-up of his realm, he was able to take Hellenization

28. Philo *Leg. Gai.* 37 §§301-2.

29. See Josephus *J.W.* 2.9.2-4 §§169-77; *Ant.* 18.2.2 §35; 18.3.1-2 §§55-62; 18.4.1-2 §§85-89; Philo *Leg. Gai.* 38 §§299-305; Luke 13:1; E. Mary Smallwood, *The Jews under Roman Rule: From Pompey to Diocletian*, SJLA 20 (Leiden: Brill, 1976) 160-74.

30. Tacitus *Ann.* 15.44.4.

31. *Pace* Joseph A. Fitzmyer, *The Gospel according to Luke: Introduction, Translation, and Notes*, 2 vols., AB28-28A (Garden City: Doubleday, 1981/85) 1:453.

32. Josephus *Ant.* 18.2.3 §§36-38; *Life* §§65-66.

33. See Josephus *Ant.* 18.5.2 §§116-19.

much farther than his contemporaries to the south. Almost nothing is known of Lysanias, who reigned over Abilene, located to the north of the Sea of Galilee, from *ca.* 28 CE to *ca.* 29-37 CE. It may be that they are mentioned because they help to extend the local geographical references to include the Gentile world of the empire in a more pointed way.

A further puzzle arises in 3:2a with the mention of "the high priesthood [singular] of Annas and Caiaphas [plural]." Annas was high priest from 6-15 CE; following him in this office were his five sons, his son-in-law Joseph Caiaphas (18-36/37 CE), and, perhaps, a grandson.[34] Hence, even though Caiaphas would have been the high priest during the period in question, the continuing presence of Annas throughout this period must have been ominous. His near-dynastic control of the office would explain Luke's usage here. This would also suggest that the real point of interest here is not the office per se, but the power resident in these individuals who controlled the temple and its machinations (cf. Acts 4:6). The role of the temple as the socioreligious focal point of Israel is important to recognize in this context. As the head of the temple and its cult, Caiaphas and Annas would have exercised virtually unrivaled power and privilege among the Jewish people.

Luke's synchronism in 3:1-2a thus provides more than a historical setting or local color for the narrative. Rather it bespeaks a particular tension-filled, top-heavy, sociohistorical milieu. Read in light of 1:5–2:52, these geopolitical references can be taken in no way other than in a negative light, for the rich and mighty have been located on the side of the opponents of God's purpose. That this is a viable reading is immediately confirmed in the Lukan narrative itself — most markedly by the opposition to John leading to his arrest by Herod (3:19-20), but also by the pronounced contrast between these rulers and John's appearance: They carry the legitimation of the ruler cult or the imprimatur of the empire or both, they possess wealth, and they represent the urban elite. But he has been empowered by God and is located in the wilderness.

The wilderness is reminiscent of the formative event in Israel's life as a nation, the exodus, and biblical and extrabiblical tradition came to associate the wilderness with a new exodus.[35] This tradition encourages an

---

34. Josephus *Ant.* 18.2.1-2 §§26-34; 18.2.2 §35; 18.4.3 §95; 18.5.3 §123; 19.6.4 §§313-16; 20.9.1 §§197-98; 20.9.7 §223.

35. E.g., Isa 35:1-2; 40:3-5; Ezek 20:33-44; Hos 2:14-23; Mic 7:15; CD 8:12-16; 1QS 9:20; Ulrich W. Mauser, *Christ in the Wilderness: The Wilderness Theme in the Second*

association of John's prophetic ministry with eschatological deliverance and portrays the powerful of 3:1-2a as those from whom God's people would be delivered (cf. 1:68-79).

Verse 3b provides a summary description of his ministry as one of "proclaiming," using the verb κηρύσσω *(kēryssō)*, which is used occasionally in the LXX with a similar sense — namely, for the announcement of imminent, eschatological judgment.[36] In Luke-Acts the word has no particularly messianic or eschatological sense, though it is used regularly to summarize the mission of God's messengers, often with the kingdom of God or the significance of Jesus as the content of what is prolaimed.[37] Interestingly, in Acts 10:37 John's mission is again characterized as one of proclaiming, and this assists Luke's overall identification of John as the Isaianic herald of redemption (Isa 40:1-9; Luke 3:4-6). Luke, however, in no way distinguishes John's mission as qualitatively distinct from that of the Christian movement, as though it were somehow provisional or belonged to a different age in salvation history. Indeed, the fundamental elements of John's ministry — proclamation + repentance + forgiveness of sins — are paralleled in the ministry to which Jesus' followers are commissioned in Luke 24:47.

What of John's baptism? Three critical issues deserve mention. First, John's baptism is necessarily qualified as a "repentance-baptism," so that his proclamation and baptism are inseparably connected. He thus follows biblical precedent in insisting on the correlation of cleansing and moral rectitude. Second, his emphasis on repentance signals his understanding that the status quo of his sociohistorical environment has been found wanting. As such, his message constitutes a prophetic appeal for people to turn their backs on previous loyalties and commitments and align themselves fundamentally with God's purpose. Third, by definition forgiveness of sins has a profound communal dimension: As sin is the means by which persons exclude themselves from community with God's people, so forgiveness marks their restoration to the community. These points will surface in greater detail in 3:7-18, where this mission summary is illustrated with the words of John.

Gospel and Its Basis in the Biblical Tradition, SBT 39 (London: SCM, 1963) 44-58; cf. Shemaryahu Talmon, "The 'Desert Motif' in the Bible and in Qumran Literature," in *Biblical Motifs: Origins and Transformations,* ed. Alexander Altmann (Cambridge: Harvard University, 1966) 31-63.

36. Cf. Isa 61:1; Joel 2:1; Zeph 3:14-15; Zech 9:9.

37. Cf. 4:18-19, 44; 8:1; 9:2; 24:47; Acts 8:5; 9:20; 10:42; 19:13; 20:25; 28:31.

First, however, Luke introduces into the narrative a pause during which he provides a direct scriptural voice as an unimpeachable witness to John's significance in God's redemptive design. Luke has chosen this point to interrupt the flow of action in order to pursue his own interpretive (persuasive!) agenda. John is set within a particular sociopolitical context (3:1-2a), but he can only be understood rightly with reference to his role as the Isaianic herald. In citing Isa 40:3-5, Luke is not so concerned with presenting John as the "fulfillment" of this passage as he is in locating John and the sequence of events of which John is a part within this redemptive-historical context. In doing so, he does not extract Isa 40:3-5 from its Isaianic co-text; rather, Luke's text both absorbs and transforms the earlier text. Luke exploits Isaiah 40's concern for the advent of God and the decisive consolation of Israel; John's is the proclaiming voice and the herald of good news (cf. Isa 40:3, 9; Luke 3:3, 4, 18). Set now within the co-text of Luke's Gospel, Isaiah's words will be read in fresh ways, but precisely because these are Isaiah's words (explicitly stated in 3:4a) Luke's narrative is enriched by the Isaianic vision of eschatological salvation.

The citation of Isa 40:3-5 at this juncture is far from abrupt and is an event for which Luke has obviously prepared. As a result it picks up key terms of the narrative and both interprets and is interpreted by its co-text: (1) We have already noted the importance of the "wilderness" due to its associations with the new exodus (cf. 1:80; 3:2, 4). (2) Since the first mention of John's birth we have been aware of his role as the one who prepares the way of the Lord (1:17, 76; 3:4; cf. 2:31). By this point in the narrative, the original proposal that John's ministry would prepare for the coming of Yahweh (1:17) has undergone a crucial shift. By "Lord" we now understand "Jesus," as in 1:43, 76; 2:11. This interpretation of divine redemption along christological lines is further advanced by Luke's amendment of the Isaianic text — from "make straight the paths of our God" to "make *his* paths straight." "His" now refers to the coming one, whom we know to be Jesus, the Lord.

(3) According to 1:16-17 and 3:3, "preparation" has taken the explicit form of turning to God and embracing God's purpose — or, in this co-text, undergoing repentance-baptism and living transformed lives (3:3, 7-14). (4) Closely related is the importance of "the way," mentioned in 1:76, 79; 3:4-5,[38] but later used in an absolute sense of the church in Acts 9:2; 19:9,

---

38. Note that ὁδός (*hodos*, "road, way") in 3:5 is a Lukan innovation vis-à-vis the LXX, which reads πεδίον (*pedion*, "level place").

23; 22:4; 24:14, 22.[39] Luke's subsequent use of the term seems to be rooted here in the designation of a people who align themselves with and serve God's salvific aim. (5) The metaphorical language related to the straightening of the path in 3:5 must be understood as both an echo of earlier language of transposition in 1:52-53; 2:34 and as a reminder that John's purpose is to prepare a people ready to receive the Lord, having themselves undergone repentance (i.e., "made straight . . . and smooth").

(6) Luke's citation of Isa 40:3-5 employs the vocabulary of salvation, language with which the reader is already familiar (1:47, 69, 71, 77; 2:11; 3:6) and that therefore must be interpreted in the holistic ways encountered in, for instance, 1:46-55, 68-79. (7) Finally, the scope of God's salvation is again identified as universal (cf. 1:55, 73; 2:14, 31-32; 3:6). John's ministry may be more narrowly directed to Israel (cf. 1:16; 3:3), but it is a part of God's larger project of bringing redemption to all humanity.

In this way, the Isaianic vision of eschatological consolation has been recontextualized, focused on the events set in motion with John's appearance. With this interpretive pause complete, Luke can now return to the narration of John's activity among those who came out to participate in his ministry.

5. Suggestions for Further Reading

Perhaps the best entry into discourse analysis is provided by Gillian Brown and George Yule, *Discourse Analysis*, CTL (Cambridge: Cambridge University, 1983). One may also wish to refer to Malcolm Coulthard, *An Introduction to Discourse Analysis*, 2d ed. (London: Longman, 1985), and David Nunan, *Introducing Discourse Analysis* (Harmondsworth: Penguin, 1993).

The sociolinguistic end of discourse analysis is helpfully developed by Michael Stubbs, *Discourse Analysis: The Sociolinguistic Analysis of Language*, LS 4 (Chicago: University of Chicago, 1983), and Ralph Fasold, *Sociolinguistics of Language*, LS 6 (Cambridge: Blackwell, 1990). Other significant subdivisions of discourse analysis are covered in Stephen C. Levinson, *Pragmatics*, CTL (Cambridge: Cambridge University, 1983); and Jean Caron, *An Introduction to Psycho-Linguistics* (Toronto: University of Toronto, 1992).

How texts *and* readers shape interpretation is developed well in Um-

---

39. Cf. 1QS 9:17-18; 10:21.

berto Eco, *The Role of the Reader: Explorations in the Semiotics of Texts,* AS (Bloomington: Indiana University, 1979). The text-linguistic focus of this phenomenon has been the interest of most NT discourse analysis — cf. A. H. Snyman, "Discourse Analysis: A Semantic Discourse Analysis of the Letter to Philemon," in *Text and Interpretation: New Approaches in the Criticism of the New Testament,* ed. P. J. Hartin and J. H. Petzer, NTTS (Leiden: Brill, 1991) 83-99; and David Alan Black, et al., eds., *Linguistics and New Testament Interpretation: Essays on Discourse Analysis* (Nashville: Broadman, 1992).

For the more recent recognition of issues of power in their relation to discourse, see Pierre Bourdieu, *Language and Symbolic Power* (Cambridge: Harvard University, 1991), and the more difficult work by Diane Macdonell, *Theories of Discourse: An Introduction* (Oxford: Blackwell, 1986). Of course, the myriad works of Michel Foucault are foundational on this issue.

Finally, on the role of sociohistorical context in the generation of discourse and its cultural products and on the potential of that discourse to subvert its context, see the programmatic work of Robert Wuthnow, *Communities of Discourse* (Cambridge: Harvard University, 1989).

10. Genre Analysis

James L. Bailey

1. The Importance of Genre

Many contemporary students of the Bible underestimate the importance of genre analysis[1] for at least two reasons: First, there is little common knowledge of the patterned ways in which ancient peoples communicated. Second, since our own speech conventions appear so commonplace to us, we seldom reflect on the multiple forms we use in our own social interactions.

In any society, people interact with one another by using conventional, repeatable patterns of speech. Without these speech patterns, these "well-worn grooves of expectation,"[2] social life could not flow smoothly. When we meet or take leave of one another, for example, we utter predictable greetings and parting phrases. When we participate in a business meeting, we recognize and understand specific oral and writing forms (e.g., the

---

1. In *Literary Forms in the New Testament: A Handbook* (Louisville: Westminster/John Knox, 1992), which I coauthored with Lyle Vander Broek, we used the term "literary form" for shorter recognizable forms like pronouncement story or miracle story and "genre" for the longer, more complex literary types like apocalypse, Gospel, and letter. In this chapter, however, it seems better not to press that distinction. Instead, I use "genre" interchangeably of any recognizable and repeatable speech pattern of sufficient length, whether oral or written. German scholars use the word *Gattung* in this way.

2. I owe this description of a speech or literary generic form to James Nieman, Assistant Professor of Homiletics at Wartburg Theological Seminary.

reading of the "minutes" followed by the chair's call for corrections or additions before approval). When we attend a service of worship, we take part in a known liturgical pattern that incorporates numerous recognizable types of material (e.g., antiphonal responses, creeds, hymns, prayers and litanies, and baptismal and eucharistic rites).

Over the years scholars have learned to identify in biblical literature such "well-worn grooves of expectation" in that literature, classifying them according to specific formal types or genres. Because of the biblical cultures' foreignness to us westerners who live in the twentieth century, this is no simple task. Even today, although we can learn the grammar and vocabulary of a contemporary language, we can still miss what is going on in a foreign country because we do not recognize the generic speech patterns. We do not know the genres the persons in the other culture employ in greeting one another, in conversing with the elderly or highly respected persons, or for responding in a classroom or a liturgical service. In the same way, when reading the NT we will not appreciate what is going on with biblical texts if we do not recognize the operative genres and their specific uses.

In NT studies, the first researchers to focus on genre forms were the form critics Martin Dibelius and Rudolf Bultmann.[3] Following the lead of Hermann Gunkel's form-critical work on the stories in Genesis and on the Psalms, they sought to identify and classify the patterns of the stories and sayings material that circulated during the oral tradition before the writing of the Synoptic Gospels.[4]

---

3. See Vernon Robbins, "Form Criticism," in *ABD*, 2:841-44, for a concise summary of the form-critical contributions of Dibelius and Bultmann.

4. Martin Dibelius, *From Tradition to Gospel* (2d ed., Cambridge/London: Clarke, 1971), described six types of material in the Synoptic Gospels: sermon, paradigm (brief example story), tale, legend, passion story, and myth. In contrast, Rudolf Bultmann, *The History of the Synoptic Tradition* (Oxford: Basil Blackwell, 1963), divided the material into sayings of Jesus and narratives about Jesus. He further classified the sayings as apophthegms (brief narratives, each culminating in a saying of Jesus) and independent sayings of Jesus. He subdivided apophthegms into (1) conflict and didactic sayings and (2) biographical apophthegms; under independent sayings of Jesus he included (1) sayings representing Jesus as a wisdom teacher, (2) prophetic and apocalyptic sayings, (3) legal sayings and church rules, (4) "I" sayings such as "I have come to call not the righteous but sinners," and (5) similitudes and related forms. Bultmann's subclassifications of the narrative material included the following forms: miracle stories (with subtypes being miracles of healing and nature miracles) and historical stories and legends (which include various stories about Jesus, the passion narratives, Easter narratives, and infancy narratives).

These early form critics also conjectured about the "setting in life" (in German, *Sitz im Leben*) or social arena and the function of these sayings and stories in the early church. Dibelius suggested that the preaching of the earliest Christians was the functional arena in which these oral forms were used and preserved. Bultmann, on the other hand, argued for a multiplicity of situations including teaching and conflict settings.

The conclusions of form critics, focused solely on the shape, content, and function of oral forms, have been vital to the progress of NT study. Yet genre analysis intends to be more comprehensive in scope. Since the germinal work of Dibelius and Bultmann on the Synoptic tradition, considerable progress has been made by scholars in expanding the range and nature of analysis. For instance, they have used various methods to increase our understanding of how Jesus' sayings and parables function or how pronouncement stories or miracle stories unfold. Beyond these rather succinct forms originally investigated by form critics (aphoristic sayings, parables, pronouncement stories, miracle stories), contemporary scholars have expanded our knowledge by describing the formal features of longer literary genres such as the ancient letter, apocalypse, biography, and history. The last two have been studied with a concern for the character and function of the Gospels.

As interpreters of the NT, we engage in genre analysis whenever we seek to identify and understand the character and function of any text, whether it be short or long, simple or complex, originating in an oral or literary environment. When interpreting a lengthy NT text, we will often encounter more than one genre. When Paul dictates a letter to a community of Christians, for example, he modifies the epistolary genre known in the Hellenistic world, and he usually incorporates shorter genres such as a vice or virtue list, paraenesis (exhortation material), and liturgical and hymnic forms. In 1 Cor 11:2-34, for instance, he inserts a liturgical form that undoubtedly originated in Christian celebration of the Lord's Supper (see vv. 23b-25). Several genres are evident in the Book of Revelation, which is an apocalyptic narrative that includes both epistolary and liturgical forms. In Rev 5:1-14, for example, the apocalyptic narrative incorporates the victory song genre (vv. 9-10, 12, 13b).

2. Understanding and Identifying Genres

Before attempting to suggest a method for genre analysis of NT texts, we should explore further the character and profound importance of genre forms.

2.1 A Basic Definition of Genre

Genres are the conventional and repeatable patterns of oral and written speech, which facilitate interaction among people in specific social situations. Decisive to this basic definition are three aspects: *patternedness, social setting,* and *rhetorical impact.*

Once a genre's generalizable pattern of content and structure is established, that pattern can be conventionally repeated or modified in a significant manner. Where it is conventionally repeated, the use of the genre reinforces the expected exchange. Where the pattern is modified, its use subverts in some way the normal social interaction. For example, a young woman repeatedly writes letters to her boyfriend, beginning each letter "Dearest Eric" and closing with "All my love, Anne." Then one day Eric receives a letter from Anne that begins "Dear Eric" and simply ends "Yours truly, Anne." The modified form creates a dramatically different impact on Eric.

Normally, genres facilitate human interaction within predictable social settings. A conventional farewell is employed when parties take leave of each other, not when they meet. On the other hand, the use of a specific genre in a social setting different from what is expected alters its impact on those involved. For example, Christians expect to sing Easter hymns during the Easter season, but if they are invited to sing an Easter hymn on Christmas, this same hymnic genre will exercise quite an unusual impact on them.

In summary, then, the rhetorical impact of using a specific genre depends on both the way the genre pattern is employed and the kind of social setting in which it is used. A genre can be utilized to reinforce or to subvert the expected.

2.2 Bakhtin's Contribution to Understanding Genres

The theoretical work of Mikhail Bakhtin can help us deepen our understanding of genres.[5] Bakhtin draws the following conclusions regarding genres:

5. Mikhail Bakhtin was born in 1895 and died in 1975. Because of the repressive Stalinist years, Bakhtin's thought was not discovered and discussed, even in his own country of Russia, until the 1950s and 1960s. For a summary of Bakhtin's thoughts about genres, see "Theory of Genres" in Gary Saul Morson and Caryl Emerson, *Mikhail Bakhtin: Creation of a Prosaics* (Stanford: Stanford University, 1990) 271-305.

1. Each genre is "a specific way of visualizing a given part of reality."[6] In response to those theorists who suggested that a genre is simply a collection of linguistic devices and elements, the construction of constituent parts into a larger whole, Bakhtin argues that every genre is a way of seeing a specific aspect of experience. For example, a legal genre has as its perspective on experience the need to set ideal standards or to regulate human behavior or both. In contrast, a brief story tends to focus on the anecdotal quality of everyday experience. If, indeed, every genre is a distinctive way of viewing a particular aspect of reality, then it follows that one genre is not reducible to a set of data or simply transferrable to another genre form. Hence, a parabolic story of Jesus cannot be transformed into an explanation of what the story means without a severe loss.

Further, since every genre involves a selective way of visualizing an aspect of reality, it combines "specific blindnesses and insights."[7] An author's selection of a specific genre, thus, is a choice for some viewpoint and against another. For instance, to criticize a political leader, a newspaper editor might select an editorial or a political cartoon. The former functions by logic and persuasion, the latter by exaggerated humor. Or in the biblical literature, a discursive segment of a Pauline letter operates basically in an explanatory and persuasive mode, whereas the poetic lines of a hymn used by Paul in a letter function primarily in a celebrative mode.

2. Genres emerge from repeated social interactions within specific arenas of life and are normally employed within the same or similar social contexts. In other words, genres are socially shaped and socially located. For example, liturgical forms like hymns and benedictions develop and function within the activity of worship, legal forms within judicial settings, and wisdom forms within settings for schooling the young in traditional insights. Of course, a genre can function in a social sphere remote from its origin. The author of Revelation, for example, can use a funeral dirge form in an apocalyptic narrative (Rev 18:2-3), not the original context for its use. When this happens, the genre likely subverts normal expectations.

3. Most cultures exhibit a rich repertoire of genres, offering a wide range of particularized visions of reality. It follows that a variety of experiences and social interactions calls for a multiplicity of genre forms. Genres reveal the diverse, though interrelated, contexts in which people in a particular culture

---

6. Morson and Emerson, "Theory of Genres," 275, who note that in this basic understanding of genre Bakhtin agrees with the thinking of P. N. Medvedev.

7. Morson and Emerson, "Theory of Genres," 276.

must continually negotiate transactions and relationships — commercial, military, political, legal, familial, sexual, and cultic contexts, for example. A hymnic genre functions quite differently from a political treatise. A business contract differs from a love song. All these various genres, Bakhtin asserts, cannot be simply integrated into some theoretical system since each of them represents a specific social interaction and a distinct perspective on reality. It is the rich variety of genres in a culture that allows for creative possibilities and interplay in both speech and literature.

4. *Genres take shape over generations and even centuries,* "crystalizing" specific ways a culture comes to "see" its experiences and history.[8] Bakhtin's appreciation of the long-term development of a genre form prompts him to label genre as a key "organ of memory."[9] A genre becomes a way of transmitting previous experiences and insights from one generation to another. Because genres carry the memory of the past, they become laden with potential meaning. "Genres (of literature and speech) throughout the centuries of their life accumulate forms of seeing and interpreting particular aspects of the world."[10] The content and shape of Jesus' story of God's beloved vineyard in Mark 12:1-12 must have stirred emotion and pathos in hearers who were familiar with the "love song" genre in Isa 5:1-7. The Markan story, because of its connection with Isaiah 5, shapes the present experience of the hearers by recalling the past experience of Israel.

5. *Changes in "real social life" can modify a genre to such an extent that a new genre emerges.* In such a case, a reciprocal dynamic occurs. Changes in the actual social life coupled with new views of these experiences lead to "different genres of speech, social behavior, and literature," and then these new genres "may teach people to see aspects of reality in a new way. . . ."[11] As a contemporary example, wedding invitations and marriage ceremonies have changed due to the shift in the social role of women. No longer, for example, is the bride normally asked in the liturgy to honor and obey her husband, and this new marriage liturgy alters peoples' understandings of the marital relationship. In the NT, the Gospel narrative may provide an example of an innovative genre: It borrows features from ancient biography and historiography but finally presents a new mixed literary genre as a way to express the surprising quality of Jesus' ministry, death, and resurrection.

8. Morson and Emerson, "Theory of Genres," 278.
9. Morson and Emerson, "Theory of Genres," 280.
10. Morson and Emerson, "Theory of Genres," 288.
11. Morson and Emerson, "Theory of Genres," 277.

6. Major genre forms exhibit flexibility and can be used in surprising ways.
In a real sense, a genre pattern is a theoretical abstraction derived by scholars observing specific concrete examples. Concretizing the genre involves choices and even allows creativity on the part of the speaker or writer.

> Genres carry the generalizable resources of particular events: but specific actions or utterances must use those resources to accomplish new purposes in each unrepeatable milieu. Each utterance, each use of a genre, demands real work; beginning with the given, something different must be created.[12]

This means that when we interpret NT texts we must analyze how, for example, a legal genre, dialogue genre, or story genre is, in fact, used. Genres significant to a culture, shaped over generations, are not inflexible vessels into which content is poured. Rather, they are supple and malleable organic forms that can be shaped to convey old insights while creating new ones. In the NT, Paul's creative use of the epistolary form illustrates this dynamic. For example, the apostle revised the typical salutation by adding a "grace and peace" greeting and then changed the normal "thanksgiving" section by both Christianizing and expanding it.

Bakhtin's thinking definitely enriches our understanding of the character and function of genres in a culture. Each genre is distinct and perspectival, is socially shaped and located, plays its part in a cultural repertoire of genre forms, bears cultural memory, and is both modifiable and flexible.

2.3 The Task of Identifying and Analyzing Genres

The form and shape of every portion of the NT have resulted from genre choices made by someone or some group at some point in the development of the tradition. That choice of genre, it should be obvious, is not trivial. It carries implications for the interpretive understanding of that text, including its rhetorical impact on hearers today. Hence, it is important to arrive at a process that can provide guidance for identifying and analyzing genre forms.

1. Learning to recognize general types of literature in the New Testament.
Even a rapid reading of the NT alerts the reader to some obvious literary types. For example, a perusal of the Gospel of Matthew in the NRSV reveals a narrative style that incorporates shorter stories. Occasionally material within the larger narrative is indented, its lines presented in a parallel or

---

12. Morson and Emerson, "Theory of Genres," 291.

poetic style. Numerous quotations of texts in the Hebrew Scriptures are presented in this manner. But there are other forms as well. The beatitudes in 5:3-10 repeat a paralleling pattern. The Lord's Prayer in 6:9b-13 discloses a poetic form. The NRSV's formatting of 10:34-39, with its allusion to Mic 7:6, demonstrates that many of Jesus' sayings utilize rhythmic parallelism, a chief characteristic of Hebrew poetry.[13] Carefully shaped thought-lines in Jesus' sayings often represent synonymous or antithetical parallelism. The former, found more frequently, includes lines that express the same or similar thought in somewhat different words; the latter consists of parallel lines that voice the opposite thought. Both types of parallelism appear in Matt 10:34-39, and this cluster of Jesus' sayings can be easily lined out in the following manner to make explicit this poetic patterning:

Antithetical Parallelism

Do not think that I have come to bring peace to the earth;
> I have not come to bring peace, but a sword.

Synonymous Parallelism

For I have come to set a man against his father,
> and a daughter against her mother,
> and a daughter-in-law against her mother-in-law;
> and one's foes will be members of one's own household.

Whoever loves father or mother more than me is not worthy of me;
> and whoever loves son or daughter more than me
>> is not worthy of me;
> and whoever does not take up the cross and follow me
>> is not worthy of me.

Antithetical Reversed Parallelism (Chiasm)

Those who find their life will lose it,
> and those who lose their life for my sake will find it.

In addition to the narratives of the Gospels, which incorporate sayings material and other poetic units such as prayers or liturgical formulas, the

---

13. See "Literary Forms in the Gospels," in *The New Oxford Annotated Bible with the Apocryphal/Deuterocanonical Books,* ed. Bruce M. Metzger and Roland E. Murphy (New York: Oxford University, 1991) 398, for a brief explanation with examples of biblical parallelism.

reader also discovers the narrative form in Acts and Revelation. In Revelation, however, the narrative relates an apocalyptic vision received by a seer. Even a quick look at the NRSV translation of the Book of Revelation reveals that this apocalypse incorporates a variety of other genres: letter forms (2:1–3:22), hymnic and doxological forms (4:8b, 11; 5:9-10, 12, 13b; 7:10, 12), a funeral dirge form (18:2-3), and various prophetic forms.

Turning to the Pauline writings, the reader encounters a Hellenistic letter form, including its subgenres of salutation, thanksgiving, body, exhortation (or *paraenesis*), travelogue, greeting, doxology, blessing, and benediction. The reader should sense that the Pauline letters offer a quite different genre of literature from that of the narrative worlds of the Gospels and Acts. They involve more manifestly a style of rhetorical persuasion and argumentation. Other NT writings adopt a letter form (e.g., James, 1-2 Peter) with rather different results from the genuine letters of Paul. Hebrews offers a treatise-like genre and functions as a rather sophisticated theological argument with a pronounced hortatory element.

2. Learning to analyze the interplay between narrative and speech in the Gospels and Acts. One useful way an interpreter can analyze smaller textual units in the Synoptic Gospels, Acts, and John is to observe carefully the alternation between narration and speech in the inner development of a pericope.[14] This analysis results in the following elementary classification of forms:

- *Action Story* (including most Miracle Stories): This type of story can include limited speech, but the narration of the action clearly governs the story (e.g., Mark 7:31-37).
- *Pronouncement Story:* The initial narration of action or of a person's question (often that of an opponent) prepares the way for the concluding saying of the story's protagonist (e.g., Mark 2:23-28 culminates in Jesus' final declarations in vv. 27-28).
- *Dialogical Story:* Dialogue between two characters[15] dominates the story (e.g., the temptation story in Matt 4:1-11).
- *Monological Argument Story:* The speech of one character in the larger

14. For the basic categorization of stories that results from an analysis of the interplay between narration and speech I am indebted to Vernon Robbins of Emory University.

15. It is important to understand that a "group" such as the crowd or the Pharisees often serves as a single character in the Gospel stories. See Mark Allan Powell, *What Is Narrative Criticism?* (Minneapolis: Fortress, 1990) 51.

narrative overshadows everything else. The most obvious examples appear in the Gospel of John, even though Jesus' monologues often follow question-and-answer dialogues (e.g., John 3:1-21).

- *Dialogue:* The narration is largely or completely absent and the speech of two characters appears in the form of a dialogical exchange. Little material in the Gospels and Acts represents this type, although the "Farewell Discourses" in John 13–16 are a dialogue in which Jesus' speech surpasses in importance the questions and interjections of his disciples.
- *Monologue:* The speech of one character in the larger narrative is given singular prominence. The major segments in the Gospel of Matthew devoted to the extended speech of Jesus provide examples of this type (e.g., Jesus' teachings in Matt 5:3–7:27, typically labeled his "Sermon on the Mount").
- *Citation Story:* In this type of story, a citation of a text with clear authority for the audience occupies a central place. In the Gospels and Acts these citations are almost exclusively of texts in the Hebrew Scriptures (e.g., Matt 1:18-25).

3. Learning to recognize the NT's rich and varied repertoire of genres. At this point, it is important for the beginning interpreter of the NT to understand that repeated reading of NT writings in English translation or even a painstaking analysis of the interplay between the use of narration and speech in biblical materials will not allow one to discover all the genre forms that scholars have identified and analyzed over the years. In addition to reading and analysis, the novice in NT interpretation must also study scholarly resources that classify, describe, and provide examples of the various genres, since in many respects the Hellenistic world is alien to persons in the twentieth century.

Scholars have identified genres in the NT by studying forms in both biblical and extrabiblical literature. Many of these identified genre forms exhibit similarities with genres used in the Hebrew Scriptures. Yet it is often difficult to determine if a specific NT genre owes its patterned structure and content primarily to the Jewish tradition, to the Greco-Roman milieu, or to an interaction of these cultural worlds during the Hellenistic period.

The following list of genres is catalogued under the three major sections of the NT: Pauline letters, Gospels and Acts, and other writings.[16]

16. This list is based on David E. Aune, *The New Testament in Its Literary Environ-*

The Pauline Tradition:
- letter genre
- apocalyptic speech (relating visions of the divinely revealed future)
- other apocalyptic forms
- speech forms (judicial, deliberative, and epideictic rhetoric)
- encomium (form designed to praise a person)
- salutation
- thanksgiving
- creed and confession
- prayer
- hymnic form
- blessing and doxology
- greeting and benediction
- diatribe (a dialogical form with a moral purpose)
- midrashic form (use of an authoritative text for a later situation)
- paraenesis (a form of exhortation)
- paraenetical topoi (statements focused on particular themes and topics)
- vice and virtue lists (lists of proscribed and recommended behaviors)
- household code (or *Haustafel*)
- chiasm (form exhibiting reversed parallelism of two or more elements)
- travelogue

The Gospels and Acts:
- Gospel genre (related to ancient biography and history)
- sayings of Jesus (involves various aphorisms, including beatitudes, woes, maxims, prophetic and apocalyptic sayings, legal sayings, etc.)
- proverb (unattributed wisdom saying)
- dialogue and monologue
- parable (including similitude, parable proper, and example story)
- revelatory speech (in John's Gospel)
- pronouncement story (variously labeled as paradigm, apophthegm, and chreia)
- miracle story (including exorcism story)
- call story (related to commissioning story)
- stories about Jesus (including infancy and passion narratives)

---

ment, LEC 8 (Philadelphia: Westminster, 1987); Bailey and Vander Broek, *Literary Forms in the New Testament;* and articles in *ABD.*

- genealogy
- summary report
- hymnic form
- prayer
- liturgy
- midrashic form
- chiastic form
- symposium (dinner setting for dialogue, discourse, and other forms)

Other Writings
- apocalypse
- homily
- baptismal liturgy
- treatise

4. Identifying the Structural Features of Specific Genres. The scholarly research leading to genre identification has proceeded in at least two ways. First, scholars have identified the "family resemblances" germane to a specific genre category. Subsequent investigation often refines and sub-divides such a category on the basis of observation of elements that distinguish various types within the genre. Beginning interpreters need to familiarize themselves with the "family resemblances" that characterize a particular genre and, wherever applicable, the more sophisticated process of subdividing a genre into distinguishable subtypes. The need for such detailed knowledge is best illustrated by describing three genres, one from each of the lists noted above:

Diatribe:[17] Although the word "diatribe" has come to have a negative modern meaning, it can simply mean "discourse" or a "short ethical treatise or lecture."[18] The term was originally associated with the lectures and conversations employed in philosophical schools, but "the modern scholarly concept of the diatribe is most closely linked to the use of the word for the records, literary by-products, or imitations of such teaching activity."[19] Thus, the diatribe was a rhetorical method used for moral-ped-

---

17. See Stanley K. Stowers: *The Diatribe and Paul's Letter to the Romans,* SBLDS 57 (Chico: Scholars, 1981); *idem,* "Diatribe," in *Greco-Roman Literature and the New Testament,* ed. David. E. Aune (Atlanta: Scholars, 1988) 71-84; and *idem,* "Diatribe," in *ABD,* 2:190-93. Compare also Bailey and Vander Broek, *Literary Forms,* 38-42.

18. LSJ, 416.

19. Stowers, "Diatribe" *(ABD),* 190.

agogical purposes. The clearest examples of its use in the NT are in Romans, especially 3:1-9 and 3:27–4:2 (cf. also 6:1, 15; 7:7, 13; 9:14, 19; 11:1, 19).

As Stowers notes, the diatribe style combines smoothly with Paul's epistolary style. The diatribe pursues a conversation in which the author's direct address is aimed at an imaginary "discussion partner."[20] The conversation normally proceeds with the imaginary partner expressing objections in the form of questions, which provide the author the opportunity to supply answers to the objections. Sometimes the questions arise from false inferences drawn from the teacher's words. The teacher can use irony and sarcasm. The diatribe form is appropriate to a variety of topics relating to morality and manner of life, and often takes on a hortatory tone.

Pronouncement Story:[21] This term is used of a brief story that culminates in a saying (and sometimes an action) of Jesus. Such a story has two main parts, the setting for the pronouncement and the pronouncement itself, that is, "the response and the situation provoking the response."[22] Often in the Synoptic Gospels, this type of story presents an antagonistic confrontation between Jesus and his opponents.

Scholars have consistently placed eleven stories in the Synoptic Gospels within this literary genre (Mark 2:15-17, 18-22, 23-28; 3:31-34; 10:13-16, 17-22, 35-40; 12:13-17, 18-27; 14:3-9; Luke 14:1-6), but they have used different terms for this type of story: apophthegm (Bultmann), paradigm (Dibelius), and pronouncement story (Taylor). More recently, some scholars have recovered the ancient rhetorical category "chreia" (Hock, Mack, Robbins), or have used the less technical term "anecdote" (Robbins) to refer to any kind of concise story or anecdote that attributes a notable statement or action to a specific person.[23]

Because of its wide and varied use in the Hellenistic period, the chreia has significantly enlarged the working definition of what constitutes a pronouncement story so that over one hundred textual units in the Gospels and Acts are now being classified under this genre.[24] Yet at the same time some scholars have refined their analysis of pronouncement stories by distinguishing subtypes. For example, Tannehill has divided them into

20. Stowers, "Diatribe" *(ABD)*, 191.
21. Compare the two articles in *ADB* on "Apophthegm" by Vernon K. Robbins (1:307-9); and "Chreia" by Ronald F. Hock (1:912-14). See also Bailey and Vander Broek, *Literary Forms,* 114-22.
22. Robbins, "Apophthegm," 307.
23. Robbins, "Apophthegm," 307-8.
24. Robbins, "Apophthegm," 308-9.

correction stories, commendation stories, objection stories, quest stories, inquiry stories, and description stories.[25]

Apocalypse:[26] The Book of Revelation provides the best known Christian example of the apocalypse genre. Hanson suggests that the first two verses of Revelation mention the basic elements in this narrative genre: (1) a revelation given by God, (2) communicated through an "otherworldly mediator," (3) directed to a "human seer," (4) "disclosing future events," and (5) often including a clear note of admonition.[27] Apocalypse is thus the term reserved for a complex apocalyptic narrative such as the Book of Revelation, which has at its center a visionary account. But this Christian apocalypse makes use of numerous briefer genres such as letter, doxology, blessing, and victory song.

2.4 The Relationship of Genre Analysis to Other Exegetical Methods

As we have noted, genre analysis builds on the efforts of the form critics, who analyzed genre forms that originated in an oral tradition. Yet it also investigates genres that began as literary forms. Moreover, genre analysis benefits from an interplay with other methods described in this volume.

Because genre analysis views genre forms as essentially social phenomena, it can profit immensely from historical study that employs social-scientific perspectives (see ch. 4 above). The more we can learn about the cultural patterns and realities of the Hellenistic world, the more we will understand the biblical repertoire of genres. Further, increased awareness of extra-canonical Jewish texts (ch. 5) and Greco-Roman literature (ch. 6) can disclose a wide range of genres employed in both realms of literature, genres that frequently have their counterparts in the NT writings. A significant task, then, is to determine whether and how known genres were adapted or modified by NT communities and which of these known genres were neglected or ignored by NT authors and communities.[28]

25. See Bailey and Vander Broek, *Literary Forms,* 115-16, for definitions and examples of these six subtypes.

26. See Aune, *Literary Environment,* 226-52; Bailey and Vander Broek, *Literary Forms,* 201-10; and Paul D. Hanson, A. Kirk Grayson, John J. Collins, and Adela Yarbro Collins, "Apocalypses and Apocalypticism," *ADB,* 1:279-92.

27. Paul D. Hanson, "Apocalypses and Apocalypticism: The Genre," *ADB,* 1:279-80, here 279.

28. See, e.g., Shaye J. D. Cohen, *From the Maccabees to the Mishnah,* LEC 7 (Philadel-

Obviously, literary genres use the grammatical and syntactical devices of the Greek language (see ch. 8), but they also involve utterances that employ linguistic structures in larger patterns with specific perspectives on real life. Narrative criticism (ch. 12) is a comprehensive analysis that includes sensitivity to the use of incorporated genres in the Gospels or Acts or in apocalyptic narrative such as Revelation. Rhetorical criticism (ch. 13), in its analysis of an entire writing (e.g., a Pauline letter) or shorter segments, must also be aware of genre patterns. Rhetorical practices of the ancient world created or at least refined specific genres.[29]

Since genres function as "organs of memory," they have much to do with how certain texts in the OT are used in the NT (see ch. 11). Their potential for a surplus of meaning enriches the scriptural echoes.

Liberation hermeneutics (ch. 16) and feminist hermeneutics (ch. 17) have among their concerns the ideological perspective of biblical texts. Is a specific text articulated by the perspective of the controlling class or the oppressed class? Is it perhaps told from an androcentric perspective? Since every genre offers a specific perspective on some aspect of experience, that perspective can be analyzed from its ideological slant. Feminist and liberationist approaches might be used to ask how the repertoire of biblical genres is heard and received by women and oppressed peoples.

Often in the past, theologians and ethicists have attended only to the content of texts, not their literary forms. In so doing, they have missed important clues for meaning. All study of the NT texts for theological and ethical enterprises needs to take seriously the import of the genre form of texts.

Clearly, genre analysis cannot proceed in isolation from other methods, especially rhetorical and narrative criticism. And we never encounter genre forms in abstraction, but rather always as they appear in concrete textual examples. Despite its limitations, genre analysis can prove invaluable to the interpreter of NT texts.

---

phia: Westminster, 1987) 174-213, for a careful discussion of Jewish literature and the development of canon.

29. Consult, for example, Burton L. Mack, *Rhetoric and the New Testament* (Minneapolis: Fortress, 1990), and Burton L. Mack and Vernon K. Robbins, *Patterns of Persuasion in the Gospels* (Sonoma: Polebridge, 1989), for introductions to the use of rhetoric in the ancient world and its application not only to epistolary material but also to Gospel narrative texts in the NT.

3. Genre Analysis in Practice

The fruitfulness of genre analysis can only be demonstrated by examining the genre forms germane to specific NT texts. On the one hand, interpreters need to consider the genre of the entire work in which a particular text appears; on the other, they must attend to any shorter genre forms within the text itself.

Since genres exhibit considerable fluidity and flexibility, interpreters need to observe closely how the genre form is precisely executed in the text under consideration. Although the scholarly description of genres is helpful, it unavoidably involves a theoretical abstraction. In the final analysis, the interpreter's knowledge of these scholarly discussions only guides the study of the particular text by providing clues regarding the genres.

In what follows I examine three texts to determine how genre analysis produces important insights into biblical texts. The three passages are rather lengthy segments of a Synoptic Gospel (Luke 3:1-20), a Pauline letter (1 Cor 11:2-34), and a Christian apocalypse (Rev 5:1-14).

3.1 Luke 3:1-20

In the NRSV Luke 3:1-20 is presented in paragraph form except for the scriptural citation in vv. 4b-6, where the poetic form is presented in indented parallel lines. In Luke's Gospel, this narrative segment featuring John son of Zechariah in the desert follows the Lukan stories that relate the circumstances surrounding the births of John and Jesus and precedes the description of Jesus' baptism, genealogy, and temptation and the inauguration of his public ministry.

But what more can we discover about the generic character of this Lukan text? The following outline results from an analysis of the alternation between narration and speech in Luke 3:1-20:

3:1-6: Narration reminiscent of a prophetic call story
vv. 1-2a: the historical context of John's prophetic call
v. 2b: the prophetic call formula: "the word of the Lord came to John. . . ."
v. 3: resulting prophetic action: John preaches a baptism of repentance leading to forgiveness
vv. 4-6: authoritative citation: quotation of the prophet's words in Isa 40:3-5 with "in the wilderness" providing a prophetic rationale for John's presence in the wilderness

3:7-9: Monological prophetic speech story
v. 7a: the prophet John addresses the crowds coming for baptism
vv. 7b-9: John's prophetic message: calls for authentic repentance in light
    of divine judgment

3:10-14: Dialogue story in a question-and-answer format:
prophetic speech provokes reactions
vv. 10-11: first exchange: the crowds
vv. 12-13: second exchange: the tax collectors
v. 14: third exchange: the soldiers

3:15-17: Monological story: John responds
to the crowds' messianic speculation
v. 15: narrative transition
vv. 16-17: the prophet John responds to the crowd by pointing to the activity
    of the "stronger one" who is coming

3:18-20: Short narrative summary
v. 18: the prophet John preaches and exhorts the people further
vv. 19-20: Herod's hostile reaction to the prophet's indictment

This outline shows that vv. 1-6 of this Lukan narrative section is patterned according to the features of a prophetic call story: (1) It begins with a reference to the time period for the prophet's call, (2) it includes the prophetic call formula, and (3) it ends with a summary description of the prophetic preaching, providing evidence that John has accepted his call.[30]

Normally included in a prophetic call story is the content of the "word of the Lord" (see, e.g., Jeremiah 1). In the Lukan narrative, the authoritative citation in 3:4-6 likely plays this role of announcing God's direct speech. The quotation of Isa 40:3-5, with its synonymous parallel couplets, provides a prophetic rationale for John's presence in the wilderness, describes his prophetic role in terms of preparing the way of the Lord, and thus pictures him as the eschatological prophet anticipating the long-awaited arrival of God's salvation.

Then, in 3:7-9, the narrative employs what could be termed "prophetic speech." This monological form efficiently announces the prophet's mes-

---

30. See Claus Westermann, *Basic Forms of Prophetic Speech* (Philadelphia: Westminster, 1967).

sage of judgment, which provokes reactions from three groups: the crowds, the tax collectors, and the soldiers. These responses to the prophet's call for repentance are narrated in the form of a dialogue story that fashions the three exchanges according to a question-and-answer device. Clearly, the prophet John's preaching is having its effect, and probably in the three reactions the author intends to represent the full range of responses to John's message.

Next, 3:15-17 provides a brief narrative transition to a new topic, the crowds' messianic speculation about John. This unit is designed as a monologue story because the prophet John alone speaks. He uses antithetical lines to contrast his baptism by water with the Coming One's baptism by the Holy Spirit and fire (hints of the Messiah's judging activity).

This Lukan narrative about John concludes with a short narrative summary that describes the prophet's preaching and Herod's hostile reaction to John's indictment of the ruler. Herod's imprisonment of John prepares for the baptism, temptation, and public ministry of Jesus.

Luke thus casts this narrative about John in prophetic genres (prophetic call story, prophetic judgment-speech, etc.) and so reintroduces familiar scriptural forms laden with meaning and authority. They bear the memory of the past into the present. For two or more centuries, the Jews had experienced a cessation of the classical prophets, so that now these genres, with their claim for John's prophetic activity and message, would have had a surprising impact on a first-century audience. But the prophetic forms are applied to a changed situation. God calls John as a final prophet in the time of Roman rulers and Jewish high priests and not Jewish kings, in the wilderness of Judea along the Jordan River and not in the city of Jerusalem near the temple. Nonetheless, the genres authorize John as an intermediary between God and the people, as one who speaks God's potent word, which creates crisis for the hearers. They confer on the activity of this strange figure in the Judean wilderness, already executed by Herod Antipas, their perspective that God acts decisively to shape and reshape historical events. The genre's perspective puts the hearer's life under divine scrutiny, yet also offers new hope for divine deliverance through repentance and trust in the promised Messiah.

3.2 1 Corinthians 11:2-34

Obviously, the major form employed here by Paul is that of a letter genre. This genre permits the apostle a wide range of rhetorical options for instructing his hearers and persuading them to think and behave in ways appropriate to the gospel that he shared with them. In this section of the letter, Paul is responding to a number of problematic situations in the Corinthian community. The text under consideration can be divided into two topical segments, 11:2-16 and 11:17-34.

Although 11:2-16 is notoriously difficult for contemporary readers to interpret, it is clear that Paul's argument seeks to persuade certain women to change their practice of praying and prophesying with their heads uncovered. To do so, he argues from Scripture by alluding to Genesis 1–2. Within his epistolary style, he thus employs another genre form. His argumentation is midrashic in character. Midrash[31] is a term for an investigation or interpretation of a scriptural text, "a type of literature, oral or written, which has its starting point in a fixed canonical text, considered the revealed word of God by the midrashist and his audience, and in which this original verse is explicitly cited or clearly alluded to."[32] The identification of midrashic argumentation is significant in the interpretation of this Pauline segment because the key to the midrashic genre is the belief that texts in the Hebrew Scriptures hold utmost authority for the community. An appeal to specific scriptural texts can establish the persuasiveness of one's argument.

Yet in some situations there can be a conflict of scriptural interpretation between two parties appealing to the same canonical text. In this passage Paul's use of the midrashic form may suggest just such a contest over the meaning of specific texts. Perhaps as a counter to the practice of certain Corinthian women who are exercising leadership roles in worship with their heads uncovered, Paul appeals in 11:8-12 to authoritative texts, Gen 1:26-27 and 2:18-23, to develop his theological case. These women may be asserting their right to behave as they do in light of their understanding of a claim in a baptismal formula that gender inequalities have been abolished in Christ (see Gal 3:27-28; 1 Cor 12:13; Col 3:10-11). Since this early baptismal formula, especially the form in Gal 3:27-28, intimates a new understanding of male and female in relationship to the image of God, it is possible that the women are also implicitly appealing to Gen 1:26-27. If this is the case, then Paul is here engaged in an exegetical battle over the meaning of the Genesis text.[33]

31. See Bailey and Vander Broek, *Literary Forms,* 42-49; Gary G. Porton, "Midrash," *ABD,* 4:818-22.

32. Porton, "Midrash," 819.

33. Antoinette Clark Wire, *The Corinthian Women Prophets* (Minneapolis: Fortress, 1990) 116-34, spells out more fully the case for this possibility.

The Corinthian women prophets are assuming one interpretation of that text, whereas in this instance the apostle Paul is pursuing another one that views the man as the "head" of the woman.

Turning to 11:17-34, Paul's words in v. 17 ("Now in the following instructions I do not commend you . . .") recall for us his commendation in v 2 ("I commend you . . ."). Although it is obvious that the apostle is troubled about the way the Corinthians are celebrating the Lord's Supper, some attention to genre can sharpen our understanding of how Paul goes about addressing the situation.

This passage subdivides easily into three sections. In 11:17-22 Paul describes two problems that are evident when the Christians gather in one place ("house") to share their ritual meal together — namely, the division between rich and poor and the neglect of the poor by the rich. Next, in 11:23-26, Paul reminds his hearers of the essential purpose of the eucharistic meal by quoting words undoubtedly repeated during the enactment of the meal. Finally, in 11:27-34, Paul suggests solutions for the glaring disunity manifested when they gather for the Lord's Supper.

But, more precisely, what can genre analysis contribute to our understanding of this passage? Paul's use in 11:23b of the technical words for "receiving" and "transmitting" an established tradition makes clear that in 11:23b-25 he is inserting a liturgically formulated genre:

> the Lord Jesus on the night when he was betrayed
> > took a loaf of bread,
> and when he had given thanks,
> he broke it and said,
> > > "This is my body that is for you.
> > > Do this in remembrance of me."
> In the same way he took the cup also,
> > after supper, saying,
> > > "This cup is the new covenant in my blood.
> > > Do this, as often as you drink it,
> > > > in remembrance of me."

This short narrative, which recalls Jesus' actions and words on the night of his betrayal, is a liturgical formula developed and shaped in early Christian worship. It recalls the defining communal ritual that links their life together with the life and death of the Lord Jesus. This liturgical genre possesses the highest authority for the community since it reenacts their Lord's last supper that anticipated his ultimate sacrifice of his own body and blood for the forgiveness of human sins. By referring to this liturgical formula, Paul appeals to the ritual activity that defines who his readers are as the new family of God. It is like quoting an oft-repeated family story that everyone knows points to the very identity of the family.

By quoting these liturgical words in his letter, Paul puts them in a new context for the Corinthians. They hear these words repeated whenever they worship together, but now they are invited to discover a fresh significance as the words are read from Paul's letter. Paul raises up this high-authority liturgical genre, so laden with poignant memories of Jesus' last supper with his disciples, including all the denials and betrayals, to prompt them to reexamine their practices associated with the meal, which contribute to their disunity.

Within the larger argument, Paul uses the familiar words used in enacting the Lord's Supper not only to critique practices of certain Corinthians when the church assembles to share the Supper, but also to provide a remedy for their disunity. As they all should understand, it is Jesus' death that makes the difference for the community. The gift of his body makes possible unity among those who represent his body as the church (cf. 10:16). Therefore, when Paul invites them to "discern the body" in 11:29, he surely implies not only their awareness of the sacramental body of Christ in the meal but also their need to acknowledge one another as members of the communal body.

Moreover, as many scholars have noted,[34] it seems likely that Paul adds his own explanation in 11:26 to the liturgical tradition. This addition, "For as often as you eat this bread and drink the cup, you proclaim the Lord's death until he comes," seeks to convince the Corinthians that the character of their communal life provides a powerful proclamation of the purpose of Jesus' death: to create unity among people whose economic and social circumstances are quite different. Hence, Paul uses the form repeated in the worshiping community (11:23b-25), but he also breaks it open to new meaning by adding his word of interpretation (11:26).

3.3 Revelation 5:1-14

This final text represents what is central to the apocalyptic genre — a revelatory vision of the future that God has planned to a human being,

---

34. So, for example, Charles H. Talbert, *Reading Corinthians* (New York: Crossroad, 1987) 78.

mediated by a divine figure. Apocalyptic literature characteristically contains allegorical features, a code language that communicates more to insiders than to those not privy to the intended meaning. Here John depicts his experience as both visual and auditory: "I looked, and there in heaven was an open door. And the first voice, which I had heard speaking to me like a trumpet, said, 'Come up here, and I will show you what must take place hereafter'" (4:1).

Thereupon, 4:2–5:14 unfolds the first majestic vision in Revelation, that of the heavenly throne room where the destiny of human beings will be decided. The awesome vision in 4:2-11 of the One sitting on the throne (a clear allusion to God) sets the stage for the symbolic vision of Christ in 5:1-14. The reader soon discovers more than surface meaning in the details of the vision: for instance, a scroll written on both sides and sealed with seven seals, the lamb standing yet as if slain, its seven horns and seven eyes, the four living creatures, and the twenty-four elders, each with a golden bowl full of incense. The narrative itself assists the reader by explaining that the lamb's horns and eyes represent "the seven spirits of God sent out into all the earth" (5:6) and that the bowls of incense held by the elders represent "the prayers of the saints" (5:8). In addition, the reader is invited to ponder the significance of the various numbers — four, seven, and twenty-four. Numerology plays a part in the apocalyptic genre.

The drama of ch. 5 begins with the seer's observation of the scroll, sealed with seven seals, in the right hand of the One seated on the throne (5:1) and the appearance of a mighty angel who voices the decisive question, "Who is worthy to open the scroll and break its seals?" (5:2). When apparently no one in the entire cosmos is worthy to do this, the seer himself becomes a direct participant in the throne scene. As he weeps on hearing the sad news, one of the elders addresses him by announcing that it is the Lion of the tribe of Judah who is worthy to open the seals. But at this point in the vision, there is great irony. The "Lion" is none other than the Lamb, slain yet standing. It is the Lamb who goes to the One on the throne to take the scroll.

This action provides the dramatic climax for the vision. The Lamb's action prompts the introduction of a victory song genre into the apocalyptic narrative. The "new song" (cf. Isa 42:10) acclaims Christ, the Lamb, as the One worthy to open the scroll of judgment because he alone accomplished redemption by his death:

You are worthy to take the scroll and to open its seals,
for you were slaughtered

and by your blood you ransomed for God
saints from every tribe and language and people and nation;
you have made them to be a kingdom and priests serving our God,
and they will reign on earth.

"You are worthy . . . because of . . . (what you have accomplished)" suggests a pattern for a victory song that could have been used in the ancient world to ascribe honor and praise to gods, conquerors, heroes, and rulers. In the ancient Greek world the term *hymnos* implied a song of praise to a god or some extraordinary human figure whose accomplishments altered the condition of life for the masses.[35]

In 5:11-12 the chorus is expanded. Now the angels, living creatures, and elders join in the victory song until "myriads of myriads and thousands of thousands" are "singing with full voice":

Worthy is the Lamb that was slaughtered
to receive power and wealth and wisdom
and might and honor and glory and blessing!

This majestic song to Christ is characterized by a sevenfold (complete) ascription of praise. But even this is not the end of praise. Finally, the chorus is expanded to include all who have voice to praise; the unimaginable is described as all creatures in heaven, on earth, under the earth, and in the sea gather up the praise of ch. 4 with that of ch. 5. This universal chorus sounds forth a fourfold praise to God and to the Christ:

To the One seated on the throne and to the Lamb
be blessing and honor and glory and might
forever and ever!

"Amen" is added by the four living creatures, and the elders worship.

These song genres of adulation and praise, situated as they are in the throne room, might have prompted Christians in Asia Minor to recall adulation directed to earthly rulers, especially the Roman emperor. But they would have to conclude that no earthly emperor could compare to their crucified Christ, in whose praise the entire universe breaks forth. For the first-century audience of Revelation, probably caught in conflict with Roman imperial power, these victory songs must have exercised a powerful

35. See M. Alfred Bichsel, "Hymns, Early Christian," *ABD*, 3:350-51.

and lasting effect. This breathtaking worship, with its soaring victory hymns that end the chapter, celebrates the crucified Christ as "King of kings and Lord of lords" (19:16) even in the midst of their struggle with the power and demands of the Roman Empire.

Songs and hymns build communal solidarity, particularly for a Christian community under pressure. A victory song in praise of God and Jesus Christ offers a needed perspective to persecuted worshippers: It is not earthly rulers but Jesus, the Lord of lords, who possesses the ultimate power and is to be feared. When Christians fear the worst from evil rulers and experience their own impotence to defend themselves, hymns and songs ("We Shall Overcome," for instance) have amazing power to engender in them hope in God and perseverance under pressure.

4. Suggestions for Further Reading

Within the last decade, an increasing number of books have focused on NT genres. All this research is indebted to the much earlier work of form critics, for example, Martin Dibelius, *From Tradition to Gospel* (2d ed., Cambridge/London: Clarke, 1971); Rudolf Bultmann, *The History of the Synoptic Tradition* (New York: Harper and Row, 1963); and Vincent Taylor, *The Formation of the Gospel Tradition* (2d ed., London: Macmillan, 1935).

A relatively short book by Amos N. Wilder (*The Language of the Gospel* [New York: Harper and Row, 1964]) did much to spark renewed interest in the various modes and genres of NT speech. Wilder analyzed the use of dialogue, story, parable, poem, and myth. Until recently Mikhail Bakhtin's germinal work on genres was largely unknown to the western world. For a helpful analysis and summary of his thought on the nature and function of genres, see Gary Saul Morson and Caryl Emerson, "Theory of Genre," in *Mikhail Bakhtin: Creation of a Prosaic* (Stanford: Stanford University, 1990) 271-305.

Various recent volumes offer comprehensive treatments of NT genres. David E. Aune, *The New Testament in Its Literary Environment*, LEC 8 (Philadelphia: Westminster, 1987), discusses the major literary genres: the Gospels in light of ancient biography and historiography, letters, and apocalypse. Aune has also edited a volume (*Greco-Roman Literature and the New Testament: Selected Forms and Genres* [Atlanta: Scholars, 1988]) that includes essays by different authors on the following genres: chreia, household code, ancient Jewish synagogue homily, diatribe, ancient Greek letter,

Greco-Roman biography, and Greek novel. James L. Bailey and Lyle D. Vander Broek, *Literary Forms in the New Testament: A Handbook* (Louisville: Westminster/John Knox, 1992), provides definitions of over thirty literary forms, examples of their use in the NT, and comments regarding the value of genre recognition for interpretation. The most comprehensive survey in German of the variety and use of genres in the NT is Klaus Berger, "Hellenistische Gattungen im Neuen Testament," *ANRW*, 2.25.2:1031-1432. Finally, for up-to-date articles on genres (apocalypse, apophthegm, aretology, beatitude, biography, blessing and curse, call story, chreia, dialogue, diatribe, epistle, genealogy, Gospel, historiography, homily form, household code, [early Christian] hymn, infancy narrative, letter, logion, midrash, miracle, myth [and mythology], [Hebrew] narrative, [Greek and Latin] novel, oracle, parable, parenesis and protreptic, thanksgiving, virtue and vice list, and woe), see *ABD*.

See George A. Kennedy, *New Testament Interpretation through Rhetorical Criticism* (Chapel Hill: University of North Carolina, 1984), for the work of a classicist who introduces the reader to ancient rhetoric and its use in analyzing texts in the NT. Burton L. Mack and Vernon K. Robbins, in *Patterns of Persuasion in the Gospels* (Sonoma: Polebridge, 1989), demonstrate how knowledge of the ancient chreia is helpful in interpreting the pronouncement stories in the Gospels and Acts.

John Dominic Crossan's work on aphorisms has notably advanced understanding of the sayings of Jesus (*In Fragments: The Aphorisms of Jesus* [San Francisco: Harper and Row, 1983]). A comprehensive analysis of Jesus' parables according to structure and function is done by Bernard Brandon Scott in *Hear Then the Parable* (Minneapolis: Fortress, 1989). Gerd Theissen's *The Miracle Stories of the Early Christian Tradition* (Philadelphia: Fortress, 1983) provides a comprehensive investigation of the NT miracle stories. Finally, for treatments of epistolary literature of the Hellenistic world, including the Pauline letters, see William G. Doty, *Letters in Primitive Christianity,* GBS (Philadelphia: Fortress, 1973), and Stanley K. Stowers, *Letter Writing in the Greco-Roman World,* LEC 5 (Philadelphia: Westminster, 1986). For other secondary works on the various genres in the NT, see the selected bibliographies in the volumes by Aune and Bailey and Vander Broek and in the relevant articles in *ABD*.

11. *The Use of the Old Testament by New Testament Writers*

Richard B. Hays and Joel B. Green

1. The Gospel and the Scriptures

How is the gospel related to the Scriptures of Israel? The earliest Christian confession known to us declares that the death and resurrection of Jesus happened "in accordance with the Scriptures":

> For I handed on to you as of first importance what I in turn had received: that Christ died for our sins *in accordance with the scriptures,* and that he was buried, and that he was raised on the third day *in accordance with the scriptures,* and that he appeared to Cephas, then to the twelve. (1 Cor 15:3-4, NRSV)

This traditional confession, received by Paul in the early Christian community and handed on to the Corinthian believers, must have been formulated within the short period of time (perhaps three years) between the crucifixion of Jesus and Paul's call to apostleship.[1] Thus, from its earliest beginnings, the Christian movement located its proclamation in continuity with Israel's Scriptures and interpreted God's saving action in relation to Israel's story.

The first followers of Jesus, as Jews looking for the appearing of God's kingdom, sought to understand the meaning of the remarkable events that had been accomplished among them by meditating on Israel's Scriptures,

---

1. Cf. Hans Conzelmann, *A Commentary on the First Epistle to the Corinthians,* Hermeneia (Philadelphia: Fortress, 1975) 251-54.

222

which the church came later to call the Old Testament. Their fundamental conviction was that God had acted in an unexpected way to fulfill the promises made to Israel, to bring to completion the whole history of God's dealings with this people. With transformed eyes, they read and reread Scripture, discovering there prefigurations of the grace of God they had come to experience. The biblical texts, in turn, provided a storehouse of images and categories out of which the gospel proclamation took shape. Thus, from the earliest stages of the Christian movement — indeed, even during Jesus' own lifetime — Scripture was integral to the formation of the identity and teaching of the community of Jesus' followers.

2. Two Initial Problems

In what specific ways were the NT writers dependent on the OT? Prior to investigating this question two issues regarding the identification of relevant data require clarification.

2.1 What Is the "Old Testament"?

References in this chapter to the "Old Testament" and even to "Israel's Scriptures" make use of a kind of shorthand that cloaks complex issues related to a nebulous history. First, there are the problems in the use of the expression "Old Testament" itself. Since in the first century CE there was no "New" Testament, strictly speaking there could be no "Old" Testament. In *historical* discussion, then, "Old Testament" is an anachronism, though in the current context the problem is hardly overcome by reference to the "Hebrew Bible" or the "Hebrew Scriptures." On the one hand, simply to refer to the Hebrew Scriptures may too easily mask an assumption that a set of "Scriptures" had become formalized by around the mid-first century CE. This is debated, even if it is possible to presume that during this period the canon of the OT was fixed *de facto*.[2] New Testament writers can none-

---

2. In this connection, one may refer to the reference in the prologue of the deutero-canonical/apocryphal book, Wisdom of Ben Sira (= Ecclesiasticus) to "the reading of the Law and the Prophets and the other books" (second century BCE; cf. Luke 24:44). On the other hand, rabbinic discussions on some books continued well after the dawning of the Christian movement, and evidence from the Dead Sea Scrolls for a normative Scripture continues to be discussed. See, e.g., Roger Beckwith, *The Old Testament Canon of the New Testament Church and Its Background in Earliest Judaism* (Grand Rapids:

theless refer to OT books and texts as "Scripture" (γραφή, *graphē;* cf., e.g., Matt 21:42; Luke 4:21; Rom 4:3; 1 Pet 2:6), and this suggests that the authority of Scripture was established even when the extent of the canon might not have been.[3] Importantly, most of the passages quoted by NT authors come from texts within the boundaries of the later rabbinic canon, though one finds occasional citations whose source is either uncertain or extracanonical (e.g., 1 Cor 2:9; 9:10).

On the other hand, use of the expression "Hebrew Bible" in discussions of early Christian use of the OT stumbles on the fact that in the NT writings Christians more often than not cite from the Greek Old Testament, that is, the Septuagint (LXX), which had been available from the third and second centuries BCE onward. For many early Christians the "Bible" was not in Hebrew.[4]

Other problems surface when NT quotations from the OT depart from the text form available to us in the Masoretic Text of the Hebrew Bible or from the LXX.[5] Divergences in text form between the Testaments underscore, first, our limited knowledge of the Hebrew text(s) available in the first century CE. After all, the best, fully extant manuscript, the Leningrad Codex, is dated to the early eleventh century CE. In addition, evidence from the Dead Sea Scrolls at least raises the question to what degree one can assume a fixed text form for the MT during the period of earliest Christianity. Second, it is evident that the LXX was itself the object of ongoing recension, with the result that it is difficult to know with certainty what version(s) of the Greek OT might have been employed in the writing of, say, Luke-Acts. Hence, our references to the OT beg the question, Which textual form of the OT?

Eerdmans, 1985); F. F. Bruce, *The Canon of Scripture* (Downers Grove: InterVarsity, 1988) 25-114; Schnayer Z. Leiman, *The Canonization of Hebrew Scripture: The Talmudic and Midrashic Evidence,* Transactions of the Connecticut Academy of Arts and Sciences (Hamden: Archon, 1976); Lee McDonald, *The Formation of the Christian Biblical Canon* (Nashville: Abingdon, 1988).

3. Cf. Hans Hübner, "γραφή," *EDNT,* 1:260-64, here 261-62.

4. Furthermore, in terms of canonical shaping, the Hebrew Bible arranges its thirty-nine books in a different order than does the Christian OT, and the LXX contains books in addition to those found in the MT.

5. Direct citations are conveniently arranged in parallel columns — Masoretic Text/Septuagint/New Testament — in Gleason L. Archer and Gregory Chirichigno, *Old Testament Quotations in the New Testament* (Chicago: Moody, 1983), even if the apologetic posture of the commentary on these citations weakens the overall usefulness of the book.

A further complicating factor has to do with the possible influence of targums or at least targumic traditions — that is, interpretive renderings of the Hebrew Scriptures into Aramaic for the purpose of teaching in the synagogue. Because Aramaic served as the *lingua franca* in the Near East, public reading of the Hebrew Bible would presumably have been followed by oral translation[6] (or paraphrase) into Aramaic. Over the course of time, these interpretive traditions were fixed and preserved in literary form.[7] Although the question of the precise form(s) of targumic material that might have been available in the first century remains debated, the possibility remains that NT writers utilized the OT in its emerging Aramaic formulations. For example, the scriptural citation of Ps 68:18 in Eph 4:8 reflects more closely the Targum on the Psalms than either the Hebrew or Greek texts: "He gave gifts to people" (rather than "you received gifts from people") is similar to the targumic "you have given it [i.e., Torah] as gifts to people."[8] A further example of note is a targumic rendering of Lev 22:28 — "My people, children of Israel, since our Father is merciful in heaven, so should you be merciful on the earth"[9] — a reading that may be echoed in Luke 6:36: "Be merciful, just as your Father is merciful."

A number of factors, then, complicate any straightforward discussion of the use of the OT by NT writers. These include both problems with the status of the OT canon in the first century and a range of issues related to the texts available to and used by NT writers. They quote texts in various ways, which show eclectic freedom to select from among various available text forms the readings most suitable for the purpose at hand; in this way, they provide historical precursors for modern-day preachers and teachers who select from among various English translations of the Bible the rendering of a passage that most lends itself to their homiletical and pedagogical aims. One must also allow for the possibility that NT authors worked from memory in citing some texts. Moreover, as well shall see, NT writers shaped their quotations of OT texts — even amending the language of the OT — so as to work at the interpretive task already in the way the text is cited.[10]

---

6. Aramaic תַּרְגּוּם, *targûm*, "translation."

7. See the helpful essay by Bruce D. Chilton, "Targums," in *DJG*, 800-4.

8. Andrew T. Lincoln (*Ephesians*, WBC 42 [Dallas: Word, 1990] 242-43) notes that, given the relatively late date of the Targum on the Psalms, it is likely in this case that both the written targum and Ephesians witness an earlier interpretive tradition.

9. *Tg. Ps.-J.* Lev 22:28.

10. Christopher D. Stanley (*Paul and the Language of Scripture: Citation Technique*

2.2 Forms of Dependence

Virtually every writing of the NT bears the signs of its dependence on the OT, but the pattern of that dependence can vary widely.

1. Among the ways in which NT texts are linked to Israel's Scriptures, the most obvious is the *direct citation,* which may or may not be introduced with an introductory formula. For example, in Luke 3:3-6 the ministry of John is said to be continuous with the prophecy of Isa 40:3-5:

> He went into all the region around the Jordan, proclaiming a baptism of repentance for the forgiveness of sins, *as it is written in the book of the words of the prophet Isaiah,*
> "The voice of one crying out in the wilderness:
> 'Prepare the way of the Lord,
>   make his paths straight.
> Every valley shall be filled,
>   and every mountain and hill shall be made low,
> and the crooked shall be made straight,
>   and the rough ways made smooth;
> and all flesh shall see the salvation of God.'" (NRSV)

Accordingly, in Luke's view, John is understood best as the Isaianic herald (cf. already Luke 1:17, 76); the Evangelist thus locates John and his ministry within the Isaianic vision of eschatological salvation. Luke's citation of the Isaianic "good news" follows the LXX closely but not absolutely. For example, Luke substitutes "make *his* paths straight" for an original "make straight the paths *of our God.*" This allows a reading that identifies the coming one as *Jesus,* who has already been referred to as "Lord" in the Lukan narrative (1:43, 76; 2:11). In addition, ὁδός (*hodos,* "road, way") in 3:5 has replaced πεδίον (*pedion,* "level place") in the LXX.[11] Luke has already used this expression, "the way" (1:76, 79), and he will use it later to designate the church (e.g., Acts 9:2). The Evangelist employs the term generally to designate a people who identify with God's purpose; here in Luke 3 this Isaianic text has been enlisted to serve the development of this motif.

---

in the Pauline Epistles and Contemporary Literature, SNTSMS 69 [Cambridge: Cambridge University, 1992]) observes the relative freedom with which ancient authors engaged in interpretive renderings of other texts.

11. Codex Alexandrinus (LXX^A) reads ὁδοὺς λείας (*hodous leias,* "rough ways"), as does Luke.

Later in the Gospel of Luke, Jesus cites the OT with no introductory formula or explicit mention of the Scripture's fulfillment: "Father, into your hands I commend my spirit" (Luke 23:46; cf. Ps 31:5). In this case, the text form on which Luke depends is not so clear, as the version in Luke is similar to and departs from both the MT and the LXX.[12] In either case, Jesus' address to God as "Father" has been added. It is of interest, then, that "Father" is Jesus' normal address for God in the Gospel of Luke; here it highlights all the more Jesus' sense of unbroken relationship with God.[13]

2. In other cases, the NT writer's dependence on the OT is evident in *summaries of OT history and teaching*. The sermon of Paul in Acts 13:16-41 is of interest in this regard. Here, in the context of a manifestly Jewish audience ("You Israelites and others who fear God," v. 16), Paul quickly surveys the history of Israel from the time of exodus to the present, underscoring particularly the providential and salvific activity of God throughout Israel's story. In this way, the sermon is allowed (1) to establish that the appearance of Jesus, a Savior, to Israel was one more in a long line of efforts on God's part to redeem Israel and, indeed, the fulfillment of God's promise; and (2) to highlight the need for Paul's (and Luke's) audience to respond positively to the gospel of forgiveness. That is, by means of this rehearsal of the history of salvation, Luke situates the contemporary mission of the church and especially of Paul in the ongoing story of God's intervention on behalf of Israel while at the same time interpreting that ongoing story by showing that it has reached its climax in the offer of forgiveness through Jesus.

Other summaries of OT history and teaching are sprinkled throughout the NT — for example, in 1 Cor 10:1-13 and in the narrative structure of the Book of Revelation.[14]

3. The influence of the OT is also seen in the use of *type-scenes* in NT narratives. Type-scenes constitute a form of repetition in biblical narrative, an episode composed of a fixed sequence of motifs, often associated with recurrent themes. They reiterate similar events — say, the announcement of birth or the trial in the wilderness — by drawing on a common inventory of actions. In the case of a birth announcement, for example, the following

---

12. Cf. Joel B. Green, *The Death of Jesus: Tradition and Interpretation in the Passion Narrative*, WUNT 2/33 (Tübingen: Mohr, 1988) 97-98.

13. Compare the citation of Ps 22:1 in Mark 15:34!

14. Cf. Robert G. Hall, *Revealed Histories: Techniques for Ancient Jewish and Christian Historiography* (Sheffield: JSOT, 1991).

elements are typical: announcement of the birth, name of the child, and future of the child.[15]

Another example is found in John 4:1-42, an illustration of the type-scene of "the betrothal by the well." In this case the pattern recounts the meeting of future spouses who then play a central role in salvation history.[16] As with type-scenes in general, so in this case audiences might be expected not only to register the similarities of this episode with other well-known scenes, but also to detect sometimes small but revealing differences that provide new meanings.[17] Thus, in the Johannine text, it is surely of interpretive significance that, unexpectedly in a scene of this type, Jesus offers water to the woman rather than receiving it from her.

4. Finally, the dependence of NT writers on the OT is recognized in *allusions* or *linguistic echoes*. For example, in 1 Cor 11:7-10 Paul alludes to the creation story of Genesis 1–2 in support of his argument that women should keep their heads covered in worship. The allusion is clear (even if its logical soundness is not), but there is no explicit quotation of the Genesis text. In attuning our ears to register OT echoes in NT texts, we account for the way in which the great stories of Israel have served the writer as a trove of symbols and metaphors that shape the author's understanding and representation of the world and of God's salvific activity.[18]

From the vantage point of literary criticism, we thus draw attention to the phenomenon of *intertextuality*. This is the notion that every text embodies the interplay of other texts and so exists as a node within a larger literary and interpretive network.[19]

On the one hand, one might inquire into how a NT writer like Paul has worked deliberately to invite his audience into a kind of echo chamber so as to hear in the current text reverberations of other texts. In this way

15. Cf. Gen 16:7-13; 17:1-21; 18:1-15; Judg 13:3-20; Matt 1:20-21; Luke 1:11-20, 26-37; 2:9-12; Edgar W. Conrad, "The Annunciation of Birth and the Birth of the Messiah," *CBQ* 47 (1985) 656-68; Robert Alter, "How Convention Helps Us Read: The Case of the Bible's Annunciation Type-Scene," *Prooftexts* 3 (1983) 115-30.

16. Cf. Gen 24:10-61; 29:1-20; Exod 2:16-22; P. Joseph Cahill, "Narrative Art in John IV," *Religious Studies Bulletin* 2 (1982) 44-47.

17. See Robert Alter, *The Art of Biblical Narrative* (New York: Basic, 1981) 96-97.

18. See Richard B. Hays, *Echoes of Scripture in the Letters of Paul* (New Haven: Yale University, 1989) 14-21, here 16. Robert Bellah laments the erosion of biblical language (including stories and metaphors) in modern American culture in "The Recovery of Biblical Language," *RADIX* 19 (1988) 4-7, 29-31.

19. Cf. Michel Foucault, *The Archaeology of Knowledge*, WM (London: Routledge, 1972) 23.

we can see Paul inscribing himself into the tradition, grounding his theological efforts in the solid granite of Israel's past. Hence, as we seek to understand a Pauline text we can ask: On what OT texts is this Pauline text built? This is not to say, however, that via the phenomenon of intertextuality a NT writer simply agrees with and builds on an earlier writing. Rather, his engagement with the OT might be parodic, repeating an old pattern or echoing ancient metaphors to signal difference at the very heart of similarity. As he narrates his birth narrative (Luke 1–2), for example, Luke does not simply draw attention to the pattern and content of the story of God's promise to Abraham; he interprets it, pointing to its fulfillment in the good news of Jesus' birth.[20]

On the other hand, one cannot simply inquire into the intentionality of the author, as though Paul knew at every point where he was dependent on the OT and purposely wove that dependence into the text. Readers — especially contemporary readers less well-trained in the Scriptures of Israel, but also first-century Christian audiences — may miss Pauline echoes of the OT, but they may also hear echoes Paul did not explicitly propose.

Whether the relation to an OT precursor is explicit or implicit, the task of interpretation demands careful attention to the way in which NT texts draw on earlier scriptural material. Thus, recent NT study has seen a growing interest in the literary and theological problems surrounding the use of the OT in the NT. These problems are challenging because the hermeneutical strategies employed by the NT writers frequently seem to produce surprising readings of the scriptural texts, surprising because some are at variance with what most modern critics might regard as the original sense of the OT text.

3. Interpretive Approaches

There are, broadly speaking, two distinguishable approaches to these questions. On the one hand, NT critics have continued to refine their understanding of ancient Jewish exegetical practices and to place the NT writers within, or against, the interpretive conventions of first-century Judaism.[21]

20. Joel B. Green, "The Problem of a Beginning: Israel's Scriptures in Luke 1-2," *BBR* 4 (1994) 61-85.

21. E.g., Carol Kern Stockhausen, *Moses' Veil and the Glory of the New Covenant: The Exegetical Substructure of II Cor. 3,1–4,6*, AnBib 116 (Rome: Pontifical Biblical Institute, 1989); E. Earle Ellis, *The Old Testament in Early Christianity: Canon and Interpretation in the Light of Modern Research*, WUNT 54 (Tübingen: Mohr, 1991) esp.

On the other hand, some NT critics have taken their cues from literary-critical approaches to intertextuality, arguing that the use of the OT by NT writers may be clarified by tuning our ears to the metaphorical significations produced when a literary text echoes voices from earlier texts.[22] These two approaches, historical and literary, are by no means mutually exclusive; indeed, the most illuminating exegesis employs them together in a complementary fashion.

3.1 Basic Assumptions

No fixed method for analyzing the use of the OT by NT writers exists, but certain basic presuppositions and procedures may be outlined.

1. First, it must always be kept clearly in mind that for the church in the first century and into the second, there was no NT; hence, there was no OT conceived as a first and incomplete portion of the Bible. Rather, ἡ γραφή (*hē graphē*, "scripture") simply meant the sacred texts of Israel that we now call the OT. (The first hints of the collection of a new body of authoritative writings begin to appear only in the latest strata of the NT itself, such as in 2 Pet 3:15-16, which presupposes that a collection of Pauline letters is circulating in the church.) Consequently, for the NT writers, theological argumentation had to proceed from the OT as the basis of authority. Paul, for example, constantly argues his case on the basis of Scripture, while very rarely appealing directly to traditions about the teaching of Jesus.

2. As we have noted, the text and canon of the OT were not precisely fixed during the first century CE. As a working principle, this leaves open the question of what text forms the various NT writers might have known.

3. Within first-century Judaism, a great variety of interpretive methods and traditions were known and practiced. These traditions were to some extent in competition with one another. One should not speak of "Jewish exegesis" or even "rabbinic exegesis" as though it were a monolithic phenomenon. The philosophically oriented allegorical exegesis of Philo (a Hellenistic Jewish philosopher of first-century Alexandria) developed

---

part 3; Charles A. Kimball, *Jesus' Exposition of the Old Testament in Luke's Gospel*, JSNTSS 94 (Sheffield: JSOT, 1994) esp. ch. 2.

22. E.g., Sipke Draisma, ed., *Intertextuality in Biblical Writings: Essays in Honour of Bas van Iersel* (Kampen: Kok, 1989); Hays, *Echoes of Scripture*; Green, "Problem of a Beginning."

alongside the apocalyptic sectarian exegesis of the Dead Sea Scrolls, which in turn must be distinguished from the halakhic exegetical traditions of emergent Pharisaic-rabbinic Judaism. Indeed, Philo himself situates his mode of exegesis over against both those who overspiritualize the Scriptures and those who have an eye only for the literal meaning of Scripture.[23]

4. The NT writers represent a distinct creative hermeneutical development, emerging within first-century Judaism simultaneously with these other interpretive communities. As Jews and as Gentiles associated with first-century Judaism, early Christians would have shared the assumptions and practices of other Jewish communities. For example, like those responsible for the Dead Sea Scrolls, some NT writers worked with an eschatological hermeneutic that allowed ancient texts to be read as directly related to contemporary events: "This (the outpouring of the Holy Spirit and glossolalia at Pentecost) is that about which the prophet Joel spoke . . ." (Acts 2:16). Particularly with regard to their christological hermeneutic — that is, their proclivity for reading OT texts through interpretive eyes provided them by the life, death, and resurrection of Jesus and their experience of him as the Risen Lord — however, early Christians distinguished their exegesis from that of their Jewish contemporaries.

At the same time, even within the NT divergent interpretive strategies are at work. Matthew does not read Scripture in the same way as the author of Hebrews does. Luke subordinates Scripture to the all-encompassing authority of "the purpose of God."[24] And so on. Thus, any analysis of the use of the OT in the NT must take into account the interpretive tendencies and concerns of each individual NT writer.

5. A corollary of these observations is that the NT writers' use of the OT can rarely be explained simply by discovering parallels in contemporary sources, though such parallels may provide an interesting counterpoint. This latter possibility is of special consequence if it can be seen that the NT writer is participating in an ongoing tradition of exegesis of certain OT material.[25]

---

23. Philo *Migr.* 89-93.

24. Compare, e.g., Mark 14:21 (where the emphasis falls on what "is written of him") and Luke 22:22 (where the emphasis falls on what "has been determined"). Cf. Joel B. Green, *The Theology of the Gospel of Luke*, NTT 3 (Cambridge: Cambridge University, 1995) ch. 2.

25. Cf. Craig A. Evans, *To See and Not to Perceive: Isaiah 6.9-10 in Early Jewish and Christian Interpretation*, JSOTSS 64 (Sheffield: JSOT, 1989); Donald Juel, *Messianic Exegesis: Christological Interpretation of the Old Testament in Early Christianity* (Philadelphia: Fortress, 1988).

One particular cul-de-sac into which concerns for parallelism have led is the use of the term "midrash." In spite of its repeated use in attempts to characterize the imaginative readings of Scripture by NT writers, "midrash" actually explains very little. The term simply means "interpretation," and it is notoriously difficult to give a formal definition of it. When a NT writer interprets a text in a peculiar way, to describe this usage as "midrash" often brings the process of interpretation to a premature halt. In fact, we ought to be asking substantive questions about the way in which the NT writer's interpretation works: What makes these imaginative connections possible? What effects are produced in the writer's unfolding argument? How are the readers thus invited to respond?

3.2 Basic Questions

In light of these considerations, one may suggest a basic list of questions to be asked when studying particular NT texts:

1. What OT texts are cited or alluded to in this NT passage? Is there a pattern that characterizes this NT writer's choice of OT references — for example, Matthew's preference for citing prophetic texts or Luke's partiality for Isaiah, the Psalms, and Genesis?

2. Does the text of the NT citation correspond exactly to any known textual tradition of the OT passage? Does it follow the MT or the LXX, or neither? Does it appear that the NT writer has modified the quotation? If so, are there any evident reasons for this modification?

3. What is the original content of the passage in its OT setting? Does the writer's interpretation of the text appear to reflect a recognition of that original setting?

4. What can be learned about traditions of interpretation of the passage in ancient Jewish sources outside the NT — for example, in the OT itself, in the Dead Sea Scrolls, in Philo's writings, in the Targums, in rabbinic texts, etc.? Does the NT writer's use of the passage appear to reflect either the form or the content of these traditional interpretations?

5. How does the OT passage function in the argument or narrative of the NT writer? In other words, what is the NT writer using the text *for?*

6. What does the use of the text suggest about the NT writer's understanding of the relation between Israel and the church?

4. A Sample: Luke 3:7-9

The most prominent use of the OT by Luke in the material on John is the direct citation of Isa 40:3-5 in Luke 3:4-6. The importance of the OT and especially of the prophetic tradition in the opening verses of Luke 3 is also signaled by the geopolitical markers of 3:1-2 and by the statement that "the word of God came to John" (3:2).[26] Not so obvious is the abundant use of OT language and images in the subsequent characterization of John's ministry; here our focus is narrowed to the warnings John pronounces to the crowds that come out to meet him:

> [7]John said to the crowds that came out to be baptized by him, "You offspring of vipers! Who warned you to flee from the coming wrath? [8]Bear fruits worthy of repentance. Do not begin to say to yourselves, 'We have Abraham as our father,' for I tell you, God can raise up children for Abraham from these stones. [9]Even now the ax is lying at the root of the trees. Therefore every tree that does not bear good fruit is cut down and thrown into the fire." (Luke 3:7-9, NRSV)

John announces two warnings to the people, both of which follow hard upon his declaration that their privileged status as children of Abraham is now insecure. First, he reminds them that they can be replaced: "God can raise up children for Abraham from these stones." With these words, John draws on several potent images rooted in the Scriptures of Israel.

First, Luke assembles a number of motifs that serve the larger theme in this passage of Abraham as the father of many nations. Luke's distinct interest in steering attention to the Abrahamic material has already been developed in the birth narrative — first with references to "our father Abraham" and concern with the "covenant" in 1:55 and 73[27] but also with numerous allusions to the story of Abraham in Genesis 11–21.[28] In Luke 1–2, Luke is struggling with his understanding that Abraham was not made the progenitor of many nations; through his use of the Abrahamic story Luke urges the belief that the divine promise is now being actualized

---

26. See above, ch. 9.

27. Cf. Nils A. Dahl, "The Story of Abraham in Luke-Acts," in *Studies in Luke-Acts,* ed. Leander E. Keck and J. Louis Martyn (Philadelphia: Fortress, 1966) 139-58. Dahl notes Luke's interest in Abraham throughout Luke-Acts and highlights Luke's interest in Abraham as "the primary recipient of God's promise to the fathers" (142).

28. This influence is documented in Green, "Problem of a Beginning."

through divine activity that both recalls that covenant-making and also gathers up its possibilities in divine consummation. Now Luke turns his attention more to the question of the nature of the heirs of God's promise to Abraham.

That is, it is precisely as a result of the *volume* of the reverberations of the Abrahamic material in Luke 1–2 that we are encouraged in our reading of Luke 3 to hear further rumblings of that ancient story. Thus, even as God has been bringing to fruition his promises to Abraham in the Lukan birth narrative, so God is revealing his ability to raise up children — first, sons to Elizabeth and Mary and now, more broadly, children to Abraham (cf. Gen 18:14).

Who are Abraham's children? Luke builds on the notion that children reflect their parentage and thus draws a startling contrast between "children" of poisonous snakes and children of Abraham. The claim, "We have Abraham as our father," then, refers to more than Abraham as "progenitor,"[29] and certainly to more than Abraham as "ancestor" (*pace* NRSV): What is underscored are the character and practices of Abraham, which are to be replicated in the lives of Abraham's children.

In order to make this point, Luke interweaves the two OT streams prevalent thus far in his account of John — namely, the eschatological coming of salvation in Isaiah and the Abrahamic covenant. This is done implicitly by the repetition of the word ποιέω (*poieō*, "make, do") — borrowed from Isa 40:3/Luke 3:4 (ποιεῖτε, *poieite*, "make") — in 3:8-14: "Bear (ποιήσατε, *poiēsate*) fruits worthy of repentance" (v. 8); "bear (ποιοῦν, *poioun*) good fruit" (v. 9); "what then should we do (ποιήσωμεν, *poiēsōmen*)?" (v. 10); "do (ποιείτω, *poieitō*) likewise" (v. 11); "teacher, what should we do (ποιήσωμεν, *poiēsōmen*)?" (v. 12); and "and we, what should we do (ποιήσωμεν, *poiēsōmen*)?" (v. 14). True children of Abraham are *those who behave like* true children of Abraham, those who make straight the paths of the Lord.

That Luke might use Isaiah in this way and anticipate that others will hear such echoes in his writing is suggested by the degree to which he is dependent on Isaiah throughout his work. In the Third Gospel, the narrator cites Isaiah directly only three times: in 3:4-6 (Isa 40:3-5); 4:18-19 (Isa 61:1-2; 58:6); and 22:37 (Isa 53:12). But significant allusions appear elsewhere: in 2:30-32 (Isa 52:10; 42:6; 49:6); 7:22 (Isa 26:19; 29:18; 35:5-6; 61:1); 8:10 (Isa 6:9-10); 19:46 (Isa 56:7); 20:9 (Isa 5:1-2),[30] and this is not

29. Cf., e.g., Gen 12:1-2; *Ps. Sol.* 18:3.
30. James A. Sanders, "Isaiah in Luke," in Craig A. Evans and James A. Sanders,

even to begin to count the myriad echoes of Isaianic material in the Third Gospel.

What are we to make of John's reference to "stones"? One may be able to hear faint echoes of the election of God's people — that is, of the election and shaping of a nation, God's people, in the exodus and crossing of the Jordan, together with the stones used to memorialize this event (cf. Joshua 4).[31] Or perhaps the stones are simply a metaphor for what is lifeless (cf. Luke 19:40; Acts 17:29).

Perhaps of greater interest, however, is the way in which these three — Isaiah's vision of salvation, Abrahamic parentage, and the stone motif are brought together in a further Isaianic text, Isa 51:1b-2 (NRSV):

> Look to the rock from which you were hewn,
>   and to the quarry from which you were dug.
> Look to Abraham your father
>   and to Sarah who bore you;
> for he was but one when I called him,
>   but I blessed him and made him many.

With an analogous conglomeration of images, John communicates God's capacity, even intent, to make a new people, to arouse life from the lifeless — including persons in the crowds who have come out to John. He further highlights the fundamental importance of *behavior* that identifies one as authentically Abrahamic. Hence, while the situation facing these "offspring of vipers" is severe, it is not without hope, for God can do the impossible and bring forth life from the lifeless. "Children to Abraham," however, will be those who embrace God's purpose and act accordingly (cf. 16:24-31).

A second warning follows — namely, the prospect of judgment. John employs two graphic images to convey the immediacy of his message. First, unfruitful trees will be cut down — a metaphor of judgment also found in Isa 10:33-34; Wis 4:3-5; Sir 6:3 and used later by Jesus (13:6-9). "Even now" underscores the necessity of immediate response, for divine judgment is imminent.

A second metaphor on which John draws is that of fire, an image that is also known to us from the OT. Of particular interest are Mal 4:1, where

---

Luke and Scripture: The Function of Sacred Tradition in Luke-Acts (Minneapolis: Fortress, 1993) 14-25 (19-20).

31. Cf. Oscar J. F. Seitz, " 'What Do These Stones Mean?' " *JBL* 79 (1960) 247-54.

the day of the Lord is likened to a burning oven, in which "all the arrogant and all evildoers" will be burned up so that "neither root nor branch" remains, and Isa 66:24, echoed more strongly in 3:18, where it is said that those who have rebelled against God will be judged with an unquenchable fire. In each case, those judged are regarded as opponents of God's purpose and for this reason are cut off and burned up in the fires of judgment. By linking these images to the present as John does and by insisting that those who have truly aligned themselves with God's purpose manifest appropriate behaviors, John accentuates the necessity of readiness *now*. He provokes a crisis, raising the concern in his audience regarding the nature of those behaviors, those fruits.

Even by narrowing the scope of our probe to these few verses we are able to gain some sense of the degree to which the OT is in the air we breathe while reading Luke 3:1-20 as a whole, and this is indicative of what we might find throughout Luke and, indeed, the NT. In this particular instance, OT echoes function in a variety of ways. They help to secure John's identity as a prophet, in line with the ancient prophets as they are known through OT texts. They are useful in establishing Luke's understanding of the "time": The mission of John is continuous with the ongoing project of God, but it also participates in the time of consummation of that project.

With these OT reverberations, Luke continues the theological affirmation he has begun so significantly in Luke 1–2, tying the story of the beginning of the Jesus movement firmly to the ongoing narration of God's one redemptive purpose. The story of God's purpose has not been forgotten, nor have his promises been declared null and void. Instead, that story continues to be written, here in Luke's own hand, as those promises themselves come to fruition. The movement in which Luke's audience participates, the broader Christian community, is nothing more nor less than the manifestation of God's ancient purpose.

5. Suggestions for Further Reading

Among significant reference texts by which students may gain entry into the study of the use of the OT by NT writers is Martin J. Mulder, ed., *Mikra: Text, Translation, Reading, and Interpretation of the Hebrew Bible in Ancient Judaism and Early Christianity*, CRINT 2/1 (Assen: Van Gorcum/Philadelphia: Fortress, 1988). In addition, D. A. Carson and H. G. M. Williamson have edited a useful volume containing discussions of interpretive approaches in ancient Israel and in Second Temple Jewish communities, along with chapters on each of the NT writers: *It Is Written: Scripture Citing Scripture. Essays in Honour of Barnabas Lindars* (Cambridge: Cambridge University, 1988). Bradley H. McLean provides an index of *Citations and Allusions to Jewish Scripture in Early Christian and Jewish Writings through 180 C.E.* (Lewiston/Queenston/Lampeter: Edwin Mellen, 1992) — a helpful beginning point, even if other readers may hear other scriptural echoes in these Christian and Jewish texts.

Among the many studies of the use of the OT by NT writers in this century, three "classics" may be mentioned: C. H. Dodd, *According to the Scriptures: The Sub-Structure of New Testament Theology* (London: Nisbet, 1952); Barnabas Lindars, *New Testament Apologetic: The Doctrinal Significance of the Old Testament Quotations* (Philadelphia: Westminster, 1961); and Leonard Goppelt, *Typos: The Theological Interpretation of the Old Testament in the New* (German: 1939; ET: Grand Rapids: Eerdmans, 1982).

Work on the use of the OT by NT writers has tended to accord privilege to explicit quotations and obvious allusions. Representative works include: Robert H. Gundry, *The Use of the Old Testament in St. Matthew's Gospel with Special Reference to the Messianic Hope,* NovTSup 18 (Leiden: Brill, 1967); Joel Marcus, *The Way of the Lord: Christological Exegesis of the Old Testament in the Gospel of Mark* (Louisville: Westminster/John Knox, 1992); Darrell L. Bock, *Proclamation from Prophecy and Pattern: Lucan Old Testament Christology,* JSNTSS 12 (Sheffield: JSOT, 1987); Craig A. Evans and James A. Sanders, *Luke and Scripture: The Function of Sacred Tradition in Luke-Acts* (Minneapolis: Fortress, 1993); Willard M. Swartley, *Israel's Scripture Traditions and the Synoptic Gospels: Story Shaping Story* (Peabody: Hendrickson, 1993); William L. Schutter, *Hermeneutic and Composition in I Peter,* WUNT 2/30 (Tübingen: Mohr, 1989); and Christopher D. Stanley, *Paul and the Language of Scripture: Citation Technique in the Pauline Epistles and Contemporary Literature,* SNTSMS 69 (Cambridge: Cambridge University, 1992).

In varying degrees these studies are historical in their orientation. That is, they are concerned with how the OT was used for first-century audiences, and they typically locate NT writers within, or against, the interpretive conventions of first-century Judaism. With reference to the Gospels, this brief is taken up more generally in Douglas J. Moo, *The Old Testament in the Gospel Passion Narratives* (Sheffield: Almond, 1983); and R. T. France and David Wenham, ed., *Studies in Midrash and Historiography,* GP 3 (Sheffield: JSOT, 1983), both of which are concerned especially with whether the

Evangelists might have "created" historical narrative by means of reflection on OT texts without reference to historical knowledge or tradition. One may refer more generally to E. Earle Ellis, *The Old Testament in Early Christianity: Canon and Interpretation in the Light of Modern Research*, WUNT 54 (Tübingen: Mohr, 1991).

The theological import of OT exegesis in NT writings has been explored especially along two lines. Of these the more prominent has featured the use of the OT in christological argument and reflection; see, for example, the titles of the volumes by Gundry, Marcus, and Bock mentioned above. This is also the focus of Donald Juel's examination of *Messianic Exegesis: Christological Interpretation of the Old Testament in Early Christianity* (Philadelphia: Fortress, 1988). But now an alternative voice has been provided by Richard B. Hays; in *Echoes of Scripture in the Letters of Paul* (New Haven: Yale University, 1989) he contends that, at least in the case of Paul's approach to the Scriptures of Israel, the central concern is with the nature of the community of God's people as prefigured in the OT.

Literary theory and criticism has in the last two decades highlighted the relation of texts to other texts both at the level of the generation of meaning and at the level of interpretation. This "literary turn" and its promise for the practice of reading is developed in, for example, Thais E. Morgan, "Is There an Intertext in This Text? Literary and Interdisciplinary Approaches to Intertextuality," *AJS* 3 (1985) 1-40; John Hollander, *The Figure of Echo: A Mode of Allusion in Milton and After* (Berkeley: University of California, 1981); and Jonathan Culler, *The Pursuit of Signs: Semiotics, Literature, Deconstruction* (London: Routledge, 1981) ch. 5.

In biblical studies, the potential of a focus on intertextuality has been demonstrated more broadly by Michael A. Fishbane, *Biblical Interpretation in Ancient Israel* (Oxford: Clarendon/New York: Oxford University, 1985). In NT studies, one may refer to Gail R. O'Day, "Jeremiah 9:22-23 and 1 Corinthians 1:26-31: A Study in Intertextuality," *JBL* 109 (1990) 259-67; and again to Hays, *Echoes of Scripture.*

12. *Narrative Criticism*

MARK ALLAN POWELL

Narrative criticism focuses on stories in biblical literature and attempts to read these stories with insights drawn from the secular field of modern literary criticism. The goal is to determine the effects that the stories are expected to have on their audience.

In NT studies, narrative criticism is practiced with primary reference to the four Gospels and the Book of Acts.[1] No one will doubt that these books relate stories, but until recently literary-critical insights regarding stories and storytelling were largely ignored by scholars who studied these books.

Under the dominance of historical-critical scholarship, books of the Bible were often treated more as resources for historical reconstruction than as works of literature in their own right.[2] By using such methods as source criticism, form criticism, and redaction criticism, Gospel scholars were able to learn about the life and teaching of Jesus and to gain insight into the interests and concerns of the early Christians who produced the texts we now have concerning him. In the 1980s, however, the interests of these scholars expanded to include inquiry into the function of these texts as literature — that is, as forms of communication that affect those who receive or experience them.

For the most part, narrative criticism has not become a domain for those who reject the processes or conclusions of historical-critical scholar-

1. Epistles may also be studied in terms of the stories that lie behind the letters. See Norman R. Peterson, *Rediscovering Paul: Philemon and the Sociology of Paul's Narrative World* (Philadelphia: Fortress, 1985).

2. See Hans W. Frei, *The Eclipse of Biblical Narrative: A Study in Eighteenth and Nineteenth Century Hermeneutics* (New Haven: Yale University, 1974).

ship but has attracted those who feel that something other than historical criticism ought also to be done. Granted that the Gospels may function referentially as records of significant history, might they not also function poetically as stories that fire the imagination, provoke repentance, inspire worship, and so on? Or to put it another way, historical criticism may be said to treat biblical narratives as windows that enable us to learn something about another time and place; narrative criticism treats these same texts as mirrors that invite audience participation in the creation of meaning.[3] For the narrative critic, texts shape the way readers understand themselves and their own present circumstances.

1. Some Basic Principles

When Bible scholars turn to secular literary theory for guidance, they may encounter a frustrating cacophony of voices. The field of modern literary criticism encompasses a vast array of systems and methods that are based in turn on diverse hermeneutical conceptions concerning language and communication. The narrative criticism that is currently practiced in NT studies is an eclectic discipline that borrows from a number of areas, including rhetorical criticism, structuralism, and reader-response criticism. The method is still undergoing development, but some widely-accepted principles can be identified.

1.1 Implied Author

Narrative criticism seeks to interpret texts with reference to their implied authors rather than with reference to their actual, historical authors. By "implied author," narrative critics mean the perspective from which the work appears to have been written, a perspective that must be reconstructed by readers on the basis of what they find in the narrative. In secular studies, the concept of the implied author was first developed by formalist critics who wished to interpret stories on their own terms without reference to anything extrinsic to the text itself.[4] Biographical information concerning

3. Murray Krieger, *A Window to Criticism: Shakespeare's Sonnets and Modern Poetics* (Princeton: Princeton University, 1964) 3.

4. Wayne C. Booth, *The Rhetoric of Fiction* (2d ed., Chicago: University of Chicago, 1983) 66-67.

the author's agenda or personality should not be imposed on the story. We may know that Jonathan Swift was concerned with the relations of Protestants and Catholics in Ireland, but since this issue is not explicitly addressed in *Gulliver's Travels* the meaning of that work should not be circumscribed by so limited an application. In fact, in literary studies, a "classic" is by definition a work that continues to be meaningful in times and places that were not originally envisioned by the author.

The concept of the implied author is significant for interpreting works that have multiple authors or are anonymous. Even a work that has no real author — such as a tale that developed over a period of time by being passed down from generation to generation — can be studied according to the perspective of its implied author.[5] Regardless of the process through which a narrative comes into being, it will always evince particular values, beliefs, and perceptions that can be described as representative of its implied author.

For narrative critics, then, questions concerning whether Luke's Gospel was written by a companion of Paul or whether the Evangelist drew some of his material from the Gospel of Mark or from a now lost Q document are irrelevant. These questions are significant for historical critics who wish to make judgments concerning the historical reliability of Luke's work or who want to determine the theological agenda of the Gospel's redactor. But they are not significant for appreciating and understanding Luke's Gospel as a completed work of literature that must, in any case, be interpreted from the perspective of its implied author.

1.2 Implied Readers

Narrative criticism seeks to determine the expected effects of stories on their implied readers, without taking into account all of the possible effects that stories may have on actual readers. The concept of the implied reader parallels that of the implied author. The implied reader is one who actualizes the potential for meaning in a text, who responds to it in ways consistent with the expectations that we may ascribe to its implied author.

The concept of the implied reader is a heuristic construct that allows critics to limit the subjectivity of their analysis by distinguishing between their own responses to a narrative and those that the text appears to invite.

---

5. Seymour Chatman, *Story and Discourse: Narrative Structure in Fiction and Film* (Ithaca: Cornell University, 1978) 140.

Most of us already know how to do this in daily life. We may be offended by a story that we consider to be in poor taste and say, "I was supposed to think it was funny, but I didn't." Or we may be bored by a novel and say "I am supposed to find it scary, but I don't." In such instances we determine that we are expected to respond to these texts differently than we actually do. In literary terms, we are able to identify how the implied reader would respond even though our own responses as actual readers may be different.

On what basis do we make such determinations? We do not need the author to tell us outright that he or she expects us to find the story amusing or frightening. Rather, our perception of expected response is based on the recognition that stories intended to be funny or scary are usually told in particular ways. Similarly, narrative critics believe that attention to literary cues enables them to determine the effects that NT literature is expected to have on its implied readers.

Narrative critics differ from historical critics in that the latter usually seek to determine the effects that a document was intended to have on a particular set of actual readers, namely the community to which it was originally addressed. This focus on original readers typically defines the meaning of the text with more specificity than the approach of narrative criticism. When narrative critics determine the effects that a text is expected to have on its implied readers they often discover a range of meaning that may have diverse applications in a variety of contexts. Narrative criticism is therefore generally more open to *polyvalence* (plurality of meaning) than is historical criticism, though the concept of the implied reader places limits on this concept.

If historical criticism defines meaning with reference to the intended effect of a text on one particular set of readers, some schools of reader-response criticism seek to define meaning in ways that encompass all of the possible effects that a text may have on those who read it in any number of different contexts or situations. Narrative criticism occupies a middle ground on this continuum, seeking to define the range of potential meaning for the text's implied reader.

1.3 Normative Process of Reading

In exploring the expected effects of texts on their implied readers, narrative critics make some assumptions about a normative process of reading. They assume, for instance, that the narrative is to be read sequentially and completely with all its parts being related to the work as a whole. Thus we cannot determine the expected effects of a passage from Luke's Gospel by considering the passage as an isolated pericope but only by considering the role that the passage plays in the narrative as a whole. And we can assume that readers desire consistency and make connections necessary to resolve apparent tensions within a text in favor of the most consistent interpretation.[6]

A normative process of reading also assumes that readers know certain things. To determine the effects that Luke's Gospel is expected to have on its readers we must assume that these readers know what a Samaritan is, what a centurion does, how much a denarius is worth, and so on. On the other hand, determination of the expected effects of a work is often contingent on assuming that the readers do not know certain things. Readers of Mark's Gospel, for instance, are not expected to have read the Gospel of Luke and, therefore, the implied reader of Mark's Gospel does not think of Jesus as one who has been born of a virgin.

Normative reading involves an implicit contract by which the reader agrees to accept the dynamics of the story world that are established by the implied author. If a story features talking animals, we are expected to suspend our disbelief and to accept that, in this story, that is the way things are. In the story world of Luke's Gospel, God speaks audibly from heaven, fantastic miracles are commonplace, and human beings interact freely with spiritual creatures like angels and demons. Narrative criticism opposes any attempt to "demythologize" such elements by determining what actual historical occurrences might have inspired the tales. Rather, the expected effects of the story can only be determined if we adopt the perspective of readers who accept these and other elements of the story as real, at least as "real" within the world of the story.

In the same vein, narrative criticism interprets stories from the perspective of implied readers who may be assumed to accept the value system that undergirds the stories they read. Many readers today would be offended by stories that present cowboys as good and Indians as bad, yet we recognize that this response is shaped by perceptions that the implied readers of such stories are not expected to share. We are free to critique or reject stories that evince values and beliefs contrary to our own, but if we wish to understand these stories we must at least pretend to adopt these values in order to determine the effects they are expected to produce on readers who

6. Wolfgang Iser, *The Act of Reading: A Theory of Aesthetic Response* (Baltimore: Johns Hopkins University, 1974).

are assumed to think this way. Assumptions undergirding the NT Gospels include the beliefs that God's point of view defines truth and that the Hebrew Scriptures can be a reliable guide for determining this divine perspective. Since narrative criticism demands that texts be interpreted from the faith perspective that their readers are assumed to hold, narrative critics may be required to focus their imagination in the opposite direction of that required for historical critics. Whereas historical critics are expected to suspend faith commitments temporarily in order to interpret texts from the perspective of objective, disinterested historians, narrative critics may be expected to adopt faith commitments temporarily in order to determine how texts are expected to affect their implied readers.

2. Narrative Analysis

In practice narrative criticism is a complex process that calls for attention to numerous literary dynamics. We will list a few of the most significant matters and then observe how consideration of some of these may affect interpretation of a typical biblical passage.

2.1 Ordering of Events

The order in which a narrative relates events is important because readers are expected to consider each new episode in light of what has gone before. Sometimes narratives report events "out of order" by presenting flashbacks concerning what happened earlier (Mark 6:17-29) or by including predictions or allusions that foreshadow what is still to come (Luke 2:34-35).

2.2 Duration and Frequency of Events

Readers' perceptions concerning the events of a narrative may be influenced by the amount of space given to reporting individual episodes or by the number of times that a particular event is referenced in the narrative. A narrative may pass quickly over events that transpire over several years (Luke 2:52) and then relate in some detail matters that take only a few minutes or hours (Luke 23:26-49). Similarly, a narrative may tell us with a single reference that something happens repeatedly (Luke 22:39) or make several references to something that happens only once (Luke 9:22, 44; 18:31-34; 24:7).

2.3   Causal Links

In making sense of a narrative readers are especially attentive to links that are established between the events that are related. Typical links include explicit or implicit indications that one event causes another to happen or at least makes the occurrence of the subsequent event possible or likely. In some literature (including NT narratives), such causal links may be teleological in that present events are influenced not only by what has happened in the past but also by what must happen in the future (Luke 24:26).

2.4   Conflict

Practically all narratives contain elements of conflict that drive the plot and involve the readers in adjudication of opposing tendencies. The manner in which these conflicts are developed and resolved has a significant effect on the readers' experience of the story. To cite but one example, conflict that is left unresolved tends to impinge directly on the readers so that they are left to decide what they would do if the matter were left to them. Thus readers of Luke 15:25-32 are not told how an elder son responds to his father's words concerning welcome of the prodigal younger brother but are expected to ask themselves, "What would I do if I were he?"

2.5   Characters

The manner in which characters are presented in a narrative is especially significant for determining the effect that the narrative is expected to have on its readers. Characters may be flat and predictable like the Pharisees in most of our Gospel stories, or they may exhibit a wide variety of traits, such as Jesus' disciples, who are presented as enlightened in one instance (Luke 8:10) and yet as lacking insight in another (Luke 9:44-45). Characters may remain much the same throughout the narrative, or they may develop and change in response to what transpires as the story progresses.

2.6   Characterization

Narrative critics are interested not only in what we know about the characters in a story but also in how we know this. Readers' perceptions concerning characters may be shaped by comments from the narrator (Luke 1:6), by reports of the characters' own words, deeds, or perceptions (Luke

1:8-12), or by reports of the words, deeds, or perceptions of others (Luke 1:22).

2.7 Empathy

The effects that a narrative has on its readers are often determined by the empathy that these readers feel with particular characters in the narrative. Empathy may be realistic in that readers believe they really are like these characters, or idealistic in that the characters have qualities or experiences the readers wish to emulate. The actual empathy of real readers with characters is impossible to predict, but literary cues sometimes indicate the characters with which readers are expected to empathize. For example, when Jesus tells the parable of the Good Samaritan (Luke 10:30-37), the explicit identification of his audience as a legal expert (10:25) encourages readers to hear the story from this perspective and to identify with the characters in the story that this person would most likely empathize with (the priest and the Levite, who like the legal expert are religious leaders).

2.8 Point of View

Narratives typically present diverse perspectives concerning what is transpiring in the story, and readers are expected to regard some of these as more reliable than others. In NT narratives, God's point of view is normative for truth and the perspective of the narrators is always reliable.[7] When God declares that Jesus is the "Beloved Son" (Luke 3:21) or when the narrator of Luke's Gospel says that Jesus is "full of the Holy Spirit" (Luke 4:1), the readers are not expected to wonder whether these things are really so. Similarly, the perspectives of angels, prophets, and Jesus himself are all shown to be reliable in the Gospel of Luke because they always concur with the point of view evinced by God and by the narrator. But when the crowds proclaim that Jesus is a prophet (Luke 7:16) readers may be expected to regard this point of view with some ambiguity since the crowds also think that Jesus is John the Baptist risen from the dead, a point of view that is clearly wrong (Luke 9:7, 19).

---

7. On reliable narrators in literature, see Booth, *Rhetoric of Fiction,* 3-4, 70-76; Chatman, *Story and Discourse,* 147-49.

2.9 Settings

The spatial, temporal, and social locations of events may be significant for how readers construe what is reported in a narrative. Readers may respond differently to the story if an event occurs on a mountain (Luke 9:28-36) or in a boat (Luke 5:3-11), on a sabbath (Luke 6:1-5) or in the evening (Luke 4:40), in private (Luke 6:12), or among a crowd (Luke 6:17-18).

2.10 Symbolism

Narratives often employ figures of speech and other symbolic language that readers are expected to understand in a way that transcends the most literal application (Luke 17:37). Thus, "bearing the cross" may signify the life of self-denial that is to be a mark of all those who follow Jesus, not just those who suffer literal martyrdom through crucifixion (Luke 9:23). Settings may also be imbued with symbolic meaning, such that a wedding may signify joy or festivity (Luke 5:34) and winter may become a symbol for the ardors of apocalyptic travail (Mark 13:18; Luke 21:29-31).

2.11 Irony

Narratives are said to be ironic when they contain literary cues that indicate readers are expected to interpret the story in ways that run contrary to what might initially appear to be the obvious interpretation. For example, an ironic parable in Luke's Gospel presents a Pharisee who thanks God he is not like a certain tax collector without realizing that it is the tax collector whom God considers justified (18:9-14).

2.12 Intertextuality

Sometimes narratives assume that readers are already familiar with other texts and so borrow freely from motifs that these texts employ. The readers of Luke's Gospel are assumed to be familiar with the writings of the OT and may be expected to recognize allusions to those writings even when explicit citations are not made. Thus, Luke's implied readers may be expected to understand Jesus' raising of a widow's son in 7:11-17 as a miracle reminiscent of miracles performed by Elijah and Elisha in 1 Kgs 17:17-24 and 2 Kgs 4:32-37.

2.13 Structural Patterns

Readers' responses to a narrative may also be affected by the patterns of discourse through which the story is told.[8] Such patterns may be poetic, employing repetition, meter, rhyme, or alliteration. They may also take the form of a logical ordering of content based on a scheme of generalization, particularization, or the like. In Luke's Gospel, for instance, four sayings that begin with the word "Blessed" (6:20-22) are contrasted with four sayings that began with the word "Woe" (6:24-26).

3. A Sample Text: Luke 3:1-20

3.1 Some Literary Features

The portion of Luke's narrative that modern Bibles designate as "chapter 3" begins with the story of John the Baptist's ministry to Israel. A number of this story's literary features are significant.

With regard to *ordering of events,* the story concludes, not as we would expect, with John's baptism of Jesus, but with John being imprisoned by Herod (3:19-20). Although Jesus' baptism must have occurred before John was arrested, we are not told about it until later (3:21). One effect of relating the events in this order is to create a definite break for readers between the stories of John and Jesus. The story of Jesus' ministry does not begin until that of John's is essentially complete. Thus, we are encouraged to view the work of these two as complementary rather than competitive.

With regard to *settings,* the temporal setting for John's ministry is defined with great precision (3:1-2), while the spatial setting is given simply as "all the region around the Jordan" (3:3). The designation of the temporal setting, furthermore, includes references to many geographical areas, telling us who the rulers of Rome, Judea, Galilee, Iturea and Trachonitis, and Abilene were. Luke's readers are expected to realize that what is reported here is of monumental significance for history — and not only for the history of those who live in the region around the Jordan but for the history of the whole world (cf. 3:6).

Symbolism is evident in the words from Isaiah that the narrator cites

---

8. For description of several such patterns see David R. Bauer, *The Structure of Matthew's Gospel: A Study in Literary Design,* JSNTSS 31 (Sheffield: Almond, 1988).

as descriptive of John's work (3:4-6). Luke's readers do not imagine that John is literally advocating the razing of hills or the filling of valleys but recognize that these images symbolize what he means by repentance: a reordering of human lives as preparation for receiving God's salvation (3:6). But symbols are by nature ambiguous and invite the readers' consideration of more than one possible application. Elsewhere in Luke, language of raising and lowering is used of social upheaval (1:52), community hospitality (14:11), and the justification of individuals before God (18:14). Along these lines, Luke's implied readers are probably expected to translate these symbols anew into contexts appropriate for their own worlds outside the story. Thus, Luke's readers are invited to consider what, for them, constitute the valleys, mountains, crooked places, or rough ways that need to be transformed.

An element of *irony* is introduced when John, whose role is to prepare Israel to receive its Messiah (cf. Acts 19:4), is actually mistaken for the Messiah himself (3:15). This irony is doubled later in the narrative when the Messiah really does come and is mistakenly identified as John the Baptist (Luke 9:7, 19).

Intertextuality is obviously a prominent feature of this story since the book of Isaiah is explicitly quoted in a way that assumes that the story's readers will not only be familiar with these words but will accept them as reliable and authoritative (3:4-6; cf. Isa 40:3-5). Less obvious intertextual allusions may also be found. The expression "the word of God came to John" in 3:2 recalls similar statements scattered throughout the OT (Jer 1:2; Hos 1:1; Joel 1:1; Jonah 1:1; Mic 1:1; Zeph 1:1; Hag 1:1; Zech 1:1). Luke's readers are expected to be familiar with this language and to realize that it marks John as a prophet (cf. Luke 1:76; 7:26). And the reference to the "region around the Jordan" (3:3) is expected to bring to mind OT imagery of the Jordan River as the entrance to the promised land (Joshua 3). Thus, the spatial setting for this story is invested with subtle symbolism through an intertextual connection: John's baptism of repentance allows people to enter into the realm of God's promise and prepares them to receive something greater than what he himself is able to offer (3:16).

These literary observations regarding Luke 3:1-20 may be interesting, each in its own right, but ultimately a narrative-critical analysis would hope to produce a sustained reading of the text that articulates its overall impact. To do this with this particular passage, attention to two matters seems imperative.

3.2 The Relationship of the Story to the Narrative as a Whole

Luke's readers do not encounter John the Baptist for the first time in this story. They have already formed impressions and expectations concerning him from material presented earlier in the accounts of his birth (1:5-25, 57-80). Many of those expectations are now fulfilled. Readers heard previously that John would be a prophet (1:76), and the presentation of him now as one to whom the word of the Lord comes confirms this (3:2). Readers heard that he would prepare the Lord's way (1:76), and now the narrator cites Isaiah's words to indicate that this is precisely what he is doing (3:4). Readers heard he would give people "knowledge of salvation by the forgiveness of their sins" (1:77), and, sure enough, John is now preparing people for the salvation of God (3:6) by offering a baptism of repentance "for the forgiveness of sins" (3:3).

Numerous connections can also be seen between what is presented here and what is to come later in this narrative. John warns people against substituting an appeal to Abraham for repentance (3:8), and later we will hear a rich man do exactly that (16:24, 27, 30). John introduces the image of fruitless trees being cut down (3:9), which will be used again in the parables of Jesus (13:6-9). John commends the sharing of possessions (3:11), a characteristic that will later mark the Jerusalem Christians in the book of Acts (2:44-45). John tells tax collectors to collect only what is due them (3:12-13), and later we will encounter a tax collector who offers to repay any whom he has defrauded (19:8).

In addition to these specific links, John the Baptist is presented in this passage as making promises or predictions regarding events that are still to come. John speaks of a more powerful one who is coming (3:16), a prediction that in some sense is fulfilled almost immediately when Jesus is baptized and begins his ministry. But John specifically promises that this one will baptize people with the Holy Spirit, and this part of the promise is not fulfilled until the second volume of the narrative (Acts 2:4). Finally, John also speaks of the coming one as a judge who will separate the wheat from the chaff (3:17), an image that Luke's reader will associate with the role Jesus is to exercise at the end of time (Acts 10:42). John's words thus offer a foreshadowing of what is to come in this story, in its sequel, and in still another story yet to be told.[9]

---

9. Narrative critics debate whether Luke and Acts should be read as one continuous

The reader, then, is expected to regard Luke 3:1-20 as providing major impetus to the overall plot of the narrative. What happens here sets in motion the events with which the remainder of the two-volume work will be concerned, the events that "turn the world upside down" (Acts 17:6). Evidence that this is the case may be adduced from such passages as Acts 1:22 and 10:37, where the ministry of John the Baptist is used to date the beginning of what comes to be accomplished through Jesus and his followers.

The plot of Luke's two-volume work is largely concerned with God's plan to bring salvation to all people.[10] Perhaps the greatest impediment to this plan in Luke's story is the false confidence or self-righteousness of religious leaders who do not think they need the salvation that God offers and who do not wish to see that salvation offered to others (5:30-32; 7:29-30; 18:9). Already in this passage, we find the theme of the two-volume work articulated clearly, namely "that all flesh might see the salvation of God" (3:6). But also already the potential for conflict is raised by John's curious warning, "Do not begin to say to yourselves, 'We have Abraham as our ancestor'" (3:8). In the immediate context, this warning makes little sense, since no one is saying this. But as Luke's story continues readers will realize that John identified from the very beginning what would prove to be a central conflict throughout the narrative.

3.3 Character Identification

Luke's readers are presented with a full range of characters in 3:1-20. At one extreme is John the Baptist, to whom the word of God comes (3:3), and at the other is Herod, to whom the narrator attributes "evil deeds" (3:19). Readers are obviously expected to regard John as the protagonist (the hero) and Herod as the antagonist (the villain) in this part of the tale. But what of the crowds, the characters who seem to occupy a neutral ground somewhere between these two extremes? On the one hand, the crowds come to John for baptism (3:7) and seem genuinely concerned with learning what they ought to do (3:10). On the other hand, they are the recipients of harsh words spoken by John (3:7-9), and they seem to miss the point when they wonder whether he is the Messiah (3:15).

---

story or as two related stories by the same author. See Mikeal C. Parsons and Richard I. Pervo, *Rethinking the Unity of Luke and Acts* (Minneapolis: Fortress, 1993).

10. Robert C. Tannehill, *The Narrative Unity of Luke-Acts: A Literary Interpretation*, 2 vols. (Philadelphia/Minneapolis: Fortress, 1986, 1990).

The crowds embody potential for either positive or negative development and so are the characters in this episode with whom readers will empathize most realistically. Such empathy is not complete. The fact that Luke's readers know things that these crowds do not — such as that Jesus is the Messiah (2:11) — places the readers in a privileged position that allows them to distance themselves from the crowds. Still, Luke's readers are expected to hear John's words from the crowds' point of view and to ask along with them "What then should we do?" The offering of three sample answers to this question (3:11, 13, 14) entices readers to consider other possible replies. If this is what John said to people with surplus goods, to tax collectors, and to soldiers, what might he have said to us? How should we prepare the way of the Lord? What "fruits worthy of repentance" are expected of us? Sometimes, narrative criticism can detect "gaps" in a narrative that readers are expected to notice and to attempt to fill, though narrative criticism may not be able to predict the manner in which readers will actually fill these gaps.[11] So in this case narrative criticism is able to detect the questions that Luke's implied readers are expected to ask themselves, though it cannot predict the answers that real readers will actually supply when they ask themselves these things.

John the Baptist is also presented as a character who invites reader identification in this episode. He serves as a model character for what is known as "idealistic empathy." Readers may not feel that they are very much like John the Baptist, but the assumption underlying the narrative is that they would like to be. Notably, Luke's Gospel lacks any mention of John wearing camel's hair or eating locusts and wild honey (Mark 1:6), details that might make him appear strange and might distance him from Luke's readers. Rather, in this story, he appears as a prototype of a typical Christian evangelist.[12] He preaches the gospel (3:18) and offers people salvation through the forgiveness of sins (3:3, 6). Indeed, later Christian missionaries will appear to be copying John when they set about proclaiming "repentance and forgiveness of sins" (24:47) and when they urge people to "repent and be baptized" (Acts 2:38) or to "do works worthy of repentance" (Acts 26:20; cf. Luke 3:8). Like John, they will be called on to shun glory wrongly attributed to them (Acts 10:25-26; 14:11-18). Like John, they will have to be bold in confronting evil rulers, to bring testimony before kings and

11. On "gaps," see Iser, *Act of Reading*.

12. Charles H. Talbert, *Reading Luke: A Literary and Theological Commentary on the Third Gospel* (New York: Crossroad, 1982) 27.

governors (21:12). John's work is described in the literal Greek of Luke 7:27 as being to "go as a messenger before the Lord's face" and these same words are used to describe the work of Jesus' disciples in Luke 9:52 and 10:1. Though Luke's readers may know that historically John the Baptist was not a Christian, the story of Luke's Gospel presents him in a way that allows him to function as a hero for Christian readers. He is an inspiring figure whom Christians will wish to emulate.

4. What Narrative Criticism Does and Does Not Do

Narrative criticism is best understood as one key among several that are available to biblical interpreters. Used properly, it is able to open some doors and grant access to certain kinds of insight that may not be otherwise attainable. But it will not open all the doors or answer all the questions that people ask about the Bible and about the meaning of biblical material.

Objections to narrative criticism usually focus on what the method is not able to do. Historical critics sometimes complain that it treats texts as mere stories rather than as records of significant moments in history. Reader-oriented literary critics may find the notion of an implied reader too limiting and accuse narrative critics of ignoring the vast panoply of potential responses that real readers actually bring to texts. Such criticisms are based on accurate observations regarding what narrative criticism does and does not attempt to do, but they miss the point if they assume that commitment to narrative criticism precludes one from also studying texts in other ways.

Ideological objections are sometimes leveled against narrative criticism on the grounds that adoption of the implied reader's perspective prevents dialogue with what is objectionable in texts. Thus, if the implied readers of a Gospel are expected to have a patriarchal or anti-Semitic point of view, the narrative critic will be forced to interpret the text from that perspective. But narrative critics are under no compulsion to accept personally the interpretations that their method leads them to articulate. Narrative criticism merely identifies how we as readers are expected to be affected by the text if we read it from the point of view that the text assumes that we possess. Whether we as real readers embrace, ignore, or resist the response expected of the implied reader is a matter of individual choice. Ironically, the proponents of "resistant reading" who make this charge against narrative criticism usually practice narrative criticism themselves, though unwittingly, in order to determine what it is that they want to resist.

Other objections to narrative criticism focus on the manner in which the method is actually practiced. For instance, narrative critics may be charged with anachronistically applying modern concepts to ancient literature or with treating the Gospels as though they were novels or works of fiction. Such criticisms may be valid. Narrative criticism is a relatively new discipline, and its procedures are still being tested in the crucibles of scholarship. Narrative critics themselves have found that some approaches work better than others and they are continually revising their work in light of new insights that arise.

For those who have embraced narrative criticism, a primary attraction has been the opportunity to study biblical stories on their own terms — as stories, rather than simply as sources for historical or theological reflection. For most Christians, the indispensable source of life and vitality of faith is neither a tentative historical reconstruction nor a set of scripturally derived doctrinal principles. That source is, rather, the stories of the Bible themselves, remembered, treasured, and interpreted in their narrative form.[13] By respecting the literary character of these stories, narrative criticism is able to attend to what many people think should be one dimension of the total theological task of scriptural exegesis.

5. Suggestions for Further Reading

The development of narrative criticism is one aspect of a larger movement involving application of modern literary theory to biblical studies. For a brief survey of this movement and an extensive bibliography of the literature it has produced see *The Bible and Modern Literary Criticism: A Critical Assessment and Annotated Bibliography,* by Mark Allan Powell with the assistance of Cecile G. Gray and Melissa C. Curtis (Westport: Greenwood, 1992).

For a historical overview of the development of narrative criticism by one who ultimately finds it shortsighted see Stephen D. Moore, *Literary Criticism and the Gospels: The Theoretical Challenge* (New Haven: Yale University, 1989). For a detailed description of the principles and procedures of narrative criticism as it is currently practiced in NT studies, see Mark Allan Powell, *What Is Narrative Criticism?* GBS (Minneapolis: Fortress, 1990).

13. Alan Culpepper, "Story and History in the Gospels," *RevExp* 81 (1984) 467-77, esp. 474.

Some of the most accessible works that use narrative criticism in studies of particular NT books are:

On Matthew: David R. Bauer, *The Structure of Matthew's Gospel: A Study in Literary Design,* JSNTSS 31 (Sheffield: Almond, 1988); John Paul Heil, *The Death and Resurrection of Jesus: A Narrative-Critical Reading of Matthew 26-28* (Minneapolis: Fortress, 1991); David B. Howell, *Matthew's Inclusive Story: A Study in the Narrative Rhetoric of the First Gospel,* JSNTSS 42 (Sheffield: JSOT, 1990); Jack Dean Kingsbury, *Matthew as Story* (2d ed., Philadelphia: Fortress, 1988); Dorothy Jean Weaver, *Matthew's Missionary Discourse: A Literary-Critical Analysis,* JSNTSS 38 (Sheffield: JSOT, 1990).

On Mark: Jerry Camery-Hoggatt, *Irony in Mark's Gospel: Text and Subtext,* SNTSMS 72 (Cambridge: Cambridge University, 1992); Jack Dean Kingsbury, *Conflict in Mark: Jesus, Authorities, Disciples* (Fortress, 1989); Elizabeth Struthers Malbon, *Narrative Space and Mythic Meaning in Mark* (San Francisco: Harper and Row, 1986); David Rhoads and Donald Michie, *Mark as Story: An Introduction to the Narrative of a Gospel* (Philadelphia: Fortress, 1982).

On Luke and Acts: John A. Darr, *On Character Building: The Reader and the Rhetoric of Characterization in Luke-Acts,* LCBI (Louisville: Westminster/John Knox, 1992); Robert J. Karris, *Luke, Artist and Theologian: Luke's Passion Account as Literature* (New York: Paulist, 1985); Jack Dean Kingsbury, *Conflict in Luke: Jesus, Authorities, Disciples* (Minneapolis: Fortress, 1991); William S. Kurz, *Reading Luke-Acts: Dynamics of Biblical Narrative* (Louisville: Westminster/John Knox, 1993); Steven M. Sheeley, *Narrative Asides in Luke-Acts,* JSNTSS 72 (Sheffield: JSOT, 1992); Robert C. Tannehill, *The Narrative Unity of Luke-Acts: A Literary Interpretation,* 2 vols. (Philadelphia/Minneapolis: Fortress, 1986, 1990).

On John: R. Alan Culpepper, *Anatomy of the Fourth Gospel: A Study in Literary Design* (Philadelphia: Fortress, 1983); Paul Duke, *Irony in the Fourth Gospel* (Atlanta: John Knox, 1985); Gail R. O'Day, *Revelation in the Fourth Gospel: Narrative Mode and Theological Claim* (Philadelphia: Fortress, 1986); Jeffrey L. Staley, *The Print's First Kiss: A Rhetorical Investigation of the Implied Reader in the Fourth Gospel,* SBLDS 82 (Atlanta: Scholars, 1988); Mark W. G. Stibbe, *John as Storyteller: Narrative Criticism and the Fourth Gospel,* SNTSMS 73 (Cambridge: Cambridge University, 1992).

13. *Rhetorical Criticism*

C. CLIFTON BLACK

As prophesied some years ago by Wilhelm Wuellner,[1] a tidal wave of rhetorical studies is pounding NT journals, conferences, and bibliographies. Its force is tsunamic and shows no signs of imminent ebb. For the uninitiated this must surely seem bizarre, since the "rhetoric" to which our television and newspapers commonly alert us is, in the words of *The Random House Dictionary of the English Language* (2d ed., 1987), "the undue use of exaggeration or display; bombast." If this is what NT exegetes are now expected to study, most of us would gladly lie down until the urge passes.

The problem, as one might guess, lies less with rhetoric than with its cheap connotation in our vernacular. For wherever someone attempts, in speech or in writing, to persuade others — whether from the pulpit or the Op-Ed page, in a term paper or around the kitchen table — there you will find rhetoric employed. As we will be using the term here, therefore, rhetoric generally bears on those distinctive properties of human discourse, especially its artistry and argument, by which the authors of biblical literature have endeavored to convince others of the truth of their beliefs.

---

1. Wilhelm Wuellner, "Where Is Rhetorical Criticism Taking Us?" *CBQ* 49 (1987) 448-63, esp. 452-53.

1. The Tradition of Rhetorical Practice and Study

Indeed, if the study of rhetoric appears innovative to modern biblical interpreters, then that is surely symptomatic of their philosophical amnesia. The practice of oratory is as old as Homer (ninth or eighth century BCE), whose epics are not only punctuated with heroic speeches but are themselves exquisite testimonies of the bard's own oratorical craft. By the fifth century BCE the Sicilian teachers Corax and Tisias, among others, had compiled technical handbooks on rhetoric for the use of ordinary Greek citizens in political assemblies and courts of law. Gorgias (*ca.* 480-375 BCE) and Isocrates (*ca.* 436-338 BCE) refined the sophistic approach to rhetoric, that is, the orator's skillful deployment of rhythm, rhyme, and other poetic embellishments to move or to entertain an audience. A backlash against the morally vacuous exploitation of sophistic rhetoric is evident in some dialogues of Plato (*ca.* 429-347 BCE; see, in particular, *Gorgias* and *Phaedrus*); yet it was Plato's own pupil Aristotle (384-322 BCE) who systematized the theoretical substructure of classical rhetoric and related its practice to the arts and sciences and to dialectical logic in particular.

With the Hellenization of the Mediterranean world, first by Alexander the Great (356-323 BCE) and later by imperial Rome (27 BCE–476 CE), technical rhetoric became the essence of secondary education, which prepared Roman citizens for advancement in public life.[2] Although it is impossible (and needless) to demonstrate that Jesus, the earliest apostles, or the authors of the Gospels received formal education in rhetoric, undeniably they were born into a culture whose everyday modes of oral and written discourse were saturated with a rhetorical tradition, which was mediated by such practitioners and theoreticians as Caecilius (a Sicilian Jew of the late first century BCE), Cicero (106-43 BCE), and Quintilian (*ca.* 40-95 CE). The influence of technical and sophistic rhetoric on Christian preaching, teaching, and apologetics is evident and easier to document during the patristic period, conspicuously in the Greek sermons of John Chrysostom (*ca.* 347-407) and of the great Cappadocians (Gregory of Nazianzus [*ca.* 329-389], Basil of Caesarea [*ca.* 330-379], and Gregory of Nyssa [*ca.* 330-395]). Of the eight most notable Latin fathers of the church, three (Hilary of Poitiers [*ca.* 315-367], Ambrose [*ca.* 337-397], and Jerome [*ca.* 342-420]) were thoroughly schooled in rhetoric, while five (Tertullian [*ca.* 160-225],

2. See Donald L. Clark, *Rhetoric in Greco-Roman Education* (New York: Columbia University, 1957).

Cyprian [d. *ca.* 258], Arnobius [d. *ca.* 330], Lactantius [*ca.* 240-320], and Augustine [354-430]) had been professional rhetoricians before their conversion to Christianity.[3]

Not only did the study of rhetoric pervade the early Christian tradition; it also enriched the medieval, Renaissance, and Enlightenment academic legacy of which modern theological students are beneficiaries. As barbarism fell like night on Italy, Cassiodorus Senator (*ca.* 490-585) helped to keep aflame the study of rhetoric and the other six liberal arts (grammar, dialectic, geometry, arithmetic, astronomy, and music) from his monastery at Vivarium.[4] During the European Renaissance and Reformation the renewal of biblical criticism and the recovery of Ciceronian rhetoric fit hand-in-glove in the work of such humanists as Lorenzo Valla (*ca.* 1406-1457), Desiderius Erasmus (1469-1536), Philipp Melanchthon (1497-1560), and John Calvin (1509-1564). Buoyed by the neoclassical revival of the arts in Europe and North America during the eighteenth and nineteenth centuries, rhetorical modes of NT analysis persisted, albeit fitfully, into the early twentieth century, as illustrated by the dissertation of the young Rudolf Bultmann (1884-1976)[5] and the grammar of NT Greek created by Friedrich Wilhelm Blass (1843-1907), which remains the standard work in its field.[6] Indisputably, the exercise and conceptualization of classical rhetoric has exerted profound impact, not only on the writings of the NT, but also on successive centuries of NT study.

3. As noted by George A. Kennedy, *Classical Rhetoric and Its Christian and Secular Tradition from Ancient to Modern Times* (Chapel Hill: University of North Carolina, 1980) 146. To Augustine belongs the credit for first drawing the implications of rhetorical theory for Christian belief and practice, hermeneutics, and homiletics. See *On Christian Doctrine,* The Library of the Liberal Arts (Indianapolis: Bobbs-Merrill, 1958).

4. Cassiodorus Senator, *An Introduction to Divine and Human Readings,* ed. and trans. Leslie Webber Jones (New York: W. W. Norton, 1946, 1969). See also James J. Murphy, *Rhetoric in the Middle Ages: A History of Rhetorical Theory from St. Augustine to the Renaissance* (Berkeley: University of California, 1974).

5. Rudolf Bultmann, *Der Stil der paulinischen Predigt und die kynisch-stoische Diatribe,* FRLANT 13 (Göttingen: Vandenhoeck und Ruprecht, 1910). Bultmann's study has been refined by Stanley K. Stowers, *The Diatribe and Paul's Letter to the Romans,* SBLDS 57 (Missoula: Scholars, 1981).

6. Friedrich Wilhelm Blass and Albert Debrunner, *A Greek Grammar of the New Testament,* trans. and ed. Robert W. Funk (Chicago: University of Chicago, 1961 [first German edition, 1896]).

2. Major Currents in Rhetorical Criticism

As suggested by the preceding differentiation of its technical, sophistic, and philosophical varieties, orators and their analysts have never completely agreed on how rhetoric should be defined. A similar multiformity, if not confusion, characterizes current rhetorical analyses of the Bible. Much as "literary criticism" has been applied to so broad a field of interpretive strategies that the label arguably deserves retirement from overwork,[7] "rhetorical criticism" is a sometimes cumbersome expression that describes a range of kindred yet distinguishable approaches to biblical exegesis.

2.1 Rhetorical Analysis as Study of the Bible's Literary Artistry

Among both OT and NT scholars the term "rhetorical criticism" is almost indissolubly associated with James Muilenburg (1896-1974), whose 1968 presidential address to the Society of Biblical Literature summed up his career-long interest in biblical poetics and issued a programmatic call for the study of Hebrew literary composition. Muilenburg conceived rhetorical criticism as a supplement to the work of form critics, among whom he sympathetically numbered himself, and as a corrective to some of that earlier method's exaggerated tendencies. In an era that had stressed a literary genre's typical and representative aspects, abstracted from their settings in the life of Israel, Muilenburg argued for the recovery of the particularities of any given pericope — "the many and various devices by which the predications [in a literary unit] are formulated and ordered into a unified whole" — with attention paid to the author's intention, historical context, and distinctive blending of form and content.[8]

In NT research the writings of Amos Niven Wilder (1895-1993) approximate Muilenburg's understanding of biblical rhetoric. Like Muilenburg's, Wilder's approach to biblical texts was historically grounded, regard-

---

7. During the past forty years alone, "literary criticism" has been used to refer to reconstruction of sources; analysis of poetic structure; study of a narrative's genre, plot, or characters; psycho-anthropological decoding of a text's "deep structure"; postmodernist deconstruction of a text by an individual or community of readers; and a great many other things besides. Richard Coggins, "Keeping Up with Recent Studies X: The Literary Approach to the Bible," *ExpTim* 96 (1984) 9-14, offers help in unraveling this methodological tangle.

8. James Muilenburg, "Form Criticism and Beyond," *JBL* 88 (1969) 4-8.

ing the study of their modes of discourse as complementary to historical criticism of biblical traditions. Also like Muilenburg, Wilder abjured separations between form and content: Biblical genres like dialogue, story, parable, and poem are "deeply determined by the faith or life-orientation that produced them," which themselves are governed by specific social and religious patterns.[9] More than Muilenburg, Wilder probed the phenomenological dimensions of biblical rhetoric, the ways in which human existence is experienced and interpreted through religious discourse.[10]

Whether Muilenburg and Wilder were the progenitors of a definable school of rhetorical interpretation is debatable. It is easier to assess the degree to which they reopened some convergent avenues of research into biblical rhetoric that have ended up veering appreciably from their own approaches. Typical of much scholarship that takes its bearings from Wilder and Muilenburg is an understanding of rhetoric that concentrates on the aesthetic or inherently literary properties of biblical discourse, with attention paid to its metaphorical, stylistic, and structural features.[11] This mode of rhetorical criticism frequently melts into so-called New Criticism, the method of choice among North American literary critics of the 1940s and 1950s.[12] At the point where it prescinds from considering the historical and social location of biblical texts and their authors' intent, rhetorical criticism of this kind diverges from Muilenburg's or Wilder's own interpretive inclinations.

2.2 Analysis of the New Testament according to the Canons of Classical Rhetoric

It may be that Muilenburg's and Wilder's historical interests are more deliberately fulfilled in the work of the North American classicist George A.

---

9. Amos N. Wilder, *Early Christian Rhetoric: The Language of the Gospel* (Cambridge: Harvard University, 1964) 25-26.

10. Among other works, see Wilder's *The New Voice: Religion, Literature, Hermeneutics* (New York: Herder and Herder, 1969), and compare Michael J. Hyde and Craig R. Smith, "Hermeneutics and Rhetoric: A Seen but Unobserved Relationship," *QJS* 65 (1979) 347-63.

11. See, for instance, Joanna Dewey, *Markan Public Debate: Literary Technique, Concentric Structure, and Theology in Mark 2:1–3:6*, SBLDS 48 (Chico: Scholars, 1980).

12. Thus Wayne C. Booth, *The Rhetoric of Fiction* (2d ed., Chicago: University of Chicago, 1983). David Rhoads and Donald Michie are among the many biblical interpreters who mine this vein of biblical rhetoric; see their *Mark as Story: An Introduction to the Narrative of a Gospel* (Philadelphia: Fortress, 1982). Consult also, in the present volume, the discussion of narrative criticism by Mark Allan Powell.

Kennedy (1928-). For Kennedy, rhetoric refers not so much to "literary artistry" as to the disciplined art of persuasion as practiced and theorized by Greeks and Romans of the classical and Hellenistic periods. "What we need to do is to try to hear [early Christian authors'] words as a Greek-speaking audience would have heard them, and that involves some understanding of classical rhetoric," particularly the norms of persuasive discourse that suffused the culture of Mediterranean antiquity. While Kennedy is not the first scholar to have reclaimed technical rhetoric for NT exegesis, his accessible presentation of classical concepts has probably been the most influential among English-speaking scholars.[13]

Kennedy's method of rhetorical criticism can be summarized in six steps, the first of which is determining the rhetorical unit to be analyzed. As form critics (like Muilenburg) identify discrete pericopes, so also rhetorical critics like Kennedy search for evidence of *inclusio,* opening and closure, in a unit of discourse with some magnitude. An attempt is made, second, to define the rhetorical situation, that is, the complex of persons, events, and relations that generates pressure for a verbal response. With this one might compare the form critic's discovery of a genre's *Sitz im Leben* or setting in life. Third, the primary rhetorical problem addressed by the discourse is identified. Kennedy suggests two classical frameworks within which this identification can be made: One may pinpoint the *stasis* or specific question at issue (which, as Kennedy argues, can be crucial for interpreting Paul's letters, the speeches in Acts, or Jesus' controversies with Pharisees). Alternatively, the critic can ascertain the kind of judgment that the audience of the discourse is asked to render: whether it is a *judicial* assessment of past circumstances (for instance, the character of Paul's early ministry in Corinth, to which much of 2 Corinthians refers), a *deliberative* reckoning of actions that might be expedient or beneficial for the listeners' future performance (thus the Sermon on the Mount in Matthew 5–7), or the *epideictic* instillation and enhancement of particular beliefs or values in the present (for example, Jesus' farewell address to his disciples in John 14–16).

Consideration of the arrangement *(taxis)* of the parts into a unified

13. George A. Kennedy, *New Testament Interpretation through Rhetorical Criticism* (Chapel Hill/London: University of North Carolina, 1984) 10. Kennedy's approach is based on ancient rhetorical handbooks that are all available, with English translation, in the LCL: Aristotle's *The "Art" of Rhetoric;* Cicero's *De inventione; Rhetorica ad Herennium* (of disputed authorship); and Quintilian's *Institutio Oratoria.*

discourse is the fourth of Kennedy's critical steps. Compared with the structure of deliberative and epideictic address, judicial oratory displays the most elaborate conventional arrangement: an introductory *proem*, followed by the *narration* of background information, the *proposition* to be proved, the *proof*, a *refutation* of contrary views, and a concluding *epilogue*. The fifth step is analysis of the invention and style of the discourse. Invention *(heurēsis)* pertains to the crafting of arguments based on proofs: *ēthos*, the persuasive power of the speaker's authoritative character (cf. Mark 1:22); *pathos*, the emotional responses generated among the listeners (cf. Acts 2:37); and *logos*, the deductive or inductive arguments of the discourse itself (e.g., Heb 1:1–2:14). Style *(lexis)* refers to the text's choice of words and their formulation in "figures of speech" and "figures of thought." Sixth, reviewing the whole analysis, the critic evaluates the unit's rhetorical effectiveness.

To date, rhetorical criticism in this classical mode has stimulated so much NT research that this research defies easy summary. Nevertheless, some basic avenues are discernible. One, notably pursued by Duane F. Watson,[14] is the intensive application of Kennedy's six-stage method to various canonical documents (usually epistles). Second, and perhaps most fruitful to date for interpreting the Gospels, is the study of *chreiai*, that is, didactic anecdotes, the nonbiblical counterparts of which were developed by Hermogenes of Tarsus (late second century CE) and other rhetoricians for training pupils in composition and orations.[15] Third, as exemplified by Margaret M. Mitchell's constructive argument for the unity of 1 Corinthians,[16] classical rhetoric has been employed to throw fresh light on some longstanding questions of NT exegesis. Fourth, classical rhetoric has been adopted by theorists who aim to reformulate tradition-historical forms of interpretation like form criticism.[17] Fifth, and perhaps most provocatively,

14. Representative of Watson's several investigations is his *Invention, Arrangement, and Style: Rhetorical Criticism of Jude and 2 Peter*, SBLDS 104 (Atlanta: Scholars, 1988).

15. Consult Burton L. Mack and Vernon K. Robbins, *Patterns of Persuasion in the Gospels*, FF: Literary Facets (Sonoma: Polebridge, 1989). Generations of North American children have been schooled in honesty through a modern *chreia* popularized by Parson Weems: young George Washington's confession that he had chopped down a cherry tree.

16. Margaret M. Mitchell, *Paul and the Rhetoric of Reconciliation: An Exegetical Investigation of the Language and Composition of 1 Corinthians* (Louisville: Westminster/John Knox, 1991).

17. Klaus Berger, *Formgeschichte des Neuen Testaments* (Heidelberg: Quelle und Meyer, 1984).

ancient rhetorical precepts and practices are used by some scholars as a springboard for revising the concepts of rhetoric and rhetorical analysis themselves. And with that, we are led into yet another mode of rhetorical criticism.

2.3 Rhetoric Appraised as an Instrument for the Consolidation of Power and Cohesion within Communities of Readers

Another rhetorical strain of NT interpretation concentrates neither on ancient poetics nor on classical modes of persuasion. Indeed, for some engaged in "the reinvention of rhetoric," diachronic pursuit of the intentions of biblical authors is regarded as evidence of "the devastating grip of [historical-critical] positivism in our discipline," which should yield to the text's argumentative function for any reader in any age.[18] Similarly, narrow preoccupation with biblical stylistics is viewed as "the [academic] ghetto," "the Babylonian captivity" from which rhetorical study must be liberated.[19] So what, properly understood, is the role of rhetoric and its criticism? Elisabeth Schüssler Fiorenza has proposed one answer:

> Whereas the poetic work attempts to create and to organize imaginative experience, rhetoric seeks to persuade and to motivate people to *act right*. Rhetoric seeks to instigate a change of attitudes and motivations, it strives to persuade, to teach and to engage the hearer/reader by eliciting reactions, emotions, convictions, and identifications. The evaluative criterion for rhetoric is not aesthetics, but praxis.[20]

For proponents of so-called New Rhetoric, the seminal work is surely that of Chaim Perelman (1912-1984) and Lucie Olbrechts-Tyteca. In the view of these two theorists, ancient rhetoric offers the modern critic not so much interpretive norms to be repristinated as a foundational, if flawed, theory to be revised, accenting the inducement or enhancement of an audience's adherence to particular values by means of various strategies of practical reasoning. For Perelman and Olbrechts-Tyteca the key to rhetoric lies in "the

18. Jan Botha, "On the 'Reinvention' of Rhetoric," *Scriptura* 31 (1989) 14-31, here 27; Lauri Thurén, *The Rhetorical Strategy of 1 Peter, with Special Regard to Ambiguous Expressions* (Åbo: Åbo Akademis, 1990).

19. Wuellner, "Where Is Rhetorical Criticism Taking Us?" 457, 462.

20. Elisabeth Schüssler Fiorenza, "Rhetorical Situation and Historical Reconstruction in 1 Corinthians," *NTS* 33 (1987) 386-403, here 387.

social aspect of language, which is an instrument of communication and influence on others."[21] Thus there is an irreducibly *practical* and *social* thrust to rhetorical criticism: A text's arguments are to be evaluated less in terms of their persuasive intent or logical validity and more with respect to the implied values of their social context and the capacity of those arguments to secure commitment and to motivate action. Similarly, though in treatises less systematic and more allusive, Kenneth Burke (1897-1993) stresses the capacity of oral and written discourse to induce social cohesion or transformation by projecting comprehensive, symbolic visions of reality.[22]

Of all the currents in rhetorical analysis, the New Rhetoric of Burke, Perelman, and others may be the most difficult to classify. Among practitioners within the biblical guild, its center of gravity resides in the text's power to move an audience or community of readers, whether ancient or modern. Grounded in the social experience of reading, the New Rhetoric usually moves beyond aesthetic or historical analysis, deliberately and often eclectically expanding the classical tradition of rhetoric into such areas as twentieth-century social psychology, hermeneutics, and semiotics (the study of sign-using behavior). When a rhetorical critic of this stripe explores the intricate creation and subversion of a reader's expectations by a biblical text, the outcome may resemble an ahistorical, reader-response interpretation.[23] Nevertheless, other New Rhetorical analyses of the NT exhibit a greater measure of historical interest.

Wilhelm Wuellner (1927-) is known for a body of work produced over many years and may be considered an exponent of the New Rhetorical approach. While his analyses of NT texts typically intersect with the tradition of classical rhetoric, increasingly his musings on rhetoric seem impatient with historical questions, instead emphasizing the intrinsically rhetorical constitution of human beings and the role of discourse as a practical exercise of power.[24] In Wuellner's own words, "Rhetorical criticism is taking

21. Chaim Perelman and Lucie Olbrechts-Tyteca, *The New Rhetoric: A Treatise on Argumentation* (Notre Dame: University of Notre Dame, 1969) 513.

22. Kenneth Burke, *A Rhetoric of Motives* (New York: Prentice-Hall, 1950); *idem*, *The Rhetoric of Religion: Studies in Logology* (Berkeley: University of California, 1970).

23. See, e.g., Jeffrey Lloyd Staley, *The Print's First Kiss: A Rhetorical Investigation of the Implied Reader in the Fourth Gospel*, SBLDS 82 (Atlanta: Scholars, 1988). Consult also, in this volume, the chapters on discourse theory and theories of reading by Joel Green and Kevin Vanhoozer.

24. See, e.g., his "Hermeneutics and Rhetorics: From 'Truth and Method' to 'Truth and Power,'" *Scriptura Special Issue* 3 (1989) 1-54.

us beyond hermeneutics and structuralism to poststructuralism and post-hermeneutics."[25]

3. Rhetorical Criticism Applied:
Three Trips to a Samaritan Well

Let us put this variegated rhetorical criticism to the test in reading John 4:1-42. A full-scale analysis of this material is obviously out of the question. Fortunately, for our purposes so complete an examination is unnecessary. All that can and need be accomplished here are some appreciative tastings of the current vintage and different varieties of rhetorical analysis.

3.1 In a Manner of Speaking

Jesus' comments in John 4 are exchanges in a dialogue with a Samaritan woman, not an uninterrupted oration. To subject this discourse to all six of Kennedy's rhetorical-critical questions would probably be unwise, even if such interrogation could be accommodated in this essay. Still, we can profitably touch on some aspects of a traditional approach to rhetorical analysis.

Kennedy's understanding of *"the rhetorical situation"* (which, as such, is not a classical notion but a modern abstraction)[26] offers us a useful way of positioning John 4:1-42 in its literary context. So if we ask what conditions have created pressure for Jesus' declarations at this point in the Fourth Gospel, we might recall such things as (1) his departure from Judea and return to Galilee, in the wake of controversy (2:13-21) and incomprehension (3:1-21); (2) the (divine?) necessity of his passing through Samaria (4:4; cf. 3:14); (3) attestations of Jesus' importance from John the baptizer (1:19-35; 3:25-36), Jesus' own disciples (1:36-51), and the Gospel's narrator (1:1-18); and (4) the Evangelist's reminder that Jesus is prescient in his dealings with people (2:23-25). Within this framework Jesus and the woman's responses to one another are striking. Jesus is forthcoming about his identity (4:26) and initiates and sustains with her a theologically serious and educational dialogue (4:7-26). For her part, she proves to be a quick study: Markedly responsive to "the gift of God" (4:10; cf. 3:3-4), she ad-

25. Wuellner, "Where Is Rhetorical Criticism Taking Us"? 449.
26. For this concept Kennedy is indebted to Lloyd F. Bitzer, "The Rhetorical Situation," *Philosophy and Rhetoric* 1 (1968) 1-14.

vances so far in her understanding of Jesus' significance (4:9, 11, 19, 29) that by the story's end she bears witness of it to others (4:28-30, 39).

Following Kennedy's lead, one may inquire about *the overriding rhetorical problem* or issue implied by John 4. Most of Jesus' remarks to the woman seem intended neither to elicit her judgment about past events nor to spur her future action, but rather to clarify her present understanding of some religious matters of fundamental importance (see especially 4:10, 21-24, 26). The force of Jesus' discourse is, therefore, primarily epideictic, which admittedly entails for this woman a judicial reconsideration of previously held beliefs as well as a deliberative decision, by the pericope's end, to missionize on the strength of her encounter with Jesus.

The distinctive *style* of Jesus' discourse in John 4 invites exploration by means of classical canons. Once readers have cultivated an ear for it, Jesus' manner of speech in the Fourth Gospel presents one of the most striking differences between John and the Synoptics. Even in English translation the Johannine Jesus' remarks are less terse and conversational, more exalted and almost operatic: "But the hour is coming, and now is here, when the true worshipers will worship the Father in spirit and truth, for the Father seeks such as these to worship him. God is spirit, and those who worship him must worship in spirit and truth" (John 4:23-24; see also 4:13-14, 21-22). On Jesus' lips seemingly innocent turns of phrase in John can be galvanized with double entendre. For instance, ὕδωρ ζῶν (*hydōr zōn*, 4:10) can mean "running water" (as the woman takes Jesus' comment, v. 11) but is surely intended to suggest "living water" (see also 6:35; cf. Jer 2:13; Zech 14:8; Sir 24:21).[27] From the Johannine Jesus' utterances flows a heavenly force that rolls over the heads of his earthbound interlocutors (John 4:7-10, 16-18, 31-34). In ch. 4, as throughout the Gospel, Jesus' speech displays the other-worldly discernment of one who does not originate from this world but transcends it (cf. 3:31-32; 6:31-59; 7:35, 46; 8:22-23).

Several stylistic traits are peculiarly associated with religious themes in antiquity: sublimity *(hypsos, hypsēgoria)*, solemnity *(semnotēs)*, and obscurity *(asapheia, obscuritas)*.[28] In the writings of "Longinus" (first

---

27. Another example of supercharged double meaning occurs in 4:26 with Jesus' acknowledgment of his messiahship: ἐγώ εἰμι *(egō eimi)*, "I am," functions in John's Gospel as an expression of Jesus' oneness with God (see also 6:20; 8:24, 28, 58; 13:19; cf. Exod 3:14; Isa 43:10-11, 25; 51:12).

28. For the following observations I am indebted to Frank Thielman, "The Style of the Fourth Gospel and Ancient Literary Critical Concepts of Religious Discourse,"

century CE) and others, *sublimity* refers not to refined locution but to an inspired form of human utterance that "contains much food for reflection" (*On the Sublime* 7.3; see also 13.2; 36.1). For Hermogenes (*On Types* 242.1–246.1), *solemnity* is especially appropriate for expressing general thoughts about the gods and aspects of humanity that intersect with divinity, such as righteousness and the soul's immortality. Whereas *obscurity* could be regarded as a stylistic fault (e.g., Aristotle *Rhetoric* 3.3.3), in other contexts (such as pronouncements by the oracle at Delphi) *asapheia* could be considered appropriate to religion's mysterious character (so Demetrius *On Style* 2.101). Since *sublimity* and *solemnity* could be characteristic of the merely wise or noble, these stylistic properties were potentially but not necessarily indicative of proximity to the divine (Philo *The Worse Attacks the Better* 43-44, 79; Hermogenes *On Types* 246.1-9).

The relationship between these considerations and John's depiction of Jesus should be obvious. In the Fourth Gospel, Jesus, while recognizably human (1:14; 4:6-7), speaks in a way suggestive of divinity, according to classical conventions of style. Interlocutors like the Samaritan woman and the disciples are attuned to only the lower level of Jesus' polyvalent discourse, the divine nuances of which are pitched at a frequency that is inaudible without a boost from God. The exalted tenor of Jesus' remarks is satisfyingly intelligible, however, to one who has read the stylistically similar prologue to the Gospel, since John 1:1-18 affords the reader information about Jesus' transcendent origin, to which the story's characters (except God and Jesus himself) are not privy. As Amos Wilder has observed, Johannine style attempts to portray "the dialogue between heaven and earth," and "it is the feature of distortion, perhaps only slight, which is the sign of genuine religious immediacy and creativeness."[29]

3.2 Poetics at Noonday

Considering the rhetoric of John 4 in the manner of Muilenburg invites scrutiny of the text's bonds and bounds, its internal arrangement and repetitive features. Viewed under this magnifying glass, John's account of

---

in *Persuasive Artistry: Studies in New Testament Rhetoric in Honor of George A. Kennedy*, ed. Duane F. Watson, JSNTSS 50 (Sheffield: JSOT, 1991) 169-83.

29. Wilder, *Early Christian Rhetoric*, 50-51.

Jesus and the woman at the well exhibits a fuguelike entwining of (A) request, (B) resistance, (C) explanation, and (D) belief:

A Structural Analysis of John 4:7-42

First movement: Jesus and an unexpected disciple (4:7-26)

    First theme: A taste of eschatological water (4:7-15)

    First interchange: Requests for a drink (4:7-10)

        A. Jesus' request of water from the Samaritan woman (4:7-8)

        B. The woman's rejection of his request, in the form of a guarded question (4:9)

        C. Jesus' response to her rejection (4:10)

            i. Were she to recognize her interlocutor's identity (4:10a),

            ii. She would ask him for a drink (4:10b).

    Second interchange: Confusion over "water" (4:11-15)

        B. The woman's misunderstanding of the water mentioned by Jesus (4:11-12)

        C. Jesus' explanation: he speaks of spiritual, not mundane, water (4:13-14)

        A. The woman's request of water from Jesus (4:15; fulfilling 4:10b)

    Second theme: A taste of eschatological worship (4:16-26)

    Third interchange: Request for the woman's husband (4:16-18)

        A. Jesus' request that the woman call her husband (4:16)

        B. The woman's oblique rejection of this request (4:17a)

        C. Jesus' discerning affirmation of her response (4:17b-18)

    Fourth interchange: Confusion over Jesus' identity (4:19-26)

        D. The woman's partial perception of Jesus' identity (4:19-20)

        C. Jesus' explanation: genuine worship is spiritual (4:21-24)

        D. The woman's leaning toward an accurate identification of Jesus (4:25), which he accepts (4:26; fulfilling 4:10a)

Second movement: Jesus and his other followers (4:27-42)

Third theme: A taste of eschatological food (4:27-38)

Fifth interchange: Invitations to leave (4:27-30)

B. Arriving, Jesus' disciples implicitly question the woman's presence (4:27).

D. Leaving, the woman explicitly invites the city to witness Jesus (4:28-29).

D. Accepting the woman's invitation, the city leaves in search of Jesus (4:30).

Sixth interchange: An imminent harvest (4:31-38)

A. The disciples' request that Jesus eat (4:31)

C. Jesus' explanation: He has food unknown to them (4:32)

B. The disciples' misunderstanding of food mentioned by Jesus (4:33; cf. 4:11-12)

C. Jesus' explanation: he speaks of spiritual, not mundane, food (4:34-38)

    i. First proverb: No interval between sowing and harvest (4:35-36)

    ii. Second proverb: The sower's end-time dispatch of the reapers (4:37-38)

Fourth theme: A taste of eschatological knowledge (4:39-42)

D. The city believes what the woman says about Jesus (4:39; cf. 4:29).

C. Accepting the citizens' invitation, Jesus stays in the city (4:40; cf. 4:30).

D. Because of Jesus' word the city believes "the Savior of the world" (4:41-42).

For all the distortion generated by any outline, the elegant architecture of John 4:7-42 remains clear. Obviously, the story oscillates between the themes of drink and worship (in 4:4-26) and of food and missionary acclamation (in 4:27-42; cf. 6:1-59). The woman's and the disciples' requests, misunderstandings, and partial realizations repeatedly crack open larger theological issues. These in turn stimulate an apparent escalation of belief about Jesus, who is addressed as "a Jew" (4:9), "sir" (4:11, 15, 19), "greater than our ancestor Jacob" (4:12), "a prophet" (4:19), "Messiah" or "Christ" (4:25, 29), "rabbi" (4:31), and finally "the Savior of the world" (4:42). The text's internal unity is tightly stitched with numerous verbal threads: "drink" (πίνειν [pinein] and its cognates, 4:7, 9, 10a, 12, 13, 14), "water" (ὕδωρ [hydōr], 4:7, 13, 14, 15), which soon shades into "living water" (ὕδωρ ζῶν [hydōr zōn], 4:10, 11) and "eternal life" (ζωὴν αἰώνιον [zōēn aiōnion], 4:14; cf. 7:37-38), "worship" (προσκυνεῖν [proskynein] and its cognates, 4:20, 21, 22, 23, 24), "seek" (ζητεῖν [zētein], 4:23, 27), "harvest" (θερισμός [therismos] and its cognates, 4:35, 36, 37, 38), "believe" (πιστεύειν [pisteuein], 4:21, 39, 41, 42), and "truth" (ἀλήθεια [alētheia] and its cognates, 4:18, 23, 24, 37, 42).

Muilenburg's brand of rhetorical criticism, we should recall, intends to recover a text's unique features, which have been clothed in a traditional form. And so we are reminded that John 4 replicates a familiar type-scene from the OT, the betrothal. Whether its characters are Isaac's servant and Rebekah (Gen 24:10-20), Jacob and Rachel (Gen 29:1-14), or Moses and Zipporah (Exod 2:15b-21), the betrothal scene unfolds in a predictable though mutable way. Upon leaving his family circle and journeying to a foreign land, a prospective bridegroom encounters a marriageable woman at a well. After water has been drawn from the well and news of his arrival has been hurriedly reported to the woman's home, the stranger is invited to dinner. Soon thereafter, the couple is betrothed. Robert Alter has argued that contemporary audiences of these ancient stories — who were as familiar with their conventions as we are with those of detective mysteries or westerns — would have been gratified by their skillful adaptation: "As is true of all original art, what is really interesting is not the schema of convention but what is done in each individual application of the schema to give it a sudden tilt of innovation or even to refashion it radically for the imaginative purposes at hand."[30]

In this light John 4:4-42 dances recognizably and mischievously, even stunningly. All of the familiar elements of the betrothal scene are in play: On leaving his "family circle" ("the Jews" of John 2:13-25; 4:1-3) and journeying to a foreign land (Samaria, 4:4), a "bridegroom" named Jesus (3:29; see also 2:1-11) encounters a woman at a well (4:6-7a). After a request to draw water from the well (4:7b), news of the stranger's arrival is hurriedly reported back home (4:28-29), and he is invited to stay (4:40). John's

30. Robert Alter, *The Art of Biblical Narrative* (New York: Basic, 1981) 47-62, here 52.

adoption of this ancient *form* intimates the *content* of Jesus' forthright announcement in 4:22-23: that the same God who established the rhythm of Israel's history is the Father of Jesus and of the Samaritan woman. Yet the Fourth Evangelist has twisted the type-scene to potent theological effect: Now it is *Jesus* who gives to those who believe in him "living water, gushing up to eternal life" (4:14). The result is a very different betrothal — not in marriage but in worship (4:21-24) and mission (4:35-42).[31]

3.3 What Is a Reader to Do?

Since the New Rhetoricians have apparently not yet reached a consensus on method, any attempt to offer a representative interpretation of some portion of John 4 from this subdisciplinary point of view is surely hopeless. It is on *general outcome* that the New Rhetoricians tend more evidently to concur: Because the experience of reading is tethered to the socially situated experience of a reader, the fundamental criterion for rhetorical analysis is practical, not aesthetic.

Following the lead of Perelman and Wuellner, we might begin with the proposition that the story of Jesus and the Samaritan woman is presented in John for essentially the same purpose as the Gospel's other components: "so that you may come to believe [or "continue to believe"] that Jesus is the Messiah, the Son of God, and that through believing you may have life in his name" (20:31). John 4:4-42 is explicitly concerned to induce or to enhance belief in precisely these values. Just here in the Fourth Gospel, Jesus does what the Jews will demand of him in 10:24: He plainly acknowledges that he is the Messiah (4:26). Trust that Jesus is the Christ, the agent of indestructible life for the world, is the ultimate destination to which Jesus' discourse is intended to lead not only the Samaritan woman and her fellow citizens (4:10, 14, 26, 36, 41-42) but also the audience of John's narrative.[32]

Perelman and Olbrechts-Tyteca categorize four general techniques of argumentation: (1) quasi-logical arguments, which operate in the domain of common sense, (2) arguments that, by appealing to customary relationships of cause and effect, derive from assumptions about the structure of

---

31. For a closer inspection of textual echoes that reverberate between the Testaments, see ch. 11 above.

32. The conjunction of John's rhetoric and missionary interests is probed by Teresa Okure, *The Johannine Approach to Mission: A Contextual Study of John 4:1-42*, WUNT 2/31 (Tübingen: Mohr: 1988).

reality, (3) arguments that seek to establish the structure of reality by extrapolating general principles from particular cases, and (4) arguments that, by dissociating concepts, attempt to reformulate reality and to provoke new understanding.[33] If we view the conversation described in John 4:7-26 through this analytical prism, two things become clear. First, *both* Jesus *and* the woman are engaged in rhetorical performance. She is not the speechless pupil, nor he the imperious lecturer who will entertain no questions from the audience. Here we have *two* interlocutors, the one attempting to persuade the other.[34]

Second, the woman is inclined toward the first, more deductive set of strategies, common sense and cause and effect; Jesus tends toward the second, more inductive pair of techniques, pertaining to general principles and dissociation of concepts. Her comments tend to move in the realm of common sense ("Sir, you haven't got a bucket, and the well's deep" [4:11]) and longstanding custom ("You're a Jew, I'm a Samaritan" [4:9]; "Our ancestors worshiped on Gerizim, you people on Zion" [4:20]). Through the use of oblique metaphors ("the gift of God" [4:10], "running/living water" [4:10], "eternal life" [4:14]), Jesus is, by contrast, making a case for the structure of reality. More than that, Jesus' argument to the woman — and, by implication, to the reader — proceeds from and instantiates, as Perelman and Olbrechts-Tyteca put it, "another outlook and another criterion of reality,"[35] namely, the tolling of an hour when God is worshiped "in spirit and in truth" (4:23-24). Ultimately, worship is dissociated from the practice of both Samaritans and Jews (4:21) and is reconceived as praise of God that participates in the transforming energy, mediated by Jesus, that offers access to authentic reality.

The transaction that mysteriously propels the encounter at Jacob's well beyond rhetorical stalemate involves Jesus' request for the woman's husband (John 4:16), her response (4:17), and his rejoinder (4:18). Oceans of ink have been spilled over the question of whether this exchange is to be taken literally or symbolically (for example, as a veiled reference to Samaria's "adulterous" idolatry [2 Kgs 17:13-34]). One could as easily ask the same about Jesus' initial request for a drink (4:7): The question, in both

---

33. Perelman and Olbrechts-Tyteca, *The New Rhetoric,* 187-92.

34. So also Sandra M. Schneiders, *The Revelatory Text: Interpreting the New Testament as Sacred Scripture* (San Francisco: HarperCollins, 1991) 189, 191, 194. See below, ch. 17.

35. Perelman and Olbrechts-Tyteca, *The New Rhetoric,* 436.

cases, may be a red herring. Ultimately the central issue is no more the woman's sexual history than the Samaritans' alleged apostasy (neither of which is developed in the conversation). As the story unfolds, the crux of the matter is whether Jesus may be trusted as the revealer of the truth about human life and the life of God. This is the concern intimated by the woman's common-sense (and therefore contracted) acknowledgment of Jesus as a prophet (4:19), perhaps the Messiah (4:29), "who told me everything I have ever done" (4:29, 39). The same concern is indicated by the city's more expansive response to Jesus (4:39-40) and by their conviction, based on unmediated access to his word, "that this is truly the Savior of the world" (4:41-42).

If we accept the proposition of Wuellner, among others, that rhetorical criticism entails the personal and social identification, even transformation, of the critic, in what such directions might the rhetoric of John 4 lead us? Clearly, Jesus is no more disqualified from interaction with the woman because he is a Jew (contrary to her assumption in 4:9) than she is disqualified from interchange with him because she is a woman (contrary to the disciples' assumption in 4:27). Arguably, the egalitarian force of this rhetorical analysis has been insufficiently appreciated by those readers who, for instance, have seized on Jesus' statements in John 4:17-18 to castigate the woman's moral turpitude (about which the text is altogether silent). Arguably, as well, the christological force of this rhetorical analysis has been insufficiently appreciated by other commentators who have seized on the woman's evangelism (4:28-29) to extol her womanhood as such (about which the text is equally mute). If rhetorical interpretation of John 4 exposes the lack of faith attaching to our presuppositions about race or sex and instead invites us as readers to faith in Jesus Christ as "the Savior of the world," then such analysis is not only political but also theological in its critical bearing.

4. Some Rhetorical Questions

4.1 Is There a Rhetorical-Critical Method?

As described and illustrated here, *how coherent are the different expressions of rhetorical criticism?* Are we dealing with a unified method or with three disparate approaches, each of which styles itself as "rhetorically critical"? At present no unanimity exists among rhetorical critics themselves. Although the various forms of rhetorical study are reconcilable for some, for others the attempt to blend, say, the classical tradition with a modern, praxis-oriented understanding of rhetoric courts hermeneutical confusion.[36]

While granting that particular formulations of rhetorical criticism may be philosophically at odds with others, we can conceive of the enterprise of rhetorical criticism in a way that responsibly coordinates the several approaches that we have observed. Heuristically drawing on classical theory, one might consider rhetorical interpretation a three-legged stool, one on which many different critics may sit, with each applying more weight to one leg than to the others. Muilenburg's approach leans on *logos*, the structure and style of a biblical text. Kennedy's version, emphasizing authorial intent and technique, inclines toward the text's underlying *ēthos*. Perelman's stress on the text's reception by an audience recalls that dimension of rhetoric described by the ancients as *pathos*. I see no reason, in principle, why biblical interpreters may not tilt the critical stool in whichever direction their interests incline them. I suppose that one could go further, in theory, and advocate a radical redesign of the stool by sawing off any two of its legs that seem nonsupportive of one's particular interests. In that case the result would be a very wobbly stool, on which it would be hard for any reader to maintain interpretive equilibrium. For this reason, the current multiformity of NT rhetorical criticism is probably a healthy development, the overall effect of which is to balance its various tendencies and to restrain the potential of each for exegetical distortion.

4.2 Is Rhetorical Criticism Compatible with Historical Criticism?

This question, too, is disputed among theorists. For some, rhetorical criticism complements traditional analyses of the NT. For others, historical research and rhetorical study are impassably divided by a big ugly ditch.[37]

Some expressions of rhetorical criticism may indeed be impossible to harmonize philosophically with a historical frame of reference. It seems to

36. Contrast the procedures of Robert Jewett, *The Thessalonian Correspondence: Pauline Rhetoric and Millenarian Piety*, FF (Philadelphia: Fortress, 1986) 63-87; and Mitchell, *Paul and the Rhetoric of Reconciliation*, 1-19.

37. Contrast the assessments of Kennedy, *New Testament Interpretation*, 3-12, 157-60; and Dennis L. Stamps, "Rhetorical Criticism and the Rhetoric of New Testament Criticism," *JLT* 6 (1992) 268-79.

me, however, that historical and rhetorical inquiries are, at root, cooperative and not contesting. Philosophically, most forms of historical and rhetorical criticism known to me presuppose a shared model of communication that attempts to triangulate (1) the intent of an author (2) in the formulation of a text (3) that forms or informs a reader.[38] It should also be noted that all interpretive approaches to the Bible are byproducts of intellectual traditions and other cultural influences; hence even the most adamantly ahistorical brands of rhetorical criticism are themselves historically conditioned. Practically, it is hard for me to imagine a well-rounded rhetorical analysis of a NT text that could completely ignore its historical characteristics and assumptions. Much of the rhetorical force of John 4 turns on awareness of ancient aversions — of some rabbis toward protracted conversation with women (cf. v. 27) and of Jews and Samaritans toward one another (cf. v. 9) — and these are irrecoverable apart from historical reconstruction.[39]

4.3 What Are the Drawbacks of Rhetorical Criticism?

Each type of rhetorical study has its peculiar liabilities, some of which I have mentioned. Common to all forms of rhetorical criticism (and to all interpretive strategies, for that matter) is a tendency among some practitioners to absolutize the insights of their favored approach and, in the process, to lose clear sight of the text itself. For rhetorical critics this danger often manifests itself in the imposition of some ideal construct — whether it be a chiastic structure, classical taxonomies of invention, or a theory of the irreducibly rhetorical character of human behavior — on a particular biblical passage or book that resists all such preset patterns. Sensitivity to the multiple dimensions of NT texts and their interpretation, which this volume is intended to encourage, remains the best precaution against all sorts of "cookie-cutter criticism," rhetorical or otherwise.[40]

38. An analogous conclusion has been drawn, in another connection, by M. C. de Boer, "Narrative Criticism, Historical Criticism, and the Gospel of John," *JSNT* 47 (1992) 35-48.

39. Relevant primary texts are discussed by C. K. Barrett, *The Gospel according to St. John: An Introduction with Commentary and Notes on the Greek Text* (2d ed., Philadelphia: Westminster, 1978) 232-33, 240.

40. This warning is sounded in a trenchant review of Hans Dieter Betz's commentary on Galatians by Paul W. Meyer (*RelSRev* 7 [1981] 318-23, esp. 319). Betz's work is referred to in the bibliography below.

4.4 What Is Gained by Rhetorical Criticism?

In the academic marketplace of ideas, the study of rhetoric has proven to be a site for lively exchange among biblical interpreters of many methodological allegiances: historical critics and literary analysts, linguists and social scientists, philosophers and theologians. For biblical teachers and preachers, rhetorical criticism may also offer a forum in which the complex dynamics of religious discourse are considered. From its beginnings Christian proclamation has necessarily availed itself of reasoned argument and stylistic conventions; yet preaching has indulged in neither logic nor aesthetics for its own sake. The prime movers of the early church were the *ēthos* of Christ and the *pathos* of a Spirit-imbued life. Creatively fusing form and content, the church's *kerygma* was designed to construe the Christian experience, to express its power and to persuade others of its truth. To the degree that rhetorical criticism helps to clarify these aspects of the NT, it illumines the text to be interpreted and challenges its modern interpreters.

5. Suggestions for Further Reading

5.1 Surveys and Theoretical Essays

The history of rhetoric is perceptively summarized by George A. Kennedy, *Classical Rhetoric and Its Christian and Secular Tradition from Ancient to Modern Times* (Chapel Hill: University of North Carolina, 1980). Heinrich Lausberg, *Handbuch der literarischen Rhetorik: Eine Grundlegung der Literaturwissenschaft* (3d ed., Stuttgart: Steiner, 1990), is the standard modern handbook in the field, systematic in presentation and encyclopedic in scope. As a reconsideration of the classical tradition, the monograph by Chaim Perelman and Lucie Olbrechts-Tyteca, *The New Rhetoric: A Treatise on Argumentation* (Notre Dame: University of Notre Dame, 1969), has proved important. Adopting a broad definition of their topic, Duane F. Watson and Alan J. Hauser tabulate thousands of investigations of biblical rhetoric in *Rhetorical Criticism of the Bible: A Comprehensive Bibliography with Notes on History and Method*, BibIntS 4 (Leiden: Brill, 1994).

5.2 Surveys of New Testament Rhetoric

James Muilenburg, "Form Criticism and Beyond," *JBL* 88 (1969) 1-18, and Amos N. Wilder, *Early Christian Rhetoric: The Language of the Gospel* (Cambridge: Harvard University, 1964), are landmark statements that fostered the twentieth-century renaissance of biblical literary criticism. Some implications of the recovery of classical rhetoric have been explored in George Kennedy's influential introduction, *New Testament Interpretation through Rhetorical Criticism* (Chapel Hill: University of North Carolina, 1984). Wilhelm Wuellner, "Hermeneutics and Rhetorics: From 'Truth and Method' to 'Truth and Power,' " *Scriptura Special Issue* 3 (1989) 1-54, is the fullest presentation of that scholar's New Rhetorical approach. A useful survey of the critical landscape, illustrated with brief analyses of biblical texts, is provided by Burton L. Mack, *Rhetoric and the New Testament*, GBS (Minneapolis: Fortress, 1990).

5.3 Rhetorical Analyses of New Testament Writings

As its components have been characterized in this essay, the spectrum of NT rhetorical criticism is represented in three book-length treatments of Paul's letters. Indebted to Wilder's approach is Robert W. Funk, *Language, Hermeneutic, and Word of God: The Problem of Language in the New Testament and Contemporary Theology* (New York: Harper and Row, 1966), which also considers the parables of Jesus. Hans Dieter Betz, *Galatians: A Commentary on Paul's Letter to the Churches in Galatia,* Hermeneia (Philadelphia: Fortress, 1979), is, to date, the most important recent commentary on a Pauline epistle to have appropriated the tradition of classical rhetoric. Explicitly predicated on the judgments of Perelman and Olbrechts-Tyteca is Antoinette Clark Wire's attempt to infer the activity and theology of women prophets in the Corinthian church: *The Corinthian Women Prophets: A Reconstruction through Paul's Rhetoric* (Minneapolis: Fortress, 1990).

14. *Presuppositions in New Testament Study*

EDGAR V. MCKNIGHT

New Testament interpretation today is influenced decisively by different presuppositions concerning what is real (ontology), how the real is known (epistemology), and the relationship between the two. The question in this essay concerns not what is referred to at the superficial level of language (theme or topic) but what is referred to at a more ultimate level. Believing interpreters are confident that what the text is saying is related to a more ultimate "aboutness" or reference that informs meanings and references at less ultimate levels. How this reference is conceptualized and related to NT study has been influenced by philosophical, theological, and literary study. This essay will trace assumptions regarding truth and human knowledge from the classical age through postmodern critiques of the rationalism developed in the Enlightenment. A central section explicates the different presuppositions of scholars in the hermeneutical tradition.

Readers will observe throughout this chapter the assumption that all methods are philosophically committed and historically located. Moreover, as we will see, such commitments do not obviate or negate meaning and significance. The hermeneutical tradition in philosophy and theology, indeed, provides a rationale and resources for determining means for readers that are not merely solipsistic. Although our interests, commitments, and meanings do not exhaust meaning, they are not without genuine meaning.

1. The Classical Period

The views of Plato (*ca.* 427-347 BCE) and Aristotle (387-322 BCE) were primary in the classical period. For Plato, the artist (including the writer) makes a copy of the material world, which is itself a copy of the eternal world of Ideas. Art is, then, an inferior activity compared to artisanship (the making of useful objects), not only because copies are involved but also because the artist needs only knowledge of the appearance of things. A variant on this view is that of Plotinus (a neo-Platonic philosopher of the 3d century CE). Plotinus saw the artist as imitating the Ideas as they were embodied in the material world. A statue of Zeus, then, is not a copy of a flesh and blood human being but a representation of power — what the concepts of power and majesty might look like if those concepts could be visible.

For Aristotle the artist captures in language not Ideas or copies of Ideas but the general principles of human action. Aristotle did not believe in an eternal world of Ideas but rather saw everything as involved in process, growth, and change. Artists, then, are not merely copying; they are imitating human action. In the artistic work, the accidental and the incidental are eliminated, and action is unified into a plot and beautified with expressive language. Moreover the artistic work has the capacity of commanding the emotions, and through a complex imitation it can cleanse the individual and serve the state. (Plato was fearful of the corrupting power of the artistic work because of its distance from the truth.)

Along with Plato and Aristotle, two other classical views must be noted. The Sophists held that opinion alone — not truth — is possible. In this tradition, art is not conceived of as imitation of Ideas or of human action but as a skill. Humankind is the measure of all things for the Sophists, and the natural ability of humans may be developed by art. For Democritus (*ca.* 460-370 BCE), on the other hand, all things — the world and all that occurs in it, natural and artificial — result from the modification in shape and arrangement of eternal atoms, of which all things are composed. Change is the movement and redistribution of atoms in the void. Art operates in the same way: by modifying the shape and arrangement of material objects.

These different views of the relationship between art and what art represents result in different ways of conceiving and discussing art itself.[1]

1. The present analysis is dependent on Richard McKeon, *Thought, Action and*

In the dialectical approach of Plato and Plotinus, the forms of expression or of art objects are imitations of the eternal forms, which exist separately from the objective world. In analysis the structures of the world of matter are related analogically to the world of Ideas.

Aristotle's method of inquiry distinguished questions according to the different disciplines in which they are asked and answered. In art, as we have seen, the form is related to human action, which is the object of imitation. The problems of art have to do with the best use of parts in the construction of wholes that are artful and different in each of the various forms of art. Analysis demonstrates the role of parts in the artistic unity and the unifying effect of form. The dramatic tragedy, for example, is an organic whole in which the various parts are brought together into a unity of structure with the resources of character and thought by means of language and linguistic devices.

The approach of the Sophists gives attention to the form provided by words and the manner of expression. Orator, historian, poet, and philosopher are comparable in the way they treat problems of form or expression. Analysis deals with content, form, and the relationships between content and form.

In the logistic approach of Democritus, the problems of art focus on the relation of knowledge to emotion and of nature to appearance. The analysis of art has to do with psychological insight into the perception of pleasure and its accompaniments or with the analysis of structures of the material of art as causes of pleasure.

2. The Ancient and Medieval Church

Plato and Aristotle became important for the church as Western philosophy and the church developed a symbiotic relationship. The Platonic tradition was dominant in the church for the first millennium. Augustine (354-430) reflected a Platonic position, and Augustine's influence in the church insured continuing domination of the Platonic tradition. Although knowledge stems from our sensations, they do not teach us truth. It is something

---

Passion (Chicago: University of Chicago, 1954) 115-18. In his introduction to *The Critical Tradition: Classic Texts and Contemporary Trends* (New York: St. Martin's, 1989) 12-14, David H. Richter shows the relationship of McKeon's scheme to other maps of criticism.

in us that is purely intelligible, necessary, motionless, and eternal that teaches us truth. This is divine illumination.

The Aristotelian tradition succeeded that of Plato as the dominant philosophical tradition in the thirteenth century. Thomas Aquinas (1225-74) is responsible for making the philosophy of Aristotle the speculative framework for systematic thinking about the Christian view of reality. The method of Aristotle became the method of Scholasticism. Scholasticism was a project of reflection based on assumptions about the nature of authoritative texts, the nature of reason, and the grounds of rational pedagogy. The procedure was this: A question would be posed, evidence would be cited (Scripture, the opinions of the Fathers, philosophical arguments), the problem would be resolved through rational argument, and the solution would be defended by responses to contrary opinions.

3. The Enlightenment

The Enlightenment facilitated movement from and replacement of the dogmatic assumptions of the ancient and medieval church. The work of René Descartes (1596-1650) and John Locke (1632-1704) prepared the way. These two may be seen as recapitulating in the area of epistemology what Plato and Aristotle did in ontology. Two different epistemological approaches developed, one holding that universal ideas are innate (Plato) and the other that universal ideas are obtained through the senses (Aristotle).

The roots of Descartes's thought go back to Augustine's differentiation between knowledge of corporeal things gained through the bodily senses and knowledge of incorporeal things gained through the mind's knowledge of itself[2] and Galileo's distinction between primary qualities (the constant characteristics of the experienced world, such as form and magnitude) and secondary qualities (the subjective effects of these primary characteristics on our senses). Descartes's position may be termed "epistemological idealism" in that he stressed innate ideas over against the position that ideas derive from the senses.

John Locke opposed what had become the "received doctrine" that people "have native ideas, and original characters, stamped on their minds in their very first being" and defended the proposition that "all ideas come from sensation or reflection." External material things are the objects of

2. *De Trinitate* 9.3.3.

sensation, and the operations of our minds (perceiving, thinking, doubting, believing, and so on) are the objects of "internal sense" or reflection. The power that produces the idea is the quality of the object.[3]

The history of the Enlightenment is the history of shifts back and forth between epistemological idealism and realism. Immanuel Kant (1724-1804) shifted the center of philosophical inquiry to an examination of the concepts and categories in terms of which we think and reason. Kant disagreed with a severe empiricism by holding that there are a priori elements in cognition. These a priori concepts are indispensable for knowledge of objects. In *Critique of Pure Reason*, Kant states the thesis in the form of an inquiry:

> Now the question arises whether there are not also antecedent concepts *a priori*, forming conditions under which alone something can be, if not seen, yet thought as an object in general; for in that case all empirical knowledge of objects would necessarily conform to such concepts, it being impossible that anything should become an object of experience without them.[4]

Kant made a basic epistemological distinction between knowledge of phenomena (empirical data) and understanding of transcendental noumenal realities. His dualism was epistemological, not ontological. This epistemological distinction, however, became an ontological dualism. Phenomenal reality became distinct from noumenal reality. Developments after Kant may be seen as expressions of an inability to accommodate transcendence in any traditional sense whatsoever. The noumenal world of Kant disappears. Such things as purposes, meanings, and intrinsic and normative values also disappear.

4. The Hermeneutical Tradition

The modern hermeneutical tradition began at the conjunction of (1) the completion and general acceptance of a worldview emphasizing rational argument and reflection, (2) the movement of Romanticism with its dis-

---

3. *Essay Concerning Human Understanding* 2.1.1-2.
4. "Transcendental Deduction of the Categories," in *Critique of Pure Reason*; ET in Lewis White Beck, ed., *Eighteenth Century Philosophy* (New York: Free/London: Collier-Macmillan, 1966) 255-56.

trust of the severely cerebral rationalism of the Enlightenment, (3) the adoption of the historical-critical approach to the Bible by biblical scholars (supplementing earlier philological achievements), and (4) questions about the conditions for the possibility of knowledge introduced by Kant.

4.1 F. D. E. Schleiermacher

Schleiermacher (1768-1834) made the decisive move whereby the preconditions for understanding in itself became the object of study. His hermeneutics may be summarized in seven interdependent arguments.[5] The first four relate thinking, speaking, and the social and personal aspects of language: (1) Hermeneutics is philosophical because it is part of the art of thinking. Because it presupposes shared experiences and language, thinking is not merely an individual phenomenon. Speaking is the "outer side" of thinking. (2) Thinking entails both general and particular aspects — the general includes inherited concepts and shared conventions of language and speech; the particular grows out of the distinctive individuality of an author. (3) Grammatical hermeneutics (concerned with language) may be contrasted with psychological hermeneutics (which is concerned with the expressions of thought of persons). They are equal and interdependent. The nature of the text and the concerns of the interpreter influence the relative importance of the grammatical and psychological sides of interpretation. (4) Neither grammatical nor psychological interpretation is able to achieve a final or complete result. Since complete knowledge is impossible in both cases, "it is necessary to move back and forth between the grammatical and psychological sides, and no rules can stipulate exactly how to do this."[6]

The final three arguments explore the cyclical nature of interpretation involving the interdependent relationship between parts and the whole, the comparative (critical) and the divinatory, and the author's intention and the contribution of the reader: (5) Complete knowledge involves an apparent circle with each part understood in terms of the whole and the whole understood in terms of the parts. (6) This circular process moves not only

5. In *New Horizons in Hermeneutics: The Theory and Practice of Transforming Biblical Reading* (Grand Rapids: Zondervan, 1992) 216-26, Anthony C. Thiselton has discussed these arguments in great detail.

6. F. D. E. Schleiermacher, *Hermeneutics: The Handwritten Manuscripts*, ed. H. Kimmerle (Missoula: Scholars, 1977) 100.

between the grammatical and psychological and the general and the particular, but also between the divinatory and the comparative. Schleier-macher associates the divinatory (the creative and intuitive capacity) with the feminine:

> Divinatory knowledge is the feminine strength in knowing people: comparative knowledge, the masculine . . . the divinatory is based on the assumption that each person is not only a unique individual in his own right, but that he has a receptivity to the uniqueness of every other person.[7]

(7) The meaning of a text is rooted in its original historical situation and determined by its historical and linguistic context; but the contemporary interpreter has the capacity to grasp the meaning of a text better than its author. The interpreter is able to gather data of which the author was only dimly conscious because a work is never able fully and completely to embody the creative spirit behind it.

4.2 Wilhelm Dilthey

Schleiermacher's philosophical presupposition, in the perspective of Wilhelm Dilthey (1831-1911), was such that historical development is only formal change, that what happens in the history of an individual shows what he or she was in the beginning.[8] Dilthey was not interested in any timeless principle embodied in humankind but in humankind's social and historical situation. He attempted to find a theoretical universality of interpretation in face of the finite historical nature of human beings and their understanding by giving attention to poetics or to the creative nature of humankind. He held language and meaning (ranging from denotation of individual terms to life itself) together in creative tension in a comprehensive systematic approach centered in the mental structure of humans. This mental structure is a continuously developing system integrating and equilibrating various stages of inner and outer development.

Because of the relationship of meaning to understanding, Dilthey sees a real analogy between meaning in sentences and the meaning involved in

---

7. Schleiermacher, *Hermeneutics*, 150.

8. For a fuller discussion of the hermeneutics of Dilthey and its relationship to the structuralist and formalist traditions, see Edgar V. McKnight, *Meaning in Texts: The Historical Shaping of a Narrative Hermeneutics* (Philadelphia: Fortress, 1978) 7-38. See also Thiselton, *New Horizons in Hermeneutics*, 237-53.

life. He defines this relationship in six assertions: (1) In the understanding of the sentence, the simplest understanding of meaning is evident. It is from the meaning or reference of individual words that understanding of the sentence takes place. But there is a reciprocal relationship between the sentence and the word. The various possibilities of word meanings make the meaning of the sentence indeterminant. (2) In the process of life, the meaning or signification of life is the result of the relationship between the meaning or reference of the parts and the whole. (3) The individual events that build the course of life have a relation to something to which they refer. The coherence of these experiences gives the meaning of the course of life. (4) The idea of meaning exists only when we relate it to the experience of understanding. In this case, what is considered is the relationship of an external, or an observable reality, to the inner reality of which it is an expression. The relationship is not a grammatical relationship, for the expression is not simply the reference of the words. (5) Meaning in this highest sense — understanding, the meaning of life and history — does not speak of references and does not point to events that are to be understood through the inner structure. (6) What we seek is the meaning of life itself. The various manifestations refer to something that belongs to life but what we seek is life itself, which does not mean something else. For Dilthey, meaning is not ultimately an intellectual relationship, not simply a rational process. "Meaning is obtained from life itself."[9]

4.3 Martin Heidegger

Heidegger's (1889-1976) estimation of the philosophical importance of Dilthey gave a focus to his own work, for Dilthey's importance was "in the fact that in all this," that is, in Dilthey's attempts to understand the experiences of life in their structural and developmental inner connections, "he was, *above all*, on his way toward the question of 'life.' "[10] Heidegger himself is interested in the human *(Dasein)* as a means of questioning Being. Instead of "How do we know?", the question is "What is the mode of being of that being who only exists through understanding?" When this approach is related to textual understanding, the result is that the understanding of the text does not involve finding an inner meaning contained in the text. To

9. Wilhelm Dilthey, *Gesammelte Schriften,* VII (5th ed., Göttingen: Vandenhoeck und Ruprecht, 1968) 233-34, 240.

10. Martin Heidegger, *Being and Time* (Oxford: Basil Blackwell, 1973) 46.

understand a text is to unfold the possibility of being that is indicated by that text.

In the later work of Heidegger, the questioning of *Dasein* for the sake of Being is no longer the procedure. Language is the equivalent of Being. Being itself is the explanation for language and the essence of language is Being's self-expression. Being is the creative explanation, Being is the text, Being is the meaning.

In the essay on "Language" in *Unterwegs zur Sprache* Heidegger says that the speaking of language should be sought in what is spoken purely, and he declares that "what is spoken purely is the poem." The basis of this assertion is not given in theoretical terms at all. The basis is experience. We may assert that "what is spoken purely is the poem" if "we succeed in hearing in a poem something that is spoken purely." "What is important is learning to live in the speaking of language." Human speaking, indeed, is a response of hearing, so the way that humans learn "to live in the speaking of language" is to "examine constantly whether and to what extent we are capable of what genuinely belongs to responding."[11]

4.4 *Rudolf Bultmann*

Rudolf Bultmann (1884-1976) recognized the possibility and legitimacy of using the Scriptures for historical and aesthetic purposes. But as Word of God, the Bible is to be interpreted so that it speaks as Word, for only in this way are faith and new understanding possible. To speak as Word to modern individuals is to speak in terms of human existence. "I think I may take for granted that the right question to frame with regard to the Bible — at any rate within the Church — is the question of human existence." Two reasons are given for this assumption: First, "I am driven to that by the urge to inquire existentially about my own existence." Second, "the Church's proclamation refers me to the Scriptures as the place where I shall hear things about my own existence that vitally concern me."[12]

Bultmann's observation that the philosophy of existence is necessary for interpretation was made when he became aware of the possible use of the conceptualization and terminology of Heidegger for the relevant con-

11. Martin Heidegger, *Poetry, Language, Thought* (New York: Harper, 1971) 194, 192, 210.

12. Rudolf Bultmann, "Bultmann Replies to His Critics," *Kerygma and Myth*, vol. 1, ed. Hans Werner Bartsch (New York: Harper and Row, 1961) 191-92.

cepts for speaking of human existence. Bultmann denies that he is suggesting a "final philosophical system" or that exegesis is to "take over the actual answers that philosophy gives to the existential question of the meaning of my own particular existence." What is important is that Heidegger has "worked out an appropriate terminology for the understanding of existence, an understanding involved in human existence itself."[13]

It is in his treatment of myth that Bultmann comes to see the radical relativity of language as an objectifying of understanding, the objectification in myth being contrary to the understanding seeking expression in it. The need to move from language back to meaning, according to Hans Jonas, a student of Heidegger and Bultmann, "derives from an unavoidable fundamental structure of the mind as such." "The innermost nature of the mind" is "symbolistic." That is, it interprets itself in objective formulas and symbols. In order to come to itself, it must not get lost in the detour of the symbol and take the substitute as ultimate. "Only in a long procedure of working back, after an exhausting completion of that detour, is a demythologized consciousness able terminologically to approach directly the original phenomena hidden in this camouflage."[14]

Bultmann, on the basis of his conclusion as to the subject matter of Scripture, finds that myth, instead of really intending to give an objective worldview or to tell of divine powers, expresses the way humans understand themselves in their world, and he finds justification for demythologizing and a procedure for demythologizing in the work of Jonas.

4.5 The New Hermeneutic and Ordinary Language Analysis

The New Hermeneutic is the name given to a movement associated with students of Bultmann, especially Ernst Fuchs and Gerhard Ebeling, which changes the hermeneutical dialectic from myth versus understanding of existence to language versus language-event.

The language that the New Hermeneutic sees as the key to the task of theology is not merely the creation of humanity. "Language," according to Fuchs, "consists not only in a statement of meaning that is heard. Language is indeed not merely discourse. Language is rather primarily a sign or a

---

13. Bultmann, "Bultmann Replies to His Critics," 193.
14. Hans Jonas, *Gnosis und spätantiker Geist,* vol. 2/1: *Von der Mythologie zur mystischen Philosophie* (Göttingen: Vandenhoeck und Ruprecht, 1954) 67.

letting be, a meaning in the active sense." He affirms that "where meaning is, there is also language." But the meaning of something is "only an abbreviation of language."[15]

The translation of the language-event in biblical texts is what is important. The translator must form the room the text sought to form when the Spirit spoke in it. The content and form of the translation must unite to allow the life of the text to appear. Proclamation is the true translation of the text, not because the NT text was necessarily originally proclamation, but because of the nature of the Word itself.[16]

4.6 Ordinary Language Analysis and the New Hermeneutic

Ordinary language analysis, associated with the work of Ludwig Wittgenstein (1889-1951) and J. L. Austin (1911-60), parallels the move of the New Hermeneutic to a view of language exceeding the conveyance of information. Paul Ricoeur delineated "permanent and fruitful" conditions of the functioning of language that are uncovered by ordinary language analysis: the variability of semantic values, the sensitivity of semantic values to contexts, and the irreducibly polysemic character of lexical terms. On the basis of the work of Wittgenstein and Austin, Ricoeur judged ordinary language to be "a kind of conservatory for expressions that have preserved the highest descriptive power as regards human experience."[17] Anthony C. Thiselton points out that in the language-event of Fuchs and the performative utterance of Austin "the issuing of the utterance is the performing of an action." Thiselton does criticize Fuchs for ignoring the function of language on the purely cognitive level and suggests that the work of the later Wittgenstein may help to bridge the gap between the function of language on the purely cognitive level and the function of language on the deeper level, the function of "exposing or reorienting attitudes and presuppositions."[18]

15. Ernst Fuchs, *Marburger Hermeneutik* (Tübingen: Mohr, 1968) 177-78.

16. Ernst Fuchs, *Studies of the Historical Jesus* (London: SCM, 1964) 192-96.

17. Paul Ricoeur, "From Existentialism to the Philosophy of Language," *Philosophy Today* 17 (1973) 95-96.

18. Anthony C. Thiselton, "The Parables as Language-Event: Some Comments on Fuch's Hermeneutics in the Light of Linguistic Philosophy," *SJT* 23 (1970) 466. See Ludwig Wittgenstein, *Philosophical Investigations* (Oxford: Blackwell, 1958) §§ 108, 316-94.

4.7 Hans-Georg Gadamer

Wilhelm von Humboldt viewed language as an unbordered creative power of thought and speech making unlimited use of limited materials. Gadamer (1900-) makes use of this understanding to develop a hermeneutics that gives attention to historical consciousness and expanding hermeneutical options beyond the romanticism of Schleiermacher and Dilthey and the existentialism of Heidegger and his heirs. Humboldt had said that learning a foreign language must achieve a new standpoint in a person's worldview, but also that this achievement is not complete because one carries to the foreign language one's own worldview. Gadamer sees this carrying of one's worldview to a language not as a limitation but as the means by which the hermeneutical experience exercises its power, and he declares that Humboldt's meaning for hermeneutics is precisely his affirmation of the view of language as the view of the world *(Sprachansicht als Weltansicht)*.

In the hermeneutics of Gadamer, there is a legitimate application of criticism, but with criticism there is an experience of being grasped, being carried by tradition, participating with the creators of discourse. We do not simply question the work with our scientific methods *or* simply see in the work what we bring; we come to the work participating in the same structure of being that is the basis for our understanding of what was intended in the work. The work of art, then, allows a "world" to be encountered, but because of the nature of the work this is not a foreign universe. The interpreter does not come to a text as an empty vessel; the interpreter comes with a horizon of meaning that is broadened to become fused with that of the text. The possibility of a fusion of horizons is based on the grounding of text and interpreter in being.

Gadamer finds mediation of the two poles — tradition and the "I" — in language. Tradition brings itself to language, and human consciousness is linguistic. In this mediation, human consciousness is not dissolved. Indeed, Gadamer emphasizes that

> there is no possible consciousness . . . in which the "object" that is handed down would appear in the light of eternity. Every assimilation of tradition is historically different: which does not mean that every one represents only an imperfect understanding of it. Rather, every one is the experience of a "view" of the object itself.[19]

19. Hans-Georg Gadamer, *Truth and Method* (New York: Seabury, 1975) 430.

289

4.8 Paul Ricoeur

In his career Ricoeur (1913-) has operated with different assumptions and understandings of the hermeneutical task. An early phenomenological approach sought to extract the essential meanings of structures of purpose, motive, and ability from lived experience. These can be spoken of in direct language. Later, when dealing with evil, Ricoeur saw the need for indirect language. Evil is spoken of indirectly in metaphors such as estrangement, errancy, burden, and bondage. These symbols are embedded in mythical narratives that tell the story of how evil began. Ricoeur at that time identified hermeneutics with the art of deciphering indirect meanings.[20]

A broader view of hermeneutics came when Ricoeur considered psychological perspectives. Psychoanalysis reduces symbols, explaining them as the results of unconscious factors. The psychoanalytic revolution requires suspicion because it has shown that the ego is not master in its own house. Ricoeur's problem of uniting psychological approaches with an approach seeking to recover the original meaning of the symbol broadened his view of hermeneutics. A hermeneutics of suspicion, as well as of retrieval, became necessary. But suspicion is not the final answer. It is subject to the task of retrieval.[21]

In later writings Ricoeur emphasizes the creative power of language. Hermeneutics, from this perspective, has the task of bringing "back to discourse the written text, if not as spoken discourse, at least as speech-act actualized in the act of reading." The object of hermeneutics, then, is not the text but "the text as discourse or discourse as the text." Discourse appears as a work because of modes of discourse that impose a form on discourse. Hermeneutics uses the dialectics of discourse and work to reconstitute message or discourse. Hermeneutics identifies the message through the codes (the modes of discourse) that generate it as a work of discourse. As a code, genre is important in Ricoeur's hermeneutics because it not only establishes communication and preserves the message from distortion, but it also may start the process of "'decontextualization' which opens the message to fresh reinterpretation according to new contexts of discourse and of life."[22]

In the hermeneutical decontextualization, a redefinition of author,

---

20. Ricoeur "From Existentialism," 91.
21. Ricoeur, "From Existentialism," 92.
22. Paul Ricoeur, "Biblical Hermeneutics," *Semeia* 4 (1975) 66-68, 71.

audience, and situation takes place. This makes it possible for a work "to transcend its psycho-sociological conditions of production and to be open to an unlimited series of readings, themselves situated within different socio-cultural contexts." What is the reference of the text in its new context? Ricoeur sees the experience of literature as relevant. In literature, where reference is abolished because concrete conditions for the act of pointing something out do not exist, reference to the given world is abolished. "The language seems to glorify itself without depending on the referential function of ordinary discourse." Ricoeur, however, is not willing to abolish the role of reference. The abolition of "first order reference" in poetic literature is "the condition of possibility for the liberation of a second order of reference that reaches the world not only at the level of manipulative objects, but at the level Husserl designated by the expression *Lebenswelt* [life-world] and Heidegger by 'being-in-the-world.' "[23]

Ricoeur sees interpretation no longer as the search for persons and psychological intentions hidden behind the text but as the explication of a sort of being-in-the-world unfolded in front of the text. Ricoeur, in his treatment of parable, suggests how the "sense" of narrative implies its metaphorical "referent." He indicates that the beginning point is a conviction that the narrative has a referent or even a "participation in the referent." This is possible because "the narrative stands metaphorically for the poetic experience that comes to language."[24]

In the essay, "Biblical Hermeneutics," Ricoeur deals with the question of what is redescribed in biblical language: "What it redescribes is human experience. In this sense we must say that the ultimate referent of the parables, proverbs, and eschatological sayings is not the Kingdom of God but human reality in its wholeness."[25] How does one know? How does one get beyond the hermeneutical circle? In a discussion toward the end of *The Symbolism of Evil*, Ricoeur suggests how we are able to get beyond the circle. Ricoeur says that this is possible in interpretation by "transforming it into a *wager*."

23. Paul Ricoeur, "The Hermeneutical Function of Distanciation," *Philosophy Today* 17 (1973) 133, 140. The first naïveté is an uncritical consciousness dismissing myth and symbol because of a supposed incompatibility with modern science and history. The second naïveté is a critical consciousness purging symbols and myths of literalism but listening to their message.
24. Ricoeur, "Biblical Hermeneutics," 96.
25. Ricoeur, "Biblical Hermeneutics," 127.

I wager that I shall have a better understanding of man and of all beings if I follow the *indication* of symbolic thought. That wager then becomes the task of *verifying* my wager and saturating it, so to speak, with intelligibility.[26]

5. The Contemporary Theoretical Context

5.1 The Hermeneutical Debate

In the contemporary context, different hermeneutical assumptions are possible. No one worldview has become so universal in its intellectual and emotional appeal that it has become a "given" and directs unconsciously the way that we think and act. One assumption would essentially ignore the entire history of hermeneutics. It would avoid theoretical questions or attempt to give a theoretical basis for an approach that ignores historical consciousness. E. D. Hirsch represents this position. His purpose in *Validity in Interpretation* is to show that meaning is separated from the historical being of the reader. The determinacy of meaning is a result of the author's will because verbal meaning is what the author has willed to convey by a particular sequence of linguistic signs.[27]

Within the hermeneutic tradition a broader base than Enlightenment rationality is sought by such scholars as Jürgen Habermas, Karl-Otto Apel, and Wolfhart Pannenberg. They do not deny that truth always and of necessity exceeds method, but they posit some kind of provisional notion of the universal to serve as basis for a metacriticism that is able to acknowledge and contain the relativity of Enlightenment rationalism.

Habermas has provided different ways of conceiving of a metacritical perspective from which critical activities of the human subject may be understood. In *Knowledge and Human Interests* he distinguishes between three different cognitive interests: technical, practical, and emancipatory. Empirical or positivistic knowledge, then, is only one type of knowledge.

---

26. Paul Ricoeur, *The Symbolism of Evil* (Boston: Beacon, 1967) 355.

27. E. D. Hirsch, *Validity in Interpretation* (New Haven: Yale University, 1967) 3, 67. Elliott E. Johnson has defended the work of Hirsch as a theoretical model for biblical interpretation in *Expository Hermeneutics: An Introduction* (Grand Rapids: Zondervan, 1990) 54-69. See Edgar V. McKnight, *The Bible and the Reader: An Introduction to Literary Criticism* (Philadelphia: Fortress, 1985) 94-100, for a fuller discussion and criticism of the work of Hirsch.

This knowledge answers only instrumental interests and is related in a dialectical fashion to "practical" knowledge, which involves interests of interpersonal understanding and social cooperation. Habermas finds a place for a metacriticism, a transcendental critique. The "interest" governing this transcendental critique is emancipatory. It would provide liberation "from dependence on hypostatized powers. Self-reflection is determined by an *emancipatory cognitive interest.*"[28]

The question as to how engagement in specific social struggles can be identified with universal conditions of knowledge remained a problem in *Knowledge and Human Interests.* In *The Theory of Communicative Action* Habermas develops a linguistic-behavioral paradigm that transforms the question. For interpersonal understanding and cooperative behavior in the life world, a standpoint is required that transcends contextual-behavioral features. Remaining at the level of life world, we are under the illusion that language conveys only its surface meaning, that language is transparent. This is a hermeneutic of innocence. A more comprehensive system of language and social practice provides a frame or dimension for ideology and social critique.[29]

Karl-Otto Apel, like Habermas, seeks to expand and not to undermine traditional epistemology. Before Habermas's *The Theory of Communicative Action,* Apel had expounded a three dimensional conceptualization involving "scientistics," "hermeneutics," and "the critique of ideology." Apel does not deny the actual pragmatic function of communities of interpreters, but he does deny that a particular community of interpreters is unrelated to universal norms. Apel, then, seeks a transcendental dimension that is not merely contextually internal to particular societies but will allow a critique of particular societies. Apel here is dependent on a hypothesis of universal commensurability whereby languages are intertranslatable and "language games" overlap, merge, fall apart, and reintegrate. The historically constituted life form of a given society (language) is

> not only the normatively binding "institution of institutions," . . . it is also the "meta-institution" of all dogmatically established institutions. As a *meta*-institution, it represents the instance of criticism for all unreflected

28. Jürgen Habermas, *Knowledge and Human Interests* (2d ed., London: Heinemann, 1978) 308, 310.

29. Jürgen Habermas, *The Theory of Communicative Action: The Critique of Functionalist Reason* (2 vols.; Cambridge: Polity, 1984, 1987).

social norms, and . . . it does not abandon the individual persons to their merely subjective reasoning.[30]

Wolfhart Pannenberg finds a modified version of Hegel's philosophy of history useful in developing a unitary theory of knowledge and a universal foundation for knowledge that transcends particular and contingent expressions of knowledge. Pannenberg acknowledges human historical finitude and the hermeneutical dimensions of understanding involved in knowledge. But Pannenberg develops a conception of universal history that preserves the intrinsic validity of the particular. The key is the future that is still hidden from the world but already revealed in Jesus. The end of history, which gathers history into a whole, is known provisionally. The meaning of the entirety of history is anticipated in the eschatological activity and destiny of Jesus of Nazareth.[31]

Another move is possible, a move that parallels the efforts of E. D. Hirsch at the skeptical pole. It has been characterized by one of its most able advocates as the transformation of hermeneutics from a way of knowing to a way of coping.[32] Richard Rorty is perhaps the most thoroughgoing critic of the search for a transcontextual or transcendental critique of the social community. With Rorty, epistemological skepticism is turned into ontology. A universal claim is made not only for the absence of a means of achieving knowledge on a level transcending particular social groups but also for the absence of any such level of knowledge. Anthony Thiselton has compared the attitude of scholars such as Rorty and scholars such as Habermas and Apel by showing that they represent different reactions to the loss of the ideal of "some absolutized foundationalism outside time, place, and history." Rorty places a priority on "historical contingency and contextualism" while his opponents see a "positive dialectical relation between contextual contingency and ongoing metacritical exploration and testing in the form of an open system." The problem is the "possibility of such a system in which neither contingent life-world nor explanatory system has the last word, but contribute to some interactive whole."[33]

30. Karl-Otto Apel, *Toward a Transformation of Philosophy* (London/Boston: Routledge, 1980) 119.

31. Wolfhart Pannenberg, *Basic Questions in Theology*, vol. 3 (London: SCM, 1970) 15.

32. Richard Rorty, *Philosophy and the Mirror of Nature* (Princeton: Princeton University, 1979, 1980) 356.

33. Thiselton, *New Horizons in Hermeneutics*, 401.

5.2 The Literary Turn

At the same time that continental scholars in the hermeneutical tradition were attempting to correlate explanation, understanding, and metacriticism, a move was being made by American scholars to transform biblical study in general and hermeneutics in particular into a form of literary criticism, more particularly a form of reading understood in terms of literary conventions. The tradition of literary studies offers rich possibilities for hermeneutics. M. H. Abrams traced the history and practice of criticism prior to reader-oriented approaches in terms of the dominance of one of the four elements in the comprehensive situation of a work of art: the work, the artist, the universal imitated in the work, and the audience.[34]

An early type of criticism, mimetic criticism, views the literary work as an imitation *(mimesis)* of the world and human life. This form of criticism was associated with the classical age, but it is also characteristic of contemporary theories of literary realism. The second type was the rhetorical. This type of criticism was dominant from the poet Horace (first century BCE) through the eighteenth century and emphasized the pleasure and instruction that the work offers the audience. The recent revival of rhetorical criticism recapitulates rhetorical (or pragmatic) criticism's emphasis on the strategies used by an artist in engaging and influencing the response of readers.

Theories of expressive criticism (Romanticism) proliferated during the late eighteenth and most of the nineteenth centuries. Romanticism was an important factor in the hermeneutics of Schleiermacher and Dilthey. It defines the literary work in terms of the operation of the artist's imagination on his or her perception. Contemporary psychologically oriented critics retain concerns of expressive criticism, looking in the work for indications of the particular temperament and experiences of the author. The fourth type (Formalism/New Criticism) developed around the beginning of the twentieth century and became dominant in the mid-twentieth century. In these formal theories, the literary work becomes its own world and transcends the facts of composition, the imitated universe, the nature and character of the author, and the effect on the audience.

In the contemporary period, reader-oriented theories are becoming dominant. Reader-oriented criticism is akin to hermeneutics in that it views

---

34. M. H. Abrams, *The Mirror and the Lamp: Romantic Theory and the Critical Tradition* (New York: Norton, 1953).

literature in terms of readers and their values, attitudes, and responses. The nature and role of the reader vary in the different forms of reader-oriented criticism, but in all forms there is a movement away from the view of interpretation as the determination by an autonomous reader of *the* meaning of an autonomous text.

The community influences the attention given by the reader and the kind of "actualization" made by the reader. To some extent, then, criticism involves determining the perspective from which reading will proceed and becomes a matter of persuasion as well as of demonstration. Interest in and appreciation of "interpretive communities" in literary study may provide appreciation for and insight into the way that different religious communities read the NT.

The literary turn was prepared for in the attempt of Rudolf Bultmann and the New Hermeneutic to prolong the text hermeneutically by attention to its linguistic dimensions. Preoccupation with existential categories and lack of interaction with genuine literary criticism hindered the task. In his 1964 publication, *The Language of the Gospel,* Amos Wilder advocated a move that takes advantage of literary insights. He expounds the NT as "language event" in terms of literary form with the conviction that "behind the particular NT forms lies a particular life-experience and a language-shaping faith." Wilder explicitly criticizes Bultmann's restriction of meaning to existential concepts. The view that the NT "tells us about ourselves, not about 'things' and the way they are and the way they happen," according to Wilder, results in a disparagement of "the whole story of man and salvation as the Bible presents it." The literary criticism that is appropriate for NT study does not remain confined to forms and conventions. There is reference in the text, but the reference is not the same as in conventional study of the Gospels. Students of the NT can learn about its literary language and reference from students of poetry: "This kind of report of reality — as in a work of art — is more subtle and complex and concrete than in the case of a discursive statement, and therefore more adequate to the matter in hand and to things of importance."[35]

35. Amos Wilder, *The Language of the Gospel: Early Christian Rhetoric* (New York: Harper, 1964) 133.

6. Conclusion

The presuppositions of the classical age concerning the reference of the literary work and the methods of interpretation are essentially the options we have today. New variations have been offered in the history of philosophy, literary criticism, and biblical study, but nothing has been offered that has effectively altered the pluralism of interpretation.

I have suggested in other writings that a literary or literary-like paradigm is appropriate for biblical study in the contemporary epoch. It allows faithfulness to the nexus of linguistic and literary relationships in the text, maintains consistency with the worlds of the readers, and permits interpreters (as individuals and in community) to make sense of biblical texts that is faithful to their needs and competence.

I would suggest that such an approach is consistent with approaches followed by believing interpreters throughout the ages. This results from an assumption of a commensurability of approaches or "language games." In our contemporary approaches we are recapitulating in our own time and place what other interpreters have accomplished in their times and places. They were "wrong" and we are "wrong" — from some time and place removed from human limitations — because they and we cannot transcend history in some final fashion. But they were and we are "right" as we imaginatively construct meanings that touch us intellectually, emotionally, and spiritually.

The appreciation we are able to muster for past approaches and meanings is appropriate for the multiplicity of approaches of the present time. Richard McKeon saw the different approaches exemplifying the classical period as commensurable:

> It is obvious that the analysis in which "form" and content are taken as basic [the operational approach] will find some place to treat transcendent values [the dialectical approach], organic unities [the problematic approach], and pleasures [the logistic approach], as consequences of style and what is expressed.[36]

An assumption of a commensurability of approaches will allow us to proceed with our own interests and projects without feeling that our interests and projects either exhaust all meaning or are meaningless. There have

36. McKeon, *Thought, Action and Passion*, 117.

been and will be other and different meanings. This fact and these meanings may enhance rather than detract from our meanings.

7. Suggestions for Further Reading

The following books together serve as guide to the complex field of literary studies in general and to hermeneutics in particular.

According to David H. Richter, editor of *The Critical Tradition: Classic Texts and Contemporary Trends* (New York: St. Martin's, 1989), "Wave after wave of European thought has found readers and shaped disciples within the human sciences in general and critical theory in particular" (v). As a result, "the critical tradition" has shifted, expanded, and contracted as new writers have entered the discourse and old ones have moved from the margins to the center.

The first third of *The Critical Tradition* is composed of "classic texts," ranging from the work of Plato to that of Susan Sontag, and the final two-thirds is composed of texts representing "contemporary trends" (Marxist criticism, psychological criticism, formalism, structuralism and semiotics, poststructuralism, feminist literary criticism, reader-response criticism, and two issues under debate: the canon and authorial intention). For every literary selection, Richter has composed an introductory essay containing a selected bibliography.

Steven Greenblatt and Giles Gunn have edited an engaging collection of essays on *Redrawing the Boundaries: The Transformation of English and American Literary Studies* (New York: MLA, 1992). The twenty-four contributors to this volume were asked to concentrate on "what is most challenging and, at the same time, disquieting about this present period in English and American literary studies" (9). Although no one critical ideology has achieved dominance of the New Criticism, many of the major critical schools share a "hermeneutics of suspicion," which seems entirely natural and inevitable. In spite of that, the critical orientations associated with poststructuralism have not placed all things in doubt. Greenblatt and Gunn applaud this situation, "for the goal in literary studies is not to seal off the frontier completely but to keep it conceptually alive; what is sought are not closed boundaries but regulated thresholds, controlled passageways" (8).

In *Postmodern Use of the Bible: The Emergence of Reader-Oriented Criticism* (Nashville: Abingdon, 1988), Edgar V. McKnight builds on antifoundationalist philosophy and argues for the right of readers to make sense of texts for themselves while remaining in dialogue with critical assumptions and approaches. The hermeneutical circle should expand from original intent to the literary relationships of the parts to the whole of the text and to its progressive context in the consciousness of individual readers and in communities of readers over the centuries.

Also focusing on the interface of contemporary hermeneutical theory and biblical studies is Sandra M. Schneiders in *The Revelatory Text: Interpreting the New Testament as Sacred Scripture* (San Francisco: HarperCollins, 1991). The first part of this "second-level reflection on the meaning of interpretation itself" (13) is a theological inquiry, a study of the theological and ecclesial claims made for the Bible in general and the NT in particular. An intellectually reputable access to the theological dimension of the NT is sought. The second part takes seriously the historical, literary and linguistic, and religious-spiritual character of the NT. These aspects of the NT are discussed in relation to the character of the NT as revelatory text.

Kurt Mueller-Vollmer has edited *The Hermeneutics Reader: Texts of the German Tradition from the Enlightenment to the Present* (New York: Continuum, 1985). This volume contains seminal works of thirteen different scholars ranging from Johann Martin Chladenius of the eighteenth century and Friedrich D. E. Schleiermacher of the nineteenth century to Jürgen Habermas and Karl-Otto Apel of the twentieth century. The introductory essay is entitled "Language, Mind, and Artifact: An Outline of Hermeneutic Theory Since the Enlightenment" and contains introductions to the works of the thirteen authors. A short biographical essay is included with each author's work.

Finally attention should be brought to Anthony C. Thiselton, *New Horizons in Hermeneutics: The Theory and Practice of Transforming Biblical Reading* (Grand Rapids: Zondervan, 1992), the title of which indicates the breadth of Thiselton's interests in a threefold word play. First, reading produces effects on readers that can enlarge their horizons. Second, new horizons have been opened in the development of hermeneutics as an interdisciplinary study over the past two decades. Third, the book attempts to open new horizons beyond those already established within the discipline.

Thiselton evaluates the variety of hermeneutical proposals from the earliest beginnings to the contemporary period from the standpoint of Gadamer's hermeneutics, which he sees as taking an ontological turn toward language. Actualization of reality occurs only in changing, historically finite events. But the provisional aspect of the actualizations must be distinguished from the reality of the broad linguistic tradition that comes to expression. Thiselton, therefore, disavows the possibility of arriving at a complete and coherent theoretical absolute that can be articulated fully either deductively or inductively. Very clearly, however, he denies that this radical incompleteness must result in the incoherence of an irrational or arational relativism or anarchism. The existence of rationality does not demand complete and coherent metatheoretical articulation.

15. The Reader in New Testament Interpretation

KEVIN J. VANHOOZER

1. Why "the Reader" in New Testament Study?

A chapter that treats the reader in NT study may appear, at first sight, to be singularly inappropriate in a volume devoted to contemporary NT interpretation. After all, there have been readers of the NT from the very beginning: "The reader you have with you always." Does not the reader figure in every approach to biblical interpretation insofar as it is the reader who chooses a particular method — be it historical criticism, structuralism, etc. — and puts it into practice on specific texts? Did not Aristotle study the effect of texts on readers in his *Rhetoric?*

Recently, however, the reader has come to the forefront in discussion of literary theory and biblical interpretation alike. Indeed, some critics speak of a reader's liberation movement. What is it that readers have hitherto not been free to do? The answer of an increasing number of literary theorists is: "make meaning." Reading is not merely a matter of perception but also of production; the reader does not discover so much as create meaning. At the very least, there would be no meaning at all if there were no readers reading. What is in the text is only the potential for meaning. Meaning is actualized not by the author at the point of the text's conception but by the reader at the point of the text's reception. If we compare the text to a well, to what should we liken meaning: to the water in the well, to the ways in which the water is drawn, or to the drinking of the water? In this chapter I will examine a number of contemporary approaches to interpretation that accord a privileged role to the reader's "response." I first examine the reasons, both literary and philosophical, for the reader's new-found fame and freedom.

1.1 Reading as Theory Laden: The Philosophical Explanation

The philosophical roots for reader-response criticism ultimately go back to Kant's "Copernican Revolution." Whereas Descartes had defined knowledge in terms of a "mind" apprehending an "object," Kant argued that the knower contributes something to the object of knowledge. The mind does not simply mirror but constructs its object, processing sensations outside the mind with the mind's own concepts. As Copernicus suggested that the sun does not revolve around the earth but the earth around the sun, so Kant suggested that the mind does not correspond to the world but the world to the mind. The mind actively participates in the construction of knowledge. This was the essence of Kant's critique of metaphysics, that search for the true description — the single correct conceptual interpretation — of ultimate reality. But whereas Kant believed that all human beings interpret the world with the same set of categories, today most philosophers hold there is no one conceptual framework that yields absolute truth or a God's-eye view of the world. What one draws from the well of the world depends on the type of bucket one uses.

The analogy with literary interpretation is exact: We do not perceive the text as it is in itself, but only the text as construed and constructed by the human mind. Kant's critique has been directed by literary theorists against the "metaphysics" of meaning. Hermeneutical realism — the notion that there is something that precedes reading to which reading must corre-spond — has become increasingly difficult to defend. Thomas Kuhn, a philosopher of science, argues that all observation is theory-laden. Every scientist belongs to some community or other whose research is oriented by a particular "paradigm" or interpretive framework. For Kuhn, the context of the scientist in a particular community influences the kinds of questions that will be asked.[1] The hermeneutical anti-realist insists that there are many equally valid sets of interpretive categories with which to process texts and produce meaning. If all reading is historically conditioned and theory-laden, then no reading is objective and the reader becomes, almost by default, the determining factor in interpretation.

1. Thomas S. Kuhn, *The Structure of Scientific Revolutions* (Chicago: University of Chicago, 1970).

1.2 The Three Ages of Criticism: The Literary Explanation

Of course, it was not always so. Literary criticism has only gradually perceived the significance of these philosophical and scientific revolutions. The traditional reader, more Cartesian than Kantian in inclination, believed that objectivity in interpretation was possible. David J. A. Clines comments that the end of Cartesian thinking is only now beginning to be felt in biblical studies: "Most active scholars appear to write as if they were still engaged in a quest for objectively determinate meanings."[2] What was the mind-independent or reader-independent something to which good reading had to correspond? Most biblical commentators from the Reformation on held that it was the author's intention. It was the author's will to mean this rather than that, with such and such a verbal sequence in such and such a historical context, that was considered the determining factor of textual meaning and the object of the interpreter's quest. In short, determinate textual meaning, that is, meaning that is anchored and fixed, was a function of authorial activity. Consequently, this "first age" of criticism belonged to the author.

Kant's Copernican Revolution complicated this quest. So did the subsequent realization that humans are historical beings. We are, as readers, distant from the author, both temporally and in our ability to know. And there is yet a third element that comes between the reader and the author: language.

These three elements — the mind, time, language — comprise, for many, an impenetrable screen. But it is a screen on which readers "project" their image or construction of what they think the author (and his or her intention) is like. According to Roland Barthes, the "author" is a convenient fiction that provides the illusion of a stable sense and a determinate meaning. Instead of cause, the author is for Barthes an *effect* of the text.

An illusory author is, however, no better than no author at all. Barthes thus pronounces the author "dead," echoing Nietzsche's earlier declaration of the death of God. Indeed, the two deaths are related, insofar as they are both variations on the theme of antirealism. Feuerbach argued that "God" was merely the projection of human thought; Barthes, similarly, argues that "the author's intention" is a projection of reading. It was Nietzsche who saw the implications of this antirealism most clearly: If we cannot discover

---

2. David J. A. Clines, "Possibilities and Priorities of Biblical Interpretation: An International Perspective," *BibInt* 1 (1993) 75.

the nature of reality, we must invent it. Barthes agrees: "Once the Author is removed, the claim to decipher a text becomes quite futile. . . . The birth of the reader must be at the cost of the death of the Author."[3]

What now functions as the norm of interpretation after the author's demise? Is meaning really there, somehow "in" the text? Is there anything independent of the process of reading that can now hold the reader responsible? Does truth lie at the bottom of the well, or is it interpretation all the way down? Is there still a way, after the author, to judge interpretations bad or good? Or, to paraphrase Dostoyevsky, if there is no Author, is everything (in interpretation) permitted? Beginning with New Criticism in the 1940s and continuing through structuralism in the 1960s, literary critics have attempted to find a principle for determinate meaning based on the text alone, considered as an entity autonomous from its author. Since the late 1960s, however, attention has focused on the reader's role in decoding and using the text. In the 1970s, Hans Robert Jauss argued that literary historians should turn their attention away from authors and their works to study the reader and the expectations and interests the reader brings to texts. We cannot study the text as it is in itself, but only the history of how readers have received it.[4] If meaning is not somehow "in" texts, then reading is like "dropping buckets into empty wells" (Cowper). With this thought, Kant's Copernican Revolution is complete.

2. What Is the Role of the Reader?

2.1 Readers and Reading: Some Presuppositions

Philosophical developments have served as midwife to the birth of the reader. What exactly has been born? Why do readers read and what do they do beyond moving their eyes from left to right across the page? The traditional answer is that we read in order to understand — to grasp the author's meaning. Reader-response criticism, on the other hand, relates meaning to the ways in which texts are received by readers: Meaning is not simply reproduced but produced.

---

3. Roland Barthes, "Death of the Author," in *The Rustle of Language* (New York: Hill and Wang, 1986) 53-55.

4. Hans Robert Jauss, "Literary History as a Challenge to Literary Theory," *NLH* 2 (1970) 7-37.

1. *The Place of the Reader: Who? When? Where?* The reader is neither a detached Cartesian mind nor a *tabula rasa*. It was Rudolf Bultmann who first alerted NT interpreters to the importance of the "place" of the reader by arguing that exegesis without presuppositions is not possible.[5] For Bultmann, the most pressing question readers have concerns their own temporal existence and its meaning. His suggestion that the reader's ontological context is the decisive context has not been accepted, but what has proved to be of more lasting significance is his notion of the reader's "horizon," the set of interests and expectations that affects what the reader looks for, and finds, in the NT texts. Hans-Georg Gadamer views the process of understanding as an encounter between the text and reader, an encounter that he describes as a "fusion" of two horizons.[6]

On the traditional author-oriented view, understanding meant occupying the same place and perspective as the author. Objective interpretation required the interpreter to leave his or her prejudices behind. The death of the author, however, deregulates interpretation. Readers need no longer apologize either for their location or their interests. Indeed, according to John Barton and Robert Morgan, the text has no aims or interests.[7] There is no one thing that readers must do with texts. Readers will have any number of interests, depending on their place and context. Some readers may show interest in a text's formal structure, others in the events that lay behind the text or gave rise to its production, still others in the relevance of the text in the light of contemporary social questions. On this view, the most important context for interpretation is thus not the original historical context of the text but the present context of the reader. The traditional goal of disinterested reading has given way to "interested" readings. The birth of the reader accounts for the current plethora of interpretive schools (feminist, Marxist, Freudian, liberation, etc.), each derived from a dominant interest. The place where the reader stands, far from being considered an obstacle to interpretation, has today become holy ground.

2. *The Indeterminacy of Meaning.* If the place of the reader determines what he or she gets out of a text, then meaning is indeterminate. However, one can understand indeterminacy of meaning in two different ways. Some reader-response critics point to certain "gaps" in the text that call for filling

---

5. Rudolf Bultmann, "Is Exegesis without Presuppositions Possible?" in *Existence and Faith,* ed. Schubert M. Ogden (New York: Living Age, 1960) 289-96.

6. Hans-Georg Gadamer, *Truth and Method* (New York: Seabury, 1975) 269-74.

7. Robert Morgan and John Barton, *Biblical Interpretation* (London/New York: Oxford University, 1988) 7.

in by the reader. On this view, indeterminacy refers to an unfinished meaning that the reader completes by following authorial instructions and textual indications. Indeterminacy also has a more radical sense, according to which the reader determines what to make of the text. On this view, texts do not have a fixed "meaning." Reading is so theory-laden that what we claim to discover in texts and then dignify by calling it "the meaning" is actually the result of a certain way of reading.

Jeffrey Stout proposes that we drop the term "meaning" altogether and speak rather of what readers wish to do with texts. Some readers, it is true, try to reconstruct the author's intention, but other readers have other interests. Why, asks Stout, should we equate only the interest of the first group with "the meaning" of the text? The "goodness" of an interpretation depends on the interpreter's aim and interest. Talk of interpretive aims thus replaces talk of textual meaning. The interests of the reader drive the process of interpretation. The text thus assumes the character of a wishing well, from which readers may draw what they like. Stout rejects the idea of a hermeneutical equivalent of Kant's moral imperative, a single duty or rule that should govern all reading. There is no one thing that makes a reading "good." On the contrary: "Good commentary is whatever serves our interests and purposes."[8] Clines agrees, noting the importance of the reader's context: "There is no one authentic meaning that we must all try to discover, no matter who we are or where we happen to be standing."[9] The myth of objectivity dies hard, however. Stephen Moore states the challenge now facing biblical interpreters: "Today, it is not our biblical texts that need demythologizing so much as our ways of reading them."[10]

3. *The Nature of Interpretation: Two Types of Reader-Response.* At the heart of the contemporary debate in the third age of criticism is the question whether or not there are normative aims for reading. If there are no norms, as Stout contends, does it follow that there can be no such thing as a misinterpretation? Reader-response critics are currently divided over how to respond to such questions. Umberto Eco distinguishes between "closed" texts, which evoke a predetermined, calculated response, and "open" texts, which invite the reader's participation in the production of meaning.[11] In

8. Jeffrey Stout, "What Is the Meaning of a Text?" *NLH* 14 (1982) 6.

9. Clines, "Possibilities and Priorities," 78.

10. Stephen D. Moore, *Literary Criticism and the Gospels* (New Haven: Yale University, 1989) 66.

11. Umberto Eco, *The Role of the Reader: Explorations in the Semiotics of Texts* (Bloomington: Indiana University, 1979).

order to make sense of the role of the reader in contemporary NT interpretation, we must make a similar distinction between readings that attempt to *reproduce* a meaning that is, in some sense, already "there" and readings that attempt to *produce* a meaning *ex libris*.

Early reader-response critics tended to be "conservative," acknowledging the role of the reader in the process of making meaning but focusing on the dynamics and direction of the text, on the various ways in which the rhetorical strategies of the text itself invite the reader to participate in the production of meaning. As early as the 1920s, I. A. Richards's *Principles of Literary Criticism* stressed the power of poetry to evoke feelings and affect the reader. The emphasis in this view is on uncovering the rhetorical mechanisms by which the text induces and produces in the reader these effects. "Understanding" is still the end of the interpretive process, though the means to that end involve active reader participation. Reading is, on this view, essentially an *obedient* activity. Its aim is to let the author and the text manipulate the reader so that he or she gradually comes to experience and adopt the ideology (the worldview) of the text. Again, the emphasis is squarely on understanding, on discovering and embracing the ideology of the text.

"Radical" reader-response critics, on the other hand, privilege the ideology or position of the reader rather than that of the text. The text becomes the opportunity for the reader to pursue his or her own interests and agenda. Such readers do more than respond: They react. Reactionary readers lobby for their respective causes and points of view. Since nothing is really "there" in the text, they try to undo traditional interpretations by claiming that they reflect the interests of some institutional authority — a State, a Church, or a School.

In some cases, where the text itself displays an unwelcome ideology (e.g., patriarchy), reactive readers must read against the text: Poisoned wells must be politically purified. At other times, reactive reading goes against the history of a text's interpretation. We could here speak of reader-rejection rather than reader-reception of a text, and of "strong-willed" readers who unapologetically impose their own ideologies onto that of the text. They are more interested in "overstanding" — in pursuing their own aims and interests and questions — than in understanding a text. Literary criticism here moves beyond describing a text and its ideology to an outright critique of it.

Given the increasing number of contexts in which the Bible is being read, what should the interpreter do? Clines espouses a "market philosophy of interpretation." In recognition of the pluralistic intellectual marketplace, he believes interpreters should "devote themselves to producing interpretation they can sell."[12] In the absence of absolute meanings, the interpreter can still hope to produce *attractive* readings.

Given the ideologically divided and market-driven situation in literary theory at present, it is hardly surprising that the issue of the ethics of interpretation has come to the fore. In the wake of authorial antirealism and interpretive relativism, the reader's interests become the determining factors in interpretation. There is no innocent reading; rather, all reading is interested, and to the extent that these are vested interests, all reading is ideological. Our choice of interpretive aim is ultimately a political decision. How could it be otherwise, if there is no such thing as a "disinterested" reading?

2.2 Making Meaning: The Procedures

Reader-response critics "make" meaning in two very different ways.

1. *Conservative Reader-Response: Reader-Respect.* According to Wolfgang Iser, texts are unfinished objects whose "gaps" and indeterminacies call out for completion by the reader. What, for instance, should one "make" of the silence of the women at the end of the Gospel of Mark (16:8)? Only the "act" of reading produces patterns and realizes meaning. Reading is the process of filling in the blanks, of making connections. Iser draws an analogy between two readers and two stargazers "who may both be looking at the same collection of stars, but one will see the image of a plough, and the other will make out a dipper. . . . The 'stars' in a literary text are fixed; the lines that join them are variable."[13]

It is unclear to many, however, whether Iser wishes to give the reader the right to connect the dots as he or she may see fit, or whether he regards the text as giving instructions for the reader's actualizations. According to his detractors, the reader to whom Iser gives birth is underdeveloped. Though Iser studies the reader's response, he construes this response as an effect of the text. The implied reader "embodies all those predispositions necessary for a literary work to exercise its effect."[14] The implied reader is thus not only an effect of the text but an unchanging textual property.

12. Clines, "Possibilities and Priorities," 80.
13. Wolfgang Iser, *The Implied Reader: Patterns of Communication in Prose Fiction from Bunyan to Beckett* (Baltimore: Johns Hopkins University, 1974) 282.
14. Wolfgang Iser, *The Act of Reading: A Theory of Aesthetic Response* (Baltimore: Johns Hopkins University, 1978) 34.

Consequently, though real readers are active, their activity is limited to performing a pre-scripted role laid down in the text — so much so that Jeanrond worries that Iser's "act of reading" may turn into a "slavery to the text."[15]

Paul Ricoeur also stresses the importance of the reader "realizing" textual meaning. Interpretation is shortcircuited, he believes, if the text is only "explained." As written discourse, texts are unfulfilled until they are appropriated or applied by readers; discourse ("someone saying something about something *to* someone") is incomplete without a recipient. What the reader receives according to Ricoeur is not the author's intention but the "world of the text" — that is, a proposed way of being-in-the-world. Reading is the process by which the world of the text intersects with the world of the reader. Interpretation is fulfilled only when the "world" is appropriated through the words. The act of reading is thus a war of the worlds: "Reading is, first and foremost, a struggle with the text."[16]

The text is inert until reactivated by the reader. As Ricoeur puts it, "reading is like the execution of a musical score; it marks the realization, the enactment, of the semantic possibilities of the text."[17] The analogy with music is apt: Like a musical score, readers perform texts. Interpretations differ as a result of the different interactions between the text's proposals and the reader's responses. No one interpretation or performance exhausts a text's interpretive possibilities.

Must we then speak of textual "worlds without end"? Is reading arbitrary? In reply, Ricoeur affirms the importance of textual constraints on interpretation as well as textual openness. Reading is a balancing act between, on the one hand, believing that each text has only one correct interpretation and, on the other, projecting ourselves into the text: "Perhaps we should say that a text is a finite space of interpretation: there is not just one interpretation, but, on the other hand, there is not an infinite number of them."[18]

Ricoeur ultimately privileges the world of the text over that of the

---

15. Werner G. Jeanrond, *Text and Interpretation as Categories of Theological Thinking* (New York: Crossroad, 1988) 110.

16. Paul Ricoeur, "World of the Text, World of the Reader," in *A Ricoeur Reader: Reflection and Imagination,* ed. Mario J. Valdes (New York/London: Harvester Wheatsheaf, 1991) 494.

17. Paul Ricoeur, *Hermeneutics and the Human Sciences,* ed. John B. Thompson (Cambridge: Cambridge University, 1981) 159.

18. Ricoeur, "World of the Text," 496.

reader. He agrees with Proust that, in interpreting texts, the reader "reads" himself or herself. That is, texts are for Ricoeur occasions to understand ourselves in a new light. The reader is active, but the reader's activity is oriented to receiving the text. In appropriating the text's world, the reader gives up (at least temporarily) his or her own self-understanding. Reading exposes the reader to new worlds and in so doing enlarges his or her sense of self. Appropriation is not a matter of making the text one's own but of surrendering oneself to the text. Insofar as interpretation thus "enlarges" human being Ricoeur can say with Francis Bacon: "Reading maketh a full man."

2. *Radical Reader-Response: Reader-Resistance.* Radical reader-response critics resist any claim — either textual or interpretive — that pretends to be authoritative, exclusive, and absolute. They see all attempts to find and fix "the meaning" of texts as covert attempts to impose an authoritarian rule on the reader. Interpretation that claims to be theoretically "correct" is judged politically incorrect. Determinate meaning threatens the freedom of the reader. There are two main varieties of reader-resistance: post-structuralist and neo-pragmatist.

Roland Barthes likens the reader to a playful producer rather than a dutiful consumer of meaning. Interpretation is a matter not of recognizing the single correct meaning of a text but of perceiving a plurality of meanings. For the consumer, reading is a safe, comfortable activity that treats the text "like a cupboard where meanings are shelved, stacked, safeguarded."[19] A creative reading, on the other hand, is a productive contribution to the economy of interpretation.

"Writerly texts" are those works that call attention to their status as complex sign-systems capable of various decodings — linguistic labyrinths. The text is "a multi-dimensional space in which are married and contested several writings, none of which is original; the text is a fabric of quotations, resulting from a thousand sources of culture."[20] Indeed, the pleasure of the text for Barthes consists in its serpentine paths: Its codes generate many levels on which the text may be traversed. The impossibility of completing or closing the process of interpretation is for him no reason for dismay; on the contrary such texts produce an ecstatic bliss insofar as they induce the thrill of losing oneself — and thus the possibility of finding oneself somewhere else.

19. Roland Barthes, *S/Z* (New York: Hill and Wang, 1974) 200-201.
20. Barthes, "Death of the Author," 53.

Barthes proclaims both the death of the Author (previously thought to be the "owner" of the text and the "authority" over interpretation) and the birth of the Reader. Because reading is a production of meaning, the class distinction dividing author and reader appears vague and arbitrary. The author simply supplies the reader with a complex code that calls for and enables multiple readings/meanings. Barthes does not hesitate to draw the conclusion: The ultimate aim in liberating the reader from bondage to "the author's intention" is to make the reader into a writer. Commentary becomes as authoritative and creative as the "original" text:

> Just as Einsteinian science compels us to include within the object studied the *relativity of reference points,* so the combined action of Marxism, Freudianism, and structuralism compels us, in literature, to relativize the relations of *scriptor,* reader, and observer (critic).[21]

Many contemporary forms of biblical criticism unapologetically advance their own ideology, their own minority and marginal interest. These "users" abandon any pretense of neutrality. Richard Rorty, the patron philosophical saint of interpretive neopragmatism, argues that texts do not have "natures," only "uses." No one use should be equated with the "right" way of reading. Instead of trying to "get it right," the neopragmatist interpreter simply wants to produce a useful or interesting reading.

It would be misleading, however, to infer that the reader's liberation movement endorses interpretive anarchy. But where do the criteria for interpretation come from? Where is the locus of interpretive authority? Stanley Fish claims that authority belongs to the "interpretive community." Every reader belongs to some community in which certain interpretive interests and procedures are shared. What a reader discovers in a text is thus the function of the community to which he or she belongs. Interpretation is thus not arbitrary, but neither is it dependent on the "myth" that meaning is "in" the text. Meaning is rather a function of the reading strategy brought to a text. As Fish puts it: "The interpretation constrains the facts rather than the other way around and also constrains the kinds of meaning that one can assign to those facts."[22] It is the community, not the canon, that constrains the reader. Both Barthes and Fish have in different ways obliterated the traditional distinction between text and reader, meaning

---

21. Barthes, "From Work to Text," in *The Rustle of Language,* 57.

22. Stanley Fish, *Is There a Text in This Class? The Authority of Interpretive Communities* (Cambridge: Harvard University, 1980) 293.

and commentary. With radical reader-response theories, Kant's Copernican Revolution reaches its apotheosis: Readers do not discover but construct meaning. The roles of text and reader have not only been revolutionized, but reversed: "Texts, like dead men and women, have no rights, no aims, no interests. They can be used in whatever way readers or interpreters choose."[23]

3. Reader-Response in Relation to Other Approaches

3.1 Historical-Critical Approaches

Critical readers since the Enlightenment have indeed been active: subjecting textual testimonies to critical assessment, taking texts apart and putting then back together in more "accurate" form, and reconstructing the history that lay behind the text and the history of the text's own composition. The reader assumed in much historical criticism was a disinterested, objective, apolitical scholar — in short, a myth. Bultmann's recognition that exegesis without presuppositions was impossible was simply an aftershock of the Kantian epistemological earthquake. All that we have access to as readers is textual phenomena; the historical "noumenon" — the thing-in-itself (the original situation, context, and reference of the text) — is unavailable. History — that is, the history we tell — is always interpreted, a product of the readerly activity, of selection, and "emplotment."[24]

3.2 Literary-Critical Approaches

Many of the same points could be made with reference to literary-critical approaches. The turn to the text (instead of its author or the history it recounts) is not yet a turn to the reading subject. The reader is often a figure in the background. Literary-critical techniques attend to the text's conventions and formal features and the processes by which it conveys sense. This would be true of structuralist, rhetorical, narrative, and canonical ap-

23. Morgan and Barton, *Biblical Interpretation,* 7.
24. So Hayden White, *Metahistory* (Baltimore: Johns Hopkins University, 1974); and Ben Meyer, "The Challenge of Text and Reader to the Historical-Critical Method," in *The Bible and Its Readers,* ed. W. A. M. Beuken, Concilium (London: SCM/Philadelphia: Trinity, 1991) 3-12.

proaches to the biblical text, for instance. These approaches, however, continue to eclipse the role of the reader in making meaning. Structuralists continue to trade on the model of objective knowledge, insisting that their approach is a "science" of the text.

3.3 Ideological Approaches

Elisabeth Schüssler Fiorenza argues that readers must ethically evaluate the text as well as respond to its initiatives.[25] The principal aim of Marxist or "materialist" readers, for instance, is to examine the relation between a text and the sociopolitical forces associated with its production and reception. Both texts and readers are viewed as sociopolitical products. Biblical stories are read with an interest in discovering something about the struggles of various classes or groups. Equally important, the contemporary reader is also situated in a class-based economic and political system. Readers are the first to be liberated by liberation theology. The assumption that only scholars in First World universities can discover the "proper" meaning of the Bible is exploded. For Carlos Mesters, the experience of poverty and oppression is just as important a "text" as Scripture itself. The place of the poor affords them special insight into the biblical message.[26] The context of the reader is just as important as the context of the text.

Ideological readers try to make the text conform to their devices and desires. Reading is a form of power. Not only what we read, but how we read, is ultimately a matter of politics. If meaning is a matter of the reader's construction, then disagreements over readings — the conflict of interpretations — are really conflicts of ideologies. But if reading is in the eye of a community of beholders (Fish), what can possibly arbitrate interpretive disputes among "believing" communities?

3.4 Deconstructive Approaches

Deconstruction is not a method of interpretation but a method for *undoing* interpretations, for exposing readings as functions of various ideological

---

25. Elisabeth Schüssler Fiorenza, "The Ethics of Biblical Interpretation: Decentering Biblical Scholarship," *JBL* 107 (1988) 3-17.

26. Carlos Mesters, "The Use of the Bible in Christian Communities of the Common People," in *The Bible and Liberation: Political and Social Hermeneutics*, ed. Norman Gottwald (New York: Orbis, 1983) 119-33.

forces. Every textual structure has to repress those elements that threaten to undo it: Patriarchy suppresses women, racism suppresses ethnic minorities, and conventional morality suppresses gays. The point of the deconstructionist critique is that every structure is, like language itself, arbitrary and conventional. No structure, no sense, is "natural." Frank Kermode writes, with reference to the parable of the good Samaritan: "My way of reading . . . seems to me natural; but that is only my way of authenticating, or claiming as universal, a habit of thought that is cultural and arbitrary. My reading would certainly not have seemed 'natural' to the church Fathers."[27] The realm of culture and interpretation is a human construct, where power is pitted against power. What deconstruction ultimately deconstructs is the accumulation of power in interpretation.[28] To deconstruct is to take issue with the text as it is constructed by the reader.

Deconstructive reading mercilessly exposes the reader's interests by undoing interpretation and by exposing the rhetoric, not logic, behind interpretation. It detoxifies the poisoned well and is the ever vigilant attempt to keep the act of reading from coming to rest in a settled interpretation, for of the making of many meanings there is no end. I agree with Werner Jeanrond's assessment: "One of Derrida's main contributions to hermeneutics lies precisely in his powerful warning against any form of absolutist or authoritarian reading of texts."[29] Of course, the deconstructionists' quasi-Reformation cry — "always rewriting" — can itself become an excuse *not* to respond to what is "there" in the text. Insofar as deconstruction renders meaning undecidable it drains away both the authority and the otherness of texts. But if nothing determinate is in the text, how can the reader respond and read responsibly?

4. Critical Remarks

Readers are indeed active in the interpretive process. The key question concerns the nature of this activity of the reader's response. Will the reader,

27. Frank Kermode, *The Genesis of Secrecy: On the Interpretation of Narrative* (Cambridge: Harvard University, 1979) 35.

28. David Jobling, "Writing the Wrongs of the World: The Deconstruction of the Biblical Text in the Context of Liberation Theologies," *Semeia* 51 (1990) 81-118, here 102.

29. Werner G. Jeanrond, *Theological Hermeneutics: Development and Significance* (London: Macmillan, 1991) 104.

confronted with a text's initatives and invitations, respect or suspect them, obey them or rebel against them? To what extent does reader-response infect (or enable) the interpretive stages of explication, understanding, and application?

4.1 Criticism, Using, and Interpreting

In the past, "criticism" referred to obtaining knowledge of a text. Today, however, "criticism" describes the reader's claim to enjoy a privileged perspective from which the text may be used or evaluated. It follows that "criticism" loses its disinterested, scholarly allure. What used to pass as "objective" description is now viewed as "subjective" or intersubjective ideological evaluation. But need it follow that we can no longer distinguish "using" from "interpreting" texts? Is "meaning" a property of texts or does it refer to what readers do with texts? Is "getting it right" strictly equivalent to "making it useful," as Rorty implies? To put it another way: Are all interpretive interests and critical perspectives equally valid?

Readers must not only respond but respond *responsibly*. There are, I believe, normative aims that readers ought to have as they approach the biblical text. One would be to seek understanding before "overstanding." That is, readers should seek to ascertain the nature of the text's communicative intent (its genre and sense) before seeking to use or evaluate it. What is the text trying to do and how is it doing it? This question must be answered with honesty and integrity. To treat a text justly is to respect it for the kind of thing it is, that is, to entertain its perspective and to heed its voice.

Of course, readers inhabit their own worlds and their interests may be different from those of the text. Readers who seek answers to their questions "overstand" the text. We might say that understanding seeks the "meaning" and overstanding the "significance" of the text. But it is crucial that readers evaluate a text's significance only after they have understood its sense. It may be that, once having grasped the text's intended sense, the reader will recoil in disgust. While some texts may give a taste of heaven, others hold horrors. But the point is that the reader's first reflex should be charitable: Understanding precedes criticism as interpretation precedes use. George Steiner goes so far as to treat critics and readers as two different species altogether: Critics function at a distance from the text, of which they are judge and master. The reader, however, "serves" the text and is its shepherd.[30]

30. George Steiner, "Critic/Reader," *NLH* 10 (1979) 423-52.

4.2 Misreading and Other Misdemeanors

Is there such a thing as a poor reading? A false one? If the reader both creates and discovers meaning, how can we maintain the distinctions between exegesis and eisegesis, text and commentary, meaning and significance, description and evaluation, the ideology of the text and the ideology of the reader? Umberto Eco, a believer in the reader's indispensable role, worries that the rights of readers have recently been exaggerated over the rights of the text.[31] Though Eco is willing to speak of a legitimate interpretive pluralism, he also speaks of the fundamental duty of protecting texts before "opening" them. There is a difference between disagreeing about what one thinks the text is trying to say and deliberately misreading the text: "Misreaders" ask neither author nor text about their intentions, but beat the text into a shape that will suit their purposes. Interpretation, on the other hand, means reading a text "in order to discover, along with our reactions to it, something about its nature."[32]

Humpty-Dumpty thought meaning was a matter of who was going to be the master, the words or the one using them: "When *I* use a word . . . it means just what I choose it to mean — nothing more, nothing less."[33] Contemporary poststructuralists and pragmatists have given Nietzsche's will to power to the reader. The Nietzschean counterpart to Humpty-Dumpty is even more hard-boiled: For the willful misreader there is no such thing as absolute meaning or a text-as-it-is-in-itself; every interpretation is the result of our aims and practices. Such strong-willed reading raises the question of interpretive violence. In the words of one American deconstructionist theologian: "Interpretation is a hostile act in which interpreter victimizes text."[34]

4.3 The Ethics of Reading

The violence of radical reader-response criticism is a function of its basic philosophical presuppositions. Its unsatisfactory ethical implications are

31. Umberto Eco, *Interpretation and Overinterpretation* (Cambridge: Cambridge University, 1992) 23.

32. Umberto Eco, *The Limits of Interpretation*, AS (Bloomington: Indiana University, 1990) 57.

33. Lewis Carroll, *Through the Looking-Glass*, in *The Philosopher's Alice*, ed. Peter Heath (New York: St Martin's, 1971) 193.

34. Mark C. Taylor, "Text as Victim," in *Deconstruction and Theology*, ed. T. Altizer (New York: Crossroad, 1982) 65.

symptomatic of its inadequate view of the nature of meaning and interpretation. Insofar as it denies that meaning is "there" in the text, radical reader-response criticism is a form of anti-realism — the philosophical view that reality is not independent but at the behest of our theories about it. While it is true that even scientists approach the world with interpretive schemes, it is not the case that our theories are hermetically sealed off from the world. On the contrary, the world does "kick back," challenging and often falsifying our ideas about it.

Similarly, there must be a realism in the realm of meaning or else anything goes in interpretation. *Gulliver's Travels* remains political satire even though some readers might mistake it for a mere children's story. If it did not continue to be so, if texts became whatever we made of them, then there would be no way in which to judge a reading false. Or, as Jeanrond says,

> a reading which claims to have interpreted the *text*, yet in reality has either only interpreted a section of a text outside of its textual context or used the text or fragments of it in order to promote the reader's own thoughts, must be considered as fraudulent.[35]

If meaning were not in some sense "there" in the text, how could texts ever challenge, inform, or transform their readers? How could texts ever criticize a dominant ideology? Without a certain "realism of reading," where meaning is independent of the interpretive process, reading would cease to be a dangerous, world-shattering prospect. One would then have not to celebrate the birth of the reader but to mourn the stillborn reader.

If the text is at the mercy of the reader, what should readers do with it? First and foremost, readers should *let it be* — not in the sense of leaving it alone but in the sense of allowing the text to fulfill its communicative aim. What the ethical reader gives to the text is, in the first instance, attention. Only then can the text give something back. Steiner depicts the ideal reader as shepherd of the text's "being." Michael LaFargue similarly sees the reader as the text's protector: "The role of the biblical scholar, as scholar, is to be a servant of the biblical text, to guard its otherness, to help make its substantive content something modern people can in some way experience and understand, in its particularity and in its otherness."[36] The

35. Jeanrond, *Text and Interpretation,* 116.
36. Michael LaFargue, "Are Texts Determinate? Derrida, Barth and the Role of the Biblical Scholars," *HTR* 81 (1988) 355.

prime interpretive interest should be to let the text have its say, that is, to heed and hearken to the text with attention, humility, and respect. We may well have a responsibility to assess and criticize a text, or to disagree with its theological or political implications. But we can only do so with integrity if we have first made the intellectual and ethical effort to receive the text on its own terms: "Whoever has ears to hear, let that person hear." The Golden Rule — for Christian ethics and interpretation alike — is "do unto others as you would have them do unto you."

5. Reader Response in Practice

What do readers do when they interpret John 4? This question demands a twofold answer, in keeping with my distinction between conservative and radical reader-response critics.

5.1 Conservative Examples: Reader-Reception

Conservative reader-response critics believe there is something in the text prior to the act of reading — gaps, indeterminacies, instructions, flags, and signals, for example — that calls for and governs their response. The reader follows invitations; like a polite guest being shown the narrative sights, the reader obliges the author by catching the cues and looking in the right direction. R. Alan Culpepper observes that by the time readers reach ch. 4 of John they should know something (on the basis of the information recorded in chs. 1-3) about Jesus and his mission. For instance, the reader of ch. 4 would already know that Jesus will be rejected by his own and believed in by some. The reader of the well story is a privileged onlooker, a guest of a reliable voice — of the so-called "omniscient" narrator — who gives the reader just enough information to make the right evaluation of the characters and the action in the story.[37]

37. J. Eugene Botha argues that the text may also "wrongfoot" readers, for example, by leading them to associate John 4 with similar man-meets-woman-at-well scenes of the OT, only to dash their expectations as the story progresses and no betrothal takes place (*Jesus and the Samaritan Woman: A Speech Act Reading of John 4:1-42* [Leiden: Brill, 1991] 191). Jeffrey Lloyd Staley speaks of the "victimization" of the implied reader by the implied author, who turns the familiar scene into "a brilliant parody of the patriarchal betrothal scenes" (*The Print's First Kiss: A Rhetorical Investigation of the Implied Reader in the Fourth Gospel* [Atlanta, Scholars, 1988] 99).

1. *Following John.* John 4 offers three examples of the way in which textual stimuli guide the reader's response. First, the text recalls a familiar type-scene from the OT: the man-meets-woman-at-the-well device. There are several recurring elements: The future bridegroom (or his surrogate) journeys to a foreign land, he meets a maiden at a well, someone draws water from the well, the maiden rushes home to bring news of the stranger, and a betrothal is arranged. The characters are, of course, unaware that they are playing out a familiar plot; the type-scene is a textual strategy for guiding the reader's understanding of what is happening in the story. In John 4, however, instead of a betrothal meal Jesus tells his disciples "My food is to do the will of him who sent me" (v. 34). Only the reader can appreciate this unexpected twist.[38] Such differences are the keys to understanding how the author is manipulating not only a literary convention but also the reader's response.

Second, Lyle Eslinger claims that the reader will recognize a number of double entendres in the conversation, all of which have sexual overtones. This ambiguity prompts the reader to wonder whether one should attribute a carnal or spiritual meaning to the dialogue. Does Jesus ask for a drink because his disciples are unavailable "or because he and the woman are alone and he can make free with her without damaging his reputation?"[39] The woman, of course, lacks the knowledge of chs. 1–3. As far as she is concerned, Jesus is being friendly, even forward. According to Eslinger, readers are invited to give a sexual connotation to Jesus' "living water" on the basis of such texts as Jer 2:13 and Prov 5:5. *5:15* The reader feels the force of the woman's interpretation, but cannot identify completely with it, being privy to additional information about Jesus' identity.

Third, though the reader has the advantage of the Prologue, which identifies Jesus with the Logos, John 4 is designed in such a way as to give the reader the same sense of confusion as to who Jesus is and what he is about. What is Jesus' motive in asking the woman for a drink? The woman "responds" to his request by hinting that he is being rather forward: Jesus is a Jew, she a Samaritan; Jesus is a man, she a woman. Eslinger believes that the text encourages the reader to share in the woman's "carnal" interpretation of Jesus' words. "To associate with" (v. 9) has sexual overtones,

---

38. Lyle Eslinger, "The Wooing of the Woman at the Well: Jesus, the Reader and Reader-Response Criticism," in *The Gospel of John as Literature: Twentieth Century Perspectives,* ed. Mark W. G. Stibbe (Leiden: Brill, 1993) 165-79.

39. Eslinger, "The Wooing of the Woman," 176.

he claims, as does "living water."[40] The reader's privileged knowledge of who Jesus is (ch. 1) and what "the gift of God" is (3:16) prevents the reader from giving free rein to the carnal interpretation: "His privilege puts him in a quandary, the experience of which gives him a direct perception of the basic problem in the gospel of John, man's misconception of Jesus and misunderstanding of what Jesus says."[41] The reader temporarily loses the omniscient narrator in the maze of the dialogue, forcing the reader to occupy the fallible human perspective of the woman at the well. "In chapter 4 the reading experience becomes an actual experience of the communication gap that the reader has already observed several times between the human characters in the story and Jesus."[42] The reader not only reads about, but undergoes, the experience of misunderstanding Jesus.

2. *Following Irony.* Misinterpreting Jesus is one of the themes of the Fourth Gospel. Culpepper notes that the misunderstandings and mistaken identities that pervade the Fourth Gospel function to teach readers how to read the Gospel correctly: "As we read, watching the encounters and forming judgments on each character, the narrator shapes the response we think we are making on our own and wins our confidence by elevating us above the characters to his position."[43] To follow the Fourth Gospel, then, the reader must be able to recognize irony.

According to Gail R. O'Day, Bultmann failed to see the dynamics of the revelatory process in the Fourth Gospel because he focused on the sheer fact of Jesus as revealer rather than on how the narrative shapes and communicates the revelation.[44] The reader must follow John's textual strategy, especially irony, in order to participate in the revelation. Irony is a form of speech in which the reader is asked to hold two meanings in tension and, as a result of moving through the tension, to arrive at what the author intends to express:

> Irony reveals by asking the reader to make judgments and decisions about the relative value of stated and intended meanings, drawing the reader into its vision of truth, so that when the reader finally understands, he or

---

40. Eslinger, "The Wooing of the Woman," 178.

41. Eslinger, "The Wooing of the Woman," 179.

42. Eslinger, "The Wooing of the Woman," 173.

43. R. Alan Culpepper, *Anatomy of the Fourth Gospel: A Study in Literary Design* (Philadelphia: Fortress, 1983) 234.

44. See Gail R. O'Day, "Narrative Mode and Theological Claim: A Study in the Fourth Gospel," *JBL* 105 (1986) 657-68.

she becomes a member of the community that shares that vision, constituted by those who have also followed the author's lead.[45]

The reader becomes the woman at the well to the extent that he or she is asked to sort through the double meanings and to move from one level of meaning to another. In v. 10 Jesus says that if the woman knew who was asking her for a drink she, in a complete role reversal, would be asking him for "water." But the woman will not be able to interpret "living water" correctly until she recognizes the identity of the one who is speaking. Jesus' clue to his true identity "is an invitation both to the woman and to the reader to grasp both levels of the conversation . . . and to move through the woman's level to Jesus."[46] By following the text's irony, therefore, the reader participates in Jesus' revelation. "Irony is an excellent example of this participation because of the type of reader response it embodies. To follow irony, one must participate and engage creatively in the text."[47] The Fourth Gospel is not just a report of Jesus as revealer but an opportunity for the reader to experience Jesus' revelation for himself or herself.

5.2 Radical Examples: Reader-Rejection?

Real readers, as opposed to ideal readers, may be less than sympathetic to the text's prompts. Accordingly, there is a history not only of text-reception but also of of text-rejection.

1. *Resisting John.* Culpepper comments that readers "dance" with the author whether they want to or not, and in the process they adopt the author's perspective on the story. But not all readers are so compliant as Culpepper believes; some prefer to lead rather than follow. Willi Braun observes that some readers do not trust the implied author. Many resist being drawn into the narrator's ideology and point of view. Braun sets forth a strategy of "resistant" reading that seeks to read the Fourth Gospel from the vantage point of those who may be marginalized by the text — Jews, for instance. These implied victims of John's irony have become real victims of Christian anti-Semitism. There is thus an "enormous incentive" to dissent from the Johannine ideology. Reading may spring not only from the

45. O'Day, "Narrative Mode," 664.
46. O'Day, "Narrative Mode," 667.
47. O'Day, "Narrative Mode," 668.

will to power, but also from "the will to clear space for oneself over against a menacingly 'strong' text."[48]

2. *Imploding Johannine Irony.* Stephen D. Moore questions the text's ability to lead readers through complications and deferrals to understanding. He claims that his reading, which is deconstructive-feminist, is "closer" than that of conservative reader-response critics. His reading is both suspicious and scrupulous inasmuch as it seeks rigorously to examine every resistance to understanding. Deconstructive reading is particularly attentive to everything that threatens the text, or interpretation, with incoherence. A hermeneutics of suspicion seeks thereby to "poison the well" and so to caution would-be readers against swallowing everything the text appears to offer.

Moore acknowledges that the text's apparent irony trades on the woman's failure to distinguish the literal and material from the figural and spiritual (v. 15). The woman is oblivious of the meaning (and the water) "from above." She is discoursing, and drawing water, "from below." As we have seen, conservative reader-response critics believe that the text's strategy is to lead the reader through irony from the lower to the "higher" meaning. Deconstruction is the dismantling of privileged hierarchical oppositions, such as male and female, spiritual and physical, figurative and literal. It is just such oppositions of higher and lower that make the woman at the well a "victim" of Jesus' irony. Moore wants his reading to overturn the text's oppositions and to show that the Samaritan woman's insight is superior to that of Jesus.

Moore notes that the complete meaning of the "living water" is not given in John 4. Jesus speaks of thirst and living water again in 7:37-38: "The one who believes in me, as the Scripture has said, 'Out of that person's heart will flow rivers of living water.'" The narrator, in an aside, informs the reader that Jesus said this "about the Spirit, which those who believe in him were to receive" (7:39). The reader is thus in a superior position to Jesus' audience, knowing something that they do not know. But Moore points out that there is a second deferral of meaning. "The figure of living water being imbibed is interpreted as the receiving of the Spirit, but its narrative representation is postponed until later: 'as yet the Spirit had not been given, because Jesus was not yet glorified' (7:39)."[49] The themes of

48. Willi Braun, "Resisting John: Ambivalent Redactor and Defensive Reader of the Fourth Gospel," *SR* 19 (1990) 64.

49. Moore, *Literary Criticism,* 160. See also his "Are There Impurities in the Living

thirsting and drinking occur once again at the scene of the crucifixion in a way that for Moore "strangely echoes" their first occurrence in ch. 4. In 19:28, however, it is Jesus who says "I thirst" — and this apparently for literal earthly, not living, water! "Expectations have been steadily raised and redirected from 4:10ff from the mundane to the supramundane. Jesus, source of the figural water, is now thrust into the very condition of the literal thirst that his discourse has led the audience to transcend."[50]

The waters become even muddier for Moore when after the satiation of Jesus' physical thirst (itself a fulfillment of Scripture — 19:28), Jesus says "It is finished" and yields up — what? his spirit? the Spirit? Moore comments: "The satiation of Jesus' physical thirst in 19:30 is an arrestingly strange precondition for the symbolic yielding up of that which is designed to satiate the supra-physical thirst of the believer."[51] Not only strange, but contradictory, since the very order of the spiritual and the physical appears to have been inverted!

> The literal, material, earthly level, hierarchically superseded in John 4:7-14 and shifted into the background, is reinstated in John 19:28-30 as the very condition (physical thirst, physical death) that enables the Spirit itself, emblem and token of the supramundane order (cf. 14:17) to effectively come into being.[52]

The opposition between the spiritual and physical on which the irony of ch. 4 depends is thus overthrown from within the text — imploded. The ostensibly superior term — living water, the Spirit — is shown to depend for its existence on the inferior term — literal water.

Jesus' death is followed by the return of the "repressed" — physical water — when the soldiers pierce Jesus' side. Upon Jesus' death, therefore, the Spirit (living water) is yielded up and material water flows from Jesus' side. What shall we make of this last flow? Moore suggests that we are left "with a symbol (the flow of water) of a metaphor (living water) for the Spirit."[53] The water that flows from Jesus' side is neither simply material nor simply spiritual; rather, it is *both* literal and figurative.

Water That the Johannine Jesus Dispenses? Deconstruction, Feminism, and the Samaritan Woman," *BibInt* 1 (1993) 207-27.

50. Moore, *Literary Criticism*, 161.
51. Moore, *Literary Criticism*, 161.
52. Moore, *Literary Criticism*, 161.
53. Moore, *Literary Criticism*, 162.

And what of the Samaritan woman? On Moore's analysis, she is closer to the truth about the water, and about Jesus, than Jesus himself. Whereas Jesus presupposes a dichotomy (and hierarchy) between the literal and figurative, physical and spiritual, the woman resists such oppositions. For her the water in the well is more than merely physical; it is water from a well dug by Jacob that has lasted centuries — it is symbolic. Far from being the victim of irony, therefore, the woman at the well has correctly recognized that all such ironies built on hierarchical oppositions eventually implode. Insofar as the woman resists the opposition between literal and figurative, she outstrips her male teacher. Such a reading is not what the text intended, but it is buried in the text's "structural unconscious." Moore argues that Jesus, insofar as he mistakenly thinks that the spiritual is "higher" than the physical, is the main ironic casualty of this undoing of the traditional interpretation of John 4. The woman at the well, far from being a victim of the author's irony, turns out to be the first deconstructive-feminist critic!

6. Conclusion: The Reader as Disciple

We are left with two opposed models for reading. Which follows the text more closely: the one that rejects or the one that respects the author's intentions and the textual strategies that embody them? Following a text means understanding the nature of its communicative activity. Following irony is not the same as following an argument, but both are forms of reader response to textual strategies. Davies says that competent readers of the Fourth Gospel need to know the Scriptures and the story of Jesus and must be part of a confessional community living out (i.e., following) the Gospel insights. "The ideal readers of the this narrative are those who can play the role of the narratees in believing that Jesus is the Christ."[54]

Finally, with regard to meaning: Do readers find it or make it? Albert Schweitzer concluded his classic *The Quest for the Historical Jesus* with a memorable image about a well: When investigators peered down into the well of Jesus' history, they managed to see only the reflection of their own faces in the water below. The reader at the literary well will come away with as great a thirst as ever if, in search of the textual Jesus, one similarly discovers only oneself. Readers who feed only on themselves are likely to

54. Margaret Davies, *Rhetoric and Reference in the Fourth Gospel* (Sheffield: JSOT, 1992) 373.

emerge from the process of interpretation unfulfilled. It is one thing to study well water, to smell it, and to analyze its chemical composition, and quite another thing to drink. One who continually suspects well water of contamination and never drinks will never quench his or her thirst.[55] The reader at the well, in order to be nourished, must draw from and drink of the text. To "drink" here means to accept and to appropriate. The reader has a responsibility to receive the text according to its nature and intention. Steiner describes good reading as responsive to its source, as resulting in a creative echo to the text.[56] One can do many things with water from a well; but in the desert of criticism, a drink should be received with eagerness and thanks.

7. Suggestions for Further Reading

7.1 Books Written by Secular Theorists

Reader-Response Criticism: From Formalism to Post-Structuralism, ed. Jane P. Tomkins (Baltimore: Johns Hopkins University, 1980), is the best single introduction to reader-oriented literary criticism. It contains, besides the editor's own excellent contribution (ix-xxvi), a number of the most important essays, all written between 1950 and 1980, that were instrumental in developing the reader-oriented approach. Authors represented include Wolfgang Iser and Stanley Fish. There is also an excellent and very useful annotated forty-page bibliography.

The Role of the Reader: Explorations in the Semiotics of Texts, by Umberto Eco (Bloomington: Indiana University, 1979), is a collection of nine early essays written between 1959 and 1978. Part One deals with "open" texts (e.g., James Joyce's *Finnegan's Wake*), those that invite the reader's participation in the production of meaning and encourage several "decodings." Part Two treats "closed" texts, which resist diverse decodings and produce predetermined responses. Part Three focuses on how the codes available to readers determine what the text means to them. More recently, in *Inter-*

---

55. On the importance of "trust" in interpretation, see Kevin J. Vanhoozer, "The Hermeneutics of I-Witness Testimony: John 21:21-24 and the 'Death' of the 'Author,'" in *Understanding Poets and Prophets,* ed. A. Graeme Auld (Sheffield: JSOT, 1993) 366-87.

56. George Steiner, "Narcissus and Echo: A Note on Current Arts of Reading," *AJS* 1 (1981) 14.

pretation and Overinterpretation (Cambridge: Cambridge University, 1992), Eco has acknowledged an intentionality inherent in the text itself. Against Richard Rorty, another contributor to the volume, Eco wants to distinguish "making it useful" and "getting it right": "If Jack the Ripper told us that he did what he did on the grounds of his interpretation of the Gospel according to Saint Luke, I suspect that many reader-oriented critics would be inclined to think that he read Saint Luke in a pretty preposterous way" (24). There *is* such a thing as misinterpretation, though Eco believes this has been lost from sight in recent years because the rights of the text have been eclipsed by the rights of the reader.

George Steiner's *Real Presences* (Chicago: University of Chicago, 1989) argues that the reader's belief in meaning is actually a wager on transcendence. This trust that there is something "in" what we say has underwritten the history of Western civilization but has been abandoned by radical reader-response critics. This powerful and beautifully written book is an eloquent plea for an "ethic of common sense": "I take it to be a moral and pragmatic fact that the poem, the painting, the sonata, are prior to the act of reception, of commentary, of valuation" (149-50). The priority of the text means the priority of the voice of the Other, a voice to which we owe an initial courtesy and respect. As with other guests, we must ask where texts come from: "The temporal, historical context of meaning, of articulate and executive forms, is integral to our possibilities of reception and response" (165).

7.2 Books Written by Biblical Scholars and Theologians

Werner G. Jeanrond's *Text and Interpretation as Categories of Theological Thinking* (New York: Crossroad, 1988) formulates a threefold concept of interpretation in dialogue with Gadamer and Ricoeur. Responsible interpretation involves not only an understanding of textual sense and an explanation of textual structure, but also an assessment or critique of textual content as well. Thanks to this last step, the reader becomes "ethically active": readers must do justice both to the text and to their situation in the world. In ch. 2 Jeanrond introduces the helpful notion of a "reading genre": Readers can read texts in different ways. Responsible reading means that the way one reads a text must be appropriate to the text. For instance, the inattentive reader who ignores the theological character of John's prologue and who assumes "that the text offers a plain 'biographical narration' acts irresponsibly" (126).

Biblical Hermeneutics: Toward a Theory of Reading as the Production of Meaning, by J. Severino Croatto (Maryknoll, New York: Orbis, 1987), is a good example of how reader-oriented criticism may be put to work in liberation theology. Croatto sees the Bible as a living word that can forge history through new, creative readings. What is relevant "is not the 'behind' of a text, but its 'ahead,' its 'forward' — what it suggests as a pertinent message for the life of the one who receives or seeks it out" (50). Croatto argues that what opens the meaning of the biblical texts is their being read in the context of a new praxis, that is, in the context of the fight against oppression. Paul's context is long gone, but the text survives. Reading is the process of recontextualizing the text for today.

The Responsibility of Hermeneutics, an interdisciplinary effort by Roger Lundin, Clarence Walhout, and Anthony C. Thiselton (Grand Rapids: Eerdmans, 1985), views writing and reading as human actions that arise within specific contexts: "To compose and to interpret texts is to engage in responsible action" (ix). The concern for right action leads the authors to make proposals concerning the ethics of interpretation. The burden of the book is to articulate an approach to reading that avoids the extremes of "objectivism" on the one hand and "subjectivism" on the other. Walhout proposes a model of literature-as-action in order to provide an intrinsic connection between text and context: "Because texts are objects produced by actions, one can speak 'objectively' about a text only in the framework of the actions that have produced the text" (43). Thiselton considers the parables as speech acts that attack, rebuke, and challenge the reader: The biblical text "performs a variety of actions on the reader, and the reader's repertoire of interpretive responses themselves constitute a varied range of action. But not all interpretive acts of reading are equally responsible" (112).

Kevin J. Vanhoozer's *Is There a Meaning in This Text? The Bible, the Reader, and the Morality of Literary Knowledge* (Grand Rapids: Zondervan, forthcoming) explores the philosophical assumptions (metaphysical, epistemological, and ethical) behind debates concerning hermeneutical realism, rationality, and responsibility. Part One examines the ways in which deconstruction and radical reader-response criticism "undo" the notions of author, text, and reader. The death of the author means that there is nothing to provide an anchor to textual meaning. The text, as a free-floating sign system, thus becomes an all-too-easy victim of ideological interpretation. Part Two seeks to "redeem" author, text, and reader by viewing meaning as something people do — as diverse kinds of communicative action. The author returns as a communicative agent, the text as a structured act governed by communicative rationality, and reading as a responsive and responsible activity governed by communicative ethics. The "morality" of text interpretation is ultimately grounded in theology. "Faith seeking understanding" applies to the work of interpretation and theology alike. If we approach the text without faith, hope, and love, we will go away as empty as we came. Consequently, the reader must be a "believer."

7.3 Books Employing This Approach to NT Texts

The Open Text: New Directions for Biblical Studies? ed. Francis Watson (London: SCM, 1993), is a stimulating collection of essays by biblical scholars and theologians united in their belief that the historical-critical method fails to do justice to the "full reality" of the biblical texts. What is needed is a variety of approaches — a "pluralist hermeneutic." Several chapters — notably those by Mark G. Brett, Francis Watson, Werner Jeanrond, and Frances Young — explore the various interests that readers bring to the text. Some of these interests are "interpretive" (e.g., interests in achieving the goal of a particular hermeneutic — structuralist, reader-response, etc.), others are "ideological" (e.g., interests in using the text in support of a particular agenda). How open do authors want to be? Should some directions in biblical studies be avoided? This volume excels in exploring new possibilities for reading the Bible, but only raises the question of which interpretive goals are ethically defensible. A concluding chapter inquires, in light of reader-response criticism, about the future of the biblical commentary: "Can the commentary be kept distinct from the propaganda weapon?" (174).

Stephen D. Moore, *Literary Criticism and the Gospels: The Theoretical Challenge* (New Haven: Yale University, 1989), is the best introduction to reader-response critical approaches to the NT now available. In Part One Moore traces the development of reader-response criticism out of literary criticism and, in particular, out of narrative analysis. Moore offers a comprehensive survey and evaluation of books and articles that use reader-oriented methods to interpret the Gospels. In Part Two he recounts the story of the Gospel reader from Robert Tannehill's 1977 study of "The Disciples in Mark" (the first appropriation of reader-response criticism for NT exegesis) to his own deconstructive reading of the Gospel of John. Of particular importance is Moore's distinction between approaches that focus on the historical readers, on the reader-in-the-text, and on real (contemporary) readers. The book includes a helpful glossary of technical terms and an equally helpful bibliography.

16. Global Perspectives on New Testament Interpretation[1]

John R. Levison and Priscilla Pope-Levison

The inclusion of a chapter on global hermeneutics in a book on NT interpretation is a salutary recognition of two developments that have a direct impact on our understanding of the Bible. The first is a hermeneutical development that arose in the First World. According to the nineteenth-century Enlightenment model, which dominated biblical scholarship for nearly two centuries, the task of the scholar was to uncover the original meaning of the Bible by means of linguistic and historical analysis. This task demanded that the interpreter jettison all bias so as not to distort the Bible's original meaning with modern questions.

This model has been seriously called into question by the recognition that no interpreter can understand any text without prejudgments formed from his or her own context.[2] In its place, another model of interpretation, based on the belief that deepest insight and relevance lie neither in the original meaning of the Bible alone nor in the contemporary context but

---

1. This article was written at the Eberhard-Karls-Universität Tübingen with the generous support of the Alexander von Humboldt Foundation. For more detailed analysis of this topic, see John R. Levison and Priscilla Pope-Levison, *Jesus in Global Contexts* (Louisville: Westminster/John Knox, 1992); *idem*, "The Use of the New Testament in Third World Christologies" *BR* 37 (1992) 32-46.

2. See "The Problem of Hermeneutics," in Rudolf Bultmann, *Essays Philosophical and Theological* (London: SCM, 1955) 234-61, esp. 252-56; *idem*, "Is Exegesis without Presuppositions Possible?" in *Existence and Faith: Shorter Writings of Rudolf Bultmann*, ed. Schubert Ogden (New York: World, 1960/London: Hodder and Stoughton, 1961) 289-96. See also ch. 14 above.

in the to-and-fro of question and answer between them, has been proferred. This model of interpretation is that of a conversation.[3] The interpreter engages the Bible as a conversation partner with specific questions that arise from his or her context. The goal of interpretation is to allow the conversation between the Bible and its interpreters to develop a life of its own. The relationship between text and context can be understood as the fusion of two horizons. The text represents the first horizon, and the context of the interpreter is the second horizon. The ultimate goal of this model of interpretation as conversation is to fuse these horizons in a way that is true to the past and relevant to the present.[4]

While this first development in biblical interpretation occurred in the First World, a second development has arisen in the Third World. Although this is one of the most important developments in Christian history, most Christians are unaware of it, and this volume is one of the first devoted to NT scholarship to recognize it. This is "nothing less than a complete change in the centre of gravity of Christianity, so that the heartlands of the Church are no longer in Europe, decreasingly in North America, but in Latin America, in certain parts of Asia, and . . . in Africa."[5] The church, both in numbers and vitality, is rapidly growing in many regions of the Third World, where the majority of the world's population lives.

Together these developments signal that biblical interpretation is incomplete without a global purview. A First World interpretation of a biblical passage, rich though it may be in linguistic and historical analysis, does not finally exhaust the meaning of a text because it ignores contexts that bring their own insights to the process of interpretation. It is necessary, therefore, to place this interpretation in conversation with interpretations from other contexts. The purpose of this article is to survey and to assess briefly some of the dominant hermeneutical trajectories in so-called Third World con-

3. Robert M. Grant and David Tracy, *A Short History of the Interpretation of the Bible* (2d ed., Philadelphia: Fortress, 1984) 154-60, 181. Here Tracy interprets Hans-Georg Gadamer, *Truth and Method* (2d ed., New York: Crossroad, 1990).

4. See Anthony C. Thiselton, *The Two Horizons: New Testament Hermeneutics and Philosophical Description with Special Reference to Heidegger, Bultmann, Gadamer, and Wittgenstein* (Grand Rapids: Eerdmans, 1980) 10-23; Gadamer, *Truth and Method*, 101-21, 293-326.

5. Andrew F. Walls, "Towards Understanding Africa's Place in Christian History," in *Religion in a Pluralistic Society*, ed. John S. Pobee (Leiden: Brill, 1976) 180; quoted by William A. Dyrness, *Learning about Theology from the Third World* (Grand Rapids: Zondervan, 1990) 13.

texts — Latin America, Asia, and Africa — and to look at a few selective interpretations of Luke 3–4 from these contexts.

1. A Survey of Approaches

1.1 Latin America

Leonardo Boff's book, *Jesus Christ Liberator*, published in 1972, provided a clarion call to contextualizing Jesus for the Latin American people.[6] To understand the use of the NT in his and other Latin American liberation theologies, we must understand the theological method of which it is a part.

In a 1968 meeting in Medellín, Colombia, Latin American bishops utilized a three-step theological method that had been delineated in the Vatican II document *Gaudium et Spes* (the Pastoral Constitution on The Church in the Modern World). The Medellín conference began with a social and economic analysis of the Latin American reality (step one), continued with biblical and theological reflection on this reality (step two), and concluded with a recommendation, among others, that the Latin American church must be in solidarity with the poor (step three). Latin American liberation theologians adopt this method with one crucial modification: They require a *pre*commitment to the poor that precedes step one and thereby influences every step. This three-step theological method serves as the pattern for their hermeneutical method, in which they reflect on the New Testament (step two) in the light of a social analysis done with a precommitment to the oppressed (step one).

Latin American liberation theologians utilize the tools of Marxist social analysis to discover the facts of their context (step one). From this perspective, they arrive at two conclusions. The first is the realization that a *class struggle* exists between the majority workers and the minority owners in Latin America. The second realization is that *liberation* is the solution to the class struggle. Their emphasis on liberation arose in part as a response to President Kennedy's "Alliance for Progress," an aid program aimed at developing Latin America.[7] Many theologians who would come to be called

---

6. Leonardo Boff, *Jesus Christ Liberator: A Critical Christology for Our Time* (Maryknoll: Orbis, 1978).

7. The word "liberation" referred to contemporary events in Latin America includ-

liberation theologians demanded instead an "integral liberation" that touches all forms of oppression: political and economic injustice, social indignity among the marginalized of society, and sin, which divides God from humankind and neighbor from neighbor.

As a reflection (step two) of this social analysis (step one), the NT becomes a resource for understanding class struggle and discerning its solution in an integral liberation. For these tasks, the Synoptic Gospels are central to a Latin American liberation hermeneutic since they tend to be more resistant to a thoroughgoing spiritualization than, for instance, Paul's letters.[8] Moreover, the hermeneutical key to interpreting the NT in general is the demand for integral liberation.

The dominant aspect of this hermeneutical key is the *political* dimension because policies of many Latin American governments have institutionalized the class struggle. For this reason, a biblical interpreter such as Juan Luis Segundo interprets Jesus' command to love in political terms. His social analysis leads to the assertion that in contemporary Latin America "love, *effective love* . . . is conditioned by all the *systems* that affect human coexistence. . . ."[9] For example, love of neighbor entails educating one's neighbor. Yet education exceeds the love of individual teachers and parents and depends, to a large extent, on the balance between military and other expenditures in a national budget. Therefore, Segundo asks,

> When it comes to the Christian understanding of love, therefore, what valid reason do we have for excluding from consideration the field in which the most crucial decisions affecting love's exercise will be made? Would it not be much more logical to take Jesus' remarks, couched in apparently more interpersonal terms in line with his own era, and translate them into political terms?[10]

---

ing the Cuban Revolution in 1959 and the death of two revolutionary figures, Camilo Torres and Ernesto "Che" Guevara, in 1966 and 1967.

8. This use of the Synoptic Gospels is not exclusive. Gustavo Gutiérrez, for instance, interprets the book of Job from a liberation perspective in *On Job: God-Talk and the Suffering of the Innocent* (Maryknoll: Orbis, 1987), and Juan Luis Segundo analyzes Romans 1–8 in *The Humanist Christology of Paul* (Maryknoll: Orbis, 1986).

9. Juan Luis Segundo, *The Historical Jesus of the Synoptics* (Maryknoll: Orbis, 1985) 81.

10. Segundo. *The Historical Jesus,* 83.

Latin American emphasis on the political dimension leads to another hermeneutical key: the *relationship between politics and religion,* since in many Latin American nations governments are buttressed by the church, which wields extraordinary power. Many liberation theologians charge that the church uses its political power to maintain intimate ties with the ruling class rather than with the poor and powerless.

The quintessential combination of politics and religion in the NT is the reign of God, and it is this notion that has obtained a preeminent place in Latin American liberation theology. Latin American biblical interpreters agree with most First World interpreters that the reign of God is central to understanding the Gospels and Jesus himself. Their analysis, however, focuses on the way in which the reign of God addresses the class struggle. The reign of God is, in its religious dimension, the reign *of God.* This God is a particular God, whose commitment to the poor is evident in Israelite law codes (e.g., Exod 22:22-24, 27b) and in the persistent prophetic plea for justice (e.g., Amos 2:6-8; Hos 6:6). In the reign of God, then, the religious dimension takes concrete form in a social, economic, and political vision of justice. The reign of God is also, in its political dimension, the *reign* of God, replete with recollections and expectations of the Davidic monarchy as expressed by the possibility, which Jesus does not deny, that Jesus is David's son (e.g., Mark 10:46-52). Jesus' proclamation that the reign of God is among people (Luke 17:21) brings together the religio-political past and future of Israel in the vision of a society characterized by concrete justice exercised on behalf of the oppressed.

Latin American liberation theologians recognize that this *annunciation* of the reign of God is only one side of the coin of liberation. The other side is *denunciation* of all that divides God from humankind and neighbor from neighbor. Therefore, when they look to the NT, liberation theologians discover a strong current of denunciation accompanying Jesus' annunciation of the reign of God. Jesus targeted any group that misused power and challenged the Pharisees for discarding justice (Matt 23:23), the lawyers for imposing unbearable burdens (Matt 23:4), the learned for stealing the keys to knowledge (Luke 11:52), the priests for transforming the temple precinct into a robber's den (Mark 11:15-17), and the rulers of this world for ruling despotically (Matt 20:26).

In summary, Latin American biblical interpreters emphasize aspects in the NT that they believe can bring about liberation from the class struggle. Of particular importance is the political dimension, which is regarded as inseparable from the religious dimension, both in first-century Palestine and twentieth-century Latin America. The inseparability between religion and politics is especially evident in the central vision of Jesus' ministry, the reign of God, which becomes in Latin America a paradigm for annunciation of hope to the oppressed and denunciation of all that oppresses.

1.2 Asia

Asia is vast and diverse, stretching from the islands of the Philippines to the Himalaya mountains, encompassing both the affluence of Tokyo and the poverty of Calcutta, and holding in tension Islam, Hinduism, Buddhism, and a variety of permutations of these religions. Despite this diversity, three hermeneutical trends, not wholly inseparable, can be discerned in this region.

Some Asian theologians begin with the *social reality* of the Asian people. For these theologians, the Asian people provide the fertile soil for theology. Asian theologians reflect theologically on the people's folktales, stories, and other artistic expressions. For instance, some Korean theologians reflect on social biographies of the *minjung* ("the mass of the people" or "the people"). Social biographies of the *minjung,* who are workers, students, poor women farmers, intellectuals, or the urban poor, reveal the present social reality of oppression. Social biographies give rise to artistic forms when the stories are enacted, as in the Korean mask dance, a dramatic portrayal in which the *minjung* ridicule their oppressors.[11]

From the perspective of what C. S. Song calls a "people hermeneutic," the Bible functions as a mirror of social biography when it is juxtaposed with popular Asian expressions.[12] The Buddhist lotus and the Christian cross, for instance, both emerge from the biographies of common people.[13] As the cross has been the focus of Christian devotion, so the image of Buddha seated cross-legged on the lotus has brought serenity to countless people. On the surface these images are different. The lotus springs peacefully from fertile water and exists harmoniously with the earth as a symbol of gentleness, while the cross is lifted defiantly from the barren earth as a symbol of brutality. Yet they are similar in many respects. Both are attempts to answer the basic question of human suffering: "Asian Buddhists enter

11. Hyun Young-Hak, "A Theological Look at the Mask Dance in Korea," in *Minjung Theology: People as the Subjects of History,* ed. Commission on Theological Concerns of the Christian Conference of Asia (Maryknoll: Orbis, 1981) 50.

12. C. S. Song, *Jesus, the Crucified People* (New York: Crossroad, 1990) 12-14.

13. C. S. Song, *Third Eye Theology: Theology in Formation in Asian Settings* (rev. ed., Maryknoll: Orbis, 1990) 119-41.

human suffering through the lotus, and Christians through the cross."[14] They are both symbols that belong not to theologians but to people in their daily struggles because they represent two storytellers who lived among common people. In addition, both symbols reinforce the protest against power: Buddha against Hinduism's oppressive caste system and Jesus against the wealthy and the Pharisees.

Because this "people hermeneutic" emerges from the Asian people, it is bereft of any biblical order or even a discernible single starting point. Nor can there be any strict hermeneutic that determines the meaning of the Bible, since the juxtaposition of Asian social biography and NT texts produces a resonance rather than a restriction of meaning.

Asian religions comprise the second aspect of the Asian reality. The scriptures of these religions, such as the Upanishads of Hindusim, the Analects of Confucius, or the Koran of Islam, are key ingredients in the mixture of Asian theology. Some Asian biblical interpreters seek to discern parallels between Christian Scriptures and other sacred writings by employing a comparative textual study. The atmosphere is one of dialogue and the goal is to engender religious harmony and the mutual elimination of texts.[15] Such studies have been undertaken between Christian Scriptures and writings from Hinduism, Buddhism, and Confucianism. One recent example is a study that traces the influence of Indian traditions on the NT. In particular, the author suggests that both Matthew's and Luke's narratives of Jesus' birth contain allusions to Buddhist and Hindu sources.[16]

The third major aspect of the Asian reality is *economics.* To analyze this dimension, some Asian theologians utilize Marxist social analysis. Still, they do not implement Marxist social analysis as wholeheartedly as their Latin American counterparts because it separates the economic factor from people's religiosity. That is, Marxism is not comprehensive enough to address the entirety of the Asian reality.[17] Therefore, Asian theologians

14. Song, *Third Eye Theology,* 141.

15. R. S. Sugirtharajah, "The Bible and Its Asian Readers," *BibInt* 1 (1993) 58.

16. See Zacharias P. Thundy, *Buddha and Christ: Nativity Stories and Indian Traditions* (Leiden: Brill, 1993). For other examples of this hermeneutic, see Sugirtharajah, "The Bible and Its Asian Readers," 55-63.

17. J. C. Duraisingh and K. C. Abraham, "Reflections from an Asian Perspective," in *Irruption of the Third World: Challenge to Theology,* ed. Virginia Fabella and Sergio Torres (Papers from the Fifth International Conference of the Ecumenical Association of Third World Theologians, August 17-29, 1981, New Delhi, India; Maryknoll: Orbis, 1983) 211.

incorporate the economic aspect of Marxism alongside the social and religious dimensions of the Asian reality. For example, one Korean *minjung* biblical interpreter considers the reality of class in his contention that Mark chose the term ὄχλος (*ochlos*, "crowd") over λαός (*laos*, "people") in order to underline the class significance of the poor and oppressed with whom Jesus spent his time.[18] Yet, *minjung* biblical interpreters also utilize social biographies and artistic expressions of the *minjung*. In this sense, Asian biblical interpretation entails, at its best, a holistic approach to the Bible that reaches the social, religious, and economic dimensions of the Asian reality. The Bible "resounds with the Word of God in the Scriptures of other religions as well as . . . permeating actions for justice and peace."[19]

In summary, Asian theologians have a wide array of issues to address. Some juxtapose the Bible with social biography and artistic expressions, while others explore the points of contact between the Bible and the scriptures of other Asian religions, and still others highlight along with these aspects the economic interpretation. It is here especially that the inseparability of these three approaches becomes apparent, for few Asian theologians are satisfied with an economic analysis that does not address the issue of Asian religions in a way that is relevant for Asia's masses.

1.3 Africa

When European colonizers came to sub-Saharan Africa[20] beginning in the fifteenth century, they succeeded in subjugating the African way of life to European political, economic, social, and religious institutions. The Bible was brought to Africa in the context of this imperialism, and understandably the hermeneutic employed to interpret its meaning reflected a Western

18. See Ahn Bung Mu, "Jesus and the Minjung in the Gospels," in *Voices from the Margin: Interpreting the Bible in the Third World,* ed. R. S. Sugirtharajah (Maryknoll: Orbis/London: SPCK, 1991) 85-103: "When we consider the fact that the *ochlos* are contrasted with the ruling class of that time and that Jesus was criticized for associating with the *ochlos,* it becomes evident that the *ochlos* were the condemned and alienated class" (90).

19. D. S. Amalorpavadass, "The Bible in Self-Renewal and Church Renewal for Service to Society," in *On Interpreting the Bible: Voices from the Third World* (EATWOT, 1987) 65.

20. This chapter reviews only theological reflection in the forty-six countries south of the Sahara desert. The five Muslim countries in northern Africa are not included because of their political, socioeconomic, and religious differences from the countries to the south.

perspective. In the wake of a rapid succession of movements for independence, African theologians attempt to glean the essence of the Bible from this Western surplus. They ask "How is it possible to sort out the Gospel of Christ from the European interpretation of Christianity?"[21] This sorting process has resulted in only a modicum of theoretical analysis of African hermeneutics. Nonetheless, an analysis of disparate biblical interpretations yields what might be called a "hermeneutic of resonance" between the NT and traditional African culture.

African theologians discern a "kindred atmosphere" connecting African traditional religion to the Hebrew Bible, with its emphasis on the pervasiveness of religion in all activities of life, the preponderence of rites and rituals, the importance of oral tradition, and the centrality of solidarity and group loyalty.[22] Elements from the NT also resonate with African traditional religion. For example, the African emphasis on community illuminates the communal dimension of the NT. In a pioneering attempt to interpret the NT from the perspective of African culture J. S. Mbiti interpreted the resurrection as a communal event in which individuality is subsumed by a corporate resurrection body.[23] Other central NT concepts such as salvation are also understood in light of the African emphasis on the need for equilibrium in community and cosmos. In this context the NT discussion of cosmic powers from whose negative influence people must be saved (e.g., Col 2:20) has a place in African theology.[24]

Because of this emphasis on community, African theologians discern a resonance between figures in African culture who function as mediators

21. Kofi Appiah-Kubi, "Why African Theology?" *AACC Bulletin* 7 (1974) 5. See also J. C. Thomas, "What Is African Theology?" *Ghana Bulletin of Theology* 4 (1973) 15. "The African realises that, laudable as the missionary endeavours are in Africa, . . . the answer to the question who Jesus is was, from the start, supplied by missionaries in their own conceptual and value-laden categories" (C. B. Okolo, "Christ, 'Emmanuel': An African Inquiry," *Bulletin de Théologie Africaine* 2 [1980] 17).

22. See Kwesi Dickson, *Theology in Africa* (Maryknoll: Orbis, 1984) 148-59; Aylward Shorter, ed., *African Christian Spirituality* (Maryknoll: Orbis/London: Chapman, 1978) 10-11; John Parratt, "African Theology and Biblical Hermeneutics," *Africa Theological Journal* 12 (1983) 88-94.

23. J. S. Mbiti, *New Testament Eschatology in an African Background: A Study of the Encounter between New Testament Theology and African Traditional Concepts* (New York/Oxford: Oxford University, 1971).

24. E.g., J. S. Mbiti "ὁ σωτὴρ ἡμῶν as an African Experience," in *Christ and Spirit in the New Testament,* ed. Barnabas Lindars and Stephen Smalley (Cambridge: Cambridge University, 1973) 397-414.

among different parts of the community, both human and divine, and NT portraits of Jesus as mediator. For example, the role of ancestors, those who have died physically but continue to live, resonates with the portrait of Jesus in the Gospel of John. As ancestors are mediators of the life-flow to their community, so Jesus is like a vine that mediates life to the branches (15:4-7). As ancestors mediate the prayers and offerings of the living to God, so Jesus is "the way, the truth, and the life" (14:6). As the ancestors provide a watchful presence over the community, so Jesus left his presence or Spirit with the community he left behind until its members, too, should enter the community of the living dead (14:18).[25]

Another key figure in African tribal life is the *nganga* or holistic healer, who, according to one Congolese theologian, can be called healer, priest, chemist, doctor, magician, prophet, and visionary.[26] Whatever the name used, the constant of African healing is its holistic quality. It requires determining the physical, spiritual, and social cause of a sickness, and therapy ranges from sacrifices to dances to restoration of social relationships.

The Synoptic Gospels are replete with accounts of Jesus' healing that share an African healer's holistic approach. Like an African healer, Jesus acknowledged a relationship between body and spirit, for, along with physical healing, Jesus absolved the unhealthy of guilt ("Your sins are forgiven," Mark 2:5) and commended the sick for their faith ("Your faith has made you well," Mark 10:52). Jesus also placed healing within the context of social reintegration to the community. Lepers had to report to the priest (Mark 1:44; Luke 17:14), the Gerasene demoniac had to go home to his friends (Mark 5:19), and Peter's mother-in-law took up her role as host immediately upon her healing (Mark 1:31). Even Jesus' methods of healing approximate those of an African healer's use of sacred objects or fetishes. He applied saliva or a mixture of saliva and dirt to the unhealthy body part (Mark 7:33; 8:23), and he made noises interpreted variously as a sigh or a snort or a groan (Mark 7:34).

These examples of a "hermeneutic of resonance" differ from the her-

25. François Kabasélé, "Christ as Ancestor and Elder Brother," in *Faces of Jesus in Africa,* ed. Robert Schreiter (Maryknoll: Orbis, 1991) 116-27; Charles Nyamiti, *Christ as Our Ancestor: Christology from an African Perspective* (Gweru: Mambo, 1984) 15-20, 23.

26. R. Buana Kibongi, "Priesthood," in *Biblical Revelation and African Beliefs,* ed. Kwesi Dickson and Paul Ellingworth (Maryknoll: Orbis/London: Lutterworth, 1969) 50. See also Matthew Schoffeleers, "Folk Christology in Africa: The Dialectics of the Nganga Paradigm," *Journal of Religion in Africa* 19 (1989) 157-83.

meneutic of liberation that characterizes the discussion among black theologians in South Africa. There, under the domination of apartheid, the exodus has become the paradigm of holistic liberation because it parallels the experience of South African blacks, who hope to jettison Afrikaaner supremacy and regain access to their ancestral land.

Two reactions to an exodus-based hermeneutic have recently been proposed. Takatso A. Mofokeng accepts the centrality of the exodus but does not think it should be utilized to rescue the entire canon of Scripture for black people. Instead, fidelity to the black tradition requires utilizing only those texts that meet the exigencies of the black struggle.[27] Itumeleng Mosala rejects the exodus altogether as the key to unlocking the Bible's relevance for South African blacks. He contends that isolating a universal, abstract word of God, such as "God's preference for the poor" or "God's liberating act," is irrelevant to working-class blacks. The starting point of their experience is "struggle," and this struggle must be the key to interpreting the Bible. Liberative biblical interpretation should be an attempt to uncover the struggles among cultures, genders, classes, and races that lie under the surface of the biblical text.[28] The fact, however, that Mofokeng and Mosala construct their hermeneutical alternatives in response to the "exodus" axis reveals how central the exodus is to South African black theology.

In summary, two hermeneutical options characterize African biblical interpretation. A "hermeneutic of resonance" juxtaposes NT conceptions with key elements and key figures in African traditional religion. A predominantly South African "hermeneutic of liberation," which has tended to emphasize the exodus, underscores elements of struggle that illuminate and reflect the Black struggle.

1.4 Assessment

The sheer variety of these approaches makes it difficult to provide a comprehensive assessment. Even the hermeneutic of liberation that spans these regions is nuanced differently. In Latin America, the political dimension of the NT is given priority because of its importance for addressing the class

27. Takatso A. Mofokeng, "Black Christians, the Bible and Liberation," in *Towards Freedom, Justice and Peace: Voices from the Third World* (EATWOT, 1987) 22.

28. Itumeleng J. Mosala, *Biblical Hermeneutics and Black Theology in South Africa* (Grand Rapids: Eerdmans, 1989) 13-42, 190-93. Micah, for instance, contains prophetic oracles that reflect a struggle among three classes: rulers, middle class, and working class.

struggle. In Asia, emphasis on this political dimension is regarded as inadequate because it does not address the meaning of the Bible in the context of other historic Asian religions, each with its own scriptures. In South Africa, the Latin American attempt to address the struggle between social classes is being displaced by the need to embrace the Black struggle and to look for that sort of struggle behind the written words of the NT. Nonetheless, despite the variety that characterizes hermeneutics in the Third World, three aspects can be isolated as areas that could be fruitfully developed.

First, Third World theologians in general agree that biblical interpretation should either take place in grassroots communities or reflect those interpretations. In Latin America, for instance, peasants often meet in base communities, in groups of twelve to fifteen people, to read the Bible and to reflect on it in the light of their context. In Africa, thousands of independent churches blend Christianity and African traditional religion, providing at the grassroots level a hermeneutic of resonance. However, despite the commitment to a shift in biblical interpretation from the elite to such grassroots communities, only a few studies of biblical interpretation within these communities are available. It would be helpful if more transcripts of their interpretations such as Ernesto Cardenal's *The Gospel in Solentiname* became available.[29] Such transcripts can be analyzed profitably to determine the relationship that exists between these readers and the biblical texts along the lines suggested above in Kevin Vanhoozer's chapter on "The Reader in New Testament Interpretation."

Second, the interplay between text and context that, on the one hand, can result in a creative fusion of horizons, can, on the other hand, lead to a collapsing of the distinction between context and text. Contemporary issues and needs can too easily be superimposed on the NT, resulting in a disregard for biblical texts that do not coincide with these needs or in a reinterpretation of those texts in a way that violates their integrity. This potential is by no means endemic to Third World hermeneutics. In 1906, Albert Schweitzer demonstrated that "each successive epoch of theology . . . found its own thoughts in Jesus" with the consequence that a modern perspective "creates the historical Jesus in its own image."[30] Particularly in a hermeneutical approach that attempts to establish a resonance between

29. Ernesto Cardenal, ed., *The Gospel in Solentiname,* 4 vols. (Maryknoll: Orbis, 1976-82).

30. Albert Schweitzer, *The Quest of the Historical Jesus: A Critical Study of Its Progress from Reimarus to Wrede* (New York: Macmillan, 1959) 4, 132.

the Bible and the modern world, it is imperative to prevent a wholesale surrender of the biblical text to the tyranny of contemporary context. For this reason, it is essential to use a social-scientific perspective, which is summarized in this volume in Stephen Barton's chapter on "Historical Criticism and Social-Scientific Perspectives in New Testament Study." By incorporating the tools of this perspective in the analysis of both ancient text and contemporary context, Third World biblical interpreters can draw significant parallels between the past and present while preserving the unique aspects that distinguish them.

A third area in which global hermeneutics can be developed is its view of Judaism. Although Third World theologians generally reflect a keen awareness of the oppression that permeates their contexts, their interpretations of the NT frequently contain a negative portrayal of Second Temple Judaism that provides the seeds of anti-Semitism. Second Temple Judaism is often utilized as a negative foil for Jesus, whose message is not "the safe and solid ground of the law" but "a universal love that is superior to all laws."[31] The Pharisees' interpretation is "a blind one that lacked any center of gravity,"[32] and the Sadducees are said to adhere to a "leisure-class spirituality."[33] To mitigate this potential for anti-Semitism, Third World biblical interpreters can turn to a massive amount of research that recognizes the rich diversity of Second Temple Judaism and refuses therefore to reduce it to a religion of legalism. Important guidelines for interpreting the NT within, rather than over against, its Jewish context are included by Richard Bauckham in this volume in "The Relevance of Extra-Canonical Jewish Texts to New Testament Study."

2. These Approaches in Practice

The variety of hermeneutical alternatives that are developing in Latin America, Asia, and Africa can be illustrated by three interpretations of Luke 3–4. Each fuses the biblical context with its own contemporary context.

31. Boff, *Jesus Christ Liberator*, 75.

32. Hugo Echegaray, *The Practice of Jesus* (Maryknoll: Orbis, 1984) 56. In addition, according to F. Eboussi Boulaga of Cameroon, the Pharisaic interpretation consists of external legalism: "plac[ing] the whole content of revelation in a corpus of usages, precepts, formulas, dispositions, and habits, which it identifies immediately with the will of God" (*Christianity without Fetishes: An African Critique and Recapture of Christianity* [Maryknoll: Orbis, 1984] 102).

33. Aloysius Pieris, *An Asian Theology of Liberation* (Maryknoll: Orbis, 1988) 63.

2.1 A Latin American Interpretation of Luke 3–4

From the perspective of Latin American liberation theology, a comparison of the two key figures that dominate Luke 3, John the Baptist and Jesus, highlights the political dimension and its relationship to the religious dimension in the context of class struggle. Luke portrays both in a manner reminiscent of the Hebrew prophet Elijah. John dressed like Elijah, was associated with Elijah by the disciples, and was even compared with Elijah by Jesus himself (Luke 7:27). Jesus healed the son of a widow of Nain, as Elijah had healed the son of a widow of Zarephath, prompting the people to cry out, "A great prophet has risen among us!" (7:11-17).

This backdrop of Elijah's activity for the lives of Jesus and John highlights the integration of the political and religious spheres since almost the entire Elijah cycle depicts Elijah as opposing the policies of Ahab.[34] On one occasion Elijah opposed Jehu's domestic policy because it oppressed the weak, such as Naboth, who lost his vineyard and his life to Ahab (1 Kgs 21:1-24). John, who was identified also as the prophetic voice of Isaiah 40 that cried in the wilderness, opposed King Herod's immoral marriage and consequently was beheaded. In an analogous way, Jesus, who was regarded as "a prophet mighty in deed and word before God and all the people" (Luke 24:19) and who called himself a prophet (Mark 6:4), initiated a succession of events that ended in crucifixion as a *political prisoner* by challenging the *religious authorities* in Jerusalem with a prophetic act of cleansing the temple.[35]

Despite their similar prophetic quality and mission, the differing demands of John and Jesus reveal two strikingly different views of the reign of God.[36] John gave very simple commands, such as to tax collectors, "Collect no more than the amount prescribed to you" (3:13), and to soldiers, "Do not extort money from anyone by threats or false accusations, and be satisfied with your wages" (3:14). These commands are like a check-

34. Segundo, *Historical Jesus,* 78. Elijah's defeat of the prophets of Baal marked a political watershed for Ahab and Jezebel, for God's next command for Elijah was political: to anoint Hazael to be king over Syria and Jehu to be king over Israel (1 Kgs 19:15-16).

35. Segundo, *Historical Jesus,* 93; see also Jon Sobrino, *Christology at the Crossroads* (Maryknoll: Orbis, 1978) 210-11; J. Severino Croatto, "The Political Dimension of Christ the Liberator," in *Faces of Jesus: Latin American Christologies,* ed. José Míguez Bonino (Maryknoll: Orbis, 1984) 116.

36. For this interpretation see Segundo, *Historical Jesus,* 90-91, 147-49.

list for different social groups to help them to prepare for the impending judgment. They are, in short, "the fruits of repentance" necessary to avoid the fiery catastrophe about to occur. There are no caveats, no nuances, no exceptions — simply the final, hurried preparation for the imminent judgment that rests like an ax at the foot of a tree (3:9).

The teaching of Jesus, in contrast, was far more complex. He utilized parables to confuse and to prod (Luke 8:9-10). He interpreted Torah with an eye to the unity of internal motivation and external action (Matt 5:17-48). This teaching reveals that he regarded the reign of God as that which was already taking root in the present rather than as an external reality about to arrive in a cosmic cataclysm. It was a present reality (Luke 17:21), effected through partial liberations — healings, exorcisms, and the rekindling of hope among the oppressed.

This essential distinction between the missions of John and Jesus can be illustrated by their table habits. John came neither eating nor drinking, but lived in a manner consistent with his expectation of judgment. Jesus ate and drank, associating with tax collectors and sinners — that is, the marginalized of first-century Palestine whom God was liberating (Luke 7:33-34). In the parties that Jesus held with these people we can see the anticipation of the final festal banquet in the reign of God, when the first will be last and the last first.

2.2 An Asian Interpretation of Luke 3–4

In Asia, christologies that address the dual Asian realities of poverty and religiosity are taking root. One such interpretation suggests that Jesus underwent a double baptism: into poverty and into religiosity.[37]

When Jesus was baptized by John, he symbolically aligned himself with two sorts of people. On the one hand, his baptism by John the Baptist symbolized his acceptance of the Baptist's prophetic asceticism. John lived in the desert, with nature, eating locusts and honey. Jesus, too, renounced the world and followed John the Baptist's way in the wilderness. On the other hand, Jesus' baptism signaled his solidarity with the rural poor who were drawn to John the Baptist's message. Theirs was a world-affirming religion that espoused the values of the countryside.

As time passed, the religiosity of the poor exerted more of an influence

37. This Asian interpretation of Luke 3–4 is espoused by Pieris of Sri Lanka in *An Asian Theology*, 46-49.

on Jesus, and his own religious ideals became more positive than John the Baptist's. For example, John cursed religious leaders and demanded radical repentance. To this Jesus added blessings and promises offered to the marginalized poor and ostracized sinners. John the Baptist preached bad news about the coming judgment, but Jesus had good news to give about imminent liberation.

The commitment to the religiosity of John the Baptist and the rural poor that Jesus made at his baptism at the Jordan River led him inevitably to a second baptism — on the cross outside Jerusalem. He took a prophetic stance in which he denounced the accumulation of wealth and worked to make the poor aware of their unique liberative role in the new order that God would bring about. This prophetic stance threatened the wealthy and powerful, who responded in rage and with death threats. In the end, they brought in the Romans, a vast colonialist power, to crucify him. This is where the journey begun at the Jordan ended. The cross represents, therefore, Jesus' second baptism on the Calvary of poverty.

This view of Jesus is particularly pertinent given the association of the Christian church with Asia's oppressive colonial past, as can be seen in a description of Vasco da Gama's arrival in India in 1498: "The captain-general's ship flew at its mast a flag on which was painted a large cross of Christ and also carried cannons, symbols of the new power entering the East."[38] For Pieris, the church of Asia must begin to emulate Jesus' double baptism, because, while the church exists *in* Asia, it is not yet a church *of* Asia. The church must be baptized into Asian religiosity by working alongside other Asian religions for mutual collaboration on Asian issues. The church must also be baptized into Asian poverty by allowing itself to be shaped by the religiosity of the poor. The doubly baptized church of Asia will be a community of Christians and non-Christians who form communities with the poor, sharing the common heritage of spirituality that poverty generates.[39]

2.3 An African Interpretation of Luke 3–4

An interpretation of Luke 3–4 that resonates with traditional African culture presents Jesus' baptism and temptation as rites of passage by which he

38. Quoted in Hans-Ruedi Weber, *Asia and the Ecumenical Movement, 1895-1961* (London: SCM/Naperville: Allenson, 1966) 18.

39. Pieris, *An Asian Theology,* 38, 125.

enters fully into the human community.[40] They are essential to an affirmation of the fullness of his humanity, without which he cannot be accepted as a full member of the African community.

In traditional African culture, being human is possible only when one is in community. An African proverb says "I am because we are." People are incorporated into community through rites of passage.[41] The rites at birth, for instance, particularly the proper disposal of the umbilical cord, symbolize that the child is now related to the community and not just to the mother who birthed it. The practice of this rite and other rites attached to birth resonates with Luke 1–2: Jesus' parents have him circumcised and, following the prescribed period of seclusion, present him at the temple with the offerings of purification prescribed by the community (2:21-24). At this juncture, devout, elderly members of the community — who in traditional African culture command the greatest respect — affirm Jesus' future role within the community (2:25-38).

These communal affirmations are followed by a story that cites Jesus' remarkable role in the community *and* his development as a human being at twelve years of age, the age of puberty, another important point of initiation (2:41-52). This rite of passage entails a new dimension: the reception of instruction from leaders in the community in the temple. It also confirms Jesus' alignment with the community and its God rather than with his biological parents: "Did you not know that I must be in my Father's house?"

Luke continues by presenting two further events that function as related rites of passage in Jesus' life, Jesus' baptism and temptation. Jesus' submission to the rite of baptism confirms his humanity because it demonstrates his solidarity with the human community. Moreover, the words from God, "You are my son," serve again to underscore that Jesus' relationship with the whole community, whose God speaks, takes priority over his relationship with his biological parents.

Baptism is followed by the journey into the wilderness for forty days. This experience is Jesus' most crucial rite of passage, and it resonates with traditional African rites of passage. First, it requires seclusion. In Africa, young members of the community often undergo a withdrawal from

40. See Anselme T. Sanon, "Jesus, Master of Initiation," in *Faces of Jesus in Africa*, ed. Robert Schreiter (Maryknoll: Orbis, 1991) 85-102.

41. For many specific examples of rites of passage, see John S. Mbiti, *African Religions and Philosophy* (Garden City: Doubleday, 1970) 143-216.

society, perhaps in the forest. Analogously, Jesus withdraws into the wilderness. Second, this dramatic seclusion symbolizes dying, living in the spirit world, and being reborn. Jesus, too, enters the world of death, where stones displace bread. He enters the realm of the spirits, led by the Spirit into the desert, tested by Satan, and emerging filled with the power of the Spirit.

In the context of traditional African culture, then, Luke 1–4 traces the rites of passage through which Jesus becomes a full member of his own community and, therefore, a full member of the human community. However, this solidarity is not an abstract theological affirmation of the humanness of Jesus. For Jesus to have a place in his community, from an African perspective, he must belong to a kinship system — that is, to a vast network that connects everyone in a tribe, clan, or family. Luke provides Jesus' place in the kinship system with a genealogy. Jesus' precise place within his human community (as Joseph's son), the ancestral community (from Heli to Adam), and the cosmos (God is the final ancestor) is firmly fixed by Luke, who places this essential kinship information at the intersection between Jesus' baptism and his seclusion in the desert, two critical and closely related rites of passage.

3. Suggestions for Further Reading

3.1 All Contexts

For an introduction to this topic, the best starting point is R. S. Sugirtharajah, ed., *Voices from the Margin: Interpreting the Bible in the Third World* (Maryknoll: Orbis, 1991), a collection of previously published articles by men and women from many Third World contexts. The volume is divided into five parts: (1) "Use of the Bible: Methods, Principles and Issues," (2) "Re-use of the Bible: Examples of Hermeneutical Explorations," consisting of miscellaneous illustrative studies, for example, an Indian interpretation of John 2:1-11, (3) "The Exodus: One Theme, Many Perspectives," in which the exodus is interpreted from the perspectives of the Korean *minjung*, Palestinians, Native Americans, and others, (4) "One Reality, Many Texts: Examples of Multi-faith Hermeneutics," articles written in light of other Asian religious traditions, and (5) "People as Exegetes," a significant section of biblical interpretations by nonscholars in Malawi, Nicaragua, Indonesia, South Africa, and China.

John S. Pobee, ed., *New Eyes for Reading: Biblical and Theological Re-*

flections by Women from the Third World (Geneva: WCC, 1986), contains brief reflections by Third World women on biblical texts in which, for the most part, women are featured. The style is conversational rather than analytical.

Recent christologies are the focus of John R. Levison and Priscilla Pope-Levison, *Jesus in Global Contexts* (Louisville: Westminster/John Knox, 1992), which analyzes portraits of Jesus in Latin American liberation theology, from Asia, from Africa, and in North American feminist and black theologies. In addition to introducing the issues faced by each context and the resulting portraits of Jesus, each chapter analyzes sources and methods used in each context, including the Bible. The conclusion also contains a summary of hermeneutical methods and biblical starting points, and a thorough bibliography is included.

3.2 Latin America

A good sense of liberation theology's approach to the Bible can be gleaned from J. Míguez Bonino, ed., *Faces of Jesus: Latin American Christologies* (Maryknoll: Orbis, 1984), particularly in the section on "Christ and Politics." Juan Luis Segundo, *The Historical Jesus of the Synoptics* (Maryknoll: Orbis, 1985), should be read only after an initial foundation in global hermeneutics and historical-critical methods is laid. Following theoretical discussion of his hermeneutics, Segundo implements the methods of historical criticism to defend the thesis that the political dimension permeated the life of Jesus.

3.3 Asia

A discussion of Asian hermeneutics should begin with R. S. Sugirtharajah, "The Bible and Its Asian Readers," *BibInt* 1 (1993) 54-66, which contains a survey, critical analyses, and a bibliography. One could also refer to *Asian Faces of Jesus*, edited by R. S. Sugirtharajah (Maryknoll: Orbis, 1993). Alongside section four of *Voices from the Margin* (above), this article provides a hermeneutical and bibliographical basis for detailed study.

3.4 Africa

As in Latin America, the central focuses of African hermeneutics can be culled from christological analyses. John S. Pobee, ed., *Exploring Afro-*

Christology, SIHC 79 (Frankfurt/New York: Lang, 1992), contains articles by black theologians in sub-Saharan Africa, North America, and the Caribbean. Robert Schreiter, ed., *Faces of Jesus in Africa* (Maryknoll: Orbis, 1991), contains survey articles on various aspects of African christology as well as specific christologies: Jesus as master of initiation (rites of passage), chief, ancestor and elder brother, and liberator. From a South African perspective, Itumeleng J. Mosala interprets Micah and Luke in *Biblical Hermeneutics and Black Theology in South Africa* (Grand Rapids: Eerdmans, 1989).

17. *Feminist Hermeneutics*[*]

SANDRA M. SCHNEIDERS

1. Situating Feminist Hermeneutics

Feminist biblical interpretation is a species of liberationist hermeneutics, which also includes class interpretation such as that which functions within Latin American theology and racial interpretation such as African American or black hermeneutics. What these types of interpretation have in common is their starting point in the experience of the oppressed, their presupposition that there is no such thing as a neutral scholarship that pursues and attains purely objective knowledge, and their goal of social transformation. For liberationist hermeneutics the goal of interpretation is not simply to ascertain "what the author intended to say" or even "what the text actually says" in some supposedly disinterested way but to integrate biblical interpretation into an agenda of personal conversion and societal transformation.

However, feminist hermeneutics differs from some of its liberationist companions, notably class hermeneutics, in one very important respect. Whereas the contemporary poor can make a fairly straightforward transfer from the divine advocacy of the poor and oppressed in the Old and New Testaments to their own situation, women who are oppressed because of their sex and the demeaning construction of gender in contemporary

---

church and society find that the Bible often underwrites their oppression by its assumption of male normativity, its presentation of sexist and even misogynist attitudes and behaviors as acceptable, and its justification of sexually based oppression as the "divine plan" for the human race. In other words, because the biblical text is not purely and simply a text of liberation for women but is itself part of the problem, the transformational agenda of feminist hermeneutics involves not only the liberation of the oppressed through the transformation of society but also the liberation of the biblical text itself from its own participation in the oppression of women, and finally the transformation of the church that continues to model, under-write, and legitimate the oppression of women in family and society on the basis of the biblical text into the discipleship of equals which it is called to be.[1]

2. Suspicion and Retrieval

Feminist biblical interpretation, as an approach, is rooted in ideology criti-cism, which starts with the assumption that the text is not "neutral" and the interpreter is not "objective."[2] In other words, it is rooted in suspicion as we have learned it from the great molders of the modern mind: Freud, Nietzsche, and Marx.

First, the text is not neutral. The biblical text, like other historical documents, was written by the "historical winners" who virtually never write *the* story but *their* story. Women are the quintessential "historical losers" in that they are the doubly oppressed of every oppressed group throughout history. The result is that women in the biblical text are often marginalized when they are not omitted entirely, pornographically reduced to their sexuality (because they are presented as they are seen by and function for men), demonized (by male projection), or trivialized (as non-

1. The expression "discipleship of equals" was coined by Elisabeth Schüssler Fiorenza in *In Memory of Her: A Feminist Theological Reconstruction of Christian Origins* (New York: Crossroad, 1983) and has been adopted by feminist interpreters and theo-logians as an expression of the goal of feminist practice in the church.

2. In the language of Jürgen Habermas, ideology produces "systematically distorted communication." For a succinct presentation of Habermas's position, see Paul Ricoeur, "Hermeneutics and the Critique of Ideology," in *Hermeneutics and the Human Sciences: Essays on Language, Action and Interpretation*, ed. John B. Thompson (Cambridge: Cam-bridge University/Paris: Maison des Sciences de l'Homme, 1981) 78-87.

participants in the spheres of male activity, which alone are deemed significant). One cannot assume, in other words, in reading the biblical text, that it gives us an accurate picture of women in the community of salvation. We get a picture of women that men created, that corresponds to the male understanding of women and their place in society at the time that these documents were written. The feminist interpreter must, therefore, presume that she or he is dealing with a distorted record from which much has been omitted and in which much that is included is unreliable.

Second, the interpreters of the biblical text have never been, and are not now, objective, if by objective one means ideologically unbiased. Until very recently virtually all biblical scholars (exegetes and teachers), pastors, and homilists have been men living in, trained for, and ruling over patriarchal churches and society. They shared the mind-set of those who produced the biblical text and so noticed nothing, or very little, amiss in its presentation of women and men.

It is characteristic of ideology that it is invisible to the one whose bias it underwrites. Usually only those who do not participate in the power system whose agenda is propagated by the ideology are aware that what seems to be simply "the way things are" is actually an oppressive conceptual, cultural, and social system. The "hermeneutical advantage" of the oppressed is precisely this ability to see, from the margins of social reality, what is second nature to those who are the beneficiaries of the social system.

Feminist interpreters must, therefore, suspect both the text and the history of its interpretation of antiwoman bias. This is not academic paranoia but realism. At the same time they must propose an alternative stance to the false objectivity whose existence (and even possibility) they deny. Feminists, with other ideologically aware scholars, know not only that there is no presuppositionless interpretation but also that there are no ideologically neutral presuppositions. In other words, everyone interprets from a perspective controlled to some extent by her or his social location, interests, and commitments. The only access to a relatively unbiased and therefore nonoppressive approach is to become self-aware of and explicit about one's social location and the effective historical consciousness to which it has contributed and then to methodically criticize and thereby neutralize as much as possible the ideological effects.

However, if feminist consciousness terminates in suspicion it must end by repudiating the biblical text as hopelessly antiwoman and therefore without salvific potential for women. Some feminists have indeed come to this conclusion.[3] Those who continue to hope that the biblical text is susceptible of a liberating hermeneutic must pass by way of suspicion to retrieval. Suspicion leads to ideology criticism. But ideology criticism is then in the service of advocacy and reconstruction. This chapter is an exercise in the hermeneutics of retrieval, the effort to face without flinching the real problems in both the text and the history of interpretation and to move through the confrontation to the liberating potential of the text for women and for society.

3. Feminist Critical Strategy

Numerous exegetical and critical strategies are employed by feminist biblical scholars in the effort to liberate the text from its own and its interpreters' ideological bias and women from the oppressive effects of this bias.[4] I will mention here five of the most common, but this list is illustrative rather than exhaustive and different methods are appropriate to different texts.

3.1 Translation

Feminist interpretation often begins by challenging translations that privilege the male/masculine at the expense of the female/feminine.[5] For example, when the masculine plural in the Greek is plainly inclusive in mean-

3. The most well known is perhaps theologian Mary Daly, who is a self-described post-Christian scholar, but an increasing number of feminist scholars in the area of religious studies have abandoned the Christian tradition for various forms of goddess-centered religious involvement; see Sandra M. Schneiders, *Beyond Patching: Faith and Feminism in the Catholic Church* (Mahwah: Paulist, 1991), esp. ch. 1, for further discussion of this phenomenon.

4. Most typologies of feminist interpretation divide current scholarship into three hermeneutical types: revisionist, liberationist, and reconstructionist. However, as feminist scholars continue to interact these classifications are breaking down. Whatever hermeneutical position a scholar embraces, certain strategies are shared. On this point, see Katherine Doob Sakenfeld, "Feminist Uses of Biblical Materials," in *Feminist Interpretation of the Bible*, ed. Letty M. Russell (Philadelphia: Westminster, 1985) 55-64. I am concerned here with strategies.

5. On the problem of translation, see Katherine Doob Sakenfeld, "Feminist Perspectives on Bible and Theology: An Introduction to Selected Issues and Literature," *Int* 42 (1988) 5-18, esp. 16-18.

ing, many modern translations (although, happily, fewer) fail to use inclusive modern language, thereby perpetuating the fixation of the imagination on males as the normative or only important participants in the drama of salvation. A case in point is the NRSV translation of John 4:12-14, in which οἱ υἱοί *(hoi huioi)* is translated as Jacob's "sons" even though, if his daughters had not also drunk of the well, there would have been very few sons! The masculine plural is used in Greek, as it often is in English, as the inclusive term for a group including both men and women — that is, for descendants, both sons and daughters in this case (cf. English "brethren"). To translate it as "sons" is, therefore, actually inaccurate, at least in modern English.

Likewise, in the RSV (happily corrected in the NRSV) Jesus is presented in the same passage as saying "whoever drinks of the water that I shall give *him* will never thirst; the water that I shall give *him* will become in *him* a spring of water welling up to eternal life" (emphasis added). The translation of αὐτῷ *(autǭ)* as masculine, given that Jesus is talking to a woman and plainly intends his message to have universal application, is literalistic and false to the meaning of the passage. Feminist consciousness recognizes and challenges the ideological agenda of rendering women textually invisible, which is an important factor in keeping them socially and ecclesially invisible.

3.2 Focusing on Texts with Liberating Potential

One of the earliest types of feminist interpretation, which still has value provided that it is not used in isolation, consists in focusing on what has been called "woman material" in the NT. In other words, feminist scholars located and exploited texts in which women figure prominently, are presented positively, or overcome actual historical or textual attempts to suppress them. The Samaritan Woman story has been used this way and John 4:27, the episode of the disciples' return from the town and their shock that Jesus is conversing with a woman, has often focused the attention of feminist interpreters. In my interpretation I will exploit this episode, but I will do so within the context of a feminist interpretation of the passage as a whole.

The danger of this focus on particular texts is that it can unconsciously support the underlying ideological presupposition that women appear in history, as in life, by way of exception. In other words, it is assumed that the biblical story, like all of human history, is basically about men. If women, by way of exception, are significant at some point, they must be singled out and raised to visibility. Thus, the question becomes: What does the Bible say about *women?* — because the story as a whole is presumed to be not about women but about men. Nevertheless, there is value in focusing on material about women in the NT text because in these texts one can see clearly what is often completely hidden in the majority of the text — namely, that women existed, participated actively, and were highly significant in Christian history from its first moments.

3.3 Raising Women to Visibility

A third strategy of feminist interpretation consists in raising to visibility the hidden feminine element in biblical texts. In other words, attention is called to the application specifically to women of texts that are obviously liberating but whose beneficiaries seem not to include women, or have been understood or interpreted as not including women. For example, the proclamation by the townspeople of Sychar that Jesus is the "Savior of the world" (John 4:42) was not merely a vindication of the claim of Samaritans to equal participation with Jews in the salvation offered by Jesus but also of the equal participation of women in that salvation. "World" is a universalist term, and the invisible subgroup of every excluded group is women.

3.4 Revealing the Text's "Secrets"

Feminist interpretation also attempts to extract from the biblical text the "secrets" about women that are buried beneath its androcentric surface, especially the hidden history of women that has been largely obscured and distorted if not erased altogether by male control of the tradition. Sometimes the feminist task involves pointing to that which is plainly in the text but has remained "unnoticed" or even been denied by exegetes. For example, there are enough ambiguities in the Fourth Gospel's few clues to the identity of the Evangelist and the Beloved Disciple to at least raise a serious question about whether one or both might have been female. The Gospel probably does not provide enough data to settle the question either way, but that in itself should suffice to undermine the nearly universal assumption that the Gospel is (of course) a male creation or that such is to be held until there is convincing evidence to the contrary.[6]

6. See Elizabeth Schüssler Fiorenza, *In Memory of Her,* 60-61: "The suggestion of

Rhetorical criticism is also used by feminist interpreters to "make the text reveal its context."[7] For example, the feminist rhetorical critic might well raise the following questions: What experience within the Johannine community would have suggested to the Evangelist to make a woman the central character in two major missionary texts, namely, the story of the evangelization of Samaria in 4:1-42 and the commission to announce the resurrection in 20:11-18? Would such stories have been acceptable in a community that restricted apostolic identity and missionary activity to males? Who might have had a stake in preserving the little episode in John 4:27 (the return of the disciples), since it plays no essential role in the story being told but clearly calls into question male hesitations about women's relationship to Jesus and to the apostolate? Would a male writer have done so or been allowed to do so by other males?

3.5 Rescuing the Text from Misinterpretation

A very important strategy of feminist interpretation consists in discerning and challenging the androcentric, patriarchal, sexist, and misogynist misinterpretations that pervade the history of NT scholarship and that have deeply affected the Christian imagination through the scholarly and homiletic tradition. For example, as I will attempt to show, the consistent identification of the Samaritan woman in John 4 as a duplicitous whore whom Jesus tricks into self-exposure and then, presumably, converts, both violates the text and allows the woman's role in the evangelization of Samaria to be minimized while the (presumably male) townspeople emerge as virtual self-evangelizers who perspicaciously recognize Jesus' true identity while dismissing the woman's testimony.

---

female authorship . . . has great imaginative-theological value because it opens up the possibility of attributing the authority of apostolic writings to women and of claiming theological authority for women" (61).

7. I take this expression from Wilhelm Wuellner, "Where Is Rhetorical Criticism Taking Us?" *CBQ* 29 (1987) 450. Elisabeth Schüssler Fiorenza elaborates the same point in her 1987 Society of Biblical Literature presidential address, "The Ethics of Biblical Interpretation: Decentering Biblical Scholarship," *JBL* 107 (1988) 3-17. The recent full-scale rhetorical study by Antoinette C. Wire of the Corinthian correspondence is an example of this type of feminist interpretation: *The Corinthian Women Prophets: A Reconstruction through Paul's Rhetoric* (Minneapolis: Fortress, 1991).

4. John 4:1-42: A Feminist Reading

Although feminist interpretation is primarily concerned with ideology criticism and reconstruction it cannot bypass the basic historical and literary-critical work whose conclusions are presuppositions in the overall interpretation.

4.1 Historical and Literary Presuppositions

In the feminist interpretation that follows I will assume that the episode in Samaria is, in all likelihood, not a historical event in the life of the earthly Jesus[8] but a reading back into Jesus' public ministry of the post-glorification conversion of Samaritans who became members of the Johannine community. The basic purpose of the Samaritan Woman story in the Gospel itself is to legitimate the Samaritan mission and to establish the full equality in the community of Samaritan Christians and Jewish Christians.

Two literary characteristics of the Samaritan Woman story are important for our purposes. First, in form the story is what has been called a "type-story" — that is, a narrative that follows a recognized biblical pattern.[9] In this case the pattern or paradigm is the story of the meeting of future spouses who then play a central role in salvation history. We find the pattern in the story of Abraham's servant finding Rebecca, the future wife of Isaac, at the well of Nahor (Gen 24:10-61), Jacob meeting Rachel at the well in Haran (Gen 29:1-20), and Moses receiving Zipporah as wife after his rescue of the seven daughters of Reuel at the well in Midian (Exod 2:16-22).

In the Johannine story Jesus meets the woman at the most famous well of all, Jacob's well in Samaria — that is, in ancient Israel. Jesus has already been identified at Cana as the true Bridegroom who supplied the good wine for the wedding feast (2:9-10) and by John the Baptist as the true Bridegroom to whom God has given the New Israel as bride (3:27-30). Now, the new Bridegroom, who assumes the role of Yahweh, the bridegroom of ancient Israel, comes to claim Samaria as an integral part of the New Israel

8. There is no evidence in the Synoptic Gospels of a Samaritan mission by the historical Jesus, and Acts 8 recounts what seems to be the first Christian mission to Samaria, which was initiated after the death of Stephen.

9. See P. Joseph Cahill, "Narrative Art in John IV," *Religious Studies Bulletin* 2 (1982) 44-47.

— namely, the Christian community and specifically the Johannine community. The marital theme is underscored by the male-female dynamic of the scene, the conversation between the woman and Jesus about marriage, and the abundant fertility and fecundity symbolism of the episode (well, water, vessel, fruitful fields, sowing and reaping, etc.).[10]

Second, the Samaritan Woman episode must be seen within the "Cana to Cana" literary development in John 2–4. This section of the Gospel, pervaded by the marital motif, begins with the wedding at Cana in ch. 2, where Jesus' Jewish disciples (presumably including his mother) come to believe in him through his signs (2:1-11) and ends with the healing of the royal official's son in Cana in ch. 4, in which a non-Jew (at least religiously, and presumably ethnically, a Gentile) and his whole household come to believe because of the word of Jesus (4:46-54). Within this literary unit the Samaritan woman is clearly contrasted with Nicodemus (3:1-15):[11] Nicodemus comes to Jesus at night and disappears into the shadows, confused by Jesus' self-revelation, but the woman encounters Jesus at high noon, accepts his self-revelation, and brings others to him by her testimony.

4.2 The Theological Focus of the Story: Mission

Although the story of the Samaritan Woman is part of the presentation of Jesus as the Bridegroom of the New Israel that pervades the first section of the Fourth Gospel, it is also clearly a missionary story. This is evident from Jesus' discourse to his disciples in vv. 31-38 as well as from the denouement of the scene, the conversion to Jesus of the Samaritan townspeople in vv. 39-42.

In the discourse that intervenes between the woman's departure to evangelize the town by recounting her encounter with Jesus and the coming of the townspeople to him, Jesus speaks to his disciples, who have returned from their errand in the town. He attaches what is occurring before their eyes to his own mission from God by declaring that his deepest hunger — namely, to do God's will — has been satisfied (v. 34) by his conversation with the woman and its consequences. He has no need of the earthly food

10. See Calum M. Carmichael, "Marriage and the Samaritan Woman," *NTS* 26 (1980) 331-46, for detailed treatment of the OT Yahweh-Israel marriage theme in John 4.

11. Mary Margaret Pazdan, "Nicodemus and the Samaritan Woman: Contrasting Models of Discipleship," *BTB* 17 (1987) 145-48.

they have brought him. Furthermore, he calls their attention to Samaria, "ripe for the harvest," and indicates that its conversion is part of the great missionary venture of the church, in which they participate but did not originate and do not control (vv. 35-38).

When the townspeople come to Jesus, they do so, the reader is explicitly told, because of "the woman's testimony" (v. 39), and they finally confess him to be "the Savior of the world" (v. 42), which is clearly a post-glorification Johannine formulation of Christian faith in Jesus. My question, then, is, What is the identity and role of the Samaritan woman in this missionary story?

4.3 The Identity and Role of the Samaritan Woman: Christian Disciple-Apostle

As anyone familiar with the major commentaries on the Fourth Gospel knows, the treatment of the Samaritan Woman in the history of interpretation is a textbook case of the trivialization, marginalization, and even sexual demonization of biblical women, which reflects and promotes the parallel treatment of real women in the church. Rather than cite the commentators and argue with them, however, I will interpret the passage as a feminist who does not assume that most women (insofar as they are interesting at all) are whores and that Jesus' paradigmatic relationship with women is centered on saving them from sexual sins, and who does not accept the assumption that Jesus called only males to apostleship or that all missionary activity in the early church was done by men. This interpretation should serve to call into question the standard approaches to this text.

The first clue to the woman's identity is her placement between Nicodemus, the Jewish authority who fails to recognize Jesus as Messiah or to accept Jesus' self-revelation, and the royal official, the (presumably) pagan authority who recognizes Jesus' life-giving power and comes to faith through and in Jesus' saving word. In other words, the woman, like Nicodemus and the official, is what Raymond Collins has called a "representative figure" — that is, a symbolic character.[12] Very often the symbolic characters in John (e.g., the mother of Jesus, the beloved disciple, the royal official, the paralytic at the pool, the man born blind) are nameless, which enhances their power

12. Raymond F. Collins, "The Representative Figures in the Fourth Gospel," Downside Review 94 (1976) 26-46, 118-32.

to represent collectivities without losing their particularity. This is the case with the Samaritan woman, one of the most sharply drawn characters in the Gospel. This woman is symbolic not only of the Samaritans who come to Jesus through the witness of the Johannine community but, as we have already seen, of the New Israel, which is given to Jesus the Bridegroom "from above." This symbolic identity should warn the reader against the sexual literalism to which so many commentators immediately leap, whether in regard to the woman's supposedly shady past or in regard to what one recent commentator described as the woman's attempt to seduce Jesus.[13]

The second clue to the woman's identity and role is her conversation with Jesus. It is important to note that the discussion, from the very first moment, is religious and even theological. The woman does not, as is often suggested, introduce extraneous theological issues as a smokescreen to distract Jesus from probing into her shameful sex life. She begins by questioning Jesus' breaking with Jewish tradition, which is indicated first by his speaking in public to a woman and asking to share utensils with a Samaritan and second by his implication, in the offer of living water, that he is on a par with the patriarch Jacob, who gave the well to Israel. Characteristic of Samaritan theology was its Mosaic-patriarchal tradition as opposed to the Davidic-monarchical tradition of the Jews. Thus, for the woman, Jesus' implicit claim to be on a par with the patriarch Jacob has enormous theological implications.

Immediately after the exchange on the five husbands (to which we will return shortly), the woman recognizes Jesus, whom she at first had identified as merely a man and a Jew, as a prophet (v. 19), and she asks him where true worship is to take place, on Mount Gerizim as the Samaritans held or in Jerusalem as the Jews believed. According to Samaritan theology the Messiah would be not a descendent of David but a prophet like Moses (as promised in Deut 18:18-19) who, on his return, would reveal all things and restore true worship, not in the temple of Jerusalem, but in Israel — that is, in the northern kingdom. In other words, the woman is pursuing a careful investigation of the identity of Jesus, who has already indicated his affinity with the patriarchs and his prophetic capacity to "tell her all things." She wants to know where he stands on the issue of true worship, which, in Samaritan theology, is not only a prophetic concern but specifically a messianic concern.

13. Lyle Eslinger, "The Wooing of the Woman at the Well: Jesus, the Reader and Reader-Response Criticism," *JLT* 1 (1987) 167-83.

When Jesus, after vindicating the claim of the Jews to be the legitimate bearers of the covenant tradition, goes on to invalidate by transcendence both the Jewish claim for Jerusalem and the Samaritan claim for Mount Gerizim in favor of worship in spirit and in truth, the woman suspects his messianic identity, that he is indeed the one who comes to restore true worship in Israel. Jesus confirms her intuition and reveals himself to her as not only the prophetic Messiah of Samaritan expectation but as ἐγώ εἰμι (egō eimi) — that is, by the very designation that the Samaritans preferred for God, the "I am" of the Mosaic revelation (Exod 3:14). This is the first use of the "I am" revelation formula in the Fourth Gospel.

Within this context of careful theological scrutiny of Jesus by the woman culminating in Jesus' self-identification as equal to and even greater than the patriarchs, the prophetic Messiah, and the Mosaic "I am" — that is, as the superabundant fulfillment of Samaritan messianic expectation — the discussion about the five husbands takes on a completely different cast from the mildly salacious one usually evoked by commentators. Either it is totally out of place, a trivial bit of moralism or even a shallow display of preternatural knowledge on the part of Jesus, or it is an integral part of this highly theological exchange.

The woman has questioned Jesus on virtually every significant tenet of Samaritan theology. Through this process she has come to suspect that he is the Messiah in and through his own self-revelation as the new prophet like Moses (significantly, not a new David), thus vindicating the Samaritan claim to be spiritually a legitimate part of the chosen people and thus of the New Israel. Jesus has pointed the way beyond the controversy between Jews and Jerusalem on the one hand and Samaritans and Mount Gerizim on the other. Both are called to transcend their particularistic traditions and to find their common identity in Jesus, who is the Truth. If this story, as I have suggested, is meant to legitimate the presence of Samaritan Christians in the Johannine community and to affirm their equality with Jewish Christians, it could not have been more artistically constructed. I would suggest, then, that the dialogue on the five husbands is integral to the discussion of Samaritan faith and theology and that the "husbands" are therefore symbolic rather than literal.[14]

14. This thesis was proposed decades ago by John Bligh in "Jesus in Samaria," *HeyJ* 3 (1962) 336. It has been regularly disputed by commentators who prefer the literal interpretation despite the context of the story and the high improbability that any Jewish or Samaritan man would marry a woman who had been divorced several times.

First, the exchange about the husbands occurs, as I have already pointed out, not as a prelude to the theological discussion but in the midst of it — that is, after the woman has perceived Jesus' implicit claim to equality with the patriarchs and before she acknowledges him to be a prophet.

Second, if the scene itself is symbolically the incorporation of Samaria into the New Israel, the bride of the new Bridegroom, which is suggested by the type-scene itself, then the adultery-idolatry symbolism so prevalent in the prophetic literature when it speaks of Israel's infidelity to Yahweh, the Bridegroom, would be a most apt vehicle for discussion of the anomalous religious situation of Samaria. Samaria's infidelity to the Mosaic covenant was symbolized by its acceptance, after the return of the remnants of the northern tribes from Assyrian captivity, of the worship of the false gods of five foreign tribes (cf. 2 Kgs 17:13-34). Samaria's Yahwism was tainted by false worship and therefore even the "husband" she now has (a reference to her relationship with the God of the Covenant) was not really her husband (v. 18) in the full integrity of the covenantal relationship. Salvation, Jesus therefore insists, is "from the Jews" (v. 22), who worship what they know — that is, whose Yahwist faith is integral and orthodox, while the Samaritans worship what they "do not know." Thus, in claiming that Samaria, in reality, has no husband, the woman is correctly (even if unwittingly) using the prophetic metaphor to describe the religious situation of her people. Jesus confirms her answer: "What you have said is true!" (v. 18).

This brings us to the third point. Jesus' revelation to the woman, who symbolizes Samaria, of her infidelity is not a display of preternatural knowledge that convinces the woman of Jesus' power (and thus her helplessness before him), embarrassing her into a diversionary tactic in an effort to escape moral exposure. Rather, it is exactly what she acknowledges it to be: "I perceive that you are a prophet" (v. 19). Jesus' declaration that Samaria "has no husband" is a classic prophetic denunciation of false worship, like Hosea's exhortation, in which the prophet, expressing God's sentiments toward unfaithful Israel, says "Plead with your mother, plead — for she is not my wife and I am not her husband — that she put away her harlotry from her face and her adultery from between her breasts" (Hos 2:2).

The woman challenges Jesus' prophetic judgment by insisting that "Our fathers," that is, the patriarchs, "worshiped on this mountain." That is, Samaritan tradition rests on the authority of the patriarchs. But Jesus vindicates his position, insisting that his prophetic judgment on Samaria is just, but also that the question of where to worship has become irrelevant because, just as Samaritan theology taught, the messianic era, which has arrived in Jesus, will be characterized by true worship of God in spirit, because God is spirit (cf. vv. 20-24). The woman is overcome by this interpretation of Samaritan faith and recognizes that Jesus may be the very Messiah who, according to Samaritan eschatological hope, would "proclaim all things to us," which is what Jesus has just done (v. 25) and what the woman will eventually offer as evidence to her fellow townspeople: "Come and see a man who told me [i.e., us] all I [i.e., we] have ever done!" (v. 29). Jesus confirms her conclusion with his lapidary and unambiguous self-identification as Messiah and as the God of Mosaic revelation, "I am" (v. 26).

In summary, the entire dialogue between Jesus and the woman is the "wooing" of Samaria to full covenant fidelity in the New Israel by Jesus, the New Bridegroom. It has nothing to do with the woman's private moral life but all to do with the covenant life of the community. Nowhere else in the Fourth Gospel is there a dialogue of such theological depth and intensity. Jesus' conversation with Nicodemus in ch. 3 ends in a long theological monologue by Jesus in which Nicodemus has ceased to participate. In ch. 6 Jesus, in response to occasional "foil lines" from his completely confused or resistant interlocutors, gives a lengthy theological monologue on faith. And at the Last Supper Jesus gives one (or several) lengthy theological discourse(s). But in this extraordinary scene the woman is not simply a "foil" feeding Jesus cue lines. She is a genuine theological dialogue partner gradually experiencing Jesus' self-revelation even as she reveals herself to him.

At the precise moment of Jesus' culminating self-revelation, the disciples, who had gone into the town to buy food, arrive. They are shocked to find Jesus talking to a woman. Interestingly enough, it is not his talking to a Samaritan that upsets them. This may well indicate that in the Johannine community, by the time this Gospel was written, the issue of Samaritan integration was long settled, while the issue of women's roles in the community was still a subject of lively debate. In any case, the disciples realize uneasily that Jesus "seeks" something in or of this woman, and they dare not question his intention.[15] The Evangelist confirms the reader's intuition that what shocks the disciples is the woman's role by inserting a detail unnecessary to the narrative over which considerable exegetical ink has

15. See Raymond E. Brown, *The Community of the Beloved Disciple* (New York: Paulist, 1979) 198.

been spilled: "Then the woman left her water jar and went back to the city."
Like the apostle-disciples in the Synoptic Gospels, whose leaving of nets,
boats, parents, or tax stall symbolized their abandonment of ordinary life
to follow Jesus and become apostles, this woman abandons her daily concerns and goes off to evangelize the town.

In the Fourth Gospel ζητέω (*zēteō*, "seek") is often used as a quasi-
technical theological term for the deep desire that finalizes religiously significant attitudes and action. Jesus' first words in the Gospel, addressed to
his first disciples, are τί ζητεῖτε *(ti zēteite),* "What do you seek?" (1:38). His
question to Mary Magdalene on the morning of the resurrection is τίνα
ζητεῖς *(tina zēteis),* "Whom do you seek?" (20:15). Throughout the Gospel
such themes as "seeking glory," "seeking to kill," "seeking the will of the one
who sent me," and "seeking the truth" emphasize the theological import of
the term by marking the ultimate motivations of various characters. In this
case the disciples are made very uneasy by what Jesus seems to seek from
this woman.

This little interlude of the return of the disciples undoubtedly tells us
more about the Johannine community than about the earthly Jesus. The
woman's theological and missionary role is profoundly unsettling to the
male disciples, who see themselves as the privileged associates of Jesus, who
nevertheless seems to have gotten along quite well without them. He does
not need the food they have brought him (vv. 31-34) because his dialogue
with the woman has satisfied both his hunger to do the will of the one who
sent him and the thirst that symbolically mediated their encounter. And
the Samaritan mission, plainly in the hands of the woman, is one in which
Jesus says they will participate as "reapers." But they do not initiate it and
it is not under their control (vv. 35-38). It seems not unlikely that whoever
wrote the Fourth Gospel had some experience of women Christians as
theologians and as apostles, was aware of the tension this aroused in the
community, and wanted to present Jesus as legitimating female participation in male-appropriated roles. Again, one cannot help wondering about
the identity of the Evangelist.

As the disciples lapse into silence, we are told that "many of the Samaritans . . . believed in him because of the woman's testimony" (v. 39).
Literally the text says διὰ τὸν λόγον τῆς γυναικὸς μαρτυρούσης *(dia ton
logon tēs gynaikos martyrousēs),* that is, "through the word of the woman
bearing witness." The Gospels come to us in the form of witness, and it is
as witness that they serve as the locus of encounter between Jesus and
postresurrection disciples. As we have noted, this scene is probably a de-

363

scription of the conversion of the Samaritans after the departure of Jesus. In 17:20, at the Last Supper, Jesus prays for his disciples on the eve of his going away. The Evangelist tells us that he prayed not just for those present with him at the Supper, "but also for those who will believe in me through their word" (ἀλλὰ καὶ περὶ τῶν πιστευόντων διὰ τοῦ λόγου αὐτῶν εἰς ἐμέ [*alla kai peri tōn pisteuontōn dia tou logou autōn eis eme*]). This woman is the first and only person (presented in the Gospel) in the public life of Jesus through whose word of witness a group of people is brought to "come and see" and "to believe in Jesus."[16]

The effectiveness of her ministry is underlined by the fact that the townspeople not only "come to Jesus," which is a Johannine expression for beginning to believe, but they entreat Jesus to "remain with them," and he "remained there two days" (v. 40). In the Fourth Gospel μένω (*menō*), "remain" or "dwell," is a quasi-technical term for union with Jesus. These new believers are presented as coming to full Johannine faith in Jesus as the Christ (as the woman has suggested in v. 29), proclaiming him as "the Savior of the world" (v. 42).

In the Fourth Gospel we repeatedly see people brought to Jesus by a disciple and coming to full faith in Jesus on the basis of his own word to them. John the Baptist (1:35-39) testified to Jesus; two of his disciples followed Jesus and remained with him that day; they came to believe in him on the basis of that interchange. One of them, Andrew (1:41-42), brought his brother Simon to Jesus. When Jesus recognized Simon and renamed him, Simon (now Peter) became a disciple. Philip (1:44-51) brought a reluctant Nathaniel to Jesus, and again Jesus' word converted his hearer into a follower. Even after the resurrection it was the testimony of Mary Magdalene that prepared the disciples to recognize Jesus when he appeared in their midst on Easter night (cf. 20:18-20), and Thomas was reprimanded for his refusal to accept the word of witness of the other disciples who claimed "We have seen the Lord" (20:25).

In each case the pattern is the same: Someone is brought to Jesus through the word of another but comes to believe in him definitively because of Jesus' own word. In a sense, there are no "second-generation disciples" in John, because all are bound to Jesus by his own word. Thus,

16. In John 1, prior to Jesus' emergence into public life at the wedding feast in Cana, John the Baptist points Jesus out to two of his followers, and they bring personal acquaintances and relatives to Jesus. But it is striking that in the Fourth Gospel Jesus does not call any "apostles" and does not send his disciples out on missionary journeys.

the role of the Samaritan Woman in the coming to faith of the townspeople is precisely the same role assigned to his disciples by Jesus himself on the night before he died. She bore witness to Jesus as the Messiah of Samaritan expectation, the "one who told me everything" as the prophet-like-Moses was to do, and through her word the hearers came to believe in him.

4.4 The Results of Feminist Interpretation

We are now in a position to summarize the results of this basically feminist exegetical-critical analysis of John 4:1-42. My inquiry began with the question about the identity and role of the woman in this episode. I began with a strong suspicion about the basic cast of much traditional exegesis of this passage, which presents the woman as a disreputable (if interesting) miscreant who, failing in her attempt to distract Jesus from her sexually disgraceful past, surrenders to his overpowering preternatural knowledge of her, alerts her fellow townspeople to his presence, and then fades from the scene as they discover him for themselves and come to believe in him. Despite this critical picture of the woman, generations of believers have been deeply religiously moved by this story and drawn to this woman, a fact that testifies to the story's literary power and spiritual substance and justifies our taking a second look at the data.

Given the male tendency, pervasive in the Bible as elsewhere, to reduce women to their sexuality and their sexuality to immorality, I entertained an alternate possibility about the woman — namely, that she was not a whore whom Jesus converted but a potential spouse whom he invited to intimacy. This hypothesis was suggested by two literary clues: the place of the episode in the Cana-to-Cana section of the Gospel and the meeting at the well type-story on which it is patterned.

The analysis of the episode from this alternative perspective revealed the woman as a symbolic figure representing the Samaritan element in the Johannine community, which understood itself as the New Israel, bride of the true Bridegroom, Jesus. In this role she engages with Jesus in a highly theological dialogue, which mediates the significant religious differences between Jews and Samaritans, differences that undoubtedly had to be resolved, and were resolved, in the Johannine community. She intuits Jesus' identity as the fulfillment of Samaritan (as well as Jewish) messianic expectations, and he confirms her intuition with the first "I am" self-revelation of the Fourth Gospel. The woman evangelizes her fellow Samaritans, who, in the classic faith pattern of the Fourth Gospel, come to Jesus, accept his word, and acknowledge him implicitly as Christ and explicitly as universal Savior. He abides with them as they come to abide in his word and thus in the Johannine community, whose theology, especially its high christology and universalism, reflects the Samaritan influence on its origins.

In this context the dialogue about the five husbands, which hardly makes sense as a historical event, since five successive marriages (as opposed to mere concubinage with several men) by a woman of that religious culture is totally implausible, assumes its theological character as symbolic discourse about the covenant. Jesus the prophet uses the familiar adultery-idolatry metaphor of the prophetic tradition to call Samaria to renounce its historical infidelity and to embrace the worship of the one God in spirit and in truth. The path to Christian identity for the Samaritans does not necessarily pass by way of Jerusalem.

This interpretation, which seems to make better sense of the pericope than the hypothesis of a long digression on the woman's morals for the sole purpose of displaying Jesus' preternatural knowledge, allows the woman to function symbolically and theologically rather than merely sexually in the episode. But this interpretation also raises a problem. Feminist biblical scholars have called attention to the underlying sexism of the prophetic tradition's marital metaphor for the covenant relationship.[17] Not only is it based on the model of patriarchal marriage, to which male domination and female subordination are intrinsic, but it always casts God as the faithful and forgiving husband and Israel as the faithless and adulterous wife, thus consolidating the entrenched tendency to divinize men and demonize women. Jesus, in this episode, does not exploit the pornographic potential of the prophetic tradition: He neither accuses nor condemns the woman but merely confirms her self-identification. But that the Evangelist uses the metaphor continues its legitimation in the Christian community.

The brief episode of the return of the disciples, looked at from a feminist perspective, reveals the all-too-familiar uneasiness of men when one of their number takes a woman too seriously, especially in the area of men's primary concern. Jesus' discourse about his mission and its extension into Samaria only serves to confirm their worst fears, that they are neither the originators nor the controllers of the church's mission. The effectiveness of the woman's evangelization of her town caps this scene, in which any

---

17. Cf. T. Drorah Setel, "Prophets and Pornography: Female Sexual Imagery in Hosea," in *Feminist Interpretation of the Bible,* ed. Letty M. Russell, 86-95.

male claim to a privileged or exclusive role in the work of Jesus is definitively undermined by Jesus' own words and deeds.

By a combination of different strategies of feminist interpretation and against the background of traditional historical and literary critical investigation, we have been able to identify and call into question the androcentric and sexist interpretation of this passage, which both denigrates women and erases their apostolic identity and role in the early Christian community (a hermeneutics of suspicion using ideology criticism). This allowed us to retrieve the liberating potential of this story for women (a hermeneutics of retrieval in the service of reconstruction). At the same time we must acknowledge that which is in the text that is not liberating and warn the reader or hearer against its subliminally negative effects.

While this text is particularly susceptible of liberating interpretation, many NT texts are not, and the moments of suspicion, critique, and rejection assume preponderance over retrieval and reconstruction. This is not an easy or pleasant conclusion for Christians whose faith is rooted in a very special way in the witness to the Gospel of Jesus that the NT constitutes. But the hermeneutics of advocacy, that is, a liberationist hermeneutics based on a commitment to the full personhood of all people, women as well as men, must affirm the priority of Jesus' disciples even in relation to the written witness to Jesus' words.

5. Suggestions for Further Reading

The student interested in pursuing feminist hermeneutics now has available an excellent selection of readily accessible materials. One might start with a *historical study* of women's engagement with the Bible in order to see how the current feminist approaches both emerged from and are different from earlier attempts by women to find a liberating message for themselves in the biblical text. See, for example, Patricia Demers, *Women as Interpreters of the Bible* (New York/Mahwah: Paulist, 1992), for a full-length study. A number of the works mentioned below contain short historical surveys or include historical sections in larger articles.

A second category of materials is individual essays or collections of essays *surveying the current situation* in the field of feminist hermeneutics. The latter usually include some articles in which feminist interpretation is applied to particular texts or topics to illustrate the theory. See J. C. Anderson, "Mapping Feminist Biblical Criticism: The American Scene, 1983-

1990," in *Critical Review of Books in Religion* 4, ed. Eldon Jay Epp (Atlanta: Scholars, 1991) 21-44; Elizabeth Johnson, "Feminist Hermeneutics," *Chicago Studies* 27 (1988) 123-35; Katherine Doob Sakenfeld, "Feminist Perspectives on Bible and Theology: An Introduction to Selected Issues and Literature," *Int* 42 (1988) 5-18. Three basic collections of essays that serve to situate the student in the current discussion are *Feminist Interpretation of the Bible*, ed. Letty M. Russell (Philadelphia: Westminster, 1985); *Feminist Perspectives on Biblical Scholarship*, ed. Adela Yarbro Collins, SBLCP (Chico: Scholars, 1985); and *The Bible and Feminist Hermeneutics*, ed. Mary Ann Tolbert, *Semeia* 28 (Chico: Scholars, 1983).

A number of good essays describe the *nature of feminist hermeneutics*, its principles and practices, its relation to other kinds of hermeneutics, the variety of types of feminist interpretation, and the objectives or goals of feminist hermeneutics. Other essays situate feminist biblical work in the broader horizon of theology and attempt to evaluate it. For example, Catherine Ogle, "The Bible and liberation: Friend or Foe? Some Issues in Feminist and Liberation Theologies," *The Way* 31 (1991) 236-47, offers a very good summary explanation of the differences between Latin American liberation theologians and feminist liberation theologians in their approach to the Bible and its interpretation, and the reasons for the differences. Anne Carr, "The New Vision of Feminist Theology: Method," in *Freeing Theology: The Essentials of Theology in Feminist Perspective*, ed. Catherine Mowry LaCugna (San Francisco: Harper, 1993) 5-29, situates feminist biblical work within the broader project of feminist theology. See also Elisabeth Schüssler Fiorenza, "Feminist Hermeneutics," *ABD* 2:783-91; Sandra M. Schneiders, "Living Word or Dead(ly) Letter: The Encounter between the New Testament and Contemporary Experience," in *The Catholic Theological Society of America: Proceedings of the Forty-Seventh Annual Convention Held in Pittsburgh 11-14 June 1992, Volume 47*, ed. Paul Crowley (Santa Clara: Santa Clara University, 1992) 45-60. A major book-length treatment of the theory and practice of feminist biblical hermeneutics is Elisabeth Schüssler Fiorenza's *Bread Not Stone: The Challenge of Feminist Biblical Interpretation* (Boston: Beacon, 1984).

The serious student will also want to look at some of the major examples of the practice of feminist hermeneutics in *actual interpretation of biblical texts*. Besides the numerous articles in some of the collections mentioned above, there now exists a one-volume commentary on the entire Bible, *The Women's Bible Commentary*, ed. Carol A. Newsom and Sharon H. Ringe (London: SPCK/Louisville: Westminster/John Knox, 1992), which

offers a feminist introduction to each book of the Bible and brief interpretations of selected passages and topics of particular interest to feminists.
Elisabeth Schüssler Fiorenza's masterwork, *In Memory of Her: A Feminist
Theological Reconstruction of Christian Origins* (New York: Crossroad,
1983), is a sustained feminist interpretation of the entire NT and is the
most important single work to date in the field of feminist hermeneutics.

A number of articles and books have been devoted to consideration of
how biblical interpretation affects *particular problems in the area of Christian
faith* — for example, women's ministry, spirituality, the gender of God, and
the sex of Jesus. See, for example, Elizabeth Johnson, "Jesus, the Wisdom
of God: A Biblical Basis for Non-Androcentric Christology," *ETL* 61 (1985)
261-94; Sandra M. Schneiders, *Women and the Word: The Gender of God in
the New Testament and the Spirituality of Women* (New York/Mahwah:
Paulist, 1986); Rosemary Radford Ruether, *Sexism and God-Talk: Toward a
Feminist Theology* (Boston: Beacon, 1983) — the first full-scale treatment
of the whole of theology from a feminist standpoint; Sally Purvis, "Christian
Feminist Spirituality," *Christian Spirituality: Post-Reformation and Modern*,
ed. L. Dupré and D. E. Saliers, *World Spirituality: An Encyclopedia of the
Religious Quest* 18 (New York: Crossroad, 1989) 500-19; Carolyn Osiek,
Beyond Anger: On Being a Feminist in the Church (New York: Paulist, 1986);
Women's Spirituality: Resources for Christian Development, ed. Joann W.
Conn (New York: Paulist, 1986); and Susan Cady, Marian Ronan, and Hal
Taussig, *Sophia: The Future of Feminist Spirituality* (San Francsico: Harper
and Row, 1986).

Finally, there is a growing body of literature concerned with the *practice*
of feminist hermeneutics through liturgical celebration, proclamation, storytelling, the rewriting of biblical narrative from a feminist perspective, and
so on. See, for example, *The Liberating Word: A Guide to Nonsexist Interpretation of the Bible*, ed. Letty M. Russell (Philadelphia: Westminster,
1976); Elisabeth Schüssler Fiorenza, *But She Said: Feminist Practices of
Biblical Interpretation* (Boston: Beacon, 1992), which was written to complement the theoretical presentation of feminist interpretation in *Bread Not
Stone*; Rosemary Radford Ruether, *Women-Church: Theology and Practice
of Feminist Liturgical Communities* (San Francisco: Harper and Row, 1985);
and Marjorie Procter-Smith, *In Her Own Rite: Constructing Feminist Liturgical Tradition* (Nashville: Abingdon, 1990).

18. *Reading the New Testament in Canonical Context*

ROBERT W. WALL

1. Current Interest in the Canon

The dramatic rise of scholarly interest in the canon of the NT in recent years has two focal points, historical and hermeneutical. Historians of the biblical canon are primarily interested in its formation in early Christianity, whether as a theological notion or as a literary collection. Although the questions addressed often imply substantial theological problems, which are sometimes recognized and considered, most of these studies specialize in the historical features of the Bible's formation or the ideology that guided the canonizing process. Thus, for example, the relationship between a book's authorship and its canonization, while theologically interesting, is typically discussed in terms of how attribution of authorship influenced the reception of a particular book both within the earliest church and then into the biblical canon.

Some interpreters of the biblical canon are especially interested in the *idea* of a biblical canon, which then provides the conceptual basis for various interpretive strategies that are typically articulated under the rubric "canonical criticism." Not only are practitioners of canonical criticism joined by a common orientation toward Scripture that provides a touchstone for their interpretation, but they also share a common criticism of the historical-critical enterprise, though to different degrees and with different concerns. Generally, however, it is felt that the methodological interests of historical criticism demote the church's more theological intentions for the Christian Bible. Thus, historical-critical analysis is primarily con-

370

cerned with the circumstances that shaped particular biblical writings at their diverse points of origin, rather than with those circumstances that subsequently shaped these same writings into a biblical canon or with the canonical hermeneutics that enable and empower the rendering of biblical writings as the word of God for today.

Actually the idea of a biblical canon includes two integral ingredients: The Christian Bible is both a canonical collection of writings and a collection of canonical writings. In the first case, emphasis is placed on the Bible's final literary form *(norma normata)*, and in the second case, emphasis is placed on its ongoing religious function *(norma normans)*.[1] The methodological interests of canonical criticism follow the lines of these two emphases, introduced by the work of two OT scholars, Brevard S. Childs and James A. Sanders. Their disagreements over hermeneutical essentials have charted the territory of canonical criticism for the guild of biblical scholars.

In brief, the "canonical approach" of Childs posits hermeneutical value in the Bible's final literary form *(norma normata)*, which supplies the normative written witness to Jesus Christ.[2] The Bible's role as Christianity's "rule of faith" presumes its trustworthy (or "apostolic") witness to him whose incarnation ultimately "norms" the community's "rule of faith." Only in this christological sense can one say that Scripture supplies both the subject matter for the church's theological reflection as well as the theological boundaries or context within which Christian theology and ethics take shape. An interpretive emphasis on the Bible as a specific and limited body of sacred writings not only values its subject matter for theological reflection and confession, but also envisages the very ordering of the Bible's subunits as the privileged, permanent expression of an intentioned, dynamic interaction between the faithful and their written rule of faith.

The canonical approach to biblical interpretation is less interested in lining up behind the reconstructed historical or linguistic intentions of a precanonical stage in the formation of a particular composition or collection. The "synchronic" interest of Childs is rather posited in a subsequent period during which the Christian Scriptures took their final literary shape

1. Cf. James A. Sanders, "The Integrity of Biblical Pluralism," in *"Not in Heaven": Coherence and Complexity in Biblical Narrative*, ed. Jason P. Rosenblatt and Joseph C. Sitterson, Jr. (Bloomington: Indiana University, 1991) 154-57, here 154-69.

2. Without question Childs's most influential work is his *Introduction to the Old Testament as Scripture* (Philadelphia: Fortress, 1979); in my opinion, he has not advanced his discussion of the "canonical approach" since its publication. See, however, Gerald Sheppard's fine essay on "Canonical Criticism," *ABD* 1:861-66.

and at the same time stabilized certain theological convictions as true in a more universal or catholic sense.[3]

No one is entirely clear why these various writings and collections, so different in theological conception and sociological origination and so fluid during their early history, eventually stabilized into the Christian Bible. Certainly, one probable reason is aesthetic: Over time, different communions of believers came to recognize one particular arrangement of books as more useful for a variety of religious services, even as the number of alternative arrangements (or "canon lists") eventually was narrowed by

3. I recognize the contested nature of what "synchronic" interpretation intends to accomplish in biblical and literary analysis; see Mark G. Brett, *Biblical Criticism in Crisis: The Impact of the Canonical Approach on Old Testament Studies* (Cambridge: Cambridge University, 1991) 104-15.

Further, there are multiple definitions of the "canonical process" in the field of canonical criticism. For Childs, the idea of a canonical process is vaguely historical and refers to the final stage in the formation of the biblical canon when the believing community "recognized" its "rule of faith" in the shape and content of a discrete form (i.e., the "final form") of its Scripture. I agree with Childs that this recognition of a biblical canon took place in history and resulted in the "fixing" of a particular shape of biblical literature. But this final stage in the formation of a discrete Scripture was largely guided by impressions of its truthfulness or intuitions of its ongoing religious utility rather than the outcome of some positivistic or rational judgment. Nor did some final redactor (or God, according to fundamentalists) wave an "editorial wand over all the disparate literature," to use Sanders's phrase, to create the church's Bible. In fact, the primacy Childs grants to the final stage of the canonical process is really an appeal to a useful metaphor for the primacy he grants to the final form of the canon.

Although Brett successfully provides Childs with the necessary epistemology to anchor his methodological interests, Sanders's notion of canonical process complements Childs's approach in a different way. Sanders's point is to describe the hermeneutics of the canonical process by which we understand more adequately *how and why* Jewish ("prophetic") and Christian ("apostolic") writings were preserved, collected, and canonized into biblical form. First, the canonizing process was a "monotheizing process" by which biblical writings became the "Word of God" brought near to God's people in relevant response to their ever-changing needs; cf. Sanders's superb summary of his account of canonical criticism in "Integrity of Biblical Pluralism." Second, however, biblical writings became God's Word by the act of biblical (i.e., rabbinic or midrashic) interpretation so that "what got picked up and read again and again, and was recommended to the children and to other communities nearby, and continued to give value and to give life, was what made it into the canon" (Sanders, "Integrity of Biblical Pluralism," 168). For Sanders, the biblical canon "norms" the community's hermeneutics, by which biblical texts are resignified into theologically relevant teachings, which help to form the community's particular identity amid the ambiguities and vicissitudes of human life and history.

disuse. In other words, a specific form of biblical literature triumphed because it facilitates or better serves its intended role within the faith community.[4] Thus, according to Childs, the final shape of the Christian Scriptures best combines and relates its subject matter to serve the church as the literary location where theological understanding is well founded and soundly framed.

The "canonical criticism" of Sanders posits value in the act of interpretation that enables the Bible to function canonically in shaping the theology and guiding the praxis of the church *(norma normans)*. The methodological interests of Sanders are more intuitive than those of Childs, emphasizing rather the interpretive calculus found at the composition's point of origin, during the canonical process, and throughout the history of interpreting the biblical canon. For Sanders, "canonical process" is not concentrated by a specific historical moment or literary product as it is for Childs; hermeneutics is not synchronic in this sense. Rather, the canonical approach of Sanders is more "diachronic" and involves the entire history of the Bible's interpretation, whenever the faith community draws on its Scriptures to "norm" its faith and life. Beginning even before biblical texts were written and continuing today, faithful interpreters contemporize the meaning of their Scriptures so that the faith community might better understand what it means to be and do what God's people ought to be and do.

For Sanders, canonical function antedates and explains canonical form even as final form facilitates those functions that the faith community intended for its canon. In my view, Childs has offered no compelling response to the objection that his interest in the Bible's final literary form is too parochial, elevating the final form of the Protestant Bible over the various other biblical canons within the Christian church. On the other hand, by shifting his attention from the Bible as *norma normata* to the Bible as *norma normans,* from its literary form to its ecclesial function, Sanders relativizes the hermeneutical importance of the Bible's final form. Since for him canonical function takes precedence over canonical form, the literary shape (or translation!) of a particular community's Bible is subsumed under the interpreter's more important vocation of adapting Scripture's meaning to the community's ever-changing life situation.

Canonical criticism, then, concentrates on how a biblical text becomes

4. This point draws upon Hans-Georg Gadamer's idea of "classical" literature; cf. *Truth and Method* (2d ed., New York: Crossroad, 1989) esp. 285-90.

canonical in the act of interpretation, when different interpreters pick up the same text again and again to "comfort the afflicted or afflict the comfortable." In the hands of faithful interpreters, past and present, Scripture acquires multiple meanings. Of course the aim of relating the canon to the faith community is to form a people who worship and bear witness to the one true God.[5] Thus, the Christian Bible is more than a canonical collection of sacred writings, shaped by religious intentions and insights into a discrete literary anthology that itself envisions patterns of hermeneutical engagement. The Bible is canonical primarily in a functional sense, with an authorized role to norm all the various norms for worship and witness of those who belong to the "one holy, catholic, and apostolic church." Under the light of this perspective toward the Bible, interpreters are led to ask additional questions about the meaning of every biblical text that attend first of all to the *theological shape* of the church's faith (in both confession and conflict) rather than to the literary shape of its biblical canon.[6]

In this sense Sanders reminds Childs that the history of the Bible's formation did more than settle on the shape of a canonical collection of sacred writings to delimit the church's "official" theology and ethics; it also evinced a species of hermeneutics that contemporizes the theological quotient of biblical teaching to give it an authoritative voice for today's community, whose worship and witness is again undermined by similar theological crises. What got picked up again and again and reread over and over were those same writings that could interpret the present crisis of faith and resolve it in a way that maintained faith and empowered life.

In fact, biblical writings were first preserved because they were sufficiently ambiguous in intent for different interpreters to mediate truth to their different audiences. At the same time, other writings were filtered out as being too narrow in sociological context or semantic intent to have a life beyond their first readers. According to Sanders, the elevation of a scriptural writing to canonical status required an inherent capacity to be reinterpreted

---

5. See James A. Sanders, *Canon and Community* (Philadelphia: Fortress, 1984).

6. While Sanders contends that the biblical canon is characterized by its textual "stability" and contextual "adaptability," his principal methodological interest has always been the Bible's adaptability (even as Childs's methodological interest has always been the Bible's stability). For Sanders, the fluidity of the biblical canon is a matter of the historical record; yet, it is also the constant experience of faithful interpreters, whose task it is to find new meanings in the same biblical texts for their new situations. It is this *experience* of interpretation that justifies this interest in Scripture's ability to adapt itself to new hearers and readers.

over and again in spiritually profitable ways by different interpreters for different situations. This sort of unrecorded hermeneutics envisages the same canonical function found in the Bible's final literary form: The Bible is formed to inform the community's understanding of God.

My own work has sought to combine and extend these insights of Sanders and Childs.[7] In doing so, I recognize the contested nature of canonical criticism within the guild of biblical scholarship. Nevertheless, the present chapter does not seek to defend the methodological interests of canonical criticism against its main competitors. Nor does it intend to provide critics with the proper epistemological credentials to lend support to my exegetical conclusions. This important work has already been undertaken by others, so that the methodological interests of canonical criticism can now be more fully exploited for fresh insight into the meaning of Scripture for today.[8]

2. The Methodological Interests of Canonical Criticism

2.1 Biblical Exegesis

Theological reflection on the Bible integrates two discrete tasks: biblical exegesis and theological interpretation. The foundational task of the hermeneutical enterprise is exegetical and is aimed at a coherent exposition of Scripture's "plain meaning." "Plain meaning" here is metaphorical and indicates that my primary interest is in the final form of the biblical canon rather than in the literary or sociological environs at its point of origin, its author, or any of its subtexts or pre-texts, however important these con-

---

7. See Robert W. Wall and Eugene E. Lemcio, *The New Testament as Canon: A Reader in Canonical Criticism,* JSNTSS 76 (Sheffield: JSOT, 1992).

8. See especially Brett, *Biblical Criticism in Crisis.* Brett's work requires supplementation in two ways: (1) to distinguish between a canonical approach specifically to NT studies, where some of the methodological problems Brett raises and responds to are not quite as important as with the OT (e.g., the duration of the canonical process) but other problems are important (e.g., the relationship between the two testaments); and (2) to show more carefully and critically how the "canonical approach" of Childs is different from and is complemented by the "canonical criticism" of Sanders. This latter point has been recently taken up in a helpful essay by Mikeal C. Parsons, "Canonical Criticism," in *New Testament Criticism and Interpretation,* ed. David A. Black and David S. Dockery (Grand Rapids: Zondervan, 1991) 253-94.

structions might be to achieve a holistic meaning.[9] Neither do I view the exegetical task as interested in privileging one particular meaning as "canonical" for all believers for all time.[10]

Moreover, I view the exegetical task as collaborative, as the shared task of a community of interpreters, whose different interests in the biblical text expose its multiple contours in pursuit of a "thickened" or holistic description of meaning. However, a methodological interest in the plain meaning of a particular text is constricted by compositional and canonical contexts within which specific texts acquire their distinctive literary and theological meaning. Plain meaning exegesis aspires to a "standard" meaning, since texts do not gather together an inclusive community of infinite meanings. Common sense and critical attention to words and patterns of words point the exegete to specific meanings. Exegetical strategies are prioritized, then, that are concerned with the meaning and arrangement of words and pericopes as well as the theological content that they convey.

Of course, Scripture has a profoundly intertextual texture, which is exploited in canonical criticism. The careful interpreter is naturally sensitive

---

9. My use of the controversial term "plain meaning" is neither naive nor courageous. It seeks rather to exploit two discussions, one medieval and another modern, the first Jewish and the second Christian. Scripture commentaries by the medieval rabbinate typically distinguished between *peshat* ("straightforward") and *derash* ("investigative") as two integral exegetical modes. If the aim of hermeneutical inquiry is *peshat,* the interpreter is concerned with a closely reasoned description of what the text actually says. In this first mode, the interpreter responds to the hermeneutical crisis of the text's incomprehensibility within a congregation of believers for whom that text is canonical. If the aim is *derash,* the interpreter is concerned with an imaginative interpretation of what the text means for its current audience. This second task, while rooted in the first, responds to a different and more important hermeneutical crisis, which is the perception of the text's theological irrelevance for its current readers. If the biblical canon intends to facilitate theological reflection, then the ultimate aim of exegesis is not *peshat* but *derash.*

My second source is the work of Raymond E. Brown, who reintroduced the idea of Scripture's *sensus plenior* into the scholarly debate over biblical hermeneutics ("The History and Development of the Theory of a *Sensus Plenior,*" *CBQ* 15 [1953] 141-62; *The* Sensus Plenior *of Sacred Scripture* [New York: Paulist, 1960]). According to Brown's more modern (and positive) definition, the *sensus plenior* or "plenary sense" of a biblical text agrees with the theological aspect of the entire biblical canon. My use of "plain meaning" includes this sense, so that the single meaning of any text bears witness to the Bible's witness to God.

10. I attempted to introduce this point in "The Relevance of the Book of Revelation for the Wesleyan Tradition," presented to the annual meeting of the Wesleyan Theological Society, Oklahoma City, November, 1993.

to the citations, allusions, and even echoes of other "subtexts" heard when reading a biblical text. And the canonical critic is inclined to value these, especially biblical, subtexts hermeneutically because they provide an implied yet normative context for the writer's own theological reflection on the events being narrated or the spiritual crisis being resolved. There is a sense in which NT writers are viewed as interpreters of their Scripture and their compositions as commentaries on Scripture. More importantly, this exegetical sensitivity to the author's intended meaning, in turn, enhances the exegete's understanding of the text's plain meaning.[11]

The scholar's search for the plain meaning of a biblical text or tradition does not mark a return to a fundamentalistic literalism that denies both the historical process that formed the Christian Scriptures and the theological diversity found in them. Rather, a concern for plain meaning guards against hermeneutical supersession. Thus, the community at work on biblical texts pursues meaning with ideological blinders on, without immediate regard for the integral wholeness of Scripture, but critical exegesis seeks to restore to full volume the voice of every biblical writer so that the whole meaning of Scripture can then be vocalized as a chorus of its various parts. To presume the simultaneity of every part of the whole without also adequately discerning the plain meaning of each in turn undermines the integral nature of Scripture and even distorts its full witness to God. Finally, however, the aim of critical exegesis, which has successfully exposed the pluriformity of Scripture, is "to put the text back together in a way that makes it available in the present and in its (biblical) entirety — not merely in the past and in the form of historically contextualized fragments."[12] In this sense, then, the plain meaning of individual writings or biblical traditions, although foundational for scriptural interpretation, has value only in relationship to a more holistic end.[13]

Even though the search for the plain meaning of Scripture concerns itself with stable texts and standard meanings, the exegetical history of every biblical text is actually quite fluid. This limitation is deepened by recognition of the inherent multivalence and intertextuality of texts. Further

---

11. In canonical criticism this exegetical sensitivity takes on a theological cast in speculation on the relationship between the two testaments of the Christian Bible: The NT is a midrash on the OT because it bears witness that the salvation promised in the first is fulfilled by the Jesus of the second.

12. Jon D. Levenson, *The Hebrew Bible, The Old Testament, and Historical Criticism* (Louisville: Westminster/John Knox, 1993) 79.

13. So esp. Brevard S. Childs, *Biblical Theology of Old and New Testaments* (Minneapolis: Fortress, 1992) 719-27.

changes in the text's "plain meaning" result from new evidence and different exegetical strategies and from interpreters shaped by diverse social and theological locations. In fact, the sort of neutrality toward biblical texts that critical exegesis envisages actually requires that such changes be made. Our experience with texts tells us that the ideal of a "standard" meaning cannot be absolutized, whether as the assured conclusion of the scholarly guild or as some meaning ordained by (and known only to) God. Thus, the fluid nature of exegesis resists the old dichotomies between past and present meanings and between authorial and textual intentions.

As a practical discipline, plain meaning exegesis clarifies the subject matter of Scripture, which supplies the conceptual freight of those theological norms and ethical principles that form Christian faith. Simply put, the straightforward meanings of the variety of biblical writings, considered holistically, help to delimit the range and determine the substance of the church's current understanding of what it means to believe and behave as it must. Yet, whenever biblical theology is still attempted, it remains (with a few notable exceptions) exclusively an exegetical enterprise, as though a careful description of the Bible's theology is sufficient to perform its canonical roles. It is in response to this misconception that I claim exegesis is the means but not the end of the hermeneutical enterprise: The plain meaning of Scripture must come to have contemporary meaning for its current readers before it can function as their Scripture.

2.2 Theological Interpretation

The interpreter's second task is *interpretation*, which in my definition aims to give the subject matter of Scripture its canonical significance for today. That is, if exegesis locates canonical authority in biblical texts, then interpretation relocates religious authority in the social contexts of the faith community where the Word of God is ultimately heard and embodied. Biblical interpretation, as I understand it, is fully contextual and aims at an imaginative (i.e., analogical) reflection on the subject matter of biblical teaching. The purpose of such reflection is to "recanonize" biblical teaching so that the faith community might know who it is as God's people and how it is to act as God's people within a new situation. While critical exegesis aims to restrict the plain meaning of a biblical text to a single standard (at least in theory), the interpretive task seeks an application of that meaning for a people whose faith and life are in constant flux. Of course, the problem to which the act of interpretation responds is the recognition that biblical writings are all occasional literature, written by particular authors for particular audiences in response to crises of a particular time and place. No biblical writing was composed for the biblical canon or for the universal readership it now enjoys.

In fact, the interpretive presupposition is that current readers will not draw out the very same meaning from a composition that might have been intended by its author or understood by its first readers. Times and places change the significance of texts for new readerships. Rather than decanonizing certain Scripture as "irrelevant" or imposing a biblical worldview on a contemporary readership, an interpretive strategy must be engaged that seeks to relate the whole witness of the biblical canon and the whole life of the faith community in fresh and meaningful ways.

In this sense, the crisis of biblical authority concerns the propriety of prior interpretations of Scripture — including those of the biblical writers — for a "new" situation. This is ultimately a theological crisis, since the subject matter of biblical revelation fails to convey God's Word to a particular people with clarity and conviction, either because they cannot understand what Scripture says or because they cannot understand its immediate relevance for life and faith.[14] In this case, then, imagination is required by the interpreter to exploit more easily the inherent polyvalency of biblical teaching in order to find new meanings for new worlds.

Thus the interpreter assumes that the agreed plain meaning of a biblical text embodies a community of analogical meanings, while at the same time recognizing that not all of these meanings hold equal significance either for a particular interpreter or for the interpreter's faith community. The interpreter's interpretations of Scripture seek to clarify and contemporize the Bible's subject matter for those who struggle to remain faithful at a particular moment in time and place. In this regard, then, the act of interpretation imagines an analogue from a range of possible meanings that renders the text's subject matter meaningfully for a people who desire to remain faithful to God in an inhospitable world.

2.3 The Role of the Interpreter

All of what has been said to this point about the exegetical and interpretive tasks implies something about the interpreter's "authority." Perhaps because

14. For this point, see Michael Fishbane, *The Garments of Torah* (Bloomington: Indiana University, 1989) 16-18.

its pioneers are located theologically in Reformed Protestantism, canonical criticism has always emphasized the authority of the Christian Bible. However, whether an interpretation satisfies the church's intentions for its Bible depends to a significant degree on the interpreter's "individual talent." The talented interpreter has the capacity to make coherent and contemporary meaning of diverse biblical traditions, each individually and together within the whole, and then to relate the canon to the faith community in ways that facilitate the hearing of God's word.

To be sure, the interpreter's talent to facilitate a meaningful conversation between canon and community is determined in part by one's vocation, whether "prophetic" or "priestly." On this basis, creative and compelling interpretations of biblical texts are made that relate the plain meaning of the biblical text to the current social context in ways that actually produce theological understanding (and so a more vital faith in God) and moral clarity (and so more faithful obedience to God's Word). In this sense, the talented interpreter renders Scripture in ways that empower the community's worship of God and witness to God in the world. Thus, the interpreter imagines what "analogical meaning" can be made of the text's "plain meaning" for the community's formation as God's people, whether to "correct and rebuke" a distorted faith (prophetic hermeneutic) or to "teach and train" a developing faith (priestly hermeneutic).

Further, the interpreter's talent is shaped by time and place. Not only does the interpreter bring a particularized perspective to the biblical text; the interpreter also brings his or her own "special" texts to the text, to participate in a conversation already under way.

2.4 A Model for Canonical Interpretation

Under the light of these methodological interests, the framework for an interpretive model can now be constructed as a sequence of three discrete though integral parts: "Canonical Context," "Canonical Content," and "Canonical Conversations." What follows is a brief description of the task apropos to each part.

1. *Canonical Context.* An interest in the final literary form of the NT leads the interpreter to an initial set of hermeneutical clues derived from consideration of both the placement and titles of NT writings, which are properties of their canonization. Quite apart from authorial intentions, the literary design of the biblical canon suggests that particular units of the NT canon (Gospel, Acts, Letter, Apocalypse) have particular roles to perform

within the whole. This consideration of the structure of the NT orients the interpreter to the subject matter found within each of those canonical units. Often the title provided each unit by the canonizing community brings to clearer focus what particular contribution each unit makes to a fully Christian faith.

In this regard, the sequence of these four units within the NT envisages an intentional rhetorical pattern — or "canon-logic" to use Albert Outler's apt phrase[15] — that more effectively orients the readership to the NT's pluriform witness to God and to God's Christ. By the logic of the final literary form of the NT canon, each unit is assigned a specific role to perform within the whole, which in turn offers another explanation for the rich diversity of theology, literature, and language that casts Scripture's subject matter. Thus, the Gospel is placed first within the NT because its narrative of the person and work of the Messiah, when taken as a fourfold whole, is theologically and morally foundational for all that follows.

Along with the final placement of writings and collections within the biblical canon, new titles were provided for individual compositions, sometimes including the naming of anonymous authors. These properties of the canonizing stage shed additional light on how these compositions and collections, written centuries earlier for congregational crises long since settled, may continue to bear witness to God and God's Christ for a nameless and future readership. The importance of any one biblical voice for theological understanding or ethical praxis is focused or qualified by its relationship to the other voices that constitute the whole canonical chorus. Extending this metaphor, one may even suppose that these various voices, before heard only individually or in smaller groups, became more impressive, invigorating, and even "canonical" for faith only when combined with other voices to sing their contrapuntal harmonies as the full chorus.

2. *Canonical Content.* A biblical text, once placed within its distinctive canonical context, acquires a potential for enhanced meaning that should help to guide the exegetical task. A canonical approach to exegesis is never solely concerned with an "objective" description of the biblical text in isolation from other biblical texts; rather, the analysis of a writer's literary artistry or theological tendencies serves the overall canonical project. The description of the text's plain meaning results from a close and critical

15. Albert C. Outler, "The 'Logic' of Canon-making and the Tasks of Canon-Criticism," in *Texts and Testaments: Critical Essays on the Bible and Early Church Fathers,* ed. W. Eugene March (San Antonio: Trinity University, 1980) 263-76.

analysis of its compositional and theological aspects (see under "Biblical Exegesis" above). In many ways, this part of the canonical critical enterprise is the most traditional. *Canonical criticism does not sponsor any new exegetical strategy; rather, it sponsors a particular orientation toward the biblical text whose principle methodological interests are the text's final literary form and canonical functions.* Naturally, the canonical interpreter is first of all drawn to those exegetical strategies that seek to make meaning out of the biblical text itself rather than its prehistory or the historical circumstances that occasioned its writing.

3. *Canonical Conversations.* The intended role of the biblical canon is to adapt its ancient teaching to contemporary life; this is also the primary objective of biblical interpretation. Under this final rubric, the results of the first two tasks are now gathered together as the subject matter of two formative and integral "conversations" about the community's life of faith. The first conversation is *intercanonical* (i.e., conversations between different biblical traditions or writers) and the second is *intercatholic* (i.e., conversations between the Bible and different faith traditions); the first "norms" and guides the second.

While a number of metaphors work well to express the Bible's theological plurality coherently and constructively, my preference for the interpreter's practical task is *conversation.* Naturally, there are different kinds of conversations. A canonical approach to the NT's pluriform subject matter envisages a conversation that is more complementary than adversarial. In one sense, the *intercanonical* conversation is very much like an intramural debate over the precise meaning of things generally agreed to be true and substantial. The purpose or outcome of debate is not to resolve firmly fixed disagreements among members of the same community or panel as though a normative synthesis were possible; rather, more often it is the sort of debate that clarifies the contested content of their common ground. Likewise, the biblical canon stabilizes and bears continuing witness to the historic disagreements between the traditions of the church's first apostles, which were often creative and instructive (cf. Acts 15:1-21; Gal 2:1-15). Not only do these controversies acquire a permanent value within Scripture, but Scripture in turn commends these same controversies to its current readers, who are invited to engage in a similar act of what Karl Popper calls "mutual criticism"[16] in order to provide

16. I learned of Popper's helpful categories for determining textual objectivity as good reason for both receiving and preserving literary texts from Brett, *Biblical Criticism,* 124-27.

more balance to parochial interests or supply instruction to clarify the theological confession of a particular faith tradition.

In fact, the point and counterpoint of this sort of conversation sometimes works better than those that seek agreement, in that they more readily expose the potential weakness of any point made *to the exclusion* of its counterpoint. In this sense, I presume that a more objective and functional meaning emerges that is neither the conception of any one biblical writer — a "canon *within* the Canon" — nor the presumption of any one expositor — a "canon *outside* of the Canon." Rather the canonical interpreter seeks to relate the different ideas of particular biblical writers and canonical units together in contrapuntal yet complementary ways, to expose the self-correcting (or "prophetic") and mutually-informing (or "priestly") whole of NT theology. In this way, the diversity of biblical theologies within the NT fashions a canon of "mutual criticism," resulting in a more objective interpretation of scriptural teaching. A NT theology thus envisaged underscores what is at stake in relating together the individual parts, whose total significance is now extended beyond their compiled meaning: The NT's diverse theologies, reconsidered holistically as complementary witnesses within the whole, actually "thicken" the meaning of each part in turn.

The midrashic character of biblical interpretation compels the contemporizing of texts, so that "new" meanings are not the result of textual synthesis but arise from contextual significance. Thus, by reconstituting these intercanonical disagreements into a hermeneutical apparatus of checks and balances, the interpreter may actually imagine a comparable dialogue that aids the church's awareness of how each part of the NT canon is important in delimiting and shaping a truly biblical religion. In fashioning a second conversation under the light of the first, therefore, the checks and balances are reimagined as *intercatholic* conversations that continue to guide the whole church in its various ecumenical conversations.

How the intercanonical conversations are arranged and then adapted to a particular faith tradition is largely intuitive and depends a great deal upon the interpreter's talent and location (see above). It should go without saying that my particular adaptation of Jas 4:13–5:6 owes a great deal to who and where I am when I come to this text and its current socioecclesial context. So I must try to listen to other interpreters, believing that true objectivity emerges out of a community of subjectivities. Thus informed, a close reading of biblical texts and ecclesial contexts can be more easily linked together, particular communions with particular NT writers, in order to define the normative checks and balances of a complementary conversation that maintains and legitimizes traditional distinctives on the one hand with the prospect of correcting a tendency toward triumphal sectarianism on the other.

3. A Canonical Interpretation of James 4:13–5:6

3.1 The Canonical Context of James

The placement of James in the multiple "letter" canon is suggestive of its significant role within the NT and therefore properly orients (or reorients) the interpreter to its subject matter.[17] According to the NT's own "canon-logic," Letter follows Gospel even as disciples follow after Jesus as their exemplar and Savior.

The fourfold narrative of Jesus' messianic career is foundational to an interpretation of the letters that follow for two reasons. First, the NT's "canon-logic" suggests that the letter articulates the holistic meaning of Christian discipleship. Even the title "letter" commends this more pastoral orientation toward these writings[18] since the role of biblical letters is comparable to the function of literary letters: to provide pastoral solutions for everyday problems that threaten Christian discipleship. Indeed, the prospect of all canonical literature is that the spiritual crisis that occasioned a particular writing is roughly comparable to the spiritual crisis that faces its future readership. It is this sensibility that orients the contemporary reader to Jas 4:13–5:6 as a normative response to a spiritual crisis that continues to undermine Christian discipleship.

17. This point is developed fully in "The Problem of the Multiple Letter Canon of the New Testament," in Wall and Lemcio, *The New Testament as Canon*, 161-83.

18. This observation is made more keen for James by its lack of epistolary form. Despite the objections of some scholars who claim that James is a letter of some sort, there remains audiovisual incongruence between James and Pauline letters: James neither "sounds" nor "looks" like Paul's compositions! The general lack of literary uniformity between the Pauline letters and some non-Pauline letters (Hebrews, James, 1 John) only underscores the value of titles as properties of canonical function rather than of literary form: James is expected to nurture the faith of the Bible's readers in a manner similar to the Pauline letters. Of course, the literary differences between the Pauline and non-Pauline members of the community of biblical letters envisage other kinds of differences as well. Thus their common canonical designation, "letter," invites the interpreter to find coherence between diverse biblical voices that nevertheless aspire to a common end.

384

Second, the Gospel supplies the letter with its narrative substructure: The biblical story of Jesus is the foundational presupposition for the practical advice given and the theological claim made in every NT letter.[19] Therefore, James not only shares its canonical role with other NT letters, including Pauline, but it shares with them a common story of God's salvation through Jesus Christ.[20]

Yet the shape of the letter canon is also tensive; after all, James is placed in a *second* collection of NT letters. While the multiplicity of Gospels has long been a topic of scholarly investigation and comment, few have considered the relationship between the NT's two groups of letters a matter of hermeneutical value. What possible relationship does the non-Pauline collection have to the Pauline collection? How might this consideration aid the interpreter in discerning what special role James has within the NT? Historically, especially in Protestantism, primary attention has been directed toward the compositions within the Pauline collection, to investigate not only the meaning of individual letters but also the relationships among them. Partial justification for this keen interest in Paul's witness to the gospel is provided by the NT's ordering of the letters, since the Pauline corpus comes first. Yet, this very Pauline priority has also led to a Pauline reductionism in study of the second, non-Pauline, collection of letters. For example, James is typically viewed as envisaging either a Pauline faith, although in other words, or an anti-Pauline faith. In either case, the more complementary character of intercanonical relationships is seriously distorted.

In my view, the canonical role of the second collection of letters, where we find James, is to provide an enhanced context for a reading of the Pauline letters. These writings, which bear witness to the faith of the "pillars" of the Jewish mission (Gal 2:7-9), provide an authorized apparatus of various

19. Richard B. Hays contends that the substructure of Paul's thought and argument consists of a "particular paradigmatic story about Jesus Christ" in *The Faith of Jesus: An Investigation of the Narrative Substructure of Galatians 3:1–4:11*, SBLDS 56 (Chico: Scholars, 1983) 5. Hays makes his point about the historical Paul; however, I would argue that the "particular paradigmatic story about Jesus Christ" is the one narrated by the fourfold Gospel, which supplies the substructure for every NT letter.

20. I would argue that this is true even though Paul's narrative of Jesus is reduced to his death and resurrection and James (with other non-Paulinists) is more interested in the exemplary and prophetic character of Jesus' life (cf. Jas 2:1-8). Others have found numerous echoes of Gospel tradition (esp. the teaching of Matthew's [or Q's] Jesus) in James. In this regard see Dean B. Deppe, *The Sayings of Jesus in the Epistle of James* (Chelsea: Bookcrafters, 1989).

checks and balances that prevents distortion of Paul and finally "thickens" the church's understanding of Paul and indeed of the full gospel.[21] In this sense, the interpreter is prepared to listen to Jas 4:13–5:6 for a different voice than is heard in reading from the Pauline corpus. But it is the voice of neither a ventriloquist nor an adversary but of a colleague, whose new perspective adds to what has already been read and owned as Christian.

3.2 The Canonical Content of James 4:13–5:6

The placement of James in the "letter" canon of the NT forms a particular orientation toward its exegesis. The interpreter of James expects to hear a distinctive voice that not only adds to the NT's witness to God and to God's Christ but also provides balance to a more Pauline understanding of Christian life. In the following comments, I am mostly interested in how Jas 4:13–5:6 understands God's relations with the pious poor, which is of special interest to James. Given its canonical context, I already anticipate that my exposition of this passage will become more meaningful when related to similar concerns in both Paul and a contemporary readership.

The main body of James (1:22–5:6) is a *halakhic* (practical) commentary on divine Wisdom, which is summarized in 1:19: "Be quick to listen" (1:22–2:26), "slow to speak" (3:1-18), and "slow to anger" (4:1–5:6).[22] In its introduction (1:2-21), James calls the faith community, besieged by "various trials" (1:2), to become wise (1:5-8) in order to pass the testing of its faith in God (1:3, 13-18) and receive God's promised blessing at the end of time (1:4, 12). The letter concludes as it began, with an exhortation to respond favorably to God's "word of truth" (5:19; cf. 1:18-19), patiently (5:10-12; cf. 1:3) and prayerfully (5:13-18; cf. 1:5) waiting for the Lord's parousia (5:7-9; cf. 1:9-11), when the promise of life will be fulfilled (5:19-20; cf. 1:4, 12, 21).

Within this compositional context, then, 4:13–5:6 concludes an extended commentary on anger (4:1; cf. 1:19c-20), which begins with an inward passion for material pleasures that one does not have (4:2-3; cf. 1:13-15) and stems from an inability to be content with one's "humble

21. See Wall and Lemcio, *The New Testament as Canon*, esp. 208-49.

22. Because of space limitations, I am unable to provide a robust exegesis of Jas 4:13–5:6 complete with a close reading of the passage, supporting argument for most observations made, and a commentary on alternative interpretations, which are many. I hope to provide these critical details in my forthcoming commentary on James from Trinity Press International.

conditions," coveting rather the material goods of others (4:4-5). The resulting spiritual crisis threatens the community's participation in God's coming triumph.

This passion for material things tests the community's dependence upon God, who resists the arrogant and "gives grace" to those of humble means (4:6; cf. 2:5). Thus, the wise community humbles itself before God (4:7-10), who alone establishes the criterion for judgment and salvation (4:11-12; cf. 2:8-13). On the other hand, the foolish indulge their self-centered passion for material profit without consideration of God's will (4:13-17); indeed, in accord with Jesus' teaching, the one who chooses Mammon over God will also choose Mammon over God's people, with the eschatological result of divine judgment rather than blessing (5:1-6; cf. Matt 6:19-33). Sharply put, the source of anger is a desire for wealth; in this sense, wealth is a spiritual problem because it tests one's faith in God.

James's interpretation of anger is actually a commentary (midrash) on Prov 3:34 (LXX), cited in Jas 4:6, which sets in opposition two classes of people, "the humble" (or pious poor) and "the arrogant" (or secular rich). "The humble" do not get angry, since they prefer God (4:7-10) to riches (4:4-6). God gives saving grace to "the humble" (4:6, 10). "The arrogant," on the other hand, are those like the merchant (4:13-17) and rich farmer (5:1-6) whose passion for pleasure first disregards God (4:13-17), who cares for the poor and powerless (2:5), and leads them to violent treatment of the pious poor (5:4, 6). Their acts against others articulate their friendship with the world order (4:4) rather than with God (cf. 2:23); and their end is divine curse (4:6; 5:5).

In my view the contrast between the proverbial poor and arrogant is concentrated where the subject shifts from "we" (4:13) to "you" (4:14): The reader ("you") is drawn to the essence of Wisdom's advice for those of "humble circumstance," who enjoy a preferential spiritual status yet aspire to the middle class: "What is the meaning of your life? It is this: You are but *mist* that appears for a little while and then vanishes." In this setting "mist" is a metaphor for a proper orientation toward God's will, which orders human life and destiny (4:15; cf. 4:7-10). The "arrogant" class make their plans as though God does not exist (4:13).

The texture of James's midrash on Prov 3:34 is "thickened" by the interpreter who recognizes that the "mist" of Jas 4:14 may well be an allusion to the "vanity" of Ecclesiastes, which defines the meaning of life by the motto "All is vanity" (1:2; 12:8, etc.). The root meaning of the Hebrew word for "vanity," הבל (*hebel*), is also "mist." Such allusions, whether intended by the author or not, link texts together. In this sense, a common definition of life as "mist" links Ecclesiastes and James together, mobilizing Ecclesiastes as a biblical source that interprets this portion of James (even as James also interprets Ecclesiastes!).

Two brief observations about the importance of the "life is mist" motto in Ecclesiastes must suffice. First, Ecclesiastes claims that worldly pleasures and wealth are "vanity" or mist-like (cf. Eccl 2:1-11; 5:8–6:12); only the fool attaches much value to brief and transitory things such as wealth and power. By comparison, the wise recognize the durability of God's purposes; this then becomes the meaning of life. Second, Ecclesiastes calls those who accumulate wealth "sinners" who subvert "good" and displease God (9:18), which will lead to a future reversal of fortunes (cf. Jas 1:9-11; 2:13), when their wealth will be given to those "wise and joyful" persons (cf. Jas 1:2-5) who please God (Eccl 2:24-26).

Against this biblical backdrop, then, the foolishness of the merchant (or any middle class aspirant) in Jas 4:13-17 is better understood. His accumulated "profit" (4:13) cannot outlive him (5:1-2). He is also foolish for living life for *his* moment, without due consideration of God's law (4:11-12, 15) and the pious poor, whom God protects and will reward at the Lord's parousia.

Appropriately, in the liturgical tradition of the Judaism of James, the biblical Ecclesiastes was read during the celebration of *sukkot* (the Feast of Tabernacles). *Sukkot*'s central symbol was the "tents" used by those who had received the promise but who had not yet entered the promised land. Since the tents provided God's people with both shelter and sanctuary, they came to symbolize God's continuing faithfulness before the restored Israel enters into its eternal Jubilee. In fact, the yearly festival corresponded with harvest and so retained this same tension between the present and the future: The good harvest of any year testified to God's present faithfulness, even though next year might bring feast or famine. Given the fragility of this life, people find meaning only when depending on the faithfulness of God rather than on their own efforts.

In my view, this further connection between Ecclesiastes and *sukkot* deepens our understanding of the harvest images of Jas 5:1-6 and therefore of the relationship between 4:13-17 and 5:1-6. The point of James's warning to the rich farmers is surely the warning implicit in *sukkot:* The next harvest may be a "day of slaughter" when the Lord judges harshly those whose wealth has been gained at the expense of the pious poor. This, too, is the verdict of Ecclesiastes, which names the "sinners" as those who gather fame and fortune at the expense of the poor (2:12-23; 8:10-17). Ironically, the fame and fortune of the rich will be taken from them by God and given to those who please God (Eccl 2:26). This eschatological reversal of fortune from rich to poor, already echoed in Jas 1:9-11, is the warning James has in mind in 5:1. Conversely, the future blessing of the pious poor at the Lord's parousia, already echoed in 2:5 and again in 4:6, is the implied promise of this passage.

3.3 James 4:13–5:6 in Canonical Conversations

1. *James 4:13–5:6 and the Pauline Voice of the NT.* In order for Jas 4:13–5:6 to function canonically, the interpreter must reflect on its meaning within the contexts of the biblical canon ("intercanonicity") and its contemporary readership ("intercatholicity"). Within the biblical canon, James's most appropriate conversation partner is Paul, an observation confirmed by the history of interpretation. Interpreters, ancient and modern, have tended to view James as Paul's adversary, resulting in the decanonizing of James in favor of a Pauline canon or in the muting of James's distinctive theological voice by emphasizing its "practical" value. In particular, the more conservative tradents of the magisterial Reformation even sought to retain James in their "inspired Scripture" by reworking it to sound a Pauline note. Most critical scholars recognize the profound and pervasive differences between Paul and James, but they seek to explain these differences by their social settings. In this way, James retains its place within the biblical canon but only as a somewhat marginal member. My contention is that the biblical canon itself envisages a more constructive conversation in which James engages Paul in "mutual criticism," forming a whole greater than the sum of its parts.

The theological differences between James and Paul over common themes are substantial and canonically important.[23] For instance, Paul conceives of the poor and powerless in theological and religious rather than in social and economic terms: The Pauline poor are all those who are outside Christ, and the powerless are all those who are without God's empowering grace. The issues at stake for Paul are covenantal and have more to do with a community's relationship with God than its relationship

---

23. A fuller discussion of the following conclusions will be found in my *A New Testament Theology of the Poor: A Canonical Critical Study,* in preparation for Abingdon Press.

with society (even though the two are fully integral in an eschatological sense for Paul). Moreover, the crisis of the Gentile mission (i.e., how Paul understands divine election and Gentile conversion) provokes a missionary response rather than a sociopolitical response from the faith community. Thus Paul defines the marginal of the world primarily in terms of their spiritual status, whether or not they are "in Christ," rather than in terms of their social status. God's preferential option is for the spiritual poor, who were alienated from the commonwealth of Israel and estranged from the covenants of promise (cf. Eph 2:12). These are evangelical and not socio-economic concerns: God calls the lost, whether rich or poor, out of the world for salvation (Rom 9:30–10:13; cf. Eph 2:11-13).

Paul's missionary preaching resists a forensic, individualistic, and ahis-torical model of divine grace. Certainly for him, spiritual transformation yields the robust transformation of individuals and their relations with each other; yet this sort of human and humane transformation results from a spiritual conversion: Love for one another is the proper work of faith in Christ (Galatians 5). Accordingly, God gives grace to those who respond favorably to "the word of faith that we proclaim: If you confess with your lips that Jesus is Lord and believe in your heart that God raised him from the dead, then you will be saved" (Rom 10:8b-9).

Given the derivative nature of social transformation in Paul's mission-ary thought, it should come as no surprise that nowhere does he renounce wealth or define God's election in terms of the socioeconomically marginal (cf. Col 3:11-12; 1 Cor 1:18-31). Nor is there any primary commitment to or identification with the poor as those especially favored by God (*contra* Jas 2:5). As a practical matter of missionary work believers must take the gospel into the mainstream of the social order and the market squares of the urban centers, where the lost are found. And the lost comprise all classes, rich and poor, male and female, Jew and non-Jew, master and slave, who are all equal in their need for God's salvation, which is offered in the proclamation of the gospel to all and received by the faith of any.

The outline of a genuine conversation between the canonical Paul and James concerning God's relations with the poor is now established. For Paul, hostility among people and between people and God is spiritually discerned and is the result of suppression of God's truth, which has been disclosed in the messianic death and resurrection of Jesus. "The arrogant" are those who seek a relationship with God on the basis of their piety rather than on the basis of Christ's. "The wise" are those who embrace the fool-ishness of God, which is Christ crucified. The hostilities found in the world and between God and sinful humanity are resolved by the preaching of "the word of faith," which calls everyone out of the world and into the risen Christ, where God's enriching grace is given.

According to Jas 4:13–5:6, hostility among people and between people and God is economically discerned and is the result of seeking after wealth rather than God's will. "The arrogant" are those who accumulate riches by exploiting the pious poor, as though God, who favors the poor, does not exist. "The wise" are those who are content with their humble circumstances and who practice God's law in preparation for their vindication at the Lord's parousia. The hostilities in the world and between God and sinful humanity are resolved by "the word of truth" (1:18), which is articulated by biblical wisdom (1:19), which is exemplified by Jesus' love for his poor neighbors (2:1-8), and which advises that the pious poor slow down their passion for pleasure, both to prevent hostility toward others and to ensure that God's grace is given to them. Whereas for Paul spiritual reconciliation issues in the end of social strife among believers, for James class conflict is the constant trial of the pious poor, whose relationship with God is tested by their inward desire for wealth.

One possible Pauline distortion was warned against by the second-century Ebionites, who were among the first champions of the biblical James.[24] Because of the Jewishness of their own Christianity, they more easily recognized the tendency of Pauline thought toward fideism and antinomianism. The result of this tendency is to define "rich" and "poor" as spiritual categories, so that the poor and powerless are those without faith in Christ. This view not only neglects the social aspect of salvation but too easily and uncritically adopts a middle-class ethos in place of a christological ethos.

Further, this same Pauline bias if unchecked by James could lead to a paternalism that views class conflict as a missionary problem that must be overcome if the gospel is to be heard and received. When the church understands itself only as a missionary community, when it understands its mission only in terms of spiritual renewal, and when it understands its missionary praxis only in terms of the principle of accommodation, the social effect tends to be the *embourgeoisement* of the church and the loss of a distinctive witness to Christ within the world order.

At the very least, Jas 4:13–5:6 reminds the Pauline interpreter that a desire for wealth is a spiritual problem and will inevitably lead to debili-

---

24. See "James and Paul in Pre-Canonical Context," in Wall and Lemcio, *The New Testament as Canon*, 250-71.

tating strife between people. Further balance is provided by James's emphasis on obedience to God's will, especially in the midst of trying circumstances, which measures the believer's devotion to God rather than *sola fide* (cf. Jas 2:24). The deeper logic of James is that submission to God and repudiation of worldly passion will result in a socially marginalized but eschatologically prepared community of believers. At the very least, a holistic appraisal of the biblical teaching concerning the poor includes a more robust idea of God's grace, which is given to both the spiritually (Pauline) and socially (James) impoverished in order to enable right relations with God and with one another. The mistake often made by the interpreter is to exclude one in favor of another, resulting in a distortion of the Bible's own theology of the poor.

2. *Jas 4:13–5:6 and the Church.* One need only survey the history of the magisterial Reformation to recognize its theological dependence on a Pauline "canon within the Canon." The resulting tendency is a theological understanding of the sort that James condemns: a confession of orthodoxy without orthopraxy (cf. 2:14-26). At the very least, the theology of James helps to maintain a creative tension between faith and faithfulness and perhaps a greater ambivalence toward the economic values and political perspectives of middle-class existence. If James's celebration of the pious poor were taken seriously without Paulinizing or platonizing it, the First World (and especially Protestant) church would become quite uncomfortable with the ease by which it has accommodated the upward economic mobility of liberal democracy while trying to follow after its downwardly mobile Lord.

Furthermore, in those faith traditions whose theological calculus is centered in sanctification (believing humanity's response to God) instead of in justification (God's response to sinful humanity), the church catholic may find a Jamesian form of Christianity that checks and balances its Pauline variety. When preaching and praxis emphasize the partnership between community and Lord, so that humanity's response to God in good works complements God's response to humanity apart from good works, only then will there be a theological basis for a complement of spiritual and social transformation. The church's solidarity with the poor is neither an option nor a means to a greater spiritual end; rather, it is a social condition that is met by the church that is blessed by God. Perhaps a recovery of Wesley's teaching of scriptural holiness, authorized by and understood by James (and other non-Pauline letters, including Revelation), is an ecumenical project. In my view, a gospel for the poor cannot be proclaimed, certainly not embodied, without it.

4. Suggestions for Further Reading

The canonical approach to biblical interpretation is a recent development and few books have been written that explain or demonstrate its merits. Brevard Childs introduced the methodological interests of canonical criticism in *Biblical Theology in Crisis* (Philadelphia: Westminster, 1970), which was written in response to objections over the "biblical theology movement." These interests are then worked out in *Introduction to the Old Testament as Scripture* (Philadelphia: Fortress, 1979); *The New Testament as Canon* (Philadelphia: Fortress, 1985); and *Biblical Theology of the Old and New Testaments* (Minneapolis: Fortress, 1993). During this same period, James Sanders introduced his version of canonical criticism in *Torah and Canon* (Philadelphia: Fortress, 1972); *Canon and Community* (Philadelphia: Fortress, 1984); and a series of influential essays collected together in *From Sacred Story to Sacred Text* (Philadelphia: Fortress, 1987). The latter concludes with a complete bibliography of the discipline through 1987.

Since then Mark Brett has published his *Biblical Criticism in Crisis* (Cambridge: Cambridge University, 1991), which has supplied the canonical approach of Childs with a compelling justification. Moreover, Rolf Rendtorff outlines a theology of the OT that is largely influenced by Childs in his *Canon and Theology*, OBT (Minneapolis: Fortress, 1993). The approaches of Sanders and Childs have been compared and integrated, with innovation and insight, by Gerald Sheppard in "Canonical Criticism," *ABD* 1:861-86.

A more synthetic application of canonical criticism to the NT has been introduced by Robert Wall and Eugene Lemcio in their *The New Testament as Canon: A Reader in Canonical Criticism*, JSNTSS 76 (Sheffield: JSOT, 1992). Among several efforts to employ a canonical approach to specific NT writings are those by Robert Wall, *Commentary on Revelation*, NIBC (Peabody: Hendrickson, 1991); D. Moody Smith, *John among the Gospels* (Minneapolis: Fortress, 1992); and William Kurz, *Reading Luke-Acts* (Louisville: Westminster/John Knox, 1993).

19. *The New Testament, Theology, and Ethics*

STEPHEN E. FOWL

1. Setting an Agenda

It may not be self-evident what a chapter entitled "The New Testament, Theology, and Ethics" ought to be about. There are so many possible ways in which to take this title that I want to spend the first part of this chapter explaining what I will and will not try to cover. In doing this I will indicate other possible ways of construing these three elements, the NT, theology, and ethics. As will become clear, I find some of these possible options misguided. Others simply represent alternative ways of thinking about these terms that I am not able to deal with here. Hence, I will devote a good deal of space at the beginning to clearing away conceptual brush and staking out a field for exploration.

I begin, therefore, by arguing about commas. In particular I want to take issue with the commas, and the separations they imply, in the title of this chapter. First, I should note that these commas are not simply the result of editorial idiosyncrasy. Within most of the academy, and all too often within the church, the NT, theology, and ethics are taken to be three separate disciplines. For anyone who wants to read the NT as a Christian theologian, however, this separation must be challenged.

The first comma I will challenge is the one that separates theology from ethics. Clearly, it is possible to study ethics apart from the particular set of narratives, convictions, and practices examined by Christian theologians. One can, for example, study Jewish ethics, liberal ethics, or environmental ethics. Ethics must, however, always be preceded by an adjective.

It was the great dream of the Enlightenment to remove the adjectives preceding ethics, to develop moral norms and behaviors that could demand the assent of all rational people at all times and places apart from their confessional convictions. As Alasdair MacIntyre has trenchantly noted, the Enlightenment's attempts to provide rational justification for morality independent of tradition-specific sets of convictions failed. In fact, as MacIntyre tells it, there was a sort of inevitability to this failure because moral demands and obligations only retain their intelligibility as part of a specific, more or less comprehensive set of convictions about the way things are.[1] It is only by finding oneself embedded in a particular historically embodied tradition of convictions and practices that one can begin to address how one ought to live in any particular situation. The various adjectives preceding the word ethics mark this connection to a particular tradition's convictions about the way the world is.

Given both this book's focus on the NT and my own commitments, this chapter will be about Christian ethics. Adding the adjective "Christian" to "ethics" ties judgments about how Christians ought to live to Christian convictions about God, humanity, and the world. Further, one (but by no means the only) way of characterizing Christian theology is to see it as the ongoing explication and exploration of this particular body of convictions and practices. On this view, theology, like ethics, also needs an adjective.[2] This necessity that moral judgments proceed out of a body of specifiable convictions and practices inextricably binds Christian ethics to Christian theology. Indeed, there is no clear and indelible line separating theology and ethics. Just as I have indicated that Christian ethics apart from reflection on the convictions and practices constitutive of Christianity is arbitrary or unintelligible, so theological reflection on what it means to think and talk like a Christian apart from some account of how this reflection should be embodied tends to be abstract and lifeless. This is why I want to blur any substantive distinction between Christian theology and Christian ethics.

Having compressed Christian ethics into theology on the one hand, we may now look at the other comma, the one separating the NT from theol-

---

1. Alasdair MacIntyre makes his strongest case against this Enlightenment vision in *After Virtue* (2d ed., Notre Dame: University of Notre Dame, 1984).

2. One should recognize that in characterizing Christian theology in this way I have made a contestable claim. Within the wide variety of ways of constituting Christian theology, my position has most affinities with the work of George Lindbeck, *The Nature of Doctrine* (Philadelphia: Westminster, 1984), and Hans Frei, *Types of Christian Theology*, ed. George Hunsinger and William C. Placher (New Haven: Yale University, 1982).

ogy. On the one hand, it has been the norm for Christians to read their Scripture theologically. That is, Christians have generally read their Scripture to guide, correct, and edify their faith, worship, and practice as part of their ongoing struggle to live faithfully before the triune God. Indeed, up until relatively recently it would have been unusual to suggest that the NT might be read for any other purposes.

This is not to say that there was ever a time when there was only one way of interpreting the NT. Christians developed and deployed a wide range of interpretive practices in their attempts to read the NT theologically. In addition, people usually recognized rough and ready distinctions between various theological tasks. These tasks, however, were all seen as part of a more or less unified theological program of articulating, shaping, and embodying convictions about God, humanity, and the world.

With the rise of modernity, however, it is possible to detect a whole new range of separations. First, a variety of critical questions and practices that came to be known as "historical criticism" began to dominate scholarly study of the Bible. One of the results of these methods of reading was to separate the practice of reading the NT in a manner geared toward historical reconstruction from the practice of developing a theologically usable reading of the NT. While most biblical scholars (of both Testaments) still continued to identify themselves as Christians, they were required at least in theory to check their theological convictions at the door when they entered the profession of biblical studies. Indeed, it is quite common to presume that those practices that we have come to know as historical criticism, while not necessarily hostile to theology, exist independently of theological concerns.[3]

In addition, theology as an academic enterprise has tended to fragment into a variety of discrete activities. These activities are largely carried out in isolation from each other. As a result, the work of NT scholars on, for example, the intricate literary relationships among the Synoptic Gospels, is generally seen by systematic theologians as both too technical and irrelevant for their own interests. Further, NT scholars tend to find the categories of systematic theology abstract and ill suited to their interests in the NT.

---

3. By saying that these practices *presume* to exist independently of theological concerns I want to draw attention to the fact that from the perspective of one who is a follower of the triune God, there is no field of inquiry that is not theological. In this I am following John Milbank's work, *Theology and Social Theory* (Oxford: Blackwell, 1990), a book that is both extremely significant and very difficult.

Another factor underwriting the separations between NT study and theology has been the professionalization of both disciplines within the structure of the modern university. To be counted as a professional within either field, one has to master such a diverse body of knowledge particular to each field that it is rare to find a scholar in one of these fields whose work is read and used by those in the other. This professionalization even influences seminaries and small liberal arts colleges to the extent that they draw their faculty from graduate programs at research universities. Further, such faculty often have professional allegiances to scholarly societies whose interests and agendas are largely shaped by concerns of the university.

Professionalization has had several important effects that are reflected more or less directly in the way the NT is taught. First, it institutionalized the separation between NT study and theology. Because there is a strong temptation in most universities to treat the work of professional scholars (whether in NT, theology, or anything else) as commodities that can be exchanged for various professional rewards (e.g., tenure, promotion, and the like), there is little incentive to take the time needed to engage seriously with the work of those outside one's own field. In fact, the commodification of scholarship works to specialize and fragment disciplines rather than to encourage the breaking down of disciplinary boundaries.

This even tends to happen in institutions like seminaries. Although seminaries should have a clear interest in overcoming divisions like those between NT and theology, their faculties are, by and large, trained in research universities, where disciplinary divisions are strictly maintained if not jealously guarded. Even if the will is there, graduate training has not equipped most scholars with the intellectual habits and conversational skills needed to engage in cross-disciplinary work. Without teachers who are accomplished in these habits and skills, the burden of integrating NT study, theology, and ethics is unfortunately shifted onto the student.

All of these are reasons why, at least at the level of the academy, there is a strong separation between NT study and theology (including ethics). Attempts at "biblical theology" have tried to overcome this gap, but without a great deal of concrete success. Indeed, most work in this field has been designed to serve a professional subdiscipline within biblical studies.[4] While there is much of an *ad hoc* nature to be learned from these works, they often exhibit less interest in exploring the issues surrounding a theological

4. This is perhaps one of the most disappointing aspects of Brevard Childs's recent *Biblical Theology of the Old and New Testaments* (Minneapolis: Fortress, 1993).

reading of Scripture in the present than in explicating the theological content of the Bible in terms taken from either dogmatic or historical theology.

It is this notion of a theological reading of Scripture that I want to focus on in this essay. When I speak of a theological reading of Scripture, I am not talking about an interpretive report on the theology or the ethics contained in the Bible. The vast majority of works under the heading of NT theology or NT ethics engage in this type of activity.[5] Rather, I am using the notion of a theological reading of Scripture to refer to the aims and practices Christians engage in when they read Scripture as part of their struggle to live faithfully before the triune God. That is, a theological reading of Scripture is one designed to shape and be shaped by the faith, worship, and practices of Christian communities. In the rest of this essay I will try to explore some issues Christians must address as they struggle to read Scripture theologically in the various contexts in which they find themselves. Clearly, in the space allotted I can only make limited gestures towards the issues surrounding a theological reading of Scripture.[6]

I will begin by arguing that the primary location for theological interpretation of Scripture is the church. This is in contrast to professional biblical studies, where the primary location is the modern research university. I will then examine two points at which this makes a difference for theological readings of Scripture. The first of these concerns ways of reading Scripture historically. The second focuses on tying the practices involved in a theological reading of Scripture to other ecclesial practices, most specifically the practices of repentance, forgiveness, and reconciliation.

Before beginning this discussion, however, I need to comment briefly on the fact that I have expanded the scope of my discussion from the NT to Scripture. While this will not make much practical difference in the content of this chapter, it is theologically important for Christians always to remember that their Scripture includes the OT as well. Anyone interested in living faithfully before the triune God cannot treat the OT as a vestigial organ that has been superseded by the NT.

---

5. Wolfgang Schrage's *Ethics of the New Testament* (Philadelphia: Fortress, 1988) and Herman Ridderbos's *Paul: An Outline of His Theology* (Grand Rapids: Eerdmans, 1975) are good examples of the type of work I am thinking of here.

6. For a more detailed account of the issues involved in a theological reading of Scripture see Stephen E. Fowl and L. Gregory Jones, *Reading in Communion: Scripture and Ethics in Christian Life* (Grand Rapids: Eerdmans, 1991).

2. Location Is Everything

By defining a theological reading of Scripture as a reading aimed at shaping and being shaped by a community's faith and practice, I have at the same time indicated a location where such reading should take place. As I have defined it, a theological reading of Scripture will take place primarily within the context of those Christian communities that seek to order their common life in accord with their interpretation of Scripture.

This is not to deny the obvious fact that many professional biblical scholars are also believing Christians. Neither is it a claim that the church should have nothing to do with the academy. Rather, it is the case that the concerns of a theological reading of Scripture presuppose a setting within Christian communities. This setting provides both the direction for theological readings of Scripture and the standards against which such readings can be judged. This means that a whole range of factors and considerations will come into play in evaluating theological readings of Scripture that do not normally constitute part of the discourse of professional biblical studies.[7] These factors have to do both with how the church is guided by its theological reading of Scripture and how the political constitution of the church can shape its reading of Scripture.

3. Ways of Being Historical

One example of how the ecclesial location of a theological reading of Scripture results in a different set of aims and interests being brought to bear on a biblical text is related to how one treats questions of history, particularly issues concerned with the historical gap that lies between the biblical text and our present day.

One of the points biblical scholars most persistently emphasize is that

---

7. In an essay explaining why Jews are not interested in biblical theology, Jon Levenson notes: "The context in terms of which a unit of literature is to be interpreted is never self-evident." After showing how different contexts of interpretation lead to different and incompatible readings of Gen 15:6 he concludes: "It is precisely the failure of the biblical theologians to recognize the limitation of the context of their enterprise that makes some of them surprised that Jews are not interested in it" (*The Hebrew Bible, The Old Testament, and Historical Criticism* [Louisville: Westminster/John Knox, 1993] 56, 61). It seems to me that many of the reasons Levenson gives might also be used to explain why Christians need not be interested in biblical theology either.

there is an enormous historical gap between the periods related in the biblical texts and our own time. Biblical scholars have generally viewed this gap as an impediment to finding the meaning of the text. As a result, much biblical scholarship over the past century and a half has been devoted to illustrating and determining historical matters surrounding both the production and the initial reading of the biblical texts. While this way of interpreting has always had its critics, these practices, which we have come to call historical criticism, came to dominate scholarly study of the Bible. Over the last fifteen to twenty years, however, historical-critical ways of reading the Bible have come under increasing attack from a wide variety of scholarly circles.[8] It is impossible to characterize the diffuse types and aims of these attacks as a single movement. There is, however, a growing dissatisfaction with both historical criticism's interests and its results.

In response to these attacks, it is common for those scholars of a historical-critical bent to argue that eliminating historical-critical practices would lead to the Bible being read in an ahistorical and therefore anarchic way.[9] On the one hand, given contemporary America's tendency to view reality as an eternal present, there may be some merit in this concern. On the other hand, both historical critics and others need to recognize that the notion of an ahistorical reading is oxymoronic. We cannot avoid giving historical interpretations. All interpretation, theological or otherwise, is always wrapped up in a whole range of historical elements. As Jon Levenson

8. See in particular Erhardt Güttgemanns, *Candid Questions concerning Gospel Form Criticism: A Methodological Sketch of the Fundamental Problems of Form and Redaction Criticism* (Pittsburgh: Pickwick, 1979); from another perspective see Hans Frei, *The Eclipse of Biblical Narrative* (New Haven: Yale University, 1977). In addition, much of Brevard Childs's work has carried on a polemic against various aspects of historical criticism.

9. While this argument is often lodged against the movement known as "structuralism," the charge of ahistorical instability is also applied to most types of literary criticism of the Bible. Structuralism has long since ceased to be a vital movement within literary criticism and never really took hold in biblical studies. For a presentation of the claim that literary approaches to the Bible are inherently unstable see John Barton, *Reading the Old Testament* (Philadelphia: Westminster, 1984). The best map in regard to current debates over historical criticism and literary critical alternatives is Stephen Moore, *Literary Criticism and the Gospels: The Theoretical Challenge* (New Haven: Yale University, 1989). Jon Levenson, however, makes the telling counter-point that an emphasis on reading Scripture in terms of its various reconstructed original contexts will result in a certain sort of theological anarchy. See his chapter "The Eighth Principle of Judaism and the Literary Simultaneity of Scripture" in *The Hebrew Bible*, 62-81.

has noted, "As soon as you treated the discolorations on the page as language, you have made a historical judgment."[10]

What is interesting about the argument against ahistorical readings, however, is not so much the chimera it attacks (i.e., ahistoricality), but what it implicitly assumes: When historical critics argue against ahistorical readings they seem to assume that the only alternative is to be a historical critic. Historical criticism, however, investigates only a very narrow range of historical issues surrounding the various stages of the production of the forms of the biblical texts that we now have. Those historical critics particularly engaged in reconstructive tasks tend to be uninterested in the biblical text once it reaches its final form. Further, by the time one gets to exploring issues regarding how subsequent generations read these texts, historical critics have largely fallen by the wayside.[11]

Christians who are interested in reading Scripture theologically need to recognize that historical criticism and "ahistorical" interpretations are not the only options.[12] The first step in moving beyond these two alternatives is to refuse to view the historical gap between biblical times and our own as an impediment to be overcome before one can understand a biblical text.

Members of any Christian community in the present must recognize that they are not the first to struggle to live faithfully before the triune God. Rather, they need to see themselves as part of an ongoing tradition extending down to the present. This is, at least in part, what is entailed when Christians regularly confess their belief in and commitment to the notion of the communion of saints and the catholicity of the church. Even by the time Paul is writing to the Corinthians, there is a sense in which fidelity to the gospel involves a "passing on" of tradition (cf. 1 Cor 11:2, 23-25). Rather than work to collapse the gap between Jesus and ourselves, Christian com-

10. Levenson, *The Hebrew Bible*, 110.

11. Historical critics are, of course, interested in what previous generations of historical critics have said. This, however, is an extremely narrow slice of the history of a text's interpretation.

12. Of course, one must recognize that even recent literary readings of the Bible are involved in historical issues. While it is the case that literary readings of the Bible often oppose themselves to historical criticism, they, too, are historical. Even if they have no explicit theological interests, literary readings of the Bible may be one of the best resources for those interested in reading Scripture theologically. One should not assume that, by engaging in literary readings, one has made an end run around historical concerns.

munities ought to find in their past rich resources for reading Scripture theologically in the present.[13] For example, American Christians struggling to understand how to live faithfully as "rich Christians in an age of hunger," might find that reading the sharp injunctions against "the rich" in Jas 5:1-6 in the light of John Chrysostom's sermons on the rich man and Lazarus (Luke 16:19-31) provides them with some insights and strategies for resisting the corrosive effects of a consumer culture.[14]

Further, as Christian communities seek to read Scripture in ways that shape and are shaped by their faith and practice they will be able to test their readings and the practices that those readings underwrite by whether or not they can construct lines of continuity between what they do and what faithful people before them have done.

Having said this, I must qualify these claims about the significant resources and standards to be found in the church's past interpretation of Scripture in two important ways. First, simply repeating what has been done before may not result in continuity with the past because even though the same action is performed, the context in which it is performed has necessarily changed over time. Hence there may be a substantial change in the significance of any particular action.

> If, in thirteenth-century Italy, you wandered around in a coarse brown gown, with a cord around your middle, your "social location" was clear: your dress said that you were one of the poor. If, in twentieth-century Cambridge, you wander around in a coarse brown gown, with a cord around your middle, your social location is curious: your dress now says, not that you are one of the poor, but that you are some kind of oddity in

---

13. Several contemporary scholars have been arguing for a theological reappropriation of the church's history of scriptural interpretation. See, e.g., David Steinmetz, "The Superiority of Pre-Critical Exegesis," *Theology Today* 37 (1980) 27-38, reprinted in *Ex Auditu* 1 (1985) 74-82 and in Donald K. McKim, *A Guide to Contemporary Hermeneutics* (Grand Rapids: Eerdmans, 1986) 65-77. George Lindbeck has recently argued that a theologically oriented history of Christian scriptural interpretation "is the theologically most crucial of all historical fields, including biblical studies, for those who think . . . that the church's future depends on its postcritical reappropriation of precritical hermeneutical strategies" (review of *Biblical Hermeneutics in Historical Perspective: Studies in Honor of Karlfried Froehlich on his Sixtieth Birthday,* ed. Mark Burrows and Paul Rorem [Grand Rapids, Eerdmans, 1991] in *Modern Theology* 10 [1994] 101-6).

14. See St. John Chrysostom, *On Wealth and Poverty* (Crestwood, New York: St. Vladimir's Seminary, 1984).

the business of "religion." Your dress now declares, not your solidarity with the poor, but your amiable eccentricity.[15]

Here Nicholas Lash is not attacking the Franciscans as much as he is pointing out that temporal and cultural change necessitates ongoing discussion and debate about how to continue a tradition. "Fidelity to tradition, in action and speech, is a risky business because it entails active engagement in a process of continual change."[16]

Second, because the history of interpretation is both exceedingly diverse and sometimes wrong (as in the case of biblical justifications for slavery), discerning what constitutes continuity with those who have preceded us in the faith will always be a matter of selective retrieval, debate, and argument. This is what MacIntyre means when he notes that a living tradition persistently engages in arguments about just what constitutes that tradition and how it needs to be construed in order for it to continue in present circumstances.[17]

For a community to be able to carry on such discussions without fragmenting or lapsing into violence not only requires some knowledge of the past, it also requires people with the imagination to see new ways of being faithful in the present. Discussions of this sort require a community schooled in the habits of disciplined conversation, prayer, and discernment. Across America, such communities are in short supply. Further, I contend that it is an absence of these types of Christian community rather than ignorance of the practices of historical criticism that will ultimately undermine Christians' ability to read Scripture theologically.

4. Sin, Repentance, and Interpretive Failure

Having just argued that communities engaged in a theological reading of Scripture will find rich resources and standards of reading in the work of previous generations, I would be naive to continue as if the church's past

15. Nicholas Lash, "What Authority Has Our Past?" in *Theology on the Way to Emmaus* (London: SCM, 1986) 54.

16. Lash, "What Authority Has Our Past?" 55.

17. "Moreover when a tradition is in good order it is always partially constituted by an argument about the goods and purposes the pursuit of which gives to that tradition its particular point and purpose" (MacIntyre, *After Virtue*, 222). MacIntyre further develops this point in *Whose Justice? Which Rationality?* (Notre Dame: Univeristy of Notre Dame, 1988).

were one unbroken stream of wise and faithfully embodied scriptural interpretation. Even a passing acquaintance with the history of Christianity will be enough to convince anyone that the church's past is extraordinarily diverse, marked, among other ways, by inspiring fidelity and by horrific and persistent sin. Almost without exception Christians have managed to find scriptural warrants for their most blatantly sinful practices.[18]

This side of the fullness of God's reign, Christians should expect nothing less than churches that are both holy and sinful. This truism, however, becomes banal and even dangerous if it does not result in an attitude of repentance and an active engagement in the practices of forgiveness and reconciliation. When, as is the case in most American churches, the practices of forgiveness and reconciliation fall into disrepair, we should not be surprised to find that instead of "bearing fruits worthy of repentance" (Luke 3:8), fruits of self-deception and cynicism prevail in the life of such Christian communities. Our past no longer becomes a resource for reading Scripture. Instead, both our past and our interpretation of Scripture tend to feed our self-deceptions, thus further distancing us from the spirit of repentance needed both to address the past and to read Scripture. As a way of explaining how this is related to theological interpretation of Scripture I want to examine briefly a text that touches on these matters.

In 1 Cor 11:17-34 Paul examines what he deems to be a lack of sound judgment, both collective and individual, in the Corinthian community. While this text has played a crucial role in Reformation and post-Reformation debates about the nature of the eucharist, its primary focus is how a heterogenous group of people is to be formed into a community capable of eating a supper whose character is determined by the Lord.[19] It appears that when the Corinthians gather for worship, they do not represent the unified body of Christ discussed in 10:16-18. Rather, their gathering for worship around what is supposed to be a shared meal has become an

18. One of the most painful examples of this for American Christians must be the use of the curse of the sons of Ham in Genesis 9 to justify the kidnapping of Africans and their enslavement in this country. For an excellent discussion of the way African American Christians turned this interpretation on its head, see Michael G. Cartwright, "Ideology and the Interpretation of Scripture in the African-American Christian Tradition," *Modern Theology* 9 (1993) 141-58.

19. While the phrase "Lord's Supper" is stylistically more elegant than "a supper whose character is determined by the Lord," it also carries a great deal of baggage. As a result I will use the less elegant phrase as a more accurate translation of the Greek κυριακὸν δεῖπνον *(kyriakon deipnon)*.

occasion for displaying disparities in wealth in the congregation.[20] Instead of a shared meal punctuated by a blessing and sharing of bread and cup, the Corinthian gathering looks like a gathering of individual groups, some well fed, others hungry and humiliated (11:21-22).[21] Even though the Corinthians seem to go through all of the proper ritual acts, they would be deceived to think that they are actually participating in a supper whose character is determined by the crucified Christ (11:20).[22]

Paul reminds them that without first discerning the proper state of the congregation and, by implication, repenting of their divisions and the material practices that led to those divisions, their ritual practice is empty.[23]

---

20. Gerd Theissen nicely summarizes the situation in Corinth:

It can be assumed that the conflict over the Lord's Supper is a conflict between poor and rich Christians. The cause of this conflict was a particular habit of the rich. They took part in the congregational meal which they themselves had made possible, but they did so by themselves — possibly separated from the others and at their own table.

Further, "The core of the problem was that the wealthier Christians made it plain to all just how much the rest were dependent on them . . ." (*The Social Setting of Pauline Christianity* [Philadelphia: Fortress, 1982] 151, 160). See also the useful article by S. Scott Bartchy, "Table Fellowship with Jesus and the 'Lord's Meal' at Corinth," in *Increase in Learning: Essays in Honor of James G. Van Buren*, ed. R. Owens and B. Hamm (Manhattan: Manhattan Christian College, 1979) 45-61, esp. 47.

21. Chrysostom lays this out quite plainly: "Perceivest thou how he [Paul] intimates that they were disgracing themselves rather? For that which is the Lord's they make a private matter: so that themselves are the first to suffer indignity, depriving their own table of its greatest prerogative." He goes on to argue that the phrase "the Lord's Supper" indicates that the food brought to this meal ought to be common on the view that what is "the Lord's" cannot belong to any individual, but to all. "So that by the Lord's' supper he expresses this, the 'community' of the feast" (Homily XXVII in *Nicene and Post Nicene Fathers*, first series, vol. 12, ed. Philip Schaff [New York: The Christian Literature Co., 1889] 159).

22. As Bartchy lays out this situation, the Corinthians presumed that their meal enabled and enhanced their personal fellowship with the exalted Christ. "In sharp contrast, Paul's expectations for this meal were rooted in the reconciling death of Christ (vs 23); and the tradition which he had 'received from the Lord' (vs 23) required that the 'Lord's Meal' demonstrate the acceptance and forgiveness between human beings made possible by that death" (Bartchy, "Table Fellowship with Jesus," 47).

23. While 1 Cor 11:27-34 implies that such penitential judgment both of individual's lives and of the common life of a community should lead to material change in the way the Corinthians relate to each other in worship, we find in Luke 3:10-14 a more direct and concrete statement of the need for material change in the lives of penitent people.

Indeed, Paul goes further to claim that such failure of judgment works ultimately to the Corinthians' condemnation. He even attributes sickness and death within the congregation to their practice of eating the "Lord's meal" apart from penitential judgment about the state of their common life (11:27-31). Paul's argument here reminds the Corinthians that they cannot separate their acts of "worship" from their concrete common life.[24] Without the courage and wisdom to "discern the body" correctly, that is, to recognize the state of the congregation, and, by implication, to repent when such discernment reveals sin, the "Lord's meal" becomes an instrument of death rather than life.

A reader of 1 Corinthians, however, already has some indication that it is precisely this wisdom that the Corinthians lack. Paul goes to great lengths in the first four chapters of the epistle to point out that the life of the Corinthian congregation indicates that they have failed to recognize that the shape of God's wisdom is cruciform.

From this Pauline judgment about the importance of penitential discernment for the practice of eating the "Lord's meal" we can derive some methodological guidelines for a theological reading of Scripture. First, and perhaps foremost, Paul's argument indicates that one aspect of the life of any particular ecclesial community cannot be separated off from the rest of the community's existence. A community's practice of partaking of the "Lord's meal" is integrally connected to other aspects of the community's common life. Distortion in one area will influence other aspects of a community's faith and practice. The ecclesial location of theological readings of Scripture entails that scriptural interpretation will also shape and be shaped by other aspects of a particular community's common life.

The health of any particular manifestation of the body of Christ is crucial to that part of the body's ability to read and embody Scripture faithfully. Christians who have been deeply shaped by the standards of individualism so common to American life might strongly resist the notion that someone's "private" life, let alone a community's corporate life, might render their interpretation unacceptable. A theological reading of Scripture, however, that seeks to shape an ecclesial community's faith and practice cannot be indifferent to the manner of life leading to or resulting from a reading of Scripture.

Second, the upshot of Paul's admonitions in 1 Cor 11:17-34 indicates

24. In this respect Paul's claim is not formally different from the claim of Amos 5:21-26.

that penitential judgment is crucial to keeping these interrelated elements of a community's life in good working order. This is particularly important as believers enter into disagreements with each other over their theological readings of Scripture. If a theological reading of Scripture ultimately aims to bring our faith, life, and worship into conformity with Scripture, then it will be essential both that we be able to recognize when these elements of our lives do not conform to the voice of Scripture and that we change ourselves accordingly.

Of course, whether or not our faith, life, and worship conform to the voice of Scripture will always be a matter of debate and discussion. We cannot escape this sort of hard work and the disagreements such work inevitably bring. We cannot advance beyond these disagreements, however, unless we are able to recognize that our cherished views are sometimes wrong. This recognition is the result of the sort of penitential judgment Paul calls for in 1 Corinthians 11 and it requires a very particular form of humility from us.

Recognizing that we have in some way failed to conform to the voice of Scripture would be a lot easier if Scripture had a voice of its own and could speak to us in the privacy of our own study. We could then dispose of our misconceptions, misunderstandings, and misdoings in the privacy of our own homes. Such events do happen, but they are rare and exceptional. More often the voice of Scripture that speaks to correct us speaks in the words of other people.[25] This is what makes the penitential judgment Paul calls for so hard. It is much easier to repent humbly before a book than before another person who knows us well.

Such humility is hard, but we have made it even harder to attain because our practices of repentance, forgiveness, and reconciliation are in such disrepair.[26] To be told that something about our life, faith, or worship is out of line with Scripture is, implicitly at least, a call to repent. We have so distorted our common life, however, that it is now difficult if not impossible to offer that call to repent and to respond with the humility that is so crucial if we are to live faithful lives. Within most ecclesial communities in this

---

25. If there were space, it would be important to develop this notion in terms of a doctrine of the Holy Spirit and of the Spirit's role in theological interpretation of Scripture. This is one of those places at which I can only point in the direction of a fuller account of a theological interpretation of Scripture.

26. For an analysis of various aspects of this disrepair see L. Gregory Jones, "The Judgement of Grace," *Pro Ecclesia* 2 (1993) 173-86.

country it has become extraordinarily hard for us to hear the voice of Scripture in the voice of another. It has become humiliating to humble ourselves when we do encounter this voice. In this situation we cannot seriously hope to nurture the sort of penitential judgment that Paul considers so important for the practice of partaking in the "Lord's meal" and that I am arguing is also essential for a theological reading of Scripture. The challenge facing Christians as they seek to read Scripture theologically is to work to establish communal contexts in which Christians can humbly correct and be corrected by one another. If we do not meet this challenge, we can expect our debates about Scripture will be (as they often are) shrill, acrimonious, and unsuccessful.

5. Conclusion: Toward an Ecclesiology for Reading Scripture

Thus far I have claimed that a theological reading of Scripture is primarily a practice of Christian communities. This ecclesial location for theological readings of Scripture means that certain issues, such as the history of a text's interpretation, will be important for theological readings of Scripture but not to professional biblical scholars. Further, theological interpretation of Scripture cannot be separated from the wider life of particular ecclesial communities. I relied on Paul's discussion of the practices surrounding the "Lord's meal" in 1 Cor 11:17-34 to illustrate this point. Moreover, following Paul's argument, I indicated that the nurture of penitential judgment and the practices related to this judgment are crucial for Christian communities as they try to shape their faith, life, and worship in accordance with their reading of Scripture.

As I have developed my argument thus far, it is clear that I consider the formation and nurture of Christian communities the crucial task for reading the NT theologically. It is important to remember, however, that such communities are not created overnight. Learning to read Scripture theologically, like learning anything else, requires time, dedication, and disciplined attention to both our successes and our failures. Becoming a wise reader of Scripture requires nothing less than the transformation of our lives and of the common life of the Christian communities in which we find ourselves.

By way of conclusion I would like to mention briefly two crucial elements in that process of transformation. First, we cannot expect to be transformed into communities of wise readers of Scripture apart from the work of the Holy Spirit. For reasons of space I have said little about the Spirit's role in scriptural interpretation. Even within the NT, however, it is clear that Paul sees himself as reading his Scripture under the guidance of the Spirit.[27] Further, a close study of Acts 10–15 shows the intimate relationship between testimony about the work of the Spirit and the testimony of Scripture as the earliest Christian communities struggled with how to include Gentiles into their midst.[28]

The second important element in the long process of being transformed into communities of wise readers of Scripture is related to Paul's discussion of the worship of the Corinthian Christians. One of the reasons that Paul is so desperately concerned about the manner in which the Corinthians partake of the Lord's meal is that he seems to understand that we are formed by our worship. One of the reasons it is so important that the common meal in which we participate adequately reflect the Lord's character is that participating in this meal shapes our character. Anyone concerned about the transformation, nurture, and sustenance of communities of Christians capable of interpreting and embodying Scripture faithfully must attend to the worship of such communities. This is very much the challenge facing the Christians in Corinth, and it remains one of the challenges facing Christians today.[29]

6. Suggestions for Further Reading

Anyone interested in reading further in the area of biblical theology (which may not be of much help for reading Scripture theologically) should grapple with the work of Brevard Childs. His most recent work, *A Biblical Theology of the Old and New Testaments* (Minneapolis: Fortress, 1993), is largely

---

27. The best discussion of Paul's Spirit-guided interpretation I have found is Richard Hays's *Echoes of Scripture in the Letters of Paul* (New Haven: Yale University, 1989). I have tried to develop some of Hays's insights about the role of the Spirit in scriptural interpretation in "Who Can Read Abraham's Story? Allegory and Interpretive Power in Gal. 4:21ff.," *JSNT* 55 (1994) 77-95.

28. A good place to begin such close study is with Luke T. Johnson's *Decision Making in the Church: A Biblical Model* (Philadelphia: Fortress, 1983).

29. I am very grateful to Andrew Adam, Margaret Adam, Jim Buckley, Joel Green, Greg Jones, Phil Kenneson, and Beverly Stratton for their comments on earlier drafts of this chapter.

disappointing. His *Introduction to the Old Testament as Scripture* (Philadelphia: Fortress, 1979) is a better place to start. The best critical engagement with Childs is Mark Brett's *Biblical Criticism in Crisis?* (Cambridge: Cambridge University, 1991). N. T. Wright is in the midst of a most promising NT theology. The first of his five volumes has been published, *The New Testament and the People of God* (Minneapolis: Fortress, 1992), with the second, *Jesus and the Victory of God,* forthcoming.

There are very few good books on the history of Christian interpretation of Scripture. Three good introductions are James Kugel and Rowan Greer, *Early Biblical Interpretation* (Philadelphia: Westminster, 1986); John Rogerson, Christopher Rowland, and Barnabas Lindars, *The Study and Use of the Bible* (Grand Rapids: Eerdmans, 1988); and Beryl Smalley, *The Study of the Bible in the Middle Ages* (reprint of 2d ed., Notre Dame: University of Notre Dame, 1964).

One of the most vigorous proponents of reading Scripture theologically was Hans Frei. His work *The Eclipse of Biblical Narrative* (New Haven: Yale University, 1977) traced the demise of a certain theological way of reading Scripture. His now out-of-print book *The Identity of Jesus Christ: The Hermeneutical Bases of Dogmatic Theology* (Philadelphia: Fortress, 1975) is a theological reading of the Gospels. Frei is hard to read and a beginning student might want to make use of the large amount of secondary literature on Frei.

The notion of a theological reading of Scripture is touched on in various ways by Robert Morgan with John Barton in *Biblical Interpretation* (Oxford: Oxford University, 1988), and Anthony C. Thiselton in *New Horizons in Hermeneutics* (Grand Rapids: Zondervan, 1992). Neither, however, stresses the importance of the ecclesial location for this reading of Scripture. One of the most provocative accounts of the relationship of historical criticism and theological interpretation is Jon Levenson's *The Hebrew Bible, The Old Testament and Historical Criticism* (Louisville: Westminster/John Knox, 1993).

Finally, most of the points in this chapter form a reprise and development of arguments first published in Stephen Fowl and L. Gregory Jones, *Reading in Communion: Scripture and Ethics in Christian Life* (Grand Rapids: Eerdmans, 1991).

20. *The Practice of Reading the New Testament*

Joel B. Green

1. Reading and Practice

The inelegance of this chapter's title is deliberate, an invitation to consider how the material of this volume might inform our use of the NT. The relationship of "reading" and "practice" can be sketched in a number of ways so as to emphasize reading the NT as transformative act.

1.1 The Aim of Reading

Most obviously "the practice of reading" has to do with *putting to use the perspectives, methods, and approaches* discussed in these pages.

But even this way of construing the title is capable of further nuance. The exercise of NT interpretation always proceeds toward an objective — say, to prepare an essay for a course assignment, to make ready a small group study, to launch the process of sermon-making, to satisfy one's curiosity regarding "what the NT says about such-and-such a topic," and so on. What is more, the aim toward which one works will determine which interpretive approach or approaches will be suitable. As Robert Morgan has asserted,

> The study of texts is always undertaken within some larger framework, whether this is recognized or not. The larger framework, constituted by interpreters' interests, determines what questions are considered impor-

tant, what methods are found appropriate, and what explanations are deemed satisfying.[1]

Morgan's insight underscores the primacy of interpretive *aim* over interpretive *method,* and so calls attention to the importance of evaluating *who* is doing the reading and *why.* Morgan himself detects a basic dichotomy of interpretive aims in contemporary readings of the Bible — that of the scholarly community, concerned with historical reconstruction or literary appreciation or both, and that of those religious communities for whom the Bible is read as Scripture.

1.2 Reading and Behavior

"The practice of reading" can be construed in a quite different way, too, in order to call attention to *a reading of the New Testament that informs our practices.* In this case, the word "practices" has to do with human behavior *(praxis)* and "reading" has to do with how our engagement with the NT might shape our behaviors. A framework for determining how this might transpire is suggested by the work of Pierre Bourdieu.[2]

In his effort to present a theory of the practical character of social interaction Bourdieu employs *habitus* as a key concept. By this means, he draws attention to a set of *dispositions* that incline people to act and react in certain ways. "The dispositions generate practices, perceptions and attitudes which are 'regular' without being consciously co-ordinated or governed by any 'rule.'"[3] For Bourdieu, these dispositions are acquired through a gradual process by which they assume the status of second nature, they reflect the social conditions within which they are acquired, they are ingrained so that they operate at a preconscious level, and they can be transposed to new settings where they might generate alternative practices. That is, *practices,* or behaviors, grow out of the interplay of *habitus* and the specific social contexts in which we find ourselves. The question is, How might our reading of the NT reform our "dispositions" and so influence in this way our practices in the world?

1. Robert Morgan with John Barton, *Biblical Interpretation* (Oxford: Oxford University, 1988) 22.
2. See esp. Bourdieu's *The Logic of Practice* (Stanford: Stanford University, 1980), and *Language and Symbolic Power* (Cambridge: Harvard University, 1991).
3. John B. Thompson, "Introduction," in Bourdieu, *Language and Symbolic Power,* 1-31, here 12.

It is clear that at this juncture we have moved far beyond the central concern of most hermeneutical reflection in this century. Hermeneutics has been occupied preeminently with how texts (and communication in general) serve to pass on *information*. Biblical interpretation has emphasized "getting the meaning right."[4] According to this second understanding of "the practice of reading," however, the focus shifts to the question of how texts might have a *transformative* role.

One way of making plain the difference with which we are concerned is to ask: What is the end of exegesis? What is the end of critical engagement with a NT text? Is it the sermon? An essay? A commentary? Or is it a people who embody its message?

Another way to address this matter is to inquire into the aims of the NT materials themselves. Given that the various books that together make up our NT took shape in the context of the struggles of God's people with their own identity and purpose before God and in ever-expanding contexts, does it not follow that these texts might also shape our similar struggles? The texts of the NT were formed in the cauldron of community formation and witness; as a consequence, interpretation of those texts that does not lead to vital discipleship and mission hardly has a claim to being *New Testament* interpretation.[5]

1.3 Reading Encouraging Reading

A third way of perceiving the relation of practice to reading merits brief attention. This is our perception that *reading the NT is itself a Christian practice.* That is, one of the *practices* nourished by the formative influence of reading Scripture is further readerly engagement with Scripture. Reading the NT not only informs our behaviors, but reading the Scriptures itself sanctions and encourages such generative reading.

---

4. Cf. Anthony C. Thiselton, *New Horizons in Hermeneutics: The Theory and Practice of Transforming Biblical Reading* (London: HarperCollins; Grand Rapids: Zondervan, 1992) 17: "Why in hermeneutical theory up to 1970 had so little attention been given to the capacity of biblical texts *to produce certain transforming effects*, rather than only to transmit certain disclosures?" (his emphasis).

5. Cf. Stephen B. Reid, "An Evangelical Approach to Scripture," *TSF Bulletin* 8 (1985) 2-5; Joel B. Green, " 'Proclaiming Repentance and Forgiveness of Sins to All Nations': A Biblical Perspective on the Church's Mission," in *The World Is My Parish: The Mission of the Church in Methodist Perspective*, ed. Alan G. Padgett, SHM 10 (Lewiston: Edwin Mellen, 1992) 13-43.

This interest is most evident in the way biblical materials reflect on other biblical materials — first in the use of earlier OT materials by later OT materials (as with the Exodus or Jubilee traditions), then with the interplay of NT with OT texts. Whether as a witness to the interpretive activity of Jesus or Paul or others, the NT writings show the degree to which people read themselves and their circumstances into and in light of the divine story. It is to the Scriptures that they turned repeatedly to grapple with their own identity as a people, their sense of mission, and the appropriate boundaries for behavior becoming to God's people.

Luke records Jesus asserting his identity publicly in the words of the prophet Isaiah (Luke 4:18-19; cf. Isa 58:6; 61:1-2), for example, and Paul uses scriptural language in identifying himself as "a person called" (cf. Gal 1:15; Jer 1:5; Isa 49:1-6). Similarly, Scripture had "a constitutive role in Jewish ethical discourse,"[6] and is employed in a variety of ways by NT writers in their own moral reasoning. A reading of the NT from this canonical perspective — that is, a reading that takes seriously the organic nature of its internal discourse — has the consequence of calling for more such reading!

2. Interested Readers

Perhaps the most fundamental lesson (and challenge) of feminist hermeneutics is its disputation of the "objective," dispassionate readings of the Bible that have been the bread and butter of twentieth-century biblical study. Not only such readings but the very prospect of such neutrality has been called into serious question. The growing recognition that we bring with us to the table of inquiry our own backgrounds, commitments, and traditions is not unique to biblical studies, of course, but has begun to infiltrate even the so-called hard sciences.

---

6. Wayne A. Meeks, *The Moral World of the First Christians*, LEC 6 (Philadelphia: Westminster, 1986) 94. Of course, exactly what constituted "Scripture" in the Second Temple period is another question — cf. the summary in Eckhard J. Schnabel, "History, Theology, and the Biblical Canon," *Catalyst* 20 (1994) 1, 4-5. J. Paul Sampley admits that the Scriptures had a central place in Paul's thought world, but deals insufficiently with their role in Paul's moral discourse (*Walking between the Times: Paul's Moral Reasoning* [Minneapolis: Fortress, 1991] esp. 92-93).

2.1 Starting with Our Questions

One may trace a line from Marx to more recent shapers of cultural under-standing, including Roland Barthes and especially Michel Foucault, to show how the ideologies of interpreters, traditions of interpretation, and inter-pretive communities have come under the spotlight. But one need not adopt a Marxist analysis to see that readers read out of their own histories, commitments, and concerns — after all, there is more to our identity and experience as humans than our relation to the means of production. Whether our inescapable embeddedness in lived reality is a blessing or bane to the hermeneutical task is not yet at issue; it is more important that we simply recognize this as anthropological reality, a part of being human. In our reading of the NT we must begin with our own lives in the world. "We must begin here because we simply cannot begin anywhere else. We cannot jump to some privileged place of neutrality or complete objectivity."[7] It is from within our life-worlds that we engage in the reading task.

For example, and speaking personally, it is easy for me to chart how my questions and approaches to NT study have been shaped by my present context. Since 1985 my office has been located across the street diagonally from Peoples' Park, a gathering point for the hungry and homeless in the South Campus area of the University of California at Berkeley. Almost daily interaction with homeless people and six years of involvement with the Berkeley Emergency Food and Housing Project raised important questions for me about the almost universally touted methods of engaging NT texts that seemed to disclose very little by way of a NT message germane to these circumstances and these lives and about the sort of message that could actually qualify as "good news to the poor" (cf. Luke 4:18-19).

As I took my *questions* about the meaning of "poor" and the substance of God's "good news" into my reading of the Scriptures, I also began searching for new *methods* that would assist my inquiry. Through a process of discovery and conversion and in continual conversation with others — some homeless, some struggling at ecclesiastical, social, or political levels with homelessness, some actively involved as service providers with the homeless, some members of the Christian fellowship to which my family and I are committed, and so on — I began seriously to question in what

7. William A. Dyrness, "How Does the Bible Function in the Christian Life?" in *The Use of the Bible in Theology: Evangelical Options,* ed. Robert K. Johnston (Atlanta: John Knox, 1985) 159-74, here 161.

ways modern definitions of "poor" (= "below such-and-such level of annual gross family income") might be significant. The experience of women and of people of color today raised for me doubts about the necessary or automatic linkage between income and status. In the same way my reading of NT texts through methodological lenses more informed by the social sciences began to bring to the surface the importance of community identity and kinship relations over questions of relative income levels or relation to the means of production. This led to my exploration of the coordinates by which we might orient the mission of the church in the presence of such need and in light of the inbreaking, imperial rule of God.[8] It also led me to a more critical analysis of the meaning of "the poor" to whom Jesus oriented his ministry in the Gospel of Luke.[9]

More broadly, one can note the way in which the experience of many in the West has led to new questions and methods regarding the status and role of women in the people of God. And in the U.S. and Germany, especially, both popular and scholarly studies at the interface of psychology and the Bible are on the rise — doubtlessly as a consequence of reconceptualizations of the nature of human beings that take with greater seriousness our emotional and subconscious selves.

The cardinal point of departure for the practice of reading the NT, then, is our own life-worlds. Not only is this the only place we can start from, but it also brings with it at least three interpretive advantages. First, beginning in this way self-consciously helps us to come clean on the interests and commitments that help to shape our reading of Scripture — interests and commitments that are operative even when they remain unacknowledged. We can thus be more honest in our reading. Second, appreciating as fully as possible the self-identities and experiences from which we interpret opens further the potential for our own experiences and commitments to come under critical scrutiny. We bring to texts preunderstandings that may require emendation, that may be judged in the reading task as parochial, egocentric, and so on. Third, this approach allows us to engage self-consciously in critical reflection on our lives in the world. We

8. Joel B. Green, *Kingdom of God: Its Meaning and Mandate* (Lexington: Bristol, 1989/Amersham-on-the-Hill: Scripture, 1990).

9. Joel B. Green, "Good News to Whom? Jesus and the 'Poor' in the Gospel of Luke," in *Jesus of Nazareth: Lord and Christ. Essays on the Historical Jesus and New Testament Christology*, ed. Joel B. Green and Max Turner (Grand Rapids: Eerdmans/Carlisle: Paternoster, 1994) 59-74.

will inquire into "the NT teaching on abortion," for example, not because we have a curiosity that needs satisfaction, not because we might need this sort of information at some future point, but because our involvement in the lives of those experiencing crisis pregnancies drives us to ask such a question.

2.2 Remaining Open to Challenge

If our own life-worlds are the starting point for reading the Bible, will we not find in its pages only that for which we are looking? By refusing to aim for a neutral reading of a NT text, have we not already compromised the objective of hearing the text? *Can we as readers have interests and still be open to challenge?* These are important questions, not least given the ease with which religious communities historically have found in their readings of the Scriptures divine legitimation for their sometimes heinous practices. A few correctives can be mentioned.

First, we must recover in an explicit way the role of the community of faith in biblical interpretation. One of the most profoundly unfortunate portraits of the practice of reading the NT today is the person awakening early in the morning for his time alone with God or the pastor sitting alone in her study bent over a desk with Bible open in preparation for Sunday's sermon. Of course, these are not really examples of reading the Bible in solo; even the person involved in an individual-centered quiet time is a representative of a tradition of interpretation. (How else will he have learned to express his piety in this way?) And the pastor, though apparently alone, is often surrounded by her commentaries and other interpretive aids, as well as her ecclesial or other traditions of reading. But such traditions of interpretation, often unacknowledged, also often go unchallenged. The practice of reading the NT is an agenda for the whole faith community.

Whose interpretive voices are allowed? Trained theological voices? Grandmotherly voices? Third World voices? Inner-city voices? Baptist voices? Third-wave charismatic voices? Young voices? Wealthy voices? To whom do we listen?

One of the insights of relatively recent work in philosophy and literary criticism is that we are able to locate a cohesive interpretation of a text only by privileging *some* components of the text over *some other* elements. Our interpretations make sense of the data *as a whole*, perhaps, but not of *each datum* taken on its own terms. We are able in this way to achieve an intelligible, perhaps even well-grounded interpretation of the text, but such an interpretation — indeed, *any* interpretation — can only be provisional, never *final*, since (at the very least) those other aspects of the text may surface to shift the weight of meaning. And it has often been the case that voices from outside one's interpretive tradition or community have been instrumental in surfacing those other elements. One example is the long-standing discussion between Calvinists and Wesleyans on NT evidence for the doctrine of "eternal security" versus evidence for the possibility of "falling away." Another is the ongoing discussion on the status and role of women in the community of God's people, with persons in different quarters emphasizing competing NT witnesses as central (paradigmatic?) to the dispute.[10] Yet another is the attempt by heirs of Martin Luther (especially Melanchton) to marginalize the NT letter of James, with its apparent emphasis on "works," over against the primacy of place given that same Epistle in the eighteenth-century Great Awakening. Indeed, we could find an example in *any* attempt to squeeze the choir of NT voices into a systematic presentation — for such attempts can only underscore the presence of a multiplicity of perspectives contained between the NT's covers.

If we are to have readerly interests (and we do) *and* remain open to being challenged by the very texts to which we bring our interests, we will need continually to adopt a position of humility in our interpretive enterprise. We will need continually to embrace the community of God's people — contemporary and historical, female and male, rural and urban, rich and poor, North and South, and so on — as conversation partners in the hermeneutical task. These hermeneutical partners will assist us in hearing countermelodies for which previously we had no ear.

Second, it follows that in our reading we will need to adopt an openness to the voices of outsiders. This includes not only other believers outside our small group of interpretive discussion (as just noted), nor only the history of interpretation of Scripture (as important as this is — see above, ch. 2), but also those whose lives seem not to be oriented around God at all. In fact, Stephen Fowl and Greg Jones insist that just such an openness is one of the discernible characteristics of authentic, believing communities.

10. Note the comment of F. F. Bruce on Gal 3:28: "Paul states the basic principle here; if restrictions on it are found elsewhere in the Pauline corpus, as in 1 Cor. 14:34f. . . . or 1 Tim 2:11f., they are to be understood in relation to Gal. 3:28, and not *vice versa* (*The Epistle to the Galatians: A Commentary on the Greek Text*, New International Greek Testament Commentary [Grand Rapids: Eerdmans, 1982] 190).

Our interpretations can take on pretensions of permanence. When our communities fall prey to this greatest of interpretive temptations, it is often only the voice of outsiders that can set us right. If we have not taken the time to cultivate the skills, habits and dispositions that allow us to hear the voices of outsiders, we will fall into a situation of interpretive arrogance. *That is, we will deceive ourselves into thinking that our words are God's word.*[11]

Of course, the Gospels and Acts are peppered with the truth to which Fowl and Jones point. Jesus himself is portrayed often enough as a relative outsider in religious discourse — such as in his reading of the Sabbath law from the standpoint of a person in need (that is, as one taking advantage of "gleaning rights" reserved for "the alien, the orphan, and the widow" — cf. Mark 2:23-28; Deut 24:19-22).[12] Repeatedly in Luke-Acts, how one *begins* the life of discipleship is ambiguous because it is not obvious when a person first joins that journey. People that we, Luke's readers, have not known, people who are in fact defined in the narrative as "outsiders," respond *as though they have already oriented their lives around the way of the Lord* (e.g., 7:1-10, 36-50; 8:43-48). We are taught by these relative outsiders the meaning of genuine response to divine visitation in Christ — and thus we are taught to listen even to those who have not earned the right to be heard. Cornelius is a Gentile, a God-fearer but not yet a Jewish proselyte and certainly not a follower of Jesus, yet God hears his prayers and Peter learns from this "outsider" the significance of Peter's own recent vision from God (Acts 10). A criminal crucified along with Jesus shows the sort of insight into Jesus' identity one would think would have been reserved for "insiders" (Luke 23:39-43). And so on.

Can we as readers have interests and be open to challenge? A third way of addressing this concern is to remember that readers are not the only ones who have interests; NT texts have them also. And "the practice of reading" involves a refusal simply to objectify the NT as though it were a commodity to be manipulated, controlled, and employed in our self-defined projects. Rather, this reading entails participation in a conversation in which the NT text is discourse partner. It entails treating the text as an

11. Stephen E. Fowl and L. Gregory Jones, *Reading in Communion: Scripture and Ethics in Christian Life* (Grand Rapids: Eerdmans/London: SPCK, 1991) 110 (emphasis added).

12. Cf. Joel B. Green, "America's Bible: Good News for All Nations?" *RADIX* 18 (1988) 8-11, 24-29.

"other." As Anthony Thiselton has urged, reading communities must resist falling prey to an immunization against a theology of the cross that de-centers individual and corporate self-interests.[13]

In person-to-person discourse, of course, this give and take can be followed more obviously:

"Are you saying . . . ?"

"Am I hearing you correctly?"

In the practice of reading NT texts, we turn and return to ask whether we have discerned its communicative intention. Have we heard its questions? Have we entertained its perspective? Have we respected its discursive aim?[14] To a significant degree, the chapters collected in this volume are oriented around assisting in this task of discernment. We can highlight important coordinates of this task by asking a series of questions.

3. "Processing" Texts

What sort of questions inform our capacity faithfully to hear the text as conversation partner? One way of ferreting out the reading process is by listening to what discourse analysts refer to metaphorically as "bottom-up" and "top-down" text processing. According to this metaphor, we may think of at least two simultaneous reading strategies along the analogy of computational modeling of language understanding. In one part of the processing, we work out the meanings of the words and structure of sentences and build up a composite meaning for the sequence of sentences (*bottom-up processing*). At the same time, we are predicting, on the basis of the context plus the composite meaning of the material already processed, what the next sentence cluster is most likely to mean (*top-down processing*).[15] As reading strategies, we may think of bottom-up and top-down modes of processing as the ongoing negotiation of the textually embedded constraints on the possible meaning of a text.

13. Thiselton, *New Horizons*, 1-29, here 28.
14. Cf. Kevin J. Vanhoozer, "Hyperactive Hermeneutics: Is the Bible Being Over-interpreted?" *Catalyst* 19 (1993) 3-4.
15. Cf. Gillian Brown and George Yule, *Discourse Analysis*, CTL (Cambridge: Cambridge University, 1983) 234-36, here 234.

The benefit of this way of reflecting on the practice of reading is that it reminds us of the artificiality of all attempts to analyze the reading moment. We do not "process" texts in discreet "steps," and the questions that follow present no attempt to provide a "technology of reading." For example, while textual criticism is clearly a "first-order method" (since establishing what text to read of necessity precedes our reading it), other aspects of the interpretive enterprise may invite us to revisit, even revise, our text-critical decisions.

3.1 What Is the Text?

The first question to ask of a text is What is it? This is not one question, however, but several.

1. *What is the text to be read?* Bottom-up reading begins by accepting as a given (especially for readers of the NT in translation) or by establishing by means of textual criticism (especially for those with facility in the Greek NT) the text to be read (see above, ch. 7).

2. *In what form is this text presented?* Umberto Eco discusses this question under the heading of *rhetorical and stylistic overcoding*.[16] He thus draws attention to the recognition of literary genres (see above, ch. 10), literary and rhetorical devices (see above, chs. 12 and 13), and other forms or conventions in texts. These conventions are functions of top-down processing since they encourage readerly anticipation. When we hear

Once upon a time . . .

or read

"Paul, called to be an apostle . . . to the church of God in . . ."

certain expectations are triggered, preparing us for what will follow. Of course, literary conventions can be manipulated so as to establish, then circumvent or subvert, such expectations.

3. *What is the discourse unit for study?* Bottom-up reading identifies textual markers denoting transitions, shifts of topic, or argumentative structure so as to determine the boundaries of the text under examination as well as to postulate its relation to previous and subsequent material. Ob-

---

16. Umberto Eco, *The Role of the Reader: Explorations in the Semiotics of Texts*, AS (Bloomington: Indiana University, 1979) 19-20.

servations of this sort prepare readers for related questions: How does the thought develop? What literary strategies does the author employ to communicate the point? (See above, chs. 9, 12, and 13.)

Students are often tempted simply to follow the units established for them by, for example, the headings provided in their versions (whether in Greek or translation) of the NT, the paragraphing of the NT books in their editions, or the divisions in lectionaries. It is well to remember, though, that Paul, for example, did not write in verses, did not use modern-day paragraphs, and certainly did not break his letters into sections with individual headings. All such attempts to present the Pauline text today are based on editorial decisions and may or may not represent well the structure of Paul's text itself. Many therefore prefer to work initially with manuscripts of NT texts devoid of all foreign markers such as verses, paragraph indentions, and the like in order to invite closer examination of the internal working of the text so as to follow its development, its argument.

3.2 How Is This Text Co-Textually Situated?

Co-text, it will be remembered, has to do with the relationship of a text to the textual material within which it is located. Two remarks are especially important here.

1. *Language is linear; texts are presented to us in a specific sequence.* In English (and Greek) we read "from left to right." On the one hand, this axiom reminds us of the prospective development of reading: What we have already read gives us a basis and builds expectations for what we what we will read (top-down processing). On the other hand, the further we read, the more certain we can be of the meaning of what we have read earlier. The linearity of language invites the retrospective clarification of meaning whereby previous ambiguities are illuminated and the range of *possible* interpretations is limited to a minimal number of *probable* interpretations (see above, chs. 9 and 12). Of course, with reference to *canonical* texts, *reading* is accompanied by *rereadings,* so that one is enabled to grasp interpretive possibilities in the ongoing interaction with a text that do not occur in a first left-to-right reading.

2. *Bottom-up processing invites co-textual considerations in how we make sense of words in the text* (see above, ch. 8). Of course, readers will both make use of the *lexicon* (including our own active memory as well as knowledge of the text's contemporary world — cf. above, chs. 4, 5, and 6) to determine the probable parameters of the meaning of words and explore

with the help of *concordances* what possible properties of words might be actualized in the present text. But the critical coordinate in word meaning is *usage in "this" co-text.*

Additionally, bottom-up reading looks for *words or concepts that occupy preeminence in the text* and thus help to focus the reader on the topic of the text. Such words or concepts are signaled by means of repetitions (cf. "census" in Luke 2:1-5), by use of words belonging to the same semantic field (cf. the language of mercy and of strength in Luke 1:46-55), or by the strategic location of a word or words (cf. the position of "poor" in Luke 4:18-19; 6:20-22; 7:21-22, etc.).

3.3 What Is the Sociohistorical Context of This Text?

In the practice of reading a NT text, the sociohistorical situation in which we locate the text helps to predetermine how we will understand that text (top-down processing). If we assume, for example, that the Book of Revelation was written for the late twentieth century, we will find in its symbolism references to the front page of the morning newspaper. If we locate it in the late first century C.E., on the other hand, we may begin to find in its pages a cultural criticism that relates first to the Roman Empire (cf. Rev 17:9) and perhaps (but only) then to all political powers that engage in the same sort of idolatrous self-deification.[17]

This focus on the communicative situation emphasizes our need to locate the NT materials within their own horizons of meaning. How are these texts drawing on church traditions, and to what end (see above, ch. 3)? Within what social world is this text located (ch. 4)? What is the relevance of contemporary Jewish and Greco-Roman literature and life for this discourse (chs. 5 and 6)?

Attention to sociohistorical context also raises the possibility that we will discern the *textual presence of paralinguistic phenomena* that contribute to textual meaning — for example, who is wearing what clothes (e.g., Luke 8:27, 35; 16:19-20), who is standing or sitting or kneeling and in whose presence (cf. Acts 10:23-26; Phil 2:10), and the like.

At the same time, we must account for the new communicative situation, that situation generated by our own contemporary reading of these same texts. And this invites reflection on our own social contexts, our own

17. Cf. Richard Bauckham, *The Theology of the Book of Revelation*, NTT (Cambridge: Cambridge University, 1993).

worlds of discourse, the contexts within which we listen to and interact with these texts (chs. 15 through 18).

3.4 On What Texts Does This Text Build?

Every text is an interplay of other texts, and the meaning of those other texts spills over into the present one; their voices are added to (just as they are shaped by) the present one. In the practice of reading, then, readers will keep an ear tuned to the phenomenon of intertextuality — that is, to the location of a text within the larger linguistic frame of reference on which it consciously or unconsciously draws for meaning. Some of these texts may be other Christian texts or traditions, others borrowed from the wider Jewish and Greco-Roman worlds; especially resonant in NT texts, though, are the reverberations of OT texts (see above, chs. 3, 5, 6, 9, and 11). Many NT writers employ Israel's Scriptures in conspicuous as well as sometimes almost nondetectable ways to inscribe their message into the ongoing story of divine redemption. They thus show their debt to the ancient story, and their texts invite their readers to hear in the present the reverberations and continuation of that story.

4. The Problem with Scripture and the Scriptural Community

"The problem with Scripture," or at least the one in view here, is that some NT texts seem so culturally embedded in the first century that they are of little or no immediate relevance. That is, although we have been exploring the practice of reading the NT in its transformative potential, we also recognize some texts from which we are distant and into whose particular image we would prefer not to be formed. Not many of us practice the holy kiss, for example, in spite of clear scriptural admonition (Rom 16:16). Nor, in spite of the clarity with which Jesus instructs his followers to do so, do many of us engage in footwashing (John 13:14). And this is not even to index those texts whose messages seem altogether to fall short of escaping their limited cultural horizons, such as the news that the 144,000 "redeemed of the earth" consists of "those who have not defiled themselves with women" (Rev 14:4).[18]

18. Our recognition that these avoiders of defilement are (1) an army of fighting men who (2) have kept themselves free of the cultic defilement incurred through sexual

4.1 The Issue of Cultural Relativity

Two ways forward may be developed here. First, we must simply acknowl-edge a hermeneutical fact: We all choose to embrace some NT texts as of particular relevance while not adopting others, at least in a literal way. So the real question is not, Do we find some biblical texts so rooted in their cultural settings that they seem of little immediate relevance to us? It is, rather, How do we determine whether a biblical directive is so rooted in its cultural setting? Three rules of thumb may be suggested.[19]

1. *Determine the relative amount of emphasis given a subject in the biblical witness.* Here we presuppose that particular issues close to the heart of what it means to be God's people will be repeated often.

2. *Determine the degree to which the biblical witnesses are uniform and consistent on a given issue.* Here we affirm the reality that the biblical materials themselves do not always speak with one voice, but must address questions in a variety of cultural settings. If in different cultural settings and sociohistorical circumstances NT voices address similar concerns in different ways, this suggests that, on the particular issue, the message is culturally rooted. One may think of the different viewpoints represented in the pages of the NT on the question (very important in the first century!) of eating meat sacrificed to idols (cf. Acts 15, Romans 14, 1 Corinthians 8, and Revelation 2–3) or of the question of the status of women in the church (cf., e.g., Romans 16; Gal 3:28; 1 Tim 2:9-15).

3. *Determine the degree to which a writer's cultural situation provides him or her with only one option (or limited options) within which to work.* Why, for example, did the early church choose from among two *male* followers of Jesus when they sought to replace Judas? Since the only crite-rion mentioned is that this person should be one who has "accompanied us during all the time that the Lord Jesus went in and out among us" (Acts 1:21-22), why were women (who met these qualifications — cf. Luke 8:1-3; 23:49, 55) not included in the selection process? Jesus and the early church, like people in other creative moments, faced what Robert Wuthnow refers

---

intercourse (cf. Richard Bauckham, *The Climax of Prophecy: Studies on the Book of Revelation* [Edinburgh: Clark, 1993] 230-31), which (3) must symbolize for John mar-tyred men *and* women and children does not detract from the problematic assumptions of this metaphor.

19. These are adapted from David M. Scholer, "Contours of an Evangelical Feminist Hermeneutics," *Catalyst* 15 (1989) 2, 4, here 2.

to as "the problem of articulation," that is, the necessity of working *within* the constraints of one's historical particularity while at the same time calling (some of) those constraints into question.[20] In a male-dominated world, could the choice of a woman as leader be "heard"? What may be of more far-reaching consequence, then, is the way issues of status, including those related to gender and sex, are generally disparaged in the Third Gospel and Acts.[21]

4.2 The Scriptural Community

Of course, "the problem of Scripture" is not only that it contains material seemingly far removed from our lives but also that we face issues about which it has nothing immediate to say. This is an interpretive obstacle only for those — whether liberal or conservative, it does not matter — who are only or most interested in the *content* of the NT ("what the NT says about such-and-such"). For others, the importance of the NT as Scripture extends further than *what* it teaches to include *how it engages in cultural and moral discourse*.

On such matters, James McClendon points in a helpful direction. Refusing some of the normal characterizations of Scripture that define its nature in and of itself, he prefers instead to discuss the nature of Scripture in relation to the community whose life is normed by it. His vision "can be expressed as a hermeneutical motto, which is shared awareness of *the present Christian community as the primitive community and the eschatological community*."[22] Among the suggestions that follow from this "motto" is the understanding that the NT is not the Christian message in frozen form. Rather, the NT provides hermeneutical coordinates for the ongoing engagement of church and world.

In a sense, the NT itself legitimizes such ongoing hermeneutical reflection. Note, for example, the presence of *four* Gospels, not one, each articulating the good news of Jesus for particular audiences; the translation of the message from predominately rural to especially urban contexts; and so on.

---

20. Robert Wuthnow, *Communities of Discourse* (Cambridge: Harvard University, 1989) esp. 1-5; cf. A. E. Harvey, *Jesus and the Constraints of History* (Philadelphia: Westminster, 1982) 6-7.

21. See Joel B. Green, *The Acts of the Apostles*, WBC 37 (Dallas: Word, forthcoming).

22. James W. McClendon, Jr., *Systematic Theology*, vol. 1: *Ethics* (Nashville: Abingdon, 1986) 31.

The practice of reading the NT, then, will interact not only with the *content* of that reading, but also with *its mode of communal and cultural discourse, its ways of engaging authorities and interacting with cultural mores.* It will ask: What mode of theologizing has already been suggested to us by NT writers? In what ways have those writers already struggled with questions of identity and purpose as God's people?

In phrasing the practice of reading this way, we have come full circle in this chapter, from an emphasis on the act of reading to a focus on the practices of the people of God fostered by that reading. What shape will Christian communities take? This can hardly be predetermined, since, as Bourdieu has suggested and as John Levison and Priscilla Pope-Levison have documented (see above, ch. 16), practices (including the practice of reading) arise in particular contexts. In our contexts, then, we join in the exploration of how our lives as God's people might be "construed via narratives that are historically set in another time and place but display redemptive power here and now."[23] Indeed, this is the aim of the practice of reading the New Testament.

23. McClendon, *Ethics,* 34.

Index of Scripture and Other Ancient Sources

Discussions of the five New Testament "set texts" used in this volume are in boldface type.

Old Testament

Pseudepigrapha

Dead Sea Scrolls

Targumim

Targum Pseudo- Jonathan on Leviticus 22:28 225	Targum on Psalm 68:18 225	Targum on Isaiah 40:6-8 99

Rabbinic Literature and Tractates

Babylonian Talmud		Beṣa 20a, b	58	Mishnah	
Baba Meṣiʿa 111a	1-4			Berakot 6:5-8	50
Berakot 42a-46a	50			Para 4:3	55

Other Ancient Authors and Writings

Alciphron		**Cassiodorus Senator**		**John Chrysostom**	
3.17.4	164	*On Divine and Human*		*Homily XXVII*	
		Readings	258		405
Aristotle				*On Wealth and*	
Rhetoric	261	**Cicero**		*Poverty*	402
3.3.3	264	*De inventione*	261		
				Josephus	
Artemidorus		**1 Clement**		*Jewish Antiquities*	
Daldiani		17:6	99	15 §417	58
Oneirocritica				18.2.1-2 §§26-34	192
1.2	170	**Demetrius**		18.2.2 §35	191-92
1.35	170	*On Style*		18.2.3 §§36-38	191
3.66	170	2.101 ·	267	18.3.1-2 §§55-62	191
				18.4.1-2 §§85-89	191
Athenaeus		**Hermas**		18.4.3 §95	192
Deipnosophists		*Similitudes*		18.4.6 § 106	189
5.179e-190a	51	7.3	167	18.5.2 §§116-19	191
5.186a	51			18.5.3 §123	192
11.462c-d	51	**Hermogenes**		19.6.4 §§313-16	192
11.462-463	51	*On Types*		20.9.1 §§197-98	192
		242.1–246.1	267	20.9.7 §223	192
Augustine		246.1-9	267		
On Christian				*Jewish War*	
Doctrine	258	**Herodotus**		1.1	121
		4.91	170	2.284	121
Callimachus				4.4.3 §261	167
Aetia		**Irenaeus**		2.9.2-4 §§169-77	191
2.46	170	*Adversus Haereses*			
		2.27	30	*Life*	
				§§65-66	191

Index of Modern Authors